AZIENDA AGRITURISTICA "Il Cortile" DI SIJTSKEN DUPON

"Il Cortile" is a typical XVIII century "courtyard" sorrounded by a southern italian garden with a spectacular magnolia grandiflora, palm trees, citrus trees, jasmines and bougainvilleas; it is a right place, in wich to linger, talking to Sijtsken, the charming owner of Dutch origins, who is an expert in flowers and plants. Moreover she is a fine cook, and may give lessons on request.
The accomodation is in two separate self-contained unite with their own secluded entrances-perfect for families with children. Meals are caten in the main part of the house or in the courtyard, and there is an inviting sitting room for guests with family antiques, confortable sofas and pictures.

Via Roma, 43 - 80033 Cicciano (NA) - Tel. +39 081 8248897
Fax +39 081 8264851 - E-mail: dupon@libero.it

Bed & Breakfast Carafa di Maddaloni

In The hearth of the historical center of Neaples, in a palace of XVI century, with the atmosphere of ancient aristocratic house. Double rooms starting from Euro 58,00

Via Maddaloni, 6 - 80134 Napoli
Tel./Fax +39 081 5513691 - +39 081 5786861

www.bb-carafa.com
E-mail: bbcarafa@bbcarafa.com

Alloggio
IL GIARDINO FIORITO

Via XX Settembre, 79 - FERRARA
Tel. 0532 742667 - Fax 0532 746133
e-mail: romvilla@tin.it - www.ilgiardinofiorito.net

Ferrara, chosen to be one of the UNESCO world heritage sites, is a town full of art treasures and history. A few yards from the national Archeological Museum, the Monastery of Sant'Antonio in Polesine and the old Jewish ghetto, "IL GIARDINO FIORITO" offers large and elegantly furnished rooms provided with private bathroom, air conditioning, kitchenette, color TV, telephone and fax. Its nice gharden is a charming place where the guests can have their breakfast and spend pleasant hours in the warm season.
- Advance booking and time of arrival are appreciated
- Covered parking is available nearby
- Credit Cards accepted

"Pianas" Bed & Breakfast

40121 Bologna - Via F. Rosselli, 13
Tel. home +39 051 524359
Uff. +39 051 221820 - Fax +39 051 224374
e-mail: romano.fiori@libero.it

Hello, we are a very friendly family and we would like to welcome you in our home that is situated in the historical centre of the city. We offer you a double room in a quiet area, with TV a private entrance, a large sitting room and private bathroom. And when you make up you will experience a home-made breakfast and genuine cooking. If you need any turistical information, no problem: we have everything you need to know about Bologna and its surroundings, one of the greenest in Europe. We have also other services available (rent a bike, transports and more, special fare to private parking) just contact us.

Bed & Breakfast
Marcello Saltalamacchia

An Aeolian-style house with the typical "epulera", 50 m from the seashore, consisting of three double rooms all with private bathroom and direct access to a large garden landscaped with lemon trees.
The traditional breakfast is made even richer with granite (crushed ice mixed with assorted fruit syrups) and brioches. The owners are at their guests' disposal for the organization of boat rides to enjoy the beautiful attractions of the island.
Pets welcome.

Via Munciarda - 09055 Isole Eolie - Lipari (Messina, Sicily)
Tel. +39 0909811692 - Fax +39 0909880541

B&B Castiglione

P.zza della Stazione Lolli, 3 - 90141 Palermo
Tel. and Fax +39 091 335300 - Cell. +39 339 7805329 - bbcastiglione@libero.it

A 19th-century apartment, located in the centre of the city, just minutes away from the port, the bus stop for the airport to city lines, and the most important city monuments.
Three rooms are reserved for our guests, each with a private bathroom, heating, and air conditioning and each is tastefully and comfortably furnished. The house has retained the charming original architectonic decorations, frescoed ceilings, ornate plaster work, and vaulted ceilings.
- Breakfast consists of freshly baked specialities and traditional Sicilian pastries, served in your room;
- Rooms are rented on a daily basis.

Daily personalised cruises aboard the historic "Maria 1899" sailboat

The trip begins in the morning when we set sail for Budelli with its splendid Pink Beach, and continues with a visit to the Porto della Madonna, also known as "Natural Pools", where we will take a long break and relax with a delicious lunch offered by the crew.
After the break, we will continue toward Spargi and round the bend toward its spectacular coves: Cala Granara and Cala Corsara with its natural sculptures. The cruise will end at around 6:00 pm when we head toward La Maddalena island.
Passengers can also board the sailboat from the Port of Palau – Cannigione – Baia Sardinia.

Tel. 338 8662906 - 339 7922263
E-Mail: info@maria1899.it

Italian
Bed & Breakfasts

Italian
Bed & Breakfasts

1,200 Special Places to Stay in Italy

TOURING CLUB OF ITALY

Touring Club Italiano
President and Chairman: Roberto Ruozi
General Manager: Guido Venturini

Touring Editore
Managing Director: Guido Venturini
General Manager: Alfieri Lorenzon
Editorial Manager: Michele D'Innella

International Department
Fabio Pittella
fabio.pittella@touringclub.it

Senior Editor: Ornella Pavone
Translation: Studio Queens srl, Milan
Photo credits: B&M archives (Corbis, Goodshoot, Iconotec, Photodisc, Stockbyte), Touring Club Italiano photographic archives, C. Concina, M. Latona, A. Maisto, L. Pessina, Realy Easy Star, A. Solazzo, T. Spagone
Cover: Zefa/Sucré Salé

Advertising Manager: Claudio Bettinelli
Local Advertising: Progetto
www.progettosrl.it - info@progettosrl.it

Printing and binding: G. Canale & C., Borgaro Torinese (Torino)

Distribution
USA/CAN - Publishing Group West
UK/Ireland - Portfolio Books

Touring Club Italiano - Corso Italia 10, 20122 Milano
www.touringclub.it

Code K5E
ISBN 88 365 2901 1

Printed in September 2003

Contents

B&B Associations and Circuits

A distinctive feature of the B&B phenomenon in Italy is the presence of numerous Associations, mainly local or regional, and some national Circuits that group Bed & Breakfasts under a single name. These organisations act as intermediaries between guests and host families, guaranteeing the former with quality standards, and the latter promotional activities and centralised booking, a filter that guarantees privacy. Some Circuits and Associations not only accept families conducting an occasional business (Bed & Breakfasts proper) as members but sometimes also guesthouses, family-run boarding houses and self-contained apartments.
It is always advisable to ask in advance as to the type and features of your chosen accommodation.

• When selecting Bed & Breakfasts to include in this book, Touring was assisted by the leading Circuits and Associations in Italy.
These organisations gave TCI the names of some of their members, allowing thorough research and the selection of the best Bed & Breakfasts for inclusion.
The following pages list all the contact details for the B&B Associations and Circuit that have contributed to this guide in alphabetical order.

• The symbol ★TCI means they have signed an agreement giving TCI members a 10% discount on rates. If you wish to join us in the TCI, please look at our website: www.touringclub.it

The 35 Associations in the guide (the abbreviations used in the guide are in brackets):

- **A casa di Parthenope**
  Galleria Umberto I 8
  80132 Naples
  infoline: tel./fax 081 7944186
  info@casadiparthenope.it
  www.casadiparthenope.it

- **ANBBA** ★TCI
  via Istria 12
  30126 Venezia Lido (VE)
  tel. 041 731429
  fax 041 2769546
  info@anbba.it
  www.anbba.it

- **Associazione Barbarossa - Bed & Breakfast nel Lodigiano**
  (Ass. Barbarossa-B&B nel Lodigiano)
  via Boccaccio 15
  20078 San Colombano al Lambro (MI)
  tel. 0371 897998
  mob. 347 8664843
  stefania.bordoni@tiscalinet.it
  http//web.tiscali.it/bordoni53

- **Associazione Bergamo B&B** ★TCI
  via Volturno 23
  24124 Bergamo
  mob. 339 7845293
  bergamobedandbreakfast@virgilio.it
  www.bedbreakfastalp.it

- **Associazione B&B Liguria... e non solo** ★TCI
  (B&B Liguria e…non solo)
  via Casaregis 23°/A canc.
  16129 Genoa
  tel. 010 3291204
  fax 010 3299774
  oltrelazzurro@libero.it
  www.bbitalia.net

- **Associazione B&B Liguria**
  via Lomellini 1/8
  16124 Genoa
  tel./fax 010 2461918
  bbliguria@hotmail.com

- **Associazione B&B Varese - Nel verde tra i Laghi** ★TCI
  (B&B Varese-Nel verde tra i laghi)
  via Amalfi 7
  21010 Cardano al Campo (VA)
  tel. 0331 260040, fax 0331 781632
  iduenoci@hotmail.com
  www.bedbreakfastalp.it

- **Associazione Calabria in famiglia** ★TCI
  viale Aldo Moro, traversa Morabito 23
  89129 Reggio di Calabria
  tel./fax 0965 626840
  info@bbcalabria.it
  www.bbcalabria.it

- **Associazione Koko Nor** ★TCI
  via Selva 5
  35135 Padua
  tel./fax 049 8643394
  mob. 338 3377912
  kokonor@bandb-veneto.it
  www.bandb-veneto.it/kokonor

- **Associazione Latte e Miele** ★TCI
  via Guglielmo Calderini 68
  00196 Rome
  tel./fax 06 3211783
  info@sleepinitaly.com
  www.sleepinitaly.com

- **Associazione Latte e Miele Salento**
  via Indipendenza 33
  73024 Maglie (LE)
  mob. 347 8182786
  salento@sleepinitaly.com
  www.sleepinitaly.com/salento

- **Associazione Ospitalità Familiare Bed and Breakfast Parchi Appennino Bolognese** ★TCI
  (Associazione Ospitalità Familiare)
  via Torreggiani 1
  40128 Bologna
  tel./fax 051 379051
  coruzzi@iol.it

- **Associazione "Sardegna Ospitale"** ★TCI
  via Cedrino 1
  07100 Sassari
  tel. 079 2595061
  fax 079 2592241
  mob. 347 7773072
  info@bbsardegna.com
  www.bbsardegna.com

- **Associazione ToscanaeOltre** ★TCI
  via Baldeschi 19
  06012 Città di Castello (PG)
  tel. 075 855986439
  mob. 328 0143471
  info@toscanaeoltre.com
  www.toscanaeoltre.com

- **Associazione Turistica Bed & Breakfast Scopripiemonte**
  (ScopriPiemonte)
  via Famolasco 50
  10060 Bibiana (TO)
  tel./fax 0121 559182
  mob. 347 3651593
  bnbscopripiemonte@tiscalinet.it

- **Associazione Turisti per Casa Bed & Breakfast** ★TCI
  (Associazione Turisti per Casa)
  via Torino 6
  40068 San Lazzaro di Savena (BO)
  tel. 0532 705052 - 051 6288619
  info@turistipercasa.it
  www.turistipercasa.it

- **Bed and Breakfast Corporation** ★TCI
  Salita Porta di Ferro 17
  04024 Gaeta (LT)
  tel./fax 0771 460025
  mob. 339 2630299
  sepes@dimensione.com

- **Bed and Breakfast Service** ★TCI
  via dei Mille 23
  10123 Turin
  tel. 011 8123675
  fax 011 8140861
  torinoservices@yahoo.it
  www.bed-breakfast.it

- **Bed & Breakfast Association of Rome**
  via A. Pacinotti 73
  (palazzina E int. 3)
  00146 Rome
  tel. 06 55302248
  fax 06 55302259
  info@b-b.rm.it
  www.b-b.rm.it

- **Bed & Breakfast in Italy**
via delle Azzorre
Lido di Ostia 352
00121 Rome
tel. 06 5640716
fax 06 5640789
res@bbitalia.com
www.bbitalia.com

- **Bed & Breakfast in Italy – Ospitalità nelle case in Friuli Venezia Giulia**
(B&B in Italy. Ospitalità nelle case)
via Sanguarzo 13
33034 Cividale (UD)
tel. 0432 731854
fax 0432 700144
bedbreakfastitaly@hotmail.com
www.bedandbreakfastfvg.com

- **Bed & Breakfast Italia**
Palazzo Sforza Cesarini
corso Vittorio Emanuele II 284
00186 Rome
tel. 06 6878618
fax 06 6878619
info@bbitalia.it
www.bbitalia.it

- **B&B Dolce Sonno**
via Egiziaca a Pizzofalcone
80132 Naples
infoline: tel. 081 2451317
mob. 338 4916755
b.bdolcesonno@tiscalinet.it

- **B&B Dolomiti - Il Bed & Breakfast nelle montagne venete - Cooperativa Il Viaggiatore**
(B&B Dolomiti nelle montagne venete)
via San Lorenzo 22
32100 Belluno
tel. 0437 949000
0437 949100

- **Case Piemontesi Bed & Breakfast Asti**
(Case Piemontesi-B&B Asti)
via Carlo Leone Grandi 5
14100 Asti
tel. 0141 670918
marzeppa@tin.it
www.bedbreakfastalp.it
www.terredasti.it/bed&breakfast.htm

- **Domus Amigas**
Via dei Partigiani 12
09010 Gonnesa (CA)
tel./fax 078 136319

- **Euganean Life International**
via Prosdocimi 14
35042 Este (PD)
tel./fax 0429 56156
mob. 347 4355474
elit@bandb-veneto.it
www.bandb-veneto.it/euganeanlife

- **ExpressRoome**
via De Gasperi 2 D
00044 Frascati (Rome)
tel./fax 06 94289163
expressroome@libero.it
www.expressroome.com
www.expressroome.it

- **Friendly Home - Gli amici del Bed & Breakfast**
(Friendly Home-Gli Amici del B&B)
via Assietta 5/5
10098 Rivoli (TO)
tel./fax 011 9536376
fhrivoli@virgilio.it
via Sant'Orsola 8
20123 Milan
tel. 02 860147
fax 02 875860
friendlymilano@dada.it

- **Home Express**
largo dell'Olgiata 15 is. 106
00123 Rome
tel./fax 06 90129063
home.express@tiscalinet.it
www.home-express.it

- **Le finestre sul Golfo Bed & Breakfast**
(Le Finestre sul Golfo B&B)
viale dei Platani 43
80040 San Sebastiano al Vesuvio (NA)
tel./fax 081 5748579
mob. 333 2440156
www.dynacom.it/finestregolfobb

- **Rome sweet home**
via della Vite 32
00187 Rome
tel. 06 69924833
info@romesweethome.it
www.romesweethome.it

- **Sardegna B&B Reservation**
via Stampa 7
09131 Cagliari
tel. 070 4520011
fax 070 4520403
bedsardegna@tiscalinet.it

- **Vacanze in famiglia**
via Casilina 4
30030 Campalto (VE)
tel./fax 041 455188, 041 900385
margherit@tin.it

- **Welcome - Bed & Breakfast in Umbria**
via degli Eucalipti 47/a
05019 Orvieto (TR)
tel. 0763 305523
fax 0763 390670
info@bbumbria.it
www.bbumbria.it

How to use this guide

- *We have collected the 1200 best Bed & Breakfasts in Italy, from Valle d'Aosta to the main islands, in 20 regional chapters.*
- *All places with one or more B&B are listed in alphabetic order by region.*
- *For every B&B we provide the booking details, a brief description and photograph, number of rooms, services offered, price bracket and any discount for Touring membership.*

B&Bs and Associations

Numerous B&Bs do not appear with their own contact details but with the name followed by the name, telephone, fax, e-mail and website details of the Association or Circuit they belong to. This follows a request for anonymity made by owners who wish only to be contacted through their organisation.

Merely contact the Association or Circuit, which will check availability, make the booking and give you details of the chosen B&B.

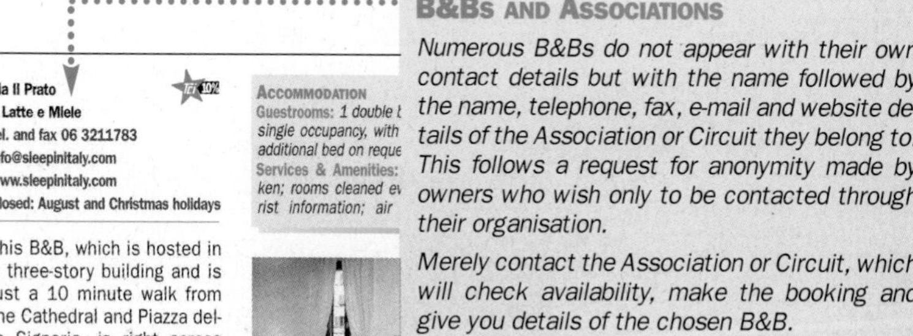

Via Il Prato
• Latte e Miele
tel. and fax 06 3211783
info@sleepinitaly.com
www.sleepinitaly.com
Closed: August and Christmas holidays

Accommodation
Guestrooms: *1 double* ...
single occupancy, with ...
additional bed on reque...
Services & Amenities: ...
ken; rooms cleaned e...
rist information; air ...

This B&B, which is hosted in a three-story building and is just a 10 minute walk from the Cathedral and Piazza della Signoria, is right across the street from the prestigious Hotel Villa Medici. The guests' large, comfortable, bright, air-conditioned double room has a private bath- ... The breakfast is the continental type.

• Bed & Breakfast Italia
Code F102
via Jacopo Nardi
tel. 06 6878618, fax 06 6878619
info@bbitalia.it
www.bbitalia.it
Closed: varies

This B&B is located in a fairly central area, on the second floor of an elegant building. It ...

Accommodation
Guestrooms: *2 (1 single, 1 double)*
Services & Amenities: *English spoken; rooms cleaned every 3 days; complimentary tourist information; private parking*
Minimum stay: *2 nights*
Rates: €€
Credit cards: *Bancomat*
Pets:

beds and a single. The guests' private bathroom has a tub. Breakfast is served in the lounge. The city's old center can be easily reached in 20 minutes by public transport.

179

Bed & Breakfast Italia codes

*B&Bs belonging to the **Bed & Breakfast Italia** circuit show an ID code, e.g.* **Code F102.** *This is used for reasons of privacy, as requested by the owners belonging to this circuit. Once contacted, the circuit's call centre will check availability, make the booking and give you details of the chosen B&B.*

Symbols

These symbols are used in the Accommodation panel:

- *no architectural barriers*
-  *pets*
- *no pets*
- VISA MC *Bancomat Credit cards accepted*

Abruzzo

Pescocostanzo (L'Aquila)

Pescocostanzo
• Dolce Sonno Bed & Breakfast
tel. 081 2451317
mob. 338 4916755
b.dolcesonno@tiscalinet.it
Open all year

This B&B is located at the town's entrance and provides a nice view of the typical mountain landscape. On the first floor of the two-story guest apartment there's a living room with a fireplace and a TV, an equipped kitchen corner, a double bed, and a bathroom wi... er. The second fl... mansard with four... the rooms have w... tain-style wooden... The town, which... minutes from the... also makes an id... going on summer ex...

Accommodation
Guestrooms: 2 (1 double bedroom, 1 quadruple, private bath)
Services & Amenities: English spoken; rooms cleaned every three days; complimentary tourist information; kitchenette
Minimum stay: 1 week
Rates: €€€-€€€€. Children under 3 free
Credit cards: not accepted
Pets: no

Pescasseroli (L'Aquila)

• Bed & Breakfast Italia
Code AB3
tel. 06 6878618, fax 06 6878619

Accommodation
Guestrooms: 3 (2 doubles, 1 triple)
Services & Amenities: English and French are spoken; rooms cleaned every three days; complimentary ... excursions; private parking
Minimum stay: 2 nights
Rates: €€
Credit cards: Bancomat
Pets: no

Tuscany

Barberino Val d'Elsa (Florence)

Il Paretaio TCI 10%
Cristina De Marchi
strada delle Ginestre 12
località San Filippo
50021 Barberino Val d'Elsa (FI)
tel. 055 8059218, mob. 338 7379626
fax 055 8059231
ilparetaio@tin.it
www.ilparetaio.it
Open all year

This B&B is located in an 18th-C working-class house situated in the heart of Chianti. There's a garden with a swimming pool, and the place is surrounded by vineyards, olive trees and a forest. The bright rooms have simple furnishings and 19th-C Tuscan furniture. The dining room with fireplace is where the buffet breakfast (with sweet items and cold cuts) is served and where guests can have dinner. There is also a ri... instructors... and expert... on dressage...

Accommodation
Guestrooms: 6 doubles, also single occupancy, with private bath
Services & Amenities: French and English are spoken; rooms cleaned every day; tourist info; horse-riding excursions; educational courses; garden; smokers welcome; parking
Minimum stay: 1 week
Rates: single €€-€€€, double €€€-€€€€
Credit cards: not accepted
Pets: yes

Borgo a Mozzano (Lucca)

La Casa Torre
via della Torre 1/g, località Diecimo
55023 Borgo a Mozzano (LU)
tel. and fax 0583 838680
mob. 338 2358327
danielabartolini@tin.it
Open all year

This B&B is hosted in a completely restored, early 13th-century tower situated in a little town called Garfagna-na, whi... lometer... has ... sphere... vençal... accomm... 2 doubl... vate bat... choose fro... which is ei... large kitch... or in the ga...

Accommodation
Guestrooms: 2 double bedrooms, with private bath
Services & Amenities: English and French are spoken; rooms cleaned every 3 days; tourist info; bike rental; terrace; garden; smokers welcome
Minimum stay: 2 nights
Rates: double €€€€. Children under 5 free
Credit cards: accepted
Pets: no

Price brackets

The Hospitality panel does not show the prices charged by each B&B, but its price bracket.

The price brackets are marked with an € and are per person.

When the price is per room, we specify single, double or triple.

These are the 5 price brackets adopted:

€	*up to 26 Euros*
€€:	*27 to 52 Euros*
€€€:	*53 to 78 Euros*
€€€€:	*79 to 103 Euros*
€€€€€:	*more than 104 Euros*

TCI discount

The symbol, TCI 10% beside the name of a B&B indicates it will offer Touring members a 10% discount. To obtain this discount please declare TCI membership when booking. For more informations, please look at our website www.touringclub.it

Trentino -
South
Tirol
Valle d'Aosta
Friuli -
Venezia
Giulia
Lombardy
Veneto
Piedmont
Emilia-Romagna
Liguria
Tuscany
Marche
Umbria
Abruzzo
Molise
Lazio
Puglia
Campania
Sardinia
Basilicata
Calabria
Sicily

Valle d'Aosta

CHÂTILLON (AOSTA)

Le Lierre
Ada Landoni
via Tour de Grange 64
11024 Châtillon (AO)
tel. and fax 0166 61521
landoni.ada@bedbreakfastalp.it
www.bedbreakfastalp.it
Closed: May

This traditional style stone and wood villa, just 20 minutes from Aosta, has a roof tiled with "lose" – a local stone. This B&B offers a wide panoramic view of the Châtillon castles. Guests have the use of a small two-story apartment that has a separate entrance from the garden. Breakfast – Italian or English – is served either in the house or outside. The town has a sports center and offers pleasurable holidays.

ACCOMMODATION
Guestrooms: *1 suite (4 beds, private bath)*
Services & Amenities: *English, French and German are spoken; rooms cleaned every day; tourist info; smokers welcome; garden*
Rates: *€€€. Children under 3 free; 3 to 5 -50%*
Credit cards: *not accepted*
Pets: 🚫

PERLOZ (AOSTA)

• Bed & Breakfast Italia
Code VA1
tel. 06 6878618, fax 06 6878619
info@bbitalia.it
www.bbitalia.it
Closed: varies

A typical Valle d'Aosta chalet, situated 850 meters above sea level, in the delighful Gressoney valley. It comprises a double room and two twin bed rooms, each with its own private bathroom with shower. Italian breakfast is served in the comfortable lounge or outside on sunny days. The B&B is 15 km from the ski slopes, 50 km from Aosta, 90 km from the French border and 75 km from the Swiss border. A car is absolutely necessary.

ACCOMMODATION
Guestrooms: *3 doubles*
Services & Amenities: *English and French are spoken; rooms cleaned every three days; complimentary tourist information; smokers welcome; private parking*
Minimum stay: *2 nights*
Rates: €€
Credit cards: VISA MC *Bancomat*
Pets: 🚫

Pollein (Aosta)

Lo Nouesse
Nadia Melidona
località Capoluogo 120
11020 Pollein (AO)
tel. 0165 53128
mob. 328 7617072
bbnadi@libero.it
www.bedbreakfastalp.it
Closed: October

This beautiful, new stone house, surrounded by grapevines and chestnut trees, is far from any traffic and just 4 km from Aosta. The hosts love wood carving and even have an atelier set up in their garage. They live on the ground floor, while the guests have the mansard. Breakfast consists of genuine local products and is served either in the living room or, when the weather's nice, in the garden. The guests have the use of a wonderful library with books on Alpine itineraries, history and local traditions.

Accommodation
Guestrooms: *3 doubles, also single occupancy, private bath; additional bed on request*
Services & Amenities: *English, French and Spanish are spoken; rooms cleaned every 3 days; tourist information; smokers welcome; terrace; garden; private parking*
Rates: *single €€, double €€€€. Additional bed supplement €*
Credit cards: *non accepted*
Pets: 🚫

Rhêmes-Saint-Georges (Aosta)

Le Boton D'Or
Idelma Anselmat
località Proussaz 14
11010 Rhêmes-Saint-Georges (AO)
tel. 0165 907659
Open all year

Once a building for storing farm equipment, this place has been very intelligently converted into an elegant, comfortable mountain home made of wood and stone. Next to it is a organic farm. The three guestrooms are furnished in wood, rustic style, and there is a nice terrace for the guests. Breakfast, consisting of natural products, is served in a reserved dining room where, on request, guests can also have dinner.

Accommodation
Guestrooms: *3 doubles, private bath; additional bed on request* ♿
Services & Amenities: *French spoken; rooms cleaned every 3 days; complimentary tourist information; smokers welcome; garden*
Rates: *double €€*
Credit cards: *not accepted*
Pets: 🚫

Saint-Christophe (Aosta)

La Fiaba
Margaretha Svenson
località Croux 11
11020 Saint-Christophe (AO)
tel. 0165 541098
svenson.margaretha@bedbreakfastalp.it
www.bedbreakfastalp.it
Closed: October and November

This beautiful house is surrounded by a garden with trees. It's located on a hill 3 km from the center of Aosta. Guests can either stay in the family home or in the small dépendance that has a kitchen and a private bath. The hostess, a Swedish lady, has preferred to furnish the house in the Scandinavian tradition. She is also more than pleased to help her guests discover the culture and legends of her native country. Her two sons give ski lessons on the slopes – paradise for skiers – that are about 20 km away. No TV.

Accommodation
Guestrooms: *2 doubles and 1 studio apartment, additional bed on request* ♿
Services & Amenities: *English, French, Spanish and Swedish are spoken; rooms cleaned every three days; complimentary tourist information; kitchenette; educational courses by request; garden; private parking*
Minimum stay: *3 nights*
Rates: *double €€, studio apartment €€€ Additional bed supplement €. Children under 3 free; 3 to 10 -50%*
Credit cards: *not accepted*
Pets: 🚫

Saint-Vincent (Aosta)

La Grisse
Paola Seris
Village de Grun 18
11027 Saint-Vincent (AO)
tel. and fax 0166 511324
seris.paola@bedbreakfastalp.it
www.bedbreakfastalp.it
Open: July to September, Easter and Christmas holidays, weekends

This traditional, 17th-century, Valle D'Aosta barn is located in a village that only has about 30 inhabitants. This is a place that time has forgotten. It still has all the atmosphere of an ancient farm village. Guests have a convenient, independent mini-apartment, which was converted from the ancient stalls. The breakfast of genuine products is served in the living room, which also has a fireplace. The hostess likes to have the guests help her make various types of marmalade.

Accommodation
Guestrooms: *1 mini-apartment with 4 beds*
Services & Amenities: *English and French are spoken; rooms cleaned every 3 days; tourist information; smokers welcome; garden*
Rates: *€€ per person. Discounts for 4 people*
Credit cards: *not accepted*
Pets:

Le Rosier
Ada Vesan
località Crotache 1
11027 Saint-Vincent (AO)
tel. and fax 0166 537726
mob. 333 2384401
vesan@libero.it
www.bedbreakfastalp.it
Open: April to October

Built in 1755 and recently restored, this traditional Val D'Aosta stone house is located at an altitude of 700 m, in a small village surrounded by vineyards. The guest accommodation, which also include a small living room, has wooden furnishings and an independent entrance. Breakfast, which also includes local products, is served in a small room which was set up in the characteristic stall with its stone, domed ceiling, and furnished with traditional Val D'Aosta furniture. This area offers many options for a pleasurable holiday.

Accommodation
Guestrooms: *2 mini-apartments*
Services & Amenities: *English and French are spoken; rooms cleaned every 3 days; complimentary tourist material; kitchenette; smokers welcome; garden; private parking*
Rates: *For 2 €€€. Additional bed supplement €. Discounts for children and extended stays*
Credit cards: *not accepted*
Pets:

Valsavarenche (Aosta)

Le Mélèze
Elisa Frassetto
località Bien 23
11010 Valsavarenche (AO)
mob. 349 7801409
lemeleze@tiscali.it
www.bedbreakfastalp.it
Open: 1 June to 1 October, Easter and Christmas holidays and weekends

Located at 1700 m, immersed in the extraordinary natural context of the Gran Paradiso National Park, this typical, 19th-century home is furnished with traditional furniture salvaged from ancient farmsteads and barns. The family shares their living room, with its fireplace and well-furnished library, with the guests. Breakfast consists of typical, genuine products. This is the ideal place for lovers of skiing or free climbing.

Accommodation
Guestrooms: *3 (1 single, 1 double bedroom and 1 double; shared bath)*
Services & Amenities: *French and English are spoken; complimentary tourist information; rooms cleaned every 3 days; smokers welcome; garden*
Rates: *single €, double €€. Children under 3 free; 3 to 10 -50%*
Credit cards: *not accepted*
Pets:

Piedmont

Albugnano (Asti)

Monastero del Rul
Maria Valencia Ardiles
località Vezzolano 57
14020 Albugnano (AT)
tel. 011 9922031, 011 9922034
mob. 335 6638834, fax 011 9922034
info@monasterodelrul.com
www.monasterodelrul.com
• **Case Piemontesi-B&B Asti**
tel. and fax 0141 670918
marzeppa@tin.it
www.terredasti.it/bed&breakfast.htm
Closed: Christmas holidays

This old farmstead, which has been restructured using original materials, is immersed in 50 acres of woods on a hill surrounded by vineyards. Guests have the use of a reading room, a game room, Internet, and hammocks in the garden, which has a superb view of Monferrato and the Alps. Breakfast consists of organic farm products and is served in the dining room. Guests can explore the surrounding hills.

Accommodation
Guestrooms: *2 doubles, private bath; additional bed on request*
Services & Amenities: *French, English, German, Spanish and Portuguese are spoken; rooms cleaned every 3 days; complimentary tourist information; bike rental; horse-riding excursions; Internet access; garden; smokers welcome; private parking*
Rates: *€€€. Additional bed supplement €. Discounts for extended stays -10%*
Credit cards: *not accepted*
Pets:

Ameno (Novara)

Casa Mari
Albina Daziano
via Strigini 15
28010 Ameno (NO)
tel. 0322 900729, mob. 338 3703226
albafri@libero.it
Closed: January, February and November

This completely restored 18th-C monastery, located at an altitude of 500 meters overlooking Lake Orta, provides three guestrooms with an independent entrance. Continental breakfast is served in the kitchen-living room on the ground floor. The host and his wife specialize in the cultivation of azaleas and rhododendrons, and put their small garden, which borders the Monte Oro botanical park, at the disposition of the guests.

Accommodation
Guestrooms: *3 doubles, private bath*
Services & Amenities: *English and German are spoken; rooms cleaned every day; complimentary tourist information; Internet access; garden; smokers welcome*
Rates: *€€ to €€€. Children under 2 free; 3 to 12 -50%*
Credit cards: *not accepted*
Pets:

ARONA (NOVARA)

il Giardino di Alice
Dario Alberto Saporiti
via Motto Mirabello 51
28041 Arona (NO)
tel. 0322 57212, fax 0322 57145
Open all year

This wooden châlet is immersed in a forest of chestnut trees on the shores of Lago Maggiore, and provides a view of the Rocca di Angera. The colors and materials of the furnishings of the rooms are in keeping with the principles of bioarchitecture. Guests have the use of a rustic room with a veranda, a living room with TV and a fireplace. They can also enjoy the furnished garden, or go mountain-biking or take a ride in a motorboat.

ACCOMMODATION
Guestrooms: *3 doubles, private bath*
Services & Amenities: *French, English and German are spoken; rooms cleaned every day; tourist information; bike rental; terrace; garden; smokers welcome; private parking*
Minimum stay: *2 nights*
Rates: *single €€, double €€; Creative hospitality programme € per day. Children under 2 free (cot on request)*
Credit cards: *Bancomat*
Pets:

ASTI

Arca Noae
Monica Roffinella
frazione Valleandona 114
località Cravera
14100 Asti
mob. 339 6233399, fax 0141 295935
• Case Piemontesi-B&B Asti
tel. and fax 0141 670918
marzeppa@tin.it
www.terredasti.it/bed&breakfast.htm
Open all year

Located on a hill near a small village, this restructured farmstead is in a natural reserve noted for its fossil finds. The B&B has three rooms with period furnishings. One of these rooms is equipped for disabled persons. The estate, which is surrounded by the vineyards and fruit trees of adjoining farm, also has a horse- riding school for lessons or excursions. A horsetherapy activity is being organized for disabled persons. Breakfast, with various marmalades and genuine biscuits, is served in a special room equipped with a bar.

ACCOMMODATION
Guestrooms: *3 doubles, private bath; additional bed on request*
Services & Amenities: *English spoken; rooms cleaned every day; tourist information; bike rental; educational courses; lunch & dinner reservations; horse-riding excursions; garden; smokers welcome; private parking*
Rates: *€ per person. Discounts for extended stays*
Credit cards: *not accepted*
Pets:

La Magnolia
Elisabetta Potenza
via Serale 34, località Valleandona
14100 Asti
tel. 0141 295100, fax 0141 295942
lamagnolia1@libero.it
• Case Piemontesi-B&B Asti
tel. and fax 0141 670918
marzeppa@tin.it
www.terredasti.it/bed&breakfast.htm
Open: March to early November and December to 6 January

This B&B – 6 km from Asti – is located among fruit trees and vineyards in the heart of the Natural Reserve of Valleandona and Val Botto. It's ideal for those who are enthusiastic about paleontology, hikes, bike excursions or horseback riding. This B&B is a restructured, typical country house, and has a courtyard, small garden and simple furniture. The generous, simple breakfast is served in a special dining room.

ACCOMMODATION
Guestrooms: *2 (1 single room and 1 suite, with private bath); additional bed on request*
Services & Amenities: *French and English are spoken; rooms cleaned every day; tourist information; kitchen use by request; bike rental; educational courses by request; garden; smokers welcome*
Rates: *single €€, double €€. Additional bed supplement €. Children under 3 free; 4 to 10 -15%. Discounts for extended stays*
Credit cards: *not accepted*
Pets:

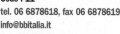

Nella Vecchia Fattoria
Maria Franca Molino
località Valletanaro
14100 Asti
tel. and fax 0141 351499
bedandbreakfastasti@libero.it
• Case Piemontesi-B&B Asti
tel. and fax 0141 670918
marzeppa@tin.it
www.terredasti.it/bed&breakfast.htm
Closed: Easter to late October
Open: November to February

This typical, completely restructured early 20th-C farmstead, is located on a hill that dominates woods and vineyards. Guests have the use of a room with satellite TV, as well as a solarium, a private park and bicycles. The furniture is plain and simple, in the traditional style. Breakfast, which has a choice of either sweet or nonsweet items, as well as an abundance of typical, natural products, is served either in the living room or in the garden. Given its name, this B&B couldn't be without its little animals, which include ducks, chickens and rabbits. Friendly atmosphere.

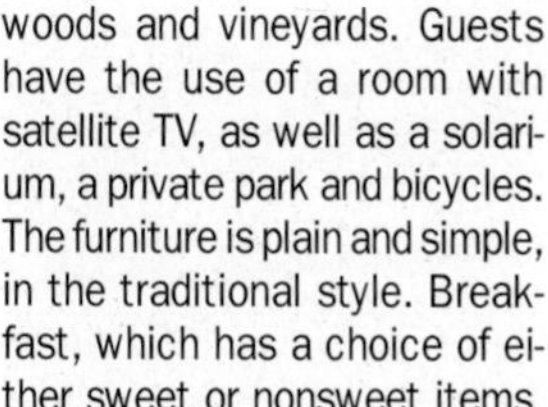

ACCOMMODATION
Guestrooms: *2 (1 double bedroom and 1 double, also single occupancy, shared bath); additional bed on request*
Services & Amenities: *Franch and English are spoken; rooms cleaned every day; tourist information; baby-sitting service; bike rental; garden; smokers welcome; private parking*
Rates: *single €€, double €€. Additional bed supplement €. Children under 3 free. Discounts for extended stays*
Credit cards: *not accepted*
Pets:

• Bed & Breakfast Italia
Code P11
tel. 06 6878618, fax 06 6878619
info@bbitalia.it
www.bbitalia.it
• Al Nido - Case Piemontesi-B&B Asti
tel. and fax 0141 670918
marzeppa@tin.it
www.terredasti.it/bed&breakfast.htm
Closed: varies

ACCOMMODATION
Guestrooms: *3 (1 single, 1 double and 1 triple room)*
Services & Amenities: *French, English and Spanish are spoken; rooms cleaned every 3 days; complimentary tourist information; bike rental; terrace; smokers welcome*
Minimum stay: *2 nights*
Rates: €€
Credit cards: VISA MC *Bancomat*
Pets:

A sloping roof apartment, independent from the rest of the villa, surrounded by 8,000 sq. m of private park nestling in a palaeontological nature reserve. All the rooms feature a large balcony and share a bathroom. The furnishings are rustic, fresh and colorful. Guests can enjoy a small swimming pool and a solarium. The hosts will arrange guided visits to nearby castles and old cellars.

BÈE (VERBANIA-CUSIO-OSSOLA)

Le Coccinelle
Marì Bonzanini
via Cascine 13
28813 Bèe (VB)
tel. 0323 56142
race2001@tiscali.it
Closed: November and Easter holidays

This B&B, located in the old center of the town, which is just outside the Val Grande National Park, has a guestroom in the main house, as well as a dépendance (fór family groups only) consisting of a bedroom, living room (with fireplace, a sofa bed, TV and library) and a bathroom. Breakfast can be served in the large family kitchen or in the garden. On request, the hostess can organize nature excursions, and also provide an English-speaking guide.

ACCOMMODATION
Guestrooms: *1 double, also single occupancy, private bath; 1 small apartment with 4 beds and private bath*
Services & Amenities: *French and English are spoken; rooms cleaned every day; complimentary tourist information; garden; smokers welcome; private parking*
Rates: *single €€, double €€€. Additional bed supplement €. Discounts for families*
Credit cards: *not accepted*
Pets:

Bibiana (Turin)

Ël Rabot
Oriana Tron
via Famolasco 50, località Famolasco
10060 Bibiana (TO)
tel. and fax 0121 559182
mob. 347 9766261
bbtronoriana@yahoo.it
www.bedandbreakfastalp.it
• ScopriPiemonte
tel. 0121 559182, mob. 347 3651593
fax 0121 559182
bnbscopripiemonte@tiscali.it
Open: 15 March to 15 November

This 18th-C farmhouse, which is surrounded by fruit trees and enjoys a panoramic view, has a large garden, a vegetable patch, and a chicken coop. The B&B part of the farmhouse is located on the ground floor and has an independent entrance. It also has a large kitchen and a common living room. Breakfast can also be served outdoors and consists of typical genuine products. Guests can consult the books in the family library to obtain information on the Valdese culture, as well as itineraries for excursion.

Accommodation
Guestrooms: *3 (1 double bedroom with private bath and 2 doubles, shared bath, also single occupancy); additional bed on request*
Services & Amenities: *English and French are spoken; rooms cleaned every day; complimentary tourist information; baby-sitting service; kitchen use by request; mountain-bike rental; Internet access; garden; smokers welcome; private parking*
Rates: *single €, double €€. Additional bed supplement. Discounts for extended stays*
Credit cards: *not accepted*
Pets:

Bra (Cuneo)

L'Ombra della Collina
Giovanni Chiesa
via Mendicità 47
12042 Bra (CN)
tel. and fax 0172 44884
Open all year

This recently restructured 18th-century house is in the center of the old part of town. The host, who restores antiques in his shop located in the courtyard, has a nice collection of period toys. He restored Giovanni Arpino's wedding bed. The name of this B&B is taken from one of Arpino's novels. Breakfast, which varies according to the preferences of the guests, is served either in the living room or in the library.

Accommodation
Guestrooms: *3 doubles, private bath, additional bed on request*
Services & Amenities: *rooms cleaned every day; tourist information; kitchen use by request; garden; smokers welcome; private parking*
Rates: *single €€€, double €€€. Additional bed supplement €. Children under 2 free. Discounts for extended stays*
Credit cards: *Bancomat*
Pets:

Bricherasio (Turin)

Il Mirtillo
Livia Laiolo
strada Basse 20
10060 Bricherasio (TO)
tel. and fax 0121 59657
www.bedandbreakfastalp.it
• ScopriPiemonte
tel. 0121 559182, 347 3651593
fax 0121 559182
bnbscopripiemonte@tiscali.it
Closed: 10 June to 26 July, 3 to 27 November and 1 to 25 January

Located in a very small, 5-family village which is 2 km from the center of Bricherasio, this 18th-century farm home is surrounded by woods and fruit trees, thus making it an ideal location for hikes and bike rides amid nature. Guests have the use of a lounge with TV that also has a library. Breakfast consists of sweet and non-sweet local products.

Accommodation
Guestrooms: *2 (1 double bedroom and 1 single, shared bath); additional bed on request*
Services & Amenities: *rooms cleaned every day; complimentary tourist information; bike rental; garden; private parking*
Rates: *single €€, double €€. Additional bed supplement €. Children under 3 -50%. Discounts for extended stays*
Credit cards: *not accepted*
Pets:

Bubbio (Asti)

La Dogliola
• Friendly Home-Gli Amici del B&B
tel. 02 860147, fax 02 875860
friendlymilano@dada.it
tel. and fax 011 9536376
fhrivoli@virgilio.it
Open: April to October

This ancient farmstead, with its country-style furniture, was so perfectly restored that it received the "Stone House 2000" award. It's the ideal place to have a complete enological experience, beginning with the panoramic view of the Langa vineyards. And no one should miss tasting the fine wines produced by the young wine-grower, including: the white and dry Ettaro, the sweet muscatel, the DOCG brachetto wine, and the Nero Vero, a wine that has received numerous awards.

Accommodation
Guestrooms: *1 double bedroom, private bath; additional bed on request*
Services & Amenities: *English and French are spoken; rooms cleaned every 3 days; complimentary tourist information; kitchenette; terrace; garden; smokers welcome*
Rates: *double €€€. Additional bed supplement €*
Credit cards: *not accepted*
Pets: ✓

Canelli (Asti)

La Casa del Ciliegio
Gabriella Morocutti
via Regione Bassano 40
14053 Canelli (AT)
tel. 02 27741429, 0141 824554
mob. 347 2213385
fax 02 29531723
gabriella.morocutti@planet.it
www.bedandbreakfast.it/lacasadelciliegio
• Case Piemontesi-B&B Asti
tel. and fax 0141 670918
marzeppa@tin.it
www.terredasti.it/bed&breakfast.htm
Closed: August
Open: 1 March to 30 November

This 19th-century, rustically-furnished farmhouse surrounded by the vegetation of the Canelli Valley, provides careful, discrete hospitality, all of which makes for a very friendly atmosphere. Guests have a small dining room for having breakfast, as well as a TV and reading room, a kitchen and a gazebo with a barbeque. The many wine cellars and excellent restaurants in the surrounding area permit planning programs for enjoying fine wine and excellent food.

Accommodation
Guestrooms: *3 doubles (2 with private baths and 1 with shared bath)*
Services & Amenities: *French and English are spoken; rooms cleaned every day; complimentary tourist information; terrace; garden; smokers welcome; private parking*
Rates: *single €€, double €€€. Discounts for children (-50%) and for extended stays (-20%)*
Credit cards: *accepted*
Pets: ✓

Cannobio (Verbania-Cusio-Ossola)

Villa Palmira
Emilia Cerutti
via Uccelli 24
28822 Cannobio (VB)
tel. and fax 0323 72347
g.madaschi@libero.it
Open all year

Located in the center of a town on the shores of Lake Maggiore, just 3 km from the Swiss border, this late-19th-C villa is furnished in local style and includes a few period pieces. Continental breakfast, including some nonsweet items, is served either in the living room or, by request, in the guestroom. The guests can also enjoy the garden, with its secular trees, and they can take some bike rides. They also have access to a well-furnished library that has books on local history and the main tourist attractions in the area.

Lake Maggiore

Accommodation
Guestrooms: *2 doubles, private bath*
Services & Amenities: *English, French and German are spoken; rooms cleaned every day; complimentary tourist information; bike rental; garden; private parking*
Rates: *single €€, double €€. Additional bed supplement €. Children under 2 free*
Credit cards: *not accepted*
Pets: ✓

Carpignano Sesia (Novara)

B&B Del Sesia
Sabrina Messineo
via per Ghemme
località Cascina Comunità 3
28064 Carpignano Sesia (NO)
tel. and fax 0321 824129
sabrmes@tin.it
Closed: September, October, November

This B&B, which is one km from the center of town, right near the Sesia River, has two guestrooms; one has Indian style furnishings and the other with modern furniture. The continental breakfast is served in the guest dining room. Guests can also enjoy the garden of this seventeenth-century farmhouse, which is surrounded by about five acres of land, part of which is cultivated, and part is for the various domestic animals and the horses.

Accommodation
Guestrooms: *2 doubles, also single occupancy, private bath*
Services & Amenities: *French and English are spoken; rooms cleaned every day; tourist info; garden; smokers welcome; private parking*
Rates: *single €€, double €€€. Additional bed supplement €. Discounts for children and extended stays*
Credit cards: *not accepted*
Pets: *on request*

Castelletto Sopra Ticino (Novara)

B&B Il Girasole
Tanya Paracchini
via Oldrina 40
28053 Castelletto Sopra Ticino (NO)
tel. 0331 971579, mob. 347 3101468
vale_tanya@libero.it
Closed: January, February, November

Located in a quiet residential neighborhood one km from the center of town, this B&B is on the ground floor of a house that dates from the '50s. Besides the bedroom, guests have the use of the living room with its TV and sofa, as well a kitchen, which is where breakfast is served. Guests also have use of the garden and its ping-pong table. The surrounding area includes the Ticino Fluvial Park protected area. Nearby, there are various sports structures and a riding-school.

Ticino Fluvial Park

Accommodation
Guestrooms: *1 double, private bath, additional bed on request*
Services & Amenities: *English, French and German are spoken; rooms cleaned every day; tourist info; kitchen use by request; garden; smokers welcome; private parking*
Rates: *€€€. Additional bed supplement €. Children under 2 free; 3 to 10 -10%*
Credit cards: *not accepted*
Pets:

B&B La Camelia
Wanda Caramella
via Trieste 10/F
28053 Castelletto Sopra Ticino (NO)
tel. 0331 972781
wancaram@tin.it
Closed: January, February, November

Accommodation
Guestrooms: *1 double bedroom, also single occupancy, private bath; additional bed on request*
Services & Amenities: *English spoken; rooms cleaned every day; complimentary tourist material; terrace; garden; private parking*
Rates: *single €, double €€. Additional bed supplement €. Children under 2 free; 3 to 12 -10%*
Credit cards: *not accepted*
Pets:

Located in the center of Castelletto Sopra Ticino, just 500 meters from the main square and the river, this small B&B villa with its little garden offers a guestroom with wicker furniture and a large terrace. The Italian breakfast is served in the family living room. The many possibilities offered by the surrounding area include boat trips on Lake Maggiore, and visits to such charming places as Rocca of Angera and the delightful Dominican sanctuary of Santa Caterina del Sasso.

Ceresole Alba (Cuneo)

• Bed & Breakfast Italia
Code P10
tel. 06 6878618, fax 06 6878619
info@bbitalia.it
www.bbitalia.it
Closed: varies

This typical rustic farmhouse is situated in the Roero woods. It is surrounded by a well-tended garden where breakfast is served in the summer; in winter, it is served in the dining room. The accommodation consists in two rooms with period country-style furniture: one quadruple room with a double bed and a bunk bed, and a double bedroom, both sharing a bathroom with shower. An extra bed for children under two can be provided on request. A car is needed to tour this area, famed for its culinary specialties and fine wines.

Accommodation
Guestrooms: *2 (1 double and 1 triple room)*
Services & Amenities: *rooms cleaned every 3 days; tourist information*
Minimum stay: *2 nights*
Rates: €
Credit cards: VISA MC *Bancomat*
Pets: no

Cortazzone (Asti)

Bricco dei Ciliegi TCI 10%
Rosa Gavello
via del Negro 22
14010 Cortazzone (AT)
tel. 0141 995270, mob. 328 7663608
bricco.ciliegi@inwind.it
• Case Piemontesi-B&B Asti
tel. and fax 0141 670918
marzeppa@tin.it
www.terredasti.it/bed&breakfast.htm
Closed: 20 to 30 July

Located on a hill, this typical Piedmont farmhouse, furnished with early 20th-C country-style furniture, has two rooms with a terrace and another room that leads directly into the garden. The hostess was a pioneer in this region as regards family hospitality. The breakfast, consisting of sweet and nonsweet items, is served in a special dining room.

Accommodation
Guestrooms: *3 (1 single, 1 double and 1 triple room), private bath; additional bed on request*
Services & Amenities: *French spoken; rooms cleaned every day; tourist information; terrace; garden; smokers welcome; private parking*
Rates: *single €€, double €€, triple €€€. Additional bed supplement €. Children under 3 free. Discounts for extended stays -10%*
Credit cards: *not accepted*
Pets: yes

La Ca' Cita TCI 10%
Elena Migliassi
via Montà 6
14010 Cortazzone (AT)
tel. and fax 0141 995176
elenamigliassi@hotmail.com
www.lacacita.supereva.it
• Case Piemontesi-B&B Asti
tel. and fax 0141 670918
marzeppa@tin.it
www.terredasti.it/bed&breakfast.htm
Open: March to December

This little villa, furnished with simple-style furniture, is located in the center of town. The Cortazzone Valleys are noted not only for their truffles but also for their religious complexes (San Secondo, Colle Don Bosco and Vezzolano) and numerous little churches that are also very interesting to visit.

Accommodation
Guestrooms: *2 doubles, also single occupancy, private bath; additional bed on request*
Services & Amenities: *English spoken; rooms cleaned every day; complimentary tourist information; babysitting service; kitchenette; bike rental; garden; smokers welcome; private parking*
Rates: *single €€, double €€. Additional bed supplement €. Discounts for extended stays*
Credit cards: *not accepted*
Pets: yes

La Fiorita
Agnes Curbis
via Vanara 37
14010 Cortazzone (AT)
tel. 0141 995287
mob. 338 9537304, 340 4765392
acurbis@katamail.com
www.bedandbreakfastalp.it
Open: 23 March to 21 June and 7 July to 31 December

ACCOMMODATION
Guestrooms: *2 (1 single and 1 double, shared bath); additional bed on request*
Services & Amenities: *English, French and Spanish are spoken; rooms cleaned every three days; complimentary tourist information; kitchen use by request; garden; smokers welcome; private parking*
Rates: *single €€, double €€€. Additional bed supplement €. Children under 3 free. Discounts for extended stays*
Credit cards: *not accepted*
Pets:

This late-19th-century country home, completely restructured by the owners according to the local traditions, is surrounded by a large garden that has nice trees and, also, a

seedling nursery. Breakfast, which is served in the kitchen-living room, consists of typical products, including sweets, salami and various types of cheese. This B&B is located 18 km from Asti, in the center of an area that has lots of interesting things to see.

COSTIGLIOLE D'ASTI (ASTI)

Casa Prunotto
Virginia Prunotto
Strada Prunotto 2
14055 Costigliole d'Asti (AT)
tel. and fax 0141 969526
mob. 348 7328957
casaprunotto@tiscalinet.it
Open: April to November
• Case Piemontesi-B&B Asti
tel. and fax 0141 670918
marzeppa@tin.it
www.terredasti.it/bed&breakfast.htm

ACCOMMODATION
Guestrooms: *2 (1 single and 1 double, private bath); additional bed on request*
Services & Amenities: *English spoken; rooms cleaned every day; complimentary tourist information; bike rental; kitchenette; garden; smokers welcome; private parking*
Rates: *single €€, double €€€. Additional bed supplement €. Discounts for extended stays*
Credit cards: *not accepted*
Pets:

A part of this recently restructured 19th-century Piedmont house, located in the Costigliole community, is equipped for providing B&B. There are two guestrooms with bath and a small room with cooking facilities, a fireplace and TV. The Piedmont style furnishings include period furniture. Breakfast, which includes typical, genuine sweets, salami and various types of local cheese, is served in the reserved dining room.

Cascina Matiot
Eugenio Fogliati
strada Bionzo 9
14055 Costigliole d'Asti (AT)
tel. 0141 968575
cascinamatiot@tin.it
digilander.iol.it/cascinamatiot
• Case Piemontesi-B&B Asti
tel. and fax 0141 670918
marzeppa@tin.it
www.terredasti.it/bed&breakfast.htm
Open all year

ACCOMMODATION
Guestrooms: *3 doubles, also single occupancy, private bath*
Services & Amenities: *English spoken; rooms cleaned every 3 days; tourist information; Internet access; garden; smokers welcome; private parking*
Rates: *single €€, double €€€. Additional bed supplement €. Children under 3 free*
Credit cards: *accepted*
Pets:

This house, surrounded by vineyards, provides a nice panoramic view of the Alta Langa hills, with the profile of the Monferrato hills in the background. Dating back to the early 20th C, this typical rural house, with its face brick, has been restructured with natural, high-quality materials. The furnishings are refined and essential, the environment is quiet and comfortable, and the breakfast is especially nice.

Craveggia (Verbania-Cusio-Ossola)

Craveggia B&B
Lora Gubetta
via Fratelli Piazza 32
28852 Craveggia (VB)
tel. 0324 98172
Open all year

This B&B (900 m asl) is just 5 minutes from the center of Craveggio. The roofs in this characteristic village are all shingled with thin slabs of the local rock, called "pioda". The village square is a sort of "Square of the Miracles" because its structure resembles Pisa. The guestrooms have modern furniture, and one of the rooms has a balcony. The continental breakfast is served in a plain room reserved for the guests. On request, guided visits of the town and naturalistic excursions can be arranged.

Accommodation
Guestrooms: *3 doubles, also single occupancy, shared bath; additional bed on request*
Services & Amenities: *rooms cleaned every day; complimentary tourist information; garden; smokers welcome; private parking*
Minimum stay: *3 nights*
Rates: *single €€, double €€. Additional bed supplement €. Discounts for groups*
Credit cards: *not accepted*
Pets: 🚫

Cremolino (Alessandria)

L'Alloro
Monica Carosio
via Belletti 53
15010 Cremolino (AL)
tel. and fax 0143 821026
monicacarosio@virgilio.it
Open: May to December

Accommodation
Guestrooms: *2 (1 double bedroom and 1 double, shared bath)*
Services & Amenities: *French and English are spoken; rooms cleaned every day; complimentary tourist information; garden; smokers welcome; private parking*
Rates: *single €, double €€. Discounts for children -20%*
Credit cards: *not accapted*
Pets: ✓

This beautiful 18th-century country house, which used to be the castle farmhouse, is surrounded by charming vineyards. The early 20th-century furniture helps create a nice friendly atmosphere. The hostess is fond of reading and pottery painting. The guests can also enjoy the garden. The Italian breakfast is served in the dining room.

Cumiana (Turin)

La Fiola
Christina Bergamasco
strada Fiola 8
10040 Cumiana (TO)
tel. 011 9058750, fax 011 9003484
giuseppebergamasco@libero.it
www.bedandbreakfastlafiola.com
• **ScopriPiemonte**
tel. 0121 559182, 347 3651593
fax 0121 559182
bnbscopripiemonte@tiscali.it
Open all year

Before it was converted into a villa by its present owner, an English lady, this B&B used to be an old, early 20th-C farmhouse. The owners live on the first floor, while the ground floor, with its entrance, three bedrooms, living room with TV and large kitchen, is reserved for the guests, who also have use of a see-saw, for the children and a barbeque. The surrounding area has lots of mushrooms.

Accommodation
Guestrooms: *3 doubles, also single occupancy, private bath*
Services & Amenities: *French, English, Spanish and Portuguese are spoken; rooms cleaned every day; complimentary tourist information; baby-sitting service; bike rental; terrace; Internet access; garden; smokers welcome; private parking*
Rates: *single €, double €€*
Credit cards: *not accepted*
Pets: 🚫

U Tej
Glady Fassetta
via Provinciale 57
10040 Cumiana (TO)
tel. 011 9059561
glady.fassetta@tiscali.it
web.tiscali.it/u_tej_bed_breakfast
• ScopriPiemonte
tel. 0121 559182, 347 3651593
fax 0121 559182
bnbscopripiemonte@tiscali.it
Open: April to September

Accommodation
Guestrooms: *3 (also single occupancy, 1 with private bath and 2 with shared bath); additional bed on request*
Services & Amenities: *French and English are spoken; rooms cleaned every day; tourist info; parking*
Rates: *single €, double €. Additional bed supplement €. Children under 3 -50%*
Credit cards: *not accepted*
Pets: ✓

This traditional farmhouse surrounded by woods, has a garden, a vegetable garden and fruit trees. Being just a short distance from the Tre Denti Mountain Park, U Tej makes the perfect starting point for trekking or bike riding. The independent part of the house reserved for the guests includes a living room with a library and TV, and a large kitchen, where the hostess offers a rich breakfast consisting of genuine products.

Cuorgnè (Turin)

La Maddalena
Giusy Bellocchi
località Ronchi Maddalena 17
10082 Cuorgnè (TO)
tel. 0124 68568, mob. 349 4640393
fax 0124 666597
www.bedandbreakfastalp.it
• ScopriPiemonte
tel. 0121 559182, mob. 347 3651593
fax 0121 559182
bnbscopripiemonte@tiscali.it
Open: mid-September to April and mid-May to late October

This simple house, which is 3 km from the center of Cuorgnè, is surrounded by woods, and also has a vegetable garden, fruit trees, and small domestic animals. Guest accommodation includes a double bedroom with fireplace. There is also a living room and a large kitchen with a wood-burning oven. Breakfast features typical, genuine products, as well as biscuits and sweet and nonsweet cakes and pies.

Accommodation
Guestrooms: *2 (1 single and 1 double bedroom, shared bath); additional bed on request*
Services & Amenities: *French and English are spoken; rooms cleaned every day; complimentary tourist information; kitchen use by request; lunch & dinner reservations; garden; smokers welcome; private parking*
Rates: *single €, double €€. Additional bed supplement €. Children under 3 free*
Credit cards: *not accepted*
Pets: ✓

Divignano (Novara)

Cascina Motto TCI 10%
Roberta Plevani
via Marzabotto 7
28010 Divignano (NO)
tel. and fax 0321 995350
david_robi@katamail.com
www.casepiemontesi_novara.vze.com
• Case Piemontesi-B&B Asti
tel. and fax 0141 670918
marzeppa@tin.it
www.terredasti.it/bed&breakfast.htm
Open: Easter to mid-November

Accommodation
Guestrooms: *1 double and 1 dépendance (2/4 beds), private bath*
Services & Amenities: *English and German are spoken; rooms cleaned every 3 days; complimentary tourist information; kitchenette; Internet access; garden; smokers welcome; private parking*
Minimum stay: *2 nights*
Rates: *double €€€, dépendance €€€-€€€€. Additional bed supplement €. Children under 2 free; 3 to 12 -30%*
Credit cards: *not accepted*
Pets: ✓

In the house itself, this old, restructured farmhouse has one guest bedroom, while in the two-story dèpendance, there's a bedroom, a small living room, a patio and a bathroom. All the rooms have plain but very nice furnishings. The continental breakfast is either served in the family dining room or outside, when the weather's nice. The guests can enjoy the large garden, which has a bocce court, volleyball facilities and a swimming pool.

Formazza (Verbania-Cusio-Ossola)

Zumsteg
Famiglia Lucia Sormani
località Ponte
28863 Formazza (VB)
tel. 0324 63080
fax 0324 63251
sormani.lucia@bedbreakfastalp.it
www.bedbreakfastalp.it
Closed: May, October and November

This traditional "walzer" house, with its typical furnishings and warm wood-paneled walls, provides the ideal opportunity for enjoying this valley's clear, clean air. The cozy living room,

which is warmed by the presence of a characteristic stone stove, is great for both spending pleasant evenings and for having breakfast, which consists of such local products as various cheeses made by the valley cooperatives and traditional baked sweets.

Accommodation
Guestrooms: *3 doubles, shared bath; additional bed on request*
Services & Amenities: *English, French and German are spoken; rooms cleaned every 3 days; complimentary tourist information; garden*
Rates: *single €, double €€. Children under 3 free; 4 to 12 - 10%*
Credit cards: *not acceppted*
Pets:

Gignese (Verbania-Cusio-Ossola)

B&B La Tavernetta
Graziella Pessina
via Mottino 36, località Alpino
28836 Gignese (VB)
tel. and fax 0323 20473
bbgraziellape@yahoo.it
www.bedbreakfastalp.it
Closed: 15 January to 15 February, October and November

Accommodation
Guestrooms: *3 doubles, also single occupancy, private bath; additional bed on request*
Services & Amenities: *French and English are spoken; room cleaned every 3 days; complimentary tourist information; kitchen use by request; bike rental; educational courses by request; garden; smokers welcome*
Rates: *single €€, double €€€. Additional bed supplement €. Children under 10 age -30%. Discounts for extended stays*
Credit cards: *not accepted*
Pets:

This B&B, a typical 1930's alpine home, is at 800 m asl, in a residential area, located 3 km from Gignese, near the intermediate Stresa-Mottarone telferage station. The guestrooms have modern furniture, flower decorations and a view of the local vegetation. Breakfast is served in a panoramic dining room reserved for the guests, who also have use of the two gardens that are furnished with deck chairs and ping-pong tables. Those who like sports can take some nice bike rides with the mountain bikes furnished by the host family. Then, nearby, there is a riding-school, tennis courts and a golf course.

Grazzano Badoglio (Asti)

Cascina Dea
Diana Scapolan
via Cascine Piccinini 6/a
14035 Grazzano Badoglio (AT)
tel. and fax 0141 921939
cascinadea@aruba.it
www.cascinadea.it
• Case Piemontesi-B&B Asti
tel. and fax 0141 670918
marzeppa@tin.it
www.terredasti.it/bed&breakfast.htm
Open all year

TCI 10%

This 18th-century farmhouse is located on a large, secular farm that also has a small, 16th-century church, which is consecrated to the patron saint of the farmers. The guestrooms, which are in the family home, have rustic or bamboo furniture. Guests have use of a fully-equipped kitchen. Then there is the small independent apartment, which also has a small kitchen. Breakfast features sweet and nonsweet items and is served on the veranda. There are also two menages on the property, a lake for sports fishing and a swimming pool.

Accommodation
Guestrooms: *3 doubles with shared bath and 1 mini-apartment; additional bed on request*
Services & Amenities: *English spoken; rooms cleaned every 3 days; tourist information; bike rental; educational courses by request; kitchen use by request; horse-riding excursions; terrace; garden; smokers welcome; private parking*
Rates: *single €€, double €€€. Discounts for children*
Credit cards: *not accepted*
Pets:

Isola d'Asti (Asti)

Casa di Rosa
via Valtiglione 53
14057 Isola d'Asti (AT)
tel. 0141 958430, fax 011 71195
mob. 328 3737488
casadirosa@inwind.it
• **Friendly Home-Gli Amici del B&B**
tel. 02 860147, fax 02 875860
friendlymilano@dada.it
tel. and fax 011 9536376
fhrivoli@virgilio.it
Open: 15 May to late October

This beautiful, spacious, independent house in the heart of Monferrato at the foot of a vineyard has a remarkable panoramic view of the gentle Asti hills: the veritable temple of Piedmont enological gastronomy. The rustic furniture helps create a very warm, friendly atmosphere. The buffet breakfast is served in the living room, which has a fireplace. Tasting the fine wines in the annexed wine cellar is highly recommended.

Accommodation
Guestrooms: *1 double, also single occupancy, private bath; additional bed on request*
Services & Amenities: *rooms cleaned every day; tourist information; terrace; garden; private parking*
Rates: *single €€, double €€. Children under 2 free*
Credit cards: *not accepted*
Pets: ✓

Le Querce
Elena Fogliotti
via Valletanaro 11
14057 Isola d'Asti (AT)
mob. 340 3483475
fogliottielena@hotmail.com
www.bedbreakfastalp.it
Open: March to November
• **Case Piemontesi-B&B Asti**
tel. and fax 0141 670918
marzeppa@tin.it
www.terredasti.it/bed&breakfast.htm

TCI 10%

This large, restructured, late-19th-century farmhouse, with it original architectural features, is located halfway between Alba and Asti. It's surrounded by large park and provides very large guestrooms with an independent entrance and a terrace. The sober, elegant rooms have classic Piedmont furniture. The typical, abundant breakfast features 100% organic products and is served either in the guestrooms or on the terrace.

Accommodation
Guestrooms: *2 doubles, also single occupancy, private bath; additional bed on request* ♿
Services & Amenities: *English and French are spoken; rooms cleaned every 3 days; complimentary tourist information; terrace; smokers welcome; garden; private parking*
Rates: *single €, double €€. Additional bed supplement €. Children under 6 free. Discounts for extended stays -20%*
Credit cards: *not accepted*
Pets: ✓

Lerma (Alessandria)

Nonna Teresa B&B
Teresa Odicino
via G.B. Baldo 3
15070 Lerma (AL)
tel. 0143 877397
nonnateresa@katamail.com
Open: 15 March to 31 October

Located on the second floor of a modern villa surrounded by a garden, this B&B is furnished with early 20th-century furniture. The villa is located in the upper part of the old town, in a hilly area on the edge of the Capanne di Marcarolo Park. The continental breakfast also includes typical sweet items and is served in a dining room with TV and fireplace reserved for the guests. Besides the several riding-schools located nearby, guests can also take bike rides and do some hunting and fishing.

Accommodation
Guestrooms: *3 double bedrooms, also single occupancy, shared bath*
Services & Amenities: *rooms cleaned every day; tourist information; garden; smokers welcome; private parking*
Rates: *single €€, double €€€. Discounts for extended stays*
Credit cards: *not accepted*
Pets: ✗

Lesa (Novara)

Villa Lidia
via Ferrari 7/9
28040 Lesa (NO)
tel. 02 58103076, 0322 7096
fax 02 34973214
patrizia.lanfranconi@consultami.com
Closed: January and February

This B&B, which is located in an early 20th-century villa surrounded by a large garden with tall trees, is 200 meters from Lake Maggiore and less than 1 km from Lesa. The three guestrooms have period furnishings and lead onto a single terrace. The abundant English-style breakfast is served in the dining room reserved for the guests. Guests are also welcome to use the family living room, which has a TV and VCR. There's a tennis club nearby that also has a swimming pool. There are also facilities for doing some sailing and canoeing.

Accommodation
Guestrooms: *3 doubles, also single occupancy, private bath; additioal bed on request*
Services & Amenities: *French, English and Spanish spoken; rooms cleaned every day; tourist info; garden; smokers welcome; parking*
Minimum stay: *2 nights*
Rates: *single €€, double €€€. Additional bed supplement €. Children under 3 free. Discounts for extended stays*
Credit cards: *accepted*
Pets:

Mappano (Turin)

Cascina Argentera
• Bed and Breakfast Service
tel. 011 8123675, fax 011 8140861
torinoservice@yahoo.it
Open: January to October

This B&B occupies part of the second floor of a large, very fascinating, 18th-C farmhouse situated in a quiet locality just 7 km from the Turin airport. The private chapel (once annexed to the convent located in one of the wings of the farmhouse), the wood-burning oven, the old country furniture and the vegetable garden, orchard and large garden, all contribute to creating an atmosphere of many years ago.

Accommodation
Guestrooms: *3 double, also single occupancy, shared bath*
Services & Amenities: *English, French and German are spoken; rooms cleaned every day; complimentary tourist information; garden; smokers welcome; private parking*
Rates: *single €€, double €€€*
Credit cards: *not accepted*
Pets:

Masera (Verbania-Cusio-Ossola)

Casa Tomà
Elena Tomà
via Menogno 5
28855 Masera (VB)
tel. and fax 0324 232084
casatoma@ossola.it
Closed: November

This house is located in the small mall of Masera, a town located in the heart of the Ossola Valleys. The town leads into the Vigezzo Valley, better known as the "valley of the painters" because of the local artistic tradition. This B&B, restored in an excellent manner, is particularly well furnished, especially as concerns the furniture and fabrics. It also has antique parquet, a fireplace and a slate-tiled roof. Guests also have the use of a convenient local laundry and a few bicycles.

Accommodation
Guestrooms: *1 double, also single occupancy, private bath; additional bed on request*
Services & Amenities: *English and French are spoken; rooms cleaned every 3 days; complimentary tourist information; kitchen use by request; bike rental; smokers welcome*
Minimum stay: *2 nights*
Rates: *single €€, double €€. Additional bed supplement €*
Credit cards: *not accepted*
Pets:

Moncalieri (Turin)

Il Piüns
Anna Maria and Francesco Calvi
strada Costalunga 6
10024 Moncalieri (TO)
tel. 011 642549, fax 011 6408505
mob. 335 6104399
fracalvi@tin.it
Open all year

This 18th-C farmhouse is situated in a quiet, sunny location surrounded by an 8,000 sq.m secular park. The B&B is set up in a rustic annex – formerly where potted lemon plants were kept – that has period furniture.

Accommodation
Guestrooms: *3 (1 suite, 2 doubles, also single occupancy, private bath)* ♿
Services & Amenities: *English and French are spoken; rooms cleaned every 3 days; tourist info; kitchen use by request; dinner reservation; horse-riding excursions; Internet access; garden; smokers welcome; private parking*
Rates: *single €€, double €€€. Discounts for extended stays*
Credit cards: *accepted*
Pets:

The owners of the house are very fond of period furniture, as well as modern art and jewelry.

Breakfast features sweet and nonsweet items on request and is served either in the dining room or on the terrace. Guests can enjoy horseback riding as well as archery.

Mongrando (Biella)

Châlet Bessa
Reana Gianola
via Martiri della Libertà 131
13888 Mongrando (BI)
tel. 015 2551270, mob. 349 4657720
bbbessa@interfree.it
Open: 1 March to 31 October

Accommodation
Guestrooms: *2 (1 double bedroom and 1 triple room, shared bath); additional bed on request*
Services & Amenities: *English and French are spoken; rooms cleaned every 3 days; complimentary tourist information; terrace; garden; smokers welcome; private parking*
Rates: *double €€, triple €€. Additional bed supplement €. Discounts for members of naturalistic associations*
Credit cards: *not accepted*
Pets:

This restructured farmhouse, with its rustic furnishings, is located on the undulating Bessa plateau, near the Bressa nature reserve, where it offers a beautiful view of the Biella Mountains. The hosts, who are nature-lovers, will gladly

help the guests plan one or more of the area's many possible hiking and mountain-bike excursions. In nearby Mongrano – the land of soft goods – guests can buy fine cloths and linens directly from the factory.

Montechiaro d'Asti (Asti)

Il Ghiro TCI 10%
Giuliana Fernicola
via Mairano 47
14025 Montechiaro d'Asti (AT)
tel. 0141 999731, mob. 328 2147394
ilghiro@virgilio.it
www.ilghiro.com
• Case Piemontesi-B&B Asti
tel. and fax 0141 670918
marzeppa@tin.it
www.terredasti.it/bed&breakfast.htm
Open: March to November

Accommodation
Guestrooms: *3 doubles, also single occupancy, private bath; additional bed on request*
Services & Amenities: *French spoken; rooms cleaned every day; complimentary tourist information; bike rental; Internet access; garden; smokers welcome; private parking*
Rates: *single €€, double €€€. Additional bed supplement €.*
Credit cards: *not accepted*
Pets:

This B&B is hosted in a modern, Piedmont rustic style house located right in the heart of the

Piedmont countryside, just a few kilometers from Asti. There are three guestrooms with an independent entrance and traditional local style furnishings. Breakfast consists of local nonsweet products and a selection of genuine sweet items.

Montemagno (Asti)

Il Monferrato
Manuela and Carla Lombardo
via Sottoripa 3
14030 Montemagno (AT)
tel. 0141 63162
manuela@monferratoturismo.it
www.monferratoturismo.it
• Case Piemontesi-B&B Asti
tel. and fax 0141 670918
marzeppa@tin.it
www.terredasti.it/bed&breakfast.htm
Open: April to December

This house, built in 1899, has been in the family for three generations. The B&B guestrooms are two large and comfortable double rooms, furnished in a simple, country style. The guests have use of Internet, a gym, a solarium terrace, a ping-pong table and bicycles.

Accommodation
Guestrooms: *2 doubles, also single occupancy, private bath. Child's bed available*
Services & Amenities: *English, French and German are spoken; rooms cleaned every day; complimentary tourist information; bike rental; terrace; garden; smokers welcome; private parking*
Rates: *single €, double €€. Additional bed supplement €. Children under 2 free, 3 to 6 -50%. Discounts for extended stays -10%*
Credit cards: *not accepted*
Pets: allowed (symbol)

Ovada (Alessandria)

Villa Schella
Maria Zagnoli
via per Molare
15076 Ovada (AL)
tel. 0143 80324, fax 0143 824343
mob. 333 4802393
schella @libero.it
Open: Easter to 15 November

This 19th-century farmhouse, which is inserted in the Dimore Storiche and Castelli Aperti circuit, is set in a secular park just two kilometers from the Ovada castle. The B&B is located in a dépendance. Guests can enjoy and relax in the park with its swimming pool; they also have the use of rental bikes, tennis courts and nearby riding-school. And there's a golf course just 10 km away.

Accommodation
Guestrooms: *3 doubles, also single occupancy, private bath; additional bed on request*
Services & Amenities: *French and English are spoken; rooms cleaned every 3 days; complimentary tourist information; bike rental; garden; smokers welcome; private parking*
Rates: *double €€€€. Additional bed supplement €. Discounts for children.*
Credit cards: *not accepted*
Pets: allowed (symbol)

Breakfast is usually served on the panoramic veranda.

Perosa Argentina (Turin)

Clara's Lodge
Clara Pagano
via Monte Grappa 7
10063 Perosa Argentina (TO)
tel. 0121 804009, mob. 338 5349613
clarapagano@alpimedia.it
• ScopriPiemonte
tel. 0121 559182, mob. 347 3651593
fax 0121 559182
bnbscopripiemonte@tiscali.it
Closed: April and from 22 September to 29 November

This B&B is located in the center of Perosa Argentina, a small village situated at the junction of the Chisone and Germanasca Valleys, not far from the skiing localities. The house is surrounded by a garden with tall trees and a pond with water lilies. Breakfast features typical products, genuine sweet items, marmalade and organic honey, and is served in the living room, the original nucleus of the building dated from the end of the 18th C The hostess is happy to act as a guide for visiting the village.

Accommodation
Guestrooms: *2 doubles, also single occupancy, private bath. Child's bed available*
Services & Amenities: *French and English are spoken; rooms cleaned every day; complimentary tourist information; garden; smokers welcome*
Rates: *single €€, double €€. Additional bed supplement €. Discounts for extended stays*
Credit cards: *not accepted*
Pets: not allowed (symbol)

Racconigi (Cuneo)

Tenuta Berroni Tci 10%
Alessandra Castelbarco
Visconti
12035 Racconigi (CN)
tel. and fax 0172 813186
tenutaberroni@brainy.it
• Bed and Breakfast Service
tel. 011 8123675, fax 011 8140861
torinoservice@yahoo.it
Open all year

This 18h-C villa with a French taste and period furniture is located in a 3 acre park, not far from the Racconigi royal palace. Countess Castelbarco Visconti organizes guided visits to the part of the villa that's open to the public. Guests have use of satellite TV, a refrigerator, a microwave oven, a boiler, a small living room, a library and a swimming pool. Breakfast is either served in the small living room or in the family kitchen. Not far away there's a golf course.

Accommodation
Guestrooms: *3 (2 double bedrooms, also single occupancy, shared bath; 1 suite, private bath); child's bed available*
Services & Amenities: *French, English and German are spoken; rooms cleaned every day; tourist information; garden; smokers welcome; private parking*
Rates: *single €€€, double €€€€, suite €€€€. Child's bed supplement €*
Credit cards: *not accepted*
Pets:

Refrancore (Asti)

Cascina La Gioia Tci 10%
Marisa Zeppa
via Cascina la Gioia 49
14030 Refrancore (AT)
tel. and fax 0141 670918
marzeppa@tin.it
www.cascinalagioia.it
• Case Piemontesi-B&B Asti
tel. and fax 0141 670918
marzeppa@tin.it
www.terredasti.it/bed&breakfast.htm
Open: March to November

This B&B, located in a panoramic position along the "wine road," is surrounded by the orchard, woods and vineyards that are on the Monferrato hills. The B&B is perfectly integrated in the Tessitore family farm, which is noted for its production of low-environmental-impact fruit. Breakfast consists of lots of typical products and is served in the living room, which has a fireplace and the same type of "grandmother" furniture that's in the guestrooms.

Accommodation
Guestrooms: *3 double, also single occupancy, private bath; additional bed on request*
Services & Amenities: *French, English and German are spoken; rooms cleaned every 3 days; complimentary tourist information; baby-sitting service; bike rental; horse-riding excursions; Internet access; garden; smokers welcome; private parking*
Rates: *single €, double €€. Additional bed supplement €. Discounts for children and extended stays*
Credit cards: *not accepted*
Pets:

Revigliasco (Turin)

Rivoira Alta Tci 10%
Marisa Massano
strada Salairolo 81
10020 Revigliasco (TO)
tel. and fax 0141 208628
• Case Piemontesi-B&B Asti
tel. and fax 0141 670918
marzeppa@tin.it
www.terredasti.it/bed&breakfast.htm
Closed: 10 December to 1 April

Accommodation
Guestrooms: *2 doubles, also single occupancy, private bath*
Services & Amenities: *French spoken; rooms cleaned every day; complimentary tourist information; terrace; garden; smokers welcome; private parking*
Rates: *single €€€€, double €€€€*
Credit cards: *not accepted*
Pets:

This B&B, located on the top of a hill, provides an all-around view of the Langhe and Monferrato. The guestrooms are in the main house and all of them have a panoramic terrace, a mini-bar and a bath with hydromassage. The park has secular trees and a swimming pool with a dressing room. The breakfast is served on the veranda. The hostess is very fond of flowers, which are present everywhere.

Robella (Asti)

Il Gelso
Sergio Corno
via Polo Nord 1
14020 Robella (AT)
tel. 0141 998154, fax 0141 530160
mob. 348 1525265
corno.c@libero.it, www.ilgelso.at.it
• Case Piemontesi-B&B Asti
tel. and fax 0141 670918
marzeppa@tin.it
www.terredasti.it/bed&breakfast.htm
Open: February to November

In 1740, this used to be the Vagiano farmstead on the ancient farm of the Robilant Counts. But, in 1893, it became the property of the Corno family. This B&B is surrounded by woods and vineyards. The guestrooms, with their period furniture and coordinated fabrics, create an elegant atmosphere. Farm holiday with a manege just 200 meters away.

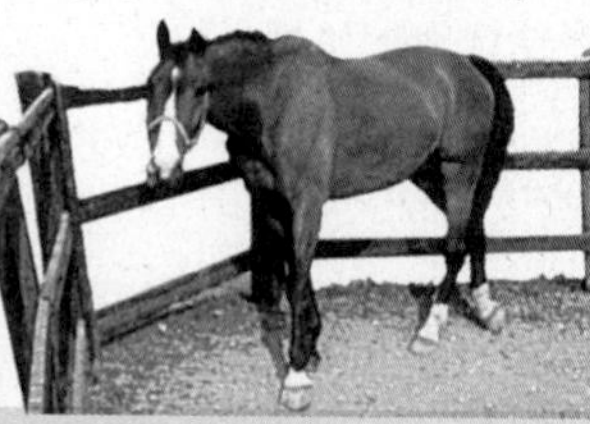

Accommodation
Guestrooms: *3 doubles, also single occupancy, private bath; additional bed on request*
Services & Amenities: *English and French are spoken; rooms cleaned every day; tourist information; dinner reservation; terrace; garden; smokers welcome; private parking*
Rates: *single €, double €€. Additional bed supplement €*
Credit cards: *not accepted*
Pets:

Rocca d'Arazzo (Asti)

Borgo Partiquilär
Davide Passarino
via Montemarzo 9-11-13
località Santa Caterina
14030 Rocca d'Arazzo (AT)
tel. and fax 0141 40823
borgopartiquilar@ridap.it
www.ridap.it/borgopartiquilar
• Case Piemontesi-B&B Asti
tel. and fax 0141 670918
marzeppa@tin.it
www.terredasti.it/bed&breakfast.htm
Open: May to late November

This typical Asti agricultural complex consisting of various 19th-C farm buildings is surrounded by the hill vegetation on a ridge that extends between Langa and Monferrato. There are two suites for the guests and an apartment with an equipped kitchen, and reading and game rooms, a hi-fi set and TV. All the rooms have classic, elegant furnishings. Also available is a sauna, an equipped gym, a swimming pool with hydromassage, a bar and games for children. The private wine cellar is very interesting, with its collection of prized wines and pantry full of preserves and local specialties.

Accommodation
Guestrooms: *2 suites, 1 mini-apartment; additional bed on request* ♿
Services & Amenities: *English, French and German are spoken; rooms cleaned every day; tourist info; kitchen use by request; terrace; garden; smokers welcome; educational courses by request; private parking*
Rates: *suite €€€, mini-apartment €€€€. Additional bed supplement €. Discounts for children and extended stays*
Credit cards: *not accepted*
Pets:

Rosignano Monferrato (Alessandria)

I Castagnoni
Filippo Bianchi
via Castagnoni 67
15030 Rosignano Monferrato (AL)
tel. 0142 488404, fax 02 70031477
icastagnoni@hotmail.com
www.icastagnoni.it
Open: 1 April to late November

Surrounded by the Monferrato vineyards, this B&B occupies part of an 18th-C villa that has frescoes, a small annexed church and an Italian garden. The guests have the use of a reading room, a fitness room, Internet and a beautiful veranda. An abundant continental breakfast, with sweet items and natural specialties, is served on this veranda. The host is an expert when it comes to fine wines.

Accommodation
Guestrooms: *2 doubles, also single occupancy, shared bath*
Services & Amenities: *English and French are spoken; rooms cleaned every day; complimentary tourist information; lunch & dinner reservations; bike rental; Internet access; garden; smokers welcome; private parking*
Rates: *single €€, double €€€. Children under 10 free*
Credit cards: *not accepted*
Pets:

Sanfrè (Cuneo)

• **Bed & Breakfast Italia**
Code P6
tel. 06 6878618, fax 06 6878619
info@bbitalia.it
www.bbitalia.it
Open: March to October

This large villa surrounded by a well-tended garden is located in Sanfrè. The guest accommodation consists in two double rooms with TV, large balcony, and private bathroom with shower. It boasts nineteenth-century Italian and French furnishings, coffered ceilings and walls with trompe l'oeil frescoes depicting architectural motifs. Extra beds for children under two are available. Pets are welcome.

Accommodation
Guestrooms: *2 doubles*
Services & Amenities: *English and German are spoken; rooms cleaned every 3 days; tourist information; terrace; private parking*
Minimum stay: *2 nights*
Rates: €€
Credit cards: VISA MC *Bancomat*
Pets: allowed

Settime (Asti)

Locanda dei Tigli
Angiola Dezzani and Alberto Bertone
via S. Rocco 2
14020 Settime (AT)
mob. 335 6450557
info@locandadeitigli.it
www.locandadeitigli.it
Open: March to December

This B&B is in a restructured, late 19th-C farmhouse, which is nicely furnished with simple furniture. It's located in a quiet spot on a plateau in a hill town just 10 km from Asti. The abundant greenery that surrounds the house includes a 100-year-old magnolia tree and linden trees. Guests have the use of a common room with fireplace, a small swimming pool and ping-pong table. There is also a manege nearby.

Accommodation
Guestrooms: *3 doubles, also single occupancy (1 with private bath, 2 with shared bath); additional bed on request*
Services & Amenities: *French and English are spoken; rooms cleaned every day; tourist info; bike rental; garden; smokers welcome; parking*
Rates: *single* €€, *double* €€€. *Additional bed supplement* €. *Discounts for extended stays*
Credit cards: *not accepted*
Pets: allowed

Stresa (Verbania-Cusio-Ossola)

Villa La Camana
Piera Murcio
via per Gignese 10
28838 Stresa (VB)
tel. and fax 032 331553
mob. 348 0354315
Open: 1 April to 30 October

This villa built in the '70s is located in the high part of the city that dominates the Borromeo Gulf. The hosts, a retired couple, are particularly proud of the 5,000 sq.m garden that surrounds the house. The two guestrooms, with direct access from the garden, have 19th and early 20th-C furniture. The continental breakfast is served either in the living room or in the garden. Guests have the use of satellite TV and a very well-furnished library. There are tennis courts nearby.

Accommodation
Guestrooms: *2 doubles, also single occupancy, private bath* ♿
Services & Amenities: *English spoken; rooms cleaned every three days; complimentary tourist information; terrace; garden; smokers welcome; private parking*
Rates: *double* €€
Credit cards: *not accepted*
Pets: not allowed

TONCO (ASTI)

Casa Porrato
Bruno Porrato
via G. Bezzzo 9
14039 Asti
tel. 0141 991313, mob. 335 6440391
fax 0141 991313
• Case Piemontesi-B&B Asti
tel. and fax 0141 670918
marzeppa@tin.it
www.terredasti.it/bed&breakfast.htm
Closed: December to late February

This B&B, which is a few kilometers from Asti, is hosted in a farmhouse that was built in the '70s. It's surrounded by a large equipped meadow. The guestrooms have modern furniture. Breakfast, which features a large selection of typical local products, is served either in the living room or on the terrace. The host knows the area very well and will gladly provide any helpful advice the guests may need.

ACCOMMODATION
Guestrooms: *2 (1 double, also single occupancy, 1 triple; private bath)*
Services & Amenities: *French, English and German are spoken; rooms cleaned every day; complimentary tourist information; bike rental; garden; terrace; private parking; smokers welcome*
Rates: *single €€, double €€€. Children under 6 free. Discounts for extended stays*
Credit cards: *not accepted*
Pets:

TURIN

Aba
Giulio Barutti
corso Regina Margherita, 240
10144 Turin
tel. and fax 011 4371988
mob. 333 2553310
Closed: 15 December to 15 January and 15 June to 15 July

This apartment is located on the ground floor of a small 5-story building dating from the early 20th C The house, which has period furnishings, is located in the San Donato quarter and is just 5 tram stops from the old center. It's also conveniently close to the ring road. Breakfast is served either in the kitchen or in the living room. On request, the guests' car can be kept in the garage.

ACCOMMODATION
Guestrooms: *1 double, also single occupancy, shared bath; additional bed on request*
Services & Amenities: *French and Spanish are spoken; rooms cleaned every 3 days; tourist info; lunch & dinner reservations; smokers welcome*
Rates: *single €, double €€. Additional bed supplement €. Discounts for children -30%*
Credit cards: *not accepted*
Pets:

B&B 'I Giandujot
Annamaria Pitta
via Asiago 13
10142 Turin
tel. and fax 011 723411
mob. 338 9256082
annamariapitta@virgilio.it
• Friendly Home-Gli Amici del B&B
tel. 02 860147, fax 02 875860
friendlymilano@dada.it
tel. and fax 011 9536376
fhrivoli@virgilio.it
Closed: July and August

This comfortable apartment is located about 20 minutes from the old center. The small guest apartment, which is next to the family home, has an independent entrance, a large bedroom with a double bed, and a living room with a small kitchen corner and a TV. The Piedmont breakfast is also suitable for persons troubled by celiac disturbances.

ACCOMMODATION
Guestrooms: *1 double bedroom, also single occupancy, private bath; additional bed on request*
Services & Amenities: *rooms cleaned every 3 days; complimentary tourist information; kitchenette; educational courses by request; smokers welcome*
Rates: *single €€, double €€€. Children under 3 free*
Credit cards: *not accepted*
Pets:

B&B Gilda
Gilda Vernetti
via S. Bernardino 12
10141 Turin
tel. 011 375241, mob. 328 1825038
bebgilda@libero.it, www.bbgilda.it
Open: 7 January to late March, 13 May to 18 August, 16 September to 14 December

Accommodation
Guestrooms: *3 doubles with shared bathroom*
Services & Amenities: *French and English are spoken; rooms cleaned every 3 days; complimentary tourist information; terrace; smokers welcome*
Rates: *single €€, double €€. Children under 4 free*
Credit cards: *not accepted*
Pets:

This B&B is in a house built in the '20s, located in a lively area and is only 15 min from the old center. The hostess lives on the 1st floor and the guestrooms, with independent entrances, are on the 2nd floor. Two of the guestrooms have a terrace and one has a balcony.

Casa Rampone Ponzano TCI 10%
• Bed and Breakfast Service
tel. 011 8123675, fax 011 8140861
torinoservice@yahoo.it
Closed: July, August and December

This beautiful apartment is on the 2nd floor of a small, early 20th-C building that's only 100 m from the old center, near the Po River and Vittorio Square. Breakfast can be served in the living room. The guestrooms have balconies and are furnished with antique furniture. The guestrooms have a TV and a collection of new and old books.

Accommodation
Guestrooms: *2 (1 single and 1 double, shared bath)*
Services & Amenities: *rooms cleaned every day; complimentary tourist information; smokers welcome*
Minimum stay: *2 nights*
Rates: *single €€, double €€€*
Credit cards: *not accepted*
Pets:

Maria Clelia Moretti TCI 10%
via Sismonda 3
10145 Turin
tel. and fax 011 7495956
• Bed and Breakfast Service
tel. 011 8123675, fax 011 8140861
torinoservice@yahoo.it
Open: 1 February to 30 July and 1 October to 31 December

This '30s villa has a garden. Guests who like to be independent have a well-organized apartment on the second floor. Its two rooms have modern, functional furniture. The large kitchen has antique copper kitchenware. The beautiful veranda overlooks the park.

Accommodation
Guestrooms: *2 (1 single and 1 double, shared bath)*
Services & Amenities: *French, English, German and Spanish are spoken; rooms cleaned every 3 days; tourist information; smokers welcome*
Rates: *single €€, double €€€€*
Credit cards: *not accepted*
Pets:

Valdengo (Biella)

Il Talucco
Valentina Aimone
via R. Sanzio 31
13855 Valdengo (BI)
tel. and fax 015 881220
v.aimone@libero.it
www.iltalucco.interfree.it
Open all year

This lovingly-restored, 17th-C house has antique furnishings and paintings by local artists. The lively family that welcomes the guests includes grandfather Gianni and grandmother Quinette, who take care of the vegetable garden and of the regular garden. The family is happy to welcome guests who want a little peace and quiet in a family environment. Breakfast, with its local flavors, includes a rich selection of various types of tea.

Accommodation
Guestrooms: *3 doubles, private bath; additional bed on request*
Services & Amenities: *French, English, Spanish and Japanese are spoken; rooms cleaned every 3 days; complimentary tourist information; terrace; Internet access; smokers welcome; private parking*
Rates: *single €€, double €€. Additional bed supplement €. Children under 5 free. Discounts for extended stays*
Credit cards: *not accepted*
Pets:

Valfenera (Asti)

Le Albizie
Valerie Lamb
via Villanova 17
14017 Valfenera (AT)
tel. and fax 0141 939712
vlamb@lycos.it, web.tiscali.it/lealbizie
• Case Piemontesi-B&B Asti
tel. & fax 0141 670918, marzeppa@tin.it
www.terredasti.it/bed&breakfast.htm
Closed: 1 to 10 August
Open: March to November

This 1862 farmstead, which is just 25 km from Alba on the road that that leads to Roero, has been faithfully restored in

local style. The guestrooms have comfortable furniture, and every detail has been given very careful attention. Guests have the use of a ping-pong table, a small soccer field and a courtesy set. The abundant buffet breakfast of products in season is served in the living room. On request, guests can enjoy wine tasting.

Accommodation
Guestrooms: *1 double, private bath; additional bed on request*
Services & Amenities: *French and English are spoken; rooms cleaned every day; complimentary tourist information; terrace; Internet access; smokers welcome; private parking*
Minimum stay: *2 nights*
Rates: *single €€, double €€. Additional bed supplement €. Children under 10 free*
Credit cards: *not accepted*
Pets:

Verbania (Verbania-Cusio-Ossola)

Villa Cordelia
Remigia Basso Bert
via al Colleggio 10
28900 Verbania
tel. 0323 557919
Open: Easter to late October and Christmas holidays

This late 18th-C historic villa has hosted many illustrious guests, including Carducci and D'Annunzio. It's located just a short walk from villa Taranto and villa San Remigio, which are visible from the B&B's windows. The guests have the use of living and dining room on the first floor, as well as the large panoramic park. The ho-

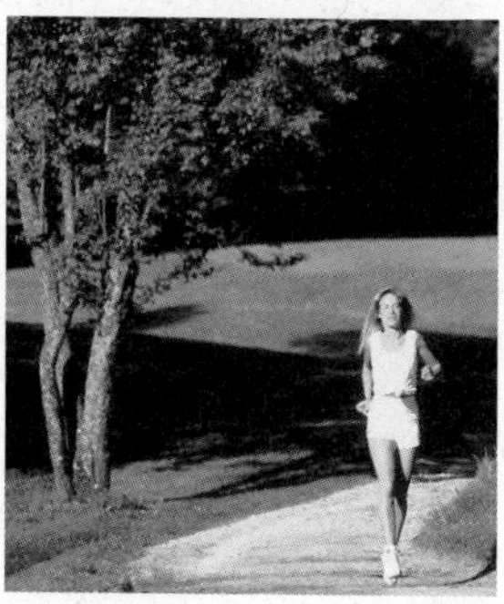

stess is fond of gardening and the history of religions.

Accommodation
Guestrooms: *3 doubles, also single occupancy, private bath; additional bed on request*
Services & Amenities: *French, English, German, Spanish and Portuguese are spoken; rooms cleaned every day; tourist information; baby-sitting service; terrace; garden; smokers welcome; private parking*
Minimum stay: *3 nights*
Rates: *single €€, double €€€. Additional bed supplement €€*
Credit cards: *not accepted*
Pets:

Villafranca d'Asti (Asti)

La Casa del Lillà
Kettou Zohra
regione Sengrado 48
14018 Villafranca d'Asti (AT)
tel. and fax 0141 942408
mob. 347 7580699
• Case Piemontesi-B&B Asti
tel. and fax 0141 670918
marzeppa@tin.it
www.terredasti.it/bed&breakfast.htm
Open: April to December

This late 19th-C farmhouse, which is just 10 minutes from the center of Asti, is located on a hill in the rural area just outside of town. The hosts manage a very dynamic farm. Guests can choose to have either sweet or nonsweet items for breakfast, which is served in the dining room. They also have the use of a common room, as well as the garden and three

or four bicycles. The guestroom, which has a TV and frigobar, also has a terrace.

Accommodation
Guestrooms: *1 double (also single occupancy, private bath); additional bed on request*
Services & Amenities: *English, French and Arabic are spoken; rooms cleaned every 3 days; tourist information; terrace; garden; smokers welcome; private parking*
Rates: *single €, double €€. Additional bed supplement €*
Credit cards: *not accepted*
Pets:

Lombardy

Bergamo

Casa di Graziella TCI 10%
Maria Grazia Ziliani
via dei Bastazi 1
24126 Bergamo
tel. 035 321622, mob. 339 8104977
mariagrazia.ziliani@libero.it
www.bedbreakfastalp.it
• Associazione Bergamo B&B
mob. 339 7845293
bergamobedandbreakfast@virgilio.it
Closed: June and July

The original sail shape of this modern condo with its private garden encloses a small, comfortable B&B. It's very close to the city airport and just a 10 minute bus ride from the city. It also makes a nice base of operations for business trips. Contributing to the informal, friendly atmosphere is the breakfast, which consists of natural cakes and biscuits.

Accommodation
Guestrooms: *2 (1 single and 1 double bedroom) shared bath; additional bed on request* ♿
Services & Amenities: *French and English are spoken; rooms cleaned every 3 days; complimentary tourist information; bike rental; terrace; smokers welcome; private parking*
Rates: *single €€, double €€€. Additional bed supplement €. Discounts for extended stays; children under 3 free*
Credit cards: *not accepted*
Pets: 🐕

Le Rondini B&B
Maria Luisa Piazzoli
via Finazzi 18
24127 Bergamo
tel. and fax 035 255812
marialuisa.piazzoli@tin.it
www.bedbreakfastalp.it
• Associazione Bergamo B&B
tel. 339 7845293
bergamobedandbreakfast@virgilio.it
Open all year

This B&B is located in a small rural spot just 10 minutes from the center of Bergamo. The restructured farm house is surrounded by vegetation, and the guests have a small, independent apartment in the upper-floor. This completely renovated apartment, in a warm rustic style, has a living room with a small kitchenette. In the summertime, guests can have breakfast on the large terrace that overlooks the garden.

Accommodation
Guestrooms: *1 mini-apartment*
Services & Amenities: *French spoken; rooms cleaned every 3 days; complimentary tourist information; kitchenette; bike rental; terrace; Internet access; garden; smokers welcome; private parking*
Rates: *single €€, double €€*
Credit cards: *not accepted*
Pets: 🐕

• **Bed & Breakfast Italia**
Code L014
tel. 06 6878618, fax 06 6878619
info@bbitalia.it
www.bbitalia.it
Closed: varies

An attic B&B located in a building in Bergamo's residential district. The spacious room has a TV, a small balcony and bathroom with shower. Completely self-contained, a staircase leads to the lower floor, where the owners live. Guests can have breakfast downstairs with the family, or privately in their room. A bus stops in front of the house which gets to the center in just 5 minutes. The ideal for tourists and business travelers.

ACCOMMODATION
Guestrooms: *1 double*
Services & Amenities: *English and Spanish are spoken; rooms cleaned every 3 days; tourist information; terrace; private parking*
Minimum stay: *2 nights*
Rates: €€
Credit cards: *Bancomat*
Pets:

BESOZZO (VARESE)

Cascina Durì
Nadia Passuello
via Massino 13 b, località Bogno
21023 Besozzo (VA)
tel. 0332 771883, mob. 347 9161011
cascinaduri@hotmail.com
www.anzwers.org/trade/cascinaduri
• **B&B Varese-Nel verde tra i laghi**
tel. 0331 260040, mob. 349 3519048
fax 0331 260040
iduenoci@hotmail.com
Open: March to November

This 18th-C farmhouse forms part of a group of farmhouses in the Val Clusone Park. The adjoining farm produces organic vegetables and cheese. Continental breakfast is served in the dining room. Modern furnishings.

ACCOMMODATION
Guestrooms: *3 doubles, also singles occupancy, private bath*
Services & Amenities: *English and German are spoken; rooms cleaned every 3 days; tourist info; smokers welcome; private parking*
Rates: *single €€, double €€€. Discounts for extended stays*
Credit cards: *not accepted*
Pets:

BORGHETTO LODIGIANO (LODI)

Mulino Sonia
località Barazzina
26812 Borghetto Lodigiano (LO)
• **Ass. Barbarossa-B&B nel Lodigiano**
tel. 0371 897998, mob. 347 8664843
stefania.bordoni@tiscali.it
http://web.tiscali.it/bordoni53
Open all year

Located in the Barazzina di Borghetto Lodigiano district, between Lodi, Piacenza and Pavia, this B&B is inside a restructured, 19th-century mill that has a large garden, is surrounded by countryside and is situated on the shore of a stream. Breakfast consists of cakes, fresh fruit, marmalades and yoghurt and gives preference to organic products. Refreshments can be provided on request, and guests also have the use of bicycles.

ACCOMMODATION
Guestrooms: *2 (1 double bedroom and 1 double, private bath); additional bed on request*
Services & Amenities: *French and English are spoken; rooms cleaned every day; complimentary tourist information; lunch & dinner reservations; bike rental; garden; smokers welcome; private parking*
Rates: *single €€, double €€€. Additional bed supplement €*
Credit cards: *accepted*
Pets:

Borgoforte (Mantua)

Corte Cascina
Chiara and Fausta Scaravelli
via San Cataldo 2
46030 Borgoforte (MN)
tel. 0376 648175, fax 0376 646189
chiarascaravelli@virgilio.it
• Associazione Turisti per Casa
tel. and fax 0532 63066
buccimg@libero.it
www.turistipercasa.it
Open all year

This old farmhouse on the shore of the Po River is surrounded by a park and is just a short drive from Mantua.

Guests have an independent area that has a breakfast room, and a living room with period furnishings and paintings done by local artists. Breakfast consists of genuine products from the area.

Accommodation
Guestrooms: *3 (1 double, private bath; 1 double, 1 double bedroom, shared bath), also single occupancy; additional bed on request*
Services & Amenities: *French and English are spoken; rooms cleaned every 3 days; complimentary tourist information; lunch & dinner reservations; bike rental; pottery courses by request; garden; private parking*
Rates: *single €€, double €€. Additional bed supplement €. Children under 2 free. Discounts for extended stays and for groups*
Credit cards: *not accepted*
Pets:

Calco (Lecco)

B&B Il Torchio
Marcella Pisacane
via Ghislanzoni 24, località Vescogna
23885 Calco (LC)
tel. 039 508724, fax 02 86453229
mattia.garrone@libero.it
Open all year

This B&B is located in a 19th-C. farm complex, just 1 km from the center of town. The apartment – converted from an old hay barn – has a living room with TV, a fireplace, a kitchen and a small private garden. Breakfast, which consists of natural products and genuine sweet items, is served in the family house. Guests have the use of the family living room, which has a period piano. Excursions can be made along the Adda River, as well as along the Bergamo bank, which can be reached by means of a rope-drawn ferry, which was a Leonardesque design.

Accommodation
Guestrooms: *2 doubles, also single occupancy, shared bath and 1 mini-apartment (3 beds)*
Services & Amenities: *English spoken; rooms cleaned every day; complimentary tourist information; kitchen use by request; garden; smokers welcome; private parking*
Rates: *single €€, double €€, triple €€€. Children under 3 free. Discounts for extended stays*
Credit cards: *not accepted*
Pets:

Cardano al Campo (Varese)

B&B La Libellula
• B&B Varese-Nel verde tra i laghi
tel. 0331 260040, mob. 349 3519048
fax 0331 260040
iduenoci@hotmail.com
Open all year

This B&B is in a tranquil, completely-restructured farmhouse, surrounded by vegetation, and is located 5 kilometers from Malpensa international airport. Guests have the use of two small, independent apartments, each of which has a large living room with a completely furnished kitchenette, and a comfortable bedroom. During the warmer months, the continental breakfast is enriched with freshly-picked fruit.

Accommodation
Guestrooms: *2 mini-apartments (6 beds)*
Services & Amenities: *French and English are spoken; rooms cleaned every day; complimentary tourist information; terrace; kitchen use by request; garden; smokers welcome; private parking*
Rates: *€€-€€€ per person. Children under 12 -50%*
Credit cards: *not accepted*
Pets:

I Due Noci
Cinzia Pedrani
via Amalfi 7
21010 Cardano al Campo (VA)
tel. and fax 0331 260040
pedrani.cinzia@bedbreakfastalp.it
www.bedbreakfastalp.it
• **B&B Varese-Nel verde tra i laghi**
tel. 0331 260040, mob. 349 3519048
fax 0331 260040
iduenoci@hotmail.com
Open: February to October

This typical, early 20th-century working-class house is located inside the Ticino Regional Park, just 5 minutes from Malpensa international airport and 40 kilometers from Milan. It has a private garden and is the ideal place for tourists just passing through or for business people who prefer a family-type arrangement rather than a hotel. Each morning, the hostess serves a rich breakfast consisting of cakes, brioches or, on request, an English breakfast.

Accommodation
Guestrooms: *1 double, also single occupancy, private bath (outside); additional bed on request*
Services & Amenities: *English spoken; rooms cleaned every 3 days; complimentary tourist information; terrace; Internet access; garden; smokers welcome; private parking*
Rates: *single €€, double €€€. Aditional bed supplement €*
Credit cards: *not accepted*
Pets: 🚫

Casalzuigno (Varese)

B&B Il Cortile
• **B&B Varese-Nel verde tra i laghi**
tel. 0331 260040, mob. 349 3519048
fax 0331 260040
iduenoci@hotmail.com
Closed: January and February

This B&B is in a restructured Lombardy farmhouse that dates from the end of the 19th C. It's located on the shores of Lake Maggiore, 10 km from Laveno. The artistic features of the house go well with the period furniture. There's the Porta Bozzolo villa nearby which belongs to the FAI and has a splendid Italian garden. The hostess organizes art courses: artistic windows, ceramic raku and engraving technique. Breakfast, which features homemade and local products, is either served in the dining room or in the garden.

Accommodation
Guestrooms: *3 (1 double and 1 double bedroom, shared bath; 1 double bedroom, private bath)*
Services & Amenities: *English and German are spoken; rooms cleaned every day; tourist information; baby-sitting service; kitchen use by request; educational courses by request; terrace; garden; smokers welcome; private parking*
Rates: *single €€, double €€ - €€€. Children under 8 free*
Credit cards: *not accepted*
Pets: 🚫

Casorate Sempione (Varese)

B&B Il Poggio
• **B&B Varese-Nel verde tra i laghi**
tel. 0331 260040, mob. 349 3519048
fax 0331 260040
iduenoci@hotmail.com
Closed: June to August

Accommodation
Guestrooms: *1 double, also single occupancy, private bath; additional bed on request*
Services & Amenities: *French and English are spoken; rooms cleaned every day; tourist information; terrace; Internet access; garden; smokers welcome; private parking*
Rates: *single €€, double €€€. Additional bed supplement €*
Credit cards: *not accepted*
Pets: 🚫

The B&B with its garden is just 5 minutes from Malpensa International airport and 40 minutes from the famous city of Milan. The villa is situated in the tranquil heart of the Ticino Regional Park. This accommodation offers an upper-floor consisting of a large, bright bedroom with private bath, and a small living room with TV. The ideal place for those who like nature tourism and for business travelers. The traditional Italian breakfast is served in the family living room.

Cemmo di Capo di Ponte (Brescia)

Casa Visnenza
via San Faustino 7
Cemmo di Ponte (BS)
tel. 0364 426112, mob. 338 2610519
fax 0364 426647
casavisnenza@fastwebnet.it

Accommodation
Guestrooms: *3 double bedrooms, also single occupancy, private bath*
Services & Amenities: *French, English and German are spoken; tourist information; bike rental; rooms cleaned every 3 days; smokers welcome; private parking*
Minimum stay: *2 nights*
Rates: €€
Credit cards: *not accepted*
Pets:

This B&B is located at an elevation of 500 meters in a very nice town in Val Camonica, which is noted for its National Park and rock engravings. The B&B is inside a 15th-century home that has rustic furnishings. Besides the bedrooms, the guests also have the use of a large living room with a fireplace, a pergola with a barbeque and a panoramic garden. The hosts organize short stays (3 or 4 days) with guided tours for discovering old towns, frescoed churches, iron mines, rural mountain communities and rock engravings.

Cogliate (Milan)

• **Bed & Breakfast Italia** TCI 10%
Code L027
tel. 06 6878618, fax 06 6878619
info@bbitalia.it
www.bbitalia.it
Closed: varies

Accommodation
Guestrooms: *2 doubles*
Services & Amenities: *French, English and German are spoken; tourist information; rooms cleaned every 3 days; bike rental; smokers welcome; private parking*
Minimum stay: *2 nights*
Rates: €€
Credit cards: VISA MC *Bancomat*
Pets:

Two-story villa surrounded by a large garden. The first floor is exclusively for guests and consists in a fully equipped kitchen, sitting room, two double rooms with bathroom, one with tub, the other with shower. Classically furnished with antiques. Breakfast is served in the lounge and in the garden in the warmer months. Guests can borrow bicycles. The house is 40 km from the airport.

Cuasso al Monte (Varese)

Rose tra gli archi
via Alberè
20080 Cuasso al Monte (VA)
tel. & fax 0332938166, 0331 518750
mob. 328 2519820
crivellari.lucia@virgilio.it
Open all year

Accommodation
Guestrooms: *3 (1 double bedroom with private bath, 1 double bedroom and 1 open-plan, additional beds on request, with private bath)*
Services & Amenities: *English and Spanish are spoken; rooms cleaned every three days; complimentary tourist information; Internet access; baby-sitting service; garden; smokers welcome*
Rates: *single €€, double €€€. Additional bed supplement*
Credit cards: *not accepted*
Pets:

An 18th-C farmhouse made of warm, local stone, located at an altitude of 550 meters, among beech and chestnut trees, in the Campo dei Fiori natural park. Large, arched windows provide a beautiful view of the Swiss Alps, in particular, Mount Generoso. The first floor, which has an independent entrance, has a bright living room, a balcony and one of the bedrooms that has bathroom. A stairway leads to the mansard where there are two other bedrooms. Guests have use of satellite TV, a fax, Internet and a garden with barbeque.

Desenzano del Garda (Brescia)

Cascina Montonale
Paola Righetti
località Rivoltella del Garda
25015 Desenzano del Garda (BS)
tel. 030 9103331
bbmontonale@libero.it
www.montonale.it
Open: March to October and Christmas holidays

An ancient stone farmhouse, which has been very carefully restructured with particular care given to the details. The furnishings are in the same style, including elegant carpets and drapes. Guestrooms are in the mansard and have a warm and friendly atmosphere. There is a large garden with an arcade, and a well-stocked library. The rich breakfast is served either in the kitchen-living room or outside. Sirmione and Desenzano are located just a few kilometers away.

Accommodation
Guestrooms: *2 (1 double and 1 triple room) shared bath; additional bed on request*
Services & Amenities: *French and English; rooms cleaned every day; complimentary tourist information; smokers welcome; private parking*
Minimum stay: *2 nights*
Rates: *double €€, triple €€€. Additional bed supplement €. Discounts for extended stays -10%; Children under 2 free*
Credit cards: *not accepted*
Pets:

Gardone Riviera (Brescia)

Dimora Bolsone
Raffaele Bonaspetti
via Panoramica 23
25083 Gardone Riviera (BS)
tel. 0365 21022, fax 0365 63367
info@bolsonedimora.com
www.bolsonedimora.com
Open all year

This ancient, charming, completely restructured home, located on a cliff overlooking the lake, offers its guests a very nice stay in its refined and elegantly furnished rooms. The very large secular park offers special theme routes. A rich English breakfast is served in the large dining room that has a fireplace. A refined dinner for two can be arranged on request.

Accommodation
Guestrooms: *3 double bedrooms, private bath*
Services & Amenities: *French and English; rooms cleaned every 3 days; complimentary tourist information; dinner reservation; bike rental; terrace; garden; smokers welcome; private parking*
Minimum stay: *2 nights*
Rates: *€€€€*
Credit cards: *Bancomat*
Pets:

Golasecca (Varese)

La Pasadita
Giovanna Crolla
via C. Battisti 16
21010 Golasecca (VA)
tel. 0331 958175
giovannapaola.crolla@bedbreakfastalp.it
www,bedbreakfastalp.it
• B&B Varese-Nel verde tra i laghi
tel. 0331 260040, mob. 349 3519048
fax 0331 260040
iduenoci@hotmail.com
Open: 15 January to 15 December

In the Ticino Regional Park, just 7 minutes from Malpensa airport, this modern villa, surrounded by a large garden with old trees, has a name that echoes a characteristic meeting place for foreigners in Puebla, Mexico. Guests have the use of a comfortable living room that has a fireplace and a billiard table. The hostess suggests visiting the Golasecca archeological site.

Accommodation
Guestrooms: *2 doubles, also single occupancy, private bath; additional bed on request*
Services & Amenities: *Spanish spoken; rooms cleaned every day; complimentary tourist information; terrace; garden; smokers welcome; private parking*
Rates: *single €€, double €€€. Additional bed supplement €*
Credit cards: *not accepted*
Pets:

Le Betulle
Imelde Fontana
via Verdi 16 - 21010 Golasecca (VA)
tel. 0331 958409
betulle16@tin.it
www.bedbreakfastalp.it
• B&B Varese-Nel verde tra i laghi
tel. 0331 260040, mob. 349 3519048
fax 0331 260040
iduenoci@hotmail.com
Open: March to September

This recently-built, two-story house has a large private garden and is very close to Malpensa airport. The guests have the exclusive use of the ground floor; it consists on one double room, a living room with TV, and a kitchen, which is where the breakfast is served. Golasecca, which only has 2,500 inhabitants, is in the Ticino Regional Park and just a short drive from Varese.

ACCOMMODATION
Guestrooms: *1 double, also single occupancy, private bath (external); additional bed on request*
Services & Amenities: *rooms cleaned every 3 days; complimentary tourist information; lunch & dinner reservations; garden; smokers welcome; private parking*
Rates: *single €€, double €€€. Additional bed supplement €. Children under 3 free*
Credit cards: *not accepted*
Pets: not allowed

LOVERE (BERGAMO)

Donizetti
Maria Grazia Rossa
via Donizetti 3
24065 Lovere (BG)
tel. 035 960989, mob. 340 607320
rossamarzia@inwind.it
• Associazione Bergamo B&B
mob. 339 7845293
bergamobedandbreakfast@virgilio.it
Closed: November

This B&B is in a modern condo located near a small port in the charming Lake Iseo bathing locality, and offers all the means for enjoying a few days of informal, complete relaxation. The host is a person with a wide range of interests. He does volunteer work, likes natural sciences, painting, and takes particular pleasure in conversing with his guests.

ACCOMMODATION
Guestrooms: *3 (1 double bedroom and 2 doubles, use as singles) shared bath; additional bed on request* ♿
Services & Amenities: *French and English are spoken; rooms cleaned every 3 days; complimentary tourist information; terrace; smokers welcome*
Rates: *single €€, double €€. Additional bed supplement €. Discounts for extended stays*
Credit cards: *not accepted*
Pets: allowed

MANDELLO DEL LARIO (LECCO)

Villa delle Rose
Armando and Maria Cristina Masarin
strada statale 125/127
23826 Mandello del Lario (LC)
tel. and fax 0341 731304
www.villadellerose.com
Closed: January

This rustic 19th-century building was restored for the first time in the '20s by the Biffi-Capalbi family of Milan before becoming the property of the Grundig family. The present owner, who restored the delightful villa, is very fond of roses and their presence is everywhere: in names of the three guestrooms which have every comfort and very carefully cared-for period furnishings, on the tables of the restaurant managed by the owners, and in the large park that faces the lake. It's a bit of paradise on "that branch of Lake Como".

ACCOMMODATION
Guestrooms: *3 double bedrooms, also single occupancy, with private bath* ♿
Services & Amenities: *French, English and German are spoken; rooms cleaned every day; complimentary tourist information; lunch & dinner reservations; garden; smokers welcome; private parking*
Rates: *single €€€, double €€€*
Credit cards: Diners, Visa, MC *Bancomat*
Pets: allowed

MILAN

Antonio e Ornella B&B

TCI 10%

Antonio Angelici and Ornella Arcari
vicolo Calusca 10/C
20123 Milan
tel. 02 8322018, fax 02 89422690
antonio1948@libero.it
Closed: July

ACCOMMODATION
Guestrooms: *1 double, also single occupancy, private bath; additional bed on request*
Services & Amenities: *French, English and Spanish are spoken; complimentary tourist information; rooms cleaned every day; lunch & dinner reservations; Internet access; private parking*
Rates: *single €€, double €€€. Additional bed supplement €. Discounts for extended stays*
Credit cards: *not accepted*
Pets:

This B&B is located in the lively Porta Ticinese quarter, which is just a 15 minute walk from the Duomo, the cathedral symbol of Milan. The guests (preferably non-smokers) have a very quiet bedroom with a double bed and a private bath. Breakfast can either be continental or as desired, and is served in the living room, which has a TV and a hi-fi system. Guests also have the use of a very convenient, private, internal parking facility.

Il Girasole

Nicola Negruzzi
via Doberdò 19
20126 Milan
tel. 02 27080738, mob. 347 1469721
fax 02 25707021
bbilgirasole@hotmail.com
web.tiscalinet.it/bbilgirasole/bbilgirasole
Closed: varies

ACCOMMODATION
Guestrooms: *3 doubles, also single occupancy, private bath ♿*
Services & Amenities: *French and English are spoken; rooms cleaned every day; complimentary tourist information; baby-sitting service; kitchen use by request; bike rental; Internet access; garden; smokers welcome; private parking*
Rates: *single €€-€€€, double €€€. Children under 12 free. Discounts for extended stays*
Credit cards: *not accepted*
Pets:

This B&B's guests are welcomed in a very friendly, personal manner and are assured functional comfort and a competitive quality/price ratio. Located in Lombardy's chief city, this B&B is very close to the Villa San Giovanni subway station. Guests have the use of a courtyard with large internal parking, a living room, a fax, a kitchen, independent rooms and a small garden. Near completion at this present time is a conference room, a sauna and a gym.

• Bed & Breakfast Italia

Code L018
via Santa Maria Valle
Carrobbio zone
tel. 06 6878618, fax 06 6878619
info@bbitalia.it
www.bbitalia.it
Closed: varies

A spacious apartment in the center of Milan on the second floor of a building with an elevator, just 5 minutes on foot from the Gothic Duomo (cathedral). Guests can use two double rooms and a triple room. Each room has TV and private bathroom with shower. The continental breakfast is served in the lounge. A subway line to the trade fair area and a tram stop are 50 m away. The lady of the house welcomes her guests offering tea and cakes

ACCOMMODATION
Guestrooms: *3 (2 doubles, 1 triple)*
Services & Amenities: *English spoken; rooms cleaned every 3 days; complimentary tourist information*
Minimum stay: *2 nights*
Rates: *€€*
Credit cards: VISA MC *Bancomat*
Pets:

• **Bed & Breakfast Italia**
Code L021
via Moisè Loria
Parco Solari zone
tel. 06 6878618, fax 06 6878619
info@bbitalia.it
www.bbitalia.it
Closed: varies

A 10-minute walk from the canal district, this apartment is located on the fourth floor of an elegant building with elevator. The guestroom, classically furnished with antiques, is equipped with TV. The private bathroom has a shower/tub. This area can be reached in 10 minutes by bus, the stops are 100 m from the B&B. The old center is within 20 minutes walking distance.

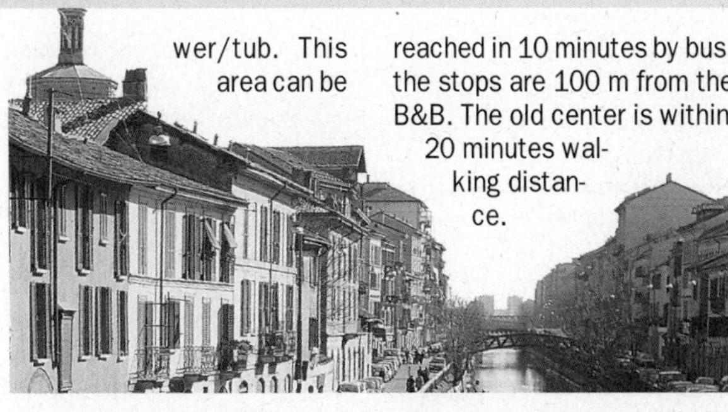

ACCOMMODATION
Guestrooms: *1 double*
Services & Amenities: *French and English are spoken; rooms cleaned every 3 days; complimentary tourist information; smokers welcome*
Minimum stay: *2 nights*
Rates: €€
Credit cards: VISA MC *Bancomat*
Pets: no pets

• **Bed & Breakfast Italia**
Code L022
via Paolo Sarpi
Parco Sempione zone
tel. 06 6878618, fax 06 6878619
info@bbitalia.it
www.bbitalia.it
Closed: varies

An elegantly furnished apartment in modern style in a district near the trade fair area. It offers two bedrooms with double beds and writing desk. Shared bathroom. Continental breakfast is offered in the kitchen or on the large balcony in summertime. The bus stop to the center is 10 m away; the tramcar stop is 30 m away. The subway green line station is within 5 minutes walking distance.

ACCOMMODATION
Guestrooms: *2 (doubles)*
Services & Amenities: *English and Spanish are spoken; rooms cleaned every 3 days; complimentary tourist information; smokers welcome*
Minimum stay: *2 nights*
Rates: €€
Credit cards: VISA MC *Bancomat*
Pets: no pets

• **Bed & Breakfast Italia**
Code L023
via Pinturicchio
Città Studi
tel. 06 6878618, fax 06 6878619
info@bbitalia.it
www.bbitalia.it
Closed: varies

ACCOMMODATION
Guestrooms: *1 single*
Services & Amenities: *French and English are spoken; rooms cleaned every 3 days; tourist information*
Minimum stay: *2 nights*
Rates: €€€
Credit cards: VISA MC *Bancomat*
Pets: no pets

This elegant apartment furnished with fine antiques is located in the university district, on the fifth floor (with elevator) of a 1930s building. It has a single room with private bathroom and shower. Continental breakfast is served in the kitchen. The subway station is a 5-minute walk away; the tramcar to the center is 200 m away. This area is full of high fashion boutiques and offers ample opportunity both for shopping and nightlife.

• Bed & Breakfast Italia
Code LO24
via Ausonio
Parco Solari zone
tel. 06 6878618
fax 06 6878619
info@bbitalia.it
www.bbitalia.it
Closed: varies

This B&B is located in the S. Ambrogio district, on the third floor of an elegant building with an elevator. The guests' accommodation consists in a simply but comfortably furnished room, with private bathroom with shower/tub, preferably available only for women guests. The continental breakfast is served in the morning. The home is 100 m from the subway station and bus and tramcar stops to the center. Smokers are welcome.

Accommodation
Guestrooms: *1 double*
Services & Amenities: *French, English, German and Spanish are spoken; rooms cleaned every 3 days; complimentary tourist information; smokers welcome*
Minimum stay: *2 nights*
Rates: €€
Credit cards: VISA MC *Bancomat*
Pets: no

• Bed & Breakfast Italia
Code LO46
viale Brianza
Loreto zone
tel. 06 6878618, fax 06 6878619
info@bbitalia.it, www.bbitalia.it
Closed: varies

This B&B is in a 2nd floor apartment of a modern building – with elevator – located in the center of Milan, in the Loreto area. Guests have a double room with classic, elegant, comfortable furnishings, air conditioning and a private bathroom with shower. The hostess serves breakfast in the family dining room. The Red-Green subway station and bus stop are 200 meters away.

Accommodation
Guestrooms: *1 double*
Services & Amenities: *English spoken; rooms cleaned every three days; tourist material; air conditioning; smokers welcome*
Minimum stay: *2 nights*
Rates: €€
Credit cards: VISA MC *Bancomat*
Pets: no

• Bed & Breakfast Italia
Code LO30
via Cola di Rienzo
Parco Solari zone
tel. 06 6878618, fax 06 6878619
info@bbitalia.it
www.bbitalia.it
Closed: varies

An elegant small villa in the trade fair area, surrounded by a well-tended garden where breakfast is served. It has two double rooms classically furnished with antiques. Each room has a private bathroom with shower. It is located 200 m from the bus and tramcar stop running to the trade fair and Piazza Duomo in 20 minutes, and to the subway station in 10 minutes. Family pets are in residence.

Accommodation
Guestrooms: *2 doubles*
Services & Amenities: *French and English are spoken; rooms cleaned every 3 days; complimentary tourist information*
Minimum stay: *2 nights*
Rates: €€€
Credit cards: VISA MC *Bancomat*
Pets: no

• Bed & Breakfast Italia
Code L031
via Tito Livio
Parco Alessandrini zone
tel. 06 6878618
fax 06 6878619
info@bbitalia.it
www.bbitalia.it
Closed: varies

A stylish loft situated on the mezzanine floor of a period building in one of Milan's semi-central districts. The guests' accommodation consists in a room with double bed and private bathroom.

Accommodation
Guestrooms: *1 double bedroom*
Services & Amenities: *English, German and Spanish are spoken; rooms cleaned every 3 days; tourist information; air conditioning*
Minimum stay: *2 nights*
Rates: €€€
Credit cards: VISA MC *Bancomat*
Pets: not allowed

The original, refined furnishings are a blend of prestigious antiques, contemporary decor and vividly painted walls. Breakfast is served in the kitchen. The subway stop is 300 m away.

Misano di Gera d'Adda (Bergamo)

Ca de Ae TCI 10%
Grazia Parolari
via Maestri 5
24040 Misano di Gera d'Adda (BG)
tel. and fax 0363 848327
mob. 329 7432699
graziap@lombardiacom.it
www.bedbreakfastalp.it
• Associazione Bergamo B&B
tel. 339 7845293
bergamobedandbreakfast@virgilio.it
Open: 15 January to 15 June and 15 August to 15 December

This modern villa – near Milan and Bergamo – is surrounded by vegetation and offers an unexpected oriental atmosphere, which is explained by the host having spent considerable time in the Arab countries. Guests are served a rich breakfast of sweet items and natural marmalades.

Accommodation
Guestrooms: *1 double, also single occupancy, private bath; additional bed on request* ♿
Services & Amenities: *French and English are spoken; rooms cleaned every day; complimentary tourist information; bike rental; terrace; garden; private parking*
Rates: *single* €€, *double* €€€. *Additional bed supplement* €€. *Discounts for more then 3 nights*
Credit cards: *not accepted*
Pets: allowed

Mozzo (Bergamo)

Amici miei TCI 10%
Dario Giuppone
via Ponchielli 7
24030 Mozzo (BG)
tel. 035 612648, mob. 320 0527108
bed012000@yahoo.it
www.web.tiscali.it/amicimieibb
• Associazione Bergamo B&B
tel. 339 7845293
bergamobedandbreakfast@virgilio.it
Open all year

This beautiful '70s villa surrounded by a charming hillside vineyard, is situated in a tranquil location just 3 km from Bergamo. The villa is just 100 m from the bus stop. Modern furnishings and a warm, friendly family atmosphere. Once a week the hosts arrange a concert of classical piano music. Breakfast is served in the living room, which has a fireplace. Guests with celiac disturbances can be served a gluten-free breakfast.

Accommodation
Guestrooms: *3 (1 double bedroom and 2 doubles, also single occupancy) private bath*
Services & Amenities: *English and German are spoken; rooms cleaned every 3 days; complimentary tourist information; lunch & dinner reservations; terrace; garden; smokers welcome; private parking*
Rates: *single* €€, *double* €€€. *Children under 12 free*
Credit cards: *not accepted*
Pets: allowed

Paladina (Bergamo)

La Casa al Brembo
Monica Pasqualini
via del Brembo 18
24030 Paladina (BG)
tel. 035 637024, mob. 335 6266460
fax 035 633800
monibb@interfree.it
www.bedbreakfastalp.it
• Associazione Bergamo B&B
tel. 339 7845293
bergamobedandbreakfast@virgilio.it
Open all year

This restructured, 20th-century farmhouse has a very nice, well-cared-for country atmosphere. Besides the guestrooms – warmly furnished in light-colored wood – the guests also have the use of comfortable, well-furnished kitchen. The small town of Paladina – an oasis of tranquility – is at the entrance to the Val Brembana and is close to Bergamo and Orio al Serio airport. Guests are greeted with a basket of products in season.

Accommodation
Guestrooms: *3 (2 doubles and 1 quadruple) private bath ♿*
Services & Amenities: *English, German and Swedish are spoken; complimentary tourist information; rooms cleaned every 3 days; kitchen use by request; bike rental; garden; smokers welcome; private parking*
Rates: *single €€, double €€€. Children under 10 free*
Credit cards: *not accepted*
Pets: 🚫

Pisogne (Brescia)

• Bed & Breakfast Italia
Code L07
tel. 06 6878618, fax 06 6878619
info@bbitalia.it
www.bbitalia.it
Closed: varies

A self-contained apartment in the villa where the hosts live at Pisogne. The small apartment includes a sitting room with sofa bed, a double bedroom, and a private bathroom with shower. Continental breakfast is served on the upper floor. It is elegantly furnished with antiques. Brescia and Bergamo are 40 km away, Venice, Padua and Verona can be reached in two hours; and the Montecampione ski resort is 12 km away.

Accommodation
Guestrooms: *2 doubles*
Services & Amenities: *French, English and German are spoken; rooms cleaned every 3 days; tourist information; private parking*
Minimum length of stay: *2 nights*
Rates: *€€*
Credit cards: VISA MC *Bancomat*
Pets: 🚫

Rovagnate (Lecco)

Bagaggera
Piero Todeschino and Paola Lazzarotto
via Bagaggera 27
23888 Rovagnate (LC)
tel. 039 5311678
fax 039 5301186
Open all year

This B&B is inserted in a nucleus of 18th-C farmhouses located in the Montevecchia Park and in Val Curone; all of these buildings have been restructured to meet bioconstruction criteria. Breakfast is served in the dining room reserved for the guests. Included in the adjoining agricultural activity is the production of vegetables and various types of organic cheese.

Accommodation
Guestrooms: *2 (1 double and 1 triple), shared bath; 1 studio (3 beds)*
Services & Amenities: *French, English and German are spoken; rooms cleaned every 3 days; complimentary tourist information; kitchenette; garden; smokers welcome; private parking*
Minimum stay: *3 nights*
Rates: *double €€, triple €€. Child's bed supplement €. Discounts for children and extended stays*
Credit cards: *not accepted*
Pets: 🚫

Rovello Porro (Como)

• Bed & Breakfast Italia
Code L026
tel. 06 6878618, fax 06 6878619
info@bbitalia.it
www.bbitalia.it
Closed: varies

Accommodation
Guestrooms: *1 double*
Services & Amenities: *English, German and Spanish are spoken; rooms cleaned every 3 days; tourist information; terrace; private parking*
Minimum stay: *2 nights*
Rates: €€
Credit cards: VISA MC *Bancomat*
Pets: no

25 km from Como and Milan, in the village of Rovello Porro, this simply and comfortably furnished apartment is located on the second floor of a modern building. The double room with large balcony is equipped with two single beds. Private bathroom with shower/tub. The continental breakfast is served by the hostess in the kitchen. It is 5 km from Rovello railway station. Family pets live in the house.

San Colombano al Lambro (Milan)

Villa Silvia
• Ass. Barbarossa-B&B nel Lodigiano
tel. 0371 897998, 347 8664843
stefania.bordoni@tiscali.it
http://web.tiscali.it/bordoni53
Closed: August

Accommodation
Guestrooms: *2 doubles, shared bath*
Services & Amenities: *French and English are spoken; rooms cleaned every day; tourist information; terrace; garden; lunch & dinner reservations; smokers welcome*
Minimum stay: *2 nights*
Rates: *double €€€*
Credit cards: *accepted*
Pets: no

This Art Nouveau-style house is located in the town's old center, and has a 19th-century furniture The two double-bed guestrooms have a bathroom in common and each has a TV. Guests can also enjoy and relax in the garden or in the terrace. The classic continental breakfast is served in the dining room. Meals provided on request.

San Giovanni Bianco (Bergamo)

Il Noce
Monica Rattighieri
via Sentino 21
24015 San Giovanni Bianco (BG)
mob. 349 8417969
monica@valbrembanaweb.com
www.bedbreakfastalp.it
• Associazione Bergamo B&B
tel. 339 7845293
bergamobedandbreakfast@virgilio.it
Open all year

TCI 10%

Accommodation
Guestrooms: *2 (1 double and 1 double bedroom, use as singles) private bath* ♿
Services & Amenities: *French, English and German are spoken; rooms cleaned every 3 days; tourist information; garden; smokers welcome; private parking*
Rates: *single €, double €€*
Credit cards: *not accepted*
Pets: no

The host family is proud of their abundant, delicious breakfast, which includes local natural specialties. The hostess is particularly careful as regards the environment and only uses strictly ecological products in

carrying out her domestic chores. This 16th-C farmhouse has a very well-cared-for country atmosphere, and the family, with its three children, is very warm and friendly. In addition to hikes along the mule trails of the Orobiche Prealps, guests can also visit the house in which Arlecchino was born, which is located in the nearby Oneta district.

Villa Arlecchino
Eugenia Caginelli
via Oneta 25, località Oneta
24015 San Giovanni Bianco (BG)
tel. 035 361893, fax 035 341094
inc@magnetictours.it
www.magnetictours.it
Open: weekends

In the small, medieval town of Oneta – 25 km from Bergamo – this B&B is hosted in a 16th-century house that faces an ancient square that has a watering trough. Its name derives from its location close to the Grataroli palace, which, according to tradition, is the house in which the 1st interpreter of Arlecchino was born. The buffet breakfast with genuine products is served in the family kitchen-living room. The hostess, who has a travel agency, is available for organizing various excursions in the area.

Accommodation
Guestrooms: *2 (1 double and 1 double bedroom, shared bath)*
Services & Amenities: *French and English are spoken; rooms cleaned every day; tourist information; horse-riding excursions; smokers welcome*
Rates: €€€
Credit cards: *accepted*
Pets:

San Pellegrino Terme (Bergamo)

Castello della Botta
Donatella Donati
via alla Vetta
24016 San Pellegrino Terme (BG)
tel. and fax 0345 23232
mob. 349 3514049
castellodellabotta@libero.it
• **Associazione Bergamo B&B**
tel. 339 7845293
bergamobedandbreakfast@virgilio.it
Open all year

Accommodation
Guestrooms: *3 doubles, also single occupancy, private bath; additional bed on request*
Services & Amenities: *French, English and German are spoken; rooms cleaned every day; tourist info; terrace; Internet access; garden; smokers welcome*
Rates: *single €€, double €€€. Additionals bed supplement €*
Credit cards: *not accepted*
Pets:

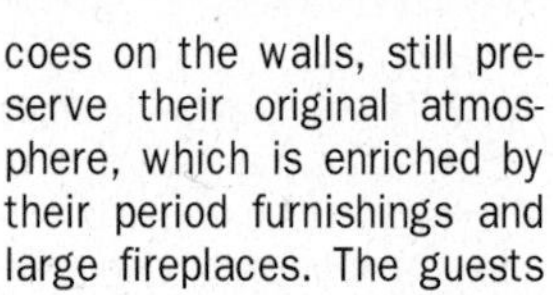

This neo-Renaissance style castle, recently reconstructed in keeping with its original architectural features, dates from the early 20th-C. The rooms, with their original frescoes on the walls, still preserve their original atmosphere, which is enriched by their period furnishings and large fireplaces. The guests can enjoy a music room, a well-furnished library and a large park complete with a pond. As a rule, the English breakfast is served in the dining room.

Santa Giuletta (Pavia)

Le Buone Terre di Castello
Daniele Marchesi
Casa Gian Pietro, località Castello
27046 Santa Giuletta (PV)
tel. 0383 899733, fax 0383 814063
marchesi.daniele@tin.it
www.azienda.agraria.marchesi.com
• **Friendly Home-Gli Amici del B&B**
tel. 02 860147, fax 02 875860
friendlymilano@dada.it
tel. and fax 011 9536376
fhrivoli@virgilio.it
Closed: 1 to 15 July

This elegant, late 19th-C villa, surrounded by the Oltrepò Pavese hills and vineyards, hosts the guests in a warm, refined atmosphere created by antique furniture of past family history. Breakfast – consisting of organic products from the farm – is either served in the dining room with fireplace or in the guestrooms. This B&B also provides the enjoyment of informal farm holiday, where guests can stop for lunch and dinner and enjoy the vegetables and wine produced by the host family. Guests can also enjoy tasting the wines.

Accommodation
Guestrooms: *3 (1 suite, private bath; 2 doubles, also single occupancy, shared bath)*
Services & Amenities: *French and English are spoken; complimentary tourist information; lunch & dinner reservations; rooms cleaned every day; educational courses by request; terrace; Internet access; garden; smokers welcome; private parking*
Rates: *single €€, double €€€. Children under 2 free. Discounts for students and seniors*
Credit cards: *Bancomat*
Pets:

Serina (Bergamo)

Casa Fiorita
Sonia Roca
via Partigiani 43
24017 Serina (BG)
tel. 0345 56719, 0345 66411
mob. 339 1360240
casafiorita.sonia@libero.it
www.bedbreakfastalp.it
• Associazione Bergamo B&B
tel. 339 7845293
bergamobedandbreakfast@virgilio.it
Open all year

Located in a small district at an elevation of 850 m, this B&B greets its guests in a friendly mountain atmosphere, with typical furniture made of the wood of the fir tree. The rich breakfast also provides a selection of various types of local cheese and is served in a living room with fireplace, where guests can enjoy and relax.

Accommodation
Guestrooms: *3 (2 double bedrooms and 1 double, also single occupancy, private bath outside)*
Services & Amenities: *French, English, German and Spanish are spoken; complimentary tourist information; bike rental; garden; rooms cleaned every 3 days; smokers welcome; private parking*
Rates: *single €, double €€*
Credit cards: *not accepted*
Pets: ✓

Sovere (Bergamo)

B&B Susanna
Susanna Lorandi
via Provinciale 14, località Sellere
24060 Sovere (BG)
tel. 035 982292
susannalorandi@libero.it
www.bedbreakfastalp.it
• Associazione Bergamo B&B
tel. 339 7845293
bergamobedandbreakfast@virgilio.it
Open all year

Just a short distance from Lovere – the Lake Iseo bathing locality – B&B Susanna welcomes its guests in a small, pink, two-story villa, which has two guestrooms in an independent apartment. The rooms, which are characterized by a different color, have modern furnishings plus two or three antique items. The Italian breakfast is served in the apartment kitchen.

Accommodation
Guestrooms: *2 (1 double and 1 quadruple, also single occupancy, shared bath)* ♿
Services & Amenities: *French and English are spoken; rooms cleaned every day; complimentary tourist information; kitchen use by request; bike rental; terrace; Internet access; garden; smokers welcome*
Rates: *single €€, double €€, quadruple €€€€. Children -50%. Discounts for extended stays*
Credit cards: *not accepted*
Pets: ✗

Stagno Lombardo (Cremona)

Cascina Lagoscuro
• Ass. Barbarossa-B&B nel Lodigiano
tel. 0371 897998, mob. 347 8664843
stefania.bordoni@tiscali.it
http://web.tiscali.it/bordoni53
Closed: August

This fascinating, 16th-century farmhouse – which, today, has the function of a organic farm – has a large park with a private pond. The house is perfectly preserved, as regards finishing and decor, and has beautiful 17th and 18th century furniture. Breakfast features the typical products of the region and is served in a beautiful dining room whose walls and ceiling have trompe-l'oeil frescoes.

Accommodation
Guestrooms: *4 (2 singles and 2 doubles, shared bath)*
Services & Amenities: *French and English are spoken; rooms cleaned every 3 days; complimentary tourist information; lunch & dinner reservations; garden; smokers welcome; private parking*
Minimum stay: *2 nights*
Rates: *single €€, double €€€*
Credit cards: *accepted*
Pets: ✓

On request, hosts can also provide meals. This B&B is 8 km from Cremona.

Tirano (Sondrio)

Ecco Casa Mia
Maria Grazia Robustellini
via Arcari 6/8
23037 Tirano (SO)
tel. 0342 705300, mob. 348 4412665
fax 0342 705050
www.geocities.com/eccocasamia
Closed: January

A name, a program: that's what the "maternal" hostess of this B&B proposes. The accordion reigns supreme in this household and smokers have to go out on the terrace. This old mansion – in the old center of the town, just a short walk from the station – used to be a slaughter house. There are steps everywhere, the furnishings are antique and the atmosphere is very friendly.

Accommodation
Guestrooms: *3 (1 double bedroom private bath, 1 double and 1 single shared bath)*
Services & Amenities: *English and German are spoken; rooms cleaned every day; tourist info; private parking*
Rates: *single €€, double €€€, double bedroom €€€. Discounts for extended stays*
Credit cards: *not accepted*
Pets: 🐕

Breakfast – with local sweet and non-sweet products – is served in the tavern or, in wintertime, in the living room.

Travedona Monate (Varese)

La Vigna
Armida Terzaghi
corso Europa 15, località Monate
21028 Travedona Monate (VA)
tel. and fax 0332 977727
terzaghi@libero.it
• **B&B Varese-Nel verde tra i laghi**
tel. 0331 260040, mob. 349 3519048
fax 0331 260040
iduenoci@hotmail.com
Closed: November
Open: March to December

This house with a private beach and large garden, is located on the shores of Lake Monate. The small guest apartment – on the ground floor – has early 20th-C furniture, includes a living room and a kitchen. Breakfast is served in the kitchen reserved for the guests and consists in sweet and non-sweet items.

Accommodation
Guestrooms: *2 doubles (also single occupancy) shared bath; additional bed on request*
Services & Amenities: *French and English are spoken; rooms cleaned every 3 days; complimentary tourist information; kitchen use by request; bike and ship rental; garden; Internet access; smokers welcome; private parking*
Minimum stay: *2 nights*
Rates: *single €€, double €€€. Additional bed supplement €. Children under 3 free. Discounts for extended stays*
Credit cards: *not accepted*
Pets: no

Valleve (Bergamo)

La Torre B & B (TCI 10%)
Marinetta Favetti
via Tegia 1
24010 Valleve (BG)
tel. 0345 78066
mfavetti@tiscali.it
www.bedbreakfastalp.it
• **Associazione Bergamo B&B**
tel. 339 7845293
bergamobedandbreakfast@virgilio.it
Open all year

This B&B has a nice, wooden Tyrolean balcony which is full of flowers in the summertime. Located in a quaint 15th-century village in the Orobie Park at an elevation of 1100 m where an old Roman lookout tower once stood, this B&B, immersed in the tranquility of a very beautiful natural setting, provides an enviable panoramic view. Guests receive a welcome basket as they are received into the warm mountain atmosphere.

Accommodation
Guestrooms: *1 quadruple*
Services & Amenities: *French, English and Spanish are spoken; complimentary tourist information; kitchen use by request; rooms cleaned every 3 days; terrace; Internet access; smokers welcome; private parking*
Rates: *single €€, quadruple €€€. Discounts for extended stays*
Credit cards: *not accepted*
Pets: no

Varese

Villa Grazia
Lucia Miraglia
via G. d'Arezzo 4
località Sant'Ambrogio Olona
21100 Varese
tel. 0332 227004
miraglia.lucia@bedbreakfastalp.it
www.bedbreakfastalp.it
• **B&B Varese-Nel verde tra i laghi**
tel. 0331 260040, mob. 349 3519048
fax 0331 260040
iduenoci@hotmail.com
Open all year

The pleasure of providing hospitality has prompted the hostess to convert her beautiful, early 20th-C home, located at the foot of Sacro Monte, into a comfortable B&B. This is the right place for guests desiring some peace and tranquility. The bright rooms, with a terrace facing the garden, still have their original furnishings. Interesting excursions can be made on Lake Maggiore or to the Villa Panza Foundation.

Accommodation
Guestrooms: *3 doubles (also single occupancy) private bath*
Services & Amenities: *French spoken; rooms cleaned every 3 days; complimentary tourist information; Internet access; garden; smokers welcome; private parking*
Rates: *single €€, double €€*
Credit cards: *not accepted*
Pets: 🚫

Verdellino (Bergamo)

Franca
Giuseppe Gritti
via Alfieri 17
24049 Verdellino (BG)
tel. and fax 035 885193
mob. 335 255636
bbfranca@ciaoweb.it
Open all year

This B&B, is located in a small modern building situated in the Bergamo countryside. It has a special feature: it also provides a special completely gluten-free breakfast for those who have celiac disturbances, and a kitchen that's completely equipped for preparing this type of food. The hostess is very happy to accompany her guests to visit the area, as well as the well-known wine cellars in the nearby Franciacorta.

Accommodation
Guestrooms: *2 (1 double and 1 double bedroom) private bath* ♿
Services & Amenities: *French, English, German and Chinese are spoken; rooms cleaned every 3 days; complimentary tourist information; bike rental; private parking*
Rates: *single €€, double €€€. Children under 2 free. Discounts for extended stays*
Credit cards: *not accepted*
Pets: 🐕

Viggiù (Varese)

B&B La Villa
rwviggiù@tin.it
• **Friendly Home-Gli Amici del B&B**
tel. 02 860147, fax 02 875860
friendlymilano@dada.it
tel. and fax 011 9536376
fhrivoli@virgilio.it
Closed: November to mid March

The authentic atmosphere of another epoch greets the guests in this late 19th-C villa in Art Nouveau-style. The rich breakfast is served in the elegant English dining room reserved for the guests. The many attractions in the area include Lake Varese, Lake Como and Lake Maggiore, as well as Lugano and Campione d'Italia. Guests can enjoy mountain biking and horseback riding, all just 50 minutes from Milan.

Accommodation
Guestrooms: *3 doubles (2 shared baths, 1 private bath), also singles*
Services & Amenities: *English and German are spoken; rooms cleaned every day; complimentary tourist information; kitchenette; garden; private parking*
Rates: *single €€€, double €€€€. Discounts for extended stays*
Credit cards: *not accepted*
Pets: 🐕

The hostess is happy to accompany her guests on visits in the surrounding area.

Trentino-South Tirol

Appiano sulla Strada del Vino/Eppan an der Weinstrasse (Bolzano)

Federer Hof
Anton Federer
via Montiggler 29,
località San Michele
39057 Appiano sulla Strada del Vino/Eppan an der Weinstrasse (BZ)
tel. and fax 0471 662048
Open: March to November

Situated in the Alto Adige's largest grape-growing area, among the vineyards and fruit groves on the hills surrounding Appiano, this house has five, classically-furnished rooms with private baths. Guests can enjoy a wonderful breakfast either on the beautiful terrace or in a reserved dining room. The garden, which is perfect for relaxing, has a ping-pong table and a children's play area.

Accommodation
Guestrooms: *5 doubles, also single occupancy, private baths; additional beds on request*
Services & Amenities: *German spoken; rooms cleaned every day; tourist information; terrace; garden; private parking*
Rates: *€ per person. Discounts for children -50%*
Credit cards: *not accepted*
Pets: 🐕

Fischerhof
Martin Mauracher
Col Terenzio 12, località Cornaiano
39057 Appiano sulla Strada del Vino/Eppan an der Weinstrasse (BZ)
tel. and fax 0471 660627
info@fischerhof/mauracher.it
Open all year

This house, surrounded by vineyards and apple trees, is located in a quiet position in the beautiful landscape of the Appiano area, just a short distance from the Col Terenzio district. Guests can enjoy a nice breakfast featuring local products in a comfortable tavern that has a ceramic stove. The large garden has a ping-pong table, bocce court and a sandbox for the kids.

Accommodation
Guestrooms: *2 doubles, also single occupancy, private baths; additional beds on request*
Services & Amenities: *German spoken; rooms cleaned every day; tourist information; dinner reservation; garden; private parking*
Rates: *single room €, double €€. Discounts for children -15%*
Credit cards: *accepted*
Pets: 🐕

Gästehaus Sanin
Therese Sanin
via M. Sparer 8
località Ganda di Sopra
39057 Appiano sulla Strada del Vino/Eppan an der Weinstrasse (BZ)
tel. and fax 0471 664547
Open all year

This large house, surrounded by greenery, is located at the foot of the rocky ramparts of the Penegal-Macaian with a view of the Dolomites. It has six Tyrolean style guestrooms, a two-level garden and a terrace with a veranda in the shade of a large cherry tree. The large, self-service breakfast, which includes natural marmalades, local products and various types of bread, can be enjoyed either in one's room or outdoors.

Accommodation
Guestrooms: *6 (1 single, 2 doubles, 2 triples, 1 quadruple, private baths)*
Services & Amenities: *German spoken; rooms cleaned every day; complimentary tourist information; kitchenette; terrace; private parking*
Rates: *€ per person. Discounts for children -30%*
Credit cards: *accepted*
Pets: 🐕

Bressanone/Brixen (Bolzano)

Haus Lasäun
famiglia Prosch
via Sant'Andrea 48/B
località Sant'Andrea
39042 Bressanone/Brixen (BZ)
tel. 0472 834841
www.lasaun.web.de
Closed: November

Just a few miles from the city, surrounded by lots of greenery, including a nearby forest of red pine, Haus Lasäun is the perfect place for special holidays, in the wintertime or summertime, since it's only a short distance from the Cima del Plose and Valcroce ski slopes. The large breakfast is in the Alto Adige tradition and is served in the dining room reserved for the guests.

Accommodation
Guestrooms: *3 doubles, also single occupancy, private baths*
Services & Amenities: *German spoken; rooms cleaned every day; tourist information; terrace; garden; private parking*
Minimum stay: *3 nights*
Rates: *double €. Children under 3 free; 3 to 10 -20%*
Credit cards: *not accepted*
Pets: 🚫

Brunico/Bruneck (Bolzano)

Haus Obermair
famiglia Obermair
in der Sandgrube 16
località Riscone
39031 Brunico/Bruneck (BZ)
tel. and fax 0474 410166
Closed: November and May

A happy, friendly atmosphere characterizes the hospitality of the Obermair family. This large house is not far from the ski slopes – a veritable paradise for skiers – which are reachable by using the free ski-bus service. The modernly furnished rooms give precedence to the warmth of wood, and the rich breakfast is served in a small room which also has games for children. Bicycles are available for the guests.

Accommodation
Guestrooms: *5 doubles, also single occupancy, private bath; additional bed on request*
Services & Amenities: *German spoken; rooms cleaned every 3 days; bike rental; terrace; garden*
Rates: *€ per person. Children under 6 -50%; 7 to 12 -30%*
Credit cards: *not accepted*
Pets: 🚫

Campo Tures/Sand in Taufers (Bolzano)

Walsterhofer Hof
Karl Achmüller
località Camminata 14
39032 Campo Tures/
Sand in Taufers (BZ)
tel. and fax 0474 678477
www.achmueller.südtirol.com
Open all year

The Wasterhofer Hof is a converted, reconstructed farm mansion with an interesting horseshoe shape. This B&B has Tyrol-decorated rooms and a rustic dining room that has a characteristic wall stove, where guests can comfortably gather to enjoy a nice

Accommodation
Guestrooms: *4 doubles, private baths; additional bed on request* ♿
Services & Amenities: *German spoken; rooms cleaned every day; tourist information; terrace; garden; private parking*
Minimum stay: *3 nights*
Rates: *double room €€. Children under 4 free*
Credit cards: *not accepted*
Pets:

breakfast featuring local specialties, including sweet and non-sweet products. The host, who is a connoisseur of the interesting local culture, is only too happy to share his knowledge with his guests.

Castelrotto/Kastelruth (Bolzano)

Haus Harderer
famiglia Tröbinger
via Platten 20
39040 Castelrotto/Kastelruth (BZ)
tel. 0471 706702
Open all year

The hosts of this B&B provide their guests with a large breakfast, that features all the local traditional and natural products. If desired, hosts will also willingly accompany their guests on hikes in the area. Furthermore, they provide a small cooking

Accommodation
Guestrooms: *3 (1 single and 2 doubles, private baths) and 1 mini-apartment (4 beds)*
Services & Amenities: *German spoken; rooms cleaned every day; complimentary tourist information; kitchenette; garden; private parking*
Minimum stay: *2 nights*
Rates: *single room €, double €€. Additional bed supplement €. Discounts for children*
Credit cards: *not accepted*
Pets:

area and refrigerator for those who would like to prepare

their own snacks. Nearby, the Buxi stop and the free bus-taxi service will take the guests to the Siusi Alps.

Cornedo all'Isarco/Karneid (Bolzano)

Haus Schönblick
Johann Vieider
località Cornedo 18
39050 Cornedo all'Isarco/Karneid (BZ)
tel. 0471 365077
Open all year

Located in a nice, quiet and out-of-the-way place, Haus Schönblick, with its friendly atmosphere – mainly created by its wood furnishings – warmly welcomes its guests, who are accommodated in a recently-restructured mansard. The large breakfast is served in a reserved dining room, and there

Accommodation
Guestrooms: *4 doubles, private baths, additional bed on request*
Services & Amenities: *German spoken; rooms cleaned every 3 days; complimentary tourist information; terrace; garden; private parking*
Rates: *double room €€. Discounts for children*
Credit cards: *not accepted*
Pets:

is a garden with tables and chairs, which makes a perfect place to relax.

Curon Venosta/Graun Im Vinschgau (Bolzano)

Haus Lechtaler
Veronika Lechtaler Punter
Neudorf 13, località Resia
39020 Curon Venosta/
Graun Im Vinschgau (BZ)
tel. and fax 0473 633202
Open all year

Haus Lechtaler offers comfortable accommodation in the center of town, right on the edge of the forest. The host personally serves the guests and maintains a typical Tyrol atmosphere both in the rooms and in the living room, where a nice breakfast featuring local products is served. In the summertime the guests can enjoy the garden and use the barbecue for grilling meat outdoors.

Accommodation
Guestrooms: *4 doubles, private baths*
Services & Amenities: *German spoken; rooms cleaned every day; complimentary tourist information; terrace; garden; smokers welcome; private parking*
Rates: *double room €€. Discounts for children*
Credit cards: *not accepted*
Pets: 🐕

Dimaro (Trento)

• Bed & Breakfast Italia
Code TR3
tel. 06 6878618
fax 06 6878619
info@bbitalia.it
www.bbitalia.it
Closed: varies

The B&B is located at Dimaro, 5 km from Marilleva and 20 km from the Stelvio and San Bernardo National Parks. There are six double rooms, all with TV, telephone, private bathroom with shower and hair dryer. The furnishings are all in wood, from the furniture to the ceilings and floors. Continental breakfast is served in the room by the hosts. The village is 15 km from Madonna di Campiglio and 4 km from the ski slopes.

Accommodation
Guestrooms: *6 doubles* ♿
Services & Amenities: *French, English and German are spoken; rooms cleaned every 3 days; complimentary tourist information; baby-sitting service; bike rental; smokers welcome; private parking*
Minimum stay: *2 nights*
Rates: *€€*
Credit cards: VISA MC *Bancomat*
Pets: 🚫🐕

Dobbiaco/Toblach (Bolzano)

Villa Kassewalder
Anna Paola Cracco
via Alemagna 8
39034 Dobbiaco/Toblach (BZ)
tel. 0474 972211
a.p.cracco@welt.it
Open all year

This B&B, located on the edge of the woods in Dobbiaco Nuova, offers four rooms with period furnishings, decorated in the colors of such flowers as forget-me-not, gentianella, arnica and rhododendron. The abundant buffet breakfast includes natural desserts and is served in either the family dining room or in the rustic living room with a large fireplace and exposed beams.

Accommodation
Guestrooms: *4 (3 double rooms and 1 triple, private baths)*
Services & Amenities: *French, English, German and Spanish are spoken; rooms cleaned every day; complimentary tourist information; garden; private parking*
Minimum stay: *3 nights*
Rates: *double room €€. Additional bed supplement €*
Credit cards: *not accepted*
Pets: 🚫🐕

Lana/Lana (Bolzano)

Haus Buabmbrunn
famiglia Santer
via del Sole 8
39011 Lana/Lana (BZ)
tel. 0473 561616
Open all year

Haus Buabmbrunn is situated in a very peaceful location, surrounded by an apple orchard; it provides five comfortable rooms with Tyrol style furnishings, and a healthy breakfast that includes local apples. The breakfast is served in a special dining room where the guests can also spend their time. The garden has a swing and a sandbox for the kids.

Accommodation
Guestrooms: *5 double rooms, also single occupancy, private baths; additional bed on request ♿*
Services & Amenities: *German spoken; rooms cleaned every day; complimentary tourist information; garden; private parking*
Rates: *single room €, double €€€. Additional bed supplement €€. Discounts for children and extended stays*
Credit cards: *accepted*
Pets: 🐾

Lasa/Laas (Bolzano)

Haus De Martin
Verena De Martin
via Venosta 95
39023 Lasa/Laas (BZ)
tel. 0473 626565
Closed: January and November

This modern building on the edge of town hosts its guests in two comfortable double rooms with private bath. The rich breakfast is served in the rustic living room, where the guests can also spend a pleasant evening. In the wintertime, it's best to make reservations. Just a few kilometers away, guests can visit Glorenza, surrounded by its square, 16th-century stone walls and three-door, corner towers.

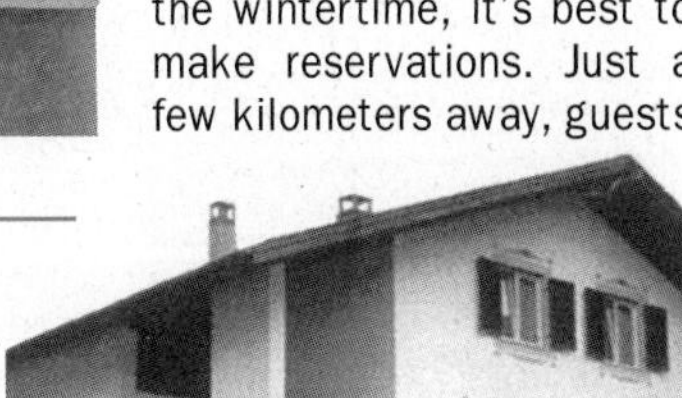

Accommodation
Guestrooms: *2 double rooms, private baths*
Services & Amenities: *German spoken; rooms cleaned every day; complimentary tourist information; garden; private parking*
Rates: *double room €€. Discounts for children and extended stays*
Credit cards: *not accepted*
Pets: 🐾

Haus Gartenblick
Franz Niederfriniger
località Tanas
39023 Lasa/Laas (BZ)
tel. 0473 739839
Open all year

A painted house in Valle di Lasa

Hospitality at an altitude of 1450 meters in a beautiful, traditionally-styled house surrounded by woods, and the availability of a bike. The typically Tyrolean breakfast, which features the house's natural sweet and non-sweet products, can be consumed autonomously. There are two independent apartments furnished in the simple style, and also a children's playground right nearby. Garden is at the guests' disposal

Accommodation
Guestrooms: *2 apartments (3 and 6 beds) ♿*
Services & Amenities: *German and English are spoken; rooms cleaned every day; complimentary tourist information; kitchen and kitchenette use by request; bike rental; terrace; garden; private parking*
Rates: *€ per person. Discounts for extended stays*
Credit cards: *not accepted*
Pets: 🐾

Niederfriniger
Gerlinde Niederfriniger
via Plur 14, località Oris
39023 Lasa/Laas (BZ)
tel. 0473 739819
niederfriniger.gerlinde@rolmail.net
Open all year

Accommodation
Guestrooms: *4 doubles, private baths*
Services & Amenities: *German spoken; rooms cleaned every day; complimentary tourist information; bike rental; terrace; garden; private parking*
Rates: *€ per person*
Credit cards: *not accepted*
Pets:

The hosts of this comfortable B&B try to meet the needs of their guests, also by putting at their disposal books, newspapers, magazine and games in the living room, and bicycles for riding around in the nearby area. The rooms, decorated in the Tyrolean style can be provided with TV and a telephone on request. The rich, abundant breakfast includes sweet products as well as Alto Adige non-sweet specialties.

Malè (Trento)

La Segosta
Filippo Endrissi
via Trento 59
38027 Malè (TN)
tel. 0463 901390
fax 0463 900675
Closed: June and October

This B&B, which is right in the center of town, is hosted by a single family and connected directly to the family restaurant of the same name.

Accommodation
Guestrooms: *8 double bedrooms, also single occupancy, private baths; additional bed on request* ♿
Services & Amenities: *English is spoken; rooms cleaned every day; complimentary tourist information; lunch & dinner reservations; terrace; Internet access; smokers welcome; private parking*
Rates: *single room €€, double €€€€. Additional bed supplement €. Discounts for children*
Credit cards: *accepted*
Pets:

This early 19th-C style house that was recently renovated and has a typical mountain atmosphere with light-wood furnishings. The well-stocked buffet breakfast is served in the restaurant.

Merano/Meran (Bolzano)

Haus Gamper
Christina Gamper
via Rosengarten 4
39012 Merano/Meran (BZ)
tel. and fax 0473 442636
Open all year

This B&B definitely stands out because it provides a rich breakfast consisting of sliced ham and salami, three types of bread, natural marmalades, creamed cottage cheese, mixtures of cereals and fresh fruit. Breakfast is served in the guest dining room (which has a refrigerator), in the summertime, out in the garden. All three guestrooms have wooden ceilings, and one has rustic style furnishings. The town of Merano is especially fascinating because of its events, which include concerts and folklore festivals, one of the most popular of which is the Grape

Accommodation
Guestrooms: *3 doubles, also single occupancy, shared bath; additional bed on request*
Services & Amenities: *German spoken; rooms cleaned every day; complimentary tourist information; terrace; garden; private parking*
Rates: *single €, double €€. Discounts for children and extended stays*
Credit cards: *not accepted*
Pets:

NATURNO/NATURNS (BOLZANO)

Stein-Hof
Agnese Götsch
via Stein 10
39025 Naturno/Naturns (BZ)
tel. and fax 0473 667451
steinhof@katamail.com
www.steinhofnaturns.com
Open all year

This Tyrolean house is surrounded by lots of greenery and an apple orchard, and is just 1 km from town. Its rooms are furnished in the local style, and it also has one independent apartment. The rich breakfast, is served in the rustic dining room and includes apples from the orchard. The B&B also has a characteristic tavern with fireplace that guests can share with the family to roast chestnuts together.

ACCOMMODATION
Guestrooms: *5 doubles, private baths and 1 apartment (4 beds)*
Services & Amenities: *German spoken; rooms cleaned every day; complimentary tourist information; dinner reservation; terrace; garden; private parking*
Rates: *double room €€, apartment €€€. Discounts for children - 30%*
Credit cards: *not accepted*
Pets: *not allowed*

NAZ SCIAVES/NATZ SCHABS (BOLZANO)

Gästehaus Klara
Klara Klement
Oelberg 111
39040 Naz Sciaves/Natz Schabs (BZ)
tel. 0472 4150122
Open all year

ACCOMMODATION
Guestrooms: *5 doubles, also single occupancy, private baths*
Services & Amenities: *German spoken; rooms cleaned every day; complimentary tourist information; terrace; garden; private parking*
Rates: *single room €, double €€. Children under 3 -30%; 3 to 12 -20%*
Credit cards: *not accepted*
Pets: *not allowed*

The town is located 9 km from Bressanone and one hour's drive from the city of Innsbruck. It is situated on a very sunny plateau at an altitude of 900 m. Gästhaus Klara, built in Tyrolean style, has five rooms availables for the guests and provides a large buffet breakfast with genuine marmalade, fresh fruit juice and different local products, all served in a large guest living room.

NOVA LEVANTE/WELSCHNOFEN (BOLZANO)

Haus Angelika
Norbert Obkircher
vicolo del Mulino 2
39056 Nova Levante/Welschnofen
tel. and fax 0471 613190
info@hausangelika.com
www.hausangelika.com
Open all year

The B&B, situated on the edge of town, is characterized by its very friendly hosts. All of the four large rooms, with their classic furnishings, have panoramic balconies. There's also a large terrace available for the guests, that has a solarium and a characteristic little wooden breakfast room. The breakfast is quite rich and features a choice of sweet and nonsweet specialties, as well as natural products.

ACCOMMODATION
Guestrooms: *4 doubles, private baths; additional bed on request*
Services & Amenities: *German spoken; rooms cleaned every day; tourist information; dinner reservation; terrace; private parking*
Rates: *double room €-€€. Children under 6 free; 6 to 12 -50%*
Credit cards: *not accepted*
Pets: *not allowed*

Haus Ratzöhlerhof
Anna Pichler Montel
vicolo Jocher 4
39056 Nova Levante/ Welschnofen (BZ)
tel. and fax 0471 613061
Open: Christmas holidays to Easter holidays and June to mid October

ACCOMMODATION
Guestrooms: *6 doubles, private bath*
Services & Amenities: *English and German are spoken; rooms cleaned every day; complimentary tourist information; terrace; garden; smokers welcome; private parking*
Rates: *double €€. Discounts for children -30%*
Credit cards: *not accepted*
Pets: not allowed

The house is located in a large field on the edge of a forest. The six guestrooms have Tyrolean furnishings and each has a balcony. Breakfast includes a choice of beverages, eggs, sliced ham and salami, and is served in a small room for the guests. The hospitality also includes a visitor's card that permits obtaining special privileges and discounts. Skiers also have free use of the skibus.

ORTISEI/SANKT ULRICH IN GRÖDEN (BOLZANO)

Sulè-Hof
famiglia Demetz Roman
via Nevel 83
39046 Ortisei/ Sankt Ulrich in Gröden (BZ)
tel. and fax 0471 797416
sule@val_gardena.com
www.val_gardena.com/sule-hof
Open all year

Sulè-Hof is an ancient, restructured 13th-century farm home run by the Demetz family. Breakfast, with its rich buffet includes local products and is served in the characteristic rustic Tyrolean living room. This room is where the guests can also spend a pleasant evening sitting on the benches around the typical wall stove. The nice, large garden has various children's playing equipment.

ACCOMMODATION
Guestrooms: *4 doubles, also single occupancy, private bath; additional bed on request*
Services & Amenities: *German spoken; rooms cleaned every day; complimentary tourist information; terrace; garden; smokers welcome; private parking*
Rates: *double €€. Discounts for children -30% and -50%*
Credit cards: *not accepted*
Pets: not allowed

PARCINES/PARTSCHINS (BOLZANO)

Haus Föhrenegg
Sig. Kasser
via Föhren 4, località Rablà
39020 Parcines/Partschins (BZ)
tel. and fax 0473 967175
Open: March to November

ACCOMMODATION
Guestrooms: *6 (2 singles and 4 doubles, 2 with shared bath and 4 with private bath)* ♿
Services & Amenities: *German spoken; rooms cleaned every day; tourist information; terrace; garden; smokers welcome; private parking*
Minimum stay: *6 nights*
Rates: *single €, double €€. Children under 10 -50%*
Credit cards: *not accepted*
Pets: not allowed

The large garden covers about 2,000 sq.meters and has a lawn chair and a ping-pong table. Five of the six rooms have a balcony. Breakfast is served in the small dining room and, every day, it features different types of white and brown bread and sliced ham and salami. The family is happy to provide any required information regarding the area, for hikes various active initiatives, entertainment and sports.

Haus Holzknecht
Gottfried Holzknecht
via Lodner 1
39020 Parcines/Partschins (BZ)
tel. and fax 0473 967316
Open: Easter holidays to early November

This modern house, in the Tyrolean style, has 4 functional rooms and a small apartment availables for guests. The breakfast features traditional Alto Adige products, various types of bread and is served in the dining room for the guests. The town is 2 km away and has a covered swimming pool and a bicycle rental service. The special artistic attraction at Naturno is the San Procolo church with its 18th and 19th-century frescos.

ACCOMMODATION
Guestrooms: *4 (1 single and 3 doubles, private bath) and 1 mini-apartment (3 beds)*
Services & Amenities: *German spoken; rooms cleaned every day; complimentary tourist information; kitchenette; terrace; garden; smokers welcome; private parking*
Rates: *single €, double €€. Discounts for children*
Credit cards: *not accepted*
Pets:

Haus Platzgummer
Elisabeth Platzgummer
via Hans-Guet 25, località Rablà
39020 Parcines/Partschins (BZ)
tel. and fax 0473 967043
Open: mid March to mid November

Located in an extremely quite place, far from the din of the traffic, Haus Platzgummer has a very nice, well-equipped garden. This Tyrolean-style B&B has recently been renovated, and has six plain, essentially furnished rooms. The breakfast is rich, as the local use, and is served in a small dining room which is also at the disposal of the guests in the evening. The host is a passionate excursionist and is only too happy to help the guests plan their outings.

ACCOMMODATION
Guestrooms: *6 (1 single and 5 doubles, private bath)*
Services & Amenities: *German spoken; rooms cleaned every day; complimentary tourist information; terrace; garden; smokers welcome; private parking*
Minimum stay: *3 nights*
Rates: *single €, double €€. Discounts for children and extended stays*
Credit cards: *not accepted*
Pets:

PINZOLO (TRENTO)

• Bed & Breakfast Italia
Code TR2

tel. 06 6878618
fax 06 6878619
info@bbitalia.it
www.bbitalia.it
Closed: varies

ACCOMMODATION
Guestrooms: *4 (2 singles, 2 doubles)*
Services & Amenities: *German spoken; rooms cleaned every 3 days; complimentary tourist information; terrace; private parking*
Minimum stay: *2 nights*
Rates: *€€*
Credit cards: *VISA MC Bancomat*
Pets:

The house is located 10 km from Madonna di Campiglio, in the heart of the Adamello-Brenta Natural Park. Recently refurbished, it is in a convenient position close to the ski lifts, ice stadium, cross-country skiing tracks, sport facilities, golf course and horse-riding club. The rooms are furnished in a Tyrolese style, and share two bathrooms with shower. Guests can also enjoy a pub-like family room and a lounge.

San Candido/Innichen (Bolzano)

Furtscheggerhof
Alois Furtschegger
via Kranzhof 7
39038 San Candido/Innichen (BZ)
tel. 0474 913433
furtschegger@tnet.it
Open all year

Furtscheggerhof is an ancient, recently restructured farm house and is not far from San Candido district. The simple, functional Alto Adige style of this house, as well as its traditional furnishings has been kept intact. Guests can enjoy the farm's production of smoked speck and relax in the rustic living room, which has a characteristic wall stove and surrounding benches.

Accommodation
Guestrooms: *4 doubles, private bath; additional bed on request*
Services & Amenities: *German spoken; rooms cleaned every day; complimentary tourist information; terrace; garden; smokers welcome; private parking*
Rates: *double €€*
Credit cards: *not accepted*
Pets: 🐕

Santa Cristina Valgardena/Sankt Christina in Gröden (Bolzano)

Haus Everest
Giuseppe Kasslatter
via Cisles 127
39047 Santa Cristina Valgardena/
Sankt Christina in Gröden (BZ)
tel. 0471 793150
Closed: April to June

This house, the property of the Kasslatter family, is at Santa Cristina and enjoys a sunny position with a beautiful view of Sasso Lungo. There are five very well-lit rooms furnished with light-colored furniture. The large buffet breakfast features Alto Adige products and is served in a room reserved for the guests. During the summertime, guests can sit out on the terrace and suntan or relax in the garden under the big trees.

Accommodation
Guestrooms: *5 (1 single and 4 doubles, private bath)* ♿
Services & Amenities: *German spoken; rooms cleaned every day; complimentary tourist information; terrace; garden; smokers welcome; private parking*
Minimum stay: *3 nights*
Rates: *single €, double €€. Discounts for children -30%*
Credit cards: *not accepted*
Pets: no

San Vigilio di Marebbe/Sankt Vigil in Enneberg (Bolzano)

Casa Brüscia
Irma Burchia Ploner
via al Plan de Sora 29/1
39030 San Vigilio di Marebbe/
Sankt Vigil in Enneberg (BZ)
tel. 0474 501191, fax 0474 501848
info@ciasabruescia.com
www.ciasabruescia.com
Open all year

The presence of a family of ski instructors and ski champions makes this B&B the ideal solution for skiers. The zone also offers mountain-bike and hiking trails among the mountains, with special rates for guests. The abundant buffet breakfast is served in the typical, rustic, Tyrolean living room with its characteristic, round wall stove with a space on top with cushions for children. Guests can also relax in the garden.

Accommodation
Guestrooms: *6 (1 single and 5 doubles, private bath)*
Services & Amenities: *German spoken; rooms cleaned every day; tourist information; smokers welcome; terrace; garden; educational courses by request; private parkinking*
Rates: *single €, double €-€€. Discounts for children -50%*
Credit cards: *not accepted*
Pets: 🐕

Sarentino/Sarntal (Bolzano)

Garni Hueber
famiglia Hueber
Nordheim 68
39058 Sarentino/Sarntal (BZ)
tel. and fax 0471 623117
hueber.jutta@rolmail.net
Open: May to early November

This B&B is located in a quiet place at an altitude of 1000 meters, in the middle of a beautiful meadow at the edge of a pine forest. The Garni Heuber's rich breakfast, which features local products, both sweet and non-sweet, is normally served in the kitchen. The large garden has a sandbox for children.

Accommodation
Guestrooms: *5 doubles, private bath; additional bed on request*
Services & Amenities: *English and German are spoken; rooms cleaned every day; complimentary tourist information; terrace; garden; smokers welcome; private parking*
Rates: *double €€. Additional bed supplement €. Children under 5 free*
Credit cards: *not accepted*
Pets: 🐕

Selva di Val Gardena/Wolkenstein in Gröden (Bolzano)

Anton Senoner
Daunëi 73
39048 Selva di Val Gardena/ Wolkenstein in Gröden (BZ)
tel. 0471 794024
senoner.a@rolmmail.net
Closed: April, May, October and November

This B&B, in a recently-constructed home with comfortable furnishings, is located in the middle of the fields of Daunëi, which is 2 km from Selva. The rich breakfast includes local products and is served in a special dining room that also provides cooking facilities. The hosts are well acquainted with the history and traditions of the valley, and are more than willing to provide any information. Guests are also welcome to use any of the books in the family library.

Accommodation
Guestrooms: *5 (3 doubles and 2 triple rooms, private bath)*
Services & Amenities: *French, English and German are spoken; rooms cleaned every three days; complimentary tourist information; kitchenette; garden; smokers welcome; private parking*
Rates: *€ per person. Discounts for children*
Credit cards: *not accepted*
Pets: 🚫🐕

Haus Seceda
famiglia Ploner
via Meisules 125
39048 Selva di Val Gardena/ Wolkenstein in Gröden (BZ)
tel. and fax 0471 795297
Open all year

This B&B is located in a quiet area not far from the church and the stores. Besides the traditional products, both sweet and non-sweet (such as speck, sliced ham and salami, various cheeses and strudel), the rich breakfast also includes Sunday cake and fresh fruit. Breakfast is served in a small comfortable dining room where guests can also relax in the evening. In wintertime, Selva offers its ice stadium and, in summertime, it's the realm of the rock-climbers.

Accommodation
Guestrooms: *6 (5 doubles and 1 triple room, private bath)*
Services & Amenities: *German spoken; rooms cleaned every day; complimentary tourist information; terrace; garden; smokers welcome; private parking*
Rates: *€ to €€ per person. Discounts for children*
Credit cards: *not accepted*
Pets: 🐕

Villa Larix
Hildegard Pezzei
strada Freina 18
39048 Selva di Val Gardena/
Wolkenstein in Gröden (BZ)
tel. and fax 0471 795318
Open all year

Accommodation
Guestrooms: *4 triples, private bath*
Services & Amenities: *French, English and German are spoken; rooms cleaned every day; tourist information; smokers welcome; garden; private parking*
Rates: *€€ per person. Discounts for children*
Credit cards: *not accepted*
Pets: ✓

Located centrally in Selva di Val Gardena, this B&B is noted for its great dedication to flowers. Breakfast, served in the special dining room for the guests, also included paté or chocolate creams, eggs and sliced ham and salami. The garden has nice lawn and is provided with lawn chairs and a ping-pong table. The hosts are happy to provide information regarding the things of natural interest in the area, including the national park. The cabin and chair lifts, located just a short distance away, takes guests to the Sella Pass, the Garden Pass, and the Cimpinoi and Siusi Alps.

Villa Prà Ronch
Erika Rabaner
via La Selva 80
39048 Selva di Val Gardena/
Wolkenstein in Gröden (BZ)
tel. and fax 0471 794064
praronch@val-gardenia.com
www.praronch.com
Open all year

A particularly fascinating stay is what Villa Prà Ronch offers to its guests: formerly an old hay barn it was converted into a romantic country house. It has elegant, refined, Tyrolean-type furnishings and most of the interiors are wainscoted. All the spacious five rooms have TV and a security box. The garden is at the guests disposal. The buffet

Accommodation
Guestrooms: *5 (4 doubles, also single occupancy, and 1 mansard, 4 beds, private bath)*
Services & Amenities: *English and German are spoken; rooms cleaned every day; tourist info; garden; smokers welcome; private parking*
Rates: *€€ per person. Discounts for children*
Credit cards: *not accepted*
Pets: ✓

breakfast, served in a special room with fireplace, includes genuine products made by the Selva farmers, as well as such typical desserts as strudel and Linzer cake.

Ultimo/Ulten (Bolzano)

Haus Elisabeth
Angelika Godio
Winkel 116, località Santa Gertrude
39016 Ultimo/Ulten (BZ)
tel. and fax 0473 798086
Open all year

Accommodation
Guestrooms: *6 (4 doubles, also single occupancy, and 2 small rooms in the mansard, private bath)*
Services & Amenities: *German spoken; rooms cleaned every day; complimentary tourist information; garden; smokers welcome; private parking*
Rates: *€€ per person. Children under 2 free. Discounts for extended stays*
Credit cards: *not accepted*
Pets: ✗

Located at the bottom of Ultimo Valley, Haus Elisabeth is surrounded by meadows and woods. It's only a 15-min drive from the ski lifts and just a 5-min walk from a cross-country ski trail. A fireplace and a Tyrolean stove at the entrance of the house create a nice atmosphere. Children can enjoy a separate area in the mansard. Breakfast provides a selection of traditional products and is served either in the special dining room or out on the terrace. The guests can also enjoy the living room with fireplace

Sunnleit
Famiglia Zöschg
Sunnleit 164
località San Pancrazio
39010 Ultimo (BZ)
tel. 0473 787130, fax 0473 787366
Open: Easter to early November

Sunnleit is located in Ultimo Valley, just 1 km from San Pancrazio. The hosts only speak German. The three guestrooms all have double beds and a balcony. One room has a private bath and the other two share a bathroom that also has a shower. The guests are served a substantial breakfast of traditional products, both sweet and non-sweet, which they have in the typical Tyrolean living room together with their hosts.

Accommodation
Guestrooms: *3 (2 doubles, 1 triple) with 2 shared baths*
Services & Amenities: *German spoken*
Rates: *€ per person.*
Credit cards: *not accepted*
Pets:

Valle Aurina/Ahrntal (Bolzano)

Gästehaus Heimatland
Annemarie Mittersteiner
località Cadipietra
39030 Valle Aurina/Ahrntal (BZ)
tel. 0474 652246
Open: Christmas to Easter holidays and June to September

Accommodation
Guestrooms: *6 doubles,private bath; additional bed on request*
Services & Amenities: *German spoken; rooms cleaned every day; complimentary tourist information; dinner reservation; garden; private parking*
Rates: *double €. Children under 7 -30%; 7 to 11 -20%*
Credit cards: *not accepted*
Pets:

This B&B, though located just off the Aurina Valley's main road, is surrounded by large fields. This accommodation offers six guestrooms, in both modern and traditional Tyrolean styles. The Italian style breakfast is served in a special dining room. The furnished garden has a beautiful pergola that's perfect for spending time enjoying some relaxation.

Varna/Vahrn (Bolzano)

Haus Wachtler
Veronika Wachter Tauber
Strada Vecchia della Pusteria 11
339040 Varna/Vahrn (BZ)
tel. 0472 837006
Open all year

Surrounded by fields and only about 3 or 4 km from Lake Varna, Haus Wachtler is close to an old 12th-century convent that has been converted into a public library. The cordial hosts provide four plain, functional rooms with bath, and an abundant breakfast. This includes a selection of various beverages, sliced ham and salami and various cheeses, white and brown bread, as well as homemade marmalade and Sunday desserts, served in a small dining room for the guests. There's also a parking area, a sandbox in the garden for the kids, and some tennis courts in Varna.

Accommodation
Guestrooms: *4 doubles, private bath*
Services & Amenities: *German spoken*
Rates: *€€ per person. Discount for additional bed -20%*
Credit cards: *not accepted*
Pets:

Veneto

Abano Terme (Padua)

Casa Ciriani
Silvana Ciriani
via Guazzi 1
35031 Abano Terme (PD)
tel. 049 715272, mob. 368 3779226
fax 049 8601422
euganenalife@job.pd.it
Closed: July

Just 4 km from the city and surrounded by a large park with trees, this B&B, which is hosted in a large, recently-built, traditionally-styled house, serves a large breakfast either in a special room or, in the summertime, under the portico that opens onto the garden. The small town of Abano, with its thermal baths, offers all types of sports and amusement facilities.

Accommodation
Guestrooms: *3 doubles, also single occupancy, private bath; additional bed on request*
Services & Amenities: *French, English and German are spoken; rooms cleaned every day; complimentary tourist information; terrace; garden; smokers welcome; private parking*
Minimum stay: *2 nights*
Rates: *single €€, double €€€. Additional bed supplement €€*
Credit cards: *not accepted*
Pets:

Agordo (Belluno)

Sòl Fiorì
Nives Pezzè
via Campo dei Fiori 11
32021 Agordo (BL)
tel. and fax 0437 63460
mob. 328 6353395
solfiori@bbdolomiti.it
• B&B Dolomiti nelle montagne venete
tel. 0437 949000, 0437 949100
info@bbdolomiti.net
www.bbdolomiti.net
Open all year

This house, with its garden, is just 5 minutes from the center of town. The B&B rooms are on the top floor mansard, which has a living room reserved for the guests. The breakfast, which is served in this living room, can also consist of non-sweet products and bacon and eggs on request.

Accommodation
Guestrooms: *3 doubles, also single occupancy, private bath.*
Services & Amenities: *English and German are spoken; rooms cleaned every 3 days; tourist information; baby-sitting service; garden; smokers welcome; private parking*
Rates: *single €, double €€. Discounts for children and extended stays*
Credit cards: *accepted*
Pets:

Asolo (Treviso)

Ca' Leda
Valy Miotto
via Frattalunga 8, località Casella
31011 Asolo (TV)
tel. 0423 55298, mob. 333 8575132
fax 0422 590973
bebbabeda@interfree.it
• Associazione Turisti per Casa
tel. and fax 0532 63066
buccimg@libero.it
www.turistipercasa.it
Open all year

This B&B is in a modern house that has a garden and is located in the countryside just

3 km from the old center. Guests have a large upper-floor, which has a living-room-studio and a view of the city and the Euganei hills. Breakfast is served on the ground-floor veranda or in the garden. Guests have the use of bicycles for riding along the special biking paths and visiting places of historical and artistic interests in the area.

Accommodation
Guestrooms: *1 double, private bath; additional bed on request*
Services & Amenities: *English and German are spoken; rooms cleaned every 3 days; complimentary tourist information; bike rental; terrace; air conditioning; garden; smokers welcome; private parking*
Rates: *€€€. Additional bed supplement €*
Credit cards: *not accepted*
Pets:

Badia Polesine (Rovigo)

B&B Adriana
Adriana Ogheri Zambruni
via Salvo D'Acquisto 66
45021 Badia Polesine (RO)
tel. 0425 51998
mob. 333 2799039
zam15@libero.it
http://digilander.iol.it/lasierl/
• Euganean Life International
tel. 0429 56156
mob. 347 4355474
fax 0429 56156
elit@bandb-veneto.it
www.bandb-veneto.it/euganeanlife
Open all year

This single-family house is located in a residential area close to one of the banks of the Adige, along which it is nice to take walks or bike rides. Breakfast, English if desired, is served either in the family kitchen or under the portico.

Accommodation
Guestrooms: *3 (2 double bedrooms, also single occupancy, 1 quadruple, shared bath)*
Services & Amenities: *English spoken; rooms cleaned every 3 days; tourist information; kitchen use by request; bike rental; garden; smokers welcome; private parking*
Rates: *single €, double €€, quadruple €€€. Children under 3 free. Discounts for extended stays*
Credit cards: *not accepted*
Pets:

Belluno

Bianco e Blu
Elga and Luisa Cardin
via San Lorenzo 22
32100 Belluno
tel. 0437 949000, 0437 949100
mob. 340 3765778, 349 4245250
biancoeblu1@bbdolomiti.net,
biancoeblu2@bbdolomiti.net
• B&B Dolomiti nelle montagne venete
tel. 0437 949000, 0437 949100
info@bbdolomiti.net
www.bbdolomiti.net
Open all year

This tranquil house, with its garden, is located on the Mus-

soi hill. It makes a good starting point for hikes or bike rides through the woods, and a good base for reaching the ski slopes. Breakfast is served either in the family living room or in the garden. Transportation by car is available to and from the railroad station.

Accommodation
Guestrooms: *2 (1 double and 1 triple, also single occupancy, private bath)*
Services & Amenities: *French and English are spoken; rooms cleaned every 3 days; complimentary tourist information; garden; smokers welcome; private parking*
Rates: *single €, double €€, triple €€€. Children under 4 free, 4 to 11 -50%. Discounts for extended stays*
Credit cards: *not accepted*
Pets:

Chioggia (Venice)

La Torre
località Sottomarina
30015 Chioggia (VE)
• Vacanze in Famiglia
tel. and fax 041 455188, 041900385
email: margherit@tin.it
Open all year

This tall, narrow house is located in an old fishing village.The guestroom, decorated with 19th-C furniture, is on the ground floor with independent entrance. Breakfast, including local sweet items, can be served on the 5th floor terrace.

Accommodation
Guestrooms: *1 double, private bath; additional bed on request*
Services & Amenities: *French and English are spoken; rooms cleaned every 3 days; tourist information; lunch & dinner reservations; bike rental; air conditioning; smokers welcome*
Minimum stay: *2 nights*
Rates: *€€€. Additional bed supplement €. Children under 3 free*
Credit cards: *not accepted*
Pets: 🐕

• Bed & Breakfast Italia
Code V17
tel. 06 6878618, fax 06 6878619
info@bbitalia.it
www.bbitalia.it
Open: April to November

Ground-floor large independent apartment in a detached house with garden. The accommodation consists in two rooms, both with a wide balcony and private bathroom with shower.

Accommodation
Guestrooms: *2 triple rooms*
Services & Amenities: *English spoken; rooms cleaned every 3 days; tourist information; terrace*
Minimum stay: *2 nights*
Rates: €€
Credit cards: VISA MC *Bancomat*
Pets: 🚫

It is a 3 minute walk to the sea and 5 minutes to the town center. Padua, Venice and Treviso are 30 minute bus rides away.

Cinto Euganeo (Padua)

B&B Della Silfa TCI 10%
Silvia Zabai
via Santa Lucia 36
35030 Cinto Euganeo (PD)
tel. and fax 0429 94672
mob. 338 7977596
zasil@libero.it
www.bedebreakfast.it/zabai
• Euganean Life International
tel. & fax 0429 56156,
mob. 347 4355474 elit@bandb-veneto.it
www.bandb-veneto.it/euganeanlife
Closed: 1 to 15 August

This late 19th-C working-class house, restructured and with wooden furniture, is located 1 km from Cinto Eugenio, inside the Colli Eugenei Regional Park. Breakfast, that is served in a tavern-room on the ground floor, consists completely of such local organic products as cakes, biscuits, marmalades and honey; Engish breakfast can be served by request.

Accommodation
Guestrooms: *2 doubles, 1 suite, also single occupancy, private bath*
Services & Amenities: *English spoken; rooms cleaned every 3 days; tourist information; garden; smokers welcome; private parking*
Minimum stay: *3 nights*
Rates: *single €€, double €€-€€€. Discounts for extended stays*
Credit cards: *not accepted*
Pets: 🐕

Codognè (Treviso)

• Bed & Breakfast Italia TCI 10%
Code V11
tel. 06 6878618, fax 06 6878619
info@bbitalia.it
www.bbitalia.it
Closed: varies

18th-C villa surrounded by a park with a swimming pool. A whole floor is used by guests and has a lounge and bedrooms. It is furnished with 19th-C pieces. The lady of the house uses natural ingredients in her homemade breakfasts.

Accommodation
Guestrooms: *3 (2 doubles, 1 triple)*
Services & Amenities: *English and German are spoken; rooms cleaned every 3 days; tourist info; parking*
Minimum stay: *2 nights*
Rates: €€
Credit cards: VISA MC *Bancomat*
Pets: 🐕

Villa Ariella
Patricia Frare
via Mazzini 11
31013 Codognè (TV)
tel. and fax 0438 795394
repatti@tin.it, www.villaariella.com
Open all year

An 18th-century manor house in extensive walled grounds, with old trees and a small swimming pool. This B&B

consists in 3 bedrooms, and a lounge. Continental breakfast, prepared with natural and genuine produce, is served in the large rustic kitchen with fireplace or in the delightful garden.

Accommodation
Guestrooms: *3 (2 doubles and 1 triple room with private bath); additional bed on request*
Services & Amenities: *English and German are spoken; rooms cleaned every 3 days; tourist information; Internet access; garden; smokers welcome; private parking*
Minimum stay: *2 nights*
Rates: *double €€-€€€. Additional bed supplement €*
Credit cards: *not accepted*
Pets: ✓

Costabissara (Vicenza)

• Bed & Breakfast Italia
Code V13
tel. 06 6878618, fax 06 6878619
info@bbitalia.it
www.bbitalia.it
Closed: varies

Accommodation
Guestrooms: *3 (1 double, 2 triples)*
Services & Amenities: *French, English and German are spoken; rooms cleaned every 3 days; tourist information; private parking*
Minimum stay: *2 nights*
Rates: €€
Credit cards: VISA MC *Bancomat*
Pets: ✓

Characteristic farmhouse nestling in vegetation. The carefully furnished bedrooms have a bathroom with shower or tub. Guests can enjoy the patio where they can breakfast in the warmer months, a lounge with a TV and fireplace. On request, the owner will make a car available.

Erbezzo (Verona)

B&B Genderli 21/23
Maria Luisa Roberti
contrada Genderli 21/23
37020 Erbezzo (VR)
tel. 045 7075219, ila.roberti@tin.it
http://space.tin.it/viaggi/ila.roberti
Open all year

TCI 10%

This very friendly B&B is located in a house made of stone and wood and is situated in a community surrounded by meadows and woods. Breakfast is served either in the family kitchen or on the terrace, that gives a nice view of the valley.

Accommodation
Guestrooms: *2 double, also single occupancy, private and shared bath*
Services & Amenities: *English spoken; complimentary tourist information; rooms cleaned every 3 days; kitchen use by request; terrace; garden; smokers welcome; parking*
Minimum stay: *2 nights*
Rates: *single €€, double €€€. Additional bed supplement €. Discounts for WWF, LIPU and ARCI members*
Credit cards: *not accepted*
Pets: ✓

• Bed & Breakfast Italia
Code V31
contrada Genderli
37020 Erbezzo (VR)
tel. 06 6878618, fax 06 6878619
info@bbitalia.it
www.bbitalia.it
Closed: varies

An old stone-roofed building situated 35 km from Verona. A double bedroom with attic-roof and fireplace, built onto an old barn, is set aside for guests.

Accommodation
Guestrooms: *1 double*
Services & Amenities: *English spoken; rooms cleaned every 3 days; complimentary tourist information; smokers welcome; private parking*
Minimum stay: *2 nights*
Rates: €€
Credit cards: VISA MC *Bancomat*
Pets: ✗

Private bathroom with shower. The ancient Contrada Genderli is located close to the Monti Lessini Nature Park on the European Path, which goes from Lake Constance to Verona. The hostess prepares delicious jams from her homegrown fruit, and guests may enjoy meals or use the barbecue in the garden.

Este (Padua)

B&B Annamaria
TCI 10%
Annamaria Capodaglio Alberti
via dei Paleoveneti 5/A
35042 Este (PD)
tel. and fax 0429 51844
alberti.annamaria@libero.it
• Euganean Life International
tel. 0429 56156, mob. 347 4355474
fax 0429 56156
elit@bandb-veneto.it
www.bandb-veneto.it/euganeanlife
Open all year

The owner of this farmstead, which has a large garden and is just 1 kilometer from the center of town, raises horses

and poultry. The B&B has its own entrance, as well as a living room and connecting kitchen. Breakfast, which consists of typical, genuine products, can be served either in the reserved kitchen or in the family living room. Besides organizing horseback rides through the surrounding area, the hosts also provide several bicycles for the guests.

Accommodation
Guestrooms: *2 doubles, also single occupancy, shared bath* ♿
Services & Amenities: *English and Portuguese are spoken; rooms cleaned every 3 days; tourist information; kitchen use by request; bike rental; horse-riding excursions; garden; smokers welcome; parking*
Rates: *single €, double €€. Discounts for children and extended stays*
Credit cards: *not accepted*
Pets: no

B&B Luisa e Franco Poeta
TCI 10%
via Prosdocimi 14
35042 Este (PD)
tel. and fax 0429 56156
mob. 347 4355474
luisa.poeta@libero.it
digilander.iol.it/lpoeta
• Euganean Life International
tel. and fax 0429 56156
mob. 347 4355474
elit@bandb-veneto.it/euganeanlife
www.bandb-veneto.it/euganeanlife
Open all year

The rooms of this B&B, which is 5 minutes from town's old center, are on the ground floor and have wrought-iron or bronze beds. The continental breakfast, which can include

organic products on request, is served in the cozy kitchen or on the veranda. The family loves music and assures a cordial atmosphere.

Accommodation
Guestrooms: *2 doubles, also single occupancy, with private bath; additional bed on request*
Services & Amenities: *French and English are spoken; rooms cleaned every 3 days; tourist info; bike rental; Internet access; garden; parking*
Rates: *single €€, double €€€. Additional bed supplement €*
Credit cards: *not accepted*
Pets: no

Galzignano Terme (Padua)

Paola Contarin
TCI 10%
via Valli 14, località Valsanzibio
35030 Galzignano Terme (PD)
tel. and fax 049 9130897
mob. 347 6552043
contarin.paola@libero.it
Open all year

Accommodation
Guestrooms: *2 (1 single and 1 double, with private bath)*
Services & Amenities: *French and German are spoken; rooms cleaned every day; tourist information; baby-sitting service; garden; smokers welcome; private parking*
Minimum stay: *3 nights*
Rates: *single €, double €€. Discounts for children and extended stays*
Credit cards: *not accepted*
Pets: yes

The independent, recently-built villa is located in a very green area. There's a golf course and a thermal bath facility nearby. This is a one-story house with English style windows, a portico and a beautiful garden. The traditional Italian breakfast is served in a kitchen that has modern furnishings.

Grezzana (Verona)

B&B "Al Gheto"
Graziano Perini
via Castellani 3, località Romagnano
37023 Grezzana (VR)
tel. 045 908936, mob. 349 5238215
lucaperini@tin.it
http://utenti.tripod.it/algheto/
Open all year

Accommodation
Guestrooms: *3 (1 single, 1 double bedroom with shared bath, 1 double bedroom with private bath)*
Services & Amenities: *French and English are spoken; rooms cleaned every 3 days; complimentary tourist information; kitchen use by request; terrace; Internet access; garden; smokers welcome; private parking*
Rates: *single €, double €€. Children under 5 -50%. Discounts for extended stays*
Credit cards: *not accepted*
Pets:

This 19th-century farmhouse, which has been recently restructured using local materials, is located in the hills at the foot of Mt. Lessini. The rooms, which were converted from what used to be the stables, hay loft and storeroom, have antique, country-style furniture. The owners of the house are happy to accompany the guests on excursions to taste the local wines and cuisine. They also offer transportation to and from the airport and the Verona railroad station.

Corte Lotrago
Maccacaro Lucia
via Lotrago 81, località Romagnano
37023 Grezzana (VR)
tel. 045 8700148
lotrago@infinito.it
Open all year

The B&B, with its comfortable, rustic atmosphere, is located inside an ancient, 18th-C, rural courtyard. The place has been completely restructured to give it its original appearance. The hostess loves viniculture and is happy to accompany her guests on excursions to the local wine cellars. She also takes care of making ticket reservations the operas given in the Arena during the opera season. Breakfast is served in the dining room reserved for the guests.

Accommodation
Guestrooms: *3 double bed rooms, also single occupancy, private bath.*
Services & Amenities: *English and German are spoken; rooms cleaned every three days; complimentary tourist information; Internet access; smokers welcome; private parking*
Rates: *single €€, double €€€. Children under 5 -50%*
Credit cards: *not accepted*
Pets:

Illasi (Verona)

The Silver Fish
Lucia Vaccà
via Ungheria 32
37031 Illasi (VR)
tel. 045 7834972
Open all year

Accommodation
Guestrooms: *3 (1 single, 1 double bedroom, 1 suite, private bath); additional bed on request*
Services & Amenities: *English, German and Spanish are spoken; rooms cleaned every 3 days; complimentary tourist information; dinner reservation; bike rental; garden; smokers welcome; private parking*
Rates: *single €, double €€, suite €€€. Children under 10 -50%. Discounts for extended stays*
Credit cards: *not accepted*
Pets:

This B&B, located in a colonial style villa near Valpolicella in the Verona countryside, has an unusual English atmosphere. Breakfast (also English, by request) is served either on the veranda, which has a view of the park, or in the kitchen. The host family organizes surprise evening entertainment with live music, ethnic dinners and guided visits in the surrounding area. The hostess is a retired schoolteacher and now writes books regarding this territory.

Longare (Vicenza)

Il Monticello Bassani
Franca Bassani Colpo
via Scodegarda 34
36023 Longare (VI)
tel. 0444 555014, mob. 333 9167202
franca.colpo@infinito.it
http: //digilander.iol.it/ilmonticello
• **Euganean Life International**
tel. 0429 56156, mob. 347 4355474
fax 0429 56156
elit@bandb-veneto.it
www.bandb-veneto.it/euganeanlife
Open all year

Il Monticello, located on the family's farmland, is a small hill that has a old park and about

200 cherry trees. Guests have the use of the main house's two auxiliary dwellings, one of which, the former lemon nursery, hosts the B&B. This place is ideal for relaxing and taking nice walks and bike rides. Breakfast, including organic products, is served either in the kitchen or in the garden.

Accommodation
Guestrooms: *1 double bedroom, private bath; additional bed on request*
Services & Amenities: *French and English are spoken; rooms cleaned every three days; tourist information; dinner reservation; garden; smokers welcome; private parking*
Rates: *€€€. Discounts for extended stays*
Credit cards: *not accepted*
Pets: ✗

Villa Secula
Isabella Stauble
via Scodegarda 24
36023 Longare (VI)
tel. and fax 0444 555115
mob. 347 1507689
• **Euganean Life International**
tel. 0429 56156, mob. 347 4355474
fax 0429 56156
elit@bandb-veneto.it
www.bandb-veneto.it/euganeanlife
Open all year

Accommodation
Guestrooms: *3 doubles, private bath; additional bed on request*
Services & Amenities: *French and English are spoken; rooms cleaned every 3 days; complimentary tourist information; kitchen use by request; lunch & dinner reservations; garden; smokers welcome; private parking*
Rates: *€ per person. Children under 2 free. Discounts for extended stays*
Credit cards: *not accepted*
Pets: ✓

This lovely, 18th-century farm villa has trompe l'oeil frescoes on the ceilings. Guests have the use of an apartment on the main floor – with living room-library and kitchen – and of a small house with living room and kitchenette. The hostess loves art history and is happy to act as a guide if the guests wish to visit the various artistic and cultural attractions of the surrounding area.

Marcon (Venice)

• **Bed & Breakfast Italia**
Code V28
tel. 06 6878618, fax 06 6878619
info@bbitalia.it
www.bbitalia.it
Closed: varies

This independent apartment of 50 square meters is situated in the small town of Marcon, 15 km from Venice, 10 km from Mestre and 7 km from Mogliano Veneto. This beautifully furnished accommodation includes two bedrooms with two bathrooms with shower and tub. The guests may also use the small kitchen area and the private car park. Frequent buses run to Venice and Mestre in 20 minutes.

Accommodation
Guestrooms: *2 (1 double, 1 triple)*
Services & Amenities: *French, English and German are spoken; rooms cleaned every three days; tourist information; private parking*
Minimum stay: *2 nights*
Rates: *€€*
Credit cards: VISA MC *Bancomat*
Pets: ✗

Miane (Treviso)

B&B Ernestina
Ernestina Rizzi
piazza Risorgimento 5
31050 Miane (TV)
tel./fax 0438 960068, mob. 348 3921137
rizziernestina@hotmail.com
ernestinarizzi@libero.it
www.prolocomiane.it/ernestina
• **Associazione Turisti per Casa**
tel. and fax 0532 63066
buccimg@libero.it
www.turistipercasa.it
Open all year

This house is located in the Treviglio foothills. Guests have the use of the family living room – with fireplace and library – where breakfast is served. The hosts are happy to accompany guests on visits to local wine cellars.

Accommodation
Guestrooms: *2 doubles, also single occupancy, private bath*
Services & Amenities: *rooms cleaned every 3 days; tourist information; kitchen use by request; air conditioning; Internet access; garden; smokers welcome; private parking*
Rates: *single €€, double €€. Additional bed supplement €*
Credit cards: *not accepted*
Pets: not allowed

Mira (Venice)

Enrico e Betta Malaguti
via Adige 1, località Oriago
30034 Mira (VE)
tel. 041 472841, mob. 328 6621749
ricobet@inwind.it
Open all year

Accommodation
Guestrooms: *1 double bedroom, shared bath; additional bed on request*
Services & Amenities: *English spoken; rooms cleaned every day; complimentary tourist information; terrace; Internet access; smokers welcome*
Rates: *€€-€€€. Additional bed supplement €*
Credit cards: *not accepted*
Pets: allowed

In their home at the entrance to the Riviera del Brenta, the hosts offer their guests hospitality in a very personalized apartment. Passionate connoisseurs of Indian culture, the hosts have decorated the guestroom with fabrics and objects collected on their trips to India. This passion is also reflected in their collection of books on the subject, as well as in the dinners, based on the gastronomic specialties of that far-off Asiatic country.

Mirano (Venice)

• **Bed & Breakfast Italia**
Codice V2
tel. 06 6878618, fax 06 6878619
info@bbitalia.it
www.bbitalia.it
Closed: varies

Recently built villa in the classic Venetian-style. The owners offer guests a double room with independent entrance and TV. The house is surrounded by a large garden, where a continental breakfast is served during summer months.

Accommodation
Guestrooms: *1 double with private bath; child's bed available*
Services & Amenities: *French, English and Spanish are spoken; rooms cleaned every 3 days; tourist information; private parking*
Minimum stay: *2 nights*
Rates: *€€*
Credit cards: VISA MC *Bancomat*
Pets: not allowed

Monselice (Padua)

Renata Barison
via Moraro 19
35043 Monselice (PD)
tel. 0429 719213, mob. 347 5633356
• Euganean Life International
tel. & fax 0429 56156, mob. 347 4355474
elit@bandb-veneto.it
www.bandb-veneto.it/euganeanlife
Open all year

This B&B is in an apartment located in the old center. It provides a panoramic view of the fortress and castle. Guests have the use of a TV, a washing machine and a refrigerator. For the breakfast, served in the kitchen, the hostess prepares whatever the guests want.

Accommodation
Guestrooms: *2 (1 single, 1 double, shared bath) and 1 apartment*
Services & Amenities: *rooms cleaned every 3 days; tourist info; kitchen use by request; terrace; smokers welcome*
Minimum stay: *3 nights*
Rates: *single €, double €€*
Credit cards: *not accepted*
Pets:

Negrar (Verona)

B&B Casa Poiega
Giuliana Andretta
via Guglielmi 1
37024 Negrar (VR)
tel. and fax 045 7501569
http://digilander.iol.it/casapoiega/
Open all year

This B&B, with its romantic atmosphere, is located in a 15th-C working-class house. This place, with its beautiful portal and large courtyard, is situated in the heart of Valpolicella, just 14 km from Verona. In addition to their bedrooms with simple furnishings, guests also have a small room for their children, as well as a common leisure room with fireplace. Breakfast, which includes natural marmalades, is either served in the garden, under the gazebo, or in the dining room.

Accommodation
Guestrooms: *3 double bedrooms, also single occupancy, private bath.*
Services & Amenities: *English spoken; rooms cleaned every 3 days; tourist information; garden; smokers welcome; private parking*
Minimum stay: *2 nights*
Rates: *single €€, double €€€, suite €€€. Discounts for children*
Credit cards: *not accepted*
Pets:

• Bed & Breakfast Italia
Code V16
tel. 06 6878618, fax 06 6878619
info@bbitalia.it, www.bbitalia.it
Closed: varies

Completely renovated apartment, located in an old Venetian-courtyard, with garden and a large portico. It has 3 bedrooms, sharing 2 bathrooms with shower, and are all furnished with wrought iron beds and antiques. Breakfast is served in the spacious lounge with fireplace. Negrar is within easy reach of Lake Garda and Monte Baldo National Park. The hosts can arrange dinner.

Accommodation
Guestrooms: *3 (1 single, 2 doubles)*
Services & Amenities: *French and English are spoken; tourist information; rooms cleaned every three days; private parking*
Minimum stay: *2 nights*
Rates: *€€*
Credit cards: VISA MC *Bancomat*
Pets:

Occhiobello (Rovigo)

• Bed & Breakfast Italia
Code V34
tel. 06 6878618, fax 06 6878619
info@bbitalia.it
www.bbitalia.it
Closed: varies

Accommodation
Guestrooms: *1 double*
Services & Amenities: *French spoken; rooms cleaned every 3 days; complimentary tourist information; bike rental; smokers welcome; private parking*
Minimum stay: *2 nights*
Rates: *€€*
Credit cards: VISA MC *Bancomat*
Pets:

This attic apartment has 2 bedrooms, a bathroom with shower, and a lounge with TV. Breakfast is served in the ground-floor dining area, or in the garden. Occhiobello is situated in the Polesine area, between the River Adige and the River Po, only 15 min from Ferrara. The other places of cultural and artistic interest are Venice, Chioggia, Padua and Bologna. On request, the hosts can arrange boat excursions on the River Po and on its canals.

Padua

Alle Piazze
• Associazione Koko Nor
tel. 049 8643394, mob. 338 3377912
fax 049 8643394
kokonor@bandb-veneto.it
www.bandb-veneto.it/kokonor
Open all year

This bright apartment in the center of Padua – right at the entrance to the Ghetto – is just a short walk from the historical squares. Entirely at the disposal of the guests, the apartment consists of a bedroom, a bathroom, and a living room that has an attic with a fireplace. It also has a kitchen that the hostess has furnished for preparing the continental breakfast.

Accommodation
Guestrooms: *1 apartment (4 beds)*
Services & Amenities: *French and English are spoken; rooms cleaned every 3 days; tourist info; kitchen use by request; smokers welcome*
Minimum stay: *2 nights*
Rates: *€€€€. Discounts for extended stays*
Credit cards: *not accepted*
Pets: 🚫

• Associazione Koko Nor
tel. 049 8643394, mob. 338 3377912
fax 049 8643394
kokonor@bandb-veneto.it
www.bandb-veneto.it/kokonor
Open all year

This B&B is hosted in a small duplex villa located in the residential section of town. It's conveniently close to various stores and restaurants and is just a short drive from the old center of town. The owners live on the upper floor and the mansard. The functional, independent bedroom has cherry wood furniture. The continental breakfast is served in the small living room.

Accommodation
Guestrooms: *1 double, private bath*
Services & Amenities: *English and Spanish are spoken; rooms cleaned every three days; complimentary tourist information; garden; smokers welcome; private parking*
Rates: *€€*
Credit cards: *not accepted*
Pets: 🚫

B&B Catai
Luisa Chelotti
via Selva 5
35135 Padua
tel. and fax 049 8643394
• Associazione Koko Nor
tel. 049 8643394, mob. 338 3377912
fax 049 8643394
kokonor@bandb-veneto.it
www.bandb-veneto.it/kokonor
Closed: August

Accommodation
Guestrooms: *2 (1 double bedroom, 1 double, also single occupancy, shared bath); additional bed on request*
Services & Amenities: *French, English, German and Chinese are spoken; rooms cleaned every day; tourist information; terrace; computer; Internet; non-smokers welcome*
Minimum stay: *2 nights*
Rates: *single €€, double €€€. Additional bed supplement €*
Credit cards: *not accepted*
Pets: 🚫

The atmosphere that characterizes this attic is the result of the numerous trips made by the hostess. For example, one of the rooms has Japanese decor, including futon. Oriental perfume permeates the rest of the house, which is in Veneto style. The buffet breakfast is either served in the Tyrolean style kitchen or in the living room, or out on the large terrace.

B&B Ezumezu
• Associazione Koko Nor
tel. 049 8643394, mob. 338 3377912
fax 049 8643394
kokonor@bandb-veneto.it
www.bandb-veneto.it/kokonor
Closed: July

This duplex villa is built in traditional Finnish style. The hostess, a lover of gastronomy and an expert on Veneto cuisine, provides information on the typical restaurants in the area and where certain gastronomic specialties can be enjoyed. Breakfast is either served in the large kitchen or in the garden.

Accommodation
Guestrooms: *1 double, also single occupancy, private bath; additional bed on request*
Services & Amenities: *French and English are spoken; rooms cleaned every three days; tourist information; garden; smokers welcome*
Minimum stay: *2 nights*
Rates: *€€ per person*
Credit cards: *not accepted*
Pets: 🚫

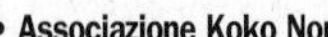

B&B Il Giardino Nascosto
• Associazione Koko Nor
tel. 049 8643394, mob. 338 3377912
fax 049 8643394
kokonor@bandb-veneto.it
www.bandb-veneto.it/kokonor
Closed: July and August

This refined, two-story building, with its terrace and large surrounding garden, is located in the center of town. There are two guestrooms: the one on the ground floor has period furnishings, the other, located in the mansard, has modern furnishings. A generous breakfast is served in the kitchen, on the ground floor. The courteous hostess makes the atmosphere particularly friendly and pleasant.

Accommodation
Guestrooms: *2 double bedroom, also single occupancy, private bath ♿*
Services & Amenities: *English and German are spoken; rooms cleaned every three days; tourist information; garden; smokers welcome; private parking*
Minimum stay: *2 nights*
Rates: *single €€, double €€€.*
Credit cards: *not accepted*
Pets: 🚫

B&B Porta Savonarola
• Associazione Koko Nor
tel. 049 8643394,
mob. 338 3377912
fax 049 8643394
kokonor@bandb-veneto.it
www.bandb-veneto.it/kokonor
Open all year

This B&B is just a short walk from ancient university, the Scrovegni Chapel (that contains a cycle of frescoes, Giotto's masterpiece) and the other buildings in the old center. Guests have the use of a small, independent apartment that has youthful, modern furnishings and sleeping facilities for four. Besides the bedroom, there's a living room with a kitchenette for having breakfast. All the rooms are air-conditioned.

Accommodation
Guestrooms: *1 mini-apartment (4 beds) ♿*
Services & Amenities: *German spoken; rooms cleaned every 3 days; tourist information; kitchenette; air conditioning; smokers welcome*
Minimum stay: *2 nights*
Rates: *€ per person. Children under 10 -20%. Discounts for extended stays*
Credit cards: *not accepted*
Pets: 🚫

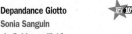

Depandance Giotto
Sonia Sanguin
via Schiaparelli 10
35136 Padua
tel. 049 8723321, mob. 339 7235574
b.b.giotto@libero.it
www.depandance-giotto.it
• Associazione Koko Nor
tel. 049 8643394, mob. 338 3377912
fax 049 8643394
kokonor@bandb-veneto.it
www.bandb-veneto.it/kokonor
Open all year

Accommodation
Guestrooms: *1 mini-apartment (2 beds); additional bed on request ♿*
Services & Amenities: *English spoken; rooms cleaned every three days; complimentary tourist information; kitchen use by request; bike rental; garden; smokers welcome; parking*
Rates: *single €€, double €€€. Additional bed supplement €. Discounts for extended stays*
Credit cards: *not accepted*
Pets: 🚫

This B&B is located in a quiet, residential area and provides its guests with a small apartment that has a furnished kitchen, a small living room with a majolica stove, a small library and a TV. And the plain, modern furnishings provide a pleasent country atmosphere. The breakfast is in Italian-style and is served in the family living room; however, on request, it can also include nonsweet items. The guests can also enjoy some pleasant relaxation in the small villa's garden.

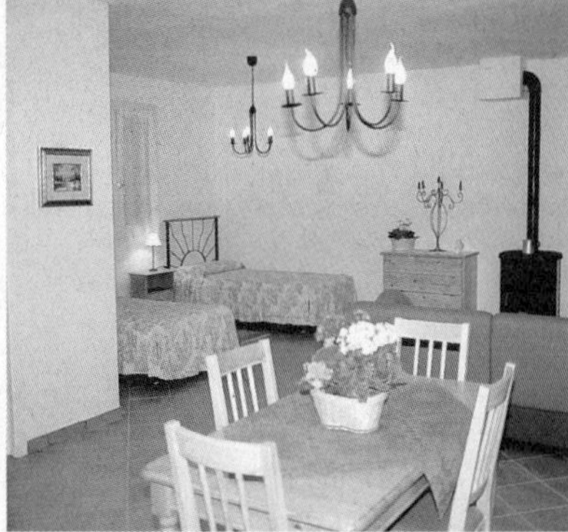

Il Glicine
TCI 10%

• **Associazione Koko Nor**
tel. 049 8643394, mob. 338 3377912
fax 049 8643394
kokonor@bandb-veneto.it
www.bandb-veneto.it/kokonor
Open all year

This B&B is located on the ground floor of a duplex situated in a quiet part of town near the ancient San Giovanni port. Guests have two bedrooms and a small dining room with kitchenette and refrigerator. Breakfast is served in this dining room. The garden has a

large wisteria, and guests can enjoy some pleasant relaxation in the shade of this splendid plant. All the rooms have just been restructured and embellished with terracotta work done by the host.

ACCOMMODATION
Guestrooms: *1 double bedroom, also single occupancy, private bath; Addictonal bed on request ♿*
Services & Amenities: *French and English are spoken; rooms cleaned every 3 days; tourist information; kitchen use by request; Internet access; garden; smokers welcome*
Minimum stay: *2 nights*
Rates: *single €€€, double €€€. Discounts for extended stays*
Credit cards: *not accepted*
Pets: 🚫

La Colorita
TCI 10%

• **Associazione Koko Nor**
tel. 049 8643394, mob. 338 3377912
fax 049 8643394
kokonor@bandb-veneto.it
www.bandb-veneto.it/kokonor
Open all year

This house with its small garden is just a short walk from Passo della Valle and from Padua's old center. The hostess is a painter, a glider pilot and an enthusiastic traveler. She also belongs to a valorization that promotes the exploitation of the city's minor artistic assets, which qualifies her for providing suggestions for visiting the city's alternative artistic and cultural attractions. Breakfast is either served in the large kitchen or under the portico or on the 1st floor terrace.

ACCOMMODATION
Guestrooms: *3 (1 single, 1 double, shared bath; 1 double, private bath); additional bed on request ♿*
Services & Amenities: *French, English and Spanish are spoken; rooms cleaned every three days; complimentary tourist information; garden; smokers welcome; private parking*
Minimum stay: *2 nights*
Rates: *single €€, double €€-€€€.*
Credit cards: *not accepted*
Pets: 🚫

• **Bed & Breakfast Italia**
Code V8
tel. 06 6878618, fax 06 6878619
info@bbitalia.it
www.bbitalia.it
Closed: varies

A beautiful villa with garden outside the walls of Padua, 2 km away from the old center. The guest accommodation includes one double and one single room, sharing a bathroom with tub. Both the rooms are simply and elegantly furnished with antique furniture. The rich breakfast is served by the owner in the reception room. The bus stop is 300 m away from the B&B. Private parking is available for the guests.

ACCOMMODATION
Guestrooms: *1 double and 1 single, shared bath*
Services & Amenities: *French spoken; rooms cleaned every 3 days; tourist information; terrace; garden; private parking*
Minimum stay: *2 nights*
Rates: €€€
Credit cards: VISA MC *Bancomat*
Pets: 🚫

Paese (Treviso)

Villa delle Meridiane
Anna Maria Mazzotti
via Zara 3, località Castagnole
31040 Paese (TV)
tel. 0422 959615
mob. 339 1804685
fax 0422 959615
villadellemeridiane@noiseplanet.com
www.noiseplanet.com/b&b.htm
• **Associazione Koko Nor**
tel. 049 8643394
mob. 338 3377912
fax 049 8643394
kokonor@bandb-veneto.it
www.bandb-veneto.it/kokonor
Open all year

This Veneto villa, which is near Treviso, is surrounded by a garden. The oldest part of the villa dates back to the 15th C. The bedrooms are very elegantly furnished. Breakfast of sweet or non-sweet items is served in the dining room which has a fireplace.

Accommodation
Guestrooms: *2 doubles, also single occupancy, private bath; additional bed on request*
Services & Amenities: *French and German are spoken; rooms cleaned every day; tourist information; Internet; garden; smokers welcome; parking*
Rates: *single €€, double €€€. Additional bed supplement €. Children under 2 free. Discounts for extended stays*
Credit cards: *not accepted*
Pets:

Peschiera del Garda (Verona)

Laghiturismo B&B da Cristina
Cristina Frigo
strada Bergamini 47
località San Benedetto di Lugana
37019 Peschiera del Garda (VR)
tel. and fax 045 7551046
mob. 339 4602847
Closed: January and February

This B&B is situated on the shores of Lake Garda. There's a large beach and a park with a group of reeds that has a lot of different types of lake birds living in it. Guests are hosted in a small modern villa that has a nice garden where they can have a pleasant Italian breakfast that also includes cakes and natural marmalades.

Accommodation
Guestrooms: *3 doubles, also single occupancy, 2 with private bath and 1 with shared bath;* ♿
Services & Amenities: *English spoken; rooms cleaned every day; tourist information; bike rental; garden; smokers welcome*
Minimum stay: *2 nights*
Rates: *single €€, double €€€. Additional bed supplement €. Children under 3 free. Discounts for students*
Credit cards: *not accepted*
Pets:

Piove di Sacco (Padua)

Palazzo Barbaro
Cinzia Borgato
via E. C. Davila 16
35028 Piove di Sacco (PD)
tel. 049 5840484, 049 9710895
fax 049 5840484
anacletomit@libero.it
http://www.piovedisacco.it/arte_pal_barbaro_lor.asp
• **Euganean Life International**
tel. 0429 56156
mob. 347 4355474
fax 0429 56156
elit@bandb-veneto.it
www.bandb-veneto.it/euganeanlife
Closed: August

Accommodation
Guestrooms: *1 mini-apartment with 4 beds.*
Services & Amenities: *French and English are spoken; rooms cleaned every 3 days; tourist information; kitchen use by request; garden; smokers welcome; private parking*
Rates: *single €€, double €€€. Discounts for extended stays*
Credit cards: *not accepted*
Pets:

This noble 16th century palace, with its old garden and adjoining tennis court, hosts a B&B made from a small, totally independent mansard that has antique furniture. Breakfast, consisting of natural sweet items, is served either in the small apartment or outdoors.

Pontecchio Polesine (Rovigo)

Bordeghina
Mirella Fortin and Enrico Maragno
via Marconi 1477
45030 Pontecchio Polesine (RO)
tel. 0425 31263
• **Euganean Life International**
tel. 0429 56156
mob. 347 4355474
fax 0429 56156
elit@bandb-veneto.it
www.bandb-veneto.it/euganeanlife
Open: mid-June to mid-September

This large 19th-C. farm mansion located in the Veneto countryside still has its typical court-

yard, a lawn garden and a vineyard at the entrance. Guests have the use of a tennis court, a small soccer field and a ping-pong table. Breakfast can be enriched by cakes and genuine sweet items as desired, and is either served in the kitchen or in one of the other large rooms.

Accommodation
Guestrooms: *2 doubles, also single occupancy, 1 with private bath and 1 with shared bath; additional bed on request*
Services & Amenities: *English spoken; rooms cleaned every day; tourist information; garden; smokers welcome; private parking*
Minimum stay: *3 nights*
Rates: *single €€, double €€€. Additional bed supplement €. Discounts for children*
Credit cards: *not accepted*
Pets: 🐾

Pove del Grappa (Vicenza)

B&B Bibi
Viviana Cavalli
via Cornon 11
36020 Pove del Grappa (VI)
tel. 0424 80235, mob. 338 4270064
vivianacavalli@libero.it
http://digilander.iol.it/VivianaCavalli
Open all year

This B&B is in a small modern villa located on a hill. Guests receive friendly treatment, beginning with the welcome basket and aperitif they are offered upon their arrival. Breakfast can either be served in the garden,

Accommodation
Guestrooms: *3 (1 single and 2 double bedrooms, also single occupancy, private bath); additional bed on request*
Services & Amenities: *French, English and Spanish are spoken; rooms cleaned every three days; tourist information; kitchen use by request; educational courses by request; terrace; Internet access; garden; smokers welcome; private parking*
Rates: *single €€, double €€€. Additional bed supplement €. Children under 5 free. Discounts for extended stays*
Credit cards: *not accepted*
Pets: 🐾

under the portico or in the living room, with fireplace. The hostess, a retired schoolteacher, gives 4-5 day intensive English courses, which include conversation and the viewing of films in the original language.

Povegliano (Treviso)

Locanda Ca' del Borgo
Liliana Bergamo
borgo S. Daniele 24
31050 Povegliano (TV)
tel. 0422 770006, mob 0422 871775
paulanus@tin.it
www.locandacadelborgo.com
Open all year

This B&B is hosted in a recently-restructured 18th-century villa, which still has the original decorations on its front side. It is surrounded by a large park that has old trees and a stream. There are

Accommodation
Guestrooms: *3 double bedrooms, also single occupancy, with private bath; additional bed on request*
Services & Amenities: *rooms cleaned every 3 days; tourist information; dinner reservation; garden; smokers welcome; private parking*
Rates: *single €€€, double €€€€. Additional bed supplement €*
Credit cards: *not accepted*
Pets: 🚫🐾

three guestrooms, all with antique furnishings. The English breakfast, enriched with natural sweet items, is served in the dining room.

Quinto di Valpantena (Verona)

• Bed & Breakfast Italia
Code V14
tel. 06 6878618, fax 06 6878619
info@bbitalia.it
www.bbitalia.it
Closed: varies

Old stone farm house recently restored to bio-building criteria. To let are one double room and a twin-bed room, both with TV and private bathroom. Breakfast is plenty of bread and natural homemade cakes, baked in the log-fire oven of

Accommodation
Guestrooms: *2 doubles*
Services & Amenities: *French and English are spoken; rooms cleaned every three days; tourist information*
Minimum stay: *2 nights*
Rates: €€
Credit cards: VISA MC *Bancomat*
Pets:

the house. Quinto is on the hills at the gateway to Verona, and where the owners run a vegetarian restaurant. A car is necessary as the area is not served by public transport.

Resana (Treviso)

Il Sole
Lucia Ferro
via Boscalto 93
31023 Resana (TV)
tel. 049 702786
ilsoleitaly@hotmail.com
luciaferro53@hotmail.com
www.geocities.com/bebitaly
Closed: December and January

Accommodation
Guestrooms: *3 doubles with shared bath; additional bed on request*
Services & Amenities: *French, English, German and Spanish are spoken; rooms cleaned every three days; tourist information; garden; smokers welcome; private parking*
Minimum stay: *2 nights*
Rates: *double* €€- €€€. *Discounts for extended stays*
Credit cards: *not accepted*
Pets:

This Veneto style villa, surrounded by vegetation, is located just a short distance from the center of town, where the bus for Padua or Treviso departs. There is one guestroom on the ground floor and two guestrooms on the upper floor, all three soberly furnished. Guests have the use of a large rustic kitchen and a living room with a library. The rich continental breakfast is served in the kitchen.

Rovolon (Padua)

Pignara
Wilma Pirolo
via Belvedere 5
35030 Rovolon (PD)
tel. 049 5226261
info@pignara.it, www.pignara.it
• Euganean Life International
tel. 0429 56156, mob. 347 4355474
fax 0429 56156
elit@bandb-veneto.it
www.bandb-veneto.it/euganeanlife
Open all year

TCI 10%

Accommodation
Guestrooms: *2 (1 double bedroom and 1 double, with private bath)*
Services & Amenities: *French and English are spoken; rooms cleaned every three days; tourist information; bike rental; Internet access; garden; smokers welcome; parking*
Rates: *single* €€, *double* €€-€€€. *Discounts for children and extended stays*
Credit cards: *not accepted*
Pets:

This country house is located inside a small vineyard surrounded by the green Colli Euganei. The two guestrooms have wooden furniture dating from the '30s. Breakfast, which consists of organic products, is served either in the garden or in the living room. The host invites the guests to try the wines of his own production.

Saccolongo (Padua)

Ca' Fucelle
Marina Favero Spandi
via Montegrappa 12
35030 Saccolongo (PD)
tel. 049 8016212, mob. 349 3780283
• Euganean Life International
tel. 0429 56156, mob. 347 4355474
fax 0429 56156
elit@bandb-veneto.it
www.bandb-veneto.it/euganeanlife
Open all year

TCI 10%

Accommodation
Guestrooms: *1 mini-apartment with 4 beds*
Services & Amenities: *French and English are spoken; rooms cleaned every three days; tourist information; kitchen use by request; garden; smokers welcome; private parking*
Rates: *€€€- €€€€*
Credit cards: *not accepted*
Pets: *not allowed*

This ancient, working-class house, with its garden, trees and lawn, is just a short drive from the center of Padua. The guests have a comfortable dépendance with living room and kitchen. Breakfast, continental or English, is served in the family living room or in the reserved kitchen. Besides taking walks along the Bacchiglione River and inside the Colli Euganei Park, guests can also enjoy playing on the nearby golf course and tennis courts.

San Pietro di Feletto (Treviso)

Casa Flaminio
Flaminio De Martin
via Pianale 61
località Santa Maria di Feletto
31020 San Pietro di Feletto (TV)
tel. and fax 0438 784090
Open all year

This B&B is hosted in an independent apartment on the 1st floor of a restructured, 19th century farmhouse located in the Treviso hills, just a few minutes from Conegliano Veneto. Particularly fond of art, the hosts have named each room after an artist that has stayed there. Breakfast consists of natural products and is served either in the family dining room or in the garden. Transportation service to and from the airport is provided.

Accommodation
Guestrooms: *3 (1 double and 2 double bedrooms, with shared bath); additional bed on request*
Services & Amenities: *French and English are spoken; rooms cleaned every three days; complimentary tourist information; terrace; garden; smokers welcome; private parking*
Rates: *double €€. Additional bed supplement €*
Credit cards: *not accepted*
Pets: *allowed*

San Pietro in Cariano (Verona)

• **Bed & Breakfast Italia**
Code V39
tel. 06 6878618, fax 06 6878619
info@bbitalia.it
www.bbitalia.it
Closed: varies

Accommodation
Guestrooms: *3 doubles*
Services & Amenities: *English and German are spoken; rooms cleaned every three days; complimentary tourist information; private parking*
Minimum stay: *2 nights*
Rates: *€€*
Credit cards: *Visa MC Bancomat*
Pets: *not allowed*

Rustic farmhouse in the Valpolicella area, 25 min from Lake Garda and 20 min from the center of Verona and the airport, also reached easily by bus (the bus stop is 400 m away). The 3 double rooms are large and offer the option of a third bed. Each room has its own bath with tub/shower. In the summer, breakfast is served on the large balcony, otherwise it is served in the dining room. A well-tended garden and private parking are available.

Santa Giustina (Belluno)

Da Flavia
Flavia Bortot
viale dei Tigli 1/A
32035 Santa Giustina (BL)
tel. 0437 888383
daflavia@bbdolomiti.net
• B&B Dolomiti nelle montagne venete
tel. 0437 949000, 0437 949100
info@bbdolomiti.net
www.bbdolomiti.net
Open all year

This small house on the outskirts of Santa Giustina, has a vegetable garden, fruit trees and a chicken coop, and is ideal for anybody who wants to spend a tranquil holiday close to nature in a simple, family atmosphere. It has one guestroom and breakfast includes organic sweet items, fresh fruit and marmalades. The nearby sports facilities and swimming pool can also be used by the disabled.

Accommodation
Guestrooms: *1 double, also single occupancy, with shared bath*
Services & Amenities: *French spoken; rooms cleaned every 3 days; complimentary tourist information; garden; smokers welcome; private parking*
Rates: *single €, double €€*
Credit cards: *not accepted*
Pets: ✗

Sommacampagna (Verona)

• Bed & Breakfast Italia TCI 10%
Code V42
tel. 06 6878618, fax 06 6878619
info@bbitalia.it
www.bbitalia.it
Closed: varies

Accommodation
Guestrooms: *1 double*
Services & Amenities: *rooms cleaned every three days; complimentary tourist information; private parking*
Minimum stay: *2 nights*
Rates: *€€*
Credit cards: *Visa MC Bancomat*
Pets: ✗

A villa surrounded by a garden, located 2 km from the center of this rural hamlet, in the province of Verona. It features a double room, with typical rural furniture, with the option of a third bed, and a private bathroom with tub and shower. Breakfast is served in the room or in the shade of the portico. The B&B is 30 km from Verona and 35 km from Lake Garda. The family places a private car park at the guests' disposal. A car is absolutely necessary.

Spinea (Venice)

• Bed & Breakfast Italia
Code V21
tel. 06 6878618, fax 06 6878619
info@bbitalia.it
www.bbitalia.it
Closed: varies

This recently built house offers accommodation in three bedrooms and shared bathroom with tub. The furnishing is modern and functional. In the summer months breakfast is served in the small garden with veranda. Spinea is 13 km from Venice, and can be reached in 20 min by bus. It is also just 35 km from the seaside resort of Jesolo, 30 min away. The hostess offers a shuttle service on request.

Accommodation
Guestrooms: *3 (1 single, 1 double and 1 triple room)*
Services & Amenities: *French, English and German are spoken; rooms cleaned every three days; tourist information; private parking*
Minimum stay: *2 nights*
Rates: *€€*
Credit cards: *Visa MC Bancomat*
Pets: ✗

Taglio di Po (Rovigo)

Ca' Zen
Maria Adelaide Avanzo
località Ca' Zen
45019 Taglio di Po (RO)
tel. and fax 0426 346469
mob. 339 8688715, 333 6572560
mary.adelaide@tiscali.it
Closed: late October to March

Accommodation
Guestrooms: *3 (1 double bedroom and 2 doubles, also single occupancy, with private bath)*
Services & Amenities: *French and English are spoken; rooms cleaned every 3 days; tourist information; garden; smokers welcome; parking*
Rates: *single €€, double €€€€. Discounts for children and extended stays*
Credit cards: *not accepted*
Pets: ✓

In the heart of the Delta del Po Park, this B&B, with its nice atmosphere, is hosted by a large, 18th-century villa, surrounded by a old park. The hostess, an Anglo-Irish lady, is very well acquainted with the bed-and-breakfast tradition and is very happy to share her knowledge of this very interesting area with her guests. Chioggia and Comacchio aren't far away, and one can also visit Venice, Ferrara and Ravenna. Upon arrival, guests are welcomed with an aperitif.

Torreglia (Padua)

I Vecchi Mulini
Fabrizio Zanetti
via Facciolati 28, 35038 Torreglia
tel. 049 5211424, mob. 335 5955070
fax 049 5211424,
fabrizio.zanetti@tin.it
www.ivecchimulini.it
• Euganean Life International
tel. 0429 56156, mob. 347 4355474
fax 0429 56156
elit@bandb-veneto.it
www.bandb-veneto.it/euganeanlife
Open: April to September

Accommodation
Guestrooms: *3 (2 double bedrooms and 1 double, with private bath)* ♿
Services & Amenities: *French, English and German are spoken; rooms cleaned every three days; complimentary tourist information; bike rental; garden; smokers welcome; parking*
Minimum stay: *2 nights*
Rates: *double €-€€. Children under 10 free. Discounts for extended stays*
Credit cards: *Visa Bancomat*
Pets: ✓

For hundreds of years, the 13th-C mills were of vital importance for the town. Today they host this B&B in the greenery of the Colli Euganei Park. The well-cared-for rooms, the breakfast with natural products (served under the wisteria pergola in summertime), and the English lawn with games, all contribute to making the guests' stay very pleasant and relaxing.

Treviso

B&B Santa Lucia
Giuliana Danieli
via Canizzano 119/I
31100 Treviso
tel. 0422 370517
bbsantalucia@hotmail.com
www.santaluciabb.it
Open all year

Accommodation
Guestrooms: *2 (1 double bedroom and 1 double, with private bath)*
Services & Amenities: *French and English are spoken; rooms cleaned every day; complimentary tourist information; kitchen use by request; terrace; Internet access; garden; smokers welcome; private parking*
Minimum stay: *2 nights*
Rates: *double €€€. Discounts for extended stays*
Credit cards: *not accepted*
Pets: ✗

This B&B, immersed in the vegetation of the countryside surrounding the city, is a recently-constructed villa located in a park. The part of the house used by the guests has an entrance, and the guests also have the use of the kitchen where they can prepare an English breakfast, which also includes fresh, organically-grown fruit. The hosts supply all the necessary ingredients.

• Bed & Breakfast Italia
Code V15
tel. 06 6878618, fax 06 6878619
info@bbitalia.it
www.bbitalia.it
Closed: varies

ACCOMMODATION
Guestrooms: *3 doubles*
Services & Amenities: *French and English are spoken; rooms cleaned every 3 days; complimentary tourist information; private parking*
Minimum stay: *2 nights*
Rates: €€
Credit cards: VISA MC *Bancomat*
Pets: not allowed

Two-story villa surrounded by a large garden with a swimming pool and tennis court. A self-contained apartment with two rooms, kitchen and bathroom with tub/shower. In the main house, the owners offer a double room with sloping roof and private bathroom with shower for guests. All the rooms are carefully furnished. Breakfast is served in the lounge or in the garden by the swimming pool. Private parking is available.

VALLE DI CADORE (BELLUNO)

Monti Pallidi
Claudia Da Rugna
via Dante 23/B
32040 Valle di Cadore (BL)
tel. 0435 500726, mob. 347 9311313
montipallidi@bbdolomiti.net
• B&B Dolomiti nelle montagne venete
tel. 0437 949000, 0437 949100
info@bbdolomiti.net
www.bbdolomiti.net
Open all year

ACCOMMODATION
Guestrooms: *2 doubles, also single occupancy, with shared bath*
Services & Amenities: *Spanish spoken; rooms cleaned every 3 days; tourist information; kitchen use by request; terrace; garden; smokers welcome; private parking*
Rates: *single €, double €€. Children under 10 -50%*
Credit cards: *not accepted*
Pets: allowed

In a fairly recent building, this mansard (with terrace), occupied by the hostess, undoubtedly makes an excellent base for quickly getting to the well-known ski localities. There are nature hiking and bicycle trails in the area, as well as sports fields and a manege. Breakfast with bread, biscuits, genuine cakes, eggs and salami, is either served in the combination kitchen/living room or on the terrace, which provides a view of the Belluno Dolomites.

VALLI DEL PASUBIO (VICENZA)

• Bed & Breakfast Italia
Code V43
tel. 06 6878618, fax 06 6878619
info@bbitalia.it
www.bbitalia.it
Closed: varies

ACCOMMODATION
Guestrooms: *2 doubles*
Services & Amenities: *French and English are spoken; rooms cleaned every three days; complimentary tourist information*
Minimum stay: *2 nights*
Rates: €€
Credit cards: VISA MC *Bancomat*
Pets: allowed

A recently restored country house located 5 km away from the center of this small hamlet. It consists of two double rooms, furnished with antiques in classic style, sharing a bathroom with shower, both with TV. The house is surrounded by a large garden, where Italian breakfast is served in summer, while in the winter months, in a nice lounge. A car is absolutely necessary.

VENICE

Al Giardino
Gianni Ferrarese
via Alfinia 119/B
località Favaro
30030 Venice
tel. and fax 041 5010556
mob. 349 4949149
algiardino@tiscali.it
www.algiardinovenezia.it
Open all year

ACCOMMODATION
Guestrooms: *3 (1 single and 2 doubles, with private bath); additional bed on request*
Services & Amenities: *French, English, German and Spanish are spoken; rooms cleaned every day; complimentary tourist information; garden; smokers welcome; private parking*
Rates: *single €€, double €€€. Children under 3 free*
Credit cards: *accepted*
Pets:

This B&B, situated on the dry-land area of Venice, is hosted in a small, 16th-century villa that has modern furniture, a garden and a sedate, warm atmosphere. Italian breakfast is served in the family combination kitchen/living room. Being only 15 minutes by bus from the old center, the villa's fortunate location avoids Venice's troublesome, inevitable, costly, parking problems.

Church of San Giorgio Maggiore.

Ca' Minù
Silvia Onda
Castello 2845/A
30122 Venice
tel. and fax 041 5287019
onda.silvano@libero.it
Open all year

This B&B, which is 10 minutes from Piazza San Marco, consists of a small suite with living room and modern furnishings, located inside a 15th-century building. This has just recently been restored with particular philological care and offers a panoramic view of the beautiful San Francesco della Vigna church, by Palladio. Breakfast, which consists of Venetian sweet specialties, is served in the family living room, which still has the original 18th-century stuccowork and decorations.

ACCOMMODATION
Guestrooms: *1 suite (4 beds), also single occupancy, with private bath*
Services & Amenities: *French and English are spoken; rooms cleaned every three days; tourist info; Internet access; garden; smokers welcome*
Rates: *single €€€, double €€€€, quadruple €€€€.*
Discounts for children
Credit cards: *not accepted*
Pets:

Ca' Orfeo
Centro Culturale "Ai Miracoli"
Cannareggio 4502
30121 Venice
tel. 041 5230616
mob. 347 826080, 333 6145740
venezia.musica@iol.it
http://vsers.iol
Closed: mid-July to mid-August and week before Christmas holidays

This B&B occupies the guestrooms of the "Ai Miracoli" Cultural Center, which is the music salon to reference when asking for information and making reservations. This B&B, with its classic, refined atmosphere, is hosted in a typically Venetian, 16th-century building that's only 5 minutes from Rialto and 10 minutes from San Marco. The guests have the use of a kitchen for their self-service breakfast. This B&B is the perfect meeting point for lovers of classical music.

ACCOMMODATION
Guestrooms: *2 double bedrooms, also single occupancy, private bath*
Services & Amenities: *French, German and Spanish are spoken; rooms cleaned every 3 days; complimentary tourist information; kitchen use by request; educational courses by request; smokers welcome*
Minimum stay: *3 nights*
Rates: *€€€- €€€€*
Credit cards: *not accepted*
Pets:

Franca Favari
via Villabona 91, località Marghera
30100 Venice
tel. 041 932839, mob. 328 4230301
francafavari@tiscali.it
http://web.tiscali.it/bandbvenice/index.html
Open all year

This tranquil and beautiful house, with its garden and orchard, is in Marghera, far from any noise. Its position permits using public transportation for getting to Venice. The abundant breakfast often includes strudel and organic marmalades and is served in the family kitchen. The family members love to play cards and enjoy having the guests participate. The family is also a good

ACCOMMODATION
Guestrooms: *2 doubles with shared bath; additional bed on request*
Services & Amenities: *French, English and German are spoken; rooms cleaned every day; tourist information; air conditioning; garden; smokers welcome; private parking*
Minimum stay: *2 nights*
Rates: *double €€€. Additional bed supplement €€*
Credit cards: *not accepted*
Pets:

source of interesting information regarding the Riviera del Brenta, which is just a few kilometers away.

Palazzo Morosini dalla Sbarra TCI 10%
tel. 041 5224521
mob. 349 5318909
bedbre@katamail.com
Open: September to May

This 16th-century building is in the old center (between the Castle and San Marco area), just 5 minutes from the connection with the railroad station, Piazzale Roma and the Lido. The well-illuminated house has prestigious furniture and antique objects. Guests have the use of the apartment located on the second floor, and of a very

ACCOMMODATION
Guestrooms: *3 (2 doubles and 1 single, with shared bath)*
Services & Amenities: *rooms cleaned every 3 days; tourist information; smokers welcome*
Minimum stay: *2 nights*
Rates: €€€€
Credit cards: *not accepted*
Pets:

large, elegantly furnished living room, which is separate from the rooms used by the hostess. The traditional Italian breakfast is served in a special dining room.

Venexia Home
Lucia Boschetto
Santa Croce 1719
30135 Venice
tel. 041 2759126, mob. 335 5291565
fax 041 2756183
l.boschetto@katamail.com
Open all year

This eclectic-character B&B is hosted in a former, restructured, 16th-C monastery with a small courtyard with trees. It is located not far from the Fontego dei Turchi, which is now the Civic Museum of Natural History. The rich Italian breakfast is served in the family living room which faces the Grand Canal.

ACCOMMODATION
Guestrooms: *1 double, also single occupancy, with shared bath*
Services & Amenities: *English spoken; rooms cleaned every three days; complimentary tourist information; air conditioning; Internet access; smokers welcome*
Minimum stay: *2 nights*
Rates: *single €€€, double €€€€*
Credit cards: *not accepted*
Pets:

Venezia B&B
Mario De Biasio
San Marco 3558
30124 Venice
tel. and fax 041 5239560
mdb192@emailfast.com
http://digilander.iol.it/bestvenice/index.html
Open all year

This B&B is located right in the middle of the old center. It's on the main floor of a 17th-century Venetian building with a private water door and a beautiful inside courtyard. The bedroom has elegant, dark-wood, period furniture, and the Italian breakfast is served in the family dining room.

Accommodation
Guestrooms: *1 double, private bath*
Services & Amenities: *French, English and Spanish are spoken; rooms cleaned every three days; complimentary tourist information; Internet access; smokers welcome*
Minimum stay: *2 nights*
Rates: *€€€€. Stays longer then 3 nights -10%*
Credit cards: *accepted*
Pets:

Villa Gabriella
Stefano Calandra
via Istria 12
30126 Venice
tel. 041 731426, mob. 347 9151158
fax 041 2769546
villagabriella@hotmail.com
www.villagabriella.net
Closed: 10 November to 20 December and 8 to 28 January

Villa Gabriella is one part of a 1907, Palladio style residence located on the verdant Lido Island, directly facing the sea. The enviable position and well-cared-for, elegant atmosphere make it very suitable for relaxing and enjoying the sea, as well as for providing a good base from which to make visits to the city. In the summertime, the abundant breakfast can be enjoyed on the octagonal terrace which provides a view of the sea and Venice.

Accommodation
Guestrooms: *3 (2 doubles and 1 suite, with shared bath)*
Services & Amenities: *French, English and Spanish are spoken; rooms cleaned every three days; complimentary tourist information; bike rental; terrace; Internet access; garden; smokers welcome*
Rates: *€€€- €€€€. Children under 3 free. Discounts for extended stays*
Credit cards: *not accepted*
Pets:

Villa Margherita
Maria Valentini
via Casilina 4, località Campalto
30030 Venice
tel. and fax 041 900385
margherit@tin.it
http://space.tin.it/associazioni/nooqv
• Vacanze in Famiglia
tel. and fax 041 455188, 041900385
email: margherit@tin.it
Open all year

This elegant, one-floor, two-family residence, situated in a park which has several trees, is very favorably located for visiting Venice, which is just 7 kilometers away. One of the guestrooms has baroque style Venetian furnishings. The abundant continental breakfast, which is served in the living room, includes yoghurt, cereals, fruit juices and excellent organic honey. The family is particularly fond of apiculture.

Accommodation
Guestrooms: *2 double bedrooms with private bath*
Services & Amenities: *French and English are spoken; rooms cleaned every day; complimentary tourist information; terrace; garden; smokers welcome; private parking*
Minimum stay: *2 nights*
Rates: *double €€€. Discounts for extended stays*
Credit cards: *not accepted*
Pets:

• **Bed & Breakfast Italia**
Code V22
calle delle Rasse
tel. 06 6878618, fax 06 6878619
info@bbitalia.it, www.bbitalia.it
Closed: varies

ACCOMMODATION
Guestrooms: *2 (1 double, 1 triple)*
Services & Amenities: *rooms cleaned every 3 days; tourist information*
Minimum stay: *3 nights*
Rates: €€
Credit cards: VISA MC *Bancomat*
Pets: no

Light and airy third floor apartment of 60 sq. m, on the upper floor of a typical three-story Venetian building without elevator, it is a 5-min walk from St. Mark's Square, near St. Mark's motor-boat station. It has a lounge with kitchenette and TV, 2 bedrooms and a bathroom with shower. The price does not include breakfast but guests have free access to the kitchen. Guests are asked to arrive between 12:00am and 6:00pm.

• **Bed & Breakfast Italia**
Code V24
Cannaregio
tel. 06 6878618, fax 06 6878619
info@bbitalia.it
www.bbitalia.it
Closed: varies

Small apartment of 50 sq.m, just a 5 min walk from St. Mark's Square. It has an entrance hall, double bedroom, lounge with double sofa bed, small kitchen and bathroom with tub. Guests may enjoy an open area, where breakfast or dinner can be served. It does not include breakfast but guests have free use of the kitchen. Guests are asked to arrive between 12am – 6pm; an extra fee is charged in case of arrival outside the check-in hours.

ACCOMMODATION
Guestrooms: *2 (1 double, 1 triple)*
Services & Amenities: *rooms cleaned every 3 days; tourist information*
Minimum stay: *3 nights*
Rates: €€
Credit cards: VISA MC *Bancomat*
Pets: no

• **Bed & Breakfast Italia**
Code V25
Castello
tel. 06 6878618, fax 06 6878619
info@bbitalia.it
www.bbitalia.it
Closed: varies

ACCOMMODATION
Guestrooms: *2 (1 double, 1 triple)*
Services & Amenities: *rooms cleaned every 3 days; tourist information*
Minimum stay: *3 nights*
Rates: €€
Credit cards: VISA MC *Bancomat*
Pets: no

Second floor apartment of 40 sq. m in an old building. It has a lounge with kitchenette and double sofa bed, a double bedroom and a bath with shower. It is a 5 min walk from St. Mark's Square. The price does not include breakfast but guests have free use of the kitchen. Guests are asked to arrive between 12:00am and 6:00pm.

• Bed & Breakfast Italia
Code V36
San Polo
tel. 06 6878618, fax 06 6878619
info@bbitalia.it
www.bbitalia.it
Closed: varies

Self-contained ground floor studio apartment (32 square meters) 5 minutes from St. Mark's Square. It includes one room with double sofa bed, bathroom with shower and kitchenette exclusively for guests. The price does not include breakfast. On request, a shuttle service is available from the airport to the B&B (additional cost).

Church and Home delle Zittelle, by Andrea Palladio.

Accommodation
Guestrooms: *1 double*
Services & Amenities: *French and English are spoken; rooms cleaned every three days; complimentary tourist information*
Minimum stay: *3 nights*
Rates: €€
Credit cards: VISA MC *Bancomat*
Pets:

• Bed & Breakfast Italia
Code V41
San Polo
tel. 06 6878618, fax 06 6878619
info@bbitalia.it
www.bbitalia.it
Closed: varies

A former inn, recently renovated, featuring a king-size bed and a single sofa bed, exposed beams and bricks, TV, and a kitchenette with provisions for breakfast. The B&B is in the old center of Venice, a 10-minute walk from the Rialto bridge.

Accommodation
Guestrooms: *1 double; additional bed on request*
Services & Amenities: *rooms cleaned every three days; complimentary tourist information; smokers welcome*
Minimum stay: *3 nights*
Rates: €€
Credit cards: VISA MC *Bancomat*
Pets:

• Bed & Breakfast Italia
Code V50
Santa Croce
tel. 06 6878618
fax 06 6878619
info@bbitalia.it
www.bbitalia.it
Closed: varies

A 200 sq. m flat on the third floor of an old mansion in the central Santa Croce district. A light-filled double bedroom with bathroom with shower and tub. The elegant and cozy furnishings featuring antiques and luminous colors lend a personal touch. St. Mark's Square is a 10 minutes' walk away. Served breakfast is not included, but guests are encouraged to use the kitchen.

Accommodation
Guestrooms: *1 double*
Services & Amenities: *English, French, German spoken; rooms cleaned every 3 days; tourist info; smokers welcome*
Minimum stay: *2 nights*
Rates: €€€
Credit cards: VISA MC *Bancomat*
Pets:

• Vacanze in Famiglia
tel. and fax 041 455188, 041900385
email: margherit@tin.it
Closed: 15 October to 15 December and January

Accommodation
Guestrooms: *1 double, shared bath; additional bed on request*
Services & Amenities: *French and English are spoken; rooms cleaned every 3 days; complimentary tourist information; smokers welcome*
Rates: *double €€- €€€*
Credit cards: *not accepted*
Pets:

The hostess and her cat are the hosts of this B&B located in a very bright apartment on the 1st floor of this condo, which is in a pedestrian area in the middle of Mestre. The place has a very cordial atmosphere, and the hostess is very happy to fix whatever the guests want for breakfast. She usually sets out fresh bread, cereals, biscuits, toasts, coffee, tea or warm milk. She's also a good source of information as regards the transportation services for the city, and can point out the best tourist attractions offered by Venice and the nearby areas.

• Vacanze in Famiglia
tel. and fax 041 455188, 041900385
email: margherit@tin.it
Open all year

Accommodation
Guestrooms: *3 (1 double bedroom, 2 with king-size beds, shared bath)*
Services & Amenities: *French, English and Spanish are spoken; rooms cleaned every three days; complimentary tourist information; bike rental; terrace; garden; smokers welcome*
Rates: *€€€€*
Credit cards: *not accepted*
Pets:

This B&B is in a large, elegant house in the center of the Lido of Venice, just 20 minutes from St. Mark's Square. All the rooms are nicely furnished, and a few of them have outstanding paintings as well as art objects and antiques. At the guests disposal are three bedrooms, but they can also make use of three small terraces plus a fourth terrace that has awnings. Breakfast, also an elegant affair, with silverware and organza tablecloths, is served in the very large living room or, when the weather is nice, in the garden.

Verona

B&B Le Cornacchie
Maria Pardini
Salita Monte Grappa 28
37126 Verona
tel. and fax 045 8342184
lecornacchie@tin.it
Open all year

Accommodation
Guestrooms: *2 mini-apartment (2 beds each); additional bed on request*
Services & Amenities: *French and English are spoken; rooms cleaned every three days; complimentary tourist information; baby-sitting service; kitchen use by request; bike rental; educational courses by request; terrace; garden; smokers welcome*
Rates: *single €€, double €€€, triple €€€€. Children under 3 free. Discounts for extended stays*
Credit cards: *not accepted*
Pets:

This B&B, located in a villa that has a large garden, is situated among the green hills in a quiet, residential part of town that's close to the center. The B&B occupies two, small, elegant, independent apartments. The Italian breakfast can either be served in the kitchen reserved for the guests, or outdoors. The informal atmosphere and nice panoramic location makes this place very pleasant and relaxing.

Ca' del Rocolo
Ilaria Corazza
via Gaspari 3, località Quinto
37034 Verona
tel. and fax 045 8700879
corazzaverona@libero.it
• Associazione Koko Nor
tel. 049 8643394, mob. 338 3377912
fax 049 8643394
kokonor@bandb-veneto.it
www.bandb-veneto.it/kokonor
Open all year

TCI 10%

This farmhouse, recently restructured, whose main part dates from 1800, is located on a 17-acre lot that has fruit and olive trees. Guestrooms are decorated with natural materials – wood and stone – and breakfast, which consists of natural, organic products, is served either in the kitchen or under the pergola. Guests who like to take short hikes have a wide range of trails to choose from. There's a manege just 2 km away for those who like horseback riding.

Accommodation
Guestrooms: *2 (1 double and 1 triple room, with private bath)*
Services & Amenities: *French and English are spoken; tourist information; rooms cleaned every 3 days; kitchen use by request; garden; smokers welcome; private parking*
Minimum stay: *2 nights*
Rates: *double €€€, triple €€€€. Discounts for children*
Credit cards: *not accepted*
Pets:

Esposito
Pierangelo Esposito
via Pindemonte 2/B
37100 Verona
tel. 045 8350557
pieranes@tin.it
www.casabellaitalia.it
Open all year

This B&B, situated in a recently-restructured, early 20th-century building located just 15 min from the town's old center, has three bright, independent rooms, each well decorated in classic style. The Italian breakfast is served in a special dining room reserved for the guests. Guests are assured absolute privacy by the discrete host who is, nonetheless, at their complete disposal.

Verona: the Romanesque church of San Zeno

Accommodation
Guestrooms: *3 doubles, also single occupancy, with private bath; additional bed on request*
Services & Amenities: *French, English and German are spoken; rooms cleaned every three days; complimentary tourist information; air conditioning; Internet access; smokers welcome; private parking*
Rates: *single €, double €€. Additional bed supplement €. Discounts for extended stays*
Credit cards: *not accepted*
Pets:

• Bed & Breakfast Italia
Code V20
tel. 06 6878618, fax 06 6878619
info@bbitalia.it
www.bbitalia.it
Closed: varies

First-floor independent apartment in a 16th-century building, located in the old center. It has two double bedrooms, both carefully furnished, with the option of a cot for children under two. Each room has its own private bathroom with tub. The guests may also use the large lounge, adorned with a red marble fireplace and a characteristic stone balcony. Venice, Padua, Treviso and Lake Garda can be easily reached by car or by train.

Accommodation
Guestrooms: *2 doubles*
Services & Amenities: *French spoken; rooms cleaned every 3 days; complimentary tourist information*
Minimum stay: *2 nights*
Rates: *€€*
Credit cards: VISA MC *Bancomat*
Pets:

• **Bed & Breakfast Italia**
Code V37
tel. 06 6878618, fax 06 6878619
info@bbitalia.it
www.bbitalia.it
Closed: varies

Third floor apartment in an old building with elevator, in the old center of Verona, 300 m from the Arena and 150 m from Juliet's House. Guests can use 3 double rooms with TV and large balcony. The rooms are carefully furnished with antiques and decorated with warm, colorful upholstery. The rooms share 2 baths with shower. Guests can use the kitchen and a reserved space in the parking lot.

Accommodation
Guestrooms: *3 doubles*
Services & Amenities: *French, English and German are spoken; rooms cleaned every three days; complimentary tourist information; baby-sitting service; smokers welcome; private parking*
Minimum stay: *2 nights*
Rates: €€
Credit cards: VISA MC *Bancomat*
Pets: no

• **Bed & Breakfast Italia**
Code V40
tel. 06 6878618, fax 06 6878619
info@bbitalia.it
www.bbitalia.it
Closed: varies

In a medieval historic area, a short distance from the Duomo and 100 meters from Piazza delle Erbe, this independent B&B on the fourth floor of an elegant building includes two double rooms, classically furnished with antiques, and sharing a private bathroom with shower. The area is well served by transport, and the bus stop is 200 m from the accommodation. Guests have free access to the kitchen and parking.

Accommodation
Guestrooms: *2 doubles*
Services & Amenities: *French, English and German are spoken; rooms cleaned every three days; tourist information; smokers welcome*
Minimum stay: *2 nights*
Rates: €€
Credit cards: VISA MC *Bancomat*
Pets: no

Vicenza

I tre Camini TCI 10%
tel. 044 868041, mob. 349 5318909
bedbre@katamail.com
Open: 1 June to 15 August

Thanks to a perfect restructuring job, this farmhouse located in the Colli Berici scenario in the Palladio villas area, has retained the characteristic features of its architecture (bare beams, terracotta floors and fireplace), as well as its rural atmosphere (it's still surrounded by the old mulberry trees that were once used for raising silk worms). However, all the modern comforts are provided, including a swimming pool. The traditional Italian breakfast is served either in the large kitchen or under the typical "tesa" (a veranda with a sloping roof supported by columns).

Accommodation
Guestrooms: *3 (1 double and 1 triple room, with shared bath, and 1 triple room with private bath)* ♿
Services & Amenities: *rooms cleaned every 3 days; tourist information; kitchen use by request; garden; smokers welcome; private parking*
Minimum stay: *3 nights*
Rates: €€€€
Credit cards: *not accepted*
Pets: no

Vicenza Villas B&B
Paolo and Janice Dal Pra
viale 10 Giugno 131-133
36100 Vicenza
tel. 0444 543087
panice@gpnet.it
Open all year

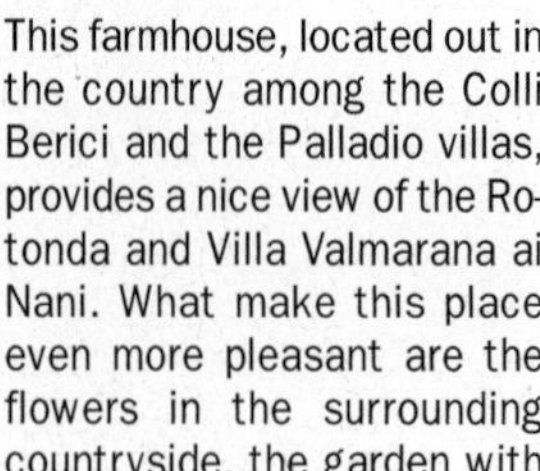

This farmhouse, located out in the country among the Colli Berici and the Palladio villas, provides a nice view of the Rotonda and Villa Valmarana ai Nani. What make this place even more pleasant are the flowers in the surrounding countryside, the garden with its fruit trees and private woods, and its large terrace and portico where the traditional breakfast, which also includes organic fruit, is served. The antique or rustic furnishings are perfectly in keeping with the style of the house.

Accommodation
Guestrooms: *3 (1 single and 2 doubles, with private bath); additional bed on request*
Services & Amenities: *French, English and German are spoken; rooms cleaned every day; tourist information; Internet access; garden; smokers welcome; private parking*
Minimum stay: *2 nights*
Rates: *single €€, double €€. Additional bed supplement €. Discounts for children*
Credit cards: *not accepted*
Pets: *not allowed*

Vigonza (Padua)

Brenta
Loretta Cacco
via Pisa 18
35010 Vigonza (PD)
tel. and fax 049 502271
mob. 347 3701287
fdino@fredomland.it
• Euganean Life International
tel. 0429 56156, mob. 347 4355474
fax 0429 56156
elit@bandb-veneto.it
www.bandb-veneto.it/euganeanlife
Open all year

The rooms in this small villa with garden, have a terrace provided with a breakfast table. Breakfast can also be consumed in the kitchen, with the family, or outside under the portico. The owner of the house also has a small boat and, on request, will be happy to take the guests for a boat ride along the canals.

Accommodation
Guestrooms: *2 doubles, also single occupancy, with shared bath; additional bed on request*
Services & Amenities: *French and English are spoken; rooms cleaned every 3 days; complimentary tourist information; kitchen use by request; terrace; Internet access; garden; smokers welcome; private parking*
Minimum stay: *2 nights*
Rates: *single €€, double €€. Additional bed supplement €*
Credit cards: *not accepted*
Pets: *not allowed*

Le Palme
• Associazione Koko Nor
tel. 049 8643394, mob. 338 3377912
fax 049 8643394
kokonor@bandb-veneto.it
www.bandb-veneto.it/kokonor
Closed: August

Accommodation
Guestrooms: *2 doubles with shared bath; additional bed on request*
Services & Amenities: *English, German, Spanish, Russian and Swedish are spoken; rooms cleaned every 3 days; tourist information; kitchen use by request; bike rental; garden; smokers welcome; private parking*
Minimum stay: *3 nights*
Rates: *€€. Discounts for extended stays*
Credit cards: *not accepted*
Pets: *allowed*

The owners of this villa – located in a quiet residential area just 3 km from Padua – turned the ground floor into an apartment with an independent entrance. The continental breakfast is served in the apartment's dining room, which opens directly onto the beautiful garden. The beginning of the Riviera del Brenta, which extends from Padua to Venice and is famous for its celebrated, historical villas, is just a very short walk from the villa. Guests also have the use of the kitchen and 2 or 3 bicycles.

Vittorio Veneto (Treviso)

Augusta Pagot
via Parravicini 14
31029 Vittorio Veneto (TV)
tel. 0438 57847, mob. 329 2173943
http/digilander.iol.it/appartamentivacanze
• **B&B in Italy. Ospitalità nelle case**
tel. and fax 0432 731854
bedbreakfastitaly@hotmail.com
www.bedandbreakfastfvg.com
Open all year

Accommodation
Guestrooms: *3 doubles, also single occupancy, with private bath*
Services & Amenities: *French and English are spoken; rooms cleaned every three days; tourist information; kitchen use by request; garden; smokers welcome; private parking*
Rates: *single €, double €€. Additional bed supplement €. Children under 6 free. Discounts for extended stays*
Credit cards: *not accepted*
Pets:

This 16th-century house, which is located in the old center of Serravalle, the old village furthest north of the two that form the city, has its original, bare-beamed ceilings and a nice garden. Breakfast, which consists of either sweet items or cold cuts and various types of cheese, as desired, is served in the large family kitchen. The three guestrooms all have fine antique furniture.

La Casa del Podestà
Francesco Rossi
piazza Giovanni Paolo I 61
31029 Vittorio Veneto (TV)
tel. 0438 53448, mob. 347 6929133
Open all year

Accommodation
Guestrooms: *3 (1 double and 2 triple room, with private bath)*
Services & Amenities: *French, English and German are spoken; rooms cleaned every 3 days; tourist info; garden; smokers welcome; parking*
Minimum stay: *2 nights*
Rates: *single €€, double €€, triple €€€. Children under 6 free.*
Credit cards: *not accepted*
Pets:

The rooms of this B&B have an independent entrance, period furnishings and wooden ceilings. The spacious breakfast room and large garden make this B&B even more pleasant. Breakfast also includes natural products.

Zermeghedo (Vicenza)

Maria Luisa
Maria Luisa Orlandi
via Mieli 12
36050 Zermeghedo (VI)
tel. 0444 685081
Open all year

Accommodation
Guestrooms: *2 doubles, also single occupancy, with shared bath*
Services & Amenities: *French, English and German are spoken; rooms cleaned every 3 days; complimentary tourist information; bike rental; terrace; air conditioning; garden; smokers welcome; private parking*
Rates: *single €€, double €€. Children under 6 - 50%. Discounts for extended stays*
Credit cards: *not accepted*
Pets:

This small villa, located in the countryside surrounding Vicenza, has 2 guestrooms, one of which is a mansard, with light-wood furnishings. Breakfast is served either in the kitchen or under the portico.

• **Bed & Breakfast Italia**
Code V27
tel. 06 6878618, fax 06 6878619
info@bbitalia.it, www.bbitalia.it
Closed: varies

Accommodation
Guestrooms: *2 (1 single, 1 double)*
Services & Amenities: *French, English and German are spoken; rooms cleaned every 3 days; tourist information; terrace; private parking*
Minimum stay: *2 nights*
Rates: €€
Credit cards: VISA MC *Bancomat*
Pets:

Small cottage with separate entrance, garden, veranda, wide balcony and private car park. The rooms are furnished in a simple and comfortable style, with private bathroom with tub. Hosts are a precious source of information for anything concerning nature, art and gastronomy in the area.

Friuli-Venezia Giulia

Attimis (Udine)

Casa Giuly
Giuliana Braidotti
via Canalutto 33, località Racchiuso
33040 Attimis (UD)
tel. 0432 789294, mob. 333 7245729
www.ursusfvg.com
• **B&B in Italy. Ospitalità nelle case**
tel. and fax 0432 731854
bedbreakfastitaly@hotmail.com
www.bedandbreakfastfvg.com
Open: April to October

Accommodation
Guestrooms: *2 (1 single with shared bath; 1 double with private bath); additional bed on request*
Services & Amenities: *French spoken; rooms cleaned every three days; tourist information; garden; smokers welcome; private parking*
Rates: *single €, double €€. Additional bed supplement €€€*
Credit cards: *not accepted*
Pets:

Guests in this ancient, restructured mill, located on the shore of a stream and surrounded by an orchard and woods, either have a single room on the same floor as the family or a comfortable mansard with an adjoining living room and library located on the third floor. Breakfast consists of pastries, organic marmalades, fruit, and wild berries from the forest.

Casa Manuela
Clara Lenchig
località Borgo Faris 28
33040 Attimis (UD)
tel. and fax 0432 728108
manuela.delfabbro@libero.it
• **B&B in Italy. Ospitalità nelle case**
tel. and fax 0432 731854
bedbreakfastitaly@hotmail.com
www.bedandbreakfastfvg.com
Open all year

This B&B is located in a traditional, restructured house situated in a village at the foot of a hill that has the Partistagno castle on it. The house is surrounded by a well equipped garden. Besides the guestrooms, there's a comfortable reading room with fireplace. The host family is in the business of growing grapes and making wine and are happy to familiarize its guests with the local wines.

Accommodation
Guestrooms: *3 doubles, also single occupancy, with private bath; additional bed on request*
Services & Amenities: *English spoken; rooms cleaned every 3 days; tourist material; bike rental; terrace; air conditioning; garden; smokers welcome; private parking*
Rates: *single €, double €€. Discounts for children and extended stays*
Credit cards: *not accepted*
Pets:

Federico Ascari e Elena Bassani
via Faedis 25/2, località Racchiuso
33040 Attimis (UD)
tel. 0432 789679
• B&B in Italy. Ospitalità nelle case
tel. and fax 0432 731854
bedbreakfastitaly@hotmail.com
www.bedandbreakfastfvg.com
Open all year

This farmhouse is located in a small village at Racchiuso di Attimis, on a grape-growing and wine-making farm known for its organic production. The B&B's large rooms are provided with all the modern comforts and have rustic furniture. Guests are invited to taste the wine and also participate in the grape harvest. The family can also take the guests on excursions in the area and provide indications for taking walks among the ancient vineyards.

Accommodation
Guestrooms: *2 (1 double and 1 triple, also single occupancy, shared bath); additional bed on request*
Services & Amenities: *English and German are spoken; rooms cleaned every day; tourist information; baby-sitting service; garden; smokers welcome; private parking*
Rates: *€ per person. Children under 3 free. Discounts for extended stays*
Credit cards: *not accepted*
Pets:

Especially noteworthy is the family's fondness for yoga gymnastics and its well-furnished library of esoteric texts.

I Pioppi
Dorigo and Mondolo
via Borgo Poiana 17
33040 Attimis (UD)
tel. and fax 0432 789758
mob. 340 2451730
jdori@libero.it
• B&B in Italy. Ospitalità nelle case
tel. and fax 0432 731854
bedbreakfastitaly@hotmail.com
www.bedandbreakfastfvg.com
Open: April and December

This three-story house is in a small locality up in the hills, surrounded by a forest of chestnut trees. The outlying areas provide trails for mountain-biking and excursions. There is also the wine road for becoming acquainted with the history of wine, as well as the Partistagno castle, the Attimis Archeological Museum and the Fossil Museum.

Accommodation
Guestrooms: *3 doubles, shared bath*
Services & Amenities: *English and German are spoken; rooms cleaned every three days; complimentary tourist information; kitchen use by request; Internet access; garden; smokers welcome*
Rates: *single €, double €€. Discounts for children*
Credit cards: *not accepted*
Pets:

Budoia (Pordenone)

Le Glicini
Armida Pitton
via Friuli 19b, 33070 Budoia (PN)
tel. 0434 654021, mob. 349 5592385
fax 0434 747905
armidapitton@libero.it
• B&B in Italy. Ospitalità nelle case
tel. and fax 0432 731854
bedbreakfastitaly@hotmail.com
www.bedandbreakfastfvg.com
Open: 7 January to 3 March, 25 March to 2 June, 30 June to 4 August and 26 August to 22 December

The hostess of this recently constructed villa with its garden, offers her guests an apartment, which has an independent entrance, two bedrooms, a bathroom and a living room with TV. The continental breakfast is served in this living room. On request, guests can have the use of a laundry and a kitchen.

Accommodation
Guestrooms: *2 (1 single and 1 double, with shared bath)*
Services & Amenities: *English spoken; rooms cleaned every three days; complimentary tourist information; kitchen use by request; garden; smokers welcome*
Rates: *single €, double €€. Discounts for children*
Credit cards: *not accepted*
Pets:

Buia (Udine)

Famiglia De Cecco
via Dobes 13, località Sopramonte
33030 Buia (UD)
tel. 0432 964022
aless.neri@libero.it
• **B&B in Italy. Ospitalità nelle case**
tel. and fax 0432 731854
bedbreakfastitaly@hotmail.com
www.bedandbreakfastfvg.com
Open: 20 April to 20 September

This typical, Friulian "L" shaped, two-story house is surrounded by a large lawn and is located on the side of a hill, in an outlying section of Sopramonte which is near the forest. The accommodation includes two guestrooms with modern furnishings. The rich breakfast provides a wide selection of natural products. The hosts love all kinds of mountain activity, and also like to engage in bike-tourism.

Accommodation
Guestrooms: *2 doubles, also single occupancy, shared bath; additional bed on request*
Services & Amenities: *English spoken; rooms cleaned every day; tourist information; terrace; garden; smokers welcome; private parking*
Rates: *€ per person. Discounts for children*
Credit cards: *not accepted*
Pets: ✓

Camino al Tagliamento (Udine)

B&B Gabri & Sante
Gabri and Sante Osso
via Andreuzza 41
33030 Camino al Tagliamento (UD)
tel. 0432 960862, mob. 338 5916256
mirella.comino@tin.it
• **B&B in Italy. Ospitalità nelle case**
tel. and fax 0432 731854
bedbreakfastitaly@hotmail.com
www.bedandbreakfastfvg.com
Closed: 15 to 30 January and November

The most pleasant characteristic of this B&B is its large park containing fir trees, trails and ponds with water-lilies. The classic wooden furnishings provide a nice, warm, welcoming atmosphere for the guests, who also have the use of a living room with a fireplace and touristic library, bicycles, a terrace-solarium and a barbecue. Breakfast, which also includes natural marmalades, is either served in the dining room or in the garden.

Accommodation
Guestrooms: *3 (2 singles, 1 double bedroom, shared bath)*
Services & Amenities: *French and English are spoken; rooms cleaned every three days; tourist information; bike rental; terrace; Internet access; garden; smokers welcome; parking*
Rates: *single €, double €€. Discounts for extended stays*
Credit cards: *not accepted*
Pets: ✓

Casa Francesca
Francesca Casaril
via Tagliamento 34
33030 Camino al Tagliamento (UD)
tel. 0432 919369, fax 0432 919482
• **B&B in Italy. Ospitalità nelle case**
tel. and fax 0432 731854
bedbreakfastitaly@hotmail.com
www.bedandbreakfastfvg.com
Open: June to September

This house is part of a late 18th-C, Venetian-style building that faces a rural courtyard that has trees. The atmosphere of this B&B is informal and friendly, and the hostess likes having her guests share the family areas. Breakfast, consisting of typical pastries or, on request, cold cuts and cheeses, is served in the characteristic Friulian kitchen with its central fireplace. Guests who are fond of sports and excursions are just a few minutes away from the nearby tennis courts and riding stables.

Accommodation
Guestrooms: *1 double bedroom, also single occupancy, shared bath*
Services & Amenities: *rooms cleaned every three days; complimentary tourist information; garden; smokers welcome*
Rates: *single €, double €€*
Credit cards: *not accepted*
Pets: ✗

Casarsa della Delizia (Pordenone)

The Cottage
Ileana Rocchi Canova
via S. D'Acquisto 11
33072 Casarsa della Delizia (PN)
tel. and fax 0434 869651
thecottage@freemail.it
www.go.to/B&BtheCottage.it
• **B&B in Italy. Ospitalità nelle case**
tel. and fax 0432 731854
bedbreakfastitaly@hotmail.com
www.bedandbreakfastfvg.com
Open all year

The guestrooms of this house, with its completely English atmosphere, are very nicely furnished, have original English wallpaper, and the bedcovers, drapes and lacquered-iron beds have coordinated colors. The rooms lead into the mansard where the guests have the use of a satellite TV, a computer and a printer. The genuine English breakfast is either served in the garden or in the mansard.

Accommodation
Guestrooms: *2 (1 double, 1 double bedroom, also single occupancy, private bath); additional bed on request*
Services & Amenities: *French and English are spoken; rooms cleaned every day; tourist information; garden; bike rental; private parking*
Rates: *single €€, double €€, triple room €€€*
Credit cards: *not accepted*
Pets: not allowed

Cividale del Friuli (Udine)

Azienda agricola Ronchi di Fornaz
Lucia Galasso
via della Fornaz 15
33043 Cividale del Friuli (UD)
tel. 0432 701462, fax 0432 730292
• **B&B in Italy. Ospitalità nelle case**
tel. and fax 0432 731854
bedbreakfastitaly@hotmail.com
www.bedandbreakfastfvg.com
Open all year

Accommodation
Guestrooms: *3 doubles, also single occupancy, with shared bath; additional bed on request*
Services & Amenities: *English and German are spoken; rooms cleaned every day; tourist info; garden; smokers welcome; private parking*
Rates: *single €, double €€. Additional bed supplement €. Discounts for children and extended stays*
Credit cards: *not accepted*
Pets: allowed

The farm is located on a hill, just a 5-minute drive from town. It has old furniture in the rustic Friulian style, and the guests have two rooms and a kitchen, where they can have their breakfast. Those who like good Friulian wine can visit the wine cellar, watch the wine-making process and taste the local wines. Guests can also take part in the grape harvest.

B&B Paola Fasano
strada del Mulino 2, località Purgessimo
33043 Cividale del Friuli (UD)
tel. 0432 730485, mob. 333 8424253
• **B&B in Italy. Ospitalità nelle case**
tel. and fax 0432 731854
bedbreakfastitaly@hotmail.com
www.bedandbreakfastfvg.com
Open: March and November

This rustic house, located in Purgessimo, which is 4 kilometers from the center of Cividale, enjoys surrounding meadows, a beautiful natural landscape, and a tranquil position on the shore of the Natisone. The guest part of the house has its own independent entrance. The rich breakfast, which features a strictly "natural" menu, also includes traditional pastries. Guests can enjoy some nice walks, especially the one that follows the old Roman road that leads to Cividale.

Accommodation
Guestrooms: *3 (1 single and 2 doubles, with shared bath)*
Services & Amenities: *rooms cleaned every 3 days; tourist information; kitchen use by request; bike rental; garden; smokers welcome; parking*
Rates: *single €, double €€. Discounts for children and extended stays*
Credit cards: *not accepted*
Pets: allowed

B&B Silvia
Marco Pittioni
via Sanguarzo 13
33043 Cividale del Friuli (UD)
tel. and fax 0432 731854
• **B&B in Italy. Ospitalità nelle case**
tel. and fax 0432 731854
bedbreakfastitaly@hotmail.com
www.bedandbreakfastfvg.com
Open: 15 March to 30 October

This B&B, which is in a well-restructured, early 20th-century house that has a garden, is located in the very green Borgo Sanguarzo village, which is about 1 kilometer from Cividale. Breakfast is served in the rustic-style kitchen. The hosts provide information regarding Cividale, which was once the seat of a Longobard dukedom and the capital of Friuli. Nice walks can be taken along the Natisone river which runs through Cividale.

Accommodation
Guestrooms: *2 (1 double bedroom,1 double, also single occupancy, shared bath); additional bed on request*
Services & Amenities: *English spoken; rooms cleaned every day; complimentary tourist information; bike rental; garden; smokers welcome*
Minimum stay: *2 nights*
Rates: *€ per person. Discounts for children*
Credit cards: *not accepted*
Pets:

Casa Fema
Nicoletta Cattelan
via Casali Grions 9
33043 Cividale del Friuli (UD)
tel. 0432 730322, mob. 328 7165923
nicolettacattelan@inwind.it
• **B&B in Italy. Ospitalità nelle case**
tel. and fax 0432 731854
bedbreakfastitaly@hotmail.com
www.bedandbreakfastfvg.com
Open: 20 March to 31 October and 19 to 31 December

Accommodation
Guestrooms: *3 doubles, also single occupancy, shared bath*
Services & Amenities: *English and Slovene are spoken; rooms cleaned every 3 days; tourist info; bike rental; garden; smokers welcome; parking*
Rates: *single €, double €€*
Credit cards: *not accepted*
Pets:

This farmhouse, which has a garden, is located in a tranquil position just 800 meters from the center of Cividale. Guests can either have a continental breakfast or a more substantial one consisting of cold cuts and cheese. Breakfast is either served in the dining room or, when the weather's nice, in the garden. The guests have the use of bicycles, provided by the family, and can also enjoy the nearby tennis courts, swimming pool and riding stables.

Casa Franca
Franca Michieli
via Adige 15
33043 Cividale del Friuli (UD)
tel. 0432 734055
• **B&B in Italy. Ospitalità nelle case**
tel. and fax 0432 731854
bedbreakfastitaly@hotmail.com
www.bedandbreakfastfvg.com
Open: March to November

Accommodation
Guestrooms: *3 (1 single and 2 doubles, with shared bath)*
Services & Amenities: *rooms cleaned every 3 days; tourist info; kitchen use by request; garden; smokers welcome*
Rates: *single €, double €€*
Credit cards: *not accepted*
Pets:

This small villa is located in a quiet, tranquil area just 10 minutes from the center of town. The guests' accommodation includes three rooms, a small garden, an independent entrance, a living room with TV, and a kitchen. The rich breakfast, which is served every morning in the guest kitchen, can either consist of pastries, brioches and yoghurt or cold cuts, cheeses and toast.

Casa Le Margherite
Rosina Vogrig
via Michele Leicht 5
33043 Cividale del Friuli (UD)
tel. 0432 733172
lienartova@libero.it
• **B&B in Italy. Ospitalità nelle case**
tel. and fax 0432 731854
bedbreakfastitaly@hotmail.com
www.bedandbreakfastfvg.com
Open: March to August and November to mid-December

This recently-built duplex, in traditional architectural style, is no more than a kilometer from the center of town. The accommodation includes one double room with private bath; there is also a garden at the guests' disposal. The breakfast, which consists of natural local products, including "gubana", a popular local pastry, can also be of the English type if so requested.

Accommodation
Guestrooms: *1 double, also single occupancy, private bath (outside)*
Services & Amenities: *German spoken; rooms cleaned every 3 days; complimentary tourist information; garden; smokers welcome; private parking*
Rates: *single €, double €€. Discounts for extended stays*
Credit cards: *not accepted*
Pets:

Casa Milena
Milena Castagnara
via De Gasperi 5
33043 Cividale del Friuli (UD)
tel. 0432 733459
• **B&B in Italy. Ospitalità nelle case**
tel. and fax 0432 731854
bedbreakfastitaly@hotmail.com
www.bedandbreakfastfvg.com
Closed: January and December

Accommodation
Guestrooms: *2 (1 single and 1 double, with shared bath)*
Services & Amenities: *French and Spanish are spoken; rooms cleaned every 3 days; tourist information; garden; smokers welcome*
Rates: *single €, double €€*
Credit cards: *not accepted*
Pets:

This B&B is in a comfortable, duplex villa that has a garden and is situated on the shore of the Natisone River, just 150 meters from the cathedral. The rich continental breakfast, consisting of pastries, biscuits and yoghurt, is usually served in the living room. This quiet, tranquil environment is ideal for guests who want to spend a nice relaxed vacation in a place that has a lot of wine-making and good-eating culture and traditions.

Francesca Gregoricchio
stretta del Mulinuss 15
33043 Cividale del Friuli (UD)
tel. 0432 701603, fax 0432 701000
• **B&B in Italy. Ospitalità nelle case**
tel. and fax 0432 731854
bedbreakfastitaly@hotmail.com
www.bedandbreakfastfvg.com
Open all year

Accommodation
Guestrooms: *3 (1 single, 1 double, 1 double bedroom, shared bath); additional bed on request*
Services & Amenities: *English spoken; rooms cleaned every day; complimentary tourist information; garden; smokers welcome*
Rates: *€ per person. Children under 10 free*
Credit cards: *not accepted*
Pets:

This small 16th-century building is located in the town's old center and is surrounded by garden closed in by a medieval wall. The building also has a hanging garden resting on a Roman tower. Guests enjoy complete autonomy and have an independent entrance. The traditional breakfast, consisting of bread, marmalades and yoghurt, can be enriched by other products on request. Guests with children are provided with every comfort.

Il Gelsomino
Francesca Dominissini
via Stretta Matteotti 11
33043 Cividale del Friuli (UD)
tel. 0432 731962
• B&B in Italy. Ospitalità nelle case
tel. and fax 0432 731854
bedbreakfastitaly@hotmail.com
www.bedandbreakfastfvg.com
Closed: 15 December to 15 January, Easter holidays, July and August

This 16th-century house, located in the old center, has a courtyard and a outside stairway made of stone. The furniture in the guestrooms date from the '30s and '40s. Breakfast, with brioches and freshly baked bread, is served in the room where the guests can also spend their evenings. The hosts are willing to use the family car for taking the guests on tours in the surrounding area.

Accommodation
Guestrooms: *2 (1 double and 1 double bedroom, also single occupancy, with shared bath)*
Services & Amenities: *English spoken; rooms cleaned every three days; complimentary tourist information; bike rental; smokers welcome*
Minimum stay: *2 nights*
Rates: *single €, double €€*
Credit cards: *not accepted*
Pets: 🚫

La Piccola Fattoria
Claudia Nadalut
33043 Cividale del Friuli (UD)
tel. 0432 731605
• B&B in Italy. Ospitalità nelle case
tel. and fax 0432 731854
bedbreakfastitaly@hotmail.com
www.bedandbreakfastfvg.com
Open all year

This 18th-century farmhouse, located in the village of Cividale, has thick walls, bare beams, plank floors and is surrounded by lots of vegetation and an old wall. There are several farm animals, including horses, in its large courtyard. Guest who like to ride also have a stall at their disposal for their horses. The guestrooms have a private courtyard entrance. The continental breakfast, which can be enriched with other items – fresh eggs, for example – is served in the ground floor dining room-kitchen that the hosts share with their guests.

Accommodation
Guestrooms: *2 (1 double and 1 quadruple room, also single occupancy, with shared bath)*
Services & Amenities: *English spoken; rooms cleaned every 3 days; tourist info; garden; smokers welcome*
Rates: *€ per person*
Credit cards: *not accepted*
Pets: 🐾

Cormons (Gorizia)

Margherita Kriza Zimic
via Riva della Torre 19 G
34071 Cormons (GO)
tel. 0481 61486
• B&B in Italy. Ospitalità nelle case
tel. and fax 0432 731854
bedbreakfastitaly@hotmail.com
www.bedandbreakfastfvg.com
Closed: 1 January to 15 March, 15 November to 1 December

This B&B, inside the rustic courtyard of a house that's located in the heart of Cormons, provides a view of the hills and has very bright, autonomous guestrooms and a sitting room. The breakfast, which can be enriched with cold cuts, cheeses and toast, is served in the living room. For guests who like good wine, the family provides information regarding the best producers, best wine cellars and best restaurants.

Accommodation
Guestrooms: *2 doubles, also single occupancy, with private bath*
Services & Amenities: *German, Slovene and Hungarian are spoken; rooms cleaned every day; complimentary tourist information; garden; smokers welcome*
Rates: *single €, double €€. Children under 6 free; 7 to 12 - 50%*
Credit cards: *not accepted*
Pets: 🐾

Villa Bianca
Thea Bassi
via Acquedotto 8, località Brazzano
34071 Cormons (GO)
tel. 0481 60464, fax 0481 630845
• B&B in Italy. Ospitalità nelle case
tel. and fax 0432 731854
bedbreakfastitaly@hotmail.com
www.bedandbreakfastfvg.com
Open: March to December

Accommodation
Guestrooms: *2 (1 double, 1 triple, also single occupancy, private bath)*
Services & Amenities: *French and English are spoken; rooms cleaned every 3 days; tourist info; kitchen use by request; bike rental; educational courses by request; garden; smokers welcome; private parking*
Minimum stay: *2 nights*
Rates: *single €, double €€, triple €€€. Children under 10 - 50%*
Credit cards: *not accepted*
Pets:

The owners of this restructured 17th-century villa, surrounded by a garden with trees, offers two very nice guestrooms with private bath, that have an independent entrance. On request, the large breakfast can be strictly vegetarian. Guests also have the use of a small kitchen, a living room, a reading room, a large terrace, and an exercise room for practicing yoga or receiving massages. Bycicles are available for the guests.

Corno di Rosazzo (Udine)

Casa Angela
Daniele Zof
località Casali Gallo 12
33040 Corno di Rosazzo (UD)
tel. 0432 759673, fax 0432 759284
info@zof.it
• B&B in Italy. Ospitalità nelle case
tel. and fax 0432 731854
bedbreakfastitaly@hotmail.com
www.bedandbreakfastfvg.com
Open: March to December

This 18th-C house, which is 2 km from town and also near a wooded area where guests can take hikes, has 2, small, independent guestrooms and a kitchen. The owners of the house leave, in the common room, the ingredients for preparing breakfast, which can be consumed in the rooms. The family winery is just a short distance away, and the guests can visit it and taste the wines.

Accommodation
Guestrooms: *3 doubles, also single occupancy, with private bath; additional bed on request* ♿
Services & Amenities: *English spoken; tourist information; rooms cleaned every 3 days; bike rental; garden; smokers welcome; parking*
Rates: *single €, double €€-€€€. Additional bed supplement €. Discounts for children and extended stays*
Credit cards: *not accepted*
Pets:

Casa Sara
Sara Zuppel
località Casali Gallo
33040 Corno di Rosazzo (UD)
tel. and fax 0432 759593
sarocchia71@yahoo.it
• B&B in Italy. Ospitalità nelle case
tel. and fax 0432 731854
bedbreakfastitaly@hotmail.com
www.bedandbreakfastfvg.com
Open all year

Accommodation
Guestrooms: *3 double rooms, also single occupancy, 1 with private bath and 2 with shared bath; additional bed on request*
Services & Amenities: *English and German are spoken; rooms cleaned every 3 days; tourist info; garden; smokers welcome; private parking*
Rates: *€-€€ per person. Children under 5 free, 6 to 12 - 50%. Discounts for extended stays*
Credit cards: *not accepted*
Pets:

This B&B is located in a large, restructured, early-19th century house, situated in front of the Trussio castle. The guestrooms have wooden floors. Breakfast can be autonomously consumed in the kitchen. However, the family is happy to share some social moments with the guests, such as preparing grilled meat or making excursions. On request, the guests can also use the swimming pool.

I due Tigli
Umberto and Mariangela Carpenetti
via San Martino 4
località Visignale dello Judrio
33040 Cormo di Rosazzo (UD)
tel. 0432 753263
fax 0481 777431
• B&B in Italy. Ospitalità nelle case
tel. and fax 0432 731854
bedbreakfastitaly@hotmail.com
www.bedandbreakfastfvg.com
Open all year

This late 18th-century manor house, which is surrounded with a large garden and is just 3 kilometers from the Slovenian border, provides a traditional Italian breakfast that can be enriched if desired. The family is happy to share their fondness for music, antiques and gardening, and can willingly accompany their guests on excursions.

Accommodation
Guestrooms: *2 (1 double bedroom and 1 double, with private bath); additional bed on request*
Services & Amenities: *English spoken; rooms cleaned every day; tourist information; bike rental; garden; smokers welcome; private parking*
Rates: *double €€. Additional bed supplement €. Discounts for children*
Credit cards: *not accepted*
Pets:

Villa Cabassi
piazza 27 Maggio 21
33040 Cormo di Rosazzo (UD)
tel. 0432 753503, fax 0432 236919
mob. 335 5665749
• B&B in Italy. Ospitalità nelle case
tel. and fax 0432 731854
bedbreakfastitaly@hotmail.com
www.bedandbreakfastfvg.com
Closed: 15 January to 15 March

Accommodation
Guestrooms: *3 doubles, 1 with private bath and 2 with shared bath; additional bed on request*
Services & Amenities: *German spoken; rooms cleaned every day; tourist info; garden; smokers welcome*
Minimum stay: *2 nights*
Rates: *double €€. Discounts for children and extended stays*
Credit cards: *not accepted*
Pets:

This 16th-century villa, which is surrounded by a large park, has been in the family for three-hundred years. The large breakfast is either served in the garden or in the traditional Friulian kitchen, which has a stone floor, wood-burning stove, and a characteristic fireplace with benches under its huge hood. Guests who are fond of good wine and good eating, will have the opportunity to become acquainted with the Friulian wine and cuisine specialties.

Dignano (Udine)

Casa Pirona
• B&B in Italy. Ospitalità nelle case
tel. and fax 0432 731854
bedbreakfastitaly@hotmail.com
www.bedandbreakfastfvg.com
Opne: May to October

This 17th-century manor house is where the abbot Jacopo Pirona was born in 1789. He was the author of the Friulian dialect vocabulary. In the back of the house, there's a large, very naturally-kept garden. The large breakfast can either be served in the dining room or in the typical Friulian kitchen, which still has a fireplace with a hood. The hostess very willingly furnishes historical information regarding the surrounding area.

Accommodation
Guestrooms: *3 doubles, also single occupancy, ensuite bathroom*
Services & Amenities: *French, English and German are spoken; rooms cleaned every 3 days; complimentary tourist information; bike rental; garden; smokers welcome*
Rates: *€ per person. Children under 2 free; 3 to 10 - 50%. Discounts for extended stays*
Credit cards: *not accepted*
Pets:

Guests can also arrange to visit the nearby winery and taste the wine.

Faedis (Udine)

Soffumbergo
Claudio Floran
via Castellame 9, località Campegli
33040 Faedis (UD)
tel. 0432 711351, mob. 388 6118191
• B&B in Italy. Ospitalità nelle case
tel. and fax 0432 731854
bedbreakfastitaly@hotmail.com
www.bedandbreakfastfvg.com
Open: 24 March to 30 October

Accommodation
Guestrooms: *2 doubles, also single occupancy, with private bath; additional bed on request*
Services & Amenities: *rooms cleaned every three days; tourist information; bike rental; garden; smokers welcome; private parking*
Rates: *single €, double €€. Additional bed supplement €. Discounts for children*
Credit cards: *not accepted*
Pets: ✓

This B&B, which gets its name from the medieval castle whose ruins are on the far side of the town, is situated inside a large plot of ground cultivated as a vineyard. The wine made from these grapes is quite exceptional, and the host is pleased to have his guests taste the wine. This tranquil, panoramic place, surrounded by woods, is ideal for taking nature hikes, as well as excursions to see the castles and fortifications.

Fontanafredda (Pordenone)

La Magnolia
famiglia Crispano
via IV Novembre 105
33074 Fontanafredda (PN)
tel. and fax 0434 998495
• B&B in Italy. Ospitalità nelle case
tel. and fax 0432 731854
bedbreakfastitaly@hotmail.com
www.bedandbreakfastfvg.com
Closed: August and 15 December to 31 January

Accommodation
Guestrooms: *2 doubles, also single occupancy, shared bath); additional bed on request*
Services & Amenities: *French, English and German are spoken; tourist information; rooms cleaned every day; air conditioning; garden; smokers welcome; private parking*
Rates: *single €, double €€. Additional bed supplement €. Discounts for extended stays*
Credit cards: *not accepted*
Pets: ✗

This B&B is located in a restructured house in the center of town. There are two guestrooms, one of which is wood-paneled mansard. Guests can have either a continental breakfast or, on request, an English breakfast. On warm days, guests can use the air conditioning system and also enjoy the beautiful garden and its flowers.

Gorizia

Palazzo Lantieri
piazza Sant'Antonio 6
34170 Gorizia
tel. 0481 531453, 0481 536740
fax 0481 531453, mob. 339 2435562
• B&B in Italy. Ospitalità nelle case
tel. and fax 0432 731854
bedbreakfastitaly@hotmail.com
www.bedandbreakfastfvg.com
Open all year

The basic nucleus of this building dates from 1200, when it was a fortress next to the city wall, parts of which are still present in the garden. In the 17th C, the building was converted into the noble residence, which is still intact, including its frescoed rooms and original furnishings. The garden has a lawn chair where guests can relax. A laundry service is provided on request.

Accommodation
Guestrooms: *3 (1 single and 1 double, private bath; 1 double, shared bath); additional bed on request*
Services & Amenities: *French, English and German are spoken; rooms cleaned every 3 days; complimentary tourist information; bike rental; garden; smokers welcome; private parking*
Rates: *single €€, double €€€€. Discounts for children*
Credit cards: *not accepted*
Pets: ✓

Villa De Baguer
Colella Elio
piazza Medaglie d'Oro 10
34170 Gorizia
tel. 0481 531241, mob. 347 8072790
villadebaguer@vaigorizia.it
• B&B in Italy. Ospitalità nelle case
tel. and fax 0432 731854
bedbreakfastitaly@hotmail.com
www.bedandbreakfastfvg.com
Open: 15 July to 15 September

This villa, built in 1929 and has a 19th-C wine cellar in the basement, is located in a large park with old trees. The window frames are painted with the colors of the Spanish flag, in honor of the home country of the noble Spanish family that had the villa built. The guest quarters, which include a kitchen and a living room, and have an independent entrance, are located on the second floor. Breakfast is served in the garden or the living room.

ACCOMMODATION
Guestrooms: *3 (1 single and 2 doubles, with shared bath)*
Services & Amenities: *rooms cleaned every three days; complimentary tourist information; garden; smokers welcome*
Rates: *single €, double €€*
Credit cards: *not accepted*
Pets: [no pets symbol]

GRADO (GORIZIA)

• **Bed & Breakfast Italia**
Code FVG1
tel. 06 6878618
fax 06 6878619
info@bbitalia.it
www.bbitalia.it
Closed: varies

The B&B is located in a renovated farmhouse in an agricultural setting. The accommodation consists in three double rooms – one with balcony – which are large and comfortable, with country style furnishings, attic roof and exposed beams. Horse riding is available on request. It is 15 km from the center of Grado. Its Venetian Republic origins are evident in the several Venetian-style buildings.

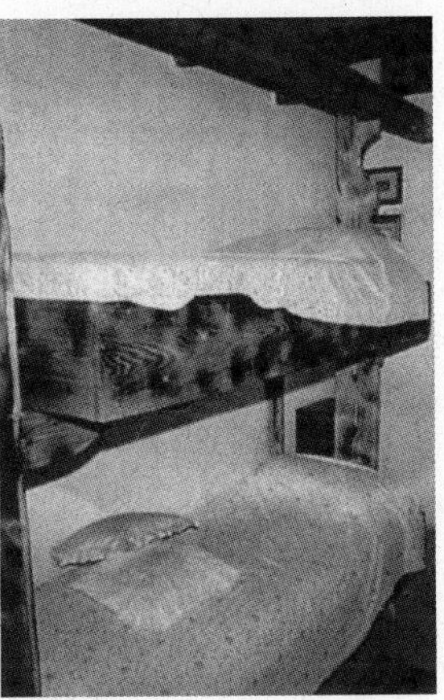

ACCOMMODATION
Guestrooms: *3 doubles*
Services & Amenities: *English spoken; rooms cleaned every three days; tourist information; horse-riding excursions; private parking*
Minimum stay: *2 nights*
Rates: *double €€*
Credit cards: VISA MC *Bancomat*
Pets: [pets symbol]

LATISANA (UDINE)

Casa Adriana
Adriana Lazzarini
via Lignano Sud 72,
località Aprilia Marittima
33053 Latisana (UD)
tel. 0431 53310, mob. 335 5471265
• B&B in Italy. Ospitalità nelle case
tel. and fax 0432 731854
bedbreakfastitaly@hotmail.com
www.bedandbreakfastfvg.com
Open: March to November

This B&B is located in a three-story, Venetian-style house, located in Aprilia Marittima, just three kilometers from the celebrated Lignano Sabbiadoro beach. Guest accommodation consists in two rooms, furnished in marine style, one of which has a big terrace. The continental breakfast, which can be enriched with cold cuts and cheese on request, is served in the villa's spacious kitchen.

ACCOMMODATION
Guestrooms: *2 doubls, also single occupancy, with shared bath*
Services & Amenities: *English and German are spoken; rooms cleaned every 3 days; complimentary tourist information; terrace; garden; smokers welcome; private parking*
Rates: *single €, double €€. Discounts for children*
Credit cards: *not accepted*
Pets: [pets symbol]

Malborghetto-Valbruna (Udine)

Casa Sinc
Monica Wedam
via Emilio Comici 10, località Valbruna
33010 Malborghetto-Valbruna (UD)
tel. 0428 60086
• B&B in Italy. Ospitalità nelle case
tel. and fax 0432 731854
bedbreakfastitaly@hotmail.com
www.bedandbreakfastfvg.com
Open: January, February,
20 March to 30 April,
June to September and December

Accommodation
Guestrooms: *3 doubles, also single occupancy, with shared bath; additional bed on request* ♿
Services & Amenities: *French and Slovene are spoken; rooms cleaned every 3 days; tourist info; garden; smokers welcome; private parking*
Rates: *single €, double €€. Discounts for children*
Credit cards: *not accepted*
Pets: 🐕

This B&B, located in the Alpi Giulie, is ideal for enjoying the natural beauties by taking hikes or going skiing. Besides the guestrooms, which have plain, traditional pine-wood furniture, guests also have a small dining room where a breakfast of pastries, brioches, yoghurt and homemade organic marmalades is served.

Monfalcone (Gorizia)

Casa del Sogno
Donatella Perazzin
via Desenibus 8
34074 Monfalcone (GO)
tel. and fax 0481 40964
www.casadelsogno@tiscali.it
• B&B in Italy. Ospitalità nelle case
tel. and fax 0432 731854
bedbreakfastitaly@hotmail.com
www.bedandbreakfastfvg.com
Open all year

This two-level attic apartment is located on the 8th floor of a condominium in the center of town. The terrace-garden, with a small kitchen, tables, umbrellas and a lawn-chair, dominates the surrounding landscape.

Accommodation
Guestrooms: *3 (1 single and 2 doubles, with shared bath)*
Services & Amenities: *French, English and German are spoken; rooms cleaned every 3 days; tourist information; baby-sitting service; terrace; smokers welcome*
Rates: *single €, double €€. Children under 3 free, 4 to 10 -50%. Discounts for extended stays*
Credit cards: *not accepted*
Pets: 🐕

There are children's games and a small swimming pool in one of the corners of the terrace. The B&B area has an independent entrance and a living room reserved for the guests.

Il Melograno
Mara Favretto
via San Gabriele 2
34074 Monfalcone (GO)
tel. 0481 482531, mob. 338 7035955
• B&B in Italy. Ospitalità nelle case
tel. and fax 0432 731854
bedbreakfastitaly@hotmail.com
www.bedandbreakfastfvg.com
Closed: December

Accommodation
Guestrooms: *1 single, 2 doubles, private bath; additional bed on request*
Services & Amenities: *French and English are spoken; rooms cleaned every day; complimentary tourist information; baby-sitting service; terrace; garden; smokers welcome*
Rates: *€ per person. Children under 3 free*
Credit cards: *not accepted*
Pets: 🚫🐕

In the characteristic section of Monfalcone, one can stay at the Melograno, a recently reconstructed house that has three guestrooms. Though simply furnished, the details of

these rooms have been very well cared for. The large breakfast, which is served in the common dining room, is enriched with homemade pastries. The hostess also arranges for a baby-sitter service for guests with children. The Monfalcone beach is close to the Melograno.

Muzzana del Turgnano (Udine)

Al Molino Vecchio
Claudine Tollon
via Mulino 40
33055 Muzzana del Turgnano (UD)
tel. 0431 697725
• **B&B in Italy. Ospitalità nelle case**
tel. and fax 0432 731854
bedbreakfastitaly@hotmail.com
www.bedandbreakfastfvg.com
Closed: 22 February to 30 November

This B&B – in the mansard of a modern house – has an independent entrance and a living room with kitchenette. Breakfast, which is prepared with natural products, is either served in the mansard living room or in the garden. Children can observe the geese, ducks, chickens, turkeys and peacocks in the area around the house. Arrangements can be made for taking boat rides in the Laguna di Marano's WWF oasis.

Accommodation
Guestrooms: *1 mansard (5 beds) with private bath*
Services & Amenities: *French, English and German are spoken; rooms cleaned every day; tourist information; kitchenette; garden; smokers welcome; bike rental; parking*
Rates: *€ per person. Children under 2 free*
Credit cards: *not accepted*
Pets: ✗

Nimis (Udine)

Casa Nongruella
Ornella Barbei
via Nongruella 7
33045 Nimis (UD)
tel. 0432 852741, fax 0432 400950
mob. 333 2668108, 335 299030
info@nongruella.com
www.nongruella.com
• **B&B in Italy. Ospitalità nelle case**
tel. and fax 0432 731854
bedbreakfastitaly@hotmail.com
www.bedandbreakfastfvg.com
Open: spring-summer

Accommodation
Guestrooms: *3 doubles, also single occupancy, with private bath*
Services & Amenities: *French and English are spoken; rooms cleaned every 3 days; tourist information; kitchen use by request; garden; smokers welcome; private parking*
Rates: *single €, double €€*
Credit cards: *not accepted*
Pets: ✗

This B&B is located in an ancient, wood and stone, Friulian house with loggias. The natural materials used in the construction and the traditional country-style furnishings create a rustic atmosphere. There are three guestrooms with a portico and an independent entrance. One of the rooms also has a small kitchen. Breakfast is either served in the room with fireplace, or under the portico.

Pagnacco (Udine)

Casa Le Magnolie
Anna Monai
via Sant'Antonio 5, località Zampis
33010 Pagnacco (UD)
tel. 0432 660708, mob. 348 3415115
anna.monai@adriacom.it
• **B&B in Italy. Ospitalità nelle case**
tel. and fax 0432 731854
bedbreakfastitaly@hotmail.com
www.bedandbreakfastfvg.com
Open: April to October, Easter and Christmas holidays

This ancient, restructured farmhouse is a 10-min drive from the center of Udine. The guests have a small sitting room on the upper floor, as well as a living room and dining room on the ground floor. All the rooms have antique fur-

Accommodation
Guestrooms: *3 (1 single and 2 doubles, with shared bath)*
Services & Amenities: *French and English are spoken; rooms cleaned every 3 days; complimentary tourist information; bike rental; garden; smokers welcome; private parking*
Rates: *single €, double €€-€€*
Credit cards: *not accepted*
Pets: ✗

niture. Breakfast is served in the dining room or in the surrounding garden. Guests can also enjoy the nearby tennis court and riding stables.

Pinzano al Tagliamento (Pordenone)

Ombretta Mingolo
via Circonvallazione 19
33094 Pinzano al Tagliamento (PN)
tel. 0432 950647
• **B&B in Italy. Ospitalità nelle case**
tel. and fax 0432 731854
bedbreakfastitaly@hotmail.com
www.bedandbreakfastfvg.com
Open: May to October

Accommodation
Guestrooms: *1 mini-apartment (4 beds); additional bed on request*
Services & Amenities: *English and German are spoken; rooms cleaned every 3 days; tourist info; kitchen; garden; smokers welcome*
Rates: *€ per person*
Credit cards: *not accepted*
Pets:

This small villa is located in the center of town and is just a short walk to the stores, bank and church. The guests have a small apartment on the ground floor, with an independent entrance, consisting of a bedroom, a living room with a sofa-bed, a bathroom and a kitchen. Guests can either prepare and have their breakfast in the kitchen or have it served in the family dining room. The many activity opportunities include canoeing, rock-climbing in the rock-climbing gym in Anduins or playing golf on the Fagagna golf course.

Porpetto (Udine)

Casa i Papaveri
tollon_claudine@libero.it
• **B&B in Italy. Ospitalità nelle case**
tel. and fax 0432 731854
bedbreakfastitaly@hotmail.com
www.bedandbreakfastfvg.com
Open all year

This recently-built house, which is near San Giorgio di Nogaro, has a small apartment with an independent entrance. The apartment also has a kitchen and a small tavern. Guests have the use of the entire ground floor, which is partially below ground level, while the family uses the upper floor. The Italian breakfast is consumed autonomously in the small tavern. There's a large garden with a pond, and there are many opportunities in the area for tasting good wine and enjoying the Friulian cuisine.

Accommodation
Guestrooms: *1 mini-apartment with 5 beds*
Services & Amenities: *English and German are spoken; rooms cleaned every 3 days; complimentary tourist information; kitchen use by request; garden; smokers welcome*
Rates: *€ per person. Children under 4 free. Discounts for extended stays*
Credit cards: *not accepted*
Pets:

Povoletto (Udine)

Domus Magna dei Partistagno TCI 10%
Chiara Pelizzo
via del Tiglio 13, località Belvedere
33040 Povoletto (UD)
tel. and fax 0432 679054
domusmagna1467@libero.it
www.domusmagna1467.ws
• **B&B in Italy. Ospitalità nelle case**
tel. and fax 0432 731854
bedbreakfastitaly@hotmail.com
www.bedandbreakfastfvg.com
Open: March to November

Accommodation
Guestrooms: *3 doubles, also single occupancy, with private bath; additional bed on request*
Services & Amenities: *English spoken; rooms cleaned every day; complimentary tourist information; kitchen use by request; Internet access; garden; smokers welcome; private parking*
Rates: *single €€, double €€€. Children under 2 free, 3 to 12 -50%*
Credit cards: *not accepted*
Pets:

This historical, very carefully restructured, 16th-century villa, which is a declared monument, is located just outside Povoletto. It's surrounded by a garden closed in by a wall, as well as by 10 acres of land on which there's a swimming pool. The continental breakfast is either served in the dining room or in the garden.

Prepotto (Udine)

Caterina da Centa
Chiara Mariotti
via Centa 76
33040 Prepotto (UD)
tel. 0432 753005
• **B&B in Italy. Ospitalità nelle case**
tel. and fax 0432 731854
bedbreakfastitaly@hotmail.com
www.bedandbreakfastfvg.com
Open: summer

This very interesting, two-story, stone house, with its rustic, traditional wooden furniture, is located in the medieval village of Prepotto and is surrounded by vineyards, olive trees and a grove of trees. The guest quarters include the bedrooms, a breakfast room and a kitchen. On request, the kitchen can also be used by the guests.

Accommodation
Guestrooms: *3 (1 double and 2 double bedrooms, also single occupancy, with shared bath)*
Services & Amenities: *French, English and German are spoken; rooms cleaned every 3 days; complimentary tourist information; garden; smokers welcome; private parking*
Rates: *single €, double €€*
Credit cards: *not accepted*
Pets:

Pulfero (Udine)

Casa Papes
Elena Fantig
via Loch 39
33046 Pulfero (UD)
tel. 0432 730322
mob. 328 7165923
Open: 1 April to 30 September

This comfortable house in Pulfero – right close to the Slovenian border – has a garden and is just a short walk from the Natisone river. It's an ideal place for going fishing or taking mountain hikes or mountain-bike excursions along one of the numerous mountain trails, accompanied by a nature guide or a mountain-bike instructor. The rich breakfast, which consists of pastries or cold cuts and cheese, as requested, is served in the family dining room.

Accommodation
Guestrooms: *3 (1 single, 1 double and 1 triple room, shared bath)*
Services & Amenities: *English and Slovene are spoken; rooms cleaned every 3 days; tourist info; garden; smokers welcome; private parking*
Rates: *single €, double €€, triple €€€*
Credit cards: *not accepted*
Pets:

Famiglia Clavora-Grava
via Cras 134
33046 Pulfero (UD)
tel. and fax 0432 709046
• **B&B in Italy. Ospitalità nelle case**
tel. and fax 0432 731854
bedbreakfastitaly@hotmail.com
www.bedandbreakfastfvg.com
Closed: February, March and November

This ancient, completely restructured house is located in Pulfero, which is 10 kilometers from Cividale del Friuli, and is the last town on the Natisone river before getting to the Slovenian border. The guest accommodation consists in a room with an independent entrance and a terrace. The traditional type of breakfast can either be consumed in the guest area or in the kitchen, together with the family.

Accommodation
Guestrooms: *1 double bedroom, also single occupancy, with private bath; additional bed on request*
Services & Amenities: *French, English, German and Slovene are spoken; rooms cleaned every day; tourist info; smokers welcome; parking*
Rates: *€ per person. Children under 2 free*
Credit cards: *not accepted*
Pets:

San Daniele del Friuli (Udine)

Casa Fernanda
Fernanda Gosparini
via Osoppo 62
33038 San Daniele del Friuli (UD)
tel. 0432 941662, mob. 347 1678620
• B&B in Italy. Ospitalità nelle case
tel. and fax 0432 731854
bedbreakfastitaly@hotmail.com
www.bedandbreakfastfvg.com
Open: 1 May to 31 July and
15 August to 31 October

This small, recently-built, one-story villa, which has a nice garden, is located 1 kilometer from the center of San Daniele. The continental breakfast is either served in the dining room or on the veranda. Guests can also have a breakfast enriched by local specialties like cold cuts and cheese.

Accommodation
Guestrooms: *2 (1 single, shared bath; 1 double bedroom, private bath); additional bed on request*
Services & Amenities: *French and English are spoken; rooms cleaned every 3 days; tourist info; kitchen and laundry use by request; garden; smokers welcome; private parking*
Rates: *single €, double €€. Additional bed supplement €. Discounts for extended stays*
Credit cards: *not accepted*
Pets: 🐕

Casa Le Ortensie
Luisa Zucchet
via Sant Andrat 16
33038 San Daniele del Friuli (UD)
tel. 0432 955610
www.infosandaniele.com/ortensie
• B&B in Italy. Ospitalità nelle case
tel. and fax 0432 731854
bedbreakfastitaly@hotmail.com
www.bedandbreakfastfvg.com
Open: April to June and
15 July to 31 October

This villa with garden, kitchen garden and small grove of trees, is located 1 km from San Daniele. The surrounding area provides the possibility of taking nature hikes, as well as mountain-bike excursions or outings on horseback. Guests have the use of a terrace with a table and chairs. The Italian breakfast is served in their rooms or on the terrace.

Accommodation
Guestrooms: *2 doubles, also single occupancy, with shared bath*
Services & Amenities: *French, English and German are spoken; rooms cleaned every 3 days; tourist information; terrace; garden; smokers welcome; private parking*
Rates: *single €, double €€. Discounts for children and extended stays*
Credit cards: *not accepted*
Pets: (not allowed)

San Floriano del Collio (Gorizia)

Casa Mattiroli
Serena Tomadin
località Scedina 1
34070 San Floriano del Collio (GO)
tel. 0481 884260, 0481 884266
serenatomadin@tiscali.it
www.golfsanfloriano.it
• B&B in Italy. Ospitalità nelle case
tel. and fax 0432 731854
bedbreakfastitaly@hotmail.com
www.bedandbreakfastfvg.com
Open: April to early November

This rustic, face-brick farmhouse, that has terracotta and wooden floors, and period furniture, is right next to the Golf Club, which makes it very convenient for golf enthusiasts. The breakfast is the buffet type. The family, that loves to cook, also provides courses in the preparation of local specialties.

Accommodation
Guestrooms: *1 double, also single occupancy, with private bath; additional bed on request*
Services & Amenities: *English spoken; rooms cleaned every day; tourist info; educational courses by request; garden; smokers welcome; parking*
Rates: *€ to €€ per person. Discounts for children and extended stays*
Credit cards: *not accepted*
Pets: 🐕

San Leonardo (Udine)

Casa Anna
località Prehot
33040 San Leonardo (UD)
• **B&B in Italy. Ospitalità nelle case**
tel. and fax 0432 731854
bedbreakfastitaly@hotmail.com
www.bedandbreakfastfvg.com
Open: May to early October

This B&B is in a old, very characteristic house, surrounded by vegetation, and was restructured under the patronage of the Superintendence. The room furnishings also reflect the spirit and rigor of the restructuring. The house is situated at an elevation of about 400 meters and is about 12 kilometers from Cividale del Friuli. It has staggered roofs, wood and stone balconies, arches, stone hinges and a 17-meter portico. Breakfast can be served under this portico.

Accommodation
Guestrooms: *3 doubles, also single occupancy, with shared bath; additional bed on request*
Services & Amenities: *Slovene spoken; rooms cleaned every 3 days; tourist info; garden; smokers welcome*
Rates: *€ per person*
Credit cards: *not accepted*
Pets:

Casa Gardenia
Ersilia Iurman
località Merso di Sotto 21
33040 San Leonardo (UD)
tel. 0432 723395
mob. 328 4726089
• **B&B in Italy. Ospitalità nelle case**
tel. and fax 0432 731854
bedbreakfastitaly@hotmail.com
www.bedandbreakfastfvg.com
Open: March to mid-October

Accommodation
Guestrooms: *1 triple, with private bath; additional bed on request*
Services & Amenities: *French and English are spoken; rooms cleaned every 3 days; tourist info; garden; smokers welcome; private parking*
Rates: *€ per person*
Credit cards: *not accepted*
Pets:

The mansard of this recently-built villa situated in a splendid valley surrounded by mountains has been made into a B&B with a kitchen area, leisure corner and a balcony. The continental breakfast also includes such Friulian pastries as gubana, strucchi and flat bread-cake. The guests are provided with complete information regarding the best places for tasting and buying local foods and wines.

San Pietro al Natisone (Udine)

Casa Bula
Luisa Zanini
località Ponteacco 110
33049 San Pietro al Natisone (UD)
tel. 0432 727132
• **B&B in Italy. Ospitalità nelle case**
tel. and fax 0432 731854
bedbreakfastitaly@hotmail.com
www.bedandbreakfastfvg.com
Open: February to October

Accommodation
Guestrooms: *1 double bedroom, also single occupancy, with private bath*
Services & Amenities: *Slovene spoken; rooms cleaned every 3 days; complimentary tourist information; kitchen use by request; garden; smokers welcome; private parking*
Rates: *single €, double €€. Discounts for extended stays*
Credit cards: *not accepted*
Pets:

This is a small, one-story villa surrounded by a garden with trees, a kitchen garden and an orchard. The owners raise various types of fowl and small animals. The part of the house reserved for the guests has an independent entrance and a living room-kitchen, which is where the breakfast, with homemade bread, pastry and organic marmalades, is served. On request, the hostess will be happy to act as a guide for making excursions in the area.

Casa Rosalba
Ezio Cedarmas and Rosalba Bertolutti
località Mezzana 8
33049 San Pietro al Natisone (UD)
tel. 0432 727258, mob. 347 9156964
rbertolutti@adriacom.it
• B&B in Italy. Ospitalità nelle case
tel. and fax 0432 731854
bedbreakfastitaly@hotmail.com
www.bedandbreakfastfvg.com
Closed: 15 January to late February and 1 November to 15 December

Accommodation
Guestrooms: *3 (1 single, 1 double and 1 triple room) with shared bath*
Services & Amenities: *English spoken; rooms cleaned every 3 days; tourist information; terrace; garden; smokers welcome; private parking*
Rates: *€ per person. Discounts for children*
Credit cards: *not accepted*
Pets: no

This B&B is located inside a restructured, rustic house that has stone external walls and wooden floors. It's architectural style is late-19th century and the house is surrounded by a large garden. Besides the bedrooms, the guests also have a solarium terrace that provides a panoramic view that extends all the way to the sea. The substantial traditional breakfast also includes local products.

Casa Venica
Daniela Venica
località Vernasso 8
33049 San Pietro al Natisone (UD)
tel. 0432 727390
mob. 340 4863812
• B&B in Italy. Ospitalità nelle case
tel. and fax 0432 731854
bedbreakfastitaly@hotmail.com
www.bedandbreakfastfvg.com
Open: June to September

Accommodation
Guestrooms: *2 (1 single and 1 double, with shared bath)*
Services & Amenities: *French, English and Slovene are spoken; rooms cleaned every 3 days; tourist information; bike rental; terrace; garden; smokers welcome; parking*
Rates: *single €, double €€. Discounts for children*
Credit cards: *not accepted*
Pets: yes

This traditional, restructured, two-story house is in Vernasso, a small community with only 200 inhabitants. The guestrooms have late 19th-C country furniture and an independent entrance, with a characteristic wooden portico. Guests can enjoy fishing and swimming in the nearby Natisone River, as well as the wine and gastronomic specialties of Cividale, which is 6 km away, and Slovenia, whose border is 11 km away.

Corte dei Svuanovi
Amabile Cosmacini
località Sorzento 21
33049 San Pietro al Natisone (UD)
tel. 0432 727384, 0432 727556
mob. 335 7050955
• B&B in Italy. Ospitalità nelle case
tel. and fax 0432 731854
bedbreakfastitaly@hotmail.com
www.bedandbreakfastfvg.com
Open: March to November

Accommodation
Guestrooms: *mini-apartment with 3 beds* (wheelchair accessible)
Services & Amenities: *English and Slovene are spoken; rooms cleaned every 3 days; tourist information; kitchenette; bike rental; Internet access; garden; smokers welcome; private parking*
Minimum stay: *2 nights*
Rates: *€ per person. Discounts for extended stays*
Credit cards: *not accepted*
Pets: yes

This ancient restructured house, situated inside a characteristic courtyard, has stone walls and wooden ceilings. The small B&B apartment on the ground floor, has an independent entrance, and a living room-kitchen, which is where breakfast is served. Guests can also use the kitchen, as well as the bicycles that are available for them.

Santa Maria la Longa (Udine)

Casa Boga
Adriano Boga
via San Pietro 5
località Mereto di Capitolo
33050 Santa Maria la Longa (UD)
tel. 0432 995106, mob. 347 4459731
adrianoboga@libero.it
• **B&B in Italy. Ospitalità nelle case**
tel. and fax 0432 731854
bedbreakfastitaly@hotmail.com
www.bedandbreakfastfvg.com
Open: February to October and December

This large, recently-built villa, located in a tranquil area surrounded by vegetation, is only 2 km from Palmanova and Aquileia and has a large garden with a grove of pine trees. The B&B occupies the floor reserved for the guests. It has an independent entrance and a living room-kitchen. The breakfast is the buffet type.

Accommodation
Guestrooms: *3 (1 single, 1 double and 1 triple, with shared bath)*
Services & Amenities: *English spoken; rooms cleaned every 3 days; complimentary tourist information; kitchen use by request; garden; smokers welcome; private parking*
Rates: *single €, double €€, triple €€€. Discounts for children*
Credit cards: *not accepted*
Pets: ✗

Savogna (Udine)

Casa Luisa
Luisa Battistig
località Masseris
33040 Savogna (UD)
tel. 0432 709942
• **B&B in Italy. Ospitalità nelle case**
tel. and fax 0432 731854
bedbreakfastitaly@hotmail.com
www.bedandbreakfastfvg.com
Open: May to October and weekends

Accommodation
Guestrooms: *1 double bedroom, also single occupancy, private bath*
Services & Amenities: *rooms cleaned every 3 days; tourist info; garden; smokers welcome; parking*
Minimum stay: *2 nights*
Rates: *€ per person*
Credit cards: *not accepted*
Pets: ✗

Located in a small villa in Massens at an altitude of about 750 meters, this B&B is ideal for sports enthusiasts. There's a wood behind the villa, and the starting points for several bicycle trails are nearby, including the CAI trail. Hang gliding is also practiced in the area. Breakfast includes typical, regional pastries as well as locally-made honey and organic marmalades. The host family is fond of mountain climbing.

Casa Vacanze
Giovanni Medves
via Barza 29/b
33040 Savogna (UD)
tel. 0432 759655, mob. 368 7627491
Open all year

This modern house, made of stone and wood, is located in a tranquil position, with a beautiful view of Mount Mataiur. The small guest apartment has a bedroom, a small sitting room with an attic, and a completely equipped kitchen. The apartment has wood and electrical heating and the hosts provide the wherewithal for preparing breakfast. The guests can take some very enjoyable walks in the very large area surrounding the house that has various plants and groves of trees.

Accommodation
Guestrooms: *mini-apartment with 4 beds*
Services & Amenities: *English, German, Spanish and Arabic are spoken; rooms cleaned every 3 days; tourist information; kitchen use by request; garden; smokers welcome; private parking*
Minimum stay: *1 week*
Rates: *€ per person. Discounts for extended stays*
Credit cards: *accepted*
Pets: ✗

Stregna (Udine)

Casa Angelina
Giorgio Chiabai
località Zamir 3
33040 Stregna (UD)
tel. 0432 723389
• **B&B in Italy. Ospitalità nelle case**
tel. and fax 0432 731854
bedbreakfastitaly@hotmail.com
www.bedandbreakfastfvg.com
Open: April to December

Accommodation
Guestrooms: *3 doubles, also single occupancy, with private bath*
Services & Amenities: *French and Slovene are spoken; rooms cleaned every 3 days; tourist information; kitchen use by request; garden; smokers welcome; private parking*
Rates: *single €, double €€. Children under 10 free. Discounts for extended stays*
Credit cards: *not accepted*
Pets:

This large, restructured house has a garden, a large lawn and tall trees. The part of the house reserved for the guests has an independent entrance and old, restored family furniture. Breakfast, which is usually continental but, on request, can be English, is either served in the special dining room or, when the weather's nice, in the garden.

Casa Cristina
Cristina Dugaro
località Oblizza 6
33040 Stregna (UD)
tel. 0432 711065
mob. 347 6496867
• **B&B in Italy. Ospitalità nelle case**
tel. and fax 0432 731854
bedbreakfastitaly@hotmail.com
www.bedandbreakfastfvg.com
Open: April, September and October

Oblizza is a small, tranquil, panoramic, rural community that has only 50 houses. It's located above Stregna at an altitude of 600 meters. The B&B has a nice, friendly, relaxed atmosphere. The rich continental breakfast is served by the hostess in the family kitchen and includes genuine, traditional, homemade Friulian pasties, such as gubana and strucchi, as well as flat bread-cake and apple tarts.

Accommodation
Guestrooms: *2 (1 double bedroom and 1 double, also single occupancy, with shared bath)*
Services & Amenities: *English, German and Spanish are spoken; rooms cleaned every 3 days; tourist info; garden; smokers welcome*
Rates: *single €, double €€. Discounts for children*
Credit cards: *not accepted*
Pets:

Taipana (Udine)

Casa Nadia
Nadia Sedola
località Platischis 74/A
33040 Taipana (UD)
tel. 0432 788017
• **B&B in Italy. Ospitalità nelle case**
tel. and fax 0432 731854
bedbreakfastitaly@hotmail.com
www.bedandbreakfastfvg.com
Closed: 15 January to 15 March

Accommodation
Guestrooms: *3 doubles, also single occupancy, with private bath*
Services & Amenities: *French and English are spoken; rooms cleaned every 3 days; tourist information; lunch & dinner reservations; garden; smokers welcome; private parking*
Rates: *single €, double €€. Discounts for children*
Credit cards: *not accepted*
Pets:

This small villa, which consists of a ground floor and a mansard, has a furnished garden and is immersed in an orchard. The mansard has bedrooms and a living-room/library. The owners run the adjacent bar where the guests can have a large breakfast with pastries or, if desired, cold cuts and various types of cheese. There's a riding stable nearby, and guests can make excursions in the area.

Casa Svetlana
Svetlana Malkina
località Montemaggiore 22
33040 Taipana (UD)
tel. 0432 788013, mob. 340 6877879
• **B&B in Italy. Ospitalità nelle case**
tel. and fax 0432 731854
bedbreakfastitaly@hotmail.com
www.bedandbreakfastfvg.com
Open all year

Montemaggiore is a mountain village situated at the foot of the Mataiur. In the wintertime there are only about 20 people living there, but in the summertime it attracts a lot of vacationers who like to take nice excursions and hikes. The B&B is on the upper floor and has an independent entrance. There is a trattoria on the ground floor, run by the hosts, where the guests are served breakfast.

Accommodation
Guestrooms: *3 doubles, also single occupancy, with private bath*
Services & Amenities: *French, German, Spanish and Russian are spoken; rooms cleaned every 3 days; complimentary tourist information; lunch & dinner reservations; terrace; smokers welcome*
Rates: *single €, double €€. Children under 2 free. Discounts for extended stays*
Credit cards: *accepted*
Pets:

Tarcento (Udine)

Les Bouganvilles
Donata Papinutti
via delle Viole 1
33017 Tarcento (UD)
tel. 0432 791908, mob. 333 8673451
lesbouganvilles@libero.it
• **B&B in Italy. Ospitalità nelle case**
tel. and fax 0432 731854
bedbreakfastitaly@hotmail.com
www.bedandbreakfastfvg.com
Open: May to September and Easter holidays

Accommodation
Guestrooms: *1 double, with private bath; additional bed on request*
Services & Amenities: *French, English and German are spoken; rooms cleaned every 3 days; tourist information; bike rental; garden; smokers welcome; private parking*
Rates: *single €, double €€. Children under 3 free. Discounts for extended stays*
Credit cards: *not accepted*
Pets:

The B&B is located in a fresh, tranquil, rustic, recently-restructured stone house. The accommodation consists in a guestroom on the ground floor with an independent entrance. The furniture dates from the '50s. The breakfast – either continental or English on request – is either served in the kitchen or, when the weather's nice, under the portico.

Tolmezzo (Udine)

B&B Daniela
Albina Muner
via Francesco Bonacca 47
località Terzo
33028 Tolmezzo (UD)
tel. 0433 47801
or 0433 43484
• **B&B in Italy. Ospitalità nelle case**
tel. and fax 0432 731854
bedbreakfastitaly@hotmail.com
www.bedandbreakfastfvg.com
Open: mid-June to mid-September and mid-December to mid-January

This two-story, one-family villa has a garden and guest quarters on the upper floor. The guests have a living room with a TV and a refrigerator, and an independent entrance. The atmosphere is very nice and friendly. The hostess is happy to use her car for taking the guests into the mountains, to the shepherds' huts, or to the nearby art cities.

Accommodation
Guestrooms: *2 doubles, also single occupancy, with shared bath*
Services & Amenities: *German spoken; rooms cleaned every three days; complimentary tourist information; bike rental; garden; smokers welcome; private parking*
Rates: *single €, double €€. Children under 2 free*
Credit cards: *not accepted*
Pets:

Torreano (Udine)

Bernadette Albergatti
via del Mulino 3/1
33040 Torreano (UD)
tel. and fax 0432 712302
rocciar@mail.nauta.it
• B&B in Italy. Ospitalità nelle case
tel. and fax 0432 731854
bedbreakfastitaly@hotmail.com
www.bedandbreakfastfvg.com
Open: May to September

Accommodation
Guestrooms: *2 double bedrooms, with shared bath*
Services & Amenities: *French and German are spoken; rooms cleaned every 3 days; tourist information; terrace; Internet access; garden; smokers welcome; private parking*
Rates: *€ per person*
Credit cards: *not accepted*
Pets: no

This recently-restructured, early-19th-century rural house, located in Torreano – which is just a few minutes from Cividale – is one of a group of houses that form a rustic courtyard right inside the town. The guests have two rooms, each with double beds, that have plain, but very well kept furnishings. The continental breakfast can either be served in the kitchen or, when the weather's nice, out on the large terrace.

Sara Pinto
località Canalutto 68
33040 Torreano (UD)
tel. 0432 712392
• B&B in Italy. Ospitalità nelle case
tel. and fax 0432 731854
bedbreakfastitaly@hotmail.com
www.bedandbreakfastfvg.com
Open: March to November

This isolated, mid 19th-century house, which still has its original stone walls, bare-beam ceilings and majolica stove, is located directly on a stream, which forms a small cascade that used to drive the mill's paddle wheel. The guest accommodation consists in a double room, located in the mansard, with period furniture. The rich breakfast has a lot of variety, and the hosts try to provide whatever the guests prefer. There's an animal shelter nearby.

Accommodation
Guestrooms: *1 double, also single occupancy, with shared bath*
Services & Amenities: *English spoken; rooms cleaned every day; complimentary tourist information; garden; terrace; private parking*
Rates: *€ per person*
Credit cards: *not accepted*
Pets: allowed

Trieste

Casa Franca
Giordano Furlan
via Cesare Battisti 24
34100 Trieste
tel. 040 214662
mob. 338 1446702
info@triestebedandbreakfast.it
www.triestebedandbreakfast.it
• B&B in Italy. Ospitalità nelle case
tel. and fax 0432 731854
bedbreakfastitaly@hotmail.com
www.bedandbreakfastfvg.com
Closed: 16 December to 19 January

Accommodation
Guestrooms: *3 doubles, also single occupancy, with shared bath; additional bed on request*
Services & Amenities: *French, English, German, Spanish and Serbo-Croatian are spoken; rooms cleaned every 3 days; complimentary tourist information; kitchen use by request; smokers welcome*
Rates: *single €, double €€. Additional bed supplement €*
Credit cards: *not accepted*
Pets: no

This B&B is on the fourth floor (no elevator) of an elegant, Hapsburg building, located in the center of Trieste. The large, bright guestrooms have a telephone. The continental or English breakfast is served in the reserved dining room. For extended stays, guest can also have use of the kitchen.

Le Casite
Alessandro Cannavò
località Trebiciano 100
34014 Trieste
mob. 333 2191852
hrovatib@tiscali.it
Closed: early March, early June and December

This B&B, which is located in a 19th-C house that has a large furnished courtyard, is named after the characteristic stone shepherd huts found on the Carso. The house is situated in a small 15th-C village, which is on

the Carso chain that circles Trieste and is only 10 min from its center. Besides local organic products, the Italian breakfast also includes cold cuts and various types of cheese and is served in the kitchen, which still remains at the disposal of the guests.

Accommodation
Guestrooms: *3 (1 single and 2 doubles, with private bath)* ♿
Services & Amenities: *English, German and Slovene are spoken; rooms cleaned every 3 days; complimentary tourist information; kitchen use by request; garden; terrace; private parking*
Rates: *single €, double €. Children under 6 -50%. Discounts for extended stays*
Credit cards: *not accepted*
Pets:

Udine

B&B "Friûl"
Virginia Collovati Venuti
via San Rocco 368
33100 Udine
tel. and fax 0432 232355
mob. 338 9992725
rickonline@tin.it
members.xomm.it/bb_friul
Closed: January, June and August

This B&B, located on the outskirts of town, is in a small, modern villa, surrounded by vegetation. Breakfast, which includes pastries and natural marmalades, is either served in the

dining room or, when the weather's nice, under the portico. The hosts provide the guests with bicycles, and also willingly accompany them on guided visits in the surrounding area.

Accommodation
Guestrooms: *1 double, also single occupancy, with private bath; additional bed on request*
Services & Amenities: *French and English are spoken; rooms cleaned every three days; complimentary tourist information; Internet access; garden; private parking*
Rates: *single €, double €€. Additional bed supplement €. Children under 2 free; 3 to 10 -50%. Discounts for extended stays*
Credit cards: *not accepted*
Pets:

B&B Irini
Rosina Zufferli
via Fagagna 6
33100 Udine
tel. 0432 44376
• **B&B in Italy. Ospitalità nelle case**
tel. and fax 0432 731854
bedbreakfastitaly@hotmail.com
www.bedandbreakfastfvg.com
Closed: July and August

The B&B Irini (which means "peace" in Greek) gets its name from the quiet atmosphere of the area in which the house is located. Just 20 min on foot from the center of town, this area is characterized by lots of space between the houses in the area and the many gardens with trees. The hostess prefers non-

smokers. The guestroom is on the upper floor. The university for scientific studies and a civic hospital are located nearby.

Accommodation
Guestrooms: *1 double, also single occupancy, with private bath*
Services & Amenities: *English and Slovene are spoken; rooms cleaned every three days; complimentary tourist information; kitchen use by requests; garden*
Rates: *single €-€€, double €€-€€€*
Credit cards: *not accepted*
Pets:

Casa Adele
Annamaria Chiavatti
via Madonnetta 44
33100 Udine
tel. 0432 602723
annabo.chi@libero.it
• **B&B in Italy. Ospitalità nelle case**
tel. and fax 0432 731854
bedbreakfastitaly@hotmail.com
www.bedandbreakfastfvg.com
Closed: December and January to 15 February

ACCOMMODATION
Guestrooms: *2 (1 single and 1 double bedroom, with private bath)*
Services & Amenities: *French, English and German are spoken; rooms cleaned every 3 days; tourist information; kitchen use by request; Internet access; garden; smokers welcome; private parking*
Minimum stay: *2 nights*
Rates: *single €, double €€*
Credit cards: *not accepted*
Pets: *no*

This ancient house, which is 10 min from the Udine train station, has a bare-stone front and a courtyard with trees. The B&B part has period furniture, a living room, a kitchen and an independent entrance. Breakfast, which is served in the kitchen, consists of typical products or cold cuts and cheese. On request, guests can also have the use of Internet and the kitchen.

Casa Mercedes
dennydany@yahoo.it
• **B&B in Italy. Ospitalità nelle case**
tel. and fax 0432 731854
bedbreakfastitaly@hotmail.com
www.bedandbreakfastfvg.com
Open: January, April to December

ACCOMMODATION
Guestrooms: *1 double, also single occupancy, with private bath*
Services & Amenities: *English spoken; rooms cleaned every 3 days; tourist information; kitchen use by request; bike rental; terrace; garden; smokers welcome; private parking*
Rates: *single €€, double €€*
Credit cards: *not accepted*
Pets: *no*

This B&B, located in the center of Udine near the university, is in an ancient building that has a private, internal courtyard with trees. The guests have the use of part of the apartment that's located on the upper floor, which has an independent entrance, a large living room and a furnished kitchen. On request, the hosts can provide private parking, two bicycles and meals.

Casa Paola
viale Palmanova 73 a
33100 Udine
tel. and fax 0432 602794
mob. 349 2678503
giantonu@tin.it
• **B&B in Italy. Ospitalità nelle case**
tel. and fax 0432 731854
bedbreakfastitaly@hotmail.com
www.bedandbreakfastfvg.com
Closed: January

ACCOMMODATION
Guestrooms: *3 (1 double bedroom and 2 doubles, also single occupancy, with shared bath)*
Services & Amenities: *English spoken; rooms cleaned every 3 days; tourist info; terrace; smokers welcome*
Rates: *single €, double €€*
Credit cards: *not accepted*
Pets: *no*

The two rooms of this B&B apartment, which is located in the center of town near the train station, have terraces provided with tables and chairs for having breakfast outdoors. Every morning, the hostess prepares a continental breakfast that can be served in the kitchen. Parking is provided in the condominium courtyard.

Casa Renata
Renata Beltramini
via Tissano 8
33100 Udine
tel. and fax 0432 600232
Closed: 6 to 30 January

This B&B, with its romantic atmosphere, was once an old stable with a connecting barn. Very careful restructuring has preserved the original, rustic, character of its stone and wood construction. There's a park for enjoying some nice relaxation, and bicycles for riding around the area. The rich Italian breakfast is usually served in a kitchen reserved for the guests.

ACCOMMODATION
Guestrooms: *2 (1 double bedroom and 1 double, also single occupancy, with private bath); additional bed on request*
Services & Amenities: *French and German are spoken; rooms cleaned every 3 days; tourist info; kitchen use by request; bike rental; terrace; garden; smokers welcome; parking*
Minimum stay: *2 nights*
Rates: *single €, double €€. Additional bed supplement €. Discounts for extended stays*
Credit cards: *not accepted*
Pets: 🐕

Casa Vallar
Paolo Vallar
via Amalfi 3
33100 Udine
tel. 0432 530092
info@vallar.it
www.vallar.it
• B&B in Italy. Ospitalità nelle case
tel. and fax 0432 731854
bedbreakfastitaly@hotmail.com
www.bedandbreakfastfvg.com
Open: 15 January to 15 July and 15 September to 15 December

This B&B apartment, with its friendly atmosphere, is on the upper floor of a small building that dates from the '40s. It's only a 20 min walk from the train station. Breakfast, continental or English on request, is served in the kitchen. Guests also have the use of the living room and its satellite TV. On request, they can also use the washing machine.

ACCOMMODATION
Guestrooms: *2 doubles, also single occupancy, with shared bath*
Services & Amenities: *English spoken; rooms cleaned every 3 days; tourist information; lunch & dinner reservations; smokers welcome*
Rates: *single €, double €€. Discounts for extended stays*
Credit cards: *not accepted*
Pets: no

Dimora Montegnacco
Vittorio Trombetta
via Cussignacco 48/3
33100 Udine
tel. 0432 204698
fax 0432 203619
vittorio.trombetta@tin.it
www.dimoramontegnacco.it
Closed: Easter and Christmas holidays and 15 August

This B&B is in a refined, early 20th-C residence – located in the city's old center – that has been completely restructured by its owners. The particular character of this B&B is attributable to its furnishings, which include pieces with a modern design and elements dating from 1910. The owners are happy to familiarize the guests with the beautiful features of the area. Breakfast, which also includes a selection of typical local pastries, is served in the family kitchen.

ACCOMMODATION
Guestrooms: *2 (1 single and 1 double, with private bath); additional bed on request* ♿
Services & Amenities: *English spoken; rooms cleaned every 3 days; tourist info; garden; smokers welcome*
Rates: *single €€, double €€€. Additional bed supplement €.*
Credit cards: *not accepted*
Pets: no

Liguria

Arcola (La Spezia)

Villa Ducci
Giacomo Malagamba
via Nosedro 2
19021 Monti d'Arcola (SP)
tel. and fax 0187 982918
mob. 347 2483645
www.villaducci.net
• **Bed and Breakfast Liguria**
tel. and fax 010 2461918
bbliguria@hotmail.com
Open all year

Accommodation
Guestrooms: *3 double bedrooms, with private bath*
Services & Amenities: *English and French are spoken; rooms cleaned every day; complimentary tourist information; smokers welcome; garden; private parking*
Minimum stay: *2 nights*
Rates: *€€. Children under 6 free*
Credit Cards: *not accepted*
Pets:

This completely restructured 18th-century home is surrounded by over 10 acres of land and a large garden, and is located in the hills bordering with Tuscany. It has four classic guestrooms, one of which is a small suite with a small sitting room, a large living room with a library and a drawing room in which to relax. This drawing room was once the building's private chapel. The rich breakfast, Italian or English, is served either on the terrace in the main living room.

Borgio Verezzi (Savona)

Luci sul Mare B&B
Gian Piero Biagioni
via Verezzi 20
17022 Borgio Verezzi (SV)
tel. and fax 019 610221
mob. 338 8083201
lucisulmare@libero.it
www.lucisulmare.it
Closed: 15 November to Christmas
Open: January to Easter
weekends only

This B&B, with its large garden, fruit trees and pergola, is located in the hills halfway between the sea and the artistic center of Verezzi, which has a well-known summer theater. In addition to the three bright bedrooms, each with its own personal color, guests also have a well-furnished kitchen. The rich Italian breakfast, which includes organic products as well as cakes and natural marmalades, can either be served in the dining room or in the garden.

Accommodation
Guestrooms: *3 (2 double bedrooms and 1 triple, private bath)*
Services & Amenities: *rooms cleaned every 3 days; tourist information; kitchen use by request; smokers welcome; air conditioning; terrace; garden; private parking*
Rates: *€€€*
Credit Cards: *not accepted*
Pets:

Calice Ligure (Savona)

La Bibliothèque
Joda Massa
località Prà
17020 Calice Ligure (SV)
tel. 019 65795, mob. 328 5833362
jodamassa@libero.it
Open: 15 March to 15 October

Accommodation
Guestrooms: *3 (1 double bedroom, 1 double and 1 single, with shared bath); additional bed on request.*
Services & Amenities: *English and French are spoken; rooms cleaned every 3 days; complimentary tourist information; kitchen use by request; smokers welcome; garden; private parking*
Rates: *single €€, double €€€. Additional bed supplement €. Children under 10 -10%. Discounts for groups or families.*
Credit Cards: *not accepted*
Pets:

This B&B, which is just a few kilometers from Finale Ligure's old center, gets its name from its impressive library, which also includes information for tourists. Just 15 min from the sea, this B&B, which is in a modern villa with garden, is in a quiet location that makes it ideal for taking mountain-bike rides. Breakfast, Italian or English, includes natural marmalades and Ligurian flat cake-bread, and is served on the terrace or in the dining room.

Castelnuovo Magra (La Spezia)

Montefrancio
• B&B Liguria e...non solo
tel. 010 3622003, mob. 338 8661461
fax 010 3106827
bbgenova@tiscali.it
www.bbitalia.net
Open: March to October

Accommodation
Guestrooms: *2 doubles, also single occupancy, with private bath; additional bed on request*
Services & Amenities: *English and French are spoken; rooms cleaned every day; tourist info; smokers welcome; garden; private parking*
Rates: *€€ per person. Children under 3 free*
Credit Cards: *not accepted*
Pets:

At an altitude of 160 m, in a panoramic location, this B&B provides two guestrooms, one of which is furnished in the classic style with 18th-C furniture, and the other has more plain furnishings with three or four period items. The rooms are located, respectively, on the ground floor and first floor of a 1980's farmhouse which is surrounded by 5,000 sq. m of farmland. Breakfast consists of local products and is served in the family kitchen. However it can also be served outdoors under the pergola.

Cogorno (Genoa)

B&B Il Tramonto

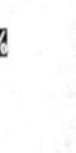

Paolo Di Matteo
via Maggiolo 35
località San Salvatore
16040 Cogorno (GE)
tel. and fax 0185 384600
mob. 338 8366330
oedem@tin.it
Open: March to November

This rustic house, located in a hilly area covered with vineyards and olive trees, is about 1 km from the center of the town. It has two guestrooms, both furnished in classic style with one or two period items. One of the rooms has a large balcony that can be provided with table and chairs. Breakfast is served in the family living room, with TV, fireplace and piano. Guests are welcome to use this living room, as well as the large garden.

Accommodation
Guestrooms: *2 (1 single and 1 double bedroom, with shared bath)*
Services & Amenities: *English, German and Spanish are spoken; rooms cleaned every day; complimentary tourist information; smokers welcome; garden; private parking*
Rates: *single €€, double €€€*
Credit Cards: *not accepted*
Pets:

Dolceacqua (Imperia)

• Bed & Breakfast Italia
Code LI7
tel. 06 6878618, fax 06 6878619
info@bbitalia.it
www.bbitalia.it
Closed: varies

A B&B in the medieval hamlet located on the first floor of a small old building without elevator. The accommodation consists in a well-renovated apartment, that includes a kitchen, a sitting room with sofa bed and TV, a double bedroom and a bathroom with shower. It is elegantly decorated with country style furniture. The lady of the house leaves breakfast in the kitchen. The village is 7 km from the sea.

Accommodation
Guestrooms: *1 mini-apartment, with 2/4 beds*
Services & Amenities: *English and French are spoken; rooms cleaned every 3 days; tourist information*
Minimum stay: *2 nigths*
Rates: €€
Credit Cards: VISA MC *Bancomat*
Pets: not allowed

Genoa

B&B Alefe
• B&B Liguria e...non solo
tel. 010 3291204
fax 010 3299774
oltrelazzurro@libero.it
www.bbitalia.net
Open all year

TCI 10%

This restructured, early 20th-C villa, surrounded by a beautiful garden with furnished areas, is located in the hills that overlook the city. The house is classically furnished, and its large living room, which has a corner for relaxing and a library, is at the guests' disposal. The buffet breakfast is either served in the living room or in the garden and includes sweet items as well as Ligurian flat cake-bread.

Accommodation
Guestrooms: *3 (1 single and 1 double bedroom, private bath – 1 double communicating, shared bath)*
Services & Amenities: *English and French are spoken; rooms cleaned every 3 days; tourist information; bike rental; smokers welcome; terrace; garden; private parking*
Rates: *single €€€, double €€€€. Discounts for children*
Credit Cards: *not accepted*
Pets: allowed

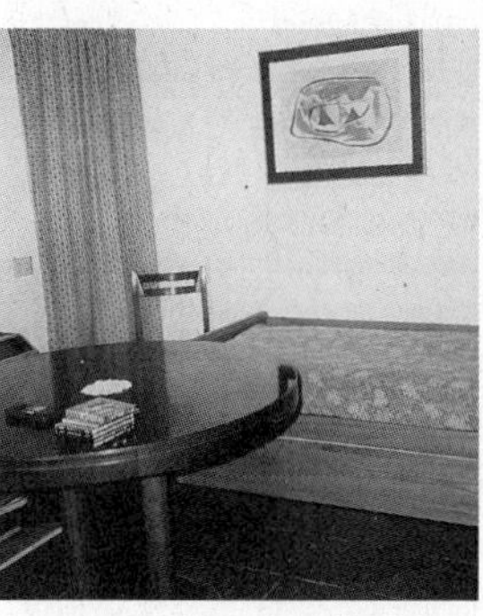

B&B Bellavista
• Bed and Breakfast Liguria
tel. and fax 010 2461918
bbliguria@hotmail.com
Closed: August

This B&B, located in a prestigious residential area, just a few minutes from the city's old center, has three guestrooms and a panoramic balcony. The rooms' darkwood dates from the '50s. The Italian breakfast, which consists of natural marmalade, Ligurian flat cake-bread and typical biscuits, is served in the living room reserved for the guests.

Genoa: a staircase detail of the San Lorenzo Cathedral.

Accommodation
Guestrooms: *3 (1 single, 2 doubles, with shared bath)* ♿
Services & Amenities: *rooms cleaned every 3 days; tourist info*
Minimum stay: *2 nights*
Rates: *single €€, double €€€*
Credit Cards: *not accepted*
Pets: not allowed

B&B Flowers
Maria Tozzi
via Lomellini 1
16124 Genoa
tel. and fax 010 2461918
mariatozzi@libero.it
www.bbflowers.it
• **Bed and Breakfast Liguria**
tel. and fax 010 2461918
bbliguria@hotmail.com
Open all year

This B&B, located right in the old center, is situated on the last floor of a 15th-century building and provides two rooms that are furnished in classical style. Both rooms are air-conditioned, have TV and lead onto a large terrace. The hostess, who loves reading, gardening and hiking, serves an abundant breakfast consisting of local products on this terrace. Guests also have the use of the living room and its TV.

Accommodation
Guestrooms: *2 double bedrooms, also single occupancy, with private bath; additional bed on request*
Services & Amenities: *English and French are spoken; rooms cleaned every day; tourist information; smokers welcome; air conditioning; Internet access; terrace*
Rates: *single €€, double €€€. Discounts for extended stays*
Credit Cards: *not accepted*
Pets:

B&B La Crociera
• **B&B Liguria e...non solo**
tel. 010 3291204
fax 010 3299774
oltrelazzurro@libero.it
www.bbitalia.net
Closed: January, February and half of November

This B&B is in a modern apartment with very nice and functional furnishings and it is located just a short distance from the fair area and the Brignole station. At guests' disposal there are three, very bright, guestrooms, one of which has a hydromassage bath facility. The Italian breakfast, which is usually served in the kitchen, is enriched with warm brioches and Ligurian flat cake-bread.

Accommodation
Guestrooms: *3 (1 single, 1 double and 1 double bedroom, with private bath); additional bed on request*
Services & Amenities: *English and French are spoken; rooms cleaned every 3 days; tourist information; smokers welcome; terrace*
Rates: *single €€, double €€€. Additional bed supplement €. Children under 3 free. Discounts for extended stays*
Credit Cards: *not accepted*
Pets:

B&B La Quercia
• **B&B Liguria e...non solo**
tel. 010 3291204
fax 010 3299774
oltrelazzurro@libero.it
www.bbitalia.net
Open all year

This B&B, located in Genoa's old center, just a short walk from the Ducal Palace, is hosted in a late 19th-century duplex villa that has a small garden. Besides the three rooms with modern furnishings, guests also have a living room with a TV and a furnished terrace. The Italian breakfast is generally served in the combination kitchen-living room.

Accommodation
Guestrooms: *3 (2 double bedrooms, also single occupancy, shared bath; 1 double). Additional bed on request*
Services & Amenities: *English spoken; rooms cleaned every 3 days; tourist info; smokers welcome; Internet access; terrace; parking*
Rates: *single €€, double €€€. Additional bed supplement €*
Credit Cards: *not accepted*
Pets:

B&B Lilliputh

TCI 10%

• B&B Liguria e...non solo
tel. 010 3291204
fax 010 3299774
oltrelazzurro@libero.it
www.bbitalia.net
Open all year

This B&B, which is just a short walk from the International Fair, the Brignole station and the waterfront, has two rooms, one in the early 20th-century style, the other in the Venetian style. Both are on the ground floor of a late 19th-century building that has a garden

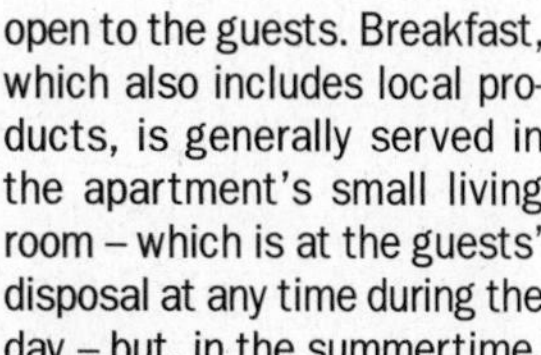

open to the guests. Breakfast, which also includes local products, is generally served in the apartment's small living room – which is at the guests' disposal at any time during the day – but, in the summertime,

it can also be served outside under the gazebo. Pets are not permitted so as to avoid possible conflicts with Luna and Pluto, the two family dogs.

ACCOMMODATION
Guestrooms: *2 (1 double and 1 double bedroom, also single occupancy, with shared bath)*
Services & Amenities: *rooms cleaned every day; complimentary tourist information; bike rental; smokers welcome; garden*
Rates: *single €€, double €€€-€€€€. Discounts for extended stays*
Credit Cards: *not accepted*
Pets:

Casa Torre

TCI 10%

• B&B Liguria e...non solo
tel. 010 3291204
fax 010 3299774
oltrelazzurro@libero.it
www.bbitalia.net
Open all year

ACCOMMODATION
Guestrooms: *3 (1 double and 2 double bedrooms, with shared bath); additional bed on request*
Services & Amenities: *English, French and Russian are spoken; rooms cleaned every 3 days; complimentary tourist information; baby-sitting service; kitchenette; bike rental; smokers welcome; Internet access; terrace; garden; private parking*
Rates: *single €€, double €€€. Additional bed supplement €. Children under 10 -50%. Discounts for extended stays*
Credit Cards: *accepted*
Pets:

This B&B is in an independent apartment situated on the ground floor of an old, completely restructured villa in the Genovese hills, 30 minutes from the center of town. This apartment, with its modern furnishings, also has a living room and a kitchen corner. Guests can visit the family apiary in the garden and taste some of the honey. The hosts are expert scuba divers and organize dives in the nearby sea area.

La Funicolare

TCI 10%

• B&B Liguria e...non solo
tel. 010 3291204
fax 010 3299774
oltrelazzurro@libero.it
www.bbitalia.net
Open all year

ACCOMMODATION
Guestrooms: *2 (1 single and 1 double bedroom, with private bath)*
Services & Amenities: *English spoken; rooms cleaned every 3 days; complimentary tourist information; smokers welcome*
Minimum stay: *2 nights*
Rates: *single €€, double €€€. Children under 3 free*
Credit Cards: *not accepted*
Pets:

This B&B is located in the Castelleto area, in a late 19th-C building, which is near the Righi funicular railway and just a few minutes from the old port and aquarium. This large, classical, refined apartment also has a reserved sitting room with a corner where guests can relax and watch

TV. The breakfast which includes typical sweet items and the famous Ligurian Focaccia (flat cake-bread), is served in the simple family kitchen.

L'Albero
via Canneto il Lungo 27/4c
16123 Genoa
tel. 010 2466807
• **Bed and Breakfast Liguria**
tel. and fax 010 2461918
bbliguria@hotmail.com
Open all year

This B&B is in the heart of the city, in an 18th-C apartment situated on the main floor of an historical building that still has its original stuccoes and decorations. The tree that gives this B&B its name is located on the large terrace where guests can have their breakfast in the summertime. In winter, breakfast is served in the beautiful dining room, which incorporates part of what used to be the building's private chapel.

ACCOMMODATION
Guestrooms: *1 double bedroom, with private bath*
Services & Amenities: *French spoken; rooms cleaned every three days; complimentary tourist information; smokers welcome; terrace*
Rates: €€€
Credit Cards: *not accepted*
Pets:

Lo Scoglio dei Mille TCI 10%
• **B&B Liguria e...non solo**
tel. 010 3291204
fax 010 3299774
oltrelazzurro@libero.it
www.bbitalia.net
• **Bed and Breakfast Liguria**
tel. and fax 010 2461918
bbliguria@hotmail.com
Open all year

This B&B is located in the Quarto dei Mille locality, which is near the railroad station and just 50 m from the sea. The two guestrooms, which are on the ground floor and have modern furnishings, are located in a building that dates from the '50s. One of the rooms communicates with the apartment's large terrace. Breakfast, which also includes local products, is served in the family dining room or outdoors. Guests also have the use of a mountain bike.

ACCOMMODATION
Guestrooms: *2 (1 single and 1 double bedroom, with shared bath); additional bed on request*
Services & Amenities: *English, French, German and Spanish are spoken; rooms cleaned every day; tourist info; smokers welcome; terrace*
Rates: *single €€, double €€€. Additional bed supplement €. Children under 10 free*
Credit Cards: *not accepted*
Pets:

LA SPEZIA

Il Gelsomino
Carla Cerretti
via Viseggi 9, località La Foce
19134 La Spezia
tel. and fax 0187 704201
ilgelsomino@inwind.it
www.bedandbreakfast.it
Closed: 15 November to 15 March

This old, restructured farmhouse, located on a panoramic hill 5 km from the city center, has three rooms with TV, furnished in classical style. Breakfast, including non-sweet items, is served in the living room or, in the summertime, on the terrace. Guests are also welcome to use the garden, as well as the living room with library. The hostess is a nature guide and she's available for arranging excursions into the surrounding area. She can also provide transportation to the railroad station and the port.

ACCOMMODATION
Guestrooms: *3 doubles, also single occupancy, 1 with private bath and 2 with shared bath; additional bed on request*
Services & Amenities: *English spoken; rooms cleaned every day; tourist information; smokers welcome; garden; private parking*
Rates: *single €€, double €€€–€€€€. Additional bed supplement €*
Credit Cards: *not accepted*
Pets:

• **Bed & Breakfast Italia**
TCI 10%
Code LI3
tel. 06 6878618, fax 06 6878619
info@bbitalia.it
www.bbitalia.it
Closed: varies

This elegant B&B is situated in the inner part of the Gulf of La Spezia. It is attractively furnished with antiques. The guests' accommodation consists in a double bedroom and a single bedroom, both spacious and light, with a shared bathroom with shower. The Cinque Terre region, the beaches of the Liguria coast and its picturesque villages surrounded by the multicoloured mediterranean vegetation, are all easily reached by car.

ACCOMMODATION
Guestrooms: *2 (1 single and 1 double, with shared bath)*
Services & Amenities: *English and French are spoken; rooms cleaned every 3 days; complimentary tourist information; private parking*
Minimum stay: *2 nights*
Rates: €€
Credit Cards: VISA MC *Bancomat*
Pets:

LERICI (LA SPEZIA)

• **Bed & Breakfast Italia**
Code LI6
tel. 06 6878618, fax 06 6878619
info@bbitalia.it
www.bbitalia.it
Closed: varies

ACCOMMODATION
Guestrooms: *2 double bedrooms*
Services & Amenities: *English and French are spoken; rooms cleaned every 3 days; tourist information*
Minimum stay: *5 nights*
Rates: €€
Credit Cards: VISA MC *Bancomat*
Pets:

This B&B is in a historic small mansion in the Lerici hills, located in the heart of the Cinque Terre region, and boasts enviable panoramic views of the Ligurian sea and of the picturesque villages in the surrounding area. The guests' accommodation consists in two double bedrooms sharing a bathroom with shower. The house is classically appointed with great attention to detail and with fine antiques. The breakfast is not cooked by the hosts: it is left in the kitchen for the guests to prepare and enjoy at their leisure. The beach is a 10 minutes' walk away.

MOCONESI (GENOA)

Il Girasole (Sunflower)
TCI 10%
• **B&B Liguria e...non solo**
tel. 010 3622003, mob. 338 8661461
fax 010 3106827
bbgenova@tiscali.it
www.bbitalia.net
• **Bed and Breakfast Liguria**
tel. and fax 010 2461918
bbliguria@hotmail.com
Closed: November

This B&B is in the ground floor apartment of a modern duplex situated in the Genovese inland hills. Guests have the use of a living room with TV and a furnished kitchen. The Italian breakfast, which, on request, can include cold cuts and various cheeses from the area, is served in this kitchen. They are also welcome to use the sunny garden, which provides pleasant relaxation.

ACCOMMODATION
Guestrooms: *2 double bedrooms, also single occupancy, shared bath*
Services & Amenities: *French spoken; rooms cleaned every 3 days; complimentary tourist information; kitchen use by request; smokers welcome; garden; private parking*
Minimum stay: *2 nights*
Rates: *single* €€, *double* €€€
Credit Cards: *not accepted*
Pets:

MONEGLIA (GENOA)

Castello di Monleone
Orietta Schiaffino
via Venino 3
16030 Moneglia (GE)
tel. 0185 49291, fax 0185 49470
info@castellodimonleone.com
www.castellodimonleone.com
• Bed and Breakfast Liguria
tel. and fax 010 2461918
bbliguria@hotmail.com
Open all year

This neo-Renaissance style building, located on a panoramic hill and surrounded by a park with statues, dates from the early 19th century. The interiors and original furnishings of this building also reflect this style. The buffet breakfast is served in the restaurant of the adjacent hotel, which also belongs to the family. Guests can also use the swimming pool, bar and relaxing room.

ACCOMMODATION
Guestrooms: *3 (1 single and 2 double bedrooms, with private bath)*
Services & Amenities: *English, French and German are spoken; rooms cleaned every day; complimentary tourist information; lunch & dinner reservations; internet access, terrace; garden; private parking*
Minimum stay: *3 nights*
Rates: *single €€€€, double €€€€. Discounts for extended stays*
Credit Cards: *accepted*
Pets: 🚫

MONTEROSSO AL MARE (LA SPEZIA)

Bed & Breakfast 7 Terre TCI 10%
• B&B Liguria e...non solo
tel. 010 3291204
fax 010 3299774
oltrelazzurro@libero.it
www.bbitalia.net
Open: March to October and weekends throught the rest of the year

This B&B is located in a modern duplex situated in the Cinque Terre Natural Park. The small duplex villa, with large garden and furnished terrace, has a welcoming atmosphere, thanks to its nice furnishings and the "treasures" collected by the hosts on their trips. The family gives culinary lessons to those who are fond of good eating, and also introduces them to Ligurian specialties. Guests can also use the barbeque and wood-burning oven that are in the garden.

ACCOMMODATION
Guestrooms: *2 (1 double and 1 double bedroom, also single occupancy, with shared bath)*
Services & Amenities: *French spoken; rooms cleaned every 3 days; tourist info; lunch & dinner reservations; educational courses by request; smokers welcome; Internet access; terrace; garden; parking*
Rates: *single €€, double €€. Children under 5 free*
Credit Cards: *not accepted*
Pets: allowed

PIEVE LIGURE (GENOA)

Hobbit's Folly
• Bed and Breakfast Liguria
tel. and fax 010 2461918
bbliguria@hotmail.com
Open: mid-May to mid-September

This 18th-C villa, whose original features have been completely restored, is surrounded by a large park and olive tree terraces. The villa provides an exceptional view of the Paradise Gulf, Portofino and Camogli. The Englishman who owns this villa has spent some time in Saudi Arabia, which is why the villa's furnishings include some items from the Middle East as well as classic furniture. The rich breakfast, which includes typical Ligurian products, is either served on the patio or in the dining room.

ACCOMMODATION
Guestrooms: *3 (1 suite, 1 double, also single occupancy, with private bath; 1 mini-apartment with 1/2 beds). Additional bed on request*
Services & Amenities: *English, French, Spanish and Arabic are spoken; rooms cleaned every day; complimentary tourist information; kitchen use by request; smokers welcome; Internet access; terrace; garden; private parking*
Minimum stay: *2 nights*
Rates: *single €€, double €€€€. Additional bed supplement €*
Credit Cards: *not accepted*
Pets: 🚫

Quiliano (Savona)

• Bed & Breakfast Italia
Code LI4
tel. 06 6878618
fax 06 6878619
info@bbitalia.it
www.bbitalia.it
Closed: varies

Accommodation
Guestrooms: *3 (2 doubles, 1 triple)*
Services & Amenities: *English, French and German are spoken; rooms cleaned every 3 days; tourist information; baby-sitting service; bike rental; smokers welcome; Internet access; private parking*
Minimum stay: *2 nights*
Rates: *€€*
Credit Cards: VISA MC *Bancomat*
Pets:

This elegant apartment is set in a carefully restored, eighteenth-century historical building. The accommodation consists in three rooms, all with TV and telephone. One double room has private bathroom with shower; the others share a bathroom. Furnished classically with antiques, each room boasts frescoed ceilings. Continental breakfast is served on a wide, panoramic balcony.

Rocchetta Nervina (Imperia)

L'Antica Macina
• B&B Liguria e...non solo
tel. 010 3291204
fax 010 3299774
oltrelazzurro@libero.it
www.bbitalia.net
Open: April to October and Christmas holidays

Accommodation
Guestrooms: *1 double bedroom, also single occupancy, with private bath; additional bed on request*
Services & Amenities: *English and French are spoken; rooms cleaned every 3 days; complimentary tourist information; kitchenette; bike rental; smokers welcome; garden; private parking*
Rates: *single €€, double €€. Additional bed supplement €. Children under 3 free. Discounts for extended stays*
Credit Cards: *not accepted*
Pets:

This single-family farmhouse has a small guestroom with a kitchenette facility and an independent entrance. The rich breakfast, which consists of natural sweet items and bread, is served in a small tavern that has various farm objects exhibited on the walls. This B&B is conveniently located from the Ventimiglia sea (only 12 kilometers) and from the Alta Via of the Ligurian mountains.

Santa Margherita Ligure (Genoa)

B&B La Mela Secca
• B&B Liguria e...non solo
tel. 010 3291204
fax 010 3299774
oltrelazzurro@libero.it
www.bbitalia.net
Open: April to October and Christmas holidays

This B&B, located in the San Lorenzo della Costa hamlet, overlooks the gulf with a view that sweeps all the way to the Portofino promontory. This old farmhouse has been completely restructured. A large expanse of green, like a balcony dominating the sea, provides the entrance to the rooms, all of which have an independent entrance. The elegant furnishings are all carefully selected, and the structure, which also acts as a farm holiday, offers the possibility of enjoying meals prepared with the use of the local farm products.

Accommodation
Guestrooms: *3 doubles with en-suite; additional bed on request*
Services & Amenities: *English and French are spoken; rooms cleaned every 3 days; complimentary tourist information; pubblic parking*
Minimum stay: *2 nights*
Rates: *€€*
Credit Cards: *not accepted*
Pets:

Sarzana (La Spezia)

Alla Vecchia Locanda 
• B&B Liguria e...non solo
tel. 010 3291204
fax 010 3299774
oltrelazzurro@libero.it
www.bbitalia.net
Open all year

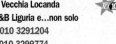

Accommodation
Guestrooms: *3 doubles, also single occupancy, with private bath; additional bed on request* ♿
Services & Amenities: *English spoken; rooms cleaned every 3 days; complimentary tourist information; bike rental; smokers welcome; garden; private parking*
Rates: *single €€, double €€€. Additional bed on request €. Discounts for children*
Credit Cards: *not accepted*
Pets:

This interesting-looking, early 19th-C, single-family home overlooks a courtyard and is near the railroad station and the public gardens. The guestrooms have their original terracotta floors and wooden ceilings. One of the rooms has a fireplace. Breakfast is served in the kitchen, that has a vaulted, brick ceiling and a wood-burning oven. Breakfast can be either the continental type or, on request, the English type, which includes a typical or homemade sweet item.

Savignone (Genoa)

A o Soâ
Claudia Crosa
via Broglio 11
16010 Savignone (GE)
tel. and fax 010 936884
mob. 335 6118766, 335 8108956
a.crosa@tin.it
• Bed and Breakfast Liguria
tel. and fax 010 2461918
bbliguria@hotmail.com
Open all year

The name of this B&B, hosted in a farmhouse in the Genova hinterland, is "A place in the sun." The house is made up of

different parts, each one constructed at a different time. The oldest part – once a chestnut drying facility – dates from the 16th C. The owners have their shops on the ground floor of the house. The period furnishings are in warm, simple style. Breakfast, with Ligurian flat cake-bread and natural marmalades, is served either in the large family kitchen or in the garden.

Accommodation
Guestrooms: *2 double bedrooms, also single occupancy, private bath*
Services & Amenities: *English, French and Spanish are spoken; rooms cleaned every 3 days; tourist info; Internet access; smokers welcome; garden; private parking*
Minimum stay: *2 nights*
Rates: *single €€, double €€€. Children under 3 free*
Credit Cards: *not accepted*
Pets:

Savona

Ca' Pramusa
Caterina Restuccia
via Santuario 105
17100 Savona
tel. 019 879522, mob. 347 1226585
pramusa@ligure.it
Closed: 5 January to 5 March

Accommodation
Guestrooms: *3 (1 double bedroom, 1 triple and 1 quadruple, shared bath)*
Services & Amenities: *English, French and Spanish are spoken; rooms cleaned every 3 days; complimentary tourist information; educational courses by request; smokers welcome; garden; private parking*
Rates: *double €€, triple €€€, quadruple €€€€. Children under 6 free. Discounts for groups*
Credit Cards: *not accepted*
Pets:

This B&B, with its plain, friendly atmosphere, is hosted in a restructured, 19th-century farmhouse located in the hills of the Savona hinterland. The guests have the use of a large garden with vegetables, a barbeque and a wood-burning oven. Breakfast, which consists of organic and natural products, is either served in the garden or in the living room. The host is a Hata Yoga and Pranajama expert, and it pleases him to share this interest with his guests.

Sestri Levante (Genoa)

B&B Andersen
Natalia Rolleri
via G. Caboto 1/1r
località Riva Trigoso
16039 Sestri Levante (GE)
tel. 0185 457467
nataliarolleri@hotmail.com
• Bed and Breakfast Liguria
tel. and fax 010 2461918
bbliguria@hotmail.com
Open all year

This B&B, which has two guestrooms with a balcony and classic style furnishings, would rather have guests who do not smoke. Located in the Riva Trigoso marine village, overlooking the Tigullio Gulf, this B&B is just a short walk from the sea and only 1 km from the center of Sestri Levante. The continental breakfast is served in the dining room or on the large apartment terrace.

Accommodation
Guestrooms: *2 (1 double bedroom and 1 double, also single occupancy, with shared bath)*
Services & Amenities: *English, French and Spanish are spoken; rooms cleaned every 3 days; tourist info; Internet access; terrace*
Minimum stay: *2 nights*
Rates: *single €€, double €€€*
Credit Cards: *not accepted*
Pets:

Sori (Genoa)

Solaria
Michela Pittaluga
via Dante Alighieri 6
16030 Sori (GE)
tel. 0185 701539, mob. 340 2347003
• Bed and Breakfast Liguria
tel. and fax 010 2461918
bbliguria@hotmail.com
Closed: mid-November to mid-December and 10 to late February

Accommodation
Guestrooms: *3 doubles, also single occupancy, with shared bath*
Services & Amenities: *English and French are spoken; rooms cleaned every day; complimentary tourist information; kitchen use by request; smokers welcome; garden*
Rates: *single €€, double €€€*
Credit Cards: *not accepted*
Pets:

The '50s villa that is situated on the Ligurian coast near Genoa and hosts this B&B is surrounded by a garden and terraces with olive trees. The hosts have dogs and a female donkey named Viola. Breakfast, which includes a choice of homemade sweet items, Ligurian flat cake-bread, cold cuts and various types of cheese, is served either in the garden or in the kitchen, as desired by the guests.

Vezzano Ligure (La Spezia)

• Bed & Breakfast Italia
Code LI5
tel. 06 6878618, fax 06 6878619
info@bbitalia.it
www.bbitalia.it
Closed: varies

A villa surrounded by a large garden located in a panoramic area. The guestrooms include a double and a single bed with private bathroom and are decorated in soft colors with elegant wood furniture. It is an ideal place from which to explore Ligurian areas of interest, such as La Spezia, the Cinque Terre region, Lerici and Porto Venere. The landlady offers warm hospitality and useful information on places to visit.

Accommodation
Guestrooms: *2 triple rooms*
Services & Amenities: *rooms cleaned every 3 days; complimentary tourist information; smokers welcome; private parking*
Minimum stay: *2 nights*
Rates: €€
Credit Cards: VISA MC *Bancomat*
Pets:

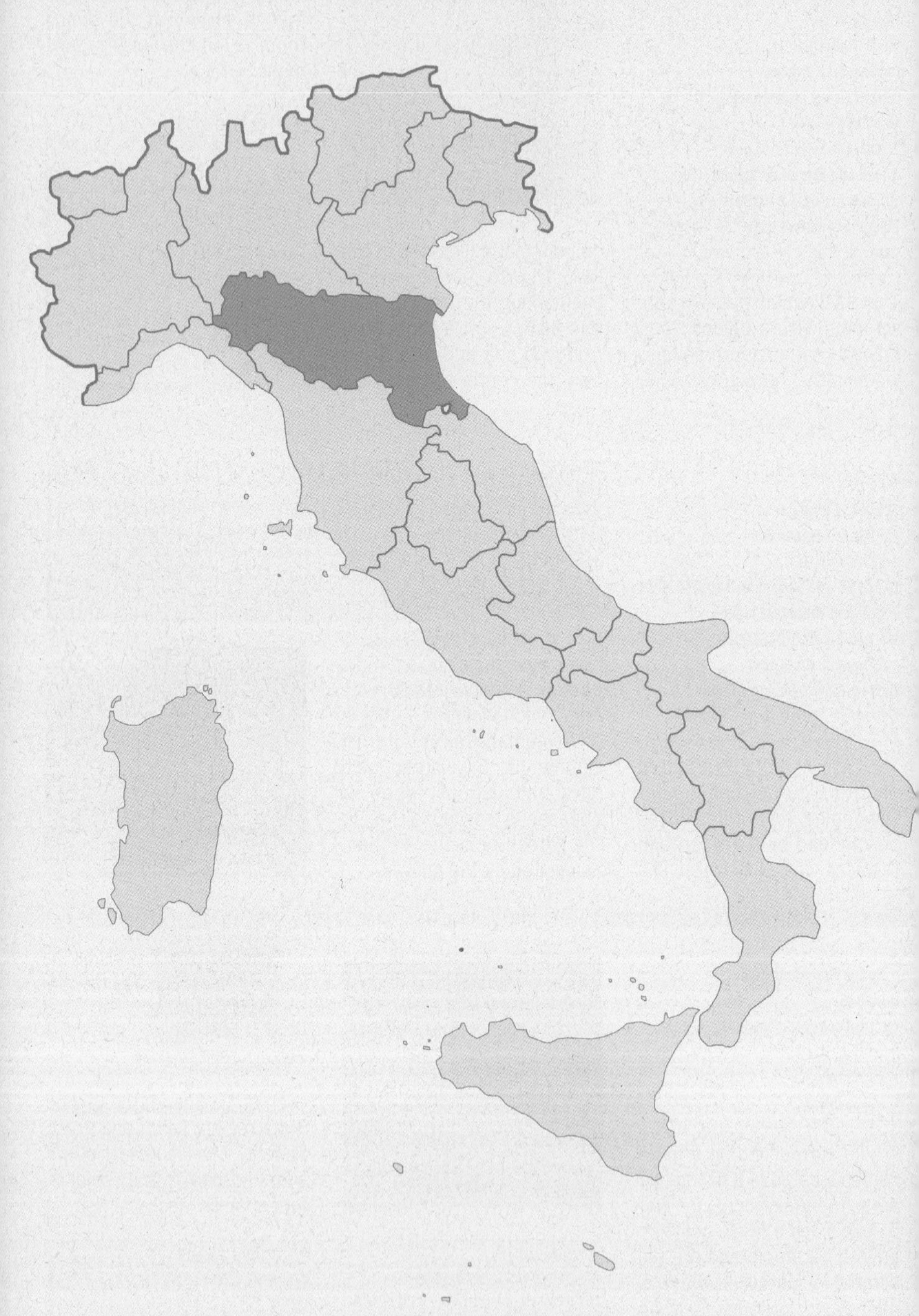

Emilia-Romagna

Alseno (Piacenza)

B&B Bellaria
via dei Gasperini, località Cortina
29010 Alseno (PC)
tel. 0523 947537
marinacazzaniga@libero.it
moving@tin.it
Open all year

This B&B, which is situated in the green Piacenza hills, has three guestrooms with double beds. One of the rooms is in the dépendance and two are in the main house, which is a rustic, completely restructured farmhouse. The rooms have a TV, a telephone and classic-style, early 20th-century furniture. Breakfast, which consists of natural products and homemade pastries, is served in the family living room. Guests can visit various wine cellars in the area.

Accommodation
Guestrooms: *3 doubles, also single occupancy, with private bath*
Services & Amenities: *French, English and German are spoken; rooms cleaned every day; tourist information; garden; smokers welcome; private parking*
Rates: *single €€, double €€€. Additional bed supplement*
Credit cards: *not accepted*
Pets:

Bagnacavallo (Ravenna)

Casa Cortesi Tci 10%
via Gloria 150, località Villanova
48012 Bagnacavallo (RA)
tel. 0545 927285, 0545 48193
mob. 349 3639571
info@casacortesi.it
www.casacortesi.it
• Associazione Turisti per Casa
tel. 0532 705052 - 051 6288619
info@turistipercasa.it
www.turistipercasa.it
Open all year

This restructured, council house, with its small garden, is in a part of the city that's being restored because of the importance of its buildings. The buffet breakfast is served in the living room, a room that the guests can also use. The small community of Villanova, which is surrounded by land that was reclaimed a long time ago and is now intensely cultivated, is 8 km from Bagnacavallo, which has an ethnographic museum of the swamp civilization.

Accommodation
Guestrooms: *4 (1 single, 2 doubles and 1 triple, private bath)*
Services & Amenities: *French, English, German and Spanish are spoken; rooms cleaned every 3 days; tourist information; garden; smokers welcome; private parking*
Rates: *single €€, double €€, triple €€. Children under 2 free*
Credit cards: *not accepted*
Pets:

Bentivoglio (Bologna)

Ben Ti Voglio
via Larghe 35, località San Marino
40010 Bentivoglio (BO)
tel. and fax 051 891000
mob. 333 4607490
• Associazione Turisti per Casa
tel. 0532 705052 - 051 6288619
info@turistipercasa.it
www.turistipercasa.it
Open all year

This restructured farmhouse, surrounded by cultivated fields and vineyards, is immersed in a very green park that also has trees and a small lake nearby.

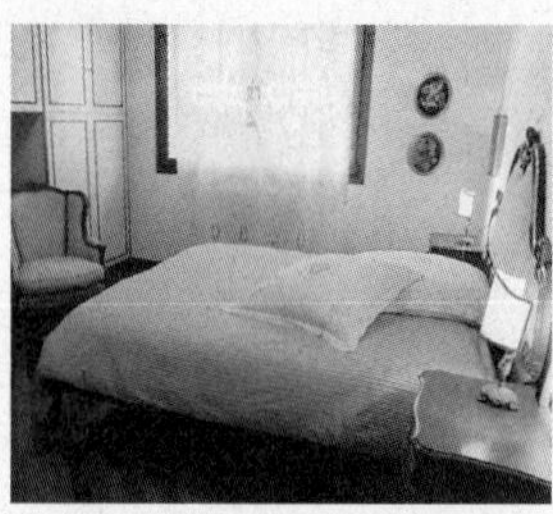

Breakfast, which consists of freshly- baked goods and homemade cakes, is either served in the kitchen-living room or, when the weather's nice, under the portico. There's an important rural civilization museum in San Marino, a small community near Bentivoglio.

Accommodation
Guestrooms: *2 (1 double and 1 double bedroom, private bath)* ♿
Services & Amenities: *French and English are spoken; rooms cleaned every 3 days; tourist information; lunch & dinner reservations; Internet access; garden; smokers welcome; private parking*
Rates: *double €€-€€€. Discounts for children and extended stays*
Credit cards: *not accepted*
Pets: 🐕

Besenzone (Piacenza)

Le Colombaie
Enrica Merli
via Bersano 33, località Bersano
29010 Besenzone (PC)
tel. 0523 830007,
fax 0523 830735
lecolombaie@colombaie.it
www.colombaie.it
Closed: mid-November to 1 March

Before you get to this B&B's rooms, all of which have a TV and a frigobar, you're met with the fragrance of a rose garden and a shady pergola. Breakfast, including pastries, and three types of fine cold cuts, is served in a converted stable that has a terracotta ceiling. The former hay barn, which has also been converted, is now a large guest living room with a fireplace. Guests also have a riding stable and a series of bicycles at their disposal.

Accommodation
Guestrooms: *3 (2 suites, 1 double, also single occupancy) private bath* ♿
Services & Amenities: *French and English are spoken; rooms cleaned every day; tourist info; bike rental; horse-riding excursions; garden; smokers welcome; private parking*
Rates: *single €€€, double €€€€. Children under 12 -30%*
Credit cards: VISA MC *Bancomat*
Pets: 🐕

Bologna

Accogliente Bologna
Maria Vecchi
via N. Sauro 26
40121 Bologna
tel. and fax 051 237498
mob. 348 6911868
• Associazione Turisti per Casa
tel. 0532 705052 - 051 6288619
info@turistipercasa.it
www.turistipercasa.it
Open all year

The guestrooms of this tranquil apartment, which has a large terrace and is located 300 m from Piazza Maggiore, has air conditioning and a TV. Breakfast consists of homemade pastries, including traditional ring-shaped cakes, as well as organic marmalades and, on request, cold cuts and various types of cheese. The hostess will also be pleased to have her guests try her typical Emilian spaghetti.

Accommodation
Guestrooms: *2 (1 single and 1 double, with shared bath); additional bed on request*
Services & Amenities: *French and English are spoken; rooms cleaned every 3 days; tourist info; lunch & dinner reservations; smokers welcome*
Minimum stay: *2 nights*
Rates: *single €€-€€€, double €€€-€€€€. Additional bed supplement €*
Credit cards: *not accepted*
Pets: 🐕

Alle Sette Chiese B&B 

Carlotta Compiani
strada Maggiore 31
40125 Bologna
tel. and fax 051 262791
• **Associazione Ospitalità Familiare**
tel. 051 379051
coruzzi@iol.it
http://users.iol.it/coruzzi/B&B
Closed: 15 December to 31 January and 15 July to 31 August

This comfortable B&B is located in a modern building situated in the old center of town, near the Santo Stefano basilica. The atmosphere is classic

and neat, and the hosts are at the complete disposal of their guests, which makes this place ideal for having a nice stay. Breakfast, which includes pastries and cold cuts, is served in the family kitchen.

ACCOMMODATION
Guestrooms: *1 triple, also single occupancy, with private bath*
Services & Amenities: *French, English and German are spoken; rooms cleaned every day; tourist info; baby-sitting service; terrace; Internet access; smokers welcome*
Minimum stay: *2 nights*
Rates: *single €€, double €€€, triple €€€€. Discounts for children and extended stays*
Credit cards: *not accepted*
Pets:

B&B "Senzanome" 

Lorenza Lucchi
via Senzanome 14
40123 Bologna
tel. and fax 051 6449245
• **Associazione Ospitalità Familiare**
tel. 051 379051
coruzzi@iol.it
http://users.iol.it/coruzzi/B&B
Closed: January, July and August

ACCOMMODATION
Guestrooms: *1 double, also single occupancy, with private bath*
Services & Amenities: *English spoken; rooms cleaned every 3 days; complimentary tourist information; smokers welcome*
Minimum stay: *2 nights*
Rates: *single €€-€€€, double €€€-€€€€*
Credit cards: *not accepted*
Pets:

This B&B is located on the first floor of a small building situated in the small Saragozza community, which is 4 kilometers from the San Luca sanctuary and just a 10-minute walk from Piazza Maggiore. The accommodation includes a double room, which has early 20th-century furniture, an independent entrance, and a private bath with a shower. The continental breakfast is served in the family dining room. There's a pay parking lot close by.

B&B di Casini Federica 

via Avesella 12
40121 Bologna
tel. 051 262001, mob. 347 7771780
fcasini@psibo.unibo.it
• **Associazione Turisti per Casa**
tel. 0532 705052 - 051 6288619
info@turistipercasa.it
www.turistipercasa.it
Open all year

ACCOMMODATION
Guestrooms: *1 double, also single occupancy, with shared bath*
Services & Amenities: *French, English and Spanish are spoken; rooms cleaned every 3 days; tourist information; smokers welcome*
Rates: *single €€, double €€€. Children under 6 free. Discounts for extended stays*
Credit cards: *not accepted*
Pets:

This quiet 2nd-floor apartment (no elevator) has a very friendly atmosphere, plain, simple furnishings, and faces a verdant, internal courtyard. It's in the center of Bologna and just 500 meters from the train station. Breakfast, which consists of organic products, homemade cakes and tarts and, on request, fresh eggs and cold cuts, is either served in the kitchen or in the living room. There's a public pay parking lot nearby.

B&B di Negroni Daniela
via Pietralata 7
40122 Bologna
mob. 347 9126506
daniela.n@libero.it
• **Associazione Turisti per Casa**
tel. 0532 705052 - 051 6288619
info@turistipercasa.it
www.turistipercasa.it
Open all year

This tranquil apartment, which is just 20 m from the bus stop, which is where one catches the bus for the train station and the trade fair, is also just a short walk from the monument area and the university. Breakfast, consisting of pastries or cold cuts, all prepared by hand according to traditional recipes, is served in the living room. Guests can use the kitchen and, if desired, can also make arrangements for lunch and dinner.

ACCOMMODATION
Guestrooms: *1 double, also single occupancy, with private bath* ♿
Services & Amenities: *English and Spanish are spoken; rooms cleaned every 3 days; complimentary tourist information; kitchen use by request; lunch & dinner reservations; smokers welcome*
Rates: *single €€, double €€€*
Credit cards: *not accepted*
Pets:

B&B di Nidi Biancamaria
via Varthema 2
40137 Bologna
tel. 051 6235219
biancamn@libero.it
• **Associazione Turisti per Casa**
tel. 0532 705052 - 051 6288619
info@turistipercasa.it
www.turistipercasa.it
Open all year

Not far from three municipal parks located near the outskirts, this B&B's bright, top-floor apartment provides a nice view of Bologna's roofs and its two celebrated towers. The hostess is strong on ecology and the breakfast she prepares has organic or, if desired, macrobiological products. Of course, guests can also have typical Emilian cheeses and cold cuts. The public transportation service is good, and it's only a 20 minute walk from the Sant'Orsola-Malpighi hospital and Bellaria complexes, and the university.

ACCOMMODATION
Guestrooms: *1 double, also single occupancy, with private bath*
Services & Amenities: *French and English are spoken; rooms cleaned every 3 days; tourist information*
Rates: *single €€, double €€€. Discounts for extended stays*
Credit cards: *not accepted*
Pets:

B&B Funivia
Anna Portolani
via Marabini 11
40134 Bologna
tel. 051 6152676, mob. 338 8664395
• **Associazione Ospitalità Familiare**
tel. 051 379051
coruzzi@iol.it
http://users.iol.it/coruzzi/B&B
Closed: June to August

This B&B, which is 3 km from the old center, is situated on the 4th floor of a modern building that's surrounded by a large garden containing games for children. The environment is very pleasant, and guestrooms have modern furnishings. Breakfast, consisting of pastries and cold cuts, is either served in the rooms or in the apartment kitchen.

ACCOMMODATION
Guestrooms: *1 double, also single occupancy, with private bath*
Services & Amenities: *French and English are spoken; rooms cleaned every 3 days; tourist information*
Rates: *single €€, double €€€. Discounts for extended stays*
Credit cards: *not accepted*
Pets:

B&B Gabriella
Signora Faccioli
via Cavaioni 4
40136 Bologna
tel. 051 589371, 051 589006
fax 051 589060
tcavaione@iol.it
• **Associazione Ospitalità Familiare**
tel. 051 379051
coruzzi@iol.it
http://users.iol.it/coruzzi/B&B
Closed: January and February

This B&B is located in a '70s villa situated in the Bologna hills. The villa, which is surrounded by a large garden that the guests can also enjoy, is just a few minutes from the old center. The four guestrooms have rustic furnishings, and two of them share a large terrace. The continental breakfast is served in the dining room reserved for the guests. There's also a public park nearby, as well as a riding stable.

Accommodation
Guestrooms: *4 (1 single and 3 doubles, 3 private baths and 1 shared bath); additional bed on request*
Services & Amenities: *French, English, German and Japanese are spoken; rooms cleaned every day; complimentary tourist information; terrace; garden; smokers welcome; private parking*
Rates: *single €, double €€. Children under 2 free*
Credit cards: *not accepted*
Pets:

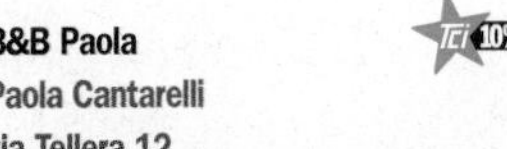

B&B Paola
Paola Cantarelli
via Tellera 12
40133 Bologna
tel. 051 6194328, mob. 339 5346218
• **Associazione Ospitalità Familiare**
tel. 051 379051
coruzzi@iol.it
http://users.iol.it/coruzzi/B&B
Open all year

This refined, very nicely furnished B&B is in a small period villa that's surrounded by a rich vegetation. It's just 2 km from the old center, which makes it ideal for both business travelers and guests wanting to visit the city. There's a choice of three different menus for breakfast, which can be served in the family kitchen.

Accommodation
Guestrooms: *1 double, also single occupancy, with shared bath*
Services & Amenities: *rooms cleaned every day; complimentary tourist information; terrace; garden; smokers welcome; private parking*
Minimum stay: *3 nights*
Rates: *single €€, double €€€*
Credit cards: *not accepted*
Pets:

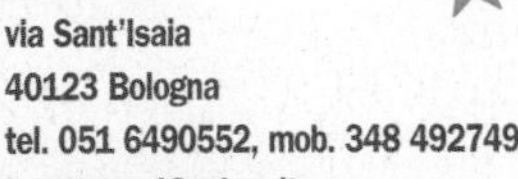

B&B S. Isaia
via Sant'Isaia
40123 Bologna
tel. 051 6490552, mob. 348 4927499
kmattarozzi@yahoo.it
• **Associazione Turisti per Casa**
tel. 0532 705052 - 051 6288619
info@turistipercasa.it
www.turistipercasa.it
Open all year

This B&B, which has a tranquil, quiet guestroom, is located in an apartment that's only a short walk from the old center and has a large terrace that faces inward. Breakfast, which consists exclusively of organic products, includes homemade yoghurt, fresh fruit, cereals, biscuits and tarts. On request, guests can also have an English breakfast. Amelia, a very nice Persian cat, is also part of the family. Baby sitting service is also available.

Accommodation
Guestrooms: *1 double, also single occupancy, private bath*
Services & Amenities: *French and English are spoken; rooms cleaned every three days; complimentary tourist information; baby-sitting service; smokers welcome*
Rates: *single €€, double €€€. Children under 5 free. Discounts for extended stays*
Credit cards: *not accepted*
Pets:

Beatrice B&B
Beatrice Marrino
via Indipendenza 56
40121 Bologna
tel. 051 246016, fax 051 4216296
mob. 338 9203407, 338 8629113
roby-bea@libero.it
• Associazione Turisti per Casa
tel. 0532 705052 - 051 6288619
info@turistipercasa.it
www.turistipercasa.it
Open all year

This B&B is in the 6th floor attic of a building located in the old center. Guests have a terrace from which they can enjoy an excellent panoramic view of the old city and the hills. For guests with a car, there's a public, indoor, pay parking facility. Breakfast includes typical pastries and is served in the living room. On request, guests can have an English breakfast. Animals are not welcome, unfortunately, because of possible problems with hosts' house cat.

Accommodation
Guestrooms: *2 (1 single and 1 double, with shared bath)*
Services & Amenities: *French and English are spoken; rooms cleaned every 3 days; tourist information; terrace; smokers welcome*
Rates: *single €€, double €€€. Discounts for children and extended stays*
Credit cards: *not accepted*
Pets:

CasAllegra
Roberto Allegra
via Montefiorino 4
40134 Bologna
tel. and fax 051 436643
mob. 333 5795690
info@casallegra.it
www.casallegra.it
• Associazione Turisti per Casa
tel. 0532 705052 - 051 6288619
info@turistipercasa.it
www.turistipercasa.it
Open all year

This B&B is in friendly, comfortable apartment located on the 3rd floor of a building situated in the center. The public transportation connections are excellent, which makes it easy to get to the city's main places of interest. Breakfast also includes flat bread-cakes and pastries prepared by the host. He is also a good source of information regarding good places to eat and drink, night clubs that feature live music and dancing, and everything else of interest that Bologna-by-night can offer.

Accommodation
Guestrooms: *2 (1 double bedroom and 1 double, with shared bath); additional bed on request*
Services & Amenities: *French, English and Spanish are spoken; rooms cleaned every 3 days; tourist information; smokers welcome*
Rates: *double €€-€€€. Children under 2 free*
Credit cards: *not accepted*
Pets:

• Bed & Breakfast Italia
Code ER11
tel. 06 6878618, fax 06 6878619
info@bbitalia.it
www.bbitalia.it
Closed: varies

The B&B is in a third-floor apartment (no elevator) and offers one double room with TV and private bathroom with shower/tub. Breakfast is served by the lady of the house in the lounge. Private parking in the grounds is available. This accommodation is in an area close to the center, on the loop that circumscribes the city, and is only a 10-minute bus ride from the central railway station.

Accommodation
Guestrooms: *1 double*
Services & Amenities: *French and English are spoken; rooms cleaned every 3 days; tourist information; smokers welcome; private parking*
Minimum stay: *2 nights*
Rates: €€€
Credit cards: *Visa MC Bancomat*
Pets:

• **Bed & Breakfast Italia**
Code ER13
tel. 06 6878618, fax 06 6878619
info@bbitalia.it
www.bbitalia.it
Closed: varies

This centrally located B&B is 100 meters from the railway station and is on the third floor of a building with an elevator. The guests' accommodation consists in a comfortable double bedroom with twin beds. The private bathroom has tub/shower. Smokers are welcome.

Accommodation
Guestrooms: *1 double*
Services & Amenities: *French and German are spoken; rooms cleaned every 3 days; complimentary tourist information; smokers welcome*
Minimum stay: *2 nights*
Rates: €€
Credit cards: VISA MC *Bancomat*
Pets: no

• **Bed & Breakfast Italia**
Code ER15
tel. 06 6878618
fax 06 6878619
info@bbitalia.it
www.bbitalia.it
Closed: varies

This accommodation in the center of Bologna is located on the fourth story of a building with elevator. It has a triple room with a double bed and a single bed available for the guests; furnishings are simple and well appointed. The bathroom has a shower. The continental breakfast is served in the kitchen or in the lounge. Is possible to use the telephone and the private parking if requested in advance. Smokers are welcome.

Accommodation
Guestrooms: *1 triple room, also single occupancy*
Services & Amenities: *French, English and German are spoken; rooms cleaned every 3 days; tourist info; baby-sitting service*
Minimum stay: *2 nights*
Rates: €€
Credit cards: VISA MC *Bancomat*
Pets: no

• **Bed & Breakfast Italia**
Code ER16
tel. 06 6878618, fax 06 6878619
info@bbitalia.it
www.bbitalia.it
Closed: varies

This B&B is located in the center of Bologna. The accommodation consists in a double room with two single beds. It is separate from the rest of the spacious house, ensuring privacy and tranquility. Furnishings are simple and tasteful; the bathroom is equipped with shower and is adjacent to the large room. The room has breakfast facilities that guests can enjoy at their leisure. The house is ideally located for touring the city on foot: the family provides information.

Accommodation
Guestrooms: *1 double*
Services & Amenities: *rooms cleaned every three days; complimentary tourist information; smokers welcome*
Minimum stay: *2 nights*
Rates: €€
Credit cards: VISA MC *Bancomat*
Pets: no

- **Bed & Breakfast Italia**

Code ER22
tel. 06 6878618, fax 06 6878619
info@bbitalia.it
www.bbitalia.it
Closed: varies

This apartment is situated in the residential area of Bologna. The center, the trade fair district and the railway station are within walking distance or can be reached in few minutes. This accommodation offers a double bedroom with two single beds and a single bedroom. Both are well lit and with TV; they are furnished in a modern, fresh style and share a bathroom with shower.

Accommodation
Guestrooms: *2 (1 single, 1 double)*
Services & Amenities: *rooms cleaned every 3 days; tourist information; smokers welcome*
Minimum stay: *2 nights*
Rates: €€
Credit cards: VISA MC *Bancomat*
Pets: 🚫

- **Bed & Breakfast Italia**

Code ER26
tel. 06 6878618, fax 06 6878619
info@bbitalia.it
www.bbitalia.it
Closed: varies

Self-contained apartment on the second floor of a building with garden. Guest accommodation includes two light airy double bedrooms, furnished in a modern and practical style, a small sitting room, a bathroom with shower and a breakfast corner. It is only 50 m from the bus stop, which is a direct 15-minute ride to the center of Bologna. Guests are given a warm welcome by the hosts, who live downstairs. Private parking on the adjacent street.

Accommodation
Guestrooms: *2 doubles*
Services & Amenities: *English spoken; rooms cleaned every three days; complimentary tourist information; private parking*
Minimum stay: *2 nights*
Rates: €€
Credit cards: VISA MC *Bancomat*
Pets: 🚫

- **Bed & Breakfast Italia**

Code ER29
tel. 06 6878618, fax 06 6878619
info@bbitalia.it
www.bbitalia.it
Closed: varies

This B&B is located in the residential area of San Lazzaro, not far from the old town and shopping center. The accommodation consists in a triple room with single beds, a private bathroom with shower, separate entrance and garden. The room decoration is simple and traditional. Breakfast items can be found in the fridge, and guests have free access to the kitchen. A bus runs to the center of Bologna in 30 minutes and stops within 7 minutes' walking distance.

Accommodation
Guestrooms: *1 triple*
Services & Amenities: *French spoken; rooms cleaned every three days; complimentary tourist information; smokers welcome*
Minimum stay: *2 nights*
Rates: €€
Credit cards: VISA MC *Bancomat*
Pets: 🚫

• Bed & Breakfast Italia
Code ER30
tel. 06 6878618, fax 06 6878619
info@bbitalia.it
www.bbitalia.it
Closed: varies

ACCOMMODATION
Guestrooms: *2 (1 single, 1 double)*
Services & Amenities: *French and English are spoken; rooms cleaned every 3 days; tourist information; terrace; air conditioning*
Minimum stay: *2 nights*
Rates: €€
Credit cards: VISA MC *Bancomat*
Pets: no

This accommodation is situated on the 4th floor of a building with elevator located in a residential area; it is stylishly furnished and comfortable with air conditioning. The bedrooms have classical furnishings. Close to the city's art attractions and conveniently located near the trade fair for those in Bologna on business. The central station can also be easily reached in 15 minutes by bus.

I Tigli
Rita Pinardi
via Mondo 4
40127 Bologna
tel. 051 510194, mob. 330 977952
fax 051 504427
• Associazione Turisti per Casa
tel. 0532 705052 - 051 6288619
info@turistipercasa.it
www.turistipercasa.it
Open all year

TCI 10%

ACCOMMODATION
Guestrooms: *1 double bedroom, also single occupancy, private bath*
Services & Amenities: *English spoken; rooms cleaned every three days; complimentary tourist information; garden; smokers welcome; private parking*
Rates: *single €€, double €€€-€€€€. Discounts for extended stays*
Credit cards: *accepted*
Pets: yes

This small villa, which has a garden with trees, is outside Porta San Donato and just a 10-minute walk to the fair. It's also just a 15-minute walk to the university area. The guestroom has a TV and a ceiling fan. Breakfast is served in the guestroom. The hostess, who is an herbalist by profession, likes to prepare breakfast using organic and natural products, but will prepare anything her guests might particularly desire. A telephone line is also available for surfing the Internet.

Open Space
Gigliola Ugelmo
via de' Coltellini 4
40122 Bologna
tel. 051 268239, fax 051 6486464
mob. 338 0082405
Open all year

This B&B is located in a beautiful, completely restructured 17th-century building in Bologna's old center. The guests accommodation consists in an independent apartment with modern, cherry-wood furniture. The rich Italian breakfast, which includes a variety of pastries and natural brioches, is served in the apartment dining room. Guests also have the use of bicycles for visiting the city's many attractions.

ACCOMMODATION
Guestrooms: *3 (1 double, also single occupancy, 1 quadruple and 1 independent suite, private bath)*
Services & Amenities: *English spoken; rooms cleaned every three days; complimentary tourist information; bike rental; smokers welcome; private parking*
Rates: *single €€, double €€€, suite €€€€. Discounts for children and extended stays*
Credit cards: *not accepted*
Pets: yes

Piana's B&B

Marco Piana
via F.lli Rosselli 13
40121 Bologna
tel. 051 221820
051 524359
fax 051 224379
romano.fiori@libero.it
• Associazione Turisti per Casa
tel. 0532 705052 - 051 6288619
info@turistipercasa.it
www.turistipercasa.it
Closed: August and December

Accommodation
Guestrooms: *1 mini-apartment with 3 beds*
Services & Amenities: *French and English are spoken; rooms cleaned every 3 days; tourist information; bike rental; smokers welcome*
Rates: *single €€€, double €€€, triple €€€€. Discounts for extended stays*
Credit cards: *not accepted*
Pets:

This B&B is in an apartment located on the 4th floor of a building that's located 600 meters from the train station. The guest quarters, which have an independent entrance, include a bedroom, a bathroom and a living room with TV and frigobar. The hostess prepares breakfast, which can be served to the guests in their living room. The B&B services also include the use of a bicycle and car transportation to and from the airport.

Budrio (Bologna)

B&B Ca' Rossa
Lucia De Col Tana
via San Zenone 14
località Maddalena
40054 Budrio (BO)
tel. and fax 051 807036
mob. 335 7116187
339 7395926
• Associazione Ospitalità Familiare
tel. 051 379051
coruzzi@iol.it
http://users.iol.it/coruzzi/B&B
Closed: 15 January to 15 February

Accommodation
Guestrooms: *2 (1 double bedroom, 1 triple, also single occupancy, shared bath); additional bed on request*
Services & Amenities: *French and English are spoken; rooms cleaned every day; complimentary tourist information; terrace; garden; smokers welcome; private parking*
Minimum stay: *2 nights*
Rates: *single €€, double €€€, triple €€€€. Additional bed supplement €. Discounts for children*
Credit cards: *not accepted*
Pets:

The B&B is located in an elegant house dates from the 30s and is surrounded by a park that has tall trees. 10 km from Bologna, it's conveniently located for persons on business trips. The breakfast, which also includes cold cuts, is served in a room reserved for the guests. In the vicinity, is a riding stable and the wherewithal for doing hang gliding.

• **Bed & Breakfast Italia**
Code ER17
località Vedrana
40054 Budrio (BO)
tel. 06 6878618, fax 06 6878619
info@bbitalia.it
www.bbitalia.it
Closed: varies

This seventeenth-century villa surrounded by rows of poplars and lawns is 30 minutes from Bologna. A double bedroom with en suite bathroom and three double bedrooms, which share a bathroom, are available for guests. On-site parking. TV, PC and fax are strictly banned, and guests can relax by the fireplace, sipping a glass of wine, or listening to a concert; candlelit dinners are served on request.

Accommodation
Guestrooms: *4 double bedrooms*
Services & Amenities: *French and English are spoken; rooms cleaned every 3 days; tourist information; smokers welcome; private parking*
Minimum stay: *2 nights*
Rates: *€€*
Credit cards: VISA MC *Bancomat*
Pets:

Calderara di Reno (Bologna)

B&B Ghelfi
Silvano Ghelfi
via Gramsci 7
40012 Calderara di Reno (BO)
tel. 051 722394
• **Associazione Ospitalità Familiare**
tel. 051 379051
coruzzi@iol.it
http://users.iol.it/coruzzi/B&B
Closed: July and August

Accommodation
Guestrooms: *2 (1 single and 1 double, with shared bath)*
Services & Amenities: *rooms cleaned every day; kitchen use by request; terrace; garden; smokers welcome; private parking*
Rates: *single €€, double €€€. Discounts for children and extended stays*
Credit cards: *not accepted*
Pets:

This functional B&B is located in a two-story house that's just 8 kilometers from Bologna, which is convenient for business visitors and others who want easy access to the city. The guests have comfortable rooms with classic furnishings. The continental breakfast is served in the family dining room.

Camugnano (Bologna)

Adriana Sgarbi
via Porranceto 144, località Barceda
40032 Camugnano (BO)
tel. 0534 91326
0534 425444
• **Associazione Ospitalità Familiare**
tel. 051 379051
coruzzi@iol.it
http://users.iol.it/coruzzi/B&B
Open: May to September

This B&B, which is located in an early 19th-century farmhouse that's at an altitude of 960 meters and is surrounded by the Two Lakes Park, has two double rooms with rustic furnishings and a shared bathroom with a shower. The rich continental breakfast, consisting of typical local products, is served in the dining room, which has a fireplace. Private parking is provided.

Accommodation
Guestrooms: *2 doubles, also single occupancy, with shared bath*
Services & Amenities: *rooms cleaned every day; complimentary tourist information; educational courses by request; garden; smokers welcome; private parking*
Minimum stay: *2 nights*
Rates: *€ per person*
Credit cards: *not accepted*
Pets:

Carignano (Parma)

Il Giardino Ritrovato
Sandra Migliavacca
strada Cava 108, località Vigatto
43010 Carignano (PR)
tel. and fax 0521 500002
mob. 333 8983020, 333 2690820
lapeonia@libero.it
www.ilgiardinoritrovato.it
Open: February to June and September to November

Accommodation
Guestrooms: *2 doubles, also single occupancy, with private bath; additional bed on request*
Services & Amenities: *French and English are spoken; rooms cleaned every 3 days; tourist information; garden; private parking*
Rates: *single €€, double €€€€. Additional bed supplement €€*
Credit cards: *not accepted*
Pets:

This solid, 18th C farmhouse, which has antique and restored furniture and almost 6 acres of an Italian park and garden (well cared for by the hostess who is an expert gardener), is located 6 kilometers from the Torrechiara castle and 4 kilometers from the Parma Golf Club. Breakfast, which consists of natural cakes and homemade black-cherry and fig marmalades, is either served in the very pleasant rooms or in the garden.

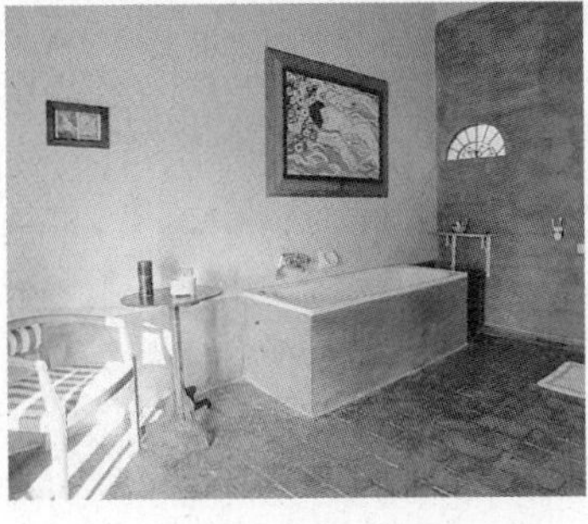

Casalfiumanese (Bologna)

• **Bed & Breakfast Italia**
Code ER6
tel. 06 6878618, fax 06 6878619
info@bbitalia.it
www.bbitalia.it
Closed: varies

Accommodation
Guestrooms: *2 (1 single, 1 double)*
Services & Amenities: *French and English are spoken; rooms cleaned every 3 days; complimentary tourist information; private parking*
Minimum stay: *2 nights*
Rates: €€
Credit cards: VISA MC *Bancomat*
Pets: allowed

This B&B is located in an area situated 15 km from Bologna. It has rustic furnishings and overlooks Bologna's hills. The guests' accommodation consists in two bedrooms: one is a double with twin beds and the other is a single. A bathroom with shower/tub is exclusively for the use of the guests. An extra bed for children under two is available. The hosts provide a shuttle service to the railway station. Pets are welcome.

Castel d'Aiano (Bologna)

B&B La Civetta TCI 10%
Valeria Vitali
via Civetta 11
località Rocca di Roffeno
40034 Castel d'Aiano (BO)
tel. 051 912717
vitalivaleria@libero.it
• **Associazione Ospitalità Familiare**
tel. 051 379051
coruzzi@iol.it
http://users.iol.it/coruzzi/B&B
Open: April to June
and September to November

This B&B, which is in a 14th-C tower, is located one hour by car from Bologna and Modena. The tower is furnished in the classical style and is located up in the hills between the Abbazia di Monteveglio and Roccamalatina Parks. The buffet breakfast, with pastries and cold cuts, is served in the dining room or in the garden. This B&B's location is ideal for those who are fond of good wine and good cuisine.

Accommodation
Guestrooms: *2 (1 single and 1 double bedroom, with shared bath); additional bed on request*
Services & Amenities: *French and English are spoken; rooms cleaned every day; tourist information; kitchen use by request; garden; smokers welcome; private parking*
Rates: *single €, double €€. Discounts for extended stays*
Credit cards: *not accepted*
Pets: not allowed

Castel San Pietro Terme (Bologna)

Borro di Sopra TCI 10%
via Paniga 1870
40024 Castel San Pietro Terme (BO)
tel. and fax 051 942444
mob. 333 3990972
cristinaverardi@libero.it
• **Associazione Turisti per Casa**
tel. 0532 705052 - 051 6288619
info@turistipercasa.it
www.turistipercasa.it
Open all year

Accommodation
Guestrooms: *4 doubles, also single occupancy, with private bath; additional bed on request*
Services & Amenities: *French spoken; rooms cleaned every 3 days; complimentary tourist information; kitchen use by request; lunch & dinner reservations; bike rental; garden; smokers welcome; private parking*
Rates: *single €€-€€€, double €€€-€€€€. Additional bed supplement €. Children under 2 free. Discounts for extended stays*
Credit cards: *not accepted*
Pets: allowed

This B&B, which is in an old, restructured farmhouse that's surrounded by a large garden, is located in the green hills and has a nice view of the valley. The guests stay in an independent pavilion, which has a living room and kitchen, both on the ground floor, and the guest bedrooms on the floor above. There are golf course, tennis courts, swimming pool and also some nice mountain-bike trails nearby. The Dozza castle, noted for it Regional Wine Collection, is of particular interest for those who are fond of good food and wine.

Castenaso (Bologna)

Marano
via della Pieve 10, località Marano
40055 Castenaso (BO)
tel. and fax 051 6060085
• Associazione Turisti per Casa
tel. 0532 705052 - 051 6288619
info@turistipercasa.it
www.turistipercasa.it
Open all year

This B&B is in a house with a small garden and is in a tranquil location, just 10 kilometers from the center of Bologna and 7 kilometers from the trade fair area. The buses don't pass very often, so it's preferable to have a car. The accommodation consists in 2 double rooms. The rich continental breakfast is usually served in the area reserved for the guests. The guests have the use of bicycles.

Accommodation
Guestrooms: *2 doubles, also single occupancy, with private bath*
Services & Amenities: *French, English, German, Spanish and Russian are spoken; rooms cleaned every day; tourist information; kitchen use by request; bike rental; garden; smokers welcome*
Rates: *single €€, double €€€. Discounts for children and extended stays*
Credit cards: *not accepted*
Pets:

Cervia (Ravenna)

• Bed & Breakfast Italia
Code ER14
tel. 06 6878618, fax 06 6878619
info@bbitalia.it
www.bbitalia.it
Closed: varies

A farmhouse set on 3,000 square meters of green park lined with trees in Cervia. A double and a single bedroom furnished with antiques are used for B&B. The two guestrooms share one bathroom with tub/shower. Guests may use telephone and fax facilities.

Accommodation
Guestrooms: *2 (1 single, 1 double)*
Services & Amenities: *French and English are spoken; rooms cleaned every 3 days; complimentary tourist information; baby-sitting service; bike rental; private parking*
Minimum stay: *2 nights*
Rates: *€€*
Credit cards: VISA MC *Bancomat*
Pets:

Private parking is available. Babysitting service on request. The seaside is 3 km away. Rimini and Ravenna are 25 km away.

Cesena (Forlì-Cesena)

• Bed & Breakfast Italia
Code ER21
tel. 06 6878618, fax 06 6878619
info@bbitalia.it
www.bbitalia.it
Closed: varies

A newly built, small detached house, with garden and private parking for guests, in a nearby suburb of Cesena. 30 km from Rimini, and 21 km from Forlì. The rustic furnishings reveal close attention to detail. A triple room and a single room are available; the triple has a double bed and a single bed. Both rooms have television. Breakfast is served either in the lounge or in the room on request.

Accommodation
Guestrooms: *2 (1 single, 1 triple)*
Services & Amenities: *French spoken; rooms cleaned every 3 days; tourist information; bike rental; smokers welcome; private parking*
Minimum stay: *2 nights*
Rates: *€€*
Credit cards: VISA MC *Bancomat*
Pets:

Coriano (Rimini)

Casa Dina
Daniela Gravina
via Mulazzano 2, località Ospedaletto
47853 Coriano (RN)
tel. 0541 656681, 0541 776171
mob. 347 4897617
mario.gravina@tin.it
Closed: October and November

This B&B, located in a rustic farm building just a few kilometers from Rimini, provides a very friendly and informal atmosphere. Guests have a kitchen and a small dining room, where the large Italian breakfast is served. They can also have grilled-meat barbecues in the garden. Bicycles are also available for guest use.

Accommodation
Guestrooms: *4 double bedrooms, also single occupancy, shared bath; additional bed on request* ♿
Services & Amenities: *German spoken; rooms cleaned every 3 days; complimentary tourist information; kitchen use by request; dinner reservation; bike rental; garden; smokers welcome; private parking*
Rates: *single €-€€, double €€€. Additional bed supplement €. Children under 4 free*
Credit cards: *not accepted*
Pets: 🐕

Cusercoli (Forlì-Cesena)

Ca' Basino Tci 10%
via San Giovanni 42
47010 Cusercoli (FC)
tel. and fax 0543 989101
cabionda@fattoriefaggioli.it
www.fattoriefaggioli.it
• **Associazione Turisti per Casa**
tel. 0532 705052 - 051 6288619
info@turistipercasa.it
www.turistipercasa.it
Open all year

This B&B is in an old, rural, stone and wood construction which has early 20th-century furniture and is part of a 150-acre farm (that also welcomes farm holidaymakers). It carries out organic farming and the raising of sheep, horses and other animals. In the surrounding area is possible to fish in the small lake, go mountain-bike riding, practice archery and, in the summertime, enjoy the swimming pool and its hydromassage. Guests can also have meals, use the kitchen facilities and be taken by car to and from the train station.

Accommodation
Guestrooms: *3 doubles, also single occupancy, with private bath*
Services & Amenities: *English spoken; rooms cleaned every three days; complimentary tourist information; kitchenette; lunch & dinner reservations; bike rental; garden; smokers welcome; private parking*
Rates: *single €€, double €€€. Children under 2 free; 3 to 8 -40%*
Credit cards: *not accepted*
Pets: 🐕

Dozza (Bologna)

B&B Maura Andreoni Tci 10%
Maura Andreoni
via XX Settembre 60
40050 Dozza (BO)
tel. 0542 679014
mob. 328 2763668
• **Associazione Ospitalità Familiare**
tel. 051 379051
coruzzi@iol.it
http://users.iol.it/coruzzi/B&B
Closed: 15 June to 15 July, Easter and Christmas holidays

This B&B is hosted in very carefully restructured medieval home located in the town's old center. The accommodation consists in a nice guestroom with wood-beam ceilings, terracotta floors and period furniture. The Italian breakfast is served in the dining room, which also has a fireplace.

Accommodation
Guestrooms: *1 double bedroom, also single occupancy, private bath*
Services & Amenities: *French, English, German, Spanish and Russian are spoken; rooms cleaned every day; tourist information; lunch & dinner reservations; terrace*
Rates: *€€ per person. Discounts for children and extended stays*
Credit cards: *not accepted*
Pets: no pets symbol

FERRARA

Corte Arcangeli
Maura Paolini
via Pontegradella 503
44100 Ferrara
tel. 0532 705052, fax 0532 758483
info@cortearcangeli.it
www.cortearcangeli.it
• Associazione Turisti per Casa
tel. 0532 705052 - 051 6288619
info@turistipercasa.it
www.turistipercasa.it
Open all year

TCI 10%

Corte Arcangeli, a former monastery that become a country residence for the Savonarola family, is now a beautiful residence that has been restored in accordance with the rules of bioarchitecture and with the use of original materials. The guestrooms provides every comfort and there are also large shared spaces and a large park. The hostess provides a large breakfast consisting of pastries and cold cuts, as well as the tasting of various wines and snacks that are the specialties of the area.

ACCOMMODATION
Guestrooms: *4 double bedrooms, also single occupancy, with private bath; additional bed on request* ♿
Services & Amenities: *French, English and German are spoken; rooms cleaned every 3 days; tourist information; baby-sitting service; kitchen use by request; lunch & dinner reservations; bike rental; horse-riding excursions; air conditioning; Internet access; garden; smokers welcome; private parking*
Rates: *single €€, double €€€. Additional bed supplement €€. Children under 2 free*
Credit cards: *accepted*
Pets: 🐾

Il Bagattino
Alessandra Maurillo
corso Porta Reno 24
44100 Ferrara
tel. 0532 241887
fax 0532 217546
info@ilbagattino.it
www.ilbagattino.it
Open all year

This B&B is located in a 16th century building that faces the city's cathedral. Guests have an independent apartment that has plain period furnishings, and every room is a different color. The large Italian breakfast, which consists of pastries and natural marmalades, is served in the small room reserved for the guests. On request, guests can have the use of bicycles.

ACCOMMODATION
Guestrooms: *4 double bedrooms, also single occupancy, private bath; additional bed on request* ♿
Services & Amenities: *French, English and Spanish are spoken; rooms cleaned every day; tourist info; bike rental; terrace; air conditioning; garden; smokers welcome*
Rates: *single €€€, double €€€€, triple €€€€. Children under 8 free; 8 to 12 -30%. Discounts for extended stays*
Credit cards: *accepted*
Pets: 🐾

Il Giardino Fiorito
Romana Villa
via XX Settembre 79
44100 Ferrara
tel. 0532 742667,
fax 0532 746133
romvilla@tin.it
www.giardinofiorito.freeweb.org
Closed: mid-July to mid-August

This B&B is located in a restructured, 18th century building situated in the old center of the city, just a short walk from the Jewish quarter. It has a large garden and a patio with trees. Guests have 3 large rooms, one of which is in the dépendance located in the garden. All the rooms have hand-painted wooden furniture, as well as a small cooking corner made of masonry. The Italian breakfast consists of natural pastries and is either served in the special small bar room or in the garden.

ACCOMMODATION
Guestrooms: *3 (1 double and 2 triple rooms, also single occupancy, with private bath)* ♿
Services & Amenities: *French, English and German are spoken; rooms cleaned every 3 days; complimentary tourist information; kitchenette; bike rental; air conditioning; garden; smokers welcome*
Rates: *single €€€, double €€€, triple €€€€*
Credit cards: *accepted*
Pets: no pets

Le Stanze di Torcicoda
Pietro Zanni
vicolo Mozzo Torcicoda 9
44100 Ferrara
tel. 0532 769389, fax 0532 798042
info@lestanze.it
www.lestanze.it
Open all year

This B&B, with its neat, romantic atmosphere, is located in an 18th-century "cassero" (a typical Ferrara building made of bricks). The four guestrooms have all the comforts, including a bath kit and a hair-drier. The large Italian (or English) breakfast is served in the reserved daytime room. Guests also have the use of the kitchen and several bicycles.

Accommodation
Guestrooms: *4 (1 single, 2 doubles and 1 triple, private bath)*
Services & Amenities: *French and English are spoken; rooms cleaned every day; tourist information; kitchen use by request; bike rental; air conditioning; smokers welcome*
Rates: *single €€€, double €€€€, triple €€€€. Discounts for extended stays*
Credit cards: *accepted*
Pets:

Gaggio Montano (Bologna)

B&B La Casa di Eolo
Claudio Sancini
via Molinaccio 77
40041 Gaggio Montano (BO)
tel. 0534 47777
• Associazione Ospitalità Familiare
tel. 051 379051
coruzzi@iol.it
http://users.iol.it/coruzzi/B&B
Open all year

This B&B is located in a small villa situated in a quiet, panoramic position. It's 30 minutes by car from Bologna and also near the Corno alle Scale ski lifts. The host family has tried to give this B&B the atmosphere of a typical English B&B. The accommodation consists in 3 rooms. The English breakfast is served in the living room. The host provides his guests with lots of information regarding the excursions that can be taken in the area, as well as the area's history and traditions.

Accommodation
Guestrooms: *3 (1 single and 1 double, with shared bath; 1 double, with private bath)*
Services & Amenities: *French, English, German and Spanish are spoken; rooms cleaned every day; tourist information; baby-sitting service; lunch & dinner reservations; bike rental; terrace; garden; smokers welcome; private parking*
Rates: *€€ per person. Discounts for children and extended stays*
Credit cards: *not accepted*
Pets:

B&B Vivienda
Giovanni Ritucci
via Porrettana 58, località Marano
40041 Gaggio Montano (BO)
tel. 0534 47137
• Associazione Ospitalità Familiare
tel. 051 379051
coruzzi@iol.it
http://users.iol.it/coruzzi/B&B
Open all year

This B&B is hosted in a small, recently-built villa, which is one hour by car from Pistoia and Bologna. It's in the vicinity of the Corno alle Scale ski lifts and Lake Suviana. The bedrooms are furnished in the classic style, and breakfast, with typical, homemade pastries and warm beverages, is served in the large kitchen. Of particular interest, the medieval villages in the area. Guests are also welcome to take their pets into the large garden.

Accommodation
Guestrooms: *2 (1 double and 1 double bedroom, also single occupancy, with shared bath)*
Services & Amenities: *English and Spanish are spoken; rooms cleaned every 3 days; complimentary tourist information; bike rental; terrace; garden; smokers welcome; private parking*
Rates: *€ per person. Discounts for children*
Credit cards: *not accepted*
Pets:

Carlo Bartoloni
vicolo della Rocca 4
40041 Gaggio Montano (BO)
tel. and fax 0534 37225
• **Associazione Ospitalità Familiare**
tel. 051 379051
coruzzi@iol.it
http://users.iol.it/coruzzi/B&B
Open all year

Accommodation
Guestrooms: *2 doubles, private bath*
Services & Amenities: *French and English are spoken; rooms cleaned every 3 days; complimentary tourist information; kitchen use by request; bike rental; garden; smokers welcome; private parking*
Rates: *€€ per person*
Credit cards: *not accepted*
Pets: ✗

This B&B, located in a 16th-century tower, which has a garden and private internal parking area that can be used by the guests, is situated just a few miles from the Porretta thermal baths. The guests have two double rooms with TV, telephone and period furniture. The continental breakfast, which consists of local products, is served in the family kitchen. On request, the hosts will gladly take their guests on guided tours of the area.

The roofs of Porretta Terme, famous for its spa waters.

Granarolo dell'Emilia (Bologna)

Villa Villani
via Porrettana 33, località Lovoleto
40057 Granarolo dell'Emilia (BO)
tel. 051 6021648, mob. 349 8626006
fax 051 6021429
villavillani@tin.it
• **Associazione Turisti per Casa**
tel. 0532 705052 - 051 6288619
info@turistipercasa.it
www.turistipercasa.it
Closed: August and Christmas holidays

This 17th-C villa, with its garden, trees and lawn, is located in Lovoleto, a tranquil rural community not far from Bologna (8 km from the trade fair area), on the road that goes from Bologna to Ferrara, which is 35 km away. The guestrooms have a TV and furnished kitchen corner. The park has a barbecue and children's games. Breakfast is served in a room that has a fireplace and is reserved for the guests. The villa also has a 20-place conference room.

Accommodation
Guestrooms: *3 mini-apartments (2-3 beds each)*
Services & Amenities: *French spoken; rooms cleaned every 3 days; tourist information; kitchen use by request; garden; smokers welcome; private parking*
Rates: *€€-€€€. Discounts for extended stays*
Credit cards: *not accepted*
Pets: ✗

Grizzana Morandi (Bologna)

Villa Arcobaleno - Country House
Paola Bizzarri
via Stanco 143, località Tavernola
40030 Grizzana Morandi (BO)
tel. and fax 051 913609
mob. 360 583149
villa.arcobaleno@libero.it
www.verdisorgenti.it
• **Associazione Ospitalità Familiare**
tel. 051 379051
coruzzi@iol.it
http://users.iol.it/coruzzi/B&B
Closed: mid-November to late February

This faithfully-restored, 18th-century country house, which is located in the ancient medieval village of Tavernola, has four double guestrooms with plain period furniture. The continental breakfast, which consists of organic products, is served in a room that has a fireplace and a library. Individual consulting and treatments regarding reikibalancing, anti-stress massage, floritherapy and chromotherapy are also available, as well as mountain bikes for taking rides through the woods located on the property.

Accommodation
Guestrooms: *4 doubles, with private bath; additional bed on request*
Services & Amenities: *French, English, German and Portuguese are spoken; rooms cleaned every day; tourist info; garden; smokers welcome*
Minimum stay: *2 nights*
Rates: *€€ per person. Discounts for groups*
Credit cards: *not accepted*
Pets: ✗

Imola (Bologna)

Shanti House TCI 10%
via Rosa Luxembourg 9/a
40026 Imola (BO)
tel. 0542 683620
mob. 347 9657021, 333 9187458
shantihouse@katamail.com
• **Associazione Turisti per Casa**
tel. 0532 705052 - 051 6288619
info@turistipercasa.it
www.turistipercasa.it
Open all year

Accommodation
Guestrooms: *1 double, private bath; additional bed on request*
Services & Amenities: *French, English and German are spoken; rooms cleaned every 3 days; tourist information; bike rental; garden; smokers welcome*
Rates: *double €€€-€€€€. Children under 6 free. Discounts for extended stays*
Credit cards: *not accepted*
Pets:

This house, whose name means "peace" in Sanscrit, is located near the Tozzoni public park and Frattoni woods on the edge of Imola. The large guest bedroom also has a table, armchairs, a TV and a hi-fi system. Moreover, it has an independent entrance and a terrace with a view of the park. The breakfast consists of typical as well as specific products requested by the guests. The services offered also include transportation to and from the train station and the making of taxi and restaurant reservations.

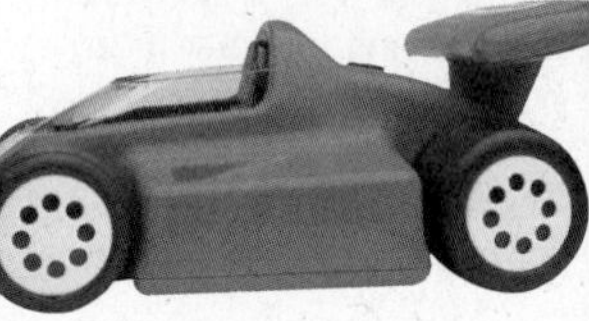

Lizzano in Belvedere (Bologna)

Villa Fedora TCI 10%
Germana Riccioni
via della Pieve 19
40042 Lizzano in Belvedere (BO)
tel. and fax 0534 51122
villafedora@cornoallescale.it
www.cornoallescale.it
• **Associazione Ospitalità Familiare**
tel. 051 379051
coruzzi@iol.it
http://users.iol.it/coruzzi/B&B
• **Associazione Turisti per Casa**
tel. 0532 705052 - 051 6288619
info@turistipercasa.it
www.turistipercasa.it
Closed: May and November

Accommodation
Guestrooms: *4 doubles, also single occupancy, private bath; additional bed on request*
Services & Amenities: *English spoken; rooms cleaned every day; complimentary tourist information; bike rental; educational courses by request; terrace; Internet access; garden; smokers welcome; private parking*
Rates: *single €€, double €€-€€€. Additional bed supplement €. Children under 3 free*
Credit cards: *not accepted*
Pets:

In the '30s, this villa, situated inside the Regional Park of the Corno alle Scale, was enlarged, transformed and made into a boarding house. It now hosts a comfortable B&B with rooms on the third floor (no elevator), a large terrace-solarium and a garden. The buffet breakfast consists of homemade pastries, marmalade and local products. The services include transportation to and from the Porretta Terme train station, bicycle rentals and the arranging of contacts with park guides and ski instructors. This B&B is part of the Legambiente's "Sustainable Tourism" project.

Misano Adriatico (Rimini)

• **Bed & Breakfast Italia**
Code ER31
tel. 06 6878618
fax 06 6878619
info@bbitalia.it
www.bbitalia.it
Closed: varies

Accommodation
Guestrooms: *5 (1 single, 4 doubles)*
Services & Amenities: *rooms cleaned every 3 days; complimentary tourist information; private parking*
Minimum stay: *2 nights*
Rates: €€
Credit cards: VISA MC *Bancomat*
Pets:

A farmhouse situated in the old center of Misano Monte. The rooms all have TV; four bathrooms, three with tub and one with shower, are shared by the rooms. The house is surrounded by a garden where guests are encouraged to relax. The landlady provides an extra bed for children under two in case of need, and bicycles on request. The bus stop to get the bus to Riccione is 200m away. A car is necessary.

Modena

• **Bed & Breakfast Italia** 
Code ER12
tel. 06 6878618, fax 06 6878619
info@bbitalia.it
www.bbitalia.it
Closed: varies

The B&B is hosted in a carefully and originally furnished prestigious house situated 6 km from the center. The accommodation consists in three large double bedrooms and two bathrooms with shower/tub. The pleasant rooms boast pretty furnishings, a four-poster bed, coffered ceilings, and lovely colors. The rich breakfast is served in the small garden surrounding the house.

Accommodation
Guestrooms: *3 doubles*
Services & Amenities: *French, English and German are spoken; rooms cleaned every 3 days; complimentary tourist information*
Minimum stay: *2 nights*
Rates: €€
Credit cards: VISA MC *Bancomat*
Pets: ✗

Monteveglio (Bologna)

Abbazia 
Liviana Balestra
via San Rocco 7
40050 Monteveglio (BO)
tel. 051 6701024, fax 051 6701835
clcandel@tin.it
• **Associazione Ospitalità Familiare**
tel. 051 379051
coruzzi@iol.it
http://users.iol.it/coruzzi/B&B
Closeda: January, February and August

This B&B, once Matilde di Canossa's defense castle, is located in the medieval village of Montevoglio. The ancient atmosphere is made more noticeable by several objects that have a modern design. Breakfast is either served in the dining room or in the garden, which is located in the back of this beautiful brick and stone house. The area has many tourist and archeological places worth visiting, as well as places for enjoying good wine and a nice cuisine.

Accommodation
Guestrooms: *4 (1 single, 3 double bedrooms, shared bath)*
Services & Amenities: *French and English are spoken; rooms cleaned every 3 days; complimentary tourist information; terrace; Internet access; garden; smokers welcome*
Rates: *single €€, double €€€.*
Credit cards: *not accepted*
Pets: ✗

B&B Casa Vivaldi 
Gianna Possati
via Vivaldi 1
40050 Monteveglio (BO)
tel. 051 6702398, mob. 339 4925269
www.casavivaldi.it
• **Associazione Ospitalità Familiare**
tel. 051 379051
coruzzi@iol.it
http://users.iol.it/coruzzi/B&B
Closed: June to August

This B&B, located in small villa situated in the hills close to the natural beauties of the Apennines, has plain furnishings and a pleasant, tranquil atmosphere. The breakfast of a wide selection of pastries and cold cuts is served in a small room that's reserved for the guests. The surrounding area has a number of places where one can enjoy good food, folklore events, village festivals and small open-air markets.

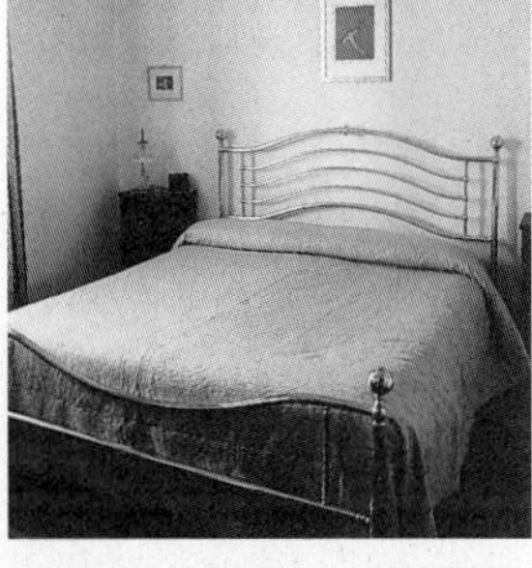

Accommodation
Guestrooms: *2 doubles, also single occupancy, shared bath; additional bed on request*
Services & Amenities: *French, English and Arabic are spoken; rooms cleaned every 3 days; tourist information; garden; smokers welcome; private parking*
Rates: *€€. Discounts for extended stays*
Credit cards: *not accepted*
Pets: ✓

B&B La Faggiola
Paola Tabanelli
via Ca' Bianca 52, località Oliveto
40050 Monteveglio (BO)
tel. and fax 051 6701012
• Associazione Ospitalità Familiare
tel. 051 379051
coruzzi@iol.it
http://users.iol.it/coruzzi/B&B
Closed: 15 December to 7 January

This B&B is located in a restructured farmhouse that has plain furnishings, is surrounded by vineyards and fruit trees, and is situated in the Oliveto hills on the edge of the Natural Park of the Monteveglio Abbey. Breakfast, consisting of organic products from the farm, is either served in the guestrooms or in the dining room. The guests have the opportunity of learning the traditional techniques for making bread, wine and marmalade. They can also enjoy taking hikes, going horseback riding and doing some archery practice.

Accommodation
Guestrooms: *1 double, also single occupancy, private bath; 1 mini-apartment (4 beds)* ♿
Services & Amenities: *English spoken; rooms cleaned every 3 days; tourist information; kitchen use by request; bike rental; horse-riding excursions; educational courses by request; garden; private parking*
Minimum stay: *2 nights*
Rates: *€€ per person. Discounts for children*
Credit cards: *not accepted*
Pets:

• **Bed & Breakfast Italia**
Code ER10
tel. 06 6878618, fax 06 6878619
info@bbitalia.it
www.bbitalia.it
Closed: varies

This B&B is located in a two-story house. The first floor and the garden are exclusively for the use of guests. It offers two rooms with all conveniences, TV and VCR. Its vicinity to Bologna makes it possible to easily reach not only Emilia's regional center, but also the lively nearby seaside resorts and the other cities of art in the region.

Accommodation
Guestrooms: *2 (1 double, 1 triple)*
Services & Amenities: *French and English are spoken; rooms cleaned every 3 days; complimentary tourist information; private parking*
Minimum stay: *2 nights*
Rates: *€€*
Credit cards: *VISA MC Bancomat*
Pets:

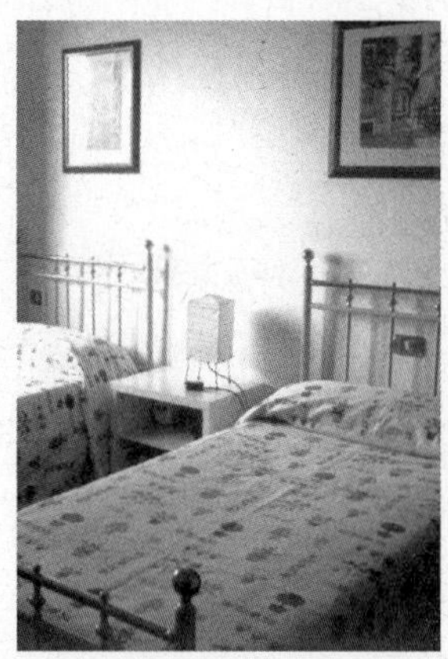

Monzuno (Bologna)

• **Bed & Breakfast Italia**
Code ER18
tel. 06 6878618, fax 06 6878619
info@bbitalia.it
www.bbitalia.it
Closed: varies

The B&B is located in a recently restored villa in stone and wood, surrounded by a garden and situated at Monzuno, 20 km from Bologna. The three guestrooms feature inlaid wooden beds and rustic furniture. The bathroom is shared by the three rooms. Parking is available. Smokers are welcome.

Accommodation
Guestrooms: *3 (1 double bedroom and 2 doubles, with shared bath)*
Services & Amenities: *French, English and German are spoken; rooms cleaned every 3 days; complimentary tourist information; smokers welcome; private parking*
Minimum stay: *2 nights*
Rates: *€€*
Credit cards: *VISA MC Bancomat*
Pets:

Pianoro (Bologna)

Elvezia Grillini
viale della Resistenza 25
40065 Pianoro (BO)
tel. 051 774095
• Associazione Ospitalità Familiare
tel. 051 379051
coruzzi@iol.it
http://users.iol.it/coruzzi/B&B
Closed: mid-June to mid-September

This B&B is situated in a single-family villa located in the first part of the Bologna hills. It's on the old Bologna-Florence road that goes over the Futa pass. The guests' accommodation consists in a small, nicely furnished apartment, including four beds, a TV, a kitchenette and an independent entrance. The kitchenette is equipped for preparing a continental breakfast.

Accommodation
Guestrooms: *1 mini-apartment with 4 beds*
Services & Amenities: *English spoken; rooms cleaned every day; complimentary tourist information; kitchenette; smokers welcome; private parking*
Rates: *€€ per person. Children under 6 free*
Credit cards: *not accepted*
Pets: ✗

I Borghetti
Ornella Tavoni Rossi
via Montecalvo 39
località Rastignano
40067 Pianoro (BO)
tel. 051 6269002, fax 051 6268042
serafino.rossi@libero.it

This place, which is located in the Gessi e Calanchi dell'Abbadessa Regional Park, has a large garden and is surrounded by olive trees and vineyards. The guest accommodation consists in three very comfortable double rooms with traditional rural furniture, all with private bath. Breakfast, which consists of both typical and organic products, is either served in the dining room or, when the weather's nice, in the garden. The excellent wine produced from the grapes grown on the property is bottled in the wine cellar. Private parking is also available for the guests.

Accommodation
Guestrooms: *3 doubles, also single occupancy, private bath; additional bed on request*
Services & Amenities: *French and English are spoken; rooms cleaned every 3 days; tourist information; Internet access; garden; smokers welcome; private parking*
Minimum stay: *2 nights*
Rates: *single €€€, double €€€€. Additional bed supplement €*
Credit cards: *not accepted*
Pets: ✗

Poggio Berni (Rimini)

La Lavanda
Floriana Raggi
via Roma 1
47824 Poggio Berni (RN)
tel. 0541 629651, mob. 348 7353799
fax 0541 687050
lavanda@libero.adhoc.net
Closed: December, January, February

With its perfumed candles, natural bubble bath and embroidery on the linen, the nice scent of lavender is this B&B's hallmark. The neat, relaxed atmosphere of this small '50s villa, which also has a beautiful garden, is characterized by the light green color, period furniture and plain, modern furnishings of the independent apartment reserved for the guests. The breakfast puts the accent on healthy organic products. Prior to departing, the guests are offered small, nicely-embroidered bags of lavender.

Accommodation
Guestrooms: *1 mini-apartment (3 beds); additional bed on request*
Services & Amenities: *French spoken; rooms cleaned every 3 days; tourist information; kitchen use by request; garden; smokers welcome; private parking*
Rates: *€€ per person. Discounts for children -10% and for extended stays*
Credit cards: *not accepted*
Pets: ✓

Reggio nell'Emilia

B&B del Vescovado
Francesca Bergomi
stradone Vescovado 1
42100 Reggio nell'Emilia
tel. 0522 430157, mob. 328 7088177
fax 0522 439311
frabergomi@yahoo.com
Closed: August

This neat, elegant, independent B&B apartment, which is in a 17th-century building, is just a short walk from the cathedral. This accommodation offers warm, light-colored modern furnishings, a few antique items, air conditioning and a telephone socket for connecting to Internet with a laptop. The large continental breakfast of pastries, natural marmalades, and a selection of typical Reggio nell'Emilia cold cuts, is either served in the dining room or in the guestrooms.

Accommodation
Guestrooms: *4 doubles, also single occupancy, private bath); additional bed on request ♿*
Services & Amenities: *English spoken; rooms cleaned every 3 days; complimentary tourist information; terrace; air conditioning; smokers welcome; private parking*
Rates: *single €€, double €€€. Additional bed supplement €. Discounts for extended stays*
Credit cards: *not accepted*
Pets: 🚫

• Bed & Breakfast Italia TCI 10%
Code ER27
tel. 06 6878618, fax 06 6878619
info@bbitalia.it
www.bbitalia.it
Closed: varies

A small three-story detached house 2 km from the old center of Reggio Emilia, with its great food and wine traditions. A small suite on the second floor is for guests' accommodation. It consists in a small sitting room with television, a double bedroom, and a bathroom with shower; breakfast is served in the room. Bicycles are provided on request; guests may use the computer.

Accommodation
Guestrooms: *1 double*
Services & Amenities: *rooms cleaned every three days; complimentary tourist information; bike rental; private parking*
Minimum stay: *2 nights*
Rates: *€€*
Credit cards: VISA MC *Bancomat*
Pets: 🚫

Rimini

Le Tre Querce
Romano and Cesarina Morganti
via Consorziale 4
località Santa Cristina
47900 Rimini
tel. 0541 767208, fax 0541 773797
letrequerce@libero.it
Closed: January to March

This B&B is in a characteristic farmhouse located in the Alta Valmarecchia hills. It's surrounded by lots of greenery and is near Santarcangelo and San Marino. The Italian breakfast, consisting of fresh fruit, natural products and traditional Romagna pastries, is either served in the living room, with fireplace, or, when the weather's nice, in the garden.

Accommodation
Guestrooms: *3 double bedrooms, also single occupancy, shared bath; additional bed on request*
Services & Amenities: *rooms cleaned every three days; complimentary tourist information; dinner reservation; garden; smokers welcome; private parking*
Rates: *single €€, double €€€. Additional bed supplement €€. Children under 4 free*
Credit cards: *not accepted*
Pets: 🐕

SALSOMAGGIORE TERME (PARMA)

• **Bed & Breakfast Italia**
Code ER28
tel. 06 6878618, fax 06 6878619
info@bbitalia.it
www.bbitalia.it
Closed: varies

The recently restored detached house is 1 km from Salsomaggiore and 3 km from Tabiano. It offers two comfortable rooms, one with a double bed and a triple room with a double bed plus a single. The private bathroom has shower/tub. Private parking on the grounds, extensive garden, playground, solarium and picnic area. The landlady prepares a hearty buffet-breakfast. Swimming pool and golf course in the area.

ACCOMMODATION
Guestrooms: *2 (1 double bedroom and 1 triple room)*
Services & Amenities: *French and English are spoken; rooms cleaned every three days; complimentary tourist information; private parking*
Minimum stay: *2 nights*
Rates: €€
Credit cards: VISA MC *Bancomat*
Pets: not allowed

SAN LAZZARO DI SAVENA (BOLOGNA)

B&B Mariangela TCI 10%
via Pio La Torre 37
40068 San Lazzaro di Savena (BO)
tel. 051 6258080
mob. 333 6420786
• **Associazione Turisti per Casa**
tel. 0532 705052 - 051 6288619
info@turistipercasa.it
www.turistipercasa.it
Open all year

This B&B occupies the attic apartment of a building of recent construction. It's located in what is now a residential section in the outskirts of Bologna, near the Villa Cicogna conference center. This accommodation offers 2 rooms with private bath. Guests can also choose between a continental or English breakfast. The hosts provide city bikes which can be used to ride along the cycling path that leads directly to the center of Bologna, which is 6 kilometers away, or for getting to the nearby Idice fluvial park.

ACCOMMODATION
Guestrooms: *2 doubles, also single occupancy, private bath*
Services & Amenities: *English and Greek are spoken; rooms cleaned every 3 days; tourist information; bike rental; terrace; garden; smokers welcome; private parking*
Rates: *single* €€, *double* €€€€. *Children under 2 free. Discounts for extended stays*
Credit cards: *not accepted*
Pets: not allowed

La Diomedea B&B TCI 10%
Anna Rita Diomede
via Torino 6
40068 San Lazzaro di Savena (BO)
tel. 051 455387, mob. 349 4786389
ar.diomede@libero.it
• **Associazione Turisti per Casa**
tel. 0532 705052 - 051 6288619
info@turistipercasa.it
www.turistipercasa.it
Open all year

This B&B is situated in a refined apartment located in a green, quiet area in the center of town, just a few kilometers from Bologna. The guests have a comfortable room, with classic furnishings, and a veranda. Breakfast, which is served on this veranda, includes pastries, cold cuts and cheese. The hostess is particularly keen about protecting the environment and thus uses ecological products in doing the housecleaning. She also organizes tours and excursions.

ACCOMMODATION
Guestrooms: *1 double, also single occupancy, private bath*
Services & Amenities: *French, English and German are spoken; rooms cleaned every 3 days; complimentary tourist information; bike rental; terrace; private parking*
Minimum stay: *2 nights*
Rates: *single* €€, *double* €€€. *Discounts for children and extended stays*
Credit cards: *not accepted*
Pets: not allowed

Murolungo
via Jussi 121 , località Fameto
40068 San Lazzaro di Savena (BO)
tel. 051 6251710, mob. 339 2886591
murolungo@libero.it
• Associazione Turisti per Casa
tel. and fax 0532 63066
buccimg@libero.it
www.turistipercasa.it
Open all year

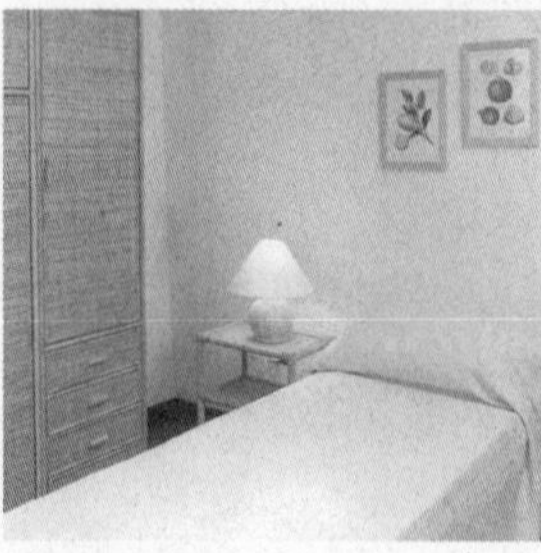

This B&B, which is part of the Legambiente "Sustainable Tourism" project, is located in a farmhouse that's surrounded by a large garden. It's just outside of San Lazzaro and is only 7 kilometers from the center of Bologna. On request, the hosts will gladly guided visits to enjoy the natural and speleological features of Abbadessa's Gessi and Calanchi Regional Park. There are several typical trattorias nearby where the guests can try some true Emilian cuisine.

Accommodation
Guestrooms: *3 (1 single and 1 double, shared bath; 1 double with private bath)*
Services & Amenities: *English spoken; rooms cleaned every three days; complimentary tourist information; garden; smokers welcome; private parking*
Rates: *single €€, double €€€. Discounts for children and extended stays*
Credit cards: *not accepted*
Pets:

Sasso Marconi (Bologna)

B&B Belvedere
via Belvedere 3
40037 Sasso Marconi (BO)
tel. and fax 051 6755043
mob. 339 1755989
• Associazione Turisti per Casa
tel. 0532 705052 - 051 6288619
info@turistipercasa.it
www.turistipercasa.it
Open all year

This single-family house, with its garden, is located in a panoramic position on a hill surrounded by chestnut trees. For breakfast, guests can have pastries and homemade cakes or local cold cuts and various types of cheese. Breakfast is

Accommodation
Guestrooms: *2 doubles, also single occupancy, private bath; additional bed on request*
Services & Amenities: *rooms cleaned every three days; complimentary tourist information; lunch & dinner reservations; garden; smokers welcome; private parking*
Rates: *single €€, double €€. Additional bed supplement €*
Credit cards: *not accepted*
Pets:

served in the dining room, but when the weather's nice it can either be served under the portico or in the garden. The hosts are always happy to let their guests try some of the various types of typical homemade Emilian spaghetti. A shuttle service to bus stop is also provided.

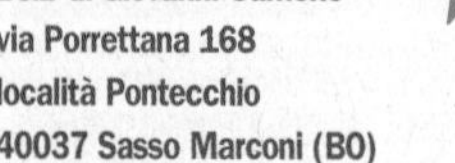

B&B di Giovanni Camerlo
via Porrettana 168
località Pontecchio
40037 Sasso Marconi (BO)
tel. 051 846249, mob. 347 4665662
• Associazione Turisti per Casa
tel. 0532 705052 - 051 6288619
info@turistipercasa.it
www.turistipercasa.it
Open: mid-January to mid-June and September to 20 December

This single-family villa and its garden planted with trees, is located in Pontecchio, a part of Sasso Marconi, in a hilly area just a few kilometers

Accommodation
Guestrooms: *3 (2 double bedroom with shared bath and 1 double with private bath, also single occupancy); additional bed on request*
Services & Amenities: *German spoken; rooms cleaned every 3 days; complimentary tourist information; garden; smokers welcome; private parking*
Rates: *single €€, double €€€. Additional bed supplement €*
Credit cards: *not accepted*
Pets:

from Bologna. The bright guestrooms are on the first floor, and breakfast is served in the family dining room. It's more convenient for the guests to have a car because, although the bus stop for Bologna is nearby, it's a fairly long wait for the bus.

B&B Hillside
Alessandro Montalbini
via Cartiera 46, località Borgonuovo
40037 Sasso Marconi (BO)
tel. 051 845318, mob. 348 7273560
info@bedandbreakfast-italy.it
www.bedandbreakfast-italy.it
• **Associazione Ospitalità Familiare**
tel. 051 379051
coruzzi@iol.it
http://users.iol.it/coruzzi/B&B
Open all year

This functional B&B is located in a nice little villa that has a garden and is located in a tranquil area that's just 8 kilometers from Bologna. This makes it convenient for going to city or for making excursions into the romantic Tuscan-Emilian Apennines. The comfortable, elegant guestrooms have satellite TV, a VCR and a hi-fi system. The continental breakfast, which provides a choice of pastries or cold cuts and cheese, is served in the family dining room.

Accommodation
Guestrooms: *2 (1 single and 1 tripla, with private bath)*
Services & Amenities: *French and English are spoken; rooms cleaned every day; tourist info; bike rental; terrace; Internet access; garden*
Minimum stay: *2 nights*
Rates: *single €€-€€€, double €€-€€€, triple €€€-€€€€. Discounts for children and extended stays*
Credit cards: *Bancomat*
Pets:

B&B La Torre di Iano
Raffaella Mazzanti
località Iano 23, 40037 Sasso Marconi
tel. and fax 051 841211
• **Associazione Ospitalità Familiare**
tel. 051 379051
coruzzi@iol.it
http://users.iol.it/coruzzi/B&B
Open all year

Accommodation
Guestrooms: *4 doubles, 1 with private bath and 3 with shared bath*
Services & Amenities: *French and English are spoken; rooms cleaned every day; complimentary tourist information; lunch & dinner reservations; educational courses by request; terrace; garden; smokers welcome; private parking*
Rates: *€€€-€€€€. Additional bed supplement €. Discounts for children*
Credit cards: *Bancomat*
Pets:

This B&B is located in a 19th-C manor house that forms part of a group of stone houses in a medieval village. Breakfast, which consists of locally-made pastries, cold cuts and cheese, is either served in the dining room or in the garden. The hosts provide lessons in photography, painting, biodance and exhibits.

• **Bed & Breakfast Italia**
Code ER20
tel. 06 6878618, fax 06 6878619
info@bbitalia.it, www.bbitalia.it
Closed: varies

A semi-detached house with garden situated in an area close to the center. It has two bedrooms and a private bathroom with shower. One is a triple with TV, and stereo; the second is a single with a balcony. Breakfast is served in the kitchen or in the lounge.

Accommodation
Guestrooms: *2 (1 single, 1 triple)*
Services & Amenities: *English spoken; rooms cleaned every 3 days; complimentary tourist information; bike rental; private parking*
Minimum stay: *2 nights*
Rates: *€€*
Credit cards: *Bancomat*
Pets:

Savignano sul Rubicone (Forlì-Cesena)

• **Bed & Breakfast Italia**
Code ER2
tel. 06 6878618, fax 06 6878619
info@bbitalia.it, www.bbitalia.it
Closed: varies

Simple functional rooms are available for guests: two twin rooms, one with double bed, and a triple room with a double and a single bed. The four rooms share two bathrooms with shower/tub. The garden surrounding the house and private parking are at the guests' disposal.

Accommodation
Guestrooms: *4 (1 double bedroom, 2 doubles and 1 triple room)*
Services & Amenities: *English, German and Spanish are spoken; rooms cleaned every 3 days; tourist info*
Minimum stay: *2 nights*
Rates: *€€*
Credit cards: *Bancomat*
Pets:

Torriana (Rimini)

Bedbreakfasttino
Anna Pazzaglia
via Sabioni 67, 47825 Torriana (RN)
mob. 340 2345698
info@bedbreakfasttino.com
www.bedbreakfasttino.com
Open all year

This B&B, with its friendly atmosphere, is located in a restructured farmhouse situated near the Marecchia River. Breakfast is prepared according to what the guests prefer. The guests also have use of the living room, with fireplace, as well as an outdoor barbecue. When it's grape-harvest time, guests can watch and participate if they so desire.

Accommodation
Guestrooms: *4 (2 single and 2 double bedroom, shared bath)*
Services & Amenities: *rooms cleaned every three days; complimentary tourist information; bike rental; garden; smokers welcome; private parking*
Rates: *single €€, double €€€*
Credit cards: *not accepted*
Pets:

Vergato (Bologna)

B&B Ca' Serra
Giuseppe Olivi
via Serra 176, località Riola
40038 Vergato (BO)
tel. 051 916222, mob. 348 2564005
• Associazione Ospitalità Familiare
tel. 051 379051, coruzzi@iol.it
http://users.iol.it/coruzzi/B&B
Open all year

TCI 10%

Accommodation
Guestrooms: *3 triple rooms, also single occupancy, with shared bath*
Services & Amenities: *English spoken; rooms cleaned every day; complimentary tourist information; baby-sitting service; kitchen use by request; lunch & dinner reservations; bike rental; educational courses by request; garden; smokers welcome; private parking*
Rates: *single and double €€, triple €€–€€€€. Discounts for children and extended stays*
Credit cards: *not accepted*
Pets:

This B&B, which is located in a small, restructured villa that has classic furnishings, is 50 km from Bologna and the airport. It's in the vicinity of the Corno alle Scale ski station and just a few minutes from the Porretta thermal baths. Breakfast, with organic pastries, cold cuts and cheese, is served in the common room. The surrounding area provides interesting visits to ancient castles and medieval villages. An interesting sight is also the church designed by Alvar Aalto.

Viano (Reggio nell'Emilia)

B&B Prà de Mandè
Carlo Bondavalli
via Prato Mandeto 4
42030 Viano (RE)
tel. 0522 383690, mob. 335 5360489
jackbond_2000@yahoo.it
www.adventurestours.com
Open: 1 April to 15 November

This B&B, is located in a stone house with warm, modern furnishings. The house is in a small 18th-C village in the back hills of Reggio nell'Emilia. The English breakfast, which consists of local products, is either served in the kitchen or in the garden. Guests have the use of a swimming pool.

Accommodation
Guestrooms: *1 mini-apartment (2 beds); additional bed on request*
Services & Amenities: *French, English and Spanish are spoken; rooms cleaned every three days; complimentary tourist information; garden; smokers welcome; private parking*
Rates: *single €, double €€, triple €€€. Discounts for children*
Credit cards: *not accepted*
Pets:

Ziano Piacentino (Piacenza)

Podere Casale
Angelo Rigamonti
via Creta, località Vicobarone
29010 Ziano Piacentino (PC)
tel. 0523 868302, fax 0523 840114
info@poderecasale.it
www.poderecasale.it
• **Benvenuti da noi**
tel. 0763 305523, fax 0763 390670
moving@tin.it
Open: April to October

Accommodation
Guestrooms: *4 doubles, also single occupancy, private bath*
Services & Amenities: *French and English are spoken; rooms cleaned every 3 days; tourist information; bike rental; Internet access; garden; smokers welcome; private parking*
Rates: *single €€-€€€, double €€€€*
Credit cards: *accepted*
Pets:

The guestrooms of this B&B are located in what used to be the stalls of an ancient, refined, 18th-C house – now an active winery surrounded by vineyards – whose original nucleus dates from the year 1000. The guestrooms have wooden ceilings, terracotta floors and rustic furniture. Breakfast consists of natural, local products and is served in the living room with fireplace. The guests can use the large swimming pool and, on request, they can also be provided with guides for visiting the outlying villages, tasting the various wines and enjoying the local cuisine.

Zola Predosa (Bologna)

B&B di Falzoni Dolci Claudia
Claudia Dolci
via San Pancrazio 10
40069 Zola Predosa (BO)
tel. and fax 051 756132
mob. 339 6660406
claudia.dol@libero.it
• **Associazione Turisti per Casa**
tel. 0532 705052 - 051 6288619
info@turistipercasa.it
www.turistipercasa.it
Closed: 15 to 30 September

Accommodation
Guestrooms: *2 (1 double bedroom and 1 quadruple room, also single occupancy, with private bath)*
Services & Amenities: *English and Spanish are spoken; rooms cleaned every three days; complimentary tourist information; baby-sitting service; kitchenette; bike rental; garden; smokers welcome; private parking*
Rates: *single €€, double €€, quadruple room €€€*
Credit cards: *not accepted*
Pets:

This B&B is located in a small duplex villa with garden and swimming pool. It's conveniently connected to Bologna by public transportation. The accommodation consists in two guestrooms with private bathroom, and one also has a kitchenette. The rich breakfast is either served in the family kitchen or in the guestroom. It can also be served in the garden. The host is always very happy to drive the guests to wherever they want to go. The hosts have two pets: a dog and a cat.

B&B Villa Leda e Romano
Romano and Leda Bisognin
via Montevecchio 16
località Ponte Ronca
40069 Zola Predosa (BO)
tel. and fax 051 757007
mob. 338 9660120
www.villaledaromano.it
• **Associazione Ospitalità Familiare**
tel. 051 379051
coruzzi@iol.it
http://users.iol.it/coruzzi/B&B
Open all year

Accommodation
Guestrooms: *3 double bedrooms, with private bath*
Services & Amenities: *French and English are spoken; rooms cleaned every day; tourist information; terrace; garden; private parking*
Rates: *€€ per person. Discounts for children*
Credit cards: *not accepted*
Pets:

This B&B with park and swimming pool is located in an elegant villa situated in the Zola Predosa hills and is an ideal place for enjoying a complete relaxation. The guestrooms have modern furniture and several period pieces. Breakfast is served on the terrace.

Anghiari (Arezzo)

Semoville
• ToscanaeOltre
tel. and fax 075 8559864
info@toscanaeoltre.com
www.toscanaeoltre.com
Open: Easter to November

This farmhouse, already farm holiday, is up on a hill surrounded by trees and fields. Guest accommodation includes four rooms, both furnished with early-20th-century and modern furniture. The atmosphere is both Spartan and quiet. The hostess teaches horseback-riding and is happy to accompany the guests on riding excursions. Breakfast, consisting of sweet items and cold cuts, is served in the large kitchen.

Accommodation
Guestrooms: *4 (2 double bedrooms and 2 doubles, with 2 private bath and 1 shared bath)*
Services & Amenities: *French spoken; rooms cleaned every 3 days; complimentary tourist information; horse-riding excursions; educational courses by request; garden; smokers welcome; private parking*
Rates: *double €€*
Credit cards: *not accepted*
Pets:

Arezzo

Il Paradisino
Augusto Casamassima
via delle Paniere 17
52100 Arezzo
fax 0575 295567, mob. 348 6412433
augie@libero.it
Open all year

This comfortable, independent, pied-à-terre is in Casa Vassari, which is located on an ancient street in the old center. It's not far from the Piero della Francesca and Cimabue masterpieces. The guests have comfortable rooms with Tuscan antique furniture and a few modern pieces, as well as a lounge. Breakfast consists of homemade sweet items and natural marmalades and can also be served in the veranda. Early reservations are recommended.

Accommodation
Guestrooms: *1 mini-apartment (4 beds); additional bed on request ♿*
Services & Amenities: *French and English are spoken; rooms cleaned every 3 days; tourist information*
Minimum stay: *2 nights*
Rates: *€ per person. Single use supplement €. Additional bed supplement €*
Credit cards: *not accepted*
Pets:

• **Bed & Breakfast Italia**
Code T49
località Rigutino
52100 Arezzo
tel. 06 6878618, fax 06 6878619
info@bbitalia.it
www.bbitalia.it
Closed: varies

ACCOMMODATION
Guestrooms: *2 doubles*
Services & Amenities: *French and English are spoken; rooms cleaned every 3 days; tourist information; baby-sitting service ; private parking*
Minimum stay: *2 nights*
Rates: €€
Credit cards: VISA MC *Bancomat*
Pets: not allowed

This B&B is an old, recently refurbished farmhouse with garden in the Arezzo area. It is a good starting point for visiting many well-known places in Tuscany. The rooms with sloping roof are spacious and complete with TV. In the summer months, breakfast is served on the terrace outside. On request, the host family arranges dinners with local produce, as well as providing a babysitting service.

• **Bed & Breakfast Italia**
Code T56
tel. 06 6878618, fax 06 6878619
info@bbitalia.it
www.bbitalia.it
Closed: varies

ACCOMMODATION
Guestrooms: *2 (1 single, 1 double)*
Services & Amenities: *English spoken; rooms cleaned every 3 days; complimentary tourist information; bike rental; smokers welcome; private parking*
Minimum stay: *2 nights*
Rates: €€
Credit cards: VISA MC *Bancomat*
Pets: not allowed

Large farmhouse used in the 11th century as a monastery to host pilgrims on their way to Arezzo, going along the Via Romea. The rooms are furnished with antiques and decorative beamed ceilings. The lady of the house will prepare a typical dinner on request. Guests can also use parking and bicycles. Arezzo, renowned for its goldsmith's art, boasts superb medieval monuments. The Fiera Antiquaria (antiques fair), held every first Saturday and Sunday in the month, is not to be missed.

AULLA (MASSA-CARRARA)

Villaggio L'Acchiappasogni
località Caprigliola
54011 Aulla (MS)
tel. 0187 414391, mob. 335 8016750
www.acchiappasogni.com
• **B&B in Italy. Ospitalità nelle case**
tel. and fax 0432 731854
bedbreakfastitaly@hotmail.com
www.bedandbreakfastfvg.com
Open all year

ACCOMMODATION
Guestrooms: *4 doubles, private bath*
Services & Amenities: *French and English are spoken; rooms cleaned every 3 days; tourist info; garden; smokers welcome; private parking*
Minimum stay: *1 week*
Rates: *double* €€€
Credit cards: *not accepted*
Pets: not allowed

This restructured, 17th-C farmhouse, surrounded by olive trees, has four rooms with personalized furnishings. Guests also have the use of a meditation room, which has carpets for practicing yoga, as well as numerous musical instruments. The hostess is an herbalist and only uses products that are organic and ecological.

Bagni San Filippo (Siena)

• **Bed & Breakfast Italia**
Code T18
tel. 06 6878618, fax 06 6878619
info@bbitalia.it
www.bbitalia.it
Closed: varies

Independent apartment, furnished in simple style. One of the rooms has an attic roof, adorned with a decorative beamed ceiling; each has TV, shower bathroom and kitchenette. Garden and private parking are available. It is situated in Val d'Orcia, on the slopes of Mt Amiata, at Bagni San Filippo. This village, 700 m asl, is known for its spa waters, in particular those of Fosso Bianco. A car is necessary.

Accommodation
Guestrooms: *2 doubles*
Services & Amenities: *English spoken; rooms cleaned every 3 days; complimentary tourist information; private parking*
Minimum stay: *2 nights*
Rates: *€€*
Credit cards: VISA MC *Bancomat*
Pets: no

Bagno a Ripoli (Florence)

Arriguccio B&B
via della Torricella 16, località Antella
50012 Bagno a Ripoli (FI)
tel. 055 620641, mob. 339 8315993
Open all year

The Arriguccio B&B is hosted in a late 19th-C, working-class house that is located in Antella, which is at an altitude of 300 m. The house has a large garden, and the two guestrooms – preferably available for couples – have period furniture and face the garden. One of the rooms has a bunk bed and an ensuite bathroom. The other has a double bed and a bath that's shared with the hosts. The continental breakfast is served in the family kitchen.

Accommodation
Guestrooms: *2 (1 double with private bath and 1 double bedroom with shared bath)* ♿
Services & Amenities: *English spoken; rooms cleaned every 3 days; tourist information; garden; smokers welcome; private parking*
Minimum stay: *2 nights*
Rates: *double €€€. Discounts for extended stays*
Credit cards: *not accepted*
Pets: no

Villa Peruzzi TCI 10%
via Peruzzi 152, località Antella
50012 Bagno a Ripoli (FI)
tel. and fax 055 621737
info@villaperuzzi.it
www.villaperuzzi.it
• **Associazione Koko Nor**
tel. 049 8643394, 338 3377912
fax 049 8643394
kokonor@bandb-veneto.it
www.bandb-veneto.it/kokonor
Open all year

Immersed in the fascinating Chianti hills, Villa Peruzzi offers a very romantic atmosphere. Over the years, several modifications have been made on the house, and the ancient tower now has two guestrooms, 1 double and 1 double bedroom. They are on different floors and each has a private bathroom, a living room and a library. One of the rooms faces the 15th-century cloister. The very carefully prepared breakfast, which includes both fresh products and cold cuts, is either served in the living room or in the lovely garden.

Accommodation
Guestrooms: *2 (1 double and 1 double bedroom, with private bath); additional bed on request*
Services & Amenities: *French, English and German are spoken; rooms cleaned every day; tourist information; Internet access; garden; smokers welcome; private parking*
Rates: *double €€€€.*
Additional bed supplement €€.
Discounts for children
Credit cards: *not accepted*
Pets: no

Barberino Val d'Elsa (Florence)

Il Paretaio
Cristina De Marchi
strada delle Ginestre 12
località San Filippo
50021 Barberino Val d'Elsa (FI)
tel. 055 8059218, mob. 338 7379626
fax 055 8059231
ilparetaio@tin.it
www.ilparetaio.it
Open all year

This B&B is located in an 18th-C working-class house situated in the heart of Chianti. There's a garden with a swimming pool, and the place is surrounded by vineyards, olive trees and a forest. The bright rooms have simple furnishings and 19th-C Tuscan furniture. The dining room with fireplace is where the buffet breakfast (with sweet items and cold cuts) is served and where guests can have dinner. There is also a riding school where instructors provide beginners and experts with instruction on dressage.

Accommodation
Guestrooms: *6 doubles, also single occupancy, with private bath*
Services & Amenities: *French and English are spoken; rooms cleaned every day; tourist info; horse-riding excursions; educational courses; garden; smokers welcome; parking*
Minimum stay: *1 week*
Rates: *single €€-€€€, double €€€-€€€€*
Credit cards: *not accepted*
Pets:

Borgo a Mozzano (Lucca)

La Casa Torre
via della Torre 1/g, località Diecimo
55023 Borgo a Mozzano (LU)
tel. and fax 0583 838680
mob. 338 2358327
danielabartolini@tin.it
Open all year

This B&B is hosted in a completely restored, early 13th-century tower situated in a little town called Garfagnana, which is just a few kilometers from Lucca. It has a romantic atmosphere, with some Provençal touches. Guest accommodation includes 2 double rooms with private bath and 5 menus to choose from for breakfast, which is either served in the large kitchen with fireplace, or in the garden.

Accommodation
Guestrooms: *2 double bedrooms, with private bath*
Services & Amenities: *English and French are spoken; rooms cleaned every 3 days; tourist info; bike rental; terrace; garden; smokers welcome*
Minimum stay: *2 nights*
Rates: *double €€€€. Children under 5 free*
Credit cards: *accepted*
Pets:

Borgo San Lorenzo (Florence)

Casa Palmira
Assunta Fiorini
via Mulinaccio 4/1, località Feriolo
50032 Borgo San Lorenzo (FI)
tel. and fax 055 8409749
palmira@cosmos.it
www.casapalmira.it
Closed: 10 January to 10 March

This B&B, located in an ancient, restructured hay barn that forms part of a medieval agricultural complex, has six guests room, one of which is a mansard. All the rooms have simple Tuscan furnishings and face the large garden. The continental breakfast, consisting of local products, is served in the large living room reserved for the guests. This room has a fireplace, a small library and a terrace. Moreover, they can also provide instruction on Tuscan cuisine and fresco painting. Transportation by a small private bus is also provided.

Accommodation
Guestrooms: *6 (3 doubles, 1 triple, private bath; 2 doubles, shared bath)*
Services & Amenities: *French and English are spoken; rooms cleaned every day; tourist information; dinner reservation; bike rental; educational courses by request; Internet access; garden; smokers welcome; private parking*
Minimum stay: *2 nights*
Rates: *double €€€, triple €€€€. Children under 3 free. Discounts for extended stays*
Credit cards: *not accepted*
Pets:

• **Bed & Breakfast Italia**
Code T54
tel. 06 6878618, fax 06 6878619
info@bbitalia.it
www.bbitalia.it
Closed: varies

The B&B is located in a large country-house; the accommodation consists in two double rooms, one single room and two private bathrooms with shower. It also includes a sitting room with fireplace and a kitchenette. Furnishings are simple and comfortable. In summer, the rich breakfast is served in the garden, where it is also possible to use the barbecue

ACCOMMODATION
Guestrooms: *3 (1 single, 2 doubles)*
Services & Amenities: *French, English and German are spoken; rooms cleaned every 3 days; tourist info*
Minimum stay: *2 nights*
Rates: €€
Credit cards: VISA MC *Bancomat*
Pets: not allowed

BUGGIANO (PISTOIA)

• **Bed & Breakfast Italia**
Code T72
tel. 06 6878618, fax 06 6878619
info@bbitalia.it
www.bbitalia.it
Closed: varies

ACCOMMODATION
Guestrooms: *5 doubles*
Services & Amenities: *French and English are spoken; rooms cleaned every 3 days; tourist information; baby-sitting service; bike rental*
Minimum stay: *2 nights*
Rates: €€
Credit cards: VISA MC *Bancomat*
Pets: not allowed

The B&B is a sixteenth-century restored house, set in a small medieval hamlet situated between Lucca and Pistoia. The five rooms are adorned with eighteenth-century frescoes and antiques, and offer a view of the hamlet and surrounding hills. Each room has its own private bathroom with shower. The railway station of Montecatini Terme is 4 km away. During summer, guests can use the outside kitchen and the owners will prepare meals on request.

CALENZANO (FLORENCE)

• **Bed & Breakfast Italia**
Code T4
tel. 06 6878618, fax 06 6878619
info@bbitalia.it
www.bbitalia.it
Closed: varies

The house is situated in a tiny medieval hamlet, nestling in a green area, 200 m above sea level. The villa is on a completely refurbished country estate, furnished with antiques in a simple, comfortable style. The two bedrooms have a private bathroom. The surrounding garden is equipped with a gazebo, deckchairs and sun loungers. On request, the owners provide a car for guests wishing to tour the surrounding area or Florence (20 km away).

ACCOMMODATION
Guestrooms: *2 (1 single, 1 double)*
Services & Amenities: *English spoken; rooms cleaned every 3 days; complimentary tourist information; private parking*
Minimum stay: *2 nights*
Rates: €€
Credit cards: VISA MC *Bancomat*
Pets: not allowed

Camaiore (Lucca)

Locanda al Colle
Massimo Lucchesi
località Santa Lucia 103
55041 Camaiore (LU)
tel. 0584 915195, fax 0584 917053
locandaalcolle@interfree.it
www.locandaalcolle.it
Open: Easter holidays to October

This B&B, with its nice, relaxing atmosphere, is hosted in a recently-restored farmhouse located between Lucca and the sea. The accommodation offers five large rooms all with its own particular furnishings with furniture ranging from period to modern. The very nice and rich Italian breakfast is either served in the garden, under the pergola, or in the kitchen. Guests can avail themselves of a massage service on request.

Accommodation
Guestrooms: *5 double bedrooms, also single occupancy, with private bath; additional bed on request*
Services & Amenities: *French, English, Spanish and Portuguese are spoken; rooms cleaned every day; complimentary tourist information; bike rental; Internet access; garden; smokers welcome; private parking*
Rates: *single €€€€, double €€€€. Additional bed supplement €€*
Credit cards: VISA MC *Bancomat*
Pets:

• Bed & Breakfast Italia
Code T57
tel. 06 6878618, fax 06 6878619
info@bbitalia.it
www.bbitalia.it
Closed: varies

Accommodation
Guestrooms: *4 (2 doubles, 2 triple)* ♿
Services & Amenities: *English spoken; rooms cleaned every 3 days; tourist info; smokers welcome; parking*
Minimum stay: *2 nights*
Rates: *€€*
Credit cards: VISA MC *Bancomat*
Pets:

This 18th-C farmhouse has been completely restored preserving the original style. There are 4 rooms, each with private bathroom with shower, featuring four-poster beds, antiques and pale colors. Guests can also enjoy swimming pool, surrounding park, library and private parking. Attached to the farm is a restaurant where to taste the local cuisine.

Villa La Bianca
Sandro and Simona Gurioli
via di Lombrici 41/45
località Lombrici
55041 Camaiore (LU)
tel. 0584 984657, fax 0584 985720
info@villalabianca.com
www.villalabianca.com
Closed: 6 January to mid-February

This 18th-C manor house, now restored to its original splendor, is located out in the country, just a few kilometers from Viareggio. Its already impressive atmosphere is further heightened by its classic, refined furnishings, which include large canopy beds. Guests have the use of a leisure room with a library, a breakfast room with a large fireplace, a swimming pool, that's surrounded by a large lawn, and a solarium. The buffet breakfast can also be served in the park. The manor house also has interesting wine and oil tasting rooms.

Accommodation
Guestrooms: *6 double bedrooms, private bath; additional bed on request* ♿
Services & Amenities: *English and Spanish are spoken; rooms cleaned every 3 days; tourist info; dinner reservation; educational courses by request; Internet access; garden; smokers welcome; private parking*
Minimum stay: *2 nights*
Rates: *double €€€€. Additional bed supplement €€€*
Credit cards: VISA MC *Bancomat*
Pets:

Capalbio (Grosseto)

• **Bed & Breakfast Italia**
Code T6
tel. 06 6878618, fax 06 6878619
info@bbitalia.it
www.bbitalia.it

Closed: varies

A small house in an ancient hamlet fortified by a double circle of 15th-century walls. The rooms have a large balcony and are furnished in a rustic style with exposed beams and terracotta floors. Capalbio, a renowned resort that conserves in its typically medieval center the St. Nicholas' parish church, built between the 12th and 13th centuries and restored in the 15th century. Inside, with its apsidal vault, it is adorned with finely sculptured Romanesque capitals and frescoes from the schools of Siena and Umbria. Montalto di Castro, Orbetello, the Argentario coast and Saturnia spa are within easy reach.

Accommodation
Guestrooms: *3 doubles*
Services & Amenities: *French and English are spoken; rooms cleaned every 3 days; tourist info; terrace*
Minimum stay: *2 nights*
Rates: €€
Credit cards: VISA MC *Bancomat*
Pets: no

• **Bed & Breakfast Italia**
Code T35
tel. 06 6878618, fax 06 6878619
info@bbitalia.it
www.bbitalia.it

Closed: varies

Accommodation
Guestrooms: *2 (1 double bedroom and 1 double)*
Services & Amenities: *English spoken; rooms cleaned every 3 days; tourist info; bike rental; private parking*
Minimum stay: *4 nights*
Rates: €€
Credit cards: VISA MC *Bancomat*
Pets: no

The whole apartment is at the disposal of guests, nestling in the WWF nature park. It includes two bedrooms, one with a double bed and one with bunk beds, bathroom with shower, sitting room with TV and fireplace. Guests have use of the kitchen, a barbecue, bicycles, and can enjoy a beautiful communal swimming pool. It is located at Marina di Capalbio, 2 km from the center. Minimum stay four nights.

Carrara

Mauro e Luisa B&B
Mauro and Luisa Gregori
via Cavaiola 29, località Avenza
54033 Carrara (MS)
tel. 0585 55975
mob. 338 8635953
• **Bed and Breakfast Liguria**
tel. and fax 010 2461918
bbliguria@hotmail.com

Closed: October and November

The hosts of this B&B, just a few kilometers from the celebrated marble quarry, have reserved a small cottage for their guests. It has a furnished kitchen, and a small living room with a fireplace. The rich breakfast consists of typical local products, including cold cuts, and is served either in the large family kitchen or in the garden. Guests have the use of bicycles for taking rides around in the area.

Accommodation
Guestrooms: *2 (1 double bedroom and 1 double, with private bath); additional bed on request* ♿
Services & Amenities: *English spoken; rooms cleaned every 3 days; tourist information; kitchen use by request; lunch & dinner reservations; Internet access; garden; smokers welcome; private parking*
Rates: *double* €€€*. Additional bed supplement* €*. Discounts for children*
Credit cards: *not accepted*
Pets: yes

Casale Marittimo (Pisa)

• **Bed & Breakfast Italia**
Code T7
tel. 06 6878618, fax 06 6878619
info@bbitalia.it
www.bbitalia.it
Closed: varies

Accommodation
Guestrooms: *1 double bedroom*
Services & Amenities: *French spoken; rooms cleaned every 3 days; complimentary tourist information; terrace; private parking*
Minimum stay: *2 nights*
Rates: €€
Credit cards: VISA MC *Bancomat*
Pets:

A recently built cottage, furnished in simple style. It is in a scenic position with a surrounding garden offering a view of the sea. Guests have a double room with private bathroom, a large balcony and independent entrance. Casale Marittimo is a charming hamlet, 10 km from the sea. Its Etruscan origins are still visible thanks to archaeological finds, including a tomb dating from the 6th century BC.

Cercina (Florence)

• **Bed & Breakfast Italia** TCI 10%
Code T50
tel. 06 6878618, fax 06 6878619
info@bbitalia.it
www.bbitalia.it
Closed: varies

Accommodation
Guestrooms: *2 doubles*
Services & Amenities: *French and English are spoken; rooms cleaned every 3 days; complimentary tourist information; bike rental; terrace; smokers welcome; private parking*
Minimum stay: *2 nights*
Rates: €€
Credit cards: VISA MC *Bancomat*
Pets:

Independent apartment, in a farmhouse with stone finishes and exposed beams, 20 min from Florence. It comprises two large comfortable double rooms with independent entrance. The private bathroom has a shower. The large balcony offers a panoramic view of Florence and the surrounding hills. Private car park and bicycles available.

Certaldo (Florence)

• **Bed & Breakfast Italia**
Code T17
tel. 06 6878618, fax 06 6878619
info@bbitalia.it
www.bbitalia.it
Closed: varies

Comfortable attic with sloping roof, furnished in a simple, functional style and including air conditioning, TV, and a balcony with a view of the village 1 km away. The room has a bathroom with shower and an independent entrance. The garden and private parking are at the guests' disposal. In July, a festival called "la Mercanzia" revives a traditional medieval market where you can buy local produce and taste old flavors. Other nearby areas of interest are Poggibonsi, Volterra and San Gimignano.

Accommodation
Guestrooms: *1 double*
Services & Amenities: *French and English are spoken; rooms cleaned every 3 days; complimentary tourist information; terrace; private parking*
Minimum stay: *2 nights*
Rates: €€
Credit cards: VISA MC *Bancomat*
Pets:

• **Bed & Breakfast Italia**
Code T46
tel. 06 6878618, fax 06 6878619
info@bbitalia.it
www.bbitalia.it
Closed: varies

A country-house, near Certaldo, an old medieval hamlet. With its country-style, comfortable and warm furnishings, it has two double rooms and a triple with single beds; each room has ensuite bathroom with shower.

ACCOMMODATION
Guestrooms: *3 (2 double bedrooms and 1 triple room)*
Services & Amenities: *English, German and Spanish spoken; rooms cleaned every 3 days; tourist info; parking*
Minimum stay: *2 nights*
Rates: €€
Credit cards: VISA MC *Bancomat*
Pets:

The spacious kitchen, stocked with breakfast provisions, is at the guests' disposal. Private parking is available for the guests.

CHIUSI (SIENA)

• **Bed & Breakfast Italia** TCI 10%
Code T40
tel. 06 6878618, fax 06 6878619
info@bbitalia.it
www.bbitalia.it
Closed: varies

ACCOMMODATION
Guestrooms: *2 (1 double and 1 triple)*
Services & Amenities: *rooms cleaned every 3 days; complimentary tourist information; private parking*
Minimum stay: *2 nights*
Rates: €€
Credit cards: VISA MC *Bancomat*
Pets:

Country-house, well appointed with comfortable furnishings in a rustic and modern style, surrounded by a large garden. It has two rooms, both with TV. The atmosphere is warm and friendly: the hostess serves breakfast with home-made cakes and sweets. The Etruscan area includes well-known locations such as Montepulciano, Cortona and Siena.

CORTONA (AREZZO)

Casa Bellavista B&B TCI 10%
Simonetta Demarchi
località Creti C.S. 40
52044 Cortona (AR)
tel. 0575 610311
info@casabellavista.it
www.casabellavista.it
• **Friendly Home-Gli Amici del B&B**
tel. 02 860147,
fax 02 875860
friendlymilano@dada.it
tel. and fax 011 9536376
fhrivoli@virgilio.it
• **ToscanaeOltre**
tel. and fax 075 8559864
info@toscanaeoltre.com
www.toscanaeoltre.com
Closed: January and February

This B&B is hosted in a restructured, 19th-century farmhouse located in the commune of Cortona. The house is surrounded by a large garden that has children's playground equipment, and olive trees (whose oil is used in making oil that the guests can taste and buy if desired). Breakfast, which includes a variety of local cold cuts, cheeses, cakes and natural marmalades, is served in the family dining room.

ACCOMMODATION
Guestrooms: *3 double bedrooms, also single occupancy, private bath*
Services & Amenities: *English spoken; rooms cleaned every day; tourist information; dinner reservation; bike rental; educational courses by request; garden; smokers welcome; private parking*
Rates: *single and double* €€€€.
Children under 2 free.
Discounts for extended stays
Credit cards: VISA MC *Bancomat*
Pets:

Il Borgo
via di Manzano 1001
località Camucia
52044 Cortona (AR)
tel. and fax 0575 601165
mob. 347 4698599
ilborgo@technet.it
www.ilborgo.it
Open all year

This B&B, which is in an ancient farmhouse surrounded by vegetation, offers four apartments with an independent entrance and a small private garden. Each apartment has a kitchen and a small living room with TV. All the rooms, which have period furniture, face the very nice internal courtyard. The continental breakfast, which also includes products from the adjoining farm, can either be served or consumed autonomously. On request, mountain-bike excursions can be organized, using bikes furnished by the hosts.

ACCOMMODATION
Guestrooms: *4 suites (2 or 4 beds)*
Services & Amenities: *French and English are spoken; rooms cleaned every 3 days; complimentary tourist information; kitchen use by request; kitchenette; bike rental; garden; smokers welcome; private parking*
Minimum stay: *2 nights*
Rates: *€€ per person. Discounts for extended stays*
Credit cards: *not accepted*
Pets:

La Badia di San Biagio
Rosalba Quaresima
località Salcotto 784
52044 Cortona (AR)
tel. 0575 630722, mob. 368 7225532
labadiadisanbiagio@hotmail.com
Closed: November and January

The restored, 17th-century Badia di San Biagio is an ancient building constructed of stone. Both a residence and a B&B, it's surrounded by olive trees, has a large garden, and provides a nice view of the church of Calcinaio. The three independent quarters for the guests have their own outdoor space, as well as a kitchen facility and traditional Tuscan period furniture. Breakfast consists of natural products and, if desired, also cold cuts and cheeses. Guests also have the use of a nice swimming pool.

ACCOMMODATION
Guestrooms: *3 mini-apartments (2 beds each); additional bed on request*
Services & Amenities: *English spoken; rooms cleaned every 3 days; complimentary tourist information; kitchen use by request; garden; smokers welcome; private parking*
Minimum stay: *in summer, 1 week*
Rates: *€€€€.*
Credit cards: *not accepted*
Pets:

EMPOLI (FLORENCE)

• Bed & Breakfast Italia

Code T59
tel. 06 6878618, fax 06 6878619
info@bbitalia.it, www.bbitalia.it
Closed: varies

Two-story country villa located at the entrance to the town, furnished with antiques and surrounded by a garden where breakfast is served. Three double rooms, one triple, two bathrooms with shower and private parking are available. Empoli, a town of Roman origin, featuring imposing ruins dating from imperial Rome, is 25 km from Florence and San Gimignano and 45 km from Lucca and Pisa.

ACCOMMODATION
Guestrooms: *4 (3 doubles, 1 triple)*
Services & Amenities: *French, English and Spanish are spoken; rooms cleaned every 3 days; tourist information; smokers welcome; private parking*
Minimum stay: *2 nights*
Rates: *€€*
Credit cards: VISA MC *Bancomat*
Pets:

Fiesole (Florence)

• **Bed & Breakfast Italia**
Code T3
tel. 06 6878618, fax 06 6878619
info@bbitalia.it, www.bbitalia.it
Closed: varies

Third floor apartment in a building in the Fiesole hills, 8 km from the center of Florence. It is furnished in a modern, simple style. The single room is large and bright, with functional furnishings. The family welcomes guests in an informal and homely atmosphere. The B&B has private parking for guests and a shared garden. The old town center can be reached in 20 minutes by bus. The nearest bus stop is 150 meters away.

Accommodation
Guestrooms: *1 single*
Services & Amenities: *French and English are spoken; rooms cleaned every 3 days; complimentary tourist information; private parking*
Minimum stay: *2 nights*
Rates: *€€*
Credit cards: VISA MC *Bancomat*
Pets:

Florence

Borgo Pinti
Borgo Pinti 31
50121 Florence
tel. 055 2480056, fax 055 2381260
beb@mail.cosmos.it
www.bnb.it/web
• **Bed & Breakfast Italia**
tel. 06 6878618, fax 06 6878619
info@bbitalia.it
www.bbitalia.it
Open all year

This B&B is located on the top floor of a historical, 17th-century building situated in the old center of Florence. All four, large, bright, guestrooms – each of which has a different color (pink, white, blue and light blue) – face the internal garden and have both classic and period furnishings. The hosts prefer women guests and would rather they didn't smoke. The American breakfast is served in a reserved, fully-equipped kitchen.

Accommodation
Guestrooms: *4 (1 single, 3 doubles)*
Services & Amenities: *French and English are spoken; rooms cleaned every day; tourist information*
Minimum stay: *2 nights*
Rates: *single €€, double €€€.*
Discounts for children -20%.
Discounts for extended stays
Credit cards: *accepted*
Pets:

Casa Pucci
Tamara Pucci
via Santa Monaca 8
50124 Florence
tel. & fax 055 216560, mob. 347 8214911
capucci@tin.it
www.primitaly.it
Open all year

This B&B, with its classic style, is in an ancient, restored 15th-century convent located just a short walk from Palazzo Pitti. The guests' accommodation consists in two large rooms (one single and one double) with private bathroom; the tablecloths have high-quality Tuscan linen, personally selected by the hostess. The rich Italian breakfast, which also includes typical cheeses, is either served in the rooms or on the patio.

Accommodation
Guestrooms: *2 (1 single and 1 double bedroom, with private bath); additional bed on request*
Services & Amenities: *French and English are spoken; rooms cleaned every 3 days; complimentary tourist information; Internet access; garden; smokers welcome*
Rates: *single €€€, double €€€€.*
Additional bed supplement €.
Children under 3 free
Credit cards: *accepted*
Pets:

Quartopiano B&B

Paolo Facetti
via Panicale 3
50123 Florence
tel. 055 287975, mob. 329 3149042
quartopiano@altavista.it
www.quartopiano.com
Open all year

The pleasant characteristic of this B&B, located in the center of Florence, is its large panoramic terrace that provides a view of the old San Lorenzo market. On sunny days, breakfast is served on this terrace. The two large

guestrooms are decorated in warm colors and have classic furnishings. The hostess loves to cook and very often makes traditional snacks for herself and her friends. Bicycles are also available.

Accommodation
Guestrooms: *2 double bedrooms, also single occupancy, private bath*
Services & Amenities: *English, German and Spanish are spoken; rooms cleaned every 3 days; complimentary tourist information; bike rental; terrace; air conditioning; Internet access; smokers welcome*
Minimum stay: *2 nights*
Rates: *single €€€, double €€€€. Children under 6 free*
Credit cards: *not accepted*
Pets:

Relais Grand Tour

Giuseppe De Flaviis
via Santa Reparata 21
50129 Florence
tel. 055 283955, fax 055 2676505
cgucciarelli@lycos.com
Closed: mid-November to mid-December, mid-January to mid-February and August

This very nice, early 20th-C building, located in the old center, once also had a small private theater. Today, it has a comfortable B&B that has a pleasant atmosphere. The guestrooms have a private bath and different color and character. This, in addition to the courteous, helpful hosts, makes this an ideal place to stay for a few restful days, rather than making a rushed visit of the Tuscan capital. Breakfast is served in the guestrooms. Smokers welcome.

Accommodation
Guestrooms: *3 double bedrooms*
Services & Amenities: *French and English are spoken; rooms cleaned every 3 days; tourist information*
Minimum stay: *3 nights*
Rates: *double €€€€*
Credit cards: *not accepted*
Pets:

Residenza Giulia

Maria Giovanna Sicari
via Porte Nuove 19
50144 Florence
tel. 055 321646, fax 055 3245149
mariella@residenzagiulia.com
www.residenzagiulia.com
Open all year

Accommodation
Guestrooms: *5 (3 doubles, also single occupancy, and 2 triple rooms, with private bath)*
Services & Amenities: *English spoken; rooms cleaned every day; complimentary tourist information; bike rental; terrace; smokers welcome*
Minimum stay: *2 nights*
Rates: *double €€€, triple €€€€. Children under 3 free. Discounts for extended stays*
Credit cards: *accepted*
Pets:

This spacious B&B, located in the center of Florence, is hosted on the 4th floor of a building that dates from the '40s. Each room has a terrace and a splendid view of the hills. Guests have use of a mini-bar and a small sitting room that

has a small library. The Italian breakfast is served in the rooms. The hostess has made arrangements whereby guests can have discounts when using the gym and sauna (located in the same building) and when renting bicycles or scooters.

Soggiorno Michelangelo 
• Latte e Miele
tel. and fax 06 3211783
info@sleepinitaly.com
www.sleepinitaly.com
Open all year

Accommodation
Guestrooms: *6 doubles, also single occupancy, private bath; additional bed on request*
Services & Amenities: *French, English and Spanish are spoken; rooms cleaned every day; tourist information; air conditioning; Internet access; smokers welcome*
Rates: *single €€€, double €€€€. Additional bed supplement €. Discounts for children*
Credit cards: VISA MC
Pets: no

This B&B has various single and double rooms, furnished in classic style, with wrought-iron beds, a telephone, TV, air conditioning and exclusive bathrooms. The B&B is located in a building that dates from the mid 19th-century. It's situated on a quiet street near Piazza della Libertà and is just 1 kilometer from Piazza della Signoria. The rich buffet breakfast, which also includes natural sweet items, is served in the dining room. Valuables can be stored in a safe.

Via Il Prato
• Latte e Miele
tel. and fax 06 3211783
info@sleepinitaly.com
www.sleepinitaly.com
Closed: August and Christmas holidays

Accommodation
Guestrooms: *1 double bedroom, also single occupancy, with private bath; additional bed on request*
Services & Amenities: *English spoken; rooms cleaned every day; tourist information; air conditioning; Internet access; smokers welcome*
Rates: *single €€€, double €€€€. Additional bed supplement €. Discounts for children*
Credit cards: *not accepted*
Pets: no

This B&B, which is hosted in a three-story building and is just a 10 minute walk from the Cathedral and Piazza della Signoria, is right across the street from the prestigious Hotel Villa Medici. The guests' large, comfortable, bright, air-conditioned double room has a private bathroom, a telephone, a minibar and a safe. Its two windows open onto the square. The breakfast is the continental type.

• Bed & Breakfast Italia
Code F102
via Jacopo Nardi
tel. 06 6878618, fax 06 6878619
info@bbitalia.it
www.bbitalia.it
Closed: varies

Accommodation
Guestrooms: *2 (1 single, 1 double)*
Services & Amenities: *English spoken; rooms cleaned every 3 days; complimentary tourist information; private parking*
Minimum stay: *2 nights*
Rates: *€€*
Credit cards: VISA MC *Bancomat*
Pets: allowed

This B&B is located in a fairly central area, on the second floor of an elegant building. It is run with discretion and warmth by a nice, elderly landlady. The house features traditional furnishings and antiques. It has two bedrooms: a double with twin beds and a single. The guests' private bathroom has a tub. Breakfast is served in the lounge. The city's old center can be easily reached in 20 minutes by public transport.

• Bed & Breakfast Italia
Code F111
via Cennini
tel. 06 6878618, fax 06 6878619
info@bbitalia.it
www.bbitalia.it
Closed: varies

This independent apartment is situated in the center of town, on the third floor of an old building with no elevator. The accommodation offers comfortable furnishings and two double rooms, a kitchen and a bathroom with a shower. A small balcony overlooks a lane. The breakfast items are left in the fridge so that guests are free to enjoy it at their leisure. The railway station is just 50 m away and the bus stop is at 30 m. A pay car park is 100 m from the house.

Accommodation
Guestrooms: *2 doubles*
Services & Amenities: *French spoken; rooms cleaned every 3 days; complimentary tourist information*
Minimum stay: *2 nights*
Rates: €€
Credit cards: VISA MC *Bancomat*
Pets: no

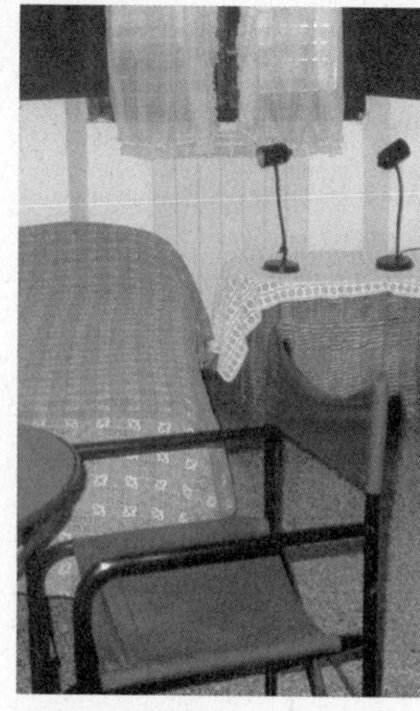

• Bed & Breakfast Italia
Code F112
via Augusto Novelli
tel. 06 6878618, fax 06 6878619
info@bbitalia.it
www.bbitalia.it
Closed: varies

This B&B is 20 min from the center of town, in a quiet area well served by public transportation. The room with two single beds is furnished in a simple modern style. The private bathroom has a shower. Breakfast is served in the lounge, where guests can also use the TV and stereo. The bus stops to and from the Duomo and Piazza della Signoria are 5 min away.

Accommodation
Guestrooms: *1 double*
Services & Amenities: *French and English are spoken; rooms cleaned every 3 days; complimentary tourist information; private parking*
Minimum stay: *2 nights*
Rates: €€
Credit cards: VISA MC *Bancomat*
Pets: no

• Bed & Breakfast Italia
Code F115
via Fossombroni
tel. 06 6878618, fax 06 6878619
info@bbitalia.it
www.bbitalia.it
Closed: varies

This B&B is just outside the old center's ancient walls within 10 min walking distance of Piazza della Signoria. It is situated on the second floor of an old building and is furnished with fine antiques. Three double rooms, two with double beds and one with single beds, are available. Two private bathrooms are shared by the three rooms. Breakfast is served by the lady of the house in the dining room.

Accommodation
Guestrooms: *3 (2 double bedrooms and 1 double)*
Services & Amenities: *French and English are spoken; rooms cleaned every 3 days; tourist information*
Minimum stay: *2 nights*
Rates: €€
Credit cards: VISA MC *Bancomat*
Pets: no

• **Bed & Breakfast Italia**
Code F212
via Caterina Ferrucci
tel. 06 6878618, fax 06 6878619
info@bbitalia.it
www.bbitalia.it
Closed: varies

The B&B is an apartment situated on the 1st floor of a building in a peaceful area. It is a nice home, light and tastefully furnished. The double bedroom with TV is furnished in a cheerful, fresh style, which reflects the landlady's character. A private bathroom with shower/tub.

Breakfast is served in the lounge. Private parking is available in the front courtyard. The bus that stops 50 m from the house takes 15 min to reach the center.

ACCOMMODATION
Guestrooms: *1 double*
Services & Amenities: *rooms cleaned every 3 days; tourist information*
Minimum stay: *2 nights*
Rates: €€
Credit cards: VISA MC *Bancomat*
Pets: not allowed

• **Bed & Breakfast Italia**
Code F214
via Bolognese
tel. 06 6878618, fax 06 6878619
info@bbitalia.it
www.bbitalia.it
Closed: varies

A two-story villa surrounded by a large park overlooking the city. It is located on an elegant street only 10 minutes from the center. Guestrooms are on the first floor: they are classically furnished with antiques and decorated in warm colors, creating a cozy atmosphere.

Breakfast is served in the large lounge or on the typical nineteenth-century patio in good weather. Bus stops to the center are 5 minutes away.

ACCOMMODATION
Guestrooms: *2 (1 double, 1 triple)*
Services & Amenities: *French and English are spoken; rooms cleaned every 3 days; complimentary tourist information; private parking*
Minimum stay: *2 nights*
Rates: €€
Credit cards: VISA MC *Bancomat*
Pets: not allowed

• **Bed & Breakfast Italia**
Code F218
borgo Santi Apostoli
tel. 06 6878618, fax 06 6878619
info@bbitalia.it, www.bbitalia.it
Closed: varies

It is an elegant apartment on the first floor of an old building with elevator in the center of Florence, 10 m from Ponte Vecchio. Four double-bedded rooms, one triple and one single are available. Each room has a private bathroom with shower. Charming accommodation that features classical furnishings with antiques, matching curtains and bedspreads. The rich breakfast is served in the rooms. The bus stops are 200 m away.

ACCOMMODATION
Guestrooms: *6 (1 single, 4 double bedrooms and 1 triple room)* ♿
Services & Amenities: *rooms cleaned every 3 days; complimentary tourist information; baby-sitting service; air conditioning; Internet access; smokers welcome*
Minimum stay: *2 nights*
Rates: €€
Credit cards: VISA MC *Bancomat*
Pets: not allowed

• **Bed & Breakfast Italia**
Code F219
via Solferino
tel. 06 6878618, fax 06 6878619
info@bbitalia.it
www.bbitalia.it
Closed: varies

This fifth-floor apartment in an elegant building with elevator is located 200 m from Piazza del Duomo and 300 m from the railway station. The guests' accommodation offers two single rooms and a double room, sharing a bathroom with shower. They are classically furnished with antiques. All the rooms face a large balcony overlooking the Cathedral's dome. The rich breakfast is served by the landlady in the family kitchen.

Accommodation
Guestrooms: *3 (2 singles, 1 double)*
Services & Amenities: *rooms cleaned every 3 days; tourist information*
Minimum stay: *2 nights*
Rates: €€
Credit cards: VISA MC *Bancomat*
Pets: no

• **Bed & Breakfast Italia**
Code F223
via Panzan
50100 Florence
tel. 06 6878618, fax 06 6878619
info@bbitalia.it
www.bbitalia.it
Closed: varies

100 meters from Piazza del Duomo, this B&B is on the third floor of an old building without elevator. The accommodation consists in a double room with simple, essential and functional furnishings, and a shared bathroom. The breakfast is offered at the nearby coffee shop. Guests can enjoy a nice view of the Duomo (one of the largest cathedrals in the Christian world) from the rooftop terrace.

Accommodation
Guestrooms: *1 double*
Services & Amenities: *French, English and German are spoken; rooms cleaned every 3 days; tourist information*
Minimum stay: *2 nights*
Rates: €
Credit cards: VISA MC *Bancomat*
Pets: no

• **Bed & Breakfast Italia**
Code F222
via Borgo Santi Apostoli
tel. 06 6878618, fax 06 6878619
info@bbitalia.it
www.bbitalia.it
Closed: varies

This fine and elegant first-floor apartment in an old building with elevator is located in the center of Florence. The accommodation consists in six double rooms: each room has a private bathroom with shower, air conditioning and telephone. This charming accommodation is classically furnished with antiques, matching curtains and bedspreads. Continental breakfast is served in the rooms. The bus stop is 200 meters away.

Accommodation
Guestrooms: *6 doubles* ♿
Services & Amenities: *French, English and Spanish are spoken; rooms cleaned every 3 days; tourist information; air conditioning; smokers welcome*
Minimum stay: *2 nights*
Rates: €€€
Credit cards: VISA MC *Bancomat*
Pets: no

• Bed & Breakfast Italia
Code F225
via San Leonardo
tel. 06 6878618, fax 06 6878619
info@bbitalia.it
www.bbitalia.it
Closed: varies

This B&B is hosted in an old 17th-century building on the Poggio Imperiale estate, located in a prestigious area called Viale dei Colli, near Piazza Michelangelo. The guests' accommodation consists in a comfortable double room with a pleasant little terrace. The antique furniture gives the house a warm and traditional atmosphere. In spring and summer, the rich breakfast is served on the "veranda". The bus stop is just 100 m away, with 10-minute links to the center.

ACCOMMODATION
Guestrooms: *1 double bedroom*
Services & Amenities: *English spoken; rooms cleaned every 3 days; tourist info; terrace; private parking*
Minimum stay: *2 nights*
Rates: €€
Credit cards: VISA MC *Bancomat*
Pets: 🐕

• Bed & Breakfast Italia
Code T66
località Trespiano
tel. 06 6878618, fax 06 6878619
info@bbitalia.it
www.bbitalia.it
Closed: varies

ACCOMMODATION
Guestrooms: *2 doubles*
Services & Amenities: *French and English are spoken; rooms cleaned every 3 days; tourist information; smokers welcome; private parking*
Minimum stay: *2 nights*
Rates: €€
Credit cards: VISA MC *Bancomat*
Pets: 🚫🐕

First-floor in an excellently refurbished stone farmhouse, 500 m asl, in a scenic position, this independent apartment consists in two double rooms and a private bathroom. Its simple and comfortable furnishings, with colored fittings and furniture in different styles, make the environment very original. Attached to the house is also a perfectly tended garden, offering a scenic view of the hills around Florence.

• Bed & Breakfast Italia TCI 10%
Code T67
via di Baroncelli
tel. 06 6878618, fax 06 6878619
info@bbitalia.it
www.bbitalia.it
Closed: varies

Restored villa lying on the hills around Florence, with a scenic view. The rooms have TV and a large balcony. The bathroom has a Jacuzzi tub. Breakfast can be served under parasols in the courtyard. The hosts will prepare delicious dishes for lunch on request. At weekends, organized guided horse-riding excursions are available. The bus stop for Florence is within walking distance. The owners will take guests to Florence free of charge on request.

ACCOMMODATION
Guestrooms: *2 (1 double, 1 triple)*
Services & Amenities: *French, English and German are spoken; rooms cleaned every 3 days; tourist info; terrace; smokers welcome; parking*
Minimum stay: *2 nights*
Rates: €€
Credit cards: VISA MC *Bancomat*
Pets: 🐕

Fosdinovo (Massa-Carrara)

Fosdinovo bed & breakfast
Simona Mulazzani
via Monte Carboli 12
54035 Fosdinovo (MS)
tel. 02 66203369, mob. 328 8962693
simogiu@libero.it
Closed: November

This B&B is located in a villa that dates from the '60s. Situated on a hill at an altitude of 575 meters, the villa is surrounded by large garden with a small orchard and vegetable garden. The accommodation offers two rooms with double beds and private bathroom, all with simple furnishings including a few period pieces. The Italian breakfast, enriched with local products, is either served in the living room, which has a fireplace, on the spacious panoramic terrace, or in the garden.

Accommodation
Guestrooms: *2 doubles, also single occupancy, with private bath; additional bed on request*
Services & Amenities: *French and English are spoken; rooms cleaned every day; tourist info; terrace; garden; smokers welcome; parking*
Rates: *single €€, double €€€. Additional bed supplement €. Children under 2 free. Discounts for extended stays and for cyclists*
Credit cards: *not accepted*
Pets: not allowed

Gavorrano (Grosseto)

• Bed & Breakfast Italia
Code T75
località Giuncarico
tel. 06 6878618, fax 06 6878619
info@bbitalia.it
www.bbitalia.it
Closed: varies

The apartment is located at Giuncarico, 20 km from Castiglione della Pescaia and 20 km from Follonica. The lady of the house offers guests a double room with double bed, furnished with classical antiques. Breakfast is usually served in the lounge. The bathroom with shower is shared with the owners. The village center is 800 m away; the railway station is 15 km away.

Accommodation
Guestrooms: *2 double bedrooms*
Services & Amenities: *French and English are spoken; rooms cleaned every 3 days; complimentary tourist information; smokers welcome*
Minimum stay: *2 nights*
Rates: *€*
Credit cards: VISA MC *Bancomat*
Pets: not allowed

Greve in Chianti (Florence)

La Cipressa Country Life in Chianti
• B&B Liguria e... non solo
tel. 010 3291204, mob. 347 26092
fax 010 3299774
oltrelazzurro@libero.it
www.bbitalia.net
Open all year

Accommodation
Guestrooms: *5 (3 double bedrooms, with private bath and 2 doubles, with shared bath); additional bed on request*
Services & Amenities: *English spoken; rooms cleaned every day; tourist information; garden; smokers welcome; private parking*
Minimum stay: *3 nights*
Rates: *double €€€€. Additional bed supplement €*
Credit cards: *not accepted*
Pets: not allowed

This restructured farmhouse, offers five panoramic rooms furnished in the classic style with 19th-C Tuscan furniture. Three of the rooms have double beds, an independent entrance and a private bath, while the other two, which also have double beds, are communicating rooms and share the same bathroom. Breakfast is generally served in the living room with fireplace. In the summertime, it can be served under the portico. There's also a large garden with cypresses, olive trees and a collection of 100 roses.

GUARDISTALLO (PISA)

I Pietrai
Donatella Botto
via Vicinale dei Poderi
56040 Guardistallo (PI)
tel. 0586 655190, mob. 335 6384714
flavia@village.it
www.iPietrai.it
Open all year

On a farm located in a panoramic position between Volterra and the sea, the hosts have restructured two agricultural buildings and made one of them a B&B. The guestrooms have period Tuscan furniture. The kitchen-living room has a fireplace and a wood-burning oven. Breakfast, which consists of sweet items and natural marmalades, is served in the kitchen. The guests are provided with linen that has been embroidered by the hostess.

ACCOMMODATION
Guestrooms: *4 (2 double bedrooms and 2 doubles, with private bath)* ♿
Services & Amenities: *English and German are spoken; rooms cleaned every 3 days; tourist info; kitchen use by request; bike rental; garden; smokers welcome; private parking*
Minimum stay: *2 nights*
Rates: *double ~~€€€-€€€€~~.*
Children under 3 free.
Discounts for extended stays
Credit cards: *not accepted*
Pets:

• Bed & Breakfast Italia
Code T76
tel. 06 6878618, fax 06 6878619
info@bbitalia.it
www.bbitalia.it
Closed: varies

An old two-story farmhouse, all built in stone. Four spacious rooms are available: a communicating triple and a double sharing a bathroom with shower, two double rooms with private bathroom. The owners also rent a self-contained apartment on the ground floor with a kitchen, sitting room with a single bed, double bedroom and bathroom with shower. Cookery classes and chamber music concerts are organized for small groups.

ACCOMMODATION
Guestrooms: *6 (1 double bedroom, 1 single, 3 doubles and 1 triple room)*
Services & Amenities: *French, English and German are spoken; rooms cleaned every 3 days; tourist information; bike rental; smokers welcome; private parking*
Minimum stay: *2 nights*
Rates: €€
Credit cards: VISA MC *Bancomat*
Pets:

INCISA IN VAL D'ARNO (FLORENCE)

• Bed & Breakfast Italia Tci 10%
Code T74
tel. 06 6878618, fax 06 6878619
info@bbitalia.it
www.bbitalia.it
Closed: varies

This villa surrounded by garden is in the Florentine countryside. The family rents a double room with private bathroom within the main house, and a self-contained apartment featuring a double room, kitchen, and an upper-level space containing a French bed, sitting room with TV, and a bathroom with shower. The valuable rustic furnishings perfectly match the Florentine farmhouse style. Breakfast is served in the garden or in the lounge. The bus stop is 900 m away and the nearest railway station is 3 km away.

ACCOMMODATION
Guestrooms: *2 (1 double and 1 triple or quadruple room)* ♿
Services & Amenities: *rooms cleaned every 3 days; tourist info*
Minimum stay: *2 nights*
Rates: €€
Credit cards: VISA MC *Bancomat*
Pets:

Lastra a Signa (Florence)

La Locandella del Poggio
Francesca Susini
via Poggio Vittorio 29
50055 Lastra a Signa (FI)
tel. 055 8721297
fax 055 8728580
info@locandella.com
www.locandella.com
Open all year

The B&B is on the ground floor of a '50s villa surrounded by a garden. The accommodation offers four double rooms with private bath, all with independent entrance, air conditioning, mini-bar and Tuscan style furnishings. Guests also have the use of a living room, which has a library, and also the use of a tavern with bar service. Breakfast is served either in this tavern, in the rooms or in the garden.

Accommodation
Guestrooms: 4 double bedrooms, also single occupancy, with private bath; additional bed on request ♿
Services & Amenities: English spoken; rooms cleaned every 3 days; complimentary tourist information; bike rental; air conditioning; Internet access; garden; smokers welcome; private parking
Rates: single €€€€, double €€€€. Additional bed supplement €€. Children under 2 free
Credit cards: accepted
Pets: allowed

Poderi Nesti e Cupoli
Enrico Villani
via Leonardo da Vinci 47/49
50055 Lastra a Signa (FI)
tel. and fax 055 8723629
agriturismo.cupoli@katamail.com
Open all year

This restructured, 18th-C working-class building, surrounded by the Florentine hills, offers six rooms, furnished in Tuscan style, with one room equipped for accommodating disabled guests. There are also a garden and swimming pool that the guests are welcome to use. Breakfast, which consists of local products, is served in a living room with TV, reserved for the guests. On request, the hosts can make arrangements, with the help of a specialized organization, for providing the guests with guided tours of Florence and naturalistic, historical and cultural excursions in the area.

Accommodation
Guestrooms: 6 doubles, also single occupancy, with private bath; additional bed on request ♿
Services & Amenities: English spoken; rooms cleaned every day; tourist information; garden; smokers welcome; private parking
Rates: single €€, double €€€. Additional bed supplement €. Children under 2 free, 2 to 10 -50%
Credit cards: Visa MC Bancomat
Pets: allowed

Villa al Piano
Alfredo Annunziata
via del Piano 23
50055 Lastra a Signa (FI)
tel. 055 8723891, fax 055 8727249
alanunn@tiscali.it and
villapiano@inwind.it
www.villa-al-piano.com
Open all year

Accommodation
Guestrooms: 5 double bedrooms, also single occupancy, with private bath; additional bed on request ♿
Services & Amenities: English and German are spoken; rooms cleaned every 3 days; complimentary tourist information; bike rental; educational courses by request; terrace; garden; smokers welcome; private parking
Rates: single €€€€, double €€€€. Additional bed supplement €€. Children €
Credit cards: accepted
Pets: not allowed

This B&B is hosted in a completely renovated villa located near Florence. The rooms have a different characters: some have period furniture, while others have modern furniture. Breakfast, which consists of a selection of sweet and non-sweet items, can either be served on the veranda or in the garden. The hosts are more than happy to open their kitchen to those who wish to learn the secrets of Tuscan cuisine and the best choice of wines in the area.

Villa Lysis

Andrea Bertini
via di Calcinaia 82/A
50055 Lastra a Signa (FI)
tel. and fax 055 8713400
mob. 338 9071640
albertini@ftbcc.it
www.livingflorence.com
Open all year

This B&B, located in the hills just outside of Florence, occupies one of the wings of a late-19th-C manor house. It offers two rooms with double beds, and one with a single bed. All three rooms have classic, period furniture. The breakfast is served in the reserved dining room. Guests also have the use of a living room, which has bare beams, a fireplace, TV and a hi-fi system, as well as a small hanging garden. The swimming pool, with its hydromassage, is perfect for relaxing. On request, the host will organize guided tours.

Accommodation
Guestrooms: *3 (1 single, with private bath and 2 doubles, also single occupancy, with shared bath)*
Services & Amenities: *French, English, German and Spanish are spoken; rooms cleaned every 3 days; tourist info; air conditioning; garden; smokers welcome; private parking*
Rates: *single €€, double €€€. Children under 2 free. Discounts for extended stays*
Credit cards: *not accepted*
Pets:

• **Bed & Breakfast Italia**
Code T1

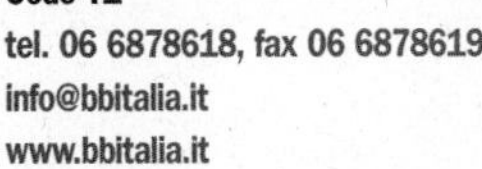

tel. 06 6878618, fax 06 6878619
info@bbitalia.it
www.bbitalia.it
Closed: varies

First-floor apartment with two rooms, in a manor house built in late 19th-century, completely refurbished and surrounded by pine trees. The apartment has a large sitting room with sofa bed, a double bedroom, a small kitchen, TV, large balcony and bathroom with shower. Furnishings are simple and functional. Private parking is available. The tiny village lies on the hills of Florence, offering a panoramic view of the surrounding valley. Scandicci is 4 km away.

Accommodation
Guestrooms: *1 double*
Services & Amenities: *French, English and German are spoken; rooms cleaned every 3 days; complimentary tourist information; private parking*
Minimum stay: *2 nights*
Rates: *€€*
Credit cards: VISA MC *Bancomat*
Pets:

Limite sull'Arno (Florence)

• **Bed & Breakfast Italia**
Code T64
tel. 06 6878618, fax 06 6878619
info@bbitalia.it
www.bbitalia.it
Closed: varies

Recently built refined B&B with all comforts and air conditioning. Bicycles and a babysitting service are available. It has a quiet, simply furnished double room complete with TV, ensuite bathroom with shower and large balcony, plus the option of an extra cot. The house is approx. 2 km from the Montelupo railway station. For guests traveling by car, the places within easy reach are Vinci, San Miniato and Scandicci.

Accommodation
Guestrooms: *1 doouble*
Services & Amenities: *English spoken; rooms cleaned every 3 days; tourist information; baby-sitting service; bike rental; air conditioning*
Minimum stay: *2 nights*
Rates: *€€*
Credit cards: VISA MC *Bancomat*
Pets:

LIVORNO

• Bed & Breakfast Italia
Code T71
località Montenero
57128 Livorno
tel. 06 6878618, fax 06 6878619
info@bbitalia.it
www.bbitalia.it
Closed: varies

This old 19th-century villa offers two double rooms with a view of the sea, furnished in a classic style with antiques. The rooms share a bathroom which has a shower. In the warmer months, breakfast is served in the garden; in the winter, it is served in the large lounge. The bus stops 100 meters away and takes guests to the center in 20 minutes. Private parking, telephone and safe are also available.

ACCOMMODATION
Guestrooms: *2 double bedrooms*
Services & Amenities: *French and English are spoken; rooms cleaned every 3 days; tourist information; smokers welcome; private parking*
Minimum stay: *2 nights*
Rates: €€
Credit cards: VISA MC *Bancomat*
Pets:

LUCCA

"Centro Storico"
Margherita Tarantino
corte Portici 16
55100 Lucca
tel. and fax 0583 490748
centrostorico@tin.it
www.affittacamerecentrostorico.com
Closed: 6 to 26 January

This comfortable B&B is located in a restructured 16th-century building situated just a few meters from Piazza San Michele. There are several guestrooms, each with rather simple, early 20th-century furnishings. The Italian breakfast, which also includes cakes, natural honey, salami and cheeses, is served in the rooms. The available services also include laundry, safe and telephone.

ACCOMMODATION
Guestrooms: *6 double bedrooms, also single occupancy, 3 with private bath and 3 with shared bath; additional bed on request*
Services & Amenities: *French, English and German are spoken; rooms cleaned every 3 days; tourist info; bike rental; Internet access; smokers welcome*
Minimum stay: *2 nights*
Rates: *single €€, double €€€. Additional bed supplement €*
Credit cards: *accepted*
Pets:

La Cappella
Pietro Monticelli
via per Camaiore, località La Cappella
55100 Lucca
tel. 0583 394347, fax 0583 395870
lacappella@lacappellalucca.it
www.domobox.it/lacappella
Open all year

ACCOMMODATION
Guestrooms: *4 doubles, also single occupancy, with private bath; additional bed on request*
Services & Amenities: *French and English are spoken; rooms cleaned every 3 days; tourist information; bike rental; horse-riding excursions; educational courses by request; garden; smokers welcome; private parking*
Rates: *single €€€-€€€€, double €€€€. Children under 5 free*
Credit cards: *accepted*
Pets:

This beautiful house, situated in a panoramic position on the ancient Via Francigena, was once an ancient, 17th-C convent. After having been neglected for many years, the convent was completely restored. The guestrooms have antique furniture and refined materials. All the furnishings have been duly "tested" by the owners of the house to assure maximum comfort. Breakfast, with homemade sweet items and Tuscan cold cuts and cheeses, is served in the large kitchen-dining room.

Lucca, Piazza Anfiteatro.

Villa Alessandra
Enrico Tosca
via Arsina 1100/B
55100 Lucca
tel. 0583 395171, fax 0583 395828
villa.ale@mailcity.com
Open all year

Situated in a panoramic position in the Lucca hills, this restructured 18th-century villa has six guestrooms, each with a double bed and private bathroom. The furnishings include both classic and period furniture. The rooms overlook the villa's large garden, which has both olive trees and fruit trees. The buffet breakfast is served either in the family dining room or outside under the portico. On request, the hostess organizes cooking courses for the guests.

Accommodation
Guestrooms: *6 doubles*
Services & Amenities: *French and English are spoken; rooms cleaned every day; complimentary tourist information; educational courses by request; garden; smokers welcome; private parking*
Minimum stay: *3 nights*
Rates: €€€€
Credit cards: VISA MC *Bancomat*
Pets:

• Bed & Breakfast Italia
Code T25
località Nozzano
55100 Lucca
tel. 06 6878618, fax 06 6878619
info@bbitalia.it
www.bbitalia.it
Closed: varies

Country-house surrounded by a 3500 sq.m garden with a sweeping view of the surrounding valley. The two double bedrooms, on the first floor, have a private bathroom with shower and an independent entrance. Furnishings are simple and functional. Breakfast includes homemade jams, cakes and fruit salads prepared by the landlady, who gathers her ingredients in the large orchard in front of the house.

Accommodation
Guestrooms: *2 double bedroms*
Services & Amenities: *English spoken; rooms cleaned every 3 days; complimentary tourist information; smokers welcome; private parking*
Minimum stay: *2 nights*
Rates: €€
Credit cards: VISA MC *Bancomat*
Pets:

• Bed & Breakfast Italia
Code T41
tel. 06 6878618, fax 06 6878619
info@bbitalia.it
www.bbitalia.it
Closed: varies

B&B completely at the disposal of guests, well appointed with modern, functional furniture and surrounded by a well-tended garden. Suitable for two people, it has a double room with TV and a private bathroom with tub. It is located in a residential area, 2 km from the center, which can be easily reached either by public transportation or on foot. The host will offer useful information on the city, the surroundings and the local restaurants.

Accommodation
Guestrooms: *1 double bedroom*
Services & Amenities: *English spoken; rooms cleaned every 3 days; tourist information; private parking*
Minimum stay: *2 nights*
Rates: €€
Credit cards: VISA MC *Bancomat*
Pets:

Magliano in Toscana (Grosseto)

San Giusto
Ovidio Umberto Croci
zona Corso 12, località Montiano
58051 Magliano in Toscana (GR)
tel. and fax 0564 589803
sangiusto@tiscalinet.it
Closed: February

This B&B is in an early 20th-C working-class building that's annexed to a farm that's out in the open countryside. The four guestrooms have bare beams, rustic style furnishings, double beds, private bathrooms, independent entrances and lead directly into the garden. The continental breakfast, consisting of organic products, is served in the large common room, which is also where dinner is served on request. Sports enthusiasts are provided with information regarding hikes and horseback riding in the area.

Foxes are common in the Maremma Nature Park.

Accommodation
Guestrooms: *4 doubles with private bath; additional bed on request* ♿
Services & Amenities: *French and English are spoken; rooms cleaned every 3 days; complimentary tourist information; dinner reservation; smokers welcome; private parking*
Rates: *double €€. Additional bed supplement €*
Credit cards: *not accepted*
Pets: 🐕

Manciano (Grosseto)

• Bed & Breakfast Italia
Code T61
tel. 06 6878618, fax 06 6878619
info@bbitalia.it
www.bbitalia.it
Closed: varies

A detached house situated in the country. Completely at the guests' disposal, it includes a double room, a lounge with double sofa bed, a fully equipped kitchen and a bathroom with shower. The French windows open onto a large garden, where guests can use the wood-burning oven to organize barbeques. It has an excellent location: 5 km from the Saturnia Baths; 30 min by car from seaside spots such as Porto Ercole and Porto Santo Stefano.

Accommodation
Guestrooms: *2 doubles*
Services & Amenities: *rooms cleaned every 3 days; complimentary tourist information; private parking*
Minimum stay: *2 nights*
Rates: €€
Credit cards: VISA MC *Bancomat*
Pets: no pets

Marina di Massa (Massa-Carrara)

• Bed & Breakfast Italia
Code T 10
tel. 06 6878618, fax 06 6878619
info@bbitalia.it
www.bbitalia.it
Closed: varies

Accommodation
Guestrooms: *3 (1 double, 2 triples)*
Services & Amenities: *French and English are spoken; rooms cleaned every 3 days; complimentary tourist information; private parking*
Minimum stay: *2 nights*
Rates: €€
Credit cards: VISA MC *Bancomat*
Pets: 🐕

Two small apartments in a villa, 600 m from the sea. One apartment has a double and a triple bedroom, a bathroom and a small kitchen; the other is a studio apartment, with kitchenette and bathroom. Both have modern, functional furnishings. The garden surrounding the villa and the private parking area are at the guests' disposal. The surrounding countryside abounds in fruit orchards. The Carrara Avenza railway station is 3 km from the B&B.

The Massa countryside

MASSA E COZZILE (PISTOIA)

Poderino Lero
via in Campo 42
51010 Massa e Cozzile (PT)
tel. and fax 0572 60218
poderinolero@yahoo.it
Open all year

This restructured farmhouse, which is situated on the hills dominating Montecatini Terme, is surrounded by vineyards, olive trees and an orchard. The three guestrooms face a large garden. The continental breakfast, which consists of organic and natural products, is served either in the reserved living room, which has a fireplace, or outside under the portico. On request, the hostess organizes courses in bio-dance, shiatsu, yoga and positive listening and communication.

ACCOMMODATION
Guestrooms: *3 (2 doubles, also single occupancy, 1 triple; private bath)*
Services & Amenities: *French, English and German are spoken; rooms cleaned every day; tourist info; educational courses by request; garden; smokers welcome; private parking*
Rates: *single €€, double €€€, triple €€€. Children under 2 free*
Credit cards: *not accepted*
Pets:

MOLAZZANA (LUCCA)

Rustico Sara
Bonacina Giuseppina
via della Chiesa 3, località Brucciano
55020 Molazzana (LU)
tel. and fax 050 818762
mob. 347 1672613
saradicorato@interfree.it
open: June to September

A thorough restructuring of this stone farm building, located in the Garfagnana hills, has converted it into a nice home. The B&B has large, characteristically rustic guestrooms with wooden ceilings, terracotta floors and period furniture, some pieces of which are 18th-C Tuscan originals. Breakfast, which also includes bread and sweet items baked in a wood-burning oven, is served in a kitchen with fireplace.

ACCOMMODATION
Guestrooms: *4 (3 double bedrooms and 1 double, also single occupancy, with shared bath)*
Services & Amenities: *French and English are spoken; rooms cleaned every 3 days; tourist information; bike rental; terrace; garden; smokers welcome; private parking*
Minimum stay: *2 nights*
Rates: *single €€€, double €€€. Children under 2 free*
Credit cards: *not accepted*
Pets:

MONTELUPO FIORENTINO (FLORENCE)

• Bed & Breakfast Italia TCI 10%
Code T27
tel. 06 6878618, fax 06 6878619
info@bbitalia.it
www.bbitalia.it
Closed: varies

This villa is surrounded by a well-tended garden. The accommodation consists in a double and single bedroom, both sunny and quiet, with simple, comfortable furnishings. The reading lounge, the outer portico where breakfast is served in the summer, the garden, the solarium and the bar service are available. A car is necessary and can be parked in front of the B&B.

ACCOMMODATION
Guestrooms: *2 (1 single, 1 double)*
Services & Amenities: *English spoken; rooms cleaned every 3 days; complimentary tourist information; smokers welcome; private parking*
Minimum stay: *2 nights*
Rates: €€
Credit cards: VISA MC *Bancomat*
Pets:

MONTEPULCIANO (SIENA)

Casale a Poggiano
Giacomo Mariotti
via di Poggiano 21, località Poggiano
53045 Montepulciano (SI)
tel. 0578 716446, 06 88588234
mob. 328 7322057, fax 0578 715231
gambinamaledetta@libero.it
casale-poggiano@libero.it
www.poggiano.com
Closed: Christmas holidays

The guestrooms of this comfortable B&B, which is located in a 19th-century farmhouse surrounded by a garden, have antique furniture as well as a few

modern pieces. Particular care is taken in the choice of the linen and in how breakfast is served. In fact, the hostess is particularly proud of the lace-trimmed, period linen and

ACCOMMODATION
Guestrooms: *4 double bedroom, also single occupancy, 3 with private bath and 1 with shared bath*
Services & Amenities: *French spoken; rooms cleaned every 3 days; tourist information; bike rental; Internet access; garden; smokers welcome; private parking*
Rates: *single €€, double €€€€. Children under 3 free*
Credit cards: *not accepted*
Pets: ✓

hand-painted china. Breakfast is served in the living room with fireplace, where the guests are also free to relax.

Casale Ortaglia
Terenzio Biscardo
strada Statale per Pienza 29
53045 Montepulciano (SI)
tel. 0578 756091, 045 7150893
fax 0578 715077, 045 7157167
tuscany@ortaglia.it
www.ortaglia.it
Closed: 7 January to 8 February

This B&B, which is in a beautiful, restructured stone farmhouse located near Montepulciano and surrounded by the famous Vino Nobile vineyards, is perfect for wine-lovers. The classic, refined furnishings include antiques and fine fabrics. The host, a wine-taster and sommelier, proposes wine-tasting ses-

ACCOMMODATION
Guestrooms: *5 (3 suites and 2 double bedrooms, with private bath); additional bed on request*
Services & Amenities: *French, English and German are spoken; rooms cleaned every 3 days; tourist information; bike rental; educational courses by request; garden; smokers welcome; private parking*
Minimum stay: *2 nights*
Rates: *double €€€€, suite €€€€. Children under 12 free*
Credit cards: *accepted*
Pets: ✗

sions. Breakfast, which consists of local sweet and non-sweet products, is served in a special room. Guests can enjoy the swimming pool, mountain-bike excursions and tours in a nine-passenger minibus.

Montorio
Stefania Savini
strada Statale per Pienza 2
53045 Montepulciano (SI)
tel. 0578 717442, fax 0578 715456
montorio@island.pi.it
www.island.pi.it/montorio
Closed: 15 November to 1 March

This 15th century country house, which is next to the San Biagio church, is located in the hills surrounding Montepulciano. It has five small guest suites that have every comfort, classic furnishings and fine fabrics. Breakfast, consist-

ACCOMMODATION
Guestrooms: *5 suites, also single occupancy; additional bed on request*
Services & Amenities: *French and English are spoken; rooms cleaned every day; tourist info; bike rental; terrace; Internet access; garden; smokers welcome; private parking*
Rates: *single €€€€, suite €€€€. Additional bed supplement €€*
Credit cards: *accepted*
Pets: ✗

ing of local sweet and non- sweet items, is served either in the garden or in a dépendance. Guests have the use of bicycles, and there's a swimming pool just 2 kilometers from the B&B.

Monterchi (Arezzo)

B&B Casanova
• Associazione Koko Nor
tel. 049 8643394, mob. 338 3377912
fax 049 8643394
kokonor@bandb-veneto.it
www.bandb-veneto.it/kokonor

This B&B is hosted in a late 19th-century stone farmhouse, which has a nice view of the valley and is located in a quiet, green, hilly area 27 kilometers from Arezzo. It has a typical arcade that's shaded by a secular wisteria vine. The accommodation offers three guestrooms with antique furniture, terracotta floors and bare ceiling beams. The rich breakfast, which consists of natural marmalades and typical local sweet items, is served in the large Tuscan kitchen.

Accommodation
Guestrooms: *3 doubles, with shared bath*
Services & Amenities: *French spoken; rooms cleaned every day; complimentary tourist information; terrace; garden; private parking*
Rates: *€-€€ per person*
Credit cards: *not accepted*
Pets:

B&B La Rocca di Monterchi
• Ass. Welcome - B&B in Umbria
tel. 0763 305523, fax 0763 390670
info@bb.umbria.it
www.bbumbria.it
Closed: varies

This B&B, in the old center of town, is located inside an ancient completely-restructured, stone construction that has 17th-century beams. The rooms are carefully furnished and include some antique pieces. The place is surrounded by a panoramic, hanging garden on the ancient wall. There's and old, rain-water well in front of entrance. The Italian breakfast is enjoyed together with the family or served in the rooms, if desired.

Accommodation
Guestrooms: *4 (3 double bedrooms and 1 suite) private bath; additional bed on request*
Services & Amenities: *French and English are spoken; rooms cleaned every day; tourist info; kitchen use by request; garden; smokers welcome*
Minimum stay: *2 nights*
Rates: *double €€€€, suite €€€€. Additional bed supplement 30%.*
Credit cards: *not accepted*
Pets:

Casa Marzocchi
Donatella Marzocchi
piazza Umberto I 18
52035 Monterchi (AR)
tel. 0575 70202 (May-October)
mob. 338 3043220, fax 0575 23921
info@casamarzocchi.com
www.casamarzocchi.com
• ToscanaeOltre
tel. and fax 075 8559864
info@toscanaeoltre.com
www.toscanaeoltre.com
Open: mid-April to mid-October

This 17th-century building located in the medieval part of town was once a castle. There are three guestrooms, two with double beds and one suite with an alcove and a fireplace. The furnishings include antique family furniture, Persian carpets and drapes. There is also a small apartment with kitchenette on the ground floor. Breakfast, which consists in sweet items, cold cuts and local homemade marmalades, is either served in the living room, which has a fireplace, or in the panoramic hanging garden.

Accommodation
Guestrooms: *3 (2 doubles and 1 suite, with private bath) and 1 mini-apartment*
Services & Amenities: *English spoken; rooms cleaned every 3 days; complimentary tourist information; kitchen use by request; kitchenette; terrace; garden; smokers welcome; private parking*
Minimum stay: *2 nights*
Rates: *double €€€€, suite €€€€. Children under 10 free. Discounts for extended stays*
Credit cards: *not accepted*
Pets:

Il Girasole
• ToscanaeOltre
tel. and fax 075 8559864
info@toscanaeoltre.com
www.toscanaeoltre.com
Closed: varies

This B&B is in a separate house, which is adjacent to the main house, and is just a short walk from the museum that has the Madonna del Parto fresco. The B&B faces the valley where Piero della Francesca painted his masterpiece. The furnishings include period furniture, and the beautiful fireplace makes the atmosphere warm and friendly. The traditional breakfast includes marmalades, honey and homemade sweet items.

ACCOMMODATION
Guestrooms: *2 doubles, also single occupancy, with shared bath*
Services & Amenities: *French and English; are spoken; rooms cleaned every 3 days; tourist information; kitchen use by request; terrace; garden; smokers welcome; private parking*
Rates: €€€-€€€€
Credit cards: *not accepted*
Pets: ⊘

MONTERONI D'ARBIA (SIENA)

Casa Bolsinina
Marcello Mazzotta
località Casale
53014 Monteroni d'Arbia (SI)
tel. and fax 0577 718477
bolsinina@bolsinina.com
www.bolsinina.com
Closed: 15 January to 15 March

ACCOMMODATION
Guestrooms: *5 double bedrooms, also single occupancy, 1 suite; private bath*
Services & Amenities: *English spoken; rooms cleaned every 3 days; tourist information; dinner reservation; bike rental; terrace; garden; smokers welcome; private parking*
Minimum stay: *3 nights*
Rates: *single and double* €€€€
Credit cards: VISA MC *Bancomat*
Pets: ⊘

This B&B is located in a restructured 18th century farmhouse that's surrounded by the chalk hills between Siena and Montalcino. The rooms, with their classic and period furnishings are located on the upper floor. The ground floor has a billiard room and a living room, which has a fireplace and is where the buffet breakfast is served. The beautiful park and swimming pool are ideal for enjoying the tranquility of this area.

MONTESPERTOLI (FLORENCE)

Il Guglierallo
Maria Grazia Pollacci
via Castiglioni 18
località Montagnana
50025 Montespertoli (FI)
tel. and fax 0571 671025
info@ilguglierallo
www.ilguglierallo.it
Closed: January to March

ACCOMMODATION
Guestrooms: *3 (2 double bedroom and 1 double, also single occupancy, with private bath); additional bed on request*
Services & Amenities: *English and German are spoken; rooms cleaned every 3 days; tourist information; terrace; garden; smokers welcome; private parking*
Rates: *single* €€, *double* €€€€. *Discounts for extended stays*
Credit cards: *not accepted*
Pets: ⊘

This restored 18th-century farmhouse, with its simple, peaceful, country atmosphere, is not far from Florence. There's a beautiful view of the Abetone from the adjacent park, which also provides a perfect play area for children. It offers 2 rooms with private bathroom. The Italian breakfast is either served on the terrace or in the kitchen.

• **Bed & Breakfast Italia**
Code T26
tel. 06 6878618, fax 06 6878619
info@bbitalia.it
www.bbitalia.it
Closed: varies

A completely refurbished country-house, part of a small family farm. The two bedrooms, a double and a triple, are furnished with inlaid period pieces, brass lights and chandeliers, coffered ceilings and typical farmhouse terracotta flooring. Each room has a private bathroom, TV, cot, independent entrance and a view of the valley. In the summer, breakfast is served in the garden in front of the house, in the kitchen in the colder months. Private parking available.

ACCOMMODATION
Guestrooms: *2 (1 double, 1 triple)*
Services & Amenities: *English spoken; rooms cleaned every 3 days; complimentary tourist information; smokers welcome; private parking*
Minimum stay: *2 nights*
Rates: €€
Credit cards: VISA MC *Bancomat*
Pets: 🐾

ORBETELLO (GROSSETO)

• **Bed & Breakfast Italia**
Code T37
tel. 06 6878618, fax 06 6878619
info@bbitalia.it
www.bbitalia.it
Closed: varies

Two 40 sq.m independent apartments. Functional and well kept, each consists in a double bedroom, lounge with sofa bed and fully equipped kitchen area, bath with shower cubicle and washing machine. Furnishings are practical and modern. Both feature self-contained heating. They are 15 minutes from the center of Orbetello and close to Porto Ercole and Porto Santo Stefano, where ferries depart for the islands of Giglio and Giannutri.

ACCOMMODATION
Guestrooms: *2 doubles*
Services & Amenities: *French spoken; rooms cleaned every 3 days; complimentary tourist information*
Minimum stay: *2 nights*
Rates: €€
Credit cards: VISA MC *Bancomat*
Pets: 🐾

PALAIA (PISA)

• **Bed & Breakfast Italia**
Code T32
località Forcoli
56036 Palaia (PI)
tel. 06 6878618, fax 06 6878619
info@bbitalia.it
www.bbitalia.it
Closed: varies

A country-house of 900 sq.m, built on the ruins of a castle owned by a very old family. This B&B offers three double rooms, all elegantly furnished, valuable carpets and upholstery, and with views of the surrounding garden. A swimming pool and private parking are available. The family welcomes guests in a friendly atmosphere. The surrounding area is full of interesting places including Livorno and Pisa (30 km), San Miniato (20 km). A golf club is 12 km away.

ACCOMMODATION
Guestrooms: *4 (3 doubles, 1 triple)*
Services & Amenities: *French, English and Spanish are spoken; rooms cleaned every 3 days; complimentary tourist information; terrace; smokers welcome; private parking*
Minimum stay: *2 nights*
Rates: €€
Credit cards: VISA MC *Bancomat*
Pets: (no pets)

Pescia (Pistoia)

Medioeval Village

• B&B Liguria e... non solo
tel. 010 3291204, mob. 347 26092
fax 010 3299774
oltrelazzurro@libero.it
www.bbitalia.net
Open all year

Accommodation
Guestrooms: *3 (1 double bedroom and 2 singles, with shared bath); additional child's bed on request*
Services & Amenities: *French, English, German and Spanish are spoken; rooms cleaned every day; tourist info; terrace; smokers welcome*
Minimum stay: *2 nights*
Rates: *single €€, double €€€. Additional child's bed supplement €*
Credit cards: *not accepted*
Pets:

This B&B is hosted in a stone house that dates from the year 1040 and is located in San Quirico, at an elevation of 560 m. The guestrooms are furnished in a simple manner, and all three share the same bathroom with bathtub. The breakfast, which also includes local products, is either served in the living room, or in the rustic kitchen or in the small tavern. During the warmer months, breakfast is served on the terrace. Guests have the use of the living room, which has a TV.

Piancastagnaio (Siena)

• Bed & Breakfast Italia
Code T33
tel. 06 6878618, fax 06 6878619
info@bbitalia.it
www.bbitalia.it
Closed: varies

Accommodation
Guestrooms: *3 (2 doubles, 1 triple)*
Services & Amenities: *French and English are spoken; rooms cleaned every 3 days; tourist information*
Minimum stay: *2 nights*
Rates: *€€*
Credit cards: VISA MC *Bancomat*
Pets:

Two small apartments, part of a farmhouse nestling on a green estate, with a view of the valley. One apartment has a double room and a triple, well appointed with period wrought iron country style furniture, TV, sitting room with fireplace and bathroom with shower. The second apartment, furnished in the same style, consists in a double room, a sitting room with double sofa bed, a small kitchen and bathroom with shower. The farmhouse is 2 km from the hamlet. Car is necessary.

Pian di Scò (Arezzo)

Villa Eleonora
Carmen Cornali
via Codilungo 49
52026 Pian di Scò (AR)
tel. and fax 055 965100
villaeleonor@tin.it
www.villaeleonora.it
Open all year

Accommodation
Guestrooms: *2 doubles, shared bath; additional bed on request*
Services & Amenities: *French and English are spoken; rooms cleaned every 3 days; complimentary tourist information; kitchen use by request; bike rental; garden; smokers welcome; private parking*
Rates: *double €€. Additional bed supplement €. Children under 3 free. Discounts for extended stays*
Credit cards: *not accepted*
Pets:

This villa, located in the upper Valdarno hills halfway between Arezzo and Florence, makes the ideal starting point for various excursions. The two guestrooms, which have traditional rustic Tuscan furniture, are in the dépendance located in the garden. The Italian breakfast is either served in the family kitchen or outdoors. During the summer months, guests can also enjoy the swimming pool.

Pisa

• **Bed & Breakfast Italia** Tci 10%
Code T77
tel. 06 6878618, fax 06 6878619
info@bbitalia.it
www.bbitalia.it
Closed: varies

An Art Nouveau villa in the center of Pisa. Guests can use three double bedrooms: one has a double bed and the other two have single beds. The classic and elegant furnishings boast antiques and frescoed ceilings. Breakfast is served in the kitchen. The bus stop is 20 m away. The center is 10 minutes away on foot. Private parking is available.

Accommodation
Guestrooms: *3 (1 double bedroom and 2 doubles)*
Services & Amenities: *French and English are spoken; rooms cleaned every 3 days; complimentary tourist information; smokers welcome; private parking*
Minimum stay: *2 nights*
Rates: €€
Credit cards: VISA MC *Bancomat*
Pets: no

Pistoia

• **Bed & Breakfast Italia** Tci 10%
Code T53
tel. 06 6878618, fax 06 6878619
info@bbitalia.it www.bbitalia.it
Closed: varies

This is a fifth-floor central apartment located in a building with elevator and furnished with antiques. The accommodation consists in a spacious room with twin beds, TV and bathroom with shower. From the bedroom window it is possible to enjoy a scenic view of the city. Guests can reach the railway station on foot. The owners organize music, cooking and Italian language courses.

A view of the roofs of Pistoia

Accommodation
Guestrooms: *1 double*
Services & Amenities: *French, English, German and Spanish are spoken; rooms cleaned every 3 days; tourist info; educational courses; Internet*
Minimum stay: *2 nights*
Rates: €€
Credit cards: VISA MC *Bancomat*
Pets: no

Pitigliano (Grosseto)

• **Bed & Breakfast Italia**
Code T38
tel. 06 6878618, fax 06 6878619
info@bbitalia.it
www.bbitalia.it
Closed: varies

Country-house surrounded by a spacious garden with two separate units; in the family part, two double rooms with private bathroom and independent entrance are available. The other apartment includes two double rooms, a private bathroom and a kitchenette. Everything has been recently renovated: elegant furnishings with antiques, brick kitchen, refined touches, charming upholstery and curtains. Swimming pool and tennis court available.

Accommodation
Guestrooms: *4 doubles; additional bed on request*
Services & Amenities: *French and English are spoken; rooms cleaned every 3 days; complimentary tourist information; terrace; private parking*
Minimum stay: *2 nights*
Rates: €€
Credit cards: VISA MC *Bancomat*
Pets: 

Pontassieve (Florence)

Casa Teano
via Stracchino 25
50065 Pontassieve (FI)
tel. and fax 055 8328301
• Bed & Breakfast Italia
tel. 06 6878618, fax 06 6878619
info@bbitalia.it
www.bbitalia.it
Open all year

This B&B is situated in a separate wing of Casa Teano – an ancient farmhouse located in an area covered with vineyards and olive trees – whose original structure dates from the 14th C. The accommodation includes two rooms and a small apartment with period furniture. The rooms share the bathroom, while the small apartment has an attic bedroom and a sitting room with TV, sofa bed and kitchenette. Breakfast is either served in the rooms, in the living room or in the large garden.

Accommodation
Guestrooms: *2 doubles, also single occupancy, with shared bath, and 1 mini-apartment (4 beds)*
Services & Amenities: *French and English are spoken; rooms cleaned every day; complimentary tourist information; kitchenette; garden; smokers welcome; private parking*
Minimum stay: *2 nights*
Rates: *single €€, double €€-€€€, mini-apartment €€€-€€€€. Additional child's bed supplement €*
Credit cards: *not accepted*
Pets: allowed

• Bed & Breakfast Italia
Code T51
tel. 06 6878618, fax 06 6878619
info@bbitalia.it
www.bbitalia.it
Closed: varies

Medici villa dating from the 16th century, situated on Florence's hills is surrounded by a perfectly tended garden with centuries-old trees and two 14th-century fountains. The house has been completely restored under the supervision of the Monuments and Fine Arts Office. The accommodation includes three bedrooms, two doubles and a single, decorated with valuable pieces of furniture, tapestries and paintings of great artistic value. The railway station is 5 km away.

Accommodation
Guestrooms: *3 doubles*
Services & Amenities: *French and English are spoken; rooms cleaned every 3 days; complimentary tourist information; private parking*
Minimum stay: *2 nights*
Rates: €€
Credit cards: VISA MC *Bancomat*
Pets: not allowed

Pontremoli (Massa-Carrara)

• Bed & Breakfast Italia
Code T73
tel. 06 6878618, fax 06 6878619
info@bbitalia.it
www.bbitalia.it
Open: June, July and September

Accommodation
Guestrooms: *2 doubles*
Services & Amenities: *French and English are spoken; rooms cleaned every 3 days; complimentary tourist information; private parking*
Minimum stay: *2 nights*
Rates: €€
Credit cards: VISA MC *Bancomat*
Pets: allowed

This B&B is hosted in an old farmhouse, completely refurbished, with a wide courtyard. The guest' accommodation consists in two large double rooms, one with twin beds, share a bathroom with shower/tub. The continental breakfast is generally served in the lounge. The railway station is 300 m away. In the nearby area there are sports facilities.

Portoferraio (Livorno)

Villa Lidia
Lidia Quintavalle
località Condotto 33
57037 Portoferraio (LI)
tel. and fax 0565 930440
Closed: mid-November to mid-December

This villa, which was recently built and is just a few minutes from Portoferraio and the beach, has large rooms furnished in the classic style and a living room that has a fireplace. The buffet breakfast, which consists of natural cakes and cold cuts, is normally served under the garden portico.

Accommodation
Guestrooms: *3 double bedrooms with private bath*
Services & Amenities: *English and German are spoken; rooms cleaned every 3 days; tourist information; bike rental; garden; smokers welcome*
Rates: *double €€€-€€€€*
Credit cards: *not accepted*
Pets: ✓

Rignano sull'Arno (Florence)

Relais Chiara e Lorenzo TCI 10%
Alberto Tozzi
località Cafaggio 74
50067 Rignano sull'Arno (FI)
tel. and fax 055 8305240
mob. 329 9150351
altox@centroin.it
www.relais_chiaraelorenzo.com
Open all year

This B&B-cum-farm holiday, which is hosted in a 16th-farmhouse, is situated in a panoramic hilly area. It has four double rooms that have classic furnishings as well as a few modern pieces. All the rooms face the garden that surrounds the house. The continental breakfast is served in a reserved dining room. On request, the guests can also have dinner. The hosts arrange cooking courses as well as guided tours of the farms and farm holiday establishments located in the area. There is also a swimming pool for children.

Accommodation
Guestrooms: *4 doubles, 3 with private bath, 1 with shared bath*
Services & Amenities: *English spoken; rooms cleaned every day; complimentary tourist information; dinner reservation; educational courses by request; Internet access; garden; smokers welcome; private parking*
Minimum stay: *2 nights*
Rates: *double €€€. Children under 2 free, 3 to 5 -50%*
Credit cards: VISA MC *Bancomat*
Pets: ✗

Roccastrada (Grosseto)

• Bed & Breakfast Italia
Code T24
tel. 06 6878618, fax 06 6878619
info@bbitalia.it
www.bbitalia.it
Closed: varies

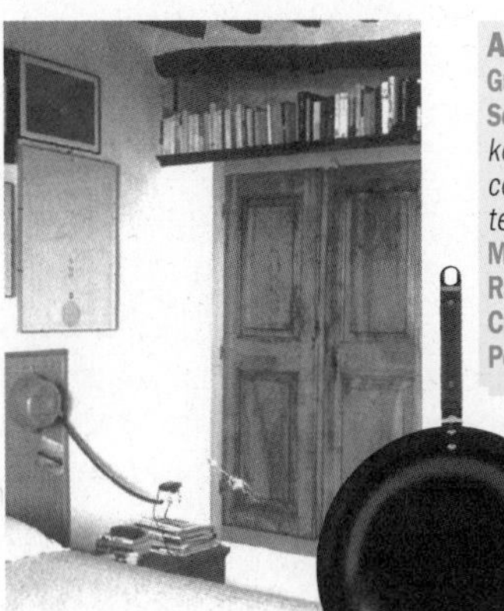

Small, 45 sq m, apartment in the old center of the village. The area available to guests has a double bedroom, private bathroom with shower, kitchenette and a large balcony with a stunning sweeping view. It is furnished in rustic style creating a warm cozy atmosphere. Roccastrada offers a choice of restaurants where you can sample the excellent cuisine and Maremma wines.

Accommodation
Guestrooms: *1 double*
Services & Amenities: *English spoken; rooms cleaned every 3 days; complimentary tourist information; terrace; smokers welcome*
Minimum stay: *2 nights*
Rates: *€€*
Credit cards: VISA MC *Bancomat*
Pets: ✗

Rosignano Marittimo (Livorno)

• Bed & Breakfast Italia
Code T52
località Castiglioncello
57016 Rosignano Marittimo (LI)
tel. 06 6878618, fax 06 6878619
info@bbitalia.it
www.bbitalia.it
Closed: varies

Detached house on a hillside 200 m above sea level. The accommodation consists in three rooms sharing a bathroom with shower, all with TV, tasteful furnishings and pastel-colored walls. PC and babysitting service are available on request. Pisa, Livorno and Lucca can be reached in 1 hour by car or train; the railway station is 300 m away. Available from April to September.

Accommodation
Guestrooms: *3 (1 single, 1 double and 1 triple room)*
Services & Amenities: *English spoken; rooms cleaned every 3 days; complimentary tourist information; baby-sitting service; private parking*
Minimum stay: *2 nights*
Rates: €€
Credit cards: VISA MC *Bancomat*
Pets: not allowed

Rufina (Florence)

Villa i Busini
Maria Rosaria Nicolodi
località Scopeti 28
50068 Rufina (FI)
tel. and fax 055 8397809
villabusini@libero.it
Closed: 15 January to late February

Accommodation
Guestrooms: *6 (1 single and 5 doubles, with shared bath); additional bed on request*
Services & Amenities: *English spoken; rooms cleaned every day; complimentary tourist information; lunch & dinner reservations; educational courses by request; garden; smokers welcome; private parking*
Minimum stay: *2 nights*
Rates: *single €€, double €€€€. Additional bed supplement €. Children under 2 free, 2 to 5 -50%*
Credit cards: VISA MC *Bancomat*
Pets: not allowed

The guestrooms of this B&B, located in an historic, 15th-century house, have classic style furnishings. The rooms face an Italian garden with swimming pool, hydromassage and bocce court. Guests also have the use of a billiard room and a reading room. The continental breakfast is served in a room that's reserved for the guests. On request, the hosts arrange cooking lessons, and visits to the local wine, gastronomic and cultural places of interest.

San Gimignano (Siena)

Villa Remignoli
Maria and Renato Faresi
località Casaglia 25
53037 San Gimignano (SI)
tel. and fax 0577 950048
mob. 335 265516
villarem@hotmail.com
Open: April to October

This ancient, elegantly-restructured farmhouse is just a short distance from San Gimignano. It has a large living room with a fireplace, and each of the five guestrooms (all with double beds) have a private bathroom. And there's a large, rustic kitchen, a terrace with panoramic view, and a large garden with swimming pool. Everything is very well kept by the owners. The rich breakfast – which is actually a brunch – includes homemade sweet items, natural cold cuts and cheeses, cereals, yoghurt and fresh eggs.

Accommodation
Guestrooms: *5 doubles, private bath*
Services & Amenities: *French and German are spoken; rooms cleaned every day; tourist info; terrace; garden; smokers welcome; parking*
Minimum stay: *2 nights*
Rates: *double €€€€*
Credit cards: *not accepted*
Pets: allowed

• **Bed & Breakfast Italia**
Code T48
tel. 06 6878618, fax 06 6878619
info@bbitalia.it
www.bbitalia.it
Closed: varies

The Castle is situated on a hill 5 min from the center. Its tower, dating from the year 1000, represents the primary construction around which the villa and the small church have been built. The style of furnishings is classic and elegant. The garden and the private parking are reserved for guests.

Meals prepared with local produce are served on request. A riding-ring, bike rental, golf course and tennis court are all a few minutes distance away.

ACCOMMODATION
Guestrooms: *3 (2 doubles, 1 triple)*
Services & Amenities: *English spoken; rooms cleaned every 3 days; tourist information; Internet access; smokers welcome; private parking*
Minimum stay: *2 nights*
Rates: €€
Credit cards: VISA MC *Bancomat*
Pets: not allowed

SAN GIULIANO TERME (PISA)

Villa Annamaria
Claudio Zeppi
strada Statale dell'Abetone 146,
località Molina di Quosa
56017 San Giuliano Terme (PI)
tel. and fax 050 850139
clazep@tin.it,
zeppi@villaannamaria.com
www.villaannamaria.com
Open all year

An 18th-century villa, surrounded by a botanical garden with tall plants, hosts this B&B, that has four double rooms with TV and telephone, and two rooms

that share the same bathroom. The rooms have frescoes and vaulted ceilings. The breakfast is either served in a reserved room or in a greenhouse. It may also be served in the garden. Guests have use of a game room, which has a billiard table, a library and a video library.

ACCOMMODATION
Guestrooms: *6 (4 doubles, also single occupancy, with private bath; 2 doubles or triples, with shared bath)* ♿
Services & Amenities: *French, English and Spanish are spoken; rooms cleaned every 3 days; tourist information; Internet access; garden; smokers welcome; private parking*
Minimum stay: *2 nights*
Rates: *single* €€, *double* €€€, *triple* €€€
Credit cards: *not accepted*
Pets: allowed

• **Bed & Breakfast Italia** TCI 10%
Code T14
località Pugnano
56017 San Giuliano Terme (PI)
tel. 06 6878618, fax 06 6878619
info@bbitalia.it
www.bbitalia.it
Closed: varies

This typical Tuscan villa lies in the valleys around the village of Pugnano. The accommodation consists in three double rooms and one triple, sharing three bathrooms, one with tub and one with shower. The furnishings are rustic and elegant and the ceilings have exposed wooden beams. Continental breakfast is served in the lounge. A car is needed.

ACCOMMODATION
Guestrooms: *4 (3 double bedrooms and 1 triple room)*
Services & Amenities: *English and German are spoken; rooms cleaned every 3 days; tourist info; parking*
Minimum stay: *2 nights*
Rates: €€
Credit cards: VISA MC *Bancomat*
Pets: not allowed

San Quirico d'Orcia (Siena)

- **Bed & Breakfast Italia**

TCI 10%

Code T11
tel. 06 6878618, fax 06 6878619
info@bbitalia.it
www.bbitalia.it
Closed: varies

This B&B is located in a villa 50 meters from the center and castle walls, offering a scenic view of Siena, Montalcino and the surrounding hillsides; the guests' accommodation consists in two apartments, each with two double bedrooms and private bathroom, kitchen, dining room, sitting room complete with TV, terrace and private parking. The surrounding garden dates from the fifties.

Accommodation
Guestrooms: *4 (2 doubles, 2 triples)*
Services & Amenities: *French and English are spoken; rooms cleaned every 3 days; tourist info; horse-riding excursions; terrace, parking*
Minimum stay: *2 nights*
Rates: €€
Credit cards: VISA MC *Bancomat*
Pets: not allowed

- **Bed & Breakfast Italia**

Code T63
tel. 06 6878618, fax 06 6878619
info@bbitalia.it
www.bbitalia.it
Closed: varies

Good standard ground floor apartment in a small medieval building on the main road, in the heart of the village. It includes one double room, a sitting room with double sofa bed, TV, kitchen with microwave oven and fridge. It has valuable period country-style furniture and decorative beamed ceilings in every room. The famed spa of Bagno Pignoni visited by such illustrious guests as Catherine of Siena, Lorenzo de' Medici and Pope Pius II are a short walk away.

Accommodation
Guestrooms: *2 doubles*
Services & Amenities: *French, English and Spanish are spoken; rooms cleaned every 3 days; tourist information; smokers welcome*
Minimum stay: *2 nights*
Rates: €€
Credit cards: VISA MC *Bancomat*
Pets: not allowed

Sansepolcro (Arezzo)

- **Bed & Breakfast Italia**

Code T9
tel. 06 6878618, fax 06 6878619
info@bbitalia.it www.bbitalia.it
Closed: varies

Accommodation
Guestrooms: *5 doubles*
Services & Amenities: *French and English are spoken; rooms cleaned every 3 days; tourist info; horse-riding excursions; smokers welcome; parking*
Minimum stay: *2 nights*
Rates: €€
Credit cards: VISA MC *Bancomat*
Pets: not allowed

The villa dates from the year 1000 and has remained unchanged throughout the centuries. The private chapel, large park with centuries-old trees, cultivated fields, surrounding woods, and the view of the valley add to the majesty of the B&B. The accommodation offers large and luminous double rooms with vaulted ceilings, antique furnishings and frescoes. Nearby there is horse riding, hiking, sailing, windsurfing, and canoeing on Lake Montedoglio.

San Vincenzo (Livorno)

- **Bed & Breakfast Italia**

Code T58
tel. 06 6878618, fax 06 6878619
info@bbitalia.it
www.bbitalia.it
Closed: varies

Two-story house, tastefully furnished in a functional style, surrounded by a garden with gazebo. It includes three double rooms and one triple, three bathrooms equipped with shower and a small kitchen. A car is necessary to explore the coast and surrounding countryside. The lady of the house is willing to accompany her guests on sightseeing tours, giving them detailed information about the area.

Accommodation
Guestrooms: *4 (3 doubles, 1 triple)*
Services & Amenities: *French, English, German and Spanish are spoken; rooms cleaned every 3 days; tourist info; smokers welcome; parking*
Minimum stay: *2 nights*
Rates: €€
Credit cards: VISA MC *Bancomat*
Pets: 🚫

Saturnia (Grosseto)

- **Bed & Breakfast Italia**

Code T62
tel. 06 6878618, fax 06 6878619
info@bbitalia.it
www.bbitalia.it
Closed: varies

A small villa with garden and a view of a private park. One wing of the house is completely at the disposal of guests and includes a double room, a sitting room with fireplace and a bathroom with shower. It is well appointed with country-style furnishings. The entrance is independent and the atmosphere is cozy and relaxing. The sea is within 40 minutes' by car and Capalbio, Porto Ercole and Porto S. Stefano are worth a visit.

Accommodation
Guestrooms: *1 double bedroom*
Services & Amenities: *English spoken; rooms cleaned every 3 days; complimentary tourist information; smokers welcome; private parking*
Minimum stay: *2 nights*
Rates: €€
Credit cards: VISA MC *Bancomat*
Pets: 🚫

Scandicci (Florence)

- **Bed & Breakfast Italia**

Code F211
tel. 06 6878618, fax 06 6878619
info@bbitalia.it
www.bbitalia.it
Closed: varies

This accommodation is a marvelous 19th-century mansion surrounded by a vineyard and an olive grove. The double bedroom boasts richly frescoed ceiling and walls, and a bathroom with shower. Bohemian style furnishings are highlighted by antiques and travel memorabilia. Breakfast is prepared with fresh local ingredients and served in the spacious kitchen.

Accommodation
Guestrooms: *1 double*
Services & Amenities: *French, English and Spanish are spoken; rooms cleaned every 3 days; tourist information; private parking*
Minimum stay: *2 nights*
Rates: €€
Credit cards: VISA MC *Bancomat*
Pets: 🚫

Scarperia (Florence)

• Bed & Breakfast Italia
Code T69
tel. 06 6878618, fax 06 6878619
info@bbitalia.it
www.bbitalia.it
Closed: varies

This small cottage with garden is at Bagnone in the Mugello area. It offers a room with a double bed and a room with twin beds, furnished with antiques. A private bathroom is shared by the two rooms, and is equipped with shower/tub. In the summer, breakfast is served in the garden or in the loggia, facing the hills; in winter, it is served in the dining room. A car is recommended.

Accommodation
Guestrooms: *2 (1 double bedroom and 1 double)*
Services & Amenities: *French and English are spoken; rooms cleaned every 3 days; tourist info; parking*
Minimum stay: *2 nights*
Rates: €€
Credit cards: VISA MC *Bancomat*
Pets: no

Siena

Villa Corazzesi
Angela Faccioli
strada del Petriccio e Belriguardo 81
53100 Siena
tel. 0577 595137, mob. 336 536369
villacorazzesi@inwind.it
spazioweb.inwind.it/villacorazzesi
Open all year

This B&B is hosted on the top floor of a large, restructured 18th-century villa that's located in a tranquil, quiet area, just a 10 minute drive from the center of Siena. The accommodation offers six guestrooms – four doubles, one triple and one single – each with bare beams and rustic style furnishings. The continental breakfast is served in a large dining room (with TV) reserved for the guests.

Accommodation
Guestrooms: *6 (1 single, 4 doubles and 1 triple, with private bath)*
Services & Amenities: *French and German spoken; rooms cleaned every day; tourist info; smokers welcome*
Rates: *single €€, double €€-€€€, triple €€€-€€€€*
Credit cards: *not accepted*
Pets: yes

Sinalunga (Siena)

Aia delle Coste
Clara Pascucci
via Cassia 146, località Bettolle
53048 Sinalunga (SI)
tel. and fax 0577 624070
mob. 347 9050723
aiadellecoste@ilr.it
Open all year

Accommodation
Guestrooms: *4 (2 doubles, with private bath, in independent apartment; 1 double bedroom, also single occupancy, with private bath; 1 suite)*
Services & Amenities: *French and English are spoken; rooms cleaned every day; complimentary tourist information; kitchen use by request; bike rental; terrace; garden; smokers welcome; private parking*
Rates: *single €€€, double €€€€. Children under 6 free. Discounts for groups and extended stays*
Credit cards: *not accepted*
Pets: yes

In this Leopoldine, 18th-C farmhouse, located in the heart of Valdichiana, the guests have a large apartment with modern furnishings, a large veranda that leads into the garden, and a living room with fireplace and library. The Italian breakfast, which consists of local sweet items, is served in the family dining room. This place is perfectly located for making one-day visits to Siena or Cortona, Montepulciano and Pienza.

Sovicille (Siena)

Borgo di Barigianino
Michela Donati
frazione Rosia, località Barigianino
53018 Sovicille (SI)
tel. and fax 0577 345644
mob. 348 5122536
barigianino@libero.it
www.barigianino.it
Open all year

This restructured farmstead, located in the Montagnola Natural Park hills, is practically a village. Its small houses, though they have their original rustic appearance, are provided with every comfort. The guest apartments, furnished in Tuscan style, have heating, independent entrances and gardens. Breakfast, is served in baskets that contain everything necessary, and is consumed in the house or in the garden. The hostess arranges courses in cuisine, ceramics and painting.

Accommodation
Guestrooms: *6 mini-apartments (2 to 4 beds each)*
Services & Amenities: *French and English spoken; rooms cleaned every 3 days; tourist info; baby-sitting service; kitchen and kitchinette; educational courses by request; garden; outdoor pool; smokers welcome; parking*
Minimum stay: *2 nights, 1 week in summer*
Rates: *double €€€. Discounts for extended stays*
Credit cards: *not accepted*
Pets:

Terranuova Bracciolini (Arezzo)

• Bed & Breakfast Italia
Code T47
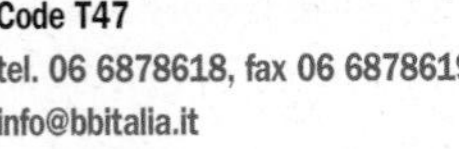
tel. 06 6878618, fax 06 6878619
info@bbitalia.it
www.bbitalia.it
Closed: varies

Detached house in a small and picturesque hamlet in the upper Arno Valley, in a scenic position in the "balze" area. The ladies of the house offer a friendly and informal stay. They offer guests a double room with private bathroom. The whole house has country-style furnishings, adorned with decorative beamed ceiling and rustic pieces of furniture. A window opening onto the old bent tile roof offers a view of the countryside and the river.

Accommodation
Guestrooms: *1 double bedroom*
Services & Amenities: *French and En-glish are spoken; rooms cleaned every 3 days; tourist info; parking*
Minimum stay: *2 nights*
Rates: *€€*
Credit cards: *Bancomat*
Pets:

Vaglia (Florence)

La Paggeria di Villa Mazzini
Paolo Verzelletti
via di Basciano 130
località Montorsoli
50030 Vaglia (FI)
tel. 055 401362, mob. 335 6266787
info@lapaggeria.com
www.lapaggeria.com
• Friendly Home-Gli Amici del B&B
tel. 02 860147, fax 02 875860
friendlymilano@dada.it
tel. and fax 011 9536376
fhrivoli@virgilio.it
Open all year

This 1850 house was formerly used to provide the services for the old Villa Mazzini. It is located on a hill just 10 kilometers from the center of Florence. The host made this house into the beautiful stone structure that it is today, using natural and ecological materials. Guests have the use of a large terrace, which provides a nice view of Florence and Fiesolo, as well as use of the garden and the living room, which has a fireplace and is also where breakfast is served.

Accommodation
Guestrooms: *3 (2 double bedrooms and 1 double, with private bath)*
Services & Amenities: *French and English are spoken; rooms cleaned every day; tourist info; terrace; garden; smokers welcome; parking*
Minimum stay: *2 nights*
Rates: *single €€€, double €€€€. Children under 3 free. Discounts for students and for honeymoon trips*
Credit cards: *not accepted*
Pets:

VARNA (FLORENCE)

Haus Wachtler
Veronika Wachter Tauber
strada Vecchia della Pusteria 11
50050 Varna (FI)
tel. 0472 837006
hauswachtler@gmx.net
Open all year

This house is located near an ancient convent that dates from 1142 and has now been converted into a public library. The B&B offers functional accommodation and a rich breakfast (various beverages, white and whole-wheat bread, cold cuts, cheeses, natural marmalade and Sunday sweet items), which is served in a small room reserved for the guests. There's a sand box in the garden for the children.

ACCOMMODATION
Guestrooms: *4 doubles, also single occupancy, with private bath; additional bed on request*
Services & Amenities: *German spoken; rooms cleaned every day; tourist information; Internet access; garden; smokers welcome; parking*
Rates: *€ per person*
Credit cards: *not accepted*
Pets:

VICCHIO (FLORENCE)

Frutti di Bosco
Bénédicte Lapere
via San Martino a Scopeto 53
50039 Vicchio (FI)
tel. and fax 055 8493568
blapere@tiscali.it
www.sottobosco.it
Open all year

This ancient, early 20th-century farmhouse, which is located in the green Mugello countryside, in the town where Giotto was born, has three rustic, comfortable guestrooms that have an independent entrance. Guests have the use of a living room that has a TV, the garden and a panoramic terrace. This terrace is where the large English breakfast is served.

ACCOMMODATION
Guestrooms: *3 (1 double bedroom with private bath, 2 doubles with shared bath, also single occupancy)*
Services & Amenities: *French, English, German and Dutch spoken; rooms cleaned every 3 days; tourist info; terrace; garden; smokers welcome; parking*
Minimum stay: *2 nights*
Rates: *double €€€-€€€€*
Credit cards: *not accepted*
Pets:

La Ripa
Meri Poli
via San Martino a Scopeto 63
50039 Vicchio (FI)
tel. and fax 055 8493519
mob. 329 8910392
laripa63@hotmail.com
Open all year

ACCOMMODATION
Guestrooms: *3 doubles, 1 also single occupancy and private bath, 2 with shared bath; additional bed on request*
Services & Amenities: *French and English are spoken; rooms cleaned every day; tourist information; garden; smokers welcome; private parking*
Minimum stay: *2 nights*
Rates: *single €€, double €€-€€€. Additional bed supplement €. Discounts for children -20%*
Credit cards: *not accepted*
Pets:

This B&B is in a stone farmhouse located in the beautiful Mugello Valley. This rustic house, surrounded by chestnut trees, is not far from Florence. The Italian breakfast is either served in the living room reserved for the guests or in the garden, when the weather's nice.

VILLA COLLEMANDINA (LUCCA)

• Bed & Breakfast Italia
Code T60
tel. 06 6878618, fax 06 6878619
info@bbitalia.it, www.bbitalia.it
Closed: varies

Villa on two levels, tucked away in the Garfagnana area. There is a double room with ensuite bathroom. Guests can enjoy a balcony, solarium, large hall, and satellite TV. Golf course and tennis court 10 km away.

ACCOMMODATION
Guestrooms: *1 double bedroom*
Services & Amenities: *English and Spanish are spoken; rooms cleaned every 3 days; tourist information; baby-sitting service; bike rental; horse-riding excursions; terrace; smokers welcome; private parking*
Minimum stay: *2 nights*
Rates: *€€*
Credit cards: *Bancomat*
Pets:

Vinci (Florence)

• **Bed & Breakfast Italia**
Code T31
tel. 06 6878618, fax 06 6878619
info@bbitalia.it
www.bbitalia.it
Closed: varies

TCI 10%

Accommodation
Guestrooms: *2 (1 single, 1 double)*
Services & Amenities: *English spoken; rooms cleaned every 3 days; tourist information; bike rental; terrace; air conditioning; Internet access; smokers welcome; private parking*
Minimum stay: *2 nights*
Rates: €€
Credit cards: VISA MC *Bancomat*
Pets: allowed

Country-house nestling in a green area with a double and single room, tastefully furnished with attention to detail, each with a large balcony. Rooms have TV and air conditioning. The host family is very friendly; on request they will organize wine and food tasting, prepare meals with local produce, and they are a source of precious information on the most interesting sites of the area.

Volterra (Pisa)

• **Bed & Breakfast Italia**
Code T39
tel. 06 6878618, fax 06 6878619
info@bbitalia.it
www.bbitalia.it
Closed: varies

Self-contained first-floor apartments in a villa with garden located 500 meters from the village's old center. The double rooms, with double or twin beds, feature comfortable, functional furnishings and TV. A third bed can be added in each room. The family offers a friendly, informal environment. A swimming pool and private parking are also at the guests' disposal. On request, is possible to use the kitchen.

Accommodation
Guestrooms: *3 (2 doubles, 1 triple)*
Services & Amenities: *French and English are spoken; rooms cleaned every 3 days; complimentary tourist information; terrace; private parking*
Minimum stay: *2 nights*
Rates: €€
Credit cards: VISA MC *Bancomat*
Pets: not allowed

• **Bed & Breakfast Italia**
Code T43
tel. 06 6878618, fax 06 6878619
info@bbitalia.it
www.bbitalia.it
Closed: varies

Accommodation
Guestrooms: *5 (3 doubles, 2 triples)* ♿
Services & Amenities: *English and German are spoken; rooms cleaned every 3 days; tourist information; smokers welcome; private parking*
Minimum stay: *2 nights*
Rates: €€
Credit cards: VISA MC *Bancomat*
Pets: allowed

A large farmhouse surrounded by a 20-hectare park of tall trees with a swimming pool. It perfectly reflects the Tuscan country-style house both inside and out. Guests are welcomed in a warm and refined environment. Five rooms are available, all with single beds and private bathrooms. The town has old origins and medieval monuments. Private parking available.

Marche

Acquaviva Picena (Ascoli Piceno)

• **Bed & Breakfast Italia**
Code MA4
tel. 06 6878618, fax 06 6878619
info@bbitalia.it
www.bbitalia.it
Closed: varies

A self-contained apartment in a small, old seventeenth-century building located within the walls of this medieval village. This accommodation offers two double bedrooms, one with TV, both with private bathroom with shower. Furnishings are modern and elegant. Guests are offered continental breakfast. This B&B is a 15-minute drive from the Adriatic coast and 20 km from San Benedetto del Tronto

Accommodation
Guestrooms: *2 double bedrooms*
Services & Amenities: *English spoken; rooms cleaned every 3 days; complimentary tourist information*
Minimum stay: *2 nights*
Rates: €€
Credit cards: VISA MC *Bancomat*
Pets: ✎

Cagli (Pesaro - Urbino)

Montescatto 12 TCI 10%
Laura Radice
località Montescatto
61043 Cagli (PU)
tel. 0721 799275
Closed: January, February and March

This B&B is located in a 16th-C farmhouse situated in the heart of the Umbria-Marche Apennines. Today, it's very nicely restructured and furnished with traditional Marche furniture and mementos that the hostess has collected on her various trips. The accommodation includes a large living room with a fireplace (with inscriptions dating from 1535), a terracotta floor and bare beams. Breakfast, which consists of organic products, including marmalades, fruit juice and genuine pastries, is served in the dining room.

Accommodation
Guestrooms: *3 (1 single, 2 doubles, 2 with private bath and 1 with shared bath)*
Services & Amenities: *French and Spanish are spoken; rooms cleaned every day; complimentary tourist information; terrace; garden; smokers welcome; private parking*
Rates: *single €, double €€. Children under 3 free; 3 to 11 -50%*
Credit cards: *not accepted*
Pets: ✎

CAMPOFILONE (ASCOLI PICENO)

Dal Capo B&B
Maria Lucia Resmini Mattioli
via Marina 3
63010 Campofilone (AP)
tel. 0734 932288, mob. 347 1623799
fax 0734 932747
omarbue@libero.it
www.primitaly.it/bb/dalcapo
www.dalcapo.it
Open all year

This B&B is in a recently-constructed villa out in the Marche countryside. It's surrounded by a garden next to an orchard and provides a nice view of the sea, which is only 1 km away. Guests have two modern style furnished rooms at their disposal, as well as a living room, which is provided with a library, a hi-fi system, and an ample collection of CD recordings of classical music. Breakfast is served on the terrace or in the kitchen.

ACCOMMODATION
Guestrooms: *2 (1 double bedroom, 1 double, also single occupancy, private bath); additional bed on request*
Services & Amenities: *rooms cleaned every 3 days; tourist information; terrace; garden; smokers welcome; private parking*
Minimum stay: *2 nights*
Rates: *single €-€€, double €€-€€€. Children under 5 free*
Credit cards: *not accepted*
Pets: 🚫

CÌNGOLI (MACERATA)

• Bed & Breakfast Italia
Code MA7
tel. 06 6878618, fax 06 6878619
info@bbitalia.it
www.bbitalia.it
Closed: varies

This old castle is situated in the center of a village, also called "the balcony of the Marche" for its stunning view over Mount Conero and the sea. Guest accommodation includes one double bedroom with twin beds and a private bathroom with shower. Guests can enjoy a well tended garden surrounding the house. This B&B boasts a very distinctive feature – a private cellar and family wine-tasting room, where local food and a fine selection of wines can be sampled.

ACCOMMODATION
Guestrooms: *1 double*
Services & Amenities: *English spoken; rooms cleaned every 3 days; complimentary tourist information*
Minimum stay: *2 nights*
Rates: *€€*
Credit cards: VISA MC *Bancomat*
Pets: 🚫

CUPRA MONTANA (ANCONA)

• Bed & Breakfast Italia
Code MA19
tel. 06 6878618, fax 06 6878619
info@bbitalia.it
www.bbitalia.it
Closed: varies

ACCOMMODATION
Guestrooms: *4 (2 double bedrooms and 2 triple rooms)*
Services & Amenities: *French, English and Spanish are spoken; rooms cleaned every 3 days; tourist information; bike rental; smokers welcome; private parking*
Minimum stay: *2 nights*
Rates: *€€*
Credit cards: VISA MC *Bancomat*
Pets: 🚫

In a small village in the province of Ancona, the hosts offer three small self-contained apartments. The accommodation consist in two triple rooms, each with a double and a single bed, and two double rooms, with a double bed. Three rooms have a private bathroom with shower. In the summertime, a continental breakfast with produce from the family farm is served in the garden. The owners provide bicycles and are happy to organize sightseeing and wine and food tours.

Fermo (Ascoli Piceno)

• Bed & Breakfast Italia
Code MA21
tel. 06 6878618, fax 06 6878619
info@bbitalia.it
www.bbitalia.it
Closed: varies

This B&B is located a short distance from the medieval walls of an old village on the hills overlooking the Adriatic coast. It consists in three bedrooms, two doubles and one single, each with independent entrance, private bathroom with shower, and TV. Private parking available since a vehicle is necessary to travel around the area. The house is 10 km from the beach at Porto San Giorgio e 15 km from San Benedetto.

Accommodation
Guestrooms: *3 (1 single and 2 double bedrooms)*
Services & Amenities: *French and English are spoken; rooms cleaned every 3 days; tourist info; private parking*
Minimum stay: *2 nights*
Rates: €€
Credit cards: VISA MC *Bancomat*
Pets: not allowed

Gagliole (Macerata)

Locanda San Rocco TCI 10%
località Collaiello 2
62020 Gagliole (MC)
tel. 0737 642324, 0737 641900
fax 0737 642324
Closed: Easter holidays, July,September

Accommodation
Guestrooms: *3 doubles, private bath; additional bed on request* ♿
Services & Amenities: *English, Spanish and Portuguese are spoken; rooms cleaned every day; tourist information; dinner reservation; bike rental; garden; smokers welcome*
Minimum stay: *2 nights*
Rates: *double* €€€€*. Additional bed supplement* €*. Children under 3 free*
Credit cards: VISA MC *Bancomat*
Pets: allowed

This rustic, 18th-C house, surrounded by the Verdicchio di Matelica vineyards, was very carefully restored and turned into an farm holiday set-up. The rooms, each of which has a different character, are provided with a private bathroom, TV and a telephone. Guests also have three nice living rooms. Breakfast consists of genuine pastries and products from the farm, and can either be served in the dining room or in the garden. Bicycles are also available.

Loro Piceno (Macerata)

Al Casale
Alma Rossini
viale della Vittoria 143
62020 Loro Piceno (MC)
tel. and fax 0733 507322
mob. 368 496279
alma@alcasale.com
www.alcasale.com
Open: May to October, holidays and weekends

This typical, converted farmhouse, with its friendly atmosphere, offers three rooms with period furniture, a living room with a fireplace, a large furnished garden and the use of several bicycles. Breakfast is either served in the dining room or outdoors. The hostess arranges mountain hikes for going on mushroom-gathering excursions, and also offers the guests the possibility of tasting some typical local products or products from the family farm.

Accommodation
Guestrooms: *3 double bedrooms, also single occupancy, private bath*
Services & Amenities: *French, English and Spanish are spoken; rooms cleaned every 3 days; tourist information; bike rental; garden; smokers welcome; private parking*
Minimum stay: *2 nights*
Rates: *single* €€*, double* €€€*. Discounts for children*
Credit cards: *not accepted*
Pets: allowed

MACERATA

• **Bed & Breakfast Italia**
Code MA22
tel. 06 6878618, fax 06 6878619
info@bbitalia.it
www.bbitalia.it
Closed: varies

This top-floor apartment with a large terrace in a modern building with elevator is located 300 m from the town's old center. The accommodation consists in two double bedrooms sharing a bathroom. The guestrooms are classically furnished with antiques. The lady of the house serves the rich continental breakfast in the lounge. The opera season held at the Sferisterio Theatre every year in July and August is highly recommended. The town is 30 minutes from Porto Recanati and Loreto, and 45 minutes from Ascoli Piceno.

ACCOMMODATION
Guestrooms: *2 double bedrooms* ♿
Services & Amenities: *French, English and Spanish are spoken; rooms cleaned every 3 days; tourist information; air conditioning; smokers welcome; private parking*
Minimum stay: *2 nights*
Rates: €€
Credit cards: VISA MC *Bancomat*
Pets: not allowed

MONTECÓSARO (MACERATA)

Europe B&B
Tiziana Matricardi
viale Europa 22, località Scalo
62010 Montecosaro (MC)
tel. and fax 0733 865859
mob. 340 0023240
tizianamat@tiscali.it, rioanni@tin.it
www.europe22.it
• **Friendly Home-Gli Amici del B&B**
tel. 02 860147, fax 02 875860
friendlymilano@dada.it
tel. and fax 011 9536376
fhrivoli@virgilio.it
Open all year

ACCOMMODATION
Guestrooms: *2 (1 double bedroom and 1 double, also single occupancy, with private bath)*
Services & Amenities: *French and English are spoken; rooms cleaned every day; complimentary tourist information; bike rental; garden*
Rates: *single €€, double €€€. Children under 6 free. Discounts for students and for honeymooners*
Credit cards: *not accepted*
Pets: not allowed

This B&B, which is hosted in a recently-built, independent house surrounded by a small, well-kept garden, is just a few kilometers from the beach and from such renowned art centers as Camerino and Fabriano. Guests have two rooms with trompe-l'oeil decorated walls and fine furnishings, as well as a quiet reading room. Breakfast consists of typical local products.

• **Bed & Breakfast Italia**
Code MA20
tel. 06 6878618, fax 06 6878619
info@bbitalia.it
www.bbitalia.it
Closed: varies

A villa set in the Marche countryside, a short distance from the center of Montecorsaro and only 6 km from the sea. A triple room with a double bed plus a single bed and a private bathroom with shower and a double bedroom with a private tub/shower bathroom are available. The rich continental breakfast is served on a large balcony under a wooden pergola. The furnishings are modern and elegant.

ACCOMMODATION
Guestrooms: *2 (1 double bedroom and 1 triple room)*
Services & Amenities: *French and English are spoken; rooms cleaned every 3 days; complimentary tourist information; bike rental; smokers welcome*
Minimum stay: *2 nights*
Rates: €€
Credit cards: VISA MC *Bancomat*
Pets: not allowed

Montedinove (Ascoli Piceno)

Il Fienile
Graziella Traini
contrada Valle, 63030 Montedinove (AP)
tel. 0736 828276, mob. 328 2263859
il.fienile@katamail.com
www.ilfienile.com
• **Friendly Home-Gli Amici del B&B**
tel. 02 860147, fax 02 875860
friendlymilano@dada.it
tel. and fax 011 9536376
fhrivoli@virgilio.it
Open all year

This typical Marches farmhouse is located in a community situated in the Sibillini Mountains. The recently-restored guestrooms have plain furnishings, as well as an independent entrance. The terrace and garden are perfect for relaxing, and bicycles are available for taking nice rides in the vicinity. Breakfast, which consists of typical local products, is served in a reserved dining room.

Accommodation
Guestrooms: *3 (2 double bedrooms and 1 double, also single occupancy, with private bath); additional bed on request ♿*
Services & Amenities: *rooms cleaned every 3 days; tourist info; kitchen use by request; bike rental; terrace; garden; smokers welcome; parking*
Rates: *single €, double €€. Additional bed supplement €. Children under 2 free. Discounts for students, seniors, disabled people and honeymooners.*
Credit cards: *not accepted*
Pets:

Morrovalle (Macerata)

B&B Il Casale
Nazzareno Salvucci
contrada Campomaggio 125
località Trodica
62010 Morrovalle (MC)
tel. 0733 865931, 0733 865560
mob. 337 634230, fax 0733 566510
info@ilcasale.org
www.ilcasale.org
Open all year

This farmhouse, built in 1780, has an independent apartment with a kitchen, three air conditioned rooms and modern furniture. The buffet breakfast, which is served in the kitchen, consists of natural pastries and local salami products. Guests are free to enjoy the swimming pool and the furnished garden, and can also use the available mountain bikes. They are also welcome to participate in some of the farm's activities, such as making marmalades and preserving food products. The host provides useful information on places to visit.

Accommodation
Guestrooms: *3 double bedrooms, also single occupancy, with private bath; additional bed on request*
Services & Amenities: *French, English and Spanish are spoken; rooms cleaned every 3 days; complimentary tourist information; kitchen use by request; bike rental; air conditioning; garden; smokers welcome; private parking*
Rates: *single €€, double €€€. Additional bed supplement €. Discounts for children and extended stays*
Credit cards: *not accepted*
Pets:

Novafeltria (Pesaro – Urbino)

B&B Pietra Salara
Alessandra Crosta
via Pietra Salara 22, località Secchiano
61015 Novafeltria (PU)
tel. 02 97290244, 0541 912344
mob. 348 5641554
Open: June to November,
Christmas and Easter holidays

The manor house, with its very beautiful garden, is in the center of this little hamlet located in the Montefeltro region. Most of the furnishings consist of family furniture and include wrought iron beds with decorated headboards and vestry cupboards. Breakfast, consists of pastries and natural marmalades, is served under the portico on the edge of the swimming pool. The hostess takes her guests on outings to gather officinal plants, as well as on walks along one of the many beaten paths.

Accommodation
Guestrooms: *2 doubles, with shared bath, and 1 mini-apartment (2 beds); additional bed on request*
Services & Amenities: *rooms cleaned every day; complimentary tourist information; garden; smokers welcome; private parking*
Minimum stay: *2 nights*
Rates: *double €€€-€€€€, mini-apartment €€€€. Additional bed supplement €*
Credit cards: *not accepted*
Pets:

Pesaro

Villa Cattani-Stuart
via Trebbiantico 67
61100 Pesaro
tel. and fax 0721 55782
villacattani@villacattani.it
www.villacattani.it
Open: May to September

This 18th-century villa is situated in the Pesaro hills, just a few kilometers from the sea. The accommodation offers three guestrooms with furnishings that are in the same style. The continental breakfast, which also includes cold cuts and cheese, is served in the room reserved for the guests. Guests also have the use of a reading room and one with a TV. They can also enjoy the park, which has a terraced Italian garden and a small grove of trees. There's also a small pond on the property.

Accommodation
Guestrooms: *3 doubles, private bath*
Services & Amenities: *French and English are spoken; rooms cleaned every day; complimentary tourist information; terrace; garden; smokers welcome; private parking*
Rates: *double €€-€€€. Children under 3 free; 3 to 10 -30%. Discounts for extended stays*
Credit cards: *not accepted*
Pets:

San Benedetto del Tronto (Ascoli Piceno)

• Bed & Breakfast Italia
Code MA1
tel. 06 6878618, fax 06 6878619
info@bbitalia.it
www.bbitalia.it
Closed: varies

This apartment is located on the mezzanine floor of a modern building. A single room with private bathroom with shower/tub is available. The B&B features simple, comfortable and fresh furnishings. Continental breakfast is served by the lady of the house in the adjacent garden in summer and in the kitchen in the cooler months. The bus stop is 100 m away. Private parking is available.

Accommodation
Guestrooms: *1 single*
Services & Amenities: *French and English are spoken; rooms cleaned every 3 days; complimentary tourist information; private parking*
Minimum stay: *2 nights*
Rates: €€
Credit cards: VISA MC *Bancomat*
Pets:

Tolentino (Macerata)

• Bed & Breakfast Italia TCI 10%
Code MA15
tel. 06 6878618, fax 06 6878619
info@bbitalia.it
www.bbitalia.it
Closed: varies

Accommodation
Guestrooms: *3 double bedrooms*
Services & Amenities: *French, English and Spanish are spoken; rooms cleaned every 3 days; complimentary tourist information; horse-riding excursions; smokers welcome; private parking*
Minimum stay: *2 nights*
Rates: €€
Credit cards: VISA MC *Bancomat*
Pets:

A thoroughly refurbished eighteenth-century farmhouse set in the Abbadia di Fiastra nature reserve. The house features typical architecture with ogival arch windows and doors, vaulted ceiling, exposed beams, terracotta and crushed stone flooring, as well as ethnic furnishings from exotic travels. This accommodation offers three double bedrooms with double beds – two share the same bathroom, the third has a private bathroom with shower. Extra bed for children available.

URBANIA (PESARO - URBINO)

• **Bed & Breakfast Italia**
Code MA8
tel. 06 6878618, fax 06 6878619
info@bbitalia.it
www.bbitalia.it
Closed: varies

This 19th-century farmhouse set in a park with swimming pool and tennis court is situated in Montefeltro, in the upper Metauro valley, 1 km from Urbania. This accommodation offers five double rooms, each with private bathroom with shower. All rooms are delightfully furnished in a personal style with antiques and wall decorations. Continental breakfast. Private parking is available.

ACCOMMODATION
Guestrooms: *5 doubles*
Services & Amenities: *rooms cleaned every 3 days; complimentary tourist information; private parking*
Minimum stay: *2 nights*
Rates: €€
Credit cards: VISA MC *Bancomat*
Pets:

URBINO

Ca' Andreana
Mauro Ferrari
via Gadana 119
località Ca' Andreana
61029 Urbino (PU)
tel. and fax 0722 327845
info@caandreana.com
www.caandreana.com
Closed: Mondays and Tuesdays, 15 January to 15 February and 20 September to 10 October

ACCOMMODATION
Guestrooms: *3 (2 doubles, also single occupancy; 1 triple, private bath)*
Services & Amenities: *French and English are spoken; rooms cleaned every day; complimentary tourist information; lunch reservation; garden; smokers welcome; private parking*
Rates: *single €€, double €€€, triple €€€. Children under 3 free*
Credit cards: *Bancomat*
Pets:

This B&B, which is hosted in a completely-restructured, 18th-century farmhouse situated in a wooded hilly area, has various, plainly-furnished rooms that face the surrounding countryside. The continental breakfast, which consists of natural products and genuine pastries, is served in a small reserved room where guests can also have dinner if desired. Guests can also enjoy taking hikes in the vicinity or go mountain-bike or horseback riding.

Ca' Maggio
Lea Luni
via Santa Maria di Pomonte 107
località Canavaccio
61029 Urbino (PU)
mob. 328 4212313
Open all year

ACCOMMODATION
Guestrooms: *3 double bedrooms, also single occupancy, private bath*
Services & Amenities: *French and English are spoken; rooms cleaned every 3 days; tourist information; bike rental; garden; smokers welcome; private parking*
Rates: *single €€€, double €€€€. Children under 4 free. Discounts for extended stays and families*
Credit cards: *accepted*
Pets:

This B&B, with its interesting, ancient atmosphere, is located in a medieval tower that's under the tutelage of the Superintendence. The house, which is surrounded by a large terrace and is just a few kilometers from the center of town, has a few mountain bikes available for guests. The Italian breakfast, consisting of typical and natural products, is either served in the covered loggia or in the large kitchen with fireplace.

Acquasparta (Terni)

La Casa nell'Oliveto
Menichella Marcucci
via Campagna 194/F
località Sant'Angelo
05021 Acquasparta (TR)
tel. and fax 0744 943480
mob. 328 2262048
casaolivo@yahoo.it
www.casaolivo.it
Open all year

This B&B, located in a small villa situated in the Umbrian countryside, 20 km from Todi, has two small independent apartments, each with early 20th-C furniture and a kitchenette. Breakfast, which includes homemade honey and fresh cottage cheese, is either served in the dining room or, if desired, in the apartments. The garden, which provides very pleasant relaxing, is surrounded by olive trees and has games for children.

Accommodation
Guestrooms: *3 (2 double bedrooms, 1 double, private bath)* ♿
Services & Amenities: *French spoken; rooms cleaned every 3 days; tourist information; kitchen use by request; bike rental; garden; smokers welcome; private parking*
Rates: *single €, double €€. Children under 6 free. Discounts for groups and extended stays*
Credit cards: *not accepted*
Pets:

• Bed & Breakfast Italia
Code U41
tel. 06 6878618, fax 06 6878619
info@bbitalia.it
www.bbitalia.it
Closed: varies

The hilltop villa is 2 km from the village. The whole first floor is available to guests. This includes two double rooms, a spacious bathroom, a sitting room with TV, a well-equipped kitchen and a parking space. Guests can enjoy the garden, equipped with a table, deckchairs, a playground and bicycles. The hostess greets her guests on arrival and provides them with useful brochures.

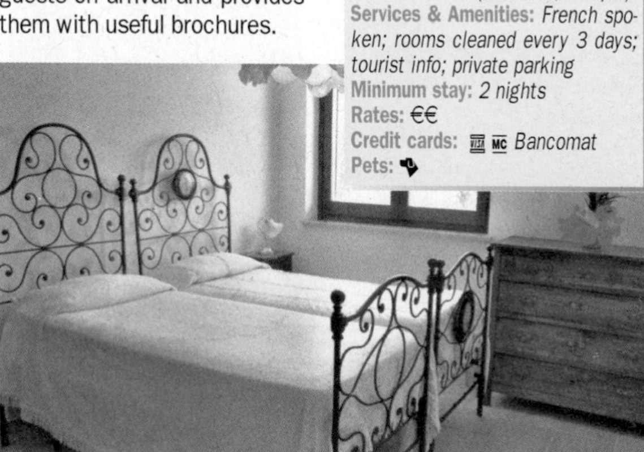

Accommodation
Guestrooms: *2 (1 double, 1 triple)*
Services & Amenities: *French spoken; rooms cleaned every 3 days; tourist info; private parking*
Minimum stay: *2 nights*
Rates: €€
Credit cards: VISA MC *Bancomat*
Pets:

Allerona (Terni)

Il Casaletto
• Ass. Welcome - B&B in Umbria
tel. 06 6878618, fax 06 6878619
info@bb.umbria.it
www.bbumbria.it
Open all year

This B&B is situated in a hilly area about 15 km from Orvieto. Two of the rooms are in the ancient, restructured farmhouse. The other is in the dépendance, which has a living room, a large kitchen and a veranda. Breakfast is either served in the family dining room, which is always at the guests' disposal, or under the portico. Both buildings are surrounded by two and one-half acres of land, part of which have olive trees and part a garden with ornamental plants and flowerbeds of lavender and roses. There's also a swimming pool.

Accommodation
Guestrooms: *3 doubles, also single occupancy, shared bath*
Services & Amenities: *French and English are spoken; rooms cleaned every day; tourist information; kitchen use by request; Internet access; garden; smokers welcome; private parking*
Rates: *single €€, double €€. Children under 3 free; 3 to 12 -35%*
Credit cards: *not accepted*
Pets:

Amelia (Terni)

• Bed & Breakfast Italia
Code U54
tel. 06 6878618, fax 06 6878619
info@bbitalia.it
www.bbitalia.it
Closed: varies

The B&B is located in an old three-story farmhouse, finely refurbished preserving its original style. It offers two well-furnished communicating rooms. The bathroom has a shower/tub. The orchard, olive grove and vineyard enclose everything. The family creates a friendly and informal environment. Private parking is available. The B&B is 1 km from Amelia, an interesting medieval hamlet.

Accommodation
Guestrooms: *2 (1 single and 1 double bedroom)* ♿
Services & Amenities: *English spoken; rooms cleaned every 3 days; complimentary tourist information; private parking*
Minimum stay: *2 nights*
Rates: €€
Credit cards: VISA MC *Bancomat*
Pets:

Arrone (Terni)

• Bed & Breakfast Italia
Code U25
tel. 06 6878618, fax 06 6878619
info@bbitalia.it
www.bbitalia.it
Closed: varies

This B&B is located in a small medieval hamlet, 15 km from the town of Terni; the villages of Piediluco and Labbro can be reached in 10 minutes. The guest accommodation consists in two twin rooms, with private bathroom with shower/tub and a large balcony. Guests can also use the garden around the house and parking. Children under two are welcome.

Accommodation
Guestrooms: *2 doubles*
Services & Amenities: *French and English are spoken; rooms cleaned every 3 days; complimentary tourist information; private parking*
Minimum stay: *2 nights*
Rates: €€
Credit cards: VISA MC *Bancomat*
Pets:

Assisi (Perugia)

• **Bed & Breakfast Italia**
Code U47
tel. 06 6878618, fax 06 6878619
info@bbitalia.it
www.bbitalia.it
Closed: varies

The suite consists in a sitting room, a double bedroom and a bathroom. The walls and ceiling are made of stone; a niche contains a modern fresco portraying St. Francis praying. The suite has also separate access to a garden with a medieval well, offering a view of Assisi and the Umbrian hills around the plain. A relaxing and distinguished environment.

The Calendimaggio historical parade.

Accommodation
Guestrooms: *1 double bedroom*
Services & Amenities: *French, English and German are spoken; rooms cleaned every 3 days; complimentary tourist information; air conditioning; smokers welcome*
Minimum stay: *2 nights*
Rates: €€€
Credit cards: VISA MC *Bancomat*
Pets: 🚫

• **Bed & Breakfast Italia**
Code U48
tel. 06 6878618, fax 06 6878619
info@bbitalia.it
www.bbitalia.it
Closed: varies

A suite in a medieval building in the very heart of the town, offering a panoramic view. Completely restored preserving its old origins, its façade boasts a 14th-C fresco portraying the Virgin Mary and Child. The accommodation features prestigious finishes, colored walls, frescoed doors and attention to detail. It includes a double bedroom, a sitting room with double sofa bed, a bathroom with shower and an independent entrance.

Accommodation
Guestrooms: *2 doubles*
Services & Amenities: *French, English and German are spoken; rooms cleaned every 3 days; complimentary tourist information; air conditioning; smokers welcome; private parking*
Minimum stay: *2 nights*
Rates: €€€
Credit cards: VISA MC *Bancomat*
Pets: 🚫

• **Bed & Breakfast Italia**
Code U49
tel. 06 6878618, fax 06 6878619
info@bbitalia.it, www.bbitalia.it
Closed: varies

Accommodation
Guestrooms: *2 (1 double bedroom and 1 double)*
Services & Amenities: *French, English and German are spoken; rooms cleaned every 3 days; tourist information; air conditioning; smokers welcome; private parking*
Minimum stay: *2 nights*
Rates: €€€
Credit cards: VISA MC *Bancomat*
Pets: 🚫

This B&B is hosted in a second floor suite in an old medieval building located in the old center. It is an attic air conditioned apartment with a large sitting room with fireplace and TV, and offers to its guests a double room and a twin, with two private bathrooms with shower. The ceiling has exposed beams and French doors open onto a large, scenic balcony with a view of the basilica of Santa Chiara and the surrounding plain. Private parking is available.

• **Bed & Breakfast Italia**
Code U50
tel. 06 6878618, fax 06 6878619
info@bbitalia.it
www.bbitalia.it
Closed: varies

First floor studio apartment in an old medieval building, completely refurbished preserving its original structure, located in the old center. It features a living area with fireplace, TV, double sofa bed, private bathroom with shower, vaulted ceiling, old frescoes on the walls and fine furnishings.

Accommodation
Guestrooms: *1 double bedroom*
Services & Amenities: *rooms cleaned every 3 days; complimentary tourist information; air conditioning; private parking*
Minimum stay: *2 nights*
Rates: €€€
Credit cards: VISA MC *Bancomat*
Pets: no

• **Bed & Breakfast Italia**
Code U51
tel. 06 6878618, fax 06 6878619
info@bbitalia.it
www.bbitalia.it
Closed: varies

Second-floor suite in a small medieval building, with a fourteenth-century fresco portraying the Virgin Mary and Child on the façade, completely restored preserving its origins and located in the very old center. The suite consists in a lounge, a double room, a single room and a bathroom with shower. It has TV and a large scenic balcony affording a view of the Basilica of Santa Chiara, the old center and the surrounding plain.

Accommodation
Guestrooms: *2 (1 single, 1 double)*
Services & Amenities: *French, English and German are spoken; rooms cleaned every 3 days; tourist information; air conditioning; smokers welcome; private parking*
Minimum stay: *2 nights*
Rates: €€€
Credit cards: VISA MC *Bancomat*
Pets: no

Baschi (Terni)

• **Bed & Breakfast Italia**
Code U12
tel. 06 6878618, fax 06 6878619
info@bbitalia.it
www.bbitalia.it
Closed: varies

The B&B features a well-tended garden and a swimming pool that overlooks the scenic hills. The rooms, three double with private bathroom, are spacious and furnished in a fresh, cheerful style. Orvieto is 10 min away by car. Its ceramics craftsmanship and well-known traditional medieval processions, including the so-called "Palombella" held in June on the day of Pentecost, are of great interest.

Accommodation
Guestrooms: *3 doubles*
Services & Amenities: *French and English are spoken; rooms cleaned every 3 days; complimentary tourist information; private parking*
Minimum stay: *2 nights*
Rates: €€
Credit cards: VISA MC *Bancomat*
Pets: yes

Bastia Umbra (Perugia)

Il Corbezzolo
• Ass. Welcome - B&B in Umbria
tel. 0763 305523, fax 0763 390670
info@bb.umbria.it
www.bbumbria.it
Closed: mid to late January and mid to late November

This B&B is in a single-family residence, located just a short distance from the center, only 3 km from Assisi. It has classic furnishings, a living room with TV and a VCR. Breakfast is either served in the kitchen or on the terrace. Guests can also enjoy relaxing in the garden. There are various churches and medieval fortresses in the vicinity well worth visiting, as well as several places for tasting good wines and enjoying fine cuisine.

Accommodation
Guestrooms: *3 (1 single and 2 doubles, with shared bath); additional child's bed on request*
Services & Amenities: *rooms cleaned every 3 days; complimentary tourist information; terrace; garden; smokers welcome; private parking*
Rates: *single €-€€, double €€-€€€*
Credit cards: *not accepted*
Pets: no

Bettona (Perugia)

La Piazzetta
• Ass. Welcome - B&B in Umbria
tel. 0763 305523, fax 0763 390670
info@bb.umbria.it
www.bbumbria.it
Closed: 6 January to 6 March and November

This stone house in the old center has 3 guestrooms with plain furnishings that also include several antiques, and a small apartment that has an equipped kitchenette. The breakfast, which also includes pastries and natural biscuits, as well as typical Umbrian flat bread-cake, is served in the living room, which is also at the disposal of the guests.

Accommodation
Guestrooms: *4 (3 double bedrooms, private bath; 1 mini-apartment)* ♿
Services & Amenities: *English spoken; rooms cleaned every day; tourist information; kitchenette; Internet access; garden; smokers welcome; private parking*
Rates: *double €€€€*
Credit cards: *accettate*
Pets: yes

Bevagna (Perugia)

Antignano
• Ass. Welcome - B&B in Umbria
tel. 0763 305523, fax 0763 390670
info@bb.umbria.it
www.bbumbria.it
Open: April to October

This B&B, located in Torre del Colle at an altitude of 400 meters, is 7 kilometers from the center. Its three double rooms, which have a TV and an independent entrance, share two bathrooms. Breakfast, which is of continental type or as desired, is either served in the guest living room or, when the weather's nice, outdoors.

Accommodation
Guestrooms: *3 double bedrooms, with shared bath*
Services & Amenities: *English spoken; rooms cleaned every 3 days; complimentary tourist information; kitchenette; garden; smokers welcome; private parking*
Rates: *single €€, double €€€. Additional bed supplement €. Children under 3 free, 3 to 12 -35%*
Credit cards: *not accepted*
Pets: yes

Cenerente (Perugia)

• **Bed & Breakfast Italia**
Code U08
tel. 06 6878618, fax 06 6878619
info@bbitalia.it
www.bbitalia.it
Closed: varies

Cenerente is a village 570 m above sea level, in a stunningly scenic position. The apartment is in a detached house in the Umbrian countryside. The guest area is made up of a triple room with a double and a single bed, a bathroom with shower, a small kitchen, a spacious balcony and independent entrance. Use of the kitchen, fully furnished and equipped, can replace breakfast service.

Accommodation
Guestrooms: *1 triple*
Services & Amenities: *French and English are spoken; rooms cleaned every 3 days; complimentary tourist information; terrace; private parking*
Minimum stay: *2 nights*
Rates: €€
Credit cards: VISA MC *Bancomat*
Pets: not allowed

Città della Pieve (Perugia)

La Fratta TCI 10%
• **Ass. Welcome - B&B in Umbria**
tel. 0763 305523, fax 0763 390670
info@bb.umbria.it
www.bbumbria.it
Open all year

This B&B, in a 30-year-old, gray-stone house located in the foothills, has three rooms with country-style furnishings, as well as a few antique items. Breakfast includes natural pastries and is served in the rustic living room with fireplace. Guests are welcome to use the family's mountain bikes, as well as the barbecue for preparing outdoor dinners.

Accommodation
Guestrooms: *3 (2 double bedrooms and 1 double, private bath)* ♿
Services & Amenities: *English and Russian are spoken; rooms cleaned every 3 days; complimentary tourist information; kitchenette; bike rental; garden; smokers welcome; private parking*
Rates: *double €€-€€€. Children under 3 free; 4 to 12 -35%*
Credit cards: *not accepted*
Pets: not allowed

• **Bed & Breakfast Italia**
Code U42
tel. 06 687861, fax 06 6878619
info@bbitalia.it
www.bbitalia.it
Closed: varies

The B&B is located in a villa nestling in a leafy, green area. The guest accommodation consists in three bedrooms, a double, a twin and a triple, all with a nice view of the surrounding park. The bathrooms, one equipped with shower and one with tub, are for the exclusive use of guests. The large garden, several bicycles, a second independent entrance and the private parking are all available for the guests.

Accommodation
Guestrooms: *3 (1 double bedroom, 1 double and 1 triple room)*
Services & Amenities: *rooms cleaned every 3 days; complimentary tourist information; bike rental; smokers welcome; private parking*
Minimum stay: *2 nights*
Rates: €€
Credit cards: VISA MC *Bancomat*
Pets: not allowed

Città di Castello (Perugia)

• **Bed & Breakfast Italia**
Code U27
tel. 06 6878618, fax 06 6878619
info@bbitalia.it
www.bbitalia.it
Closed: varies

The B&B is a self-contained apartment in a fifteenth-century building. It is furnished with antiques in a classic, elegant style. The spacious balcony with a large glass window gives a view of the old center rooftops and the hills around the village. The little town is also known for its pottery and hand-woven textiles using Renaissance techniques.

Accommodation
Guestrooms: *2 doubles*
Services & Amenities: *English spoken; rooms cleaned every 3 days; complimentary tourist information*
Minimum stay: *2 nights*
Rates: €€
Credit cards: VISA MC *Bancomat*
Pets:

Corciano (Perugia)

Il Galletto
• **Ass. Welcome - B&B in Umbria**
tel. 0763 305523
fax 0763 390670
info@bb.umbria.it
www.bbumbria.it
Open all year

This B&B, close to the walls of a medieval village, offers three guestrooms furnished in the classic style that lead directly into the villa's large garden. There are two double rooms and one with three beds, a fireplace, a living area (with TV and library) and a kitchenette. The large breakfast consists of pastries, homemade marmalades, fresh eggs, products from the family farm, flat bread-cake and various cheeses, and is either served in the guestrooms or, when the weather's nice, in the garden.

Accommodation
Guestrooms: *3 (2 doubles, also single occupancy, 1 triple room, private bath); additional bed on request* ♿
Services & Amenities: *French, English and German are spoken; rooms cleaned every 3 days; tourist info; kitchen and kitchenette use by request; garden; smokers welcome*
Rates: *single €€, double €€€, triple €€€. Additional bed supplement €. Children under 3 free; 3 to 12 -35%*
Credit cards: *not accepted*
Pets:

• **Bed & Breakfast Italia**
Code U11
tel. 06 6878618, fax 06 6878619
info@bbitalia.it
www.bbitalia.it
Closed: varies

The B&B is located in an old medieval village that has remained unchanged throughout the centuries. The apartment features a double and a quadruple room, both with TV and furnished in a cheerful, modern style. The rooms share a bathroom with shower. On request, the lady of the house provides a cot for children under the age of two. The village preserves its old wine and food traditions, as well as Etruscan remains.

Accommodation
Guestrooms: *1 double, 1 quadruple*
Services & Amenities: *French, English and German are spoken; rooms cleaned every 3 days; tourist info; terrace; private parking*
Minimum stay: *2 nights*
Rates: €
Credit cards: VISA MC *Bancomat*
Pets:

DERUTA (PERUGIA)

B&B La Pietra Filosofale
• Ass. Welcome - B&B in Umbria
tel. 0763 305523, fax 0763 390670
info@bb.umbria.it
www.bbumbria.it
Closed: 7 to 31 January

TCI 10%

This apartment, which is located in an 18th-century building in the old center of the city of ceramics, has a warm, friendly atmosphere. The accommodation consists in three double rooms and also offers the use of a VCR, a kitchen, a laundry, and bicycles. The hostess can also organize various educational courses and is happy to provide useful informations about the surrounding area.

ACCOMMODATION
Guestrooms: *3 doubles, with shared bath*
Services & Amenities: *English, German and Spanish are spoken; rooms cleaned every day; complimentary tourist information; kitchen use by request; bike rental; horse-riding excursions; educational courses by request; Internet access; garden; smokers welcome; private parking*
Rates: *double €€€. Discounts for children under 6, students, singles and honeymooners*
Credit cards: *not accepted*
Pets:

FABRO (TERNI)

Il Roseto
• Ass. Welcome - B&B in Umbria
tel. 0763 305523, fax 0763 390670
info@bb.umbria.it
www.bbumbria.it
Closed: varies

TCI 10%

ACCOMMODATION
Guestrooms: *1 double, private bath*
Services & Amenities: *English spoken; rooms cleaned every day; complimentary tourist information; terrace; Internet access; garden; smokers welcome; private parking*
Rates: *double €€-€€€*
Credit cards: *not accepted*
Pets:

This B&B is located in a recently-restructured farmhouse situated on a large estate that also has a small, ancient church. The guest accommodation consists of a double room, with plain Umbrian furniture and a private bathroom. The Italian breakfast, which includes homemade pastries and other natural specialties offered by the hostess, is served on the terrace, which is covered by a small loggia. For relaxing, there's a large garden and a portico that surround the house.

• Bed & Breakfast Italia
Code U40
tel. 06 6878618, fax 06 6878619
info@bbitalia.it
www.bbitalia.it
Closed: varies

The B&B is on the 2nd floor of a typical lodging-house. The double rooms and bathroom are equipped for the disabled. Each room has brickwork vaults and exposed beamed ceilings. The owner welcomes guests on arrival offering them a sample of mushrooms, truffles, the local Vinsanto, a sweet white raisin wine, and to finish "cantuccini", local home-made biscuits.

ACCOMMODATION
Guestrooms: *3 (1 double and 2 double bedrooms)* ♿
Services & Amenities: *rooms cleaned every 3 days; tourist information; bike rental; private parking*
Minimum stay: *2 nights*
Rates: €€
Credit cards: VISA MC *Bancomat*
Pets:

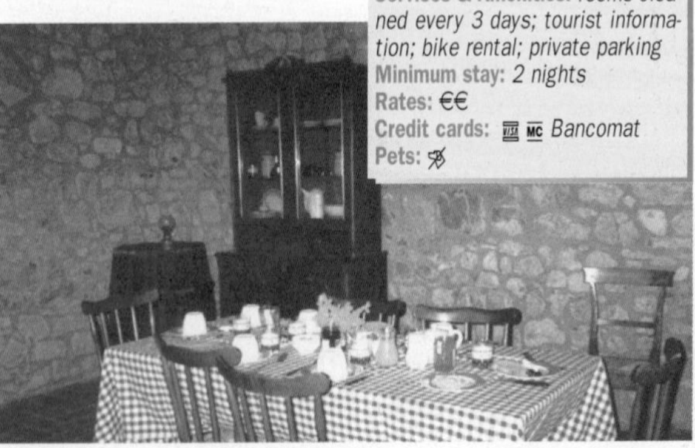

Ficulle (Terni)

• **Bed & Breakfast Italia**
Code U58
tel. 06 6878618, fax 06 6878619
info@bbitalia.it
www.bbitalia.it
Closed: varies

This B&B is located in a stone farmhouse, recently refurbished, in the Umbrian hills, within the Castello della Sala hunting reserve. The guest accommodation consists in two small apartments: one with two double rooms, bathroom with shower, kitchen and TV; the other with one double room, a kitchenette and a bathroom with shower. Both are furnished in rustic style. The bus stop is 700 m away.

Accommodation
Guestrooms: *3 doubles*
Services & Amenities: *rooms cleaned every 3 days; complimentary tourist information; smokers welcome; private parking*
Minimum stay: *2 nights*
Rates: *€€*
Credit cards: *Visa MC Bancomat*
Pets: *allowed*

Fratta Todina (Perugia)

Casale Terrarossa (TCI 10%)
• **Ass. Welcome - B&B in Umbria**
tel. 0763 305523, fax 0763 390670
info@bb.umbria.it
www.bbumbria.it
Closed: varies

Accommodation
Guestrooms: *2 doubles, also single occupancy, with shared bath; additional bed on request*
Services & Amenities: *French spoken; rooms cleaned every day; tourist information; garden; smokers welcome*
Rates: *single €€€, double €€€. Additional bed supplement 30%. Discounts for children*
Credit cards: *not accepted*
Pets: *not allowed*

This large, 18th-C, recently-restructured, stone farmhouse, which has art déco-style furnishings, is situated midway between Marsciano and Todi, just outside the old center. The French hostess serves the Italian breakfast in the family dining room.

Lugnano in Teverina (Terni)

• **Bed & Breakfast Italia**
Code U55
tel. 06 6878618, fax 06 6878619
info@bbitalia.it
www.bbitalia.it
Closed: varies

Accommodation
Guestrooms: *1 double*
Services & Amenities: *English spoken; rooms cleaned every 3 days; complimentary tourist information*
Minimum stay: *2 nights*
Rates: *€€*
Credit cards: *Visa MC Bancomat*
Pets: *not allowed*

This apartment, in a building dating from the early 20th century, is in the old center of a medieval hamlet in a scenic position in the Tiber valley. The large room has twin beds and is tastefully furnished in a simple but colorful style. The bathroom has a shower and the entrance is independent. Breakfast is prepared with typical local produce and served in the lounge. The medieval hamlet is in a strategic position for Orvieto (30 km) and Todi (60 km).

MAGIONE (PERUGIA)

• Bed & Breakfast Italia
Code U20
tel. 06 6878618, fax 06 6878619
info@bbitalia.it
www.bbitalia.it
Closed: varies

ACCOMMODATION
Guestrooms: *3 (2 doubles, 1 triple)*
Services & Amenities: *French and English are spoken; rooms cleaned every 3 days; complimentary tourist information; bike rental; horse-riding excursions; private parking*
Minimum stay: *2 nights*
Rates: €€
Credit cards: VISA MC *Bancomat*
Pets:

The farm lies on a hill not far from the Lake Trasimeno. This B&B offers comfortable apartments with independent entrance. They are located in an old, nineteenth-century farmhouse, built of so-called 'serena' stone and carefully renovated. Furnishings are classical; the bathrooms are new and have a shower. Decorative beamed ceilings and stonewalls create an old atmosphere. The owner's hospitality offers courtesy, sincerity and quality services. Private parking available. The village of Maggione is easily reached on the A1 highway.

MARSCIANO (PERUGIA)

Locanda di San Bartolomeo
Renato and Cinzia Ciccarelli
vocabolo San Bartolomeo
06055 Marsciano (PG)
tel. and fax 075 8743990
locsanbartolomeo@hotmail.com
www.umbriacountryhouse.net
Closed: Christmas holidays

ACCOMMODATION
Guestrooms: *3 doubles, private bath; additional bed on request*
Services & Amenities: *rooms cleaned every 3 days; tourist info; lunch & dinner reservations; garden; smokers welcome; private parking*
Rates: *double €€€€. Additional bed supplement €*
Credit cards: *not accepted*
Pets:

This 18th-century, recently-restructured, stone farmhouse, is situated on a hill near a forest. The accommodation offers three large, elegant, romantic rooms whose names echo the titles of great literary classics. The rich breakfast, which consists of natural, organic products, is served in a reserved dining room. The table is carefully set with fine silverware and porcelain dishes.

MONTECASTRILLI (TERNI)

• Bed & Breakfast Italia
Code U24
tel. 06 6878618, fax 06 6878619
info@bbitalia.it
www.bbitalia.it
Closed: varies

ACCOMMODATION
Guestrooms: *3 (1 single, 2 doubles)*
Services & Amenities: *French, English and Spanish are spoken; rooms cleaned every 3 days; tourist information; private parking*
Minimum stay: *2 nights*
Rates: €€
Credit cards: VISA MC *Bancomat*
Pets:

White walls decorated with stones enhance the typical country-style of this farmhouse. The simply furnished rooms face the garden. The B&B is located within 20 minutes walking distance of the small hamlet center. A car is needed to visit the hinterland.

MONTEFALCO (PERUGIA)

In Villa 
• Ass. Welcome - B&B in Umbria
tel. 0763 305523, fax 0763 390670
info@bb.umbria.it
www.bbumbria.it
Closed: varies

ACCOMMODATION
Guestrooms: *3 (2 double bedrooms and 1 double, with shared bath); additional bed on request*
Services & Amenities: *English and German are spoken; rooms cleaned every day; tourist information; kitchen use by request; garden; smokers welcome; parking*
Rates: *double €€-€€€. Additional bed supplement 30%*
Credit cards: *not accepted*
Pets: ✓

This large villa, surrounded by a park, is situated in the Belvedere area, just outside the old medieval center. The wide view takes in the hills surrounding the Umbria Valley. The house has both antique and modern furnishings. Rooms have wrought-iron beds and plain, Umbrian furniture. There is also a swimming pool. Breakfast is served in the shared room. The town's San Francesco church, which dates from the 14th C, is very well worth visiting.

• Bed & Breakfast Italia
Code U32
tel. 06 6878618, fax 06 6878619
info@bbitalia.it
www.bbitalia.it
Closed: varies

ACCOMMODATION
Guestrooms: *4 (2 single, 2 doubles)*
Services & Amenities: *English spoken; rooms cleaned every 3 days; complimentary tourist information; private parking*
Minimum stay: *2 nights*
Rates: *€€*
Credit cards: VISA MC *Bancomat*
Pets: ✗

This villa is surrounded by a large garden. The landlords offer two independent wings for B&B purposes; both consist in a single and a double room with private bathroom. The classic furnishings are enriched with colored fittings, making the environment welcoming and comfortable. To reach the accommodation by car, take the A1 highway and exit at Orte. It is 20 km from Spello and Spoleto. Private parking is available for the guests.

MONTELEONE D'ORVIETO (TERNI)

Jolly Camere
• Ass. Welcome - B&B in Umbria
tel. 0763 305523, fax 0763 390670
info@bb.umbria.it
www.bbumbria.it
Open all year

ACCOMMODATION
Guestrooms: *3 (1 single and 2 double bedrooms, with private bath); additional bed on request*
Services & Amenities: *French and English are spoken; rooms cleaned every day; tourist information; kitchenette; garden; smokers welcome; private parking*
Rates: *single €€, double €€. Additional bed supplement €€. Children under 3 free*
Credit cards: *not accepted*
Pets: ✓

This B&B is hosted by a small, recently-restructured, '50s villa, located in Monteleone d'Orvieto, near Terni. The guest accommodation consists in two double rooms, with a kitchenette, and one single room. All three have modern furnishings and private bathrooms. The rich continental breakfast is either served in the dining room or, when the weather's nice, in the garden.

The hostess can make arrangements through a specialized association for providing the guests with guided tours of the area. Guests also have the use of private, internal parking.

• Bed & Breakfast Italia
Code U31
tel. 06 6878618, fax 06 6878619
info@bbitalia.it
www.bbitalia.it
Closed: varies

The B&B is in an old building within its medieval walls. Two of the guestrooms have a large balcony and TV. The bathrooms are for the exclusive use of guests. The original settlement at Monteleone d'Orvieto dates from 1000/1100 AD. The castle, fortress, drawbridge, walls and towers are witnesses to its stormy past under the rule of many noble families.

ACCOMMODATION
Guestrooms: *4 (1 single, 1 double and 2 double bedrooms)*
Services & Amenities: *English spoken; rooms cleaned every 3 days; complimentary tourist information*
Minimum stay: *2 nights*
Rates: *€€*
Credit cards: *MC Bancomat*
Pets:

MONTONE (PERUGIA)

B&B Il Poggio delle Noci
• Ass. Welcome - B&B in Umbria
tel. 0763 305523, fax 0763 390670
info@bb.umbria.it
www.bbumbria.it
Closed: varies

This B&B is located in a beautiful house situated on a verdant hill that provides a nice panoramic view. It's just outside the city's old center and only a few km from Gubbio. The very nice, personalized furnishings also include some antiques. The Italian breakfast is served in the kitchen.

ACCOMMODATION
Guestrooms: *2 doubles with private bath; additional bed on request*
Services & Amenities: *French spoken; rooms cleaned every day; tourist information; kitchen use by request; Internet access; garden; smokers welcome; private parking*
Rates: *double €€€. Additional bed supplement 30%*
Credit cards: *not accepted*
Pets:

Il Caseto
• Ass. Welcome - B&B in Umbria
tel. 0763 305523, fax 0763 390670
info@bb.umbria.it
www.bbumbria.it
Open all year

ACCOMMODATION
Guestrooms: *2 (1 single and 1 double bedroom, with shared bath)*
Services & Amenities: *English spoken; rooms cleaned every day; complimentary tourist information; bike rental; garden; smokers welcome*
Minimum stay: *2 nights*
Rates: *single €, double €€€. Children under 3 free; 3 to 12 -35%*
Credit cards: *not accepted*
Pets:

This B&B is in a 17th-century, stone house not far from a medieval village. Each of the two guestrooms has an independent entrance and both rooms share the use of a small living room with TV, telephone and a hi-fi system. The rooms, which are furnished in the classic manner and include a few antiques, lead directly into a large garden. The rich Italian breakfast consists of local products and is either served in the living room or outdoors.

Narni (Terni)

B&B La Fenice
• Ass. Welcome - B&B in Umbria
tel. 0763 305523, fax 0763 390670
info@bb.umbria.it
www.bbumbria.it
Closed: varies

This house, located in a village near Narni, has a garden and personalized English-style furnishing. Guests have the use of a very well furnished library that includes a nice collection of international guide books. The atmosphere is cosmopolitan and quite particular. There are many interesting eating places in the vicinity that are certainly well worth visiting.

Accommodation
Guestrooms: *2 doubles with shared bath; additional bed on request*
Services & Amenities: *French spoken; rooms cleaned every day; complimentary tourist information; garden; smokers welcome*
Minimum stay: *2 nights*
Rates: *single €€, double €€€. Additional bed supplement 30%*
Credit cards: *not accepted*
Pets:

• Bed & Breakfast Italia
Code U26
tel. 06 6878618, fax 06 6878619
info@bbitalia.it
www.bbitalia.it
Closed: varies

Located in the old medieval hamlet, this B&B is a stone-finished house. Carefully maintained and comfortable, it has an independent entrance and country-style furnishings. The guest accommodation consists in two double rooms: one with a double four-poster bed and the other with twin beds. The private bathroom has a tub. The village is 12 km from Terni.

Accommodation
Guestrooms: *2 (1 double bedroom and 1 double)*
Services & Amenities: *French and English are spoken; rooms cleaned every 3 days; tourist information*
Minimum stay: *2 nights*
Rates: *€€*
Credit cards: VISA MC *Bancomat*
Pets:

• Bed & Breakfast Italia
Code U56
tel. 06 6878618, fax 06 6878619
info@bbitalia.it
www.bbitalia.it
Closed: varies

The villa, surrounded by a 500 square meter olive grove, includes a room with double bed and TV and a room with twin beds, which share a bathroom with shower/tub. The option of a cot is included. Furnishings are colorful and cheerful; the atmosphere is quiet. Breakfast can be served in the lounge or in the garden, weather permitting. Private parking is available. The town offers many opportunities including natural, art and cultural tours.

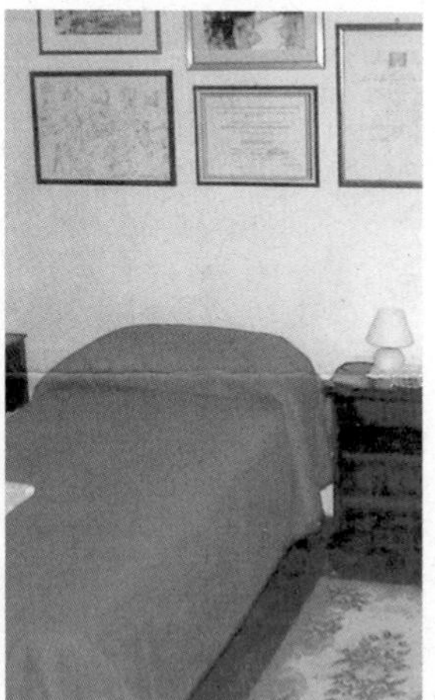

Accommodation
Guestrooms: *2 doubles*
Services & Amenities: *French and English are spoken; rooms cleaned every 3 days; complimentary tourist information; bike rental; air conditioning; private parking*
Minimum stay: *2 nights*
Rates: *€€*
Credit cards: VISA MC *Bancomat*
Pets:

Nocera Umbra (Perugia)

• **Bed & Breakfast Italia**
Code U52
tel. 06 6878618, fax 06 6878619
info@bbitalia.it
www.bbitalia.it
Closed: varies

A complex of ten apartments located in the panoramic medieval hamlet. These apartments include a small sitting room, one or two double bedrooms, private bathroom with shower and kitchenette. Swimming pool, playground for children, barbecue, and the garden are also available. The village is very quaint, with terraced houses built on different levels of the steep hill that dominates the Topino valley.

Accommodation
Guestrooms: *2 bedrooms each* ♿
Services & Amenities: *French, English and German are spoken; rooms cleaned every 3 days; complimentary tourist information; bike rental; smokers welcome; private parking*
Minimum stay: *2 nights*
Rates: €€
Credit cards: VISA MC *Bancomat*
Pets: 🚫

Orvieto (Terni)

Il Palazzo del Cardinale TCI 10%
• **Ass. Welcome - B&B in Umbria**
tel. 0763 305523, fax 0763 390670
info@bb.umbria.it
www.bbumbria.it
Closed: varies

This B&B consists of a suite, located in the dépendance of an ancient, aristocratic building, and a separate guestroom, located inside the family apartment. The suite has antique and modern furniture and a double bed located on an upper level. The room in the apartment has frescoes and period furniture. Breakfast is either served in the dining room or in the guestroom.

Accommodation
Guestrooms: *1 suite (4 beds) and 1 double*
Services & Amenities: *English, German and Spanish are spoken; rooms cleaned every day; tourist information; kitchen use by request; lunch & dinner reservations; garden; smokers welcome*
Rates: *double* €€€€, *suite* €€€€
Credit cards: *not accepted*
Pets: 🚫

La Magnolia TCI 10%
• **Ass. Welcome - B&B in Umbria**
tel. 0763 305523, fax 0763 390670
info@bb.umbria.it
www.bbumbria.it
Closed: varies

Accommodation
Guestrooms: *3 doubles, private bath*
Services & Amenities: *German and Spanish are spoken; rooms cleaned every day; complimentary tourist information; smokers welcome*
Rates: *double* €€€
Credit cards: *not accepted*
Pets: 🚫

This B&B is located in one of the city's most beautiful, ancient buildings. Its classic-style furniture is perfect in every detail. It also provides a nice panoramic view and is only a short distance from the Cathedral. Breakfast is served in the guestroom. The city's many interesting monuments include the Cathedral, the Albornozian Rocca and the St Patrick's well. One of the public events you can't miss is the historic Festa dei Corpus Domini procession.

La Rocca

• **Ass. Welcome - B&B in Umbria**

tel. 0763 305523, fax 0763 390670
info@bb.umbria.it
www.bbumbria.it

Closed: varies

This B&B, with it warm, friendly atmosphere and both plain and modern furniture, is located in a completely-restructured, bare-stone farmhouse situated in the Orvieto countryside. Breakfast is served in the guestroom. The interesting places to visit in the vicinity include the Crocefisso del Tufo's Etruscan burial sites, the Sts Severo e Martirio abbey, the Cobara Lake and the village of Civita di Bagnoregio.

Accommodation

Guestrooms: *1 double bedroom, with private bath*

Services & Amenities: *German and Spanish are spoken; rooms cleaned every day; complimentary tourist information; kitchen use by request; garden; smokers welcome*

Rates: *double €€€€*

Credit cards: *not accepted*

Pets:

The rose window adorning the façade of the Duomo of Orvieto.

Rosemarie

• **Ass. Welcome - B&B in Umbria**

tel. 0763 305523, fax 0763 390670
info@bb.umbria.it
www.bbumbria.it

Closed: varies

This B&B, with its warm atmosphere and plain, comfortable furniture, is in a modern home surrounded by a large park. It's out in the country and about 2 km from Orvieto's old center. The German hostess prepares an excellent breakfast, which she serves in the guestroom.

Accommodation

Guestrooms: *3 double bedrooms, shared bath; additional bed on request*

Services & Amenities: *German spoken; rooms cleaned every day; complimentary tourist information; kitchen use by request; Internet access; garden; smokers welcome*

Rates: *double €€. Additional bed supplement 30%*

Credit cards: *not accepted*

Pets:

Trepporte

• **Ass. Welcome - B&B in Umbria**

tel. 0763 305523, fax 0763 390670
info@bb.umbria.it
www.bbumbria.it

Closed: varies

This B&B, located in an apartment situated in this Umbrian city's medieval old center, is just a short distance from the Piazza della Repubblica, which is famous for its Municipal Building and its Sant'Andrea Church, with its 12-faced tower and mullioned windows. The accommodation offers one double room with private bath and guests also have use of the kitchen.

Accommodation

Guestrooms: *1 double, private bath*

Services & Amenities: *English, German and Spanish are spoken; rooms cleaned every day; complimentary tourist information; kitchen use by request; garden; smokers welcome*

Rates: *double €€€*

Credit cards: *not accepted*

Pets:

• **Bed & Breakfast Italia**
Code U16
tel. 06 6878618, fax 06 6878619
info@bbitalia.it
www.bbitalia.it
Closed: varies

Rustic stone farmhouse, surrounded by a rose-garden, 5 km from the center. The owners offer guests one double room with a large balcony. The bathroom with shower is shared with other guests. Breakfast is made with local produce and is served in the garden in summer, or in the lounge in the cooler months. The host family offers guests the use of the swimming pool in a nearby sports center

Accommodation
Guestrooms: *1 double bedroom*
Services & Amenities: *English spoken; rooms cleaned every 3 days; complimentary tourist information; smokers welcome; private parking*
Minimum stay: *2 nights*
Rates: €€
Credit cards: VISA MC *Bancomat*
Pets: not allowed

• **Bed & Breakfast Italia**
Code U43
tel. 06 6878618, fax 06 6878619
info@bbitalia.it
www.bbitalia.it
Closed: varies

This small independent apartment is inside a small 16th-C building, and features a vaulted ceiling in relaxing shades of blue and white. Comfortable and functional, it is suitable for a couple. It is located in the old center of Orvieto, a medieval town, dominated by the imposing magnificence of its Duomo. Here every year festivals and processions are organized.

Accommodation
Guestrooms: *1 double*
Services & Amenities: *French and English are spoken; rooms cleaned every 3 days; complimentary tourist information; smokers welcome*
Minimum stay: *2 nights*
Rates: €€
Credit cards: VISA MC *Bancomat*
Pets: not allowed

• **Bed & Breakfast Italia**
Code U53
tel. 06 6878618, fax 06 6878619
info@bbitalia.it
www.bbitalia.it
Closed: varies

Accommodation
Guestrooms: *1 double bedroom; additional bed on request*
Services & Amenities: *French and English are spoken; rooms cleaned every 3 days; complimentary tourist information; smokers welcome; private parking*
Minimum stay: *2 nights*
Rates: €€
Credit cards: VISA MC *Bancomat*
Pets: not allowed

This elegant apartment is located in a sixteenth-century frescoed building; the walls are frescoed with grotesques in the soft and warm shades of blue, green and pink, the ceiling is very high, the furnishings are antique. The guest accommodation consists in a large double room, equipped with TV, and bathroom with shower/tub. The rich continental breakfast is usually served by the lady of the house who will prepare typical Umbrian meals on request. Private parking is also available

Passignano sul Trasimeno (Perugia)

Villa Sanni

• Ass. Welcome - B&B in Umbria
tel. 0763 305523, fax 0763 390670
info@bb.umbria.it
www.bbumbria.it
Closed: varies

This B&B, located in a stone villa surrounded by a portico, has modern, comfortable furniture and a warm and friendly atmosphere. This accommodation offers three double rooms with private bath. The Italian breakfast is usually served in the living room. The interesting excursions include a boat trip to Madonna dell'Olivetto. The boat sets out toward Isola Maggior and passes by Castiglione del Lago.

Accommodation
Guestrooms: *3 doubles, private bath; additional bed on request*
Services & Amenities: *German and Spanish are spoken; rooms cleaned every day; complimentary tourist information; garden; smokers welcome*
Rates: *single €€, double €€€. Additional bed supplement 30%*
Credit cards: *not accepted*
Pets: 🚫

Penna in Teverina (Terni)

La Chioccia

• Ass. Welcome - B&B in Umbria
tel. 0763 305523, fax 0763 390670
info@bb.umbria.it
www.bbumbria.it
Closed: varies

This B&B, with its friendly, cordial atmosphere and typically Umbrian furniture, is located in a restructured, bare-stone farmhouse situated on the Lazio border. The very good Italian breakfast, prepared by the hostess, is served in the guestroom. Guests are also welcome to enjoy the garden and swimming pool.

Accommodation
Guestrooms: *3 double bedrooms, shared bath; additional bed on request*
Services & Amenities: *German and Spanish are spoken; rooms cleaned every day; tourist information; kitchen use by request; garden; smokers welcome; private parking*
Rates: *double €€€€. Additional bed supplement 30%*
Credit cards: *not accepted*
Pets: ✓

• Bed & Breakfast Italia
Code U09
tel. 06 6878618, fax 06 6878619
info@bbitalia.it
www.bbitalia.it
Closed: varies

In this villa with garden, the main section consists in two rooms, with a shower bathroom; the wing has two rooms, a single and a double, with bathroom. All four rooms are carefully furnished and feature a large balcony. The landscape is dotted with olive groves, vines and centuries-old oak and holm-oak woods. Do not miss the grape harvest festival, where one can taste the local wine and "bruschetta", toasted bread seasoned with oil, salt, pepper and garlic, and grilled meat.

Accommodation
Guestrooms: *4 (1 single, 3 doubles)*
Services & Amenities: *French and English are spoken; rooms cleaned every 3 days; complimentary tourist information; terrace; private parking*
Minimum stay: *2 nights*
Rates: *€€*
Credit cards: VISA MC *Bancomat*
Pets: 🚫

PERUGIA

Alla Residenza Domus Minervae
• Ass. Welcome - B&B in Umbria
tel. 0763 305523, fax 0763 390670
info@bb.umbria.it
www.bbumbria.it
Closed: 23 December to 1 January

This B&B, located in the center of town, in a restructured, early 20th-century building, has three double rooms, all situated on the second floor and all with early 20th-century furniture and a private terrace. The continental breakfast is served in the dining room reserved for the guests. Guests are also welcome to use the garden. On request, the hosts, who are both teachers, are available for providing lessons in "Italian Language and Cuisine for Foreigners".

ACCOMMODATION
Guestrooms: *3 doubles, also single occupancy, with private bath; additional bed on request*
Services & Amenities: *French, English and Spanish are spoken; rooms cleaned every day; complimentary tourist information; educational courses by request; terrace; smokers welcome*
Rates: *single €€, double €€€. Additional bed supplement €. Children under 3 free; 3 to 12 -35%*
Credit cards: *accepted*
Pets:

Baldassarri
• Ass. Welcome - B&B in Umbria
tel. 0763 305523, fax 0763 390670
info@bb.umbria.it
www.bbumbria.it
Closed: 15 January to 31 March and 1 to 20 November

At about 4 km from the old center, this restructured, stone farmhouse, with its extensive farmland, swimming pool, olive trees, and wheat and sunflower fields, provides 3 guestrooms, that have period furniture, a private bath, a TV and a telephone. The continental breakfast, consisting of genuine pastries and fresh products, is served in a reserved dining room.

ACCOMMODATION
Guestrooms: *3 (2 double bedrooms, also single occupancy; 1 triple, private bath). Additional bed on request*
Services & Amenities: *English spoken; rooms cleaned every day; tourist information; Internet access; garden; smokers welcome; private parking*
Rates: *single €€, double €€€, triple €€€. Additional bed supplement €. Children under 3 free*
Credit cards: *not accepted*
Pets:

Casale dei Girasoli
località San Martino in Colle
• Ass. Welcome - B&B in Umbria
tel. 0763 305523
fax 0763 390670
info@bb.umbria.it
www.bbumbria.it
Closed: varies

This 16th-century, faithfully-restructured farmhouse, located in the commune of Perugia, has a warm, friendly atmosphere and furniture whose rustic style is in keeping with that of the building. An Italian breakfast, prepared by the hostess, is served in the guestrooms. Children have the use of a very well-furnished library.

ACCOMMODATION
Guestrooms: *3 doubles, shared bath; additional bed on request*
Services & Amenities: *rooms cleaned every day; complimentary tourist information; garden; smokers welcome*
Minimum stay: *2 nights*
Rates: *single €€, double €€€. Additional bed supplement 30%. Discounts for children*
Credit cards: *not accepted*
Pets:

• **Bed & Breakfast Italia**
Code U15
tel. 06 6878618, fax 06 6878619
info@bbitalia.it
www.bbitalia.it
Closed: varies

Farm-holiday accommodation, 2 kilometers from the center of Perugia, surrounded by a large garden. It features three double rooms, a triple and a quadruple, all spacious and sunny with simple, rustic furnishings, opening onto the courtyard. Besides being renowned for its art treasures, every year Perugia hosts several important European wine and food festivals. In the surrounding area, visit Deruta, a town where famous pottery is produced.

Accommodation
Guestrooms: *5 (3 doubles, 1 triple room and 1 quadruple room)*
Services & Amenities: *English spoken; rooms cleaned every 3 days; tourist information; private parking*
Minimum stay: *2 nights*
Rates: €€€
Credit cards: VISA MC *Bancomat*
Pets: no

• **Bed & Breakfast Italia**
Code U22
località San Marco
tel. 06 6878618, fax 06 6878619
info@bbitalia.it
www.bbitalia.it
Closed: varies

This apartment, at the disposal of guests, has a sloping roof, a spacious sitting room, double bedroom and bathroom. Furnishings are in a fresh, cheerful style. A ten-minute bus ride takes guests to the center of Perugia. If necessary, a cot is available for children under two years of age. Private parking is also available.

Accommodation
Guestrooms: *1 double*
Services & Amenities: *English and Spanish are spoken; rooms cleaned every 3 days; complimentary tourist information; terrace; private parking*
Minimum stay: *2 nights*
Rates: €€
Credit cards: VISA MC *Bancomat*
Pets: no

• **Bed & Breakfast Italia** TCI 10%
Code U37
tel. 06 6878618, fax 06 6878619
info@bbitalia.it
www.bbitalia.it
Closed: varies

Accommodation
Guestrooms: *1 double bedroom*
Services & Amenities: *French and English are spoken; rooms cleaned every 3 days; complimentary tourist information*
Minimum stay: *2 nights*
Rates: €€
Credit cards: VISA MC *Bancomat*
Pets: no

Old stone building in the old center of Perugia, on two levels, one wholly at the disposal of guests. The accommodation consists in a room, with a double bed, is furnished with antiques and has exposed wooden beams. Guests can have breakfast in the dining room or in the lounge by the fireplace in winter. The heart of the town dates back more than two thousand years, and retains several testimonies of its past.

• **Bed & Breakfast Italia**
Code U46
tel. 06 6878618, fax 06 6878619
info@bbitalia.it
www.bbitalia.it
Closed: varies

This Art Nouveau building, recently restored, retains all the characteristics of the period: neo-Gothic pointed arched windows with two and three lights and original stained glass. The rooms, doubles or twins, are furnished with authentic period country style furniture. The accommodation is in a central position, right in front of the escalators going to the Paolina Fortress and the Acropolis, and 50 m from the bus stop on the route to the railway station.

ACCOMMODATION
Guestrooms: *6 (double bedrooms and singles)*
Services & Amenities: *French, English and Spanish are spoken; rooms cleaned every 3 days; tourist info; smokers welcome; private parking*
Minimum stay: *2 nights*
Rates: €€
Credit cards: VISA MC *Bancomat*
Pets: ✗

PORANO (TERNI)

Colleombroso
• **Ass. Welcome - B&B in Umbria**
tel. 0763 305523
fax 0763 390670
info@bb.umbria.it
www.bbumbria.it
Closed: varies

TCI 10%

This B&B is located in a recently-constructed villa that's just outside the center of Porano and is nicely furnished in typical, plain Umbrian style. Besides its relaxed atmosphere, this villa provides a nice panoramic view. The host prepares breakfast, which both the guests and the family enjoy together.

ACCOMMODATION
Guestrooms: *2 (1 single and 1 double, with private bath)*
Services & Amenities: *English, German and Spanish are spoken; rooms cleaned every day; tourist information; kitchen use by request; garden; smokers welcome*
Rates: *single €€, double €€€*
Credit cards: *not accepted*
Pets: ✗

PRECI (PERUGIA)

• **Bed & Breakfast Italia**
Code U13
tel. 06 6878618, fax 06 6878619
info@bbitalia.it
www.bbitalia.it
Closed: varies

ACCOMMODATION
Guestrooms: *6 (1 single, 5 doubles)*
Services & Amenities: *French and English are spoken; rooms cleaned every 3 days; complimentary tourist information; private parking*
Minimum stay: *2 nights*
Rates: €€
Credit cards: VISA MC *Bancomat*
Pets: ✓

Two self-contained apartments at Todiano di Preci, featuring independent heating, satellite TV, a large portico with a wood burning oven and barbecue, and a spacious balcony, which can be used as a solarium. The house is furnished in a simple, functional style. Norcia, a medieval village, is 12 km away. The village is considered the cradle of pork-butchery: the art of making dressed pork products, "norcineria" in Italian, takes its name from this place.

San Gemini (Terni)

• **Bed & Breakfast Italia**
Code U34
tel. 06 6878618, fax 06 6878619
info@bbitalia.it
www.bbitalia.it
Closed: varies

Accommodation
Guestrooms: *4 (1 single, 2 doubles and 1 triple)*
Services & Amenities: *English spoken; rooms cleaned every 3 days; tourist information; terrace; private parking*
Minimum stay: *2 nights*
Rates: €€
Credit cards: VISA MC *Bancomat*
Pets: no

This semi-detached house is 2 km from the medieval hamlet of San Gemini, renowned for its curative waters. It offers a triple room, two doubles and a single, a large balcony and a private bathroom with shower. The house is surrounded by a large garden with a pergola

where guests can lunch. Private parking is also available. Interesting places in the surrounding area are Narni (6 km), Todi (20 km), Spoleto and Orvieto (30 km).

Spello (Perugia)

TCI 10%

La Casa di Properzio
• **Ass. Welcome - B&B in Umbria**
tel. 0763 305523, fax 0763 390670
info@bb.umbria.it
www.bbumbria.it
Closed: varies

This B&B occupies a small, tastefully-furnished apartment in a restructured, Umbrian-style, stone farmhouse situated in a Spello hamlet in the open countryside. The accommodation consists in three mini apartments with private bath. The many interesting events to be enjoyed include

the Infiorata (the Sunday of Corpus Domini), the Olive Festival (the Sunday of Carnival), the Incontri (during the month of August), and the many contemporary art shows and performances.

Accommodation
Guestrooms: *3 mini-apartments with private bath*
Services & Amenities: *English spoken; rooms cleaned every day; complimentary tourist information; kitchen use by request; garden; smokers welcome; private parking*
Rates: *mini-apartment €€€-€€€€*
Credit cards: *not accepted*
Pets: no

Spoleto (Perugia)

TCI 10%

Casale Fusco
• **Ass. Welcome - B&B in Umbria**
tel. 0763 305523, fax 0763 390670
info@bb.umbria.it
www.bbumbria.it
Closed: 1 December to 28 February

This completely-restructured farmhouse is located in the open countryside in a hamlet that's just 12 km from Spoleto. It has a warm, friendly atmosphere and is tastefully furnished with Umbrian-style furniture and several antiques. The hostess prepares the breakfast, which both the guests and the family enjoy together.

Accommodation
Guestrooms: *3 doubles, also single occupancy, with shared bath; additional bed on request*
Services & Amenities: *rooms cleaned every day; tourist information; garden; smokers welcome*
Rates: *single €€, double €€€. Additional bed supplement 30%*
Credit cards: *not accepted*
Pets: yes

• Bed & Breakfast Italia
Code U07
tel. 06 6878618, fax 06 6878619
info@bbitalia.it
www.bbitalia.it
Closed: varies

This prestigious B&B is 3 kilometers from Spoleto, located in a typical Umbrian farmhouse, recently restored. The guest accommodation consists in three large double rooms, one a twin, with large balconies, carefully furnished with rustic antique furniture. Two bathrooms are shared. Poggiolo lies in a rich grid of olive-groves, ploughed fields, vines and meadows. The landlords will arrange dinners with local specialties on request. Private parking is available.

ACCOMMODATION
Guestrooms: *3 doubls*
Services & Amenities: *French, English and Spanish are spoken; rooms cleaned every 3 days; complimentary tourist information; private parking*
Minimum stay: *2 nights*
Rates: €€
Credit cards: VISA MC *Bancomat*
Pets:

• Bed & Breakfast Italia
Code U29
tel. 06 6878618, fax 06 6878619
info@bbitalia.it
www.bbitalia.it
Closed: varies

This B&B is located in the Umbrian countryside 7 kilometers from Spoleto. The lady of the house welcomes guests to her rustic house, featuring wood and stone furnishings and vivid colors that match the brightness of the garden. The accommodation consists in two communicating bedrooms, one double and one single, sharing a private bathroom with shower.

ACCOMMODATION
Guestrooms: *2 (1 single and 1 double bedroom)*
Services & Amenities: *English spoken; rooms cleaned every 3 days; complimentary tourist information*
Minimum stay: *2 nights*
Rates: €€
Credit cards: VISA MC *Bancomat*
Pets:

• Bed & Breakfast Italia
Code U33
tel. 06 6878618, fax 06 6878619
info@bbitalia.it
www.bbitalia.it
Closed: varies

ACCOMMODATION
Guestrooms: *2 doubles*
Services & Amenities: *French and English are spoken; rooms cleaned every three days; complimentary tourist information; smokers welcome; horse-riding excursions; private parking*
Minimum stay: *2 nights*
Rates: €€
Credit cards: VISA MC *Bancomat*
Pets:

A 16th-century villa, situated 500 meters from the center of Spoleto, surrounded by a park with high trunk trees, and a swimming pool, affording a view of the town and the surrounding countryside. The guest accommodation, which consists in two double rooms, is welcoming and comfortable, classically and simply furnished. The hostess allows guests to use the private parking, an equipped garden and swimming pool.

STRONCONE (TERNI)

• **Bed & Breakfast Italia**
Code U04
tel. 06 6878618, fax 06 6878619
info@bbitalia.it
www.bbitalia.it
Closed: varies

The B&B is hosted by a rustic farmhouse surrounded by fields, with an extensive garden, in the Umbrian hills, in the province of Terni. This accommodation offers four double rooms, two with twin beds, and two bathrooms with shower and tub respectively. Private parking is available for the guests. The old hamlet of Stroncone is renowned for the annual Nativity Play performed live every Christmas. A car is needed to tour the area.

ACCOMMODATION
Guestrooms: *4 (2 double bedrooms and 2 doubles)*
Services & Amenities: *French and English are spoken; rooms cleaned every 3 days; tourist info; private parking*
Minimum stay: *2 nights*
Rates: €€
Credit cards: VISA MC *Bancomat*
Pets:

TERNI

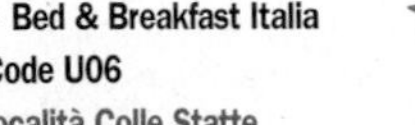

• **Bed & Breakfast Italia**
Code U06
località Colle Statte
05100 Terni
tel. 06 6878618, fax 06 6878619
info@bbitalia.it
www.bbitalia.it
Closed: varies

The B&B is located in a detached hillside house. The accommodation consists in three double rooms, two with twin beds, share a bathroom with shower/tub. Each room has a TV. The house is surrounded by a large garden, an olive-grove and a wood full of mushrooms. There is also an opportunity for extreme sports: two-level rafting on the Nera river and bungee jumping at the falls.

ACCOMMODATION
Guestrooms: *3 (1 double bedrooms and 2 doubles)*
Services & Amenities: *English spoken; rooms cleaned every 3 days; complimentary tourist information; terrace; private parking*
Minimum stay: *2 nights*
Rates: €€
Credit cards: VISA MC *Bancomat*
Pets:

• **Bed & Breakfast Italia**
Code U30
tel. 06 6878618, fax 06 6878619
info@bbitalia.it
www.bbitalia.it
Closed: varies

The B&B is hosted by a semi-detached house 3 kilometers from Terni. The guest accommodation consists in a first-floor apartment, furnished in a simple, rustic style. It includes one double room, one twin room and a single with TV. Pets are welcome. Private parking and a garden are also available. The town of Spoleto is 30 minutes away by car.

ACCOMMODATION
Guestrooms: *3 (1 single, 1 double bedroom and 1 double)*
Services & Amenities: *English spoken; rooms cleaned every 3 days; complimentary tourist information; private parking*
Minimum stay: *2 nights*
Rates: €€
Credit cards: VISA MC *Bancomat*
Pets:

Todi (Perugia)

Le Vetrate

• **Ass. Welcome - B&B in Umbria**
tel. 0763 305523, fax 0763 390670
info@bb.umbria.it
www.bbumbria.it
Closed: varies

This new apartment is located in an ancient building of the city's old center. The house has a tranquil, friendly atmosphere, as well as all the comforts and modern, refined furnishings. Guests have many opportunities for getting acquainted with the city. In fact, there's the Italian Antiques Show in April, the National Handicrafts Market Show in August, and the Todi Festival. This festival, which lasts throughout August and through the first part of September, features various plays and concerts, as well as ballet and cinema events.

Accommodation
Guestrooms: *2 doubles shared bath; additional bed on request*
Services & Amenities: *German and Spanish are spoken; rooms cleaned every day; tourist information; smokers welcome*
Rates: *single €€, double €€€€. Additional bed supplement 30%*
Credit cards: *not accepted*
Pets:

Torrechiave

• **Ass. Welcome - B&B in Umbria**
tel. 0763 305523, fax 0763 390670
info@bb.umbria.it
www.bbumbria.it
Open all year

This B&B with boxed ceilings, period furniture and independent entrances, is located in a old, restored barn. Breakfast, which consists of natural products and genuine pastries, is either served in the living room-kitchen (with fireplace, library, TV, telephone and hi-fi system) or out on the terrace, which provides a nice view of the Tevere Valley. Guests are welcome to use the large and beautiful garden with fruit trees. Private parking is also available.

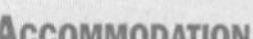

Accommodation
Guestrooms: *3 double bedrooms with private bath; additional bed on request*
Services & Amenities: *English and Spanish are spoken; rooms cleaned every 3 days; complimentary tourist information; kitchen use by request; bike rental; terrace; garden; smokers welcome; private parking*
Rates: *single €€, double €€. Additional bed supplement €. Children under 3 free; 3 to 12 -35%*
Credit cards: *not accepted*
Pets:

Villa Sobrano

Lidia Vizzino
località Sobrano, 06059 Todi (PG)
tel. 075 887127, fax 075 8870128
villasobrano@libero.it
www.villasobrano.com
Open all year

Accommodation
Guestrooms: *4 (2 suites, 1 double bedroom and 1 double, with private bath); additional bed on request*
Services & Amenities: *French, English and Spanish are spoken; rooms cleaned every 3 days; complimentary tourist information; dinner reservation; bike rental; garden; smokers welcome; private parking*
Rates: *double €€€€, suite €€€€. Children under 3 free*
Credit cards: *accepted*
Pets:

This B&B, which is just a few km from Todi, in a picturesque 19th-C country residence surrounded by the silence of Umbrian woods and countryside, has four comfortable rooms that still have almost all of their original furnishings. The buffet breakfast, which also includes products from the adjoining farm, is either served in the reserved dining room or in the guestrooms. The swimming pool adds to the relaxing pleasure already provided by the park. Local wine products are also available for tasting and purchasing, as desired.

Tuoro sul Trasimeno (Perugia)

Badia
• Ass. Welcome - B&B in Umbria
tel. 0763 305523, fax 0763 390670
info@bb.umbria.it
www.bbumbria.it
Closed: varies

Accommodation
Guestrooms: *1 mini-apartment (4 beds); additional bed on request*
Services & Amenities: *rooms cleaned every day; complimentary tourist information; garden; smokers welcome*
Rates: *single €€, double €€€. Additional bed supplement €*
Credit cards: *not accepted*
Pets:

Badia, which is located in a small farming village, is famous for having been the venue of the battle of Hannibal. The B&B is hosted in a converted convent built in the year 1290. All that's left of the convent is the bell-tower and a small church: the so-called "badia." The B&B is accessed through the family living room, which used to be the convent's refectory. The guests have a plainly-furnished apartment that sleeps four persons. Breakfast consists of typical local products and is served in the small apartment.

Umbertide (Perugia)

• Bed & Breakfast Italia
Code U38
tel. 06 6878618, fax 06 6878619
info@bbitalia.it
www.bbitalia.it
Closed: varies

This B&B is an eighteenth-century farmhouse, completely restored. The guest accommodation consists in two double rooms and one twin, furnished with antiques and wrought iron beds. The hosts produce organic foods, including the delicious jams that are served for breakfast. Gubbio and Città di Castello are 15 kilometers away. The surrounding area is full of artistic and historic sites but there are also many food-and-wine-tasting tours. Nearby there is a well equipped golf course .

Accommodation
Guestrooms: *3 (2 double bedrooms and 1 double)*
Services & Amenities: *French, English and German are spoken; rooms cleaned every 3 days; complimentary tourist information; private parking*
Minimum stay: *2 nights*
Rates: *€€*
Credit cards: VISA MC *Bancomat*
Pets:

Lazio

Amatrice (Rieti)

Villa Sanguigni B&B
Annamaria and Domenico Sanguigni
località Bagnolo
02012 Amatrice (RI)
tel. and fax 0746 821075
mob. 360 806141
sanguigni1@libero.it
www.primitaly.it/bb/villasanguigni
Closed: February and November

This B&B is in a 19th-century villa, which has been in the owner's family for a very long time, has been wonderfully restored by the owner's wife who has also furnished it with period furniture. Surrounded by a large park with old trees, the villa's position at 1050 m of altitude allows it to dominate the grandiose Monti della Laga landscape. Guests have the use of a library, an Internet access and piped classical music.

Accommodation
Guestrooms: *3 doubles, private bath*
Services & Amenities: *French and English are spoken; rooms cleaned every day; tourist information; Internet access; garden; smokers welcome; private parking*
Minimum stay: *2 nights*
Rates: *doubles €€€. Discounts for children and extended stays*
Credit cards: *not accepted*
Pets: no

Anzio (Rome)

• **Bed & Breakfast Italia**
Code L089
tel. 06 6878618, fax 06 6878619
info@bbitalia.it
www.bbitalia.it
Closed: varies

This recently built villa is surrounded by a well-tended garden where breakfast is served in summer. It has wood and wickerwork furniture in marine style. It has four rooms: a single and three doubles, each with TV and private bathroom with shower. Boats cruising to the isle of Ponza in 40 minutes leave from the small port in the village; Rome is one hour's journey by train or bus.

Accommodation
Guestrooms: *4 (1 single, 3 doubles)*
Services & Amenities: *French and English are spoken; rooms cleaned every 3 days; complimentary tourist information; air conditioning; smokers welcome; private parking*
Minimum stay: *2 nights*
Rates: *€€*
Credit cards: VISA MC *Bancomat*
Pets: yes

Aprilia (Latina)

Eucalyptus - Golf Club
Marina Tognoli
via Cogna 5
04011 Aprilia (LT)
tel. 06 92746252, fax 06 9268502
info@eucalyptusgolfclub.it
www.eucalyptusgolfclub.it
Closed: 15 January to 28 February and 1 November to 15 December

This B&B, which is located in a typical 1930's building with bare-beamed ceilings, is surrounded by a verdant, old park in the Nettuno and Anzio hinterland. Guest accommodation consists in three suites with TV and both modern and period furniture. The continental or English breakfast can either be served in the shared dining room or in the guestroom. Guests are welcome to use the video library, tennis court and swimming pool.

Accommodation
Guestrooms: *3 suites (1 single and 2 doubles, with private bath); additional bed on request*
Services & Amenities: *French, English, German and Dutch are spoken; rooms cleaned every day; tourist information; garden; smokers welcome; private parking*
Rates: *single €€, double €€€. Additional bed supplement €€*
Credit cards: *not accepted*
Pets: [no pets symbol]

Arce (Frosinone)

La Puta
Francesco Martinelli
via Puzzaca 93
03032 Arce (FR)
tel. 0776 522448
srmartinelli@hotmail.com
Closed: August and Christmas holidays

Accommodation
Guestrooms: *3 (1 single and 2 doubles, with shared bath)*
Services & Amenities: *French and English are spoken; rooms cleaned every day; complimentary tourist information; Internet access; garden; smokers welcome; private parking*
Rates: *single €€, double €€€. Discounts for extended stays*
Credit cards: *not accepted*
Pets: [pets allowed symbol]

This B&B is located in a recently-constructed farmhouse situated in the Melfa valley, 15 km from Arpino. The three guestrooms have period furniture. The continental or English breakfast includes cold cuts, pastries and brioches and can be served in the bright family living room, which has a TV and a library. Guests can also enjoy the large garden and swimming pool.

Ardea (Rome)

• Bed & Breakfast Italia
Code L098
tel. 06 6878618, fax 06 6878619
info@bbitalia.it
www.bbitalia.it
Closed: varies

This house surrounded by a well-tended garden is in a small old village 5 km from the sea. It has one double room with a double bed and is furnished in a fresh and modern style; the guests' private bathroom has a shower. It is 10 km from Anzio, 15 from Nettuno, famed for its port, and 40 km from Rome, all connected by an efficient bus service.

Accommodation
Guestrooms: *1 double*
Services & Amenities: *French, English and Spanish are spoken; rooms cleaned every 3 days; tourist information; private parking*
Minimum stay: *2 nights*
Rates: *€€*
Credit cards: VISA MC *Bancomat*
Pets: [pets allowed symbol]

Ariccia (Rome)

La Casa nel Bosco
Laura Antonelli and Giannino Mari
via dei Lecci 36/38
00040 Ariccia (RM)
tel. 06 9332292
Closed: October, November, February

This B&B is in one of 200 villas immersed in the verdant so-called Monte Gentile area, which is a private, fenced-in area with security guards. Each villa has its own grove of trees. The host family lives on the ground floor and the guestrooms, which have antique furniture and practical, built-in

wardrobes, are on the upper floor. The host takes care of small woods and the garden while the hostess looks after the guests, preparing breakfast, consisting of pastries or cold cuts and cheese, as desired, and serving it in the dining room.

Accommodation
Guestrooms: *3 (1 double bedroom with private bath and 2 additional bunk beds, 2 double bedrooms with shared bath)*
Services & Amenities: *French spoken; rooms cleaned every day; tourist info; baby-sitting service; garden; smokers welcome; private parking*
Rates: *single €€, double €€€. Discounts for extended stays. Children under 2 free; 2 to 12 -50%*
Credit cards: *not accepted*
Pets: ✓

• **Bed & Breakfast Italia**
Code L092
tel. 06 6878618, fax 06 6878619
info@bbitalia.it
www.bbitalia.it
Closed: varies

The house boasts very old origins as it was built on the ruins of an ancient Roman villa, converted into a convent in 1800. Its present owners have lived here for generations. It has two guest bedrooms: a double one with a large balcony and television, and a single. Bathroom with shower/tub. It is surrounded by a well-

kept garden, where guests may use the bocce court and tennis court.

Accommodation
Guestrooms: *2 (1 single and 1 double bedroom)*
Services & Amenities: *French and English are spoken; rooms cleaned every 3 days; tourist information; terrace; private parking*
Minimum stay: *2 nights*
Rates: €€
Credit cards: VISA MC *Bancomat*
Pets: ✓

• **Bed & Breakfast Italia** TCI 10%
Code L113
tel. 06 6878618, fax 06 6878619
info@bbitalia.it
www.bbitalia.it
Closed: varies

Located at Ariccia, the famous resort in the Castelli Romani region, this small modern house set in a leafy area is surrounded by an extensive garden and boasts antique and classic furnishings. It has three double rooms, one with a double bed, each with TV. Two bathrooms are shared by the three rooms.

Accommodation
Guestrooms: *3 (1 double bedroom and 2 doubles)*
Services & Amenities: *Spanish spoken; rooms cleaned every 3 days; tourist information; private parking*
Minimum stay: *2 nights*
Rates: €€
Credit cards: VISA MC *Bancomat*
Pets: ✗

Boville (Rome)

• **Bed & Breakfast Italia**
Code L081
località Santa Maria delle Mole
tel. 06 6878618, fax 06 6878619
info@bbitalia.it
www.bbitalia.it
Closed: varies

This accommodation consists in a semi-detached house surrounded by a well-kept courtyard and garden. It is carefully furnished with antiques and other fine details. It comprises two double rooms, one with TV and a separate entrance, decorated in the same style as the rest of the apartment, with warm colors and soft lighting. Two pets live in the house. Rome is 20 minutes away by train.

Accommodation
Guestrooms: *2 double bedrooms*
Services & Amenities: *French, English and Spanish are spoken; rooms cleaned every 3 days; tourist information*
Minimum stay: *2 nights*
Rates: €€
Credit cards: VISA MC *Bancomat*
Pets: 🐾

Bracciano (Rome)

• **Bed & Breakfast Italia**
Code L076
tel. 06 6878618, fax 06 6878619
info@bbitalia.it
www.bbitalia.it
Closed: varies

Accommodation
Guestrooms: *4 (1 double bedroom, 2 doubles and 2 triple rooms)*
Services & Amenities: *French, English and Spanish are spoken; rooms cleaned every 3 days; complimentary tourist information; private parking*
Minimum stay: *2 nights*
Rates: €€
Credit cards: VISA MC *Bancomat*
Pets: 🐾

This farmhouse set in a leafy area 1 km from Lake Bracciano is all built in stone and wood, with a garden and parking. It offers two double rooms, one with a double bed and one with twin beds, and two triple rooms. The three private bathrooms are with shower. The interiors are all decorated in wood in harmony with the outer structure. On arrival, guests are welcomed by their hosts in an amicable atmosphere.

Campagnano di Roma (Rome)

• **Bed & Breakfast Italia**
Code L085
tel. 06 6878618, fax 06 6878619
info@bbitalia.it
www.bbitalia.it
Closed: varies

Accommodation
Guestrooms: *1 double bedroom*
Services & Amenities: *French, English and Spanish are spoken; rooms cleaned every 3 days; tourist information; bike rental; horse-riding excursions; terrace; private parking*
Minimum stay: *2 nights*
Rates: €€
Credit cards: VISA MC *Bancomat*
Pets: 🐾

This B&B is hosted by a homely villa with a garden in a picturesque village in the Roman countryside. The house is well kept and cozy, with country-style furnishings, and comprises a double room with a large balcony and a bathroom with shower.

It is 20 kilometers from Rome by bus or by train; Lake Bracciano is 20 minutes away by car. Guests can arrange for horse-riding excursions and mountain bike rides.

Canino (Viterbo)

Palazzo Brenciaglia
Paolo Brenciaglia
corso Matteotti 40
01011 Canino (VT)
tel. and fax 0761 437020
mob. 339 4747046
palazzobren@palazzobren.com
Closed: 15 January to 15 March

This building, which was already a villa back in 1490, has now become integrated into the old center of Canino. It's been owned by this family since 1840. It still has its original terracotta floors and its important vaulted ceilings. One of its rooms – the so-called "Bonaparte room" – was where the Princess Maria stayed during the period that preceded her marriage to Count Valentino. Breakfast is also served in the nice garden. The host, who is also the president of the city's Archeological Group, very willingly accompanies his guests to see the various points of interest in the area.

Accommodation
Guestrooms: *3 doubles with private bath; additional bed on request*
Services & Amenities: *French and English are spoken; rooms cleaned every day; tourist info; baby-sitting service; kitchen use by request; garden; smokers welcome; parking*
Rates: *single €€, double €€€. Additional bed supplement €. Discounts for children and extended stays*
Credit cards: *not accepted*
Pets:

Capena (Rome)

Villa Maria Pia
Costantino Martini
via per Morlupo 118
00060 Capena (RM)
tel. 06 9032273
Closed: 1 to 15 January and 1 to 15 December

This villa is located in the countryside, 2 kilometers from the center of this village that's situated in the hills between the Tiberino and Flaminia roads. The couple living in this villa provides three guestrooms that have classic period furniture and lead directly into the large garden, with its olive and fruit trees. The rich breakfast is served in the family breakfast nook. Guests can enjoy the living room and its TV. The very interesting Lucus Feroniae Etruscan necropolises are very well worth visiting. Private parking available.

Accommodation
Guestrooms: *3 (1 single and 2 double bedrooms, private bath)*
Services & Amenities: *French and English are spoken; rooms cleaned every day; tourist info; garden; smokers welcome; private parking*
Rates: *single €, double €€. Discounts for children and extended stays*
Credit cards: *not accepted*
Pets:

Capranica (Viterbo)

I Castagni TCI 10%
Giuseppe Di Milia
strada Regagni 6
01012 Capranica (VT)
tel. 0761 660117, mob. 338 6687939
fax 0761 668664
gidimili@mclink.it
www.agriturismo-icastagni.com
Open all year

The guestrooms of this early 19th-C farmhouse, located in the Etruscan city with its medieval hamlet 6 km from Vico Lake, have antique furniture and paintings and an independent entrance leading in from the garden. Breakfast, which consists of local products, is served in a reserved room or outdoors, under the pergola. Guests are also welcome to use the TV room and the reading room with fireplace. Outside there's a ping-pong table and a bocce court. The vicinity also provides a riding stable and gym.

Accommodation
Guestrooms: *3 (1 double bedroom and 2 doubles, also single occupancy, with private bath)*
Services & Amenities: *English spoken; rooms cleaned every day; tourist information; garden; smokers welcome; private parking*
Rates: *single €€, double €€€. Discounts for children*
Credit cards: *not accepted*
Pets:

Caprarola (Viterbo)

• **Bed & Breakfast Italia**
Code L066
tel. 06 6878618, fax 06 6878619
info@bbitalia.it
www.bbitalia.it
Closed: varies

B&B situated amidst the hills, in a peaceful residential area, close to the village. This complex is in a nature reserve overlooking the romantic Lake Vico. The apartments can sleep two to four guests, are fully equipped and stylishly furnished with fireplace and period furniture, and are very sunny. They have separate entrances and a private garden. Rome is 40 minutes away by bus. Private parking available.

Accommodation
Guestrooms: *6 (4 doubles, 2 triples)*
Services & Amenities: *French, English and German are spoken; rooms cleaned every 3 days; tourist information; private parking*
Minimum stay: *2 nights*
Rates: €€
Credit cards: VISA MC *Bancomat*
Pets: not allowed

Cassino (Frosinone)

• **Bed & Breakfast Italia**
Code L053
tel. 06 6878618, fax 06 6878619
info@bbitalia.it
www.bbitalia.it
Closed: varies

A recently built cottage 1 kilometer from Cassino; a double room with TV and extra bed for children, and a single room, both with attic roof, are available for guests; bathroom with shower. Spacious garden and car park for guest use. Cassino is an interesting city from a cultural point of view: it is famed for its university and is also a religious destination. The Abruzzi National Park is 60 minutes away.

Accommodation
Guestrooms: *2 (1 single, 1 double)*
Services & Amenities: *French spoken; rooms cleaned every 3 days; complimentary tourist information; private parking*
Minimum stay: *2 nights*
Rates: €€
Credit cards: VISA MC *Bancomat*
Pets: not allowed

Castel Gandolfo (Roma)

• **Bed & Breakfast Italia** TCI 10%
Code L075
tel. 06 6878618, fax 06 6878619
info@bbitalia.it
www.bbitalia.it
Closed: varies

A villa set in a leafy area surrounded by Lake Castel Gandolfo, the summer residence of the Pope. This accommodation consists in five bedrooms, four doubles and a single, stylishly furnished in Venetian style, overlooking the flowered garden with a fine view of the lake. Breakfast is served in the large lounge. A shuttle service to Castelli Romani or Eternal City is provided on request; sun lovers can enjoy the lakeshore facilities at special prices.

Accommodation
Guestrooms: *5 (1 single, 4 doubles)*
Services & Amenities: *English and German are spoken; rooms cleaned every 3 days; complimentary tourist information; private parking*
Minimum stay: *2 nights*
Rates: €€
Credit cards: VISA MC *Bancomat*
Pets: not allowed

Castelnuovo di Porto (Rome)

Green House
Marisa Lene
via Giammarile 26
00060 Castelnuovo di Porto (RM)
tel. 06 9034466, mob. 338 4834500
cmlene@tin.it
Closed: 10 January to 28 February and 10 to 30 August

This 1970's villa is located north of Rome in a residential center on the Via Flaminia, 3 kilometers from Castelnuovo di Porto. This accommodation offers three, well-furnished guestrooms with an independent entrance. Guest also have the use of a large living room with TV, as well as a billiard table, game tables and a small kitchen that's equipped for preparing the continental breakfast that the guests can have in the large garden. The hosts, who love traveling and gardening, can provide their guests with all types of tourist information.

Accommodation
Guestrooms: *3 (2 double bedrooms and 1 double, also single occupancy, with shared bath); additional bed on request*
Services & Amenities: *French and English are spoken; rooms cleaned every 3 days; tourist information; kitchen use by request; garden; smokers welcome; private parking*
Rates: *single €€, double €€€. Additional bed supplement €*
Credit cards: *not accepted*
Pets: *not allowed*

• Bed & Breakfast Italia
Code L 112
tel. 06 6878618, fax 06 6878619
info@bbitalia.it
www.bbitalia.it
Closed: varies

An elegant villa on Via Tiberina, 15 km from Rome, surrounded by a 3-hectare park with a scenic view. It has five double bedrooms with classic furnishings, each with private bathroom. Guests may use the swimming pool in the garden. Several buses and a train reach the town center in 30 minutes. There is a sports club with tennis courts in the environs.

Accommodation
Guestrooms: *5 doubles*
Services & Amenities: *French, English and Spanish are spoken; rooms cleaned every 3 days; tourist information; horse-riding excursions; private parking*
Minimum stay: *2 nights*
Rates: *€€*
Credit cards: VISA MC *Bancomat*
Pets: *not allowed*

Ceprano (Frosinone)

Casa Fregellae
Felix Di Ruzza
via San Manno 42
03024 Ceprano (FR)
mob. 333 4127567
fregellae@virgilio.it
Closed: January to March

This small villa, located out in the countryside, is just 15 kilometers from the Pastena Grottos and 2 kilometers from the A1 Ceprano turn-off. The accommodation offers three guestrooms with modern furnishings. The continental breakfast is served is the bright family kitchen. Guests are also welcome to use the family living room any time during the day, as well as the garden. Parking is also provided.

Accommodation
Guestrooms: *3 (1 double with private bath, 1 double and 1 single, with shared bath)*
Services & Amenities: *English spoken; rooms cleaned every day; tourist information; garden; smokers welcome; private parking*
Rates: *single €, double €€. Discounts for children -15%*
Credit cards: *not accepted*
Pets: *allowed*

Ciampino (Rome)

Villa Valentino
via Giachino Errico 5/B
00043 Ciampino (RM)
tel. 06 7960985
Closed: 15 January to 15 February and 1 July to 31 August

This villa, which is occupied by a family of five, is located in the new Ciampino area, 100 meters from the Acqua Acetosa train station (Roma Termini-Castel Gandolfo-Albano line). The double room for the guests, which faces a large terrace, has classic-style furnishings and a sitting area with a TV and telephone. The continental breakfast is generally served in the family dining room. On request, guests can be privately accompanied by car to and from the train station or the airport.

Accommodation
Guestrooms: *1 double bedroom, with private bath*
Services & Amenities: *English spoken; rooms cleaned every 3 days; tourist information; terrace; garden; smokers welcome*
Minimum stay: *2 nights*
Rates: *€€-€€€. Discounts for children*
Credit cards: *not accepted*
Pets: ✗

Civitavecchia (Rome)

Casamica B&B
Alessandra Germoglio
via De Gasperi 1
00053 Civitavecchia (RM)
tel. 0766 31182, fax 0766 588511
casamica.cv@libero.it
www.casamicacv.it
Closed: 15 January to 28 February and 15 October to 30 November

This B&B is in a small, stone villa located on the Via Aurelia, 1 km from the port and 800 m from the train station. Guests have 3 rooms with TV, each furnished differently. One has modern furniture, one has English style furniture and one has old marine-type furniture. The continental breakfast is served in the living room reserved for the guests. This room also has satellite TV, a VCR and a piano. Guests are also welcome to use the large terrace and its solarium.

Accommodation
Guestrooms: *3 doubles, also single occupancy, private bath; additional bed on request*
Services & Amenities: *French, English and Spanish are spoken; rooms cleaned every day; tourist information; terrace; garden; smokers welcome; private parking*
Rates: *single €€, double €€€. Additional bed supplement €. Children under 2 free*
Credit cards: *not accepted*
Pets: ✓

Contigliano (Rieti)

B&B da Luigi
Luigi Tamburello
via Montisola 92
02043 Contigliano (RI)
mob. 338 9286497
ltamburello@libero.it
Closed: February

Accommodation
Guestrooms: *3 doubles, also single occupancy, with shared bath*
Services & Amenities: *English and Spanish are spoken; rooms cleaned every day; complimentary tourist information; kitchen use by request; educational courses by request; garden; smokers welcome; private parking*
Rates: *€. Discounts for children -10% and extended stays*
Credit cards: *not accepted*
Pets: ✓

This B&B, which is located in an early 20th-century rural complex that has a large garden, is situated near the Laghi Reatini Natural Reserve and is 15 kilometers from the Monte Terminillo ski lifts. The three guestrooms have rustic furniture and an independent entrance. The host, who is a water sports enthusiast and teaches canoeing, is available for providing lessons in rafting and guided excursions in the area. Where possible, the guests can also do some bird-watching. The rich continental breakfast is served in the reserved guestroom that has a fireplace.

Fara in Sabina (Rieti)

• **Bed & Breakfast Italia**
Code L156
tel. 06 6878618, fax 06 6878619
info@bbitalia.it
www.bbitalia.it
Closed: varies

A stone country house nestling in the green Sabina valleys. The hostess offers two self-contained studio apartments with country-style furnishing; colorful blankets, bedspreads and sofas create a cheerful and cozy atmosphere. Each apartment has a lounge with a sofa bed, a kitchen and a loft with a double bedroom with bathroom and shower. The surrounding land is used by the hosts to grow organic products.

Accommodation
Guestrooms: *4 doubles ♿*
Services & Amenities: *French and English are spoken; rooms cleaned every 3 days; complimentary tourist information; baby-sitting service; bike rental; Internet access; smokers welcome*
Minimum stay: *2 nights*
Rates: €€
Credit cards: VISA MC *Bancomat*
Pets: 🐕

Farnese (Viterbo)

• **Bed & Breakfast Italia**
Code L118
tel. 06 6878618, fax 06 6878619
info@bbitalia.it
www.bbitalia.it
Closed: varies

This B&B is in a former 12th-century converted bakery and has stuccoed stonewalls, vaulted ceilings, and Art Deco furniture. It has a double room with TV and a separate entrance, and bathroom with shower. It is set in the green "Selva del Lamone", which stretches for about 2,000 hectares between Lazio and Tuscany, with a fauna rich in foxes, porcupines, wild boars, and owls.

Accommodation
Guestrooms: *1 double bedroom*
Services & Amenities: *French, English and Spanish are spoken; rooms cleaned every 3 days; complimentary tourist information*
Minimum stay: *2 nights*
Rates: €€
Credit cards: VISA MC *Bancomat*
Pets: 🐕 (not allowed)

Fiano Romano (Rome)

La Spighetta
Maria Di Bonifacio
via Torino 11
00065 Fiano Romano (RM)
tel. 0765 455591
Closed: 1 January to 15 February, 15 August to 15 September and November

This B&B is on the ground floor of a small, modern villa that's surrounded by a large garden that has ornamental plants and tall trees. The villa is near the A1's north Rome exit and 4 km from the center of Fiano Romano. The guestrooms are furnished differently, in classic and in Old American style, and have a TV and a telephone. The breakfast is generally served in the room reserved for the guests but, in the summertime, it can be served on the veranda. Excursions in the surrounding area can be arranged.

Accommodation
Guestrooms: *2 (1 double bedroom and 1 double, with shared bath)*
Services & Amenities: *French and English are spoken; rooms cleaned every day; complimentary tourist information; terrace; garden; smokers welcome; private parking*
Rates: *single* €€, *double* €€€. *Children under 3 free; 4 to 12 -20%*
Credit cards: *not accepted*
Pets: 🐕 (not allowed)

• Bed & Breakfast Italia
Code L039
tel. 06 6878618, fax 06 6878619
info@bbitalia.it
www.bbitalia.it
Closed: varies

A B&B in the old center of a picturesque village. This self-contained apartment offers an attic double room with balcony, a lounge with sofa bed and TV, bathroom with shower and a kitchen corner; it is furnished in country style with attention to detail; it features exposed beams, terracotta floors and dark timber furniture. Rome is within easy traveling distance (A1 motorway exit Roma Nord).

ACCOMMODATION
Guestrooms: *2 doubles*
Services & Amenities: *English spoken; rooms cleaned every 3 days; complimentary tourist information*
Minimum stay: *2 nights*
Rates: €€
Credit cards: VISA MC *Bancomat*
Pets: 🚫

FIUMICINO (ROME)

Belvedere
Gabriella Filoni
via Portunno 23
00054 Fiumicino (RM)
tel. 06 6550524, mob. 347 4402010
Closed: June to August

This B&B is located in an attic apartment that's a 10-minute walk to the city center. The accommodation consists in two guestrooms with modern furnishings that face the terrace. The continental breakfast is prepared according to the particular preferences of the guests and is either served in the kitchen or on the veranda. However it can also be served outdoors. Private transportation by car is also available. Smokers are welcome.

ACCOMMODATION
Guestrooms: *2 (1 double and 1 double bedroom, also single occupancy, with shared bath); additional bed on request*
Services & Amenities: *French and English are spoken; rooms cleaned every day; complimentary tourist information; terrace; smokers welcome*
Rates: *single* €€, *double* €€€. *Additional bed supplement* €
Credit cards: *not accepted*
Pets: 🚫

Isola Sacra B&B
Alberto and Gigliola Boscono
via della Basilica di Sant'Ippolito 15
00054 Fiumicino (RM)
tel. and fax 06 6522488
isolasacra@libero.it
Closed: varies

ACCOMMODATION
Guestrooms: *2 doubles, also single occupancy, with shared bath; additional bed on request*
Services & Amenities: *French, English and Spanish are spoken; rooms cleaned every day; complimentary tourist information; Internet access; garden; private parking*
Rates: *single* €€, *double* €€€. *Children under 5 free. Discounts for extended stays*
Credit cards: *not accepted*
Pets: 🐾

This B&B has a name that's important for those who are fond of archeology. The hostess picks up her guests from the airport. Breakfast, which can consist of either pastries or cold cuts and cheese, as preferred, is either served in the dining room or in the patio. There's a surprise outside the villa: the garden extends to the banks of the Tiber, which is a nice place to go for enjoying some relaxation after having visited, say, the Ship Museum or the Sant'Ippolito Tower.

• Bed & Breakfast Italia
Code L095
tel. 06 6878618, fax 06 6878619
info@bbitalia.it
www.bbitalia.it
Closed: varies

Accommodation
Guestrooms: *3 doubles*
Services & Amenities: *French, English and Spanish are spoken; rooms cleaned every 3 days; complimentary tourist information; air conditioning; smokers welcome; private parking*
Minimum stay: *2 nights*
Rates: €€
Credit cards: VISA MC *Bancomat*
Pets: allowed

A villa built on the bank of the Tiber, 5 kilometers north of the Roman coast. This accommodation consists in three double bedrooms with single beds, all classically furnished, with air conditioning and TV; each has its own private bathroom with shower. It is 25 kilometers from Rome, easily reached in 30 minutes by bus or train.

Fondi (Latina)

B&B Villa Mimosa TCI 10%
• Bed & Breakfast Corporation
tel. and fax 0771 460123
mob. 339 2690299
sepes@dimensione.com
Closed: 3 January to 7 March and November

This B&B is in a small villa that's 600 meters from the center of town and 25 kilometers from Gaeta. It's surrounded by a large garden with fruit trees. There a room with a double bed and another that has both a double and a single bed. Both rooms have modern furnishings, TV, and a private bathroom with a tub. The continental breakfast is either served in the family kitchen or, when the weather's nice, outdoors. Private parking is provided. The B&B Corporation arranges guided tours of Gaeta and the vicinity. And, in collaboration with the WWF, it organizes hikes and bike trips into the Monte Orlando Regional Park. Guests are also free to use the complete library and several mountain bikes. And finally, guests can take advantage of the special agreements made with various restaurants, pizza places, bathing establishments and sailing clubs in the area.

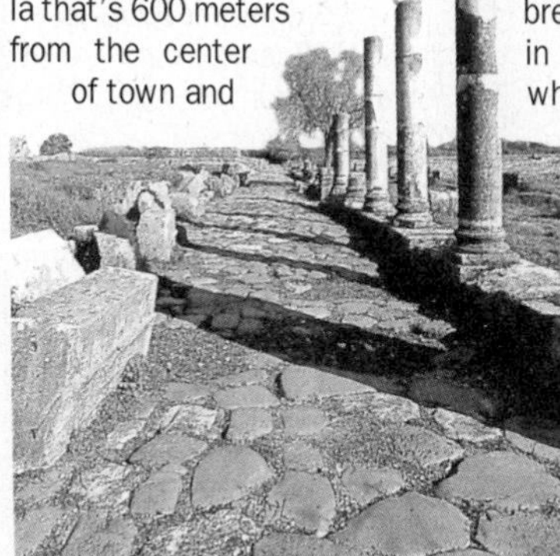

A section of the Via Appia Antica

Accommodation
Guestrooms: *2 (1 double bedroom and 1 triple, also single occupancy, with private bath)*
Services & Amenities: *English and Spanish are spoken; rooms cleaned every 3 days; complimentary tourist information; bike rental; smokers welcome; private parking*
Rates: *single* €-€€, *double* €€-€€€. *Additional bed supplement* €
Credit cards: *not accepted*
Pets: allowed

• Bed & Breakfast Italia
Code L159
tel. 06 6878618, fax 06 6878619
info@bbitalia.it
www.bbitalia.it
Closed: varies

Accommodation
Guestrooms: *3 doubles*
Services & Amenities: *English spoken; rooms cleaned every 3 days; complimentary tourist information*
Minimum stay: *2 nights*
Rates: €€
Credit cards: VISA MC *Bancomat*
Pets: not allowed

This one-story house is located in the old center of the medieval village. The accommodation includes three rooms: two doubles with queen-sized beds and private bath with shower, and a twin with a tub/shower bathroom. They have classic furnishings with antiques and a dressing room. This B&B is 8 kilometers from the sea, reached by bus or car.

Formia (Latina)

B&B Fede
• Bed & Breakfast Corporation
tel. and fax 0771 460123
mob. 339 2690299
sepes@dimensione.com
Closed: 1 February to 13 March and 19 June to 5 August

This B&B is in one of a group of small villas immersed in a pine grove. It's 100 meters from the sea, 500 meters from the center of Formia and 5 kilometers from Gaeta. The guestroom, which is a double, has a bathroom (with a tub) that the guests share with their hosts. The room has modern furniture, a TV, and leads onto a small terrace. The continental breakfast is served in the kitchen. Guests are free to use the condominium swimming pool. They can also take bike rides in and around the area. Mountain bikes are furnished by the B&B Corporation, which is always on hand to provide complete assistance for the tourists.

Accommodation
Guestrooms: *1 double bedroom, also single occupancy, shared bath; additional bed on request*
Services & Amenities: *French and English are spoken; rooms cleaned every 3 days; tourist information; bike rental; terrace; smokers welcome; private parking*
Rates: *single €, double €€. Additional bed supplement €. Discounts for families and children -10%*
Credit cards: *not accepted*
Pets:

• Bed & Breakfast Italia
Code L155
tel. 06 6878618, fax 06 6878619
info@bbitalia.it
www.bbitalia.it
Closed: varies

A large three-story villa. One floor is completely at the disposal of guests and consists in three spacious sunny rooms, two triples and a double, with a large balcony overlooking the garden. The furnishings are modern and comfortable; each room has a private bathroom with shower. The equipped beaches are 5 minutes' drive away; the railway station is 10 minutes away on foot.

Accommodation
Guestrooms: *3 (1 double and 2 triple rooms)*
Services & Amenities: *rooms cleaned every 3 days; complimentary tourist information; bike rental; Internet access; private parking*
Minimum stay: *2 nights*
Rates: €€
Credit cards: *Bancomat*
Pets:

Fregene (Rome)

Le Coin Vert
Thérèse Valenza Casano
via Porto Maurizio 86
00050 Fregene (RM)
tel. and fax 06 6685010
tereva@tin.it
www.mediazoom.com/valenza
Closed: August

This B&B is located between the sea and the Fregene pine grove. It's an ideal location for discovering both the treasures of Rome and the pleasures of the "Tyrrhenian pearl". This B&B was baptized with the name "The Green Corner" because that's the name the hostess chose to give it. Her great passions are antiques, literature and cats. In fact, she's got four of them in her house. Breakfast consists of pastries or cold cuts and cheese, as desired, and is either served in the living room or under the portico.

Accommodation
Guestrooms: *1 double, also single occupancy, shared bath*
Services & Amenities: *French, English and Spanish are spoken; rooms cleaned every 3 days; complimentary tourist information; lunch & dinner reservations; bike rental; garden; smokers welcome; private parking*
Rates: *single €€, double €€. Discounts for extended stays*
Credit cards: *not accepted*
Pets:

Gaeta (Latina)

B&B Chiostro Antico TCI 10%
• Bed & Breakfast Corporation
tel. and fax 0771 460123
mob. 339 2690299
sepes@dimensione.com
Closed: 9 January to 12 March and November

Accommodation
Guestrooms: *1 triple, also single or double occupancy, with private bath; additional bed on request*
Services & Amenities: *English spoken; rooms cleaned every 3 days; tourist info; smokers welcome*
Rates: *single €-€€, double €€-€€€, triple €€-€€€. Additional bed supplement €. Children under 10 -10%*
Credit cards: *not accepted*
Pets:

This B&B, located on the ground floor of an early 20th-century building located 500 meters from the sea and one kilometer from the old center of town - which has a lot of things to see of historical and architectural interest – provides a triple room with plain, essential furnishings, an independent entrance and a private bath with shower. The continental breakfast is served in the family kitchen.

B&B Domus Antiqua TCI 10%
• Bed & Breakfast Corporation
tel. and fax 0771 460123
mob. 339 2690299
sepes@dimensione.com
Closed: 6 November to 6 February

Accommodation
Guestrooms: *2 doubles, also single occupancy, with private bath); additional bed on request*
Services & Amenities: *rooms cleaned every 3 days; tourist information; terrace; smokers welcome*
Rates: *single €-€€, double €€ to €€€. Additional bed supplement €*
Credit cards: *not accepted*
Pets:

This B&B, located in an independent, early 20th-century house that provides a view of the old city and the sea, has two guestrooms, one with two beds and one with a double bed and a panoramic balcony. Both nicely furnished rooms have period furniture and a private bath (one has a tub and a shower, the other just a shower). The continental breakfast is served in the family kitchen. Highly recommended is the visit to the splendid castle-fortress whose imposing towers dominate the ancient village.

B&B Il Girasole TCI 10%
• Bed & Breakfast Corporation
tel. and fax 0771 460123
mob. 339 2690299
sepes@dimensione.com
Closed: 3 January to early April

Accommodation
Guestrooms: *1 double, also single occupancy, shared bath; additional bed on request*
Services & Amenities: *English spoken; rooms cleaned every 3 days; complimentary tourist information; terrace; smokers welcome*
Rates: *single €-€€, double €€-€€€. Additional bed supplement €*
Credit cards: *not accepted*
Pets:

This B&B is located on the last floor of a 1970's apartment building situated right in the center of town. The guestroom is a double with a nice view of the sea. The bathroom (with shower) is share with the hostess. The very nice room, which has marine furnishings, is provided with a TV. The continental breakfast is usually served in the kitchen but, when the weather's nice, it's served outside on the panoramic terrace. One trip well worth making is the hike to the top of Monte Orlando to see the mausoleum of Lucio Munazio Planco, one of Julius Caesar's famous generals.

B&B La Favorita
• Bed & Breakfast Corporation
tel. and fax 0771 460123
mob. 339 2690299
sepes@dimensione.com
Closed: 9 January to 12 March and November

This B&B is on the first floor of an ancient Bourbon home situated in the old center and just a short distance from the sea. Guests have two rooms – a single and a double – with a shared bath (with tub) that's reserved for the guests. The rooms are furnished in style and each has a TV, a mini-bar and a fan. One of the rooms has a terrace. The continental breakfast is served in the family kitchen. An interesting thing worth seeing is the Montagna Spaccata sanctuary, which is located in the extreme southwestern end of Monte Orlando. The sanctuary is in a high panoramic position overlooking the sea. Then, by going down a stairway, carved out of the rock, one reaches the impressive Turco rock.

ACCOMMODATION
Guestrooms: *2 (1 single and 1 double bedroom, with shared bath)*
Services & Amenities: *English spoken; rooms cleaned every 3 days; complimentary tourist information; terrace; smokers welcome*
Rates: *single €-€€, double €€-€€€. Additional bed supplement €*
Credit cards: *not accepted*
Pets:

B&B La Rosa
• Bed & Breakfast Corporation
tel. and fax 0771 460123
mob. 339 2690299
sepes@dimensione.com
Closed: 3 January to early April

This B&B is located in an apartment situated on the first floor of a 1960's building. It's just a short walk from the Gaeta Cathedral, with its splendid Norman-Moorish bell tower. This accommodation offers a double room, with modern furniture and a TV, and a private bath with a shower. The continental breakfast is served in the kitchen.

ACCOMMODATION
Guestrooms: *1 double, also single occupancy, private bath*
Services & Amenities: *English spoken; rooms cleaned every 3 days; tourist info; smokers welcome*
Rates: *single €-€€, double €€-€€€. Additional bed supplement €*
Credit cards: *not accepted*
Pets:

B&B L'Orchidea
• Bed & Breakfast Corporation
tel. and fax 0771 460123
mob. 339 2690299
sepes@dimensione.com
Closed: 3 January to early April

This B&B is located in an apartment that has a terrace facing the sea and the city's main square. The guestroom has modern furniture, TV and a private adjoining bathroom. Breakfast is generally served in the kitchen but, during the warm months, it can be served outside. The Santissima Annunziata church, with its so-called Grotta d'Oro (golden Grotto), is very well worth visiting.

ACCOMMODATION
Guestrooms: *1 double, also single occupancy, private bath*
Services & Amenities: *English spoken; rooms cleaned every 3 days; complimentary tourist information; terrace; smokers welcome*
Rates: *single €-€€, double €€-€€€. Additional bed supplement €*
Credit cards: *not accepted*
Pets:

GENZANO DI ROMA (ROME)

Garden House - Castelli Romani
Rocchina De Palma
via Francavilla 20
00045 Genzano di Roma (RM)
tel. 06 9399494, 06 9396279
mob. 338 2452251
Closed: January to March

ACCOMMODATION
Guestrooms: *2 doubles, 1 with private bath and 1 with shared bath; additional bed on request*
Services & Amenities: *French and English are spoken; rooms cleaned every day; complimentary tourist information; terrace; garden; smokers welcome*
Rates: *€-€€. Additional bed supplement €. Discounts for children and extended stays*
Credit cards: *not accepted*
Pets: no pets

This B&B, which is located on the first floor of a recently-constructed building situated in a hilly area, less than a kilometer from the center of town, has two rooms. One of them is appointed with period furniture, and each has a TV and a terrace garden. The continental breakfast is generally served in the living room but, during the summertime, it's served outside. One of the most interesting June events is the traditional Infiorata, when the streets are covered with multicolored flower petals.

A creation by the master flower-arrangers of Genzano.

• Bed & Breakfast Italia
Code L065
tel. 06 6878618, fax 06 6878619
info@bbitalia.it, www.bbitalia.it
Closed: varies

An attic double room with exposed timber beams and skylight. Breakfast is usually served in the large, tastefully furnished lounge with a stunning view over Lake Nemi, called the "looking-glass of Diana" by the ancients. The bathroom is shared with the hosts. Nature lovers can go hiking.

ACCOMMODATION
Guestrooms: *1 double bedroom*
Services & Amenities: *French, English and Spanish are spoken; rooms cleaned every 3 days; tourist info*
Minimum stay: *2 nights*
Rates: *€*
Credit cards: VISA MC *Bancomat*
Pets: pets allowed

GROTTAFERRATA (ROME)

Villa Flavia
Claudia Papetti
via Anagnina 165/167
00046 Grottaferrata (RM)
tel. 06 9410618, mob. 338 8940089
fax 06 8841665
villaflavia@tiscali.it
Closed: 10 January to 10 March and 5 November to 5 December

This B&B is in a ground-floor apartment in an early 20th-century villa situated in the center of this little town of Castelli Romani. There are three guestrooms and a living room with TV. The nicely-furnished rooms face the large garden that has a barbecue.

ACCOMMODATION
Guestrooms: *3 doubles, also single occupancy, with shared bath; additional bed on request*
Services & Amenities: *French, English, Spanish and Portuguese are spoken; rooms cleaned every day; complimentary tourist information; garden; smokers welcome; private parking*
Rates: *single €€, double €€. Children under 3 free, 4 to 10 -50%*
Credit cards: *not accepted*
Pets: pets allowed

Breakfast is generally served is the room reserved for the guests. However, during the summertime, it may be served outdoors under the portico. The nearby abbey, founded by San Nilo in 1004, is well worth a visit.

Guidonia-Montecelio (Rome)

• Bed & Breakfast Italia
Code L134
tel. 06 6878618, fax 06 6878619
info@bbitalia.it
www.bbitalia.it
Closed: varies

A cottage between Tivoli and Guidonia, 18 kilometers from Rome. The house is surrounded by a well-kept garden and has three rooms, decorated in classic style with modern furnishings. The accommodation also includes two doubles and one triple, all with single beds, TV, a large balcony and private bathroom with shower. Hadrian's Villa is nearby. A baby-sitting service is available by prior arrangement.

Accommodation
Guestrooms: *3 (2 doubles and 1 triple room)*
Services & Amenities: *French and English are spoken; rooms cleaned every 3 days; tourist info; baby-sitting service; terrace; parking*
Minimum stay: *2 nights*
Rates: €€
Credit cards: VISA MC *Bancomat*
Pets: not allowed

Isola di Ponza (Latina)

Isola di Ponza
Andrea De Bellis
via Piana, località Le Forna
04027 Ponza (LT)
tel. and fax 0771 808383
www.isoladiponzait.it
Open: March to October

This B&B is in a recently-constructed, two-story house that's surrounded by a verdant Mediterranean garden and provides a view of the Circeo promontory. All the rooms have an independent entrance from the garden. Guests also have the use of a solarium, a swimming pool with a hydromassage, and a barbecue. The hosts are available for organizing boat rides or going fishing, and can also provide skin-diving instruction.

Accommodation
Guestrooms: *3 doubles, also single occupancy, with private bath*
Services & Amenities: *French and English are spoken; rooms cleaned every 3 days; complimentary tourist information; kitchenette; garden; private parking*
Rates: €€-€€€ *per person*
Credit cards: *not accepted*
Pets: allowed

Luna Ponzese
Maria Giovanna Spugno
via Chiaia di Luna 33
04027 Ponza (LT)
tel. 0771 80402
Open: Easter to October and Christmas holidays

This B&B, which is located on the ground-floor of a two-story building situated just 50 meters from Ponza's most famous, splendid beach – the Chiaia di Luna – has two guestrooms with an independent entrance from the courtyard. The atmosphere is uncomplicated and friendly, and guests can order anything they want for breakfast, which is either served outdoors or in the guestroom, as desired. There are tennis courts nearby

Accommodation
Guestrooms: *2 (1 double and 1 triple room, with private bath)*
Services & Amenities: *English spoken; rooms cleaned every day; complimentary tourist information; lunch & dinner reservations*
Rates: *double* €€, *triple* €€€
Credit cards: *not accepted*
Pets: allowed

Turist Ponza
Maria Grazia Nuziale
via Dragonara
04027 Ponza (LT)
tel. and fax 0771 809708
turistponza@libero.it
Open: June to September

This B&B, located on the 2nd floor of a small building in Ponza, is not far from the port and only a 10-minute walk to the Chiaia di Luna: the island's most fascinating beach. The continental or English breakfast is served in the family living room. The family gladly provides any and all tourist information and relative advice, and can take care of making reservations. Private parking is also available.

ACCOMMODATION
Guestrooms: *2 doubles, shared bath; additional bed on request*
Services & Amenities: *rooms cleaned every 3 days; complimentary tourist information; private parking*
Rates: *double €€€. Additional bed supplement €€*
Credit cards: *not accepted*
Pets: 🚫

The port of Ponza in a delightful period photograph.

ITRI (LATINA)

Villa Fiorita
• Bed & Breakfast Corporation
tel. and fax 0771 460123
mob. 339 2690299
sepes@dimensione.com
Closed: 9 January to 12 March and November

TCI 10%

This B&B is in a small, single-family villa that has a garden and is situated in the fascinating scenario of the Aurunci Mountains, 5 kilometers from the center of town and from the Madonna della Civita sanctuary. The accommodation consists in a double with a private bathroom right next to it, with a shower and hydromassage. The room has modern furnishings, an independent entrance, and satellite TV. The continental breakfast is generally served in the family kitchen, but when the weather is nice, it's served out in the garden.

ACCOMMODATION
Guestrooms: *1 double with private bath; additional bed on request*
Services & Amenities: *English spoken; rooms cleaned every 3 days; complimentary tourist information; garden; smokers welcome; parking*
Rates: *single €-€€, double €€-€€€. Additional bed supplement €*
Credit cards: *not accepted*
Pets: 🚫

LADISPOLI (ROME)

Le Naiadi
via Orione 6
località Marina San Nicola
00055 Ladispoli (RM)
tel. 06 35507350, mob. 347 1720390
Closed: June to August

This B&B is located on the ground floor of a modern building that has a small garden, a swimming pool and is in the Marina San Nicola residential district. The two guestrooms have a TV and the continental breakfast is served in the family living room.

ACCOMMODATION
Guestrooms: *2 (1 double and 1 triple room, also single occupancy, with private bath)*
Services & Amenities: *rooms cleaned every 3 days; complimentary tourist information; terrace; garden; smokers welcome*
Rates: *single €€, double €€€, triple €€€€*
Credit cards: *not accepted*
Pets: 🚫

The Ladispoli coastline.

Lariano (Rome)

Casa di Angela
Angela Santarsiero
via Dante Alighieri 59
00040 Lariano (RM)
tel. 06 9648131
Closed: February and March

This B&B is in a recently-constructed, two-family villa, located in the Castelli Romani area, 1 km from the center of town. The family provides a guestroom with classic furnishings. The room faces a terrace that's interconnected with the garden. The continental breakfast in served in the family breakfast room, which has a fireplace. Guests are also welcome to use the TV room, as well as the equipped portico.

Accommodation
Guestrooms: *1 double with private bath; additional bed on request*
Services & Amenities: *English spoken; rooms cleaned every day; tourist information; garden; smokers welcome; private parking*
Minimum stay: *3 nights*
Rates: *€€. Additional bed supplement €. Discounts for children and extended stays*
Credit cards: *not accepted*
Pets: 🚫

Lubriano (Viterbo)

Le Casette di Lubriano Tci 10%
• Ass. Welcome - B&B in Umbria
tel. 0763 305523, fax 0763 390670
info@bb.umbria.it
www.bbumbria.it
Closed: varies

This B&B, which is located in a panoramic position in front of Civita di Bagnoregio and the Valle dei Calanchi, midway between Orvieto and Bolsena, has two mini-apartments. Both have a kitchen corner and one has an upper level. There is also an apartment consisting of two bedrooms, a kitchen, a living room and a terrace. All the rooms are nicely furnished and have rustic furniture. Breakfast is the buffet type.

Accommodation
Guestrooms: *3 mini-apartments*
Services & Amenities: *French and English are spoken; rooms cleaned every 3 days; kitchen; terrace; garden; smokers welcome; parking*
Rates: *€€€-€€€€. Discounts for extended stays*
Credit cards: *not accepted*
Pets: 🚫

Magliano Sabina (Rieti)

B&B I Giardini
Maria Teresa Bella Gamba
via del Giardino 2
02046 Magliano Sabina (RI)
tel. and fax 0744 919296
r.abiuso@tiscali.it
Closed: 15 to 31 July
and 15 to 31 December

Accommodation
Guestrooms: *2 (1 double with private bath, 1 single with shared bath)*
Services & Amenities: *French and English are spoken; rooms cleaned every day; complimentary tourist information; garden; smokers welcome; parking*
Rates: *single €, double €€. Discounts for extended stays*
Credit cards: *not accepted*
Pets: ✓

This B&B, which has two guestrooms with modern furnishings, is located in a 1920's building that's surrounded by a garden and is situated in an area of great historical-cultural interest on Viterbo hill. The traditional breakfast, which consists of organic products, is either served in the family living room with fireplace, or, when the weather's nice, outdoors.

Marino (Rome)

Vigne del Sole
Francesca Scavazza
via Vivaldi 9
00047 Marino (RM)
tel. and fax 06 9384342
bedandbreakfastvignedelsole@hotmail.com
Closed: 9 January to 11 April

This B&B, on the ground floor of a small, three-family villa surrounded by a green valley among vineyards and orchards, is just 200 meters from Marino's main square. The three, plainly-furnished guestrooms have an independent entrance. The hostess, who loves music and art, serves the continental breakfast in the room reserved for the guests. Guests are also welcome to use the nice garden. On request, guests can be driven to and from the station.

Multicoloured bee-eaters are present in the Lake Nemi zone.

Accommodation
Guestrooms: *3 (1 single and 2 doubles, with shared bath); additional bed on request*
Services & Amenities: *English spoken; rooms cleaned every day; tourist information; garden; smokers welcome; private parking*
Rates: *single €, double €€. Additional bed supplement €*
Credit cards: *not accepted*
Pets:

Villa Monia 1-2-3
via Colle Picchione 71
località Due Santi
00047 Marino (RM)
tel. 06 9352337
06 9352337, 06 96149303
Closed: 9 January to 28 February and 6 November to 14 December

This B&B is in a 1970's villa situated on the Appia Nuova in an area with vineyards and orchards 7 km from the center of Marino. The 3 guestrooms are on the ground floor, face the garden and have an independent entrance. Guests have the use of a room with a refrigerator and TV. The continental breakfast is generally served in a room reserved for the guests. In the summertime, breakfast can be served outdoors.

Accommodation
Guestrooms: *3 (1 single and 2 doubles, with shared bath); additional bed on request*
Services & Amenities: *English spoken; rooms cleaned every day; tourist information; garden; smokers welcome; parking*
Rates: *single €–€€, double €€€–€€€€. Additional bed supplement €*
Credit cards: *not accepted*
Pets:

A costume parade, during the local Grape Festival.

Mazzano Romano (Rome)

Guesthouse Bed&Breakfast
Giorgio Osimani
via A. Pancrazi 7
00060 Mazzano Romano (RM)
tel. and fax 06 9049086
guest.house@tiscali.it
www.gh-guesthouse.com/dove.htm
Closed: varies

This B&B is located in the attic of a two-story building that faces the city post office and is not far from the Bracciano Lake and the Valle del Treja Regional Park. The accommodation offers a bedroom, a kitchen, a bathroom and a large terrace, where the guests can have an enjoyable breakfast. Not far away is Calcata, a picturesque, very well kept medieval village where many homes and wine cellars have been converted into charming little souvenir and antique shops. Private parking is also available for the guests.

Accommodation
Guestrooms: *1 triple, also single occupancy, with private bath*
Services & Amenities: *English spoken; rooms cleaned every 3 days; complimentary tourist information; kitchen and kitchenette use by request; smokers welcome; private parking*
Rates: *single €€, double €€€, triple €€€*
Credit cards: *not accepted*
Pets:

• **Bed & Breakfast Italia**
Code L146
tel. 06 6878618, fax 06 6878619
info@bbitalia.it
www.bbitalia.it
Closed: varies

The house is in the old center of a medieval village. It is furnished in rustic country-style, and has a double room with a large balcony overlooking the valley of the Treja River, and a private bathroom with shower. If needed, an extra bed for children under two is provided by the hostess. A car is necessary to reach Viterbo, a city of art and culture, the Mount Gelato falls, Sutri and Calcata, the old place of refuge of the partisans.

ACCOMMODATION
Guestrooms: *1 double bedroom*
Services & Amenities: *French and English are spoken; rooms cleaned every 3 days; complimentary tourist information; smokers welcome*
Minimum stay: *2 nights*
Rates: €€
Credit cards: VISA MC *Bancomat*
Pets: not allowed

• **Bed & Breakfast Italia** TCI 10%
Code L153
tel. 06 6878618, fax 06 6878619
info@bbitalia.it
www.bbitalia.it
Closed: varies

A penthouse with terrace in the old center of the village with classic and functional furnishings. It features TV, hair-dryer and independent heating. This B&B offers a triple room with three single beds, a lounge and guest private bathroom with shower. Rome can be reached in 20 minutes by train. The Treja Valley and Mount Gelato falls are 10 km away.

ACCOMMODATION
Guestrooms: *1 triple room*
Services & Amenities: *English spoken; rooms cleaned every three days; complimentary tourist information; bike rental; terrace; smokers welcome; private parking*
Minimum stay: *2 nights*
Rates: €€
Credit cards: VISA MC
Bancomat
Pets: not allowed

MENTANA (ROME)

Centro Casa 2
Maria Francorsi
via Zanella 14
00013 Mentana (RM)
tel. 06 90627075, fax 06 90625433
Closed: December, January and August

This B&B, which is in a small, three-family villa that's 3 kilometers from the station, offers a guest apartment consisting of three double rooms, a room with TV and two bathrooms. The guest apartment communicates with the family apartment. All the rooms have classic furnishings and a TV, and one also has a terrace. The continental breakfast is served in the dining room.

ACCOMMODATION
Guestrooms: *3 doubles, also single occupancy, shared bath; additional bed on request*
Services & Amenities: *French and English are spoken; rooms cleaned every day; complimentary tourist information; garden; smokers welcome; private parking*
Rates: *single €-€€, double €€-€€€. Additional bed supplement €. Children under 10 -10%*
Credit cards: *accepted*
Pets: allowed

Medals in the Museo Garibaldino of Mentana.

• **Bed & Breakfast Italia**
Code L110
tel. 06 6878618, fax 06 6878619
info@bbitalia.it
www.bbitalia.it
Closed: varies

A country house set in 2000 square meters of green park with olive trees, cypresses and cedars of Lebanon. It is an estate on a hill planted with vineyards and olive trees. The accommodation offers a double room, with an independent entrance and country-style furnishings, and private bathroom with tub/shower. An extra bed can be added for children under two. Private parking is also available for the guests. Ice-rink in the environs.

Accommodation
Guestrooms: *1 double bedroom*
Services & Amenities: *French, English, German and Spanish are spoken; rooms cleaned every 3 days; complimentary tourist information; terrace; private parking*
Minimum stay: *2 nights*
Rates: €€
Credit cards: VISA MC *Bancomat*
Pets: no

Montasola (Rieti)

• **Bed & Breakfast Italia**
Code L054
tel. 06 6878618, fax 06 6878619
info@bbitalia.it
www.bbitalia.it
Closed: varies

A farmstead situated north of Rome, in the Sabina hills. It is in an ideal position to watch wild animals and sample genuine local food. This accommodation offers small apartments consisting in bedrooms, a small lounge, a kitchen corner and a private bathroom. All the rooms are tastefully furnished and carefully kept by the pleasant lady of the house. Guests can gather in the lounge. The host provides useful information on places to visit.

Accommodation
Guestrooms: *3 doubles*
Services & Amenities: *English spoken; rooms cleaned every 3 days; complimentary tourist information*
Minimum stay: *2 nights*
Rates: €€
Credit cards: VISA MC *Bancomat*
Pets: no

Montelanico (Rome)

• **Bed & Breakfast Italia**
Code L150
tel. 06 6878618, fax 06 6878619
info@bbitalia.it
www.bbitalia.it
Closed: varies

The house is located in the old center of this village in the Lepini mountains. This accommodation consists in two double rooms, one with twin beds, furnished in a modern and functional style; both have an ensuite bathroom and TV. Nature excursions, tours of the old center or the surrounding villages, horseback rides, and ancient Roman cookery courses are arranged by the hosts on request. They also provides useful tourist information.

Accommodation
Guestrooms: *2 (1 double bedroom and 1 double)* ♿
Services & Amenities: *English spoken; rooms cleaned every 3 days; tourist information; baby-sitting service; smokers welcome*
Minimum stay: *2 nights*
Rates: €€
Credit cards: VISA MC *Bancomat*
Pets: no

MONTELIBRETTI (ROME)

• Bed & Breakfast Italia
Code L036
tel. 06 6878618, fax 06 6878619
info@bbitalia.it
www.bbitalia.it
Closed: varies

This B&B is hosted by a country-style cottage with garden, located in the center of the village. The accommodation consists in two spacious bright double rooms, one with a separate entrance, furnished with antiques, precious carpets, and with

exposed timber beams, and private bathroom with shower. An extra bed or a children's cot can be added. The hosts welcome guests in a friendly and homely ambience.

ACCOMMODATION
Guestrooms: *2 doubles*
Services & Amenities: *English spoken; rooms cleaned every 3 days; complimentary tourist information; terrace; parking*
Minimum stay: *2 nights*
Rates: €€
Credit cards: VISA MC *Bancomat*
Pets: no

MONTEROTONDO (ROME)

Centro Casa 1
Marco Cutini Calisti
via Sicilia 14
00015 Monterotondo (RM)
tel. 06 90627075, fax 06 90625433
Closed: December, January and August

This B&B, on Via Salaria, is in a 1960's villa, which is surrounded by a 1000 sq. meter garden. The host family, which consists of three persons, provides three double guestrooms that have modern furniture, a TV and a telephone. One of the rooms faces a large terrace. The continental breakfast is served in the family dining room. The guests are also

ACCOMMODATION
Guestrooms: *3 doubles, also single occupancy, with shared bath; additional bed on request*
Services & Amenities: *French and English are spoken; rooms cleaned every day; tourist info; garden; smokers welcome; private parking*
Rates: *single €-€€, double €€-€€€. Additional bed supplement €. Children under 10 -10%*
Credit cards: *accepted*
Pets: yes

welcome to use the living room, which has a TV.

• Bed & Breakfast Italia
Code L101
tel. 06 6878618, fax 06 6878619
info@bbitalia.it
www.bbitalia.it
Closed: varies

This B&B is hosted by a villa with a scenic view over the hills, located in a small village in the Roman countryside. The accommodation consists in three double bedrooms with rustic furnishings, with TV and private bathroom with shower. Homely and informal ambience. Rome is 30 kilo-

meters away and can be reached by car or by train, which reaches Piazza del Popolo in 30 minutes. Private parking available. The old villages along Via Salaria deserve a visit.

ACCOMMODATION
Guestrooms: *3 double bedrooms*
Services & Amenities: *English spoken; rooms cleaned every 3 days; complimentary tourist information; terrace; private parking*
Minimum stay: *2 nights*
Rates: €€
Credit cards: VISA MC *Bancomat*
Pets: no

Morlupo (Rome)

• **Bed & Breakfast Italia**
Code L001
tel. 06 6878618, fax 06 6878619
info@bbitalia.it
www.bbitalia.it
Closed: varies

The B&B is located in a panoramic villa in Montelarco. The three guestrooms are furnished with antiques: two have a double bed and one has twin beds; two private bathrooms with shower. An extensive garden and private parking are available. This is a very green and peaceful area. Nearby Campagnano Romano is famed for its antiques market. Rome is easily reached by car in 40 minutes.

Accommodation
Guestrooms: *3 (2 double bedrooms and 1 double)*
Services & Amenities: *French and English are spoken; rooms cleaned every 3 days; complimentary tourist information; private parking*
Minimum stay: *2 nights*
Rates: €€
Credit cards: VISA MC *Bancomat*
Pets: not allowed

Nepi (Viterbo)

Le Tre Acacie
Enrica Capanna
La Corta per Ronciglione
località XXX Miglia
01036 Nepi (VT)
tel. 06 7027873
mob. 338 3572325, 333 2329295
enrica.capanna@mclink.it
www.mclink.it/personal/MC3250
Closed: November to February

This B&B has good connections for Rome and is in a villa that's surrounded by a 16 000 sq.meter park. The rooms have both modern and antique furniture. The host loves painting and there are over 200 of his paintings located throughout the house. Breakfast, which includes pastries or cold cuts and cheese, is served in the living room or in the garden. Guests have the use of a small soccer field, a gazebo and a deck chair. And there's a golf course and swimming pool nearby.

Accommodation
Guestrooms: *3 doubles, also single occupancy, 1 with private bath and 2 with shared bath*
Services & Amenities: *French, English and Spanish are spoken; rooms cleaned every day; tourist information; baby-sitting service; terrace; Internet access; garden; smokers welcome; parking*
Rates: *single €, double €€. Discounts for children and extended stays*
Credit cards: *not accepted*
Pets: not allowed

• **Bed & Breakfast Italia** (TCI 10%)
Code L147
tel. 06 6878618, fax 06 6878619
info@bbitalia.it
www.bbitalia.it
Closed: varies

Accommodation
Guestrooms: *3 (1 single, 1 double and 1 triple room)*
Services & Amenities: *French, English and Spanish are spoken; rooms cleaned every 3 days; complimentary tourist information; bike rental; private parking*
Minimum stay: *2 nights*
Rates: €
Credit cards: VISA MC *Bancomat*
Pets: not allowed

4 kilometers from Nepi, a small medieval hamlet, this house is set in a 3000 sq.m park with high trunk trees. This accommodation offers three guestrooms: a single, a double, and a triple with double bed and a single bed. The shared bathroom has tub/shower. Rome is 40 km away and can be reached using the efficient bus service to the subway station linked to the old center. The journey takes 40 minutes

NEROLA (ROME)

• **Bed & Breakfast Italia**
Code L149
tel. 06 6878618, fax 06 6878619
info@bbitalia.it
www.bbitalia.it
Closed: varies

A villa situated along the Via Salaria, in the medieval hamlet of Nerola. It has five double rooms (four with double beds), and two private bathrooms shared by all the rooms. Classic furnishings with antiques; guests are encouraged to use the well-kept garden of the villa. The Abbey of Farfa is 10 km away; a remarkable example of medieval architecture in Reatino.

ACCOMMODATION
Guestrooms: *5 (4 double bedrooms and 1 double)*
Services & Amenities: *English spoken; rooms cleaned every 3 days; tourist info; smokers welcome; parking*
Minimum stay: *2 nights*
Rates: €€
Credit cards: VISA MC *Bancomat*
Pets: not allowed

PALESTRINA (ROME)

Praeneste
Luciano D'Itri
via di Bocca Piana 10
00036 Palestrina (RM)
tel. and fax 06 9573170
mob. 338 2967236
Closed: April, July and December

This B&B is in a small, modern villa located south of Rome in a hilly area near the Castelli Romani. The two guestrooms, on the first floor, have plane, linear furnishings. The continental breakfast is generally served in the family living room, the room that guests are welcome to use at any time during the day. If the weather's nice, breakfast may be served in the small terraced garden. On request, guests may be driven privately to and from the nearby Zagarolo train station.

ACCOMMODATION
Guestrooms: *2 (1 double bedroom and 1 double, with shared bath); additional bed on request*
Services & Amenities: *rooms cleaned every day; complimentary tourist information; garden; smokers welcome; private parking*
Rates: *€€. Additional bed supplement €. Discounts for extended stays*
Credit cards: *not accepted*
Pets: allowed

POGGIO NATIVO (RIETI)

• **Bed & Breakfast Italia**
Code L024
tel. 06 6878618, fax 06 6878619
info@bbitalia.it
www.bbitalia.it
Closed: varies

A farmhouse in the leafy valley of the river Farfa. The four double rooms are furnished in country style; each has a bathroom with shower and an extra bed can be added. Guests are encouraged to use mountain-bikes, table-tennis table, billiards, and soccer pitch; meals prepared with local produce grown by the owners can be served. A sports center with swimming pool, tennis courts and a small fishing lake is 1 km away.

ACCOMMODATION
Guestrooms: *4 doubles*
Services & Amenities: *English spoken; rooms cleaned every 3 days; tourist information; horse-riding excursions; private parking*
Minimum stay: *2 nights*
Rates: €€
Credit cards: VISA MC *Bancomat*
Pets: not allowed

Pomezia (Rome)

• **Bed & Breakfast Italia**
Code L106
tel. 06 6878618, fax 06 6878619
info@bbitalia.it
www.bbitalia.it
Closed: varies

The B&B is located in an elegant, recently built villa classically furnished with antiques and offers three rooms: a double one, a twin and a single; a private bathroom is shared by all the rooms. The hosts, who offer informal and homely hospitality, will drive guests to the bus stop for Rome, the EUR district, in 30 minutes. The Anzio seaside resort is 15 minutes from Pomezia.

Accommodation
Guestrooms: *3 (1 single, 1 double bedroom and 1 double)*
Services & Amenities: *English spoken; rooms cleaned every 3 days; tourist information; parking*
Minimum stay: *2 nights*
Rates: €€
Credit cards: VISA MC *Bancomat*
Pets: ✗

Riano (Rome)

Villa Rosa TCI 10%
Rosa Tanga
via Parigi 97
00060 Riano (RM)
tel. 06 9035127, fax 06 90139182
villarosa@lcnet.it
Closed: 14 January to 28 February and 18 July to 30 August

This B&B, in a tranquil, panoramic, hilly area, 15 minutes from Rome, offers an apartment with modern furniture and an independent entrance. It has two rooms, a bathroom, and a living room with TV. The bedrooms share a balcony and face the garden, which has olive trees, fruit trees and ornamental plants. The continental breakfast is served in the reserved living room. On request, the hosts can organize guided visits to Rome and the surrounding area, including visits to see places of natural and archeological interest.

Accommodation
Guestrooms: *2 (1 double bedroom, also single occupancy, and 1 quadruple, with shared bath); additional bed on request*
Services & Amenities: *French and English are spoken; rooms cleaned every 3 days; tourist info; garden; smokers welcome; parking*
Rates: *€ per person. Additional bed supplement €. Children under 3 free*
Credit cards: *not accepted*
Pets: ✗

Rieti

• **Bed & Breakfast Italia** TCI 10%
Code L051
tel. 06 6878618, fax 06 6878619
info@bbitalia.it
www.bbitalia.it
Closed: varies

This B&B is hosted by a villa with garden, nestling in the Reatino valley, at Cerchiara. The guest accommodation, which consists in three bedrooms overlooking the valley, have rustic furniture; an extra bed can be added for children. Private parking is also available. There are horse-riding and tennis courts in the environs. Smokers are welcome.

Accommodation
Guestrooms: *3 (1 single, 2 doubles)*
Services & Amenities: *French spoken; rooms cleaned every 3 days; complimentary tourist information; horse-riding excursions; smokers welcome; private parking*
Minimum stay: *2 nights*
Rates: €€
Credit cards: VISA MC *Bancomat*
Pets: ✗

Rivodutri (Rieti)

• Bed & Breakfast Italia
Code L107
tel. 06 6878618, fax 06 6878619
info@bbitalia.it
www.bbitalia.it
Closed: varies

A recently refurbished two-room apartment situated in the center of the small medieval hamlet in the province of Rieti. It is self-contained, with period country-style furniture, and has a double bedroom (with the option of an extra bed), lounge, kitchen, and bathroom with shower. The Marmore Falls, where extreme sports, such as rafting and bungee jumping, can be practiced are reached in 30 minutes. A car is indispensable.

Accommodation
Guestrooms: *1 double bedroom*
Services & Amenities: *French and English are spoken; rooms cleaned every 3 days; tourist information*
Minimum stay: *2 nights*
Rates: €€
Credit cards: VISA MC *Bancomat*
Pets: not allowed

Rocca di Papa (Rome)

Bed & Breakfast In Villa
Roberto Maldera
via delle Barozze 71, corner via dei Laghi
00040 Rocca di Papa (RM)
tel. and fax 06 9496472
mob. 347 0748758
info@invilla.it
www.invilla.it
Closed: varies

This B&B is in a beautiful villa that's close to the Lago di Castelgandolfo. The guestrooms face a large garden that has old pine trees. The host, who was a professional actor up until 1992, has made it a point to provide his guests with certain things that are not found in hotel rooms, such as candles, anti-suffocation cushions, an aquarium, a welcoming kit, and fine Tuscan linen and antiques.

Accommodation
Guestrooms: *3 double bedrooms, also single occupancy, with private bath; additional bed on request*
Services & Amenities: *French and English are spoken; rooms cleaned every day; tourist information; Internet access; garden; smokers welcome; private parking*
Rates: *single* €€, *double* €€€. *Additional bed supplement* €. *Children under 12 free.*
Credit cards: *accepted*
Pets: allowed

• Bed & Breakfast Italia
Code L127
tel. 06 6878618, fax 06 6878619
info@bbitalia.it
www.bbitalia.it
Closed: varies

A large comfortable attic apartment with classic period furnishings. It has three double bedrooms and two private bathrooms, with the option of an extra bed for children under two. Rocca di Papa is 15 minutes from Castel Gandolfo, Grottaferrata, and Frascati. It is famous for its fine restaurants and is 15 km from Rome, easily reached on several local buses.

Accommodation
Guestrooms: *3 double bedrooms*
Services & Amenities: *French and English are spoken; rooms cleaned every 3 days; complimentary tourist information; private parking*
Minimum stay: *2 nights*
Rates: €€
Credit cards: VISA MC *Bancomat*
Pets: not allowed

- **Bed & Breakfast Italia** TCI 10%

Code L130
tel. 06 6878618, fax 06 6878619
info@bbitalia.it
www.bbitalia.it
Closed: varies

ACCOMMODATION
Guestrooms: *3 (2 double bedrooms, 1 tripla)*
Services & Amenities: *English spoken; rooms cleaned every three days; complimentary tourist information; horse-riding excursions; private parking*
Minimum stay: *2 nights*
Rates: €€
Credit cards: VISA MC *Bancomat*
Pets:

Located in the picturesque and charming village of Castelli Romani, this cozy B&B is simply furnished. This accommodation offers three rooms: two double rooms and a triple with three single beds; the private bathroom has a tub and shower. An extra bed for children under two can be added. It is just a few kilometers from Lake Albano, Lake Nemi, and Castel Gandolfo, Rome is 15 km away.

ROCCAGIOVINE (ROME)

- **Bed & Breakfast Italia**

Code L151
tel. 06 6878618, fax 06 6878619
info@bbitalia.it
www.bbitalia.it
Closed: varies

The house is located in the old center of this picturesque village in the Roman countryside. The guest accommodation consists in two double rooms – one with twin beds – and a triple with a double and a single, decorated with period country-style furniture. Each guestroom has a TV and a private bathroom. Guests may borrow mountain-bikes. The village is in the Lucretili mountain park dotted with large picnic areas. Private parking is also available.

ACCOMMODATION
Guestrooms: *3 (2 doubles, 1 triple)*
Services & Amenities: *French and English are spoken; rooms cleaned every 3 days; tourist information; baby-sitting service; smokers welcome; private parking*
Minimum stay: *2 nights*
Rates: €€
Credit cards: VISA MC *Bancomat*
Pets:

ROME

For easier identification of the numerous B&Bs in the capital city, these are listed below, divided by district, or by quarter if in the old city centre.
The name of the district, in brackets, is flanked by the geographical position with respect to the old city centre.
The number before each B&B refers to its number on the description pages.

• Appio (south east)
143. Code R1178
178. Code R1270
219. Code R2125
231. Code R49
• Ardeatino (south)
73. Maria & Paolo B&B
201. Code R2041
• Aurela Raganelli (west)
23. B&B Cris & Mapi
• Aurelio (west)
40. B&B Piccolomini
68. Il Fontanile
94. Vista di Roma
98. Code R01
115. Code R1054
121. Code R1095
154. Code R1211
156. Code R1213
175. Code R1267
213. Code R2107
• Balduina (north west)
28. Il Giardino
112. Code R1050
151. Code R12
158. Code R1220
166. Code R1239
171. Code R1252
182. Code R1279
185. Code R1283
189. Code R1287
198. Code R2018
204. Code R2047
209. Code R2077
222. Code R2135
244. Code R76
• Boccea (west)
110. Code R1038
134. Code R1155
• Campo Marzio (old center)
86. Toia's B&B
223. Code R2138
• Casal Palocco (south west)
90. Villa Chiara
236. Code R66
• Casilino (south east)
102. Code R1010
• Castro Pretorio (old center)
1. A&C Much More
17. B&B Belle Arti
26. B&B Holiday Rome
54. C&G
63. Euro
• Celio (old center)
19. B&B Appio Latino
32. B&B L'Ariete
• Esquilino (old center)
9. Anne & Mary
24. B&B Esquilin
69. Italian B&B
81. Pierri B&B
87. Tourist House
89. Vacanze Romane
99. Code R04
123. Code R1105
179. Code R1250
207. Code R2066
220. Code R2129
237. Code R68
• Eur (south)
107. Code R1029
116. Code R1071
138. Code R1164
144. Code R1179
149. Code R1196
161. Code R1224
162. Code R1226
• Flaminio (north)
10. Arti B&B
33. B&B Mancini
109. Code R1037
170. Code R1251
174. Code R1263
225. Code R2140
226. Code R2143
• Fleming (north)
21. Collina Fleming
114. Code R1052
153. Code R1208
• Foro Italico (north)
75. Millennium B&B
• Garbatella (south)
242. Code R74
• Gianicolo (old center)
5. All'ombra del Cupolone
25. B&B Gianicolo
45. B&B San Pietro
46. B&B San Pietro Cavalleggeri
60. Cupola
65. Fiori e Semi B&B
85. The Cloister
105. Code R1022
113. Code R1051
130. Code R1130
163. Code R1232
179. Code R1271
181. Code R1277
214. Code R2108
• Grotte Rosse (north)
27. B&B Igloo and Red Houses
• Laurentino (south)
71. Laurentina B&B
106. Code R1028
111. Code R1044
126. Code R1112
139. Code R1166
173. Code R1262
229. Code R37
• Monte Mario (north west)
30. B&B La Capitale
72. B&B Le Terrazze
164. Code R1236
• Montesacro (north east)
56. Casa Giardino
100. Code R1001
101. Code R1005
103. Code R1015
104. Code R1016
122. Code R1098
124. Code R1109
125. Code R1110
141. Code R1171
221. Code R2123
227. Code R23
239. Code R71
• Monteverde (west)
36. B&B Nocetta
66. Giada B&B
80. Pamphili House
108. Code R1034
120. Code R1086
137. Code R1161
183. Code R1281

192. Code R20
208. Code R2067
215. Code R2115
217. Code R2120
241. Code R73

- Monti (old center)

77. New Rome Bed & Breakfast
140. Code R1170
197. Code R2017
212. Code R2172
228. Code R25

- Nomentana-Bologna (north east)

8. Anna Lucia B&B
34. B&B Martin
119. Code R1085
132. Code R1139
133. Code R1141
159. Code R1221
160. Code R1222
172. Code R1255

- Nomentana-Trieste (north)

22. B&B Coppedè
42. B&B Regina Margherita
50. B&B via Messina (Porta Pia)
74. Metella B&B
82. Rap B&B
92. Villino Trieste
128. Code R1121
147. Code R1185
243. Code R75

- Nomentano (north east)

127. Code R1114
135. Code R1156
180. Code R1276

- Ostia (south west)

95. Code L091
96. Code L109
97. Code L114

- Parioli (north)

188. Code R1286
195. Code R2010
199. Code R2026

- Rione Pigna (old center)

224. Code R2139

- Portuense (south west)

3. A Casa di Silvana
11. Arvalia B&B - Colle del Sole
93. Virginia B&B
148. Code R1190
150. Code R1197
186. Code R1284
191. Code R13

- Ponte/Parione (old center)

18. B&B Campo de' Fiori
38. B&B Pascucci
39. B&B Pettinari - Campo de' Fiori
47. B&B Teatro
118. Code R1083
194. Code R2007
233. Code R55
240. Code R72

- Prati (north east)

2. A Casa di Serena
4. Alex's B&B (S.P.)
12. At Simona's B&B
13. B&B 4th Floor (rione B??)
14. B&B ai Musei Vaticani (S.P.)
35. B&B Massimo Zoli
37. B&B Orchidea
41. B&B Raggi
50. B&B Villino Cecilia Musei Vaticani
53. Borgo Vittorio B&B (rione B??)
59. Clodio B&B
62. Domus Tiber
84. Sogno Roma B&B
117. Code R1081
129. Code R1125
155. Code R1212
157. Code R1214
187. Code R1285
190. Code R1288
202. Code R2042
205. Code R2053
210. Code R2080
211. Code R21
216. Code R2117
218. Code R2124
245. Code R77

- Prima Porta (old center)

177. Code R1269
196. Code R2013

- Ludovisi/Sallustiano (old center)

31. B&B La Dolce Vita
48. B&B Veneto
52. Bed & Breakfast via Calabria

- Regola (old center)

55. Casa Banzo

- San Giovanni (south)

16. B&B Anna
20. B&B Colli Albani
67. Gioia B&B
70. I Tetti di Roma
83. San Giovanni B&B
131. Code R1131
136. Code R1160
145. Code R1182
152. Code R1204
203. Code R2045
234. Code R59
235. Code R63

- San Paolo (south)

51. Bed & Breakfast European
91. Villa Lucia
168. Code R1247

- Testaccio (old center)

15. B&B Angeli in Roma
57. Casa Mary B&B
165. Code R1238

- Tiburtino (north east)

142. Code R1173
146. Code R1184

- Tomba di Nerone (north west)

88. Un villino sulla Cassia

- Torre Gaia (south east)

29. B&B Infa

- Trastevere (old center)

6. A Trastevere
7. Ancient Trastevere
43. B&B Revoltella-Monteverde
61. Di Bartolomeo B&B
76. My Home Trilussa
78. Nicolini B&B Casa in Trastevere
167. Code R1240
176. Code R1268
200. Code R2036
230. Code R38
232. Code R52

- Trevi (old center)

44. B&B Rodan
58. Casa Trevi
184. Code R1282
193. Code R2006
206. Code R2058

Rome

1. A&C Much More

Americo Cavicchia
via Palestro 49
00185 Rome
tel. 06 44701152
holidayrome@yahoo.it
Closed: August, November and December

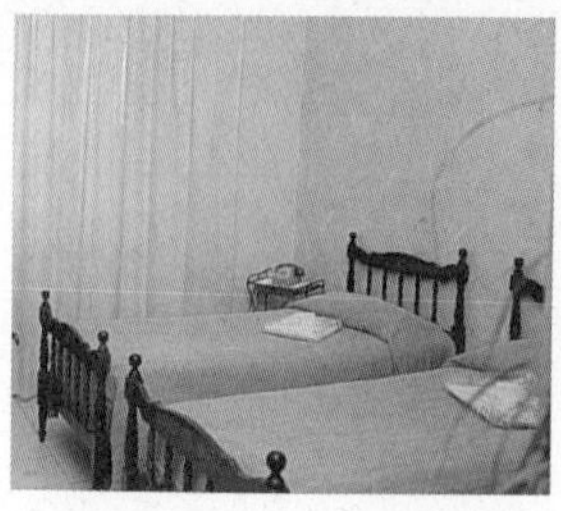

This B&B, which is on the 2nd floor of a period building, is close to the Termini train station and is also in the vicinity of Piazza Indipendenza. The guest accommodation consists in a single room and two double rooms with a TV and a receiving telephone. The rooms share a bathroom. Guests are also welcome to use the family terrace and the room where the continental type breakfast is served. The house is not suitable for children.

Accommodation
Guestrooms: *3 (1 single and 2 doubles, with shared bath)*
Services & Amenities: *French, English and German are spoken; rooms cleaned every day; tourist information; terrace; Internet access; smokers welcome*
Rates: *single €€, double €€-€€€. Discounts for extended stays*
Credit cards: *not accepted*
Pets:

2. A Casa di Serena

Serenella Mencarelli
piazzale degli Eroi (circ.ne Trionfale 1)
00193 Rome
tel. 06 39735570, mob. 336 635542
fax 06 68805586
ocelim@iol.it
www.ilbedandbreakfastaroma.com
Closed: 8 to 31 January and 5 to 23 November

For the hostess, "the pleasure of providing hospitality" means providing the details that make the difference, such as breakfast à la carte, a toilette kit, fresh flowers everywhere and a dominant color for each room, which are provided with satellite TV. The house, which is a close-up of the '20s, is bright, soundproof and air conditioned. Guests have the use of a living room with an Internet connection. All of this is just a short walk from the St. Peter's basilica and the Castel Sant'Angelo.

Accommodation
Guestrooms: *3 doubles, also single occupancy, private bath ♿*
Services & Amenities: *English spoken; rooms cleaned every 3 days; tourist information; terrace; air conditioning; Internet access; smokers welcome*
Rates: *single €€€, doubles €€€€. Children under 6 free. Discounts for extended stays*
Credit Cards: *not accepted*
Pets:

3. A Casa di Silvana

TCI 10%

• Home Express
tel. and fax 06 90129063
homeexpress@tiscalinet.it
www.home-express.it
Open all year

Accommodation
Guestrooms: *2 doubles with shared bath; additional bed on request*
Services & Amenities: *English spoken; rooms cleaned every 3 days; complimentary tourist information; smokers welcome*
Rates: *double €€€. Additional bed supplement €*
Credit cards: *not accepted*
Pets:

This B&B is hosted by a refined building located in the Via Portuense peripheral area, southwest of the center and is served by the No. 8 tram. The two double or triple guestrooms share a bathroom. The rich Italian breakfast is usually served in the apartment's dining room. The hostess, who is painter, likes giving her guests one of her nice watercolor paintings. Smokers are also welcome.

4. Alex's B&B
Alessandro Carè
via Germanico 55
00100 Rome
tel. and fax 06 39742268
mob. 338 3511373
carealex@yahoo.com
www.abbcare.com
Open all year

This B&B, in a small, restored, 19th-century building that has an inner garden, is just 100 m from St. Peter's square and the Vatican Museums. The modern furniture contributes to creating a friendly atmosphere. Breakfast is either served in the kitchen or in the dining room. There's a pay garage in the immediate vicinity.

Accommodation
Guestrooms: *3 doubles, also single occupancy, with private bath; additional bed on request*
Services & Amenities: *French and English are spoken; rooms cleaned every day; tourist information; Internet access; smokers welcome*
Rates: *single €€, double €€€. Additional bed supplement €. Discounts for children*
Credit cards: *not accepted*
Pets: ✓

5. All'Ombra del Cupolone
Walter Fiorucci
viale delle Mura Aurelie 19
00165 Rome
tel. and fax 06 9964472
mob. 347 6243501
info@alcupolone.it
www.cupolone.com
Closed: February, November and December

Accommodation
Guestrooms: *3 (2 doubles, 1 triple, also single occupancy, private bath)*
Services & Amenities: *English and Spanish are spoken; rooms cleaned every 3 days; complimentary tourist information; kitchen use by request; smokers welcome*
Minimum stay: *preferably 2 nights*
Rates: *single €€, double €€€, triple €€€. Children under 5 free*
Credit cards: *not accepted*
Pets: ✓

This B&B is on the second floor of a recently-restructured, late 19th-century building, which is located just 50 meters from the columns of St. Peter's square. This accommodation offers three rooms with modern furniture, a TV, a telephone and a private bath. The continental breakfast is either served in the guest room or in the family kitchen.

6. A Trastevere
• B&B Association of Rome
tel. 06 55302248
fax 06 55302259
info@b-b.rm.it
www.b-b.rm.it
Closed: July, August and Christmas holidays

Accommodation
Guestrooms: *2 (1 single and 1 double bedroom, with private bath)*
Services & Amenities: *rooms cleaned every 3 days; tourist information; smokers welcome*
Minimum stay: *2 nights*
Rates: *single €€, double €€€€*
Credit cards: *not accepted*
Pets: ✗

This B&B is in an apartment located on the second floor of a small, early 20th-C building. The rooms have modern furniture. Breakfast is served in the family living room.

7. Ancient Trastevere B&B
Laura Viotti
via Della Lungara 18
00165 Rome
tel. and fax 06 5819932
mob. 335 6064279
roma_accomodations@.libero.it
www.ancientrastevere.com
Open all year

Accommodation
Guestrooms: *3 suites, also single occupancy, with private bath; additional bed on request*
Services & Amenities: *French, English, Spanish and Singhalese are spoken; rooms cleaned every 3 days; tourist info; baby-sitting service; Internet access; smokers welcome*
Rates: *single €€–€€€, double €€€–€€€€. Additional bed supplement €€. Discounts for groups*
Credit cards: *not accepted*
Pets: ✓

This B&B is on the first floor of a very fascinating antique building, located just outside the historical part of town. From the windows, you can see the Farnesina gardens. The eclectic furnishings, collected by the hostess after considerable hunting among small merchants, are anything but standard.

8. Anna Lucia B&B
Vittoria Parisi
via Lucca 14
00161 Rome
tel. and fax 06 4402466
mob. 333 3237035
Closed: 1-10 January, 1-15 February, 10-20 April, 15-31 August, November and 20-31 December

Accommodation
Guestrooms: *1 single with shared bath; additional bed on request*
Services & Amenities: *French and English are spoken; rooms cleaned every day; complimentary tourist information; smokers welcome*
Rates: *€€. Additional bed supplement €€. Discounts for extended stays (2 weeks)*
Credit cards: *not accepted*
Pets: 🐾

This B&B is hosted by a recently-restructured apartment located on the second floor of a period building. It's near the La Sapienza University and 15 minutes by subway to the old center. The guest accommodation consists in a single that shares the bathroom – which has a tub and a shower – with the hosts. The room has classic furnishings, as well as a TV and a library. The rich continental breakfast is either served in the guestroom or in the apartment kitchen. Smokers welcome.

9. Anne & Mary
Silvia Moroni
via Cavour 325
00184 Rome
tel. 06 69941187, mob. 339 1103016
fax 06 6780629
info@anne-mary.com
www.anne-mary.com
Closed: February, August and November

This B&B is on the second floor of a 19th-century building that's just a short walk from the Roman Forum and the Coliseum. The house is well furnished. The guestroom has a safe and a mini-bar, as well as double windows and air conditioning. The decor and custom furniture is classic and elegant. Italian breakfast can either be served in the kitchen or, if desired, in the room. The hostess, a language teacher, allows her guests to use her Internet facility.

Accommodation
Guestrooms: *3 double bedrooms, also single occupancy, with private bath; additional bed on request*
Services & Amenities: *English spoken; rooms cleaned every day; complimentary tourist information; air conditioning; Internet access; smokers welcome*
Rates: *single €€€, double €€€€, triple €€€€. Children under 3 free. Discounts for extended stays*
Credit cards: *not accepted*
Pets: 🐾

10. Arti B&B
Anna Rosa Artizzu
via Donatello 75
00196 Rome
tel. and fax 06 3215355
mob. 339 1995575, 338 1163451
artibeb.yb.net
Closed: July and August

Accommodation
Guestrooms: *3 doubles, also single occupancy, with private bath; additional bed on request*
Services & Amenities: *French, English and Spanish are spoken; rooms cleaned every day; complimentary tourist information; smokers welcome*
Minimum stay: *2 nights*
Rates: *single €€€, double €€€€. Additional bed supplement €*
Credit cards: *not accepted*
Pets: 🐾

This B&B is on the 5th floor of a prestigious building that surrounds a small, internal cloister. It's located just a few minutes from St. Peter's, on the shore of the Tiber between Piazza del Popolo and the Italic Forum. The host apartment is quiet, has beautiful marble floors and romantic furnishings, including late 19th-C pieces and coordinated pink and green fabrics. Breakfast is served in a special room. Guests have maximum autonomy and the atmosphere is very pleasant.

11. Arvalia B&B - Colle del Sole TCI 10%

Annamaria and Gino Sabatini
via San Giovanni d'Asso 27
00148 Rome
tel. 06 6550275, 06 6551033
fax 06 6550275
Closed: 10 January to 10 March and November

This B&B, which is 500 meters from the Medici Park and 8 kilometers from the Campidoglio, has double rooms, a private bathroom with shower, a TV, a ventilator and a covered terrace. The very large continental breakfast is served in the small room reserved for the guests. Guests can park in the garden surrounding the house. On request, guests can be privately driven to and from the Magliana train station (Rome-Ostiense station-Fiumicino line) or to the bus stop for going to the city center.

Accommodation
Guestrooms: *3 double bedrooms, also single occupancy, with private bath; additional bed on request*
Services & Amenities: *English spoken; rooms cleaned every day; tourist information; terrace; garden; smokers welcome; parking*
Rates: *single €€, double €€€. Additional bed supplement €*
Credit cards: *not accepted*
Pets: ⊘

12. At Simona's B&B

Simona Bacher
viale Vaticano 52
00165 Rome
tel. 06 39734390
simbach@tiscali.it
Closed: February, August and November

This B&B is located in an apartment on the ground floor of a building dating from the time of Umberto I. It is just 5 minutes on foot from the famous Vatican Museums. Guest accommodation consists in two double rooms that have plain, functional furniture, and share a bathroom (with shower) with the hostess. One of the rooms opens onto a large terrace and a balcony, both of which provide a view of Mount Mario. The continental, buffet breakfast is generally served in the family dining room.

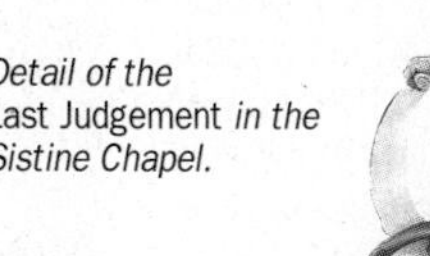

Detail of the Last Judgement *in the Sistine Chapel.*

Accommodation
Guestrooms: *2 doubles, also single occupancy, with shared bath; additional bed on request*
Services & Amenities: *French and English are spoken; rooms cleaned every day; complimentary tourist information; terrace; Internet access; smokers welcome*
Minimum stay: *2 nights*
Rates: *single €€, double €€€. Additional bed supplement €. Discounts for children*
Credit cards: *not accepted*
Pets: ⊘

13. B&B 4th Floor

via Borgo Vittorio 5
(apartment n. 13) rione Borgo
00100 Rome
tel. 06 68308186
06 39386673 (3-8pm)
fax 06 39388857
mob. 347 1103623
4th_floor@id.it
www.geocities.com/4th_floor
Closed: January, February and August

This B&B is on the top floor of a 19th-C building located in the old center just 150 m from St. Peter's. The very quiet guestroom, which faces the internal courtyard, has orthopedic beds and a shared bathroom with shower. The ethnic furnishings are a mix of decorative oriental and African elements. The continental breakfast is normally served in the dining room but, when the weather's nice, it can be served on the large terrace that's full of flowers and surrounds the entire apartment. The host, who is an author and director, offers his guests Genzano bread.

Accommodation
Guestrooms: *1 double bedroom, also single occupancy, shared bath.*
Services & Amenities: *French and English are spoken; rooms cleaned every 3 days; tourist information; terrace; smokers welcome*
Rates: *single €€, double €€€. Discounts for extended stays*
Credit cards: *not accepted*
Pets: ⊘

14. B&B ai Musei Vaticani 

Erminia Pascucci
via S. Veniero 78
00192 Rome
tel. 06 68210776, mob. 347 3851600
fax 06 68215921
bbcenter@tin.it
www.bbroma.com/venier.htm
Closed: January, February and August

This B&B, located on the 2nd floor of a building built in 1927, is just a short distance from the Vatican Museums. It has two rooms with twin beds, one of which has a private bathroom, and a room with a double bed, which shares the bathroom with shower with the other room that has the twin beds. The continental, buffet breakfast is served in the family kitchen. A specialized agency provides shuttle service to and from the airport.

ACCOMMODATION
Guestrooms: *3 doubles, also single occupancy, 1 with private bath and 2 with shared bath; additional bed on request*
Services & Amenities: *French, English and Spanish are spoken; rooms cleaned every 3 days; tourist information; smokers welcome*
Rates: *single €€, double €€€. Additional bed supplement €. Discounts for families and extended stays*
Credit cards: *not accepted*
Pets: 🚫

15. B&B Angeli in Roma

Maryan Abad
via di Villa Pepoli 20
00100 Rome
tel. and fax 06 5742208
bbangeli@hotmail.com
www.bbangeli.com
Closed: January, February and November

This B&B is located in a luxurious apartment in a villa on a quiet private road on the Aventino. Its refined atmosphere is created by the period furniture and elegant fabrics selected by the hostess. Its more frequent guests include members of the diplomatic corps because of its being close to various embassies. The rich English breakfast – which is actually a brunch – is served "with white gloves" in the guestrooms.

ACCOMMODATION
Guestrooms: *3 double bedrooms, also single occupancy, 1 with private bath and 2 with shared bath* ♿
Services & Amenities: *French, English and Spanish are spoken; rooms cleaned every 3 days; tourist information; garden; smokers welcome; private parking*
Rates: *single €€, double €€€€*
Credit cards: *not accepted*
Pets: 🚫

16. B&B Anna

• Home Express
tel. and fax 06 90129063
homeexpress@tiscalinet.it
www.home-express.it
Open all year

ACCOMMODATION
Guestrooms: *1 double bedroom, private bath; additional bed on request*
Services & Amenities: *French and English are spoken; rooms cleaned every 3 days; complimentary tourist information; terrace*
Minimum stay: *2 nights*
Rates: *€€€. Additional bed supplement €*
Credit cards: *not accepted*
Pets: 🚫

This B&B is in an attic that has a large terrace and a veranda, and it's just a few minutes from San Giovanni in Laterano. Guests have a bright, double room with modern furnishings, a living room with a TV and a beautiful veranda with fireplace. Breakfast is served in the kitchen. The area is very well served by various means of public transportation, and has a number of stores and various services. Guests are particularly reminded not to miss the Nero's Aqueduct and the Aurelian Walls.

17. B&B Belle Arti
• B&B Association of Rome
tel. 06 55302248, fax 06 55302259
info@b-b.rm.it
www.b-b.rm.it
Closed: 6 January to 3 March and 4 November to 6 December

This B&B, which is in a separate wing of an apartment located near the Porta Pia villa, just 10 minutes by bus from the old center, has two double rooms – one of which has a sitting area – air conditioning, and direct access to a large terrace, which can also be accessed from the other room. The rooms have classic style furnishings and share a bathroom that has a tub with a shower. The continental breakfast is served on the veranda reserved for the guests.

Accommodation
Guestrooms: *2 double bedrooms, also single occupancy, with shared bath; additional bed on request*
Services & Amenities: *French and English are spoken; rooms cleaned every day; complimentary tourist information; smokers welcome*
Minimum stay: *2 nights*
Rates: *single €€, double €€€. Additional bed supplement €. Discounts for extended stays*
Credit cards: *not accepted*
Pets:

18. B&B Campo de' Fiori
Giovanna De Luca
via De' Giubbonari 23
00186 Rome
tel. and fax 06 68307493
mob. 347 6604011
giodeluc@libero.it
• B&B Association of Rome
tel. 06 55302248, fax 06 55302259
info@b-b.rm.it
www.b-b.rm.it
• Friendly Home-Gli Amici del B&B
tel. 02 860147, fax 02 875860
friendlymilano@dada.it
tel. and fax 011 9536376
fhrivoli@virgilio.it
Closed: July-August

This B&B is located on the top floor of a completely-restored convent situated in one of the capital city's most fascinating, aristocratic districts. It has a large terrace with lots of splendid greenery. The character and atmosphere of this apartment, with its antique, Sicilian furniture, is very refined and cultured. The hostess is a theater artist and has all sorts of interests. The Italian breakfast is either served in an elegant living room – which is next to the bedroom – or on the terrace.

Accommodation
Guestrooms: *1 double bedroom, with private bath*
Services & Amenities: *English spoken; rooms cleaned every day; complimentary tourist information; terrace; smokers welcome*
Minimum stay: *2 nights*
Rates: *€€€€*
Credit cards: *not accepted*
Pets:

19. B&B Casa Appio Latino TCI 10%
• Associazione Koko Nor
tel. 049 8643394, mob. 338 3377912
fax 049 8643394
kokonor@bandb-veneto.it
www.bandb-veneto.it/kokonor
Open all year

Accommodation
Guestrooms: *2 doubles, with shared bath; additional bed on request*
Services & Amenities: *French and English are spoken; rooms cleaned every 3 days; complimentary tourist information; kitchen use by request; smokers welcome*
Minimum stay: *2 nights*
Rates: *single €€, double €€€. Discounts for children*
Credit cards: *not accepted*
Pets:

This B&B is in a 1940's building with an internal garden and is located in Porta Metronia, near Celio Hill. The two double guestrooms have period furniture. A fifth bed can be provided in the living room, as well as a small bed for children under 3 years of age. Breakfast, enriched with eggs and genuine marmalade, is either served in the kitchen or in the apartment's living room. Guests who stay for more than three days receive a complimentary basket of products from the Umbrian countryside.

20. B&B Colli Albani
Fulvia Giuliani
via Columba 52
00179 Rome
tel. 06 7800139, mob. 338 2055029
Closed: July, August and November

ACCOMMODATION
Guestrooms: *1 double, also single occupancy, with private bath; additional bed on request*
Services & Amenities: *French, English, Spanish are spoken; rooms cleaned every 3 days; tourist info; air conditioning; smokers welcome*
Minimum stay: *2 nights*
Rates: *single €€, double €€€. Additional bed supplement €€. Discounts for children and extended stays*
Credit cards: *not accepted*
Pets:

This B&B is on the ground floor of a modern building located in the San Giovanni area, 10 minutes from the San Pietro subway station (Line A). Guests have a double room with an adjoining private bathroom that has a tub with a shower. The room, which has period furniture, has a receiving telephone and air conditioning. The continental breakfast is served in the family kitchen. The host family consists of four persons. Guests can park in the small square that's in front of the building's main door.

21. B&B Collina Fleming
• B&B Association of Rome
tel. 06 55302248, fax 06 55302259
info@b-b.rm.it
www.b-b.rm.it
Closed: 1 to 20 January and 10 to 25 February

ACCOMMODATION
Guestrooms: *1 double bedroom, also single occupancy, private bath* ♿
Services & Amenities: *French, English and Spanish are spoken; rooms cleaned every 3 days; tourist information; terrace; Internet access; smokers welcome*
Minimum stay: *3 nights*
Rates: *single €€, double €€€*
Credit cards: *not accepted*
Pets:

This B&B is located north of the city center, in the residential area that has the same name. It's about a half-hour bus ride to the old center. The comfortable guestroom has both antique and modern furniture, and guests are welcome to use the various shared rooms in the apartment, as well as a very pleasant terrace. The Italian breakfast is served in the dining room.

22. B&B Coppedé
• B&B Association of Rome
tel. 06 55302248, fax 06 55302259
info@b-b.rm.it
www.b-b.rm.it
Closed: 15 January to 28 February and 15 July to 31 August

ACCOMMODATION
Guestrooms: *1 double bedroom, also single occupancy, with private bath; cot or child's bed available*
Services & Amenities: *French and English are spoken; rooms cleaned every day; complimentary tourist information; smokers welcome*
Minimum stay: *2 nights*
Rates: *single €€, double €€€. Discounts for children and extended stays*
Credit cards: *not accepted*
Pets:

This B&B, situated on the ground floor of a building dating from the '60s, is located in the Viale Regina Margherita area and is just a 15-minute walk south of Via Veneto and north of the Costanza mausoleum. Guests have a double room with classic-style furnishings, a private bathroom with a shower, and a telephone. The continental breakfast is served in the family dining room. Guests are welcome to use the living room, which has a TV, as well as the garden.

The mid-4th century mausoleum of St Constance is easily reached from the Coppedé district.

23. B&B Cris & Mapi
Maria Carta Cristiano
via L. Bianchi 15
00166 Rome
tel. 06 66182124, mob. 339 3465169
Closed: July, October and November

This B&B, located in a ground floor apartment in a small, modern villa situated in the Aurelia Raganelli area, just 5 minutes by bus to the Vatican, has three double rooms with TV and two bathrooms (with tubs), of which only one is reserved for the guests. The rooms face the small, private garden that completely surrounds the apartment and can be enjoyed by the guests. The continental breakfast is generally served in the kitchen but, when the weather's nice, it can be served outdoors.

13th-century mosaic kept in the Sacre Grotte.

Accommodation
Guestrooms: *3 doubles, also single occupancy, 1 with private bath and 2 with shared bath; additional bed on request*
Services & Amenities: *French and English are spoken; rooms cleaned every 3 day; tourist info; garden; smokers welcome; private parking*
Rates: *single €€, double €€-€€€. Additional bed supplement €. Discounts for children*
Credit cards: *not accepted*
Pets: ✓

24. B&B Esquilino • Latte e Miele
TCI 10%
tel. and fax 06 3211783
info@sleepinitaly.com
www.sleepinitaly.com
Closed: November to January

This B&B is located in a 19th-C building that's of considerable architectural importance. It's in the old center, not far from the Imperial Forums, the Coliseum and Santa Maria Maggiore. The large classic-style rooms, which have authentic 19th-C furnishings, are particularly impressive. The continental breakfast is served in the guestrooms.

Accommodation
Guestrooms: *2 (1 single, 1 double bedroom, private bath)*
Services & Amenities: *French, English, German and Spanish are spoken; rooms cleaned every 3 days; tourist info; smokers welcome*
Minimum stay: *2 nights*
Rates: *single and double €€€*
Credit cards: *not accepted*
Pets: ✗

25. B&B Gianicolo
Gabriella Pisani
via Fabrizi 11/B
00153 Rome
tel. 06 5813235, mob. 339 3396026
gabp@libero.it
www.bbgianicolo.com
Closed: February and August

This B&B is located on the 6th floor of a building that dates from the '20s and is situated on the Gianicolo, 15 mins from St. Peter's. There are three guestrooms. One is a double with period furniture, another is a single and the third is a double that has a private bathroom. The latter two rooms have modern furniture and each has a TV. Breakfast is generally served in the family kitchen but, when the weather's nice, it can be served on the apartment terrace that provides a view of the city. On request, with guests that stay for at least four nights, the hostess can give cooking lessons. Guests are strongly advised not to miss the nearby Palazzo Corsini botanical gardens, which has over 8,000 types of plants.

Accommodation
Guestrooms: *3 (1 single, 1 double bedroom and 1 double, 1 with private bath and 2 with shared bath); additional bed on request*
Services & Amenities: *French and English are spoken; rooms cleaned every three days; complimentary tourist information; terrace; smokers welcome*
Minimum stay: *3 nights*
Rates: *single €€€, double €€€€. Additional bed supplement €€*
Credit cards: *not accepted*
Pets: ✗

26. B&B Holiday Rome
Adalgisa Perotti
via Palestro 49
00185 Rome
tel. 06 4453024, fax 06 44701152
Closed: 1 to 13 March, 15 to 31 July, August, 1 to 15 November and 1 to 15 December

This B&B is on the 3rd floor of a period building located near the Termini train station. The guest accommodation consists in a single room and two double rooms, which share a bathroom equipped with shower. All the rooms have modern furniture, a TV and a telephone. The rich continental breakfast is generally served in the family kitchen. The house is not suitable for children. Smokers are also welcome.

Accommodation
Guestrooms: *3 (1 single and 2 double bedrooms, with shared bath)*
Services & Amenities: *French, English and German are spoken; rooms cleaned every day; complimentary tourist information; Internet access; smokers welcome*
Rates: *single €€, double €€-€€€€*
Credit cards: *not accepted*
Pets:

27. B&B Igloo and Red House
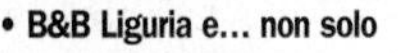
• B&B Liguria e... non solo
tel. 010 3291204
fax 010 3299774
oltrelazzurro@libero.it
www.bbitalia.net
Closed: 23rd to 30th of every month

This B&B is in a residential complex located north of Rome, 2 km from the Parioli district, and has a golf course. Guests have two small dépendances that belong to a stone manor villa surrounded by a park with tall trees. Each has a twin bed, a small living-room area, a TV, a telephone (on request) and a private bath. Breakfast is served in the small equipped kitchen of these modernly-furnished, one-room abodes. Guests are also welcome to use the family swimming pool. Private internal parking is also provided.

Accommodation
Guestrooms: *2 double bedrooms, private bath; additional bed on request*
Services & Amenities: *French, English and Spanish are spoken; rooms cleaned every day; tourist information; garden; smokers welcome; private parking*
Minimum stay: *2 nights*
Rates: *€€€€. Additional bed supplement €. Discounts for children (-10%) and extended stays*
Credit cards: *accepted*
Pets:

28. B&B Il Giardino
Vittoria Bertoni
via G. Bitossi 21
00136 Rome
tel. and fax 06 35496217
mob. 339 5771710
• B&B Association of Rome
tel. 06 55302248, fax 06 55302259
info@b-b.rm.it
www.b-b.rm.it
Closed: 7 January to 18 February, August and 10 to 25 December

This B&B is in a 1st-floor apartment of a '60s building, which is surrounded by a very old park and situated in a residential complex located northwest of Rome, in the Balduina district. The guest accommodation consists in two, very silent double rooms with period furniture and equipped with TV, receiving telephone, blower ventilator and view of the vegetation. The rich continental breakfast is generally served in the family dining room, but, when the weather's nice, it can be served on the apartment's terrace. Private internal parking is also provided.

Accommodation
Guestrooms: *2 double bedrooms, also single occupancy, private bath* ♿
Services & Amenities: *French and English are spoken; rooms cleaned every day; complimentary tourist information; terrace; air conditioning; smokers welcome*
Rates: *single €€, double €€€*
Credit cards: *not accepted*
Pets:

29. B&B Infa

Ingrid Zobernig
via Cino del Duca 76
00133 Rome
tel. and fax 06 20433193
infabb@tiscali.it
Closed: January, February and November

This B&B is situated on the 4th floor of a 1980's building located at the foot of the Castelli Romani, in a residential complex surrounded by a verdant pine grove. This accommodation offers one double room with private bath. The large continental breakfast is served in the family dining room or on the apartment's panoramic terrace. If requested, the host, who is an Austrian tourist guide, will be glad to show the guests around the city and also drive them to and from the airport or train station. Internal parking is provided.

ACCOMMODATION
Guestrooms: *1 double bedroom, private bath; additional bed on request*
Services & Amenities: *French, English, German and Spanish are spoken; rooms cleaned every day; tourist info; terrace; Internet; smokers welcome*
Minimum stay: *3 nights*
Rates: *€€. Additional bed supplement €. Discounts for children and extended stays*
Credit cards: *not accepted*
Pets: ✓

30. B&B La Capitale TCI 10%

• B&B Liguria e... non solo
tel. 010 3291204
fax 010 3299774
oltrelazzurro@libero.it
www.bbitalia.net
Closed: varies

This B&B is on the 1st floor of a 1950's building situated in the Monte Mario area, near the astronomical observatory, just 10 minutes by bus from St. Peter's. This accommodation consists in a double room, with a TV and modern furnishings, that faces a very quiet private street. The continental breakfast is generally served in the family living room. The family consists of two persons, and the guests are welcome to use the living room with its TV.

ACCOMMODATION
Guestrooms: *1 double, private bath*
Services & Amenities: *rooms cleaned every day; tourist information; smokers welcome*
Minimum stay: *3 nights*
Rates: *€€€€*
Credit cards: *not accepted*
Pets: ✗

31. B&B La Dolce Vita TCI 10%

• Home Express
tel. and fax 06 90129063
homeexpress@tiscalinet.it
www.home-express.it
Closed: February, August, November and early December

This B&B is located in a beautiful, early 20th-C building situated in Via Veneto. Some of the rooms have their original frescoes. Guests have the use of two suites, each with a small living room and a single bedroom. The two suites have different colors: one is light blue and the other is red. The wall colors match the fabric colors. Breakfast is either served in the living room or in the guestrooms.

ACCOMMODATION
Guestrooms: *2 suites (3 beds) with private bath*
Services & Amenities: *English spoken; rooms cleaned every 3 days; tourist information; kitchenette; smokers welcome*
Minimum stay: *3 nights*
Rates: *€€€€. Additional bed supplement €. Discounts for children and extended stays*
Credit cards: *not accepted*
Pets: ✗

32. B&B L'Ariete

• B&B Association of Rome
tel. 06 55302248, fax 06 55302259
info@b-b.rm.it
www.b-b.rm.it
Closed: July, August and November

This B&B is in a 1940's building located near the Celio. The guest accommodation consists in an attic with two rooms with classic furnishings, a large terrace and a beautiful, heated veranda where the Italian breakfast is served.

ACCOMMODATION
Guestrooms: *2 (1 double bedroom and 1 double, also single occupancy, with shared bath); additional bed on request* ♿
Services & Amenities: *French and English are spoken; rooms cleaned every 3 days; tourist information; terrace; smokers welcome*
Rates: *single €€, double €€€. Additional bed supplement €*
Credit cards: *not accepted*
Pets: ✓

33. B&B Mancini
• B&B Association of Rome
tel. 06 55302248, fax 06 55302259
info@b-b.rm.it
www.b-b.rm.it
Closed: 10 January to 10 March and August

ACCOMMODATION
Guestrooms: *2 (1 double, 1 triple, also single occupancy, private bath)*
Services & Amenities: *English and Spanish are spoken; rooms cleaned every day; tourist information*
Minimum stay: *2 nights*
Rates: *€€€. Discounts for extended stays*
Credit cards: *not accepted*
Pets: no pets

This refined B&B is located in a distinguished building dating from the early 20th century. It's 10 minutes by tram to the old center. The guest accommodation consists in two elegantly furnished rooms, including a few antique items. The continental breakfast is served in the large dining room with background music. The house is not suited for hosting children.

34. B&B Martin
Maria Nanni
via Grossi Gondi 13
00162 Rome
tel. and fax 06 86207784
mob. 333 4741638
Closed: 10 January to 10 March and November

ACCOMMODATION
Guestrooms: *2 doubles, also single occupancy, with shared bath; additional bed on request*
Services & Amenities: *English spoken; rooms cleaned every day; complimentary tourist information; air conditioning; smokers welcome*
Minimum stay: *2 nights*
Rates: *single €-€€, double €€-€€€. Additional bed supplement €*
Credit cards: *not accepted*
Pets: no pets

This B&B is situated on the 1st floor of a 1950's building that's near Piazza Bologna, 1 kilometer from the old center. The guest accommodation consists in a twin bed room with big terrace and a double room, both nicely furnished with modern and Venetian style furniture. The rooms have a TV and share the bathroom (with a shower) reserved for the guests. The continental breakfast is

either served in the kitchen or in the family living room. The family consists of three persons. There's a pay garage in the vicinity.

35. B&B Massimo Zoli
via T. Campanella 21
00195 Rome
tel. and fax 06 39733063
mob. 347 7366027
mzoliroma@hotmail.com
www.chez.com/zoliroma
Closed: December to February

ACCOMMODATION
Guestrooms: *3 (2 doubles, with shared bath, and 1 single, with private bath); additional bed on request*
Services & Amenities: *French, English and Portuguese are spoken; rooms cleaned every three days; complimentary tourist information; kitchen use by request; bike rental; terrace; garden; smokers welcome*
Rates: *single €€, double €€€. Additional bed supplement €. Discounts for children and extended stays*
Credit cards: *not accepted*
Pets: no pets

This B&B is in a small, period building located on Via Liberata, 300 m from the Vatican City. The apartment has wood paneling, tapestries and classic, elegant furniture. The Italian breakfast is served in the living room. The host, who is very interested in archeology and architecture, willing suggests tour itineraries.

The sarcophagus of Giunio Basso conserved in the Vatican museums.

36. B&B Nocetta
• B&B Association of Rome
tel. 06 55302248, fax 06 55302259
info@b-b.rm.it
www.b-b.rm.it
Closed: January, February and November

This B&B is located in a residential complex that has a private road and is in the vicinity of the splendid Villa Doria Pamphili park. This accommodation offers three rooms with classic style furnishings and, if requested, satellite TV. The rooms face a large garden that has tall trees. Two of these rooms are doubles and one has a private bathroom with a hydromassage. The third room is a single that shares the other double's bathroom (with tub). Guests also have the use of a third bathroom (with a sauna and Turkish bath), as well as the family living room (which has a computer connected to Internet). The continental breakfast is generally served in the very nice dining room that has beautiful period furniture. On request, the hostess will provide lessons in Mediterranean cuisine. Guests can also be privately driven to any part of the city.

Accommodation
Guestrooms: *3 (1 single and 2 double bedroom, with private bath)*
Services & Amenities: *English and Spanish are spoken; rooms cleaned every day; tourist information; Internet access; smokers welcome; private parking*
Minimum stay: *2 nights*
Rates: *single €€, double €€€€*
Credit cards: *not accepted*
Pets:

37. B&B Orchidea
• ExpressRoome
tel. and fax 06 94289163
expressroome@libero.it
www.expressroome.it
Open all year

This B&B is in an apartment located on the 4th floor of an early 20th-century building that has a garden. It's situated in the Prati district, just a few minutes away from St. Peter's Basilica. The guest accommodation consists in

three, recently-restructured, double rooms with plain furniture, air conditioning, TV and mini-bar. The Italian breakfast is either served in the guestroom or in the hosts' restaurant.

Accommodation
Guestrooms: *3 doubles with private bath*
Services & Amenities: *French and English are spoken; rooms cleaned every day; air conditioning; smokers welcome*
Rates: *€€€€. Discounts for children and extended stays*
Credit cards: *accepted*
Pets:

38. B&B Pascucci
Luciano Pascucci
via di Panico 9, 00186 Rome
tel. 06 6869054, mob. 339 2347474
lpascucci@tiscali.it
web.tiscalinet.it/lpascucci
• Bed & Breakfast Italia
tel. 06 6878618, fax 06 6878619
info@bbitalia.it, www.bbitalia.it
Closed: 15 January to 15 March and August

This B&B is located on the 1st floor of an 18th-century building that's situated in the old center, just 150 meters from Castel Sant'Angelo. The guest accommodation consists in a double room with a boxed ceiling and a private entrance, and equipped with a TV, a receiving telephone and air conditioning. The Italian breakfast is generally served in the family dining room. Guests are also welcome to use the living room, which has a fireplace and a library. Guests can make arrangement by phone for getting to and from the airport. Smokers are welcome.

Accommodation
Guestrooms: *1 double bedroom, also single occupancy, private bath*
Services & Amenities: *French, English and Spanish are spoken; rooms cleaned every day; air conditioning; smokers welcome*
Rates: *single €€€-€€€€, double €€€€. Children under 3 free. Discounts for extended stays*
Credit cards: *not accepted*
Pets:

39. B&B Pettinari - Campo dei Fiori
• Latte e Miele
tel. and fax 06 3211783
info@sleepinitaly.com
www.sleepinitaly.com
Closed: 10 January to 10 February, 15 July to 15 September

TCI 10%

This B&B is in a 17th-century building on an old street, close to Piazza Navona. And it has a nice view of the famous Palazzo Spada. Guests have a small, modernly-furnished apartment consisting of a double room and a living room with a breakfast nook. It also has a terrace and satellite TV. Breakfast is the Italian style.

Accommodation
Guestrooms: *1 mini-apartment (2 beds)*
Services & Amenities: *French, English and Spanish are spoken; rooms cleaned every day; complimentary tourist information; kitchenette; terrace; Internet access; smokers welcome*
Rates: *€€€€. Children under 1 free*
Credit cards: *not accepted*
Pets:

40. B&B Piccolomini
via Piccolomini 35
00165 Rome
tel. 06 39367672, 06 6877348
fax 06 6874881
info@b-b.rm.it
www.b-b.rm.it
• B&B Association of Rome
tel. 06 55302248, fax 06 55302259
info@b-b.rm.it
www.b-b.rm.it
Closed: June to August

This B&B is situated on the ground floor of a small, 1970's building that's located near Villa Doria Pamphili, just one bus stop from St. Peter's. This accommodation provides small family nuclei with two large communicating rooms with period furniture. One room is a double, the other is a single. They both use the same bathroom, which is reserved for the guests, that has a tub with a shower. The continental breakfast is served in the living room except in the summertime, when it's served outdoors. Smokers are welcome.

Accommodation
Guestrooms: *2 (1 double bedroom and 1 single, with shared bath); additional bed on request*
Services & Amenities: *French and English are spoken; rooms cleaned every 3 days; complimentary tourist information; smokers welcome*
Rates: *single €€-€€€, double €€€. Additional bed supplement €. Discounts for children*
Credit cards: *not accepted*
Pets:

41. B&B Raggi
• Home Express
tel. and fax 06 90129063
homeexpress@tiscalinet.it
www..home-express.it
Closed: Easter and Christmas holidays

TCI 10%

This B&B is located in a 4th floor apartment in a early 20th-century building that has a nice internal courtyard but no elevator. It's just a few minutes from the Vatican. The guest accommodation consists in a double room with modern, light-colored and lacquered furniture. The generous Italian breakfast is usually served in a small, equipped kitchen that the hosts reserved for the B&B guests. Smokers welcome.

Accommodation
Guestrooms: *1 double bedroom, private bath; additional bed on request*
Services & Amenities: *French and English are spoken; rooms cleaned every day; tourist information; kitchen use by request; terrace; smokers welcome*
Rates: *€€€€. Additional bed supplement €*
Credit cards: *not accepted*
Pets:

Michelangelo's Pietà, conserved in St. Peter's basilica.

42. B&B Regina Margherita
Giorgio Sessa
viale Regina Margherita 157
00198 Rome
tel. and fax 06 8550135
gisessa@tiscali.it
Closed: January and November

This B&B is located in a large, bright, 4th floor apartment in a 1920's building situated in the Parioli district; it is also not far from the famous Villa Borghese. The guest accommodation consists in three double rooms that share two bathrooms. The rooms are air conditioned and have plain, essential furnishings. One also has a small balcony. The continental, buffet breakfast is served in the room reserved for the guests. Guests are also welcome to use the condominium garden. The hostess, who is very fond of films, theater, music, literature and traveling, will be happy to organize city tours on request. Guests can be privately driven to and from the airport. An underground, pay parking is available nearby.

Accommodation
Guestrooms: *3 doubles, also single occupancy, with shared bath; additional bed on request*
Services & Amenities: *English and Spanish are spoken; rooms cleaned every day; tourist information; air conditioning; smokers welcome*
Rates: *single €€, double €€€. Additional bed supplement €. Discounts for children and extended stays*
Credit cards: *not accepted*
Pets: 🐾

43. B&B Revoltella-Monteverde
via Revoltella 85
00152 Rome
tel. 06 58238197, mob. 338 8304688
Closed: 7 May to 10 July and November

This B&B is in an apartment situated on the 3rd floor of small, 1970's building located in the Trastevere area, about 10 kilometers from the old center. The accommodation consists in a double room with modern furniture, TV and a private internal bathroom (with a shower). The continental breakfast is served in the guestroom. Guests also have the use of a terrace, which is accessible from the apartment kitchen. Internal parking is also available on request. A visit to the Villa Doria Pamphili park is recommended. It's the city's largest public park.

Ponte Sisto, one of the entrances to the Trastevere district.

Accommodation
Guestrooms: *1 double, also single occupancy, with private bath; additional bed on request*
Services & Amenities: *rooms cleaned every 3 days; tourist information; smokers welcome*
Rates: *single €€, double €€€. Additional bed supplement €. Discounts for children*
Credit cards: *not accepted*
Pets: (not accepted)

44. B&B Rodan
Nicola D'Azzeo
via Rasella 134
00187 Rome
tel. and fax 06 42011422
mob. 338 4936347
ndazzeo@yahoo.it
www.bbrodan.com
Closed: 13 January to 23 February and 1 November to 23 December

This B&B in on the third floor of a period building located in the old center. The guest accommodation consists in three double rooms, each of which has a private, internal bathroom (with tub and shower). The rooms have period furniture and paintings and are equipped with TV, telephone and air conditioning. The continental breakfast is usually served in a small room (with satellite TV) reserved for the guests. Guests are also welcome to use this room during the day.

Accommodation
Guestrooms: *3 doubles, also single occupancy, with private bath; additional bed on request*
Services & Amenities: *French and English spoken; rooms cleaned every day; tourist info; air conditioning; smokers welcome; private parking*
Minimum stay: *3 nights*
Rates: *single €€€€, double €€€€. Additional bed supplement +30%. Discounts for children*
Credit cards: VISA MC *Bancomat*
Pets: 🐾

45. B&B San Pietro

Anna Maria Pascucci
via della Stazione Vaticana 5
00165 Rome
tel. 06 5018930, 06 39731610
mob. 347 7053001
ampascucci@tiscali.it
www.paginegialle.it/bbsanpietro
Closed: 15 January to 15 March and November

This B&B is in on the ground floor of a 18th-century building located in the old center, facing the rear entrance of the Vatican. The house is on a dead-end street, and offers to its guests three double bedrooms, two of which overlook a garden. They all have modern furnishings, and one has a private, internal bathroom. The other two share a bathroom. The continental buffet breakfast is served in the large family kitchen. The hosts provide useful information about the city.

ACCOMMODATION
Guestrooms: *3 doubles, 1 with private bath and 2 with shared bath; additional bed on request*
Services & Amenities: *French and English are spoken; rooms cleaned every day; complimentary tourist information; kitchen use by request; smokers welcome*
Minimum stay: *3 nights*
Rates: *€€€. Additional bed supplement €*
Credit cards: *not accepted*
Pets:

46. B&B San Pietro Cavalleggeri

Elvira Di Pasquale
via dei Cavalleggeri 4
00165 Rome
tel. 06 632544, mob. 339 2178342
• **B&B Association of Rome**
tel. 06 55302248, fax 06 55302259
info@b-b.rm.it
www.b-b.rm.it
Closed: January, February, 1 to 15 March and 1 to 15 December

This B&B is on a 4th-floor apartment located in a 1950's building situated in the old center, in the shadow of the dome of St. Peter's. The guest accommodation consists in a double room with a private bathroom (with a shower), that has Mexican-style furnishings, TV, stereo and a library, which is at their complete disposal. This family of four, that loves music, literature and films, offers a rich continental breakfast, which is served in the family dining room.

ACCOMMODATION
Guestrooms: *1 double, also single occupancy, with private bath*
Services & Amenities: *English and Spanish are spoken; rooms cleaned every day; tourist information; smokers welcome*
Rates: *single €€, double €€€€. Discounts for extended stays*
Credit cards: *not accepted*
Pets:

47. B&B Teatro

• **B&B Association of Rome**
tel. 06 55302248, fax 06 55302259
info@b-b.rm.it
www.b-b.rm.it
Closed: 1 to 15 January, 10 to 25 February, August and December

This B&B is located on the 4th floor of a completely-restored 16th-century building (with no elevator) situated in the Campo de' Fiori area, just 50 meters from Piazza Navona and 10 minutes on foot from St. Peter's. The guest accommodation consists in a double room with a private bath (and a shower). The room has period furnishings. The continental type breakfast is served in a room reserved for the guests.

ACCOMMODATION
Guestrooms: *1 double bedroom, with private bath*
Services & Amenities: *French, English, German and Spanish are spoken; rooms cleaned every day; tourist information ; smokers welcome*
Minimum stay: *2 nights*
Rates: *€€€€. Discounts for extended stays*
Credit cards: *not accepted*
Pets:

48. B&B Veneto
• ExpressRoome
tel. and fax 06 94289163
expressroome@libero.it
www.expressroome.it
Closed: February, July and August

This B&B is located in a beautiful period building that faces Via Veneto. The accommodation offers a room with luxurious furnishings. The Italian breakfast is served in a reserved room. The B&B is very centrally located and very close to the Barberini subway station.

ACCOMMODATION
Guestrooms: *3 (1 double, also single occupancy; 2 triples, private bath)*
Services & Amenities: *French and English are spoken; rooms cleaned every 3 days; smokers welcome*
Minimum stay: *2 nights*
Rates: *single €€€, double €€€€, triple €€€€*
Credit cards: *not accepted*
Pets:

49. B&B via Messina (Porta Pia)
• Latte e Miele
tel. and fax 06 3211783
info@sleepinitaly.com
www.sleepinitaly.com
Closed: August

This B&B, on the top floor of a finely-refinished building located in the Porta Pia residential area, is only a short walk from the Quirinale, the Fountain of Trevi and Villa Borghese. Guests have nicely-furnished bedrooms, and the family living room is at their disposal both for breakfast and for enjoying at any time during the day. Smokers welcome.

ACCOMMODATION
Guestrooms: *3 doubles, also single occupancy, with private bath*
Services & Amenities: *French, English, Spanish are spoken; rooms cleaned every 3 days; tourist info*
Minimum stay: *3 nights*
Rates: *single €€–€€€, double €€€–€€€€. Children under 3 free; 4 to 12 -30%*
Credit cards: *not accepted*
Pets:

50. B&B Villino Cecilia Musei Vaticani
Adriana Collavini
viale Vaticano 51/E
00165 Rome
tel. and fax 06 39730143
mob. 338 1506857
a-depaola@virgilio.it
fabio.collavini@tin.it
members.xoom.it/casacecilia
Closed: August and September

This B&B offers one floor of a small, early 20th-C villa located near St. Peter's, 400 m from the Vatican Museums. The guest apartment has 3 bedrooms, a bathroom, a small living room with TV and a kitchen, which is where the continental breakfast is served. Guests are also welcome to enjoy the terrace and garden.

ACCOMMODATION
Guestrooms: *3 doubles with shared bath; additional bed on request*
Services & Amenities: *English spoken; rooms cleaned every three days; complimentary tourist information; kitchen use by request; dinner reservation; terrace; garden; smokers welcome; private parking*
Rates: *single €€, double €€€. Additional bed supplement €. Discounts for children and extended stays*
Credit cards: *not accepted*
Pets:

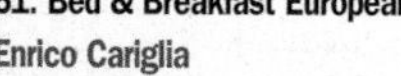

51. Bed & Breakfast European
Enrico Cariglia
via Di Valco di San Paolo 22
00146 Rome
tel. 06 59600324, mob. 328 4167403
info@bbeuropean.com
www.bbeuropean.com
Closed: February, August and December

This B&B is on the ground floor of a small, 1960's villa located 5 minutes by subway from the Coliseum. It has an independent entrance and faces a small, equipped garden that the guests are welcome to enjoy. The Italian breakfast can either be served in the room or outdoors, as desired.

ACCOMMODATION
Guestrooms: *3 doubles, also single occupancy, with private bath; additional bed on request*
Services & Amenities: *English spoken; rooms cleaned every day; complimentary tourist information; kitchenette use by request; garden; smokers welcome*
Minimum stay: *2 nights*
Rates: *single €€, double €€€. Additional bed supplement €. Children under 7 free. Discounts for extended stays*
Credit cards:
Pets:

52. Bed & Breakfast via Calabria
via Calabria 17, 00187 Rome
tel. and fax 06 42904922
mob. 328 4137775
bb/roma10@yahoo.com
• **Latte e Miele**
tel. and fax 06 3211783
info@sleepinitaly.com
www.sleepinitaly.com
Closed: February, July and August

This B&B is in an apartment located on the 3rd and 4th floors of a late 19th-C building situated in the Fiume area, just 5 mins on foot from Via Veneto. Guests have a double and a triple room, both nicely furnished, that share two bathrooms. The one with the tub is reserved for the guests and the other, which has a shower, is shared with the family. The continental breakfast is served in the living room with TV. Guests are urged to visit the nearby Santa Maria Maggiore basilica.

Accommodation
Guestrooms: *2 (1 double, 1 triple, also single occupancy, 1 with private bath and 1 with shared bath)*
Services & Amenities: *English spoken; rooms cleaned every three days; complimentary tourist information; smokers welcome*
Rates: *single €€, double €€€, triple €€€€. Discounts for extended stays*
Credit cards: *not accepted*
Pets: *not allowed*

53. Borgo Vittorio B&B
• **B&B Association of Rome**
tel. 06 55302248, fax 06 55302259
info@b-b.rm.it
www.b-b.rm.it
Closed: August, 15 November to 15 December and 15 January to 15 February

This B&B is in an 18th-century building located just 5 minutes on foot from St. Peter's. Guests have just one room, which has a modern character. The Italian breakfast, which includes pastries, is either served in the kitchen or in the room.

Accommodation
Guestrooms: *1 double bedroom, with private bath ♿*
Services & Amenities: *English spoken; rooms cleaned every three days; tourist information; Internet access; smokers welcome*
Minimum stay: *3 nights*
Rates: *€€€-€€€€. Children under 2 free*
Credit cards: *not accepted*
Pets: *not allowed*

54. C&G
Giuseppe Cavicchia
via Palestro 49
00185 Rome
tel. 06 4957223
Closed: January, February and August

This B&B is on the 2nd floor of an Umbertian-style building located in the Termini Station area, in the Castro Pretorio district. The guest accommodation consists in two double rooms with modern furniture, equipped with TV and receiving telephone, and that share the same bathroom (with shower). The continental breakfast is generally served in a breakfast nook that's reserved for the guests. The hosts will be happy to provide any tourist information about the city. The house is not suitable for children. Guarded pay parking is available in the immediate vicinity. Smokers are welcome.

Accommodation
Guestrooms: *2 (1 double bedroom and 1 double, also single occupancy, with shared bath)*
Services & Amenities: *French, English and German are spoken; rooms cleaned every day; tourist information; smokers welcome*
Rates: *single €€, double €€-€€€€*
Credit cards: *not accepted*
Pets: *not allowed*

55. Casa Banzo

Antonietta Testagrossi Tomassi
piazza Monte di Pietà 30
rione Regola Campitelli
00186 Rome
tel. 06 6833909, fax 06 6864575
Closed: February, July and August

This B&B, on the first floor of a 16th-century building located in the old center close to Piazza Navone, has three double guestrooms, each with a private bathroom (with shower) and an independent entrance. Two of the rooms have both classic and period furniture and each have a small balcony. The continental breakfast is served in the family dining room, which has frescoes, a vaulted ceiling and one wall consisting entirely of glass in the early 20th-century Art Nouveau style. On request, private parking is available. A visit to the nearby, lively, Campo de' Fiori market is particularly recommended.

Accommodation
Guestrooms: *3 doubles, also single occupancy (by request), with private bath; additional bed on request*
Services & Amenities: *English spoken; rooms cleaned every day; tourist information ; smokers welcome; private parking*
Rates: *double €€€€. Additional bed supplement €*
Credit cards: *not accepted*
Pets: 🚫

56. Casa Giardino TCI 10%

Vanna Vanni
via Adamello 6
00141 Rome
tel. and fax 06 87182503
mob. 335 5386724
Closed: January, August and December

This B&B is in a small, early 20th-C villa built in the '20s that's 20 mins from the old center and well served by the public transportation system. The two small guest apartments, with period furniture and colored windows, face a large garden that's open to the guests. One of these apartments has a small living room with a sofa bed and double room. The other consists of just one room with a double bed. Both have private bathrooms, a TV and a kitchen that's well equipped for preparing a large breakfast. A visit to the Santa Agnese Fuori le Mura basilica on Via Nomentana is recommended, especially for its splendid Byzantine mosaic decorated apse.

Accommodation
Guestrooms: *2 mini-apartments (4 and 2 beds)*
Services & Amenities: *French and English are spoken; rooms cleaned every day; complimentary tourist information; kitchen use by request; garden; smokers welcome; private parking*
Minimum stay: *2 nights*
Rates: *double €€€€. Discounts for extended stays*
Credit cards: *not accepted*
Pets: 🐾

57. Casa Mary B&B

• B&B Association of Rome
tel. 06 55302248, fax 06 55302259
info@b-b.rm.it
www.b-b.rm.it
Closed: January, February and November

This B&B is on the ground floor of a 1970's building located in the Pyramid area close to the Terme di Caracalla. The guestroom is a double and has a private bathroom (with a shower). The room has period furniture, including a brass bed, and faces a private park that has very old trees. The room can also have a TV and a telephone. The continental breakfast is served in the family dining room. The guests are welcome to use the family living room, which has a TV.

Accommodation
Guestrooms: *1 double bedroom, also single occupancy, private bath*
Services & Amenities: *English, German, Spanish and Japanese are spoken; rooms cleaned every 3 days; tourist information; smokers welcome*
Minimum stay: *2 nights*
Rates: *single €€, double €€€*
Credit cards: *not accepted*
Pets: 🚫

58. Casa Trevi
Marta Nicolini
via in Arcione 98
00187 Rome
tel. 06 69787084, mob. 3356205768
info@casaintrastevere.it
Open all year

This B&B, in an 18th-C building has two, carefully-restructured apartments with independent entrance and facing an internal garden that has orange trees, fountains and Roman ruins. One of the apartments has a living room with two single sofa beds and a kitchenette, and a double room with two bathrooms with shower. The other is a single room with a double bed, a single sofa bed, a lounge area with a kitchenette, and a large bathroom. Smokers welcome.

Accommodation
Guestrooms: *2 apartments (3 and 4 beds).*
Services & Amenities: *French and English are spoken; rooms cleaned every 3 days; kitchenette; terrace; air conditioning; garden*
Minimum stay: *4 nights*
Rates: €€€€
Credit cards: *accepted*
Pets: 🐕

59. Clodio B&B
• B&B Association of Rome
tel. 06 55302248, fax 06 55302259
info@b-b.rm.it
www.b-b.rm.it
Closed: February, August and December

This B&B, situated on the 2nd floor of a 1930's building located in the Prati area, 5 minutes from the Vatican Museums, consists of a guestroom with classic furnishings, a ventilating fan and a TV. The continental breakfast is served in the family dining room. Guests are welcome to use the family living room, which has a TV.

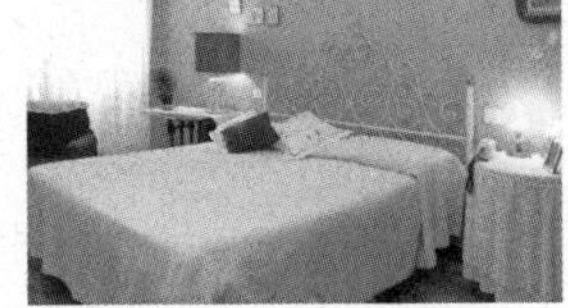

Accommodation
Guestrooms: *1 double bedroom, shared bath; child's bed available*
Services & Amenities: *French, English, Spanish spoken; rooms cleaned every day; tourist info; smokers welcome*
Minimum stay: *2 nights*
Rates: *single €€, double €€€. Child's bed supplement +30%. Discounts for extended stays*
Credit cards: *not accepted*
Pets: 🚫

60. Cupola
Maria Calaria
piazzale Gregorio VII 31, 00169 Rome
tel. 06 39386673, fax 06 39388897
bbcupola@iol.it
www.bbcupola.com
Closed: 10 January to late February, August, and 21 to 30 November

This B&B is in a modern condominium with a garden full of cats. It's located in an elegant part of town and has all the conveniences as regards public transportation and various stores. It's also conveniently located because it's right in front of St. Peter's basilica. Hosts provide what's necessary to make guests able to prepare breakfast by themselves.

Accommodation
Guestrooms: *1 double, private bath*
Services & Amenities: *French and English are spoken; rooms cleaned every day; complimentary tourist information; kitchen use by request; smokers welcome*
Rates: €€€
Credit cards: *not accepted*
Pets: 🚫

61. Di Bartolomeo B&B
Maurizio Di Bartolomeo
via Majorana 171, 00152 Rome
tel. 06 5819597, 06 5819795
fax 06 5812144
m.dibartolomeo@agora.stm.it
Closed: 1 to 15 January, February, 1 to 15 October and November

This B&B is in an apartment situated on the 7th floor of a modern building located at the foot of Gianicolo. The guestrooms have modern furniture and a TV. The continental breakfast is generally served in the kitchen. If requested, it can be served in the apartment's large living room (which has a TV and a balcony). The host will gladly act as a guide for touring the city.

Accommodation
Guestrooms: *2 doubles, also single occupancy, 1 private bath and 1 shared bath; additional bed on request*
Services & Amenities: *English spoken; rooms cleaned every day; tourist information; smokers welcome*
Rates: *single €, double €€. Additional bed supplement €. Discounts for extended stays, families and for frequent visitors*
Credit cards: *not accepted*
Pets: 🐕

62. Domus Tiber
Paolo Serpone
lungotevere De' Mellini 39
00100 Rome
serpone@hotmail.com
Open all year

This B&B is in the 4th floor apartment of a 19th-century building that provides a wide view of the Tiber. The apartment's ethnic furnishings include Indian and Indonesian items collected by the travel-loving hosts. The various colors of the walls add a happy note to this apartment's friendly atmosphere. The Italian breakfast is served in the dining room. On request, the guests can use the whole apartment, which includes an additional room and the kitchen.

Accommodation
Guestrooms: *2 (1 double and 1 double bedroom, also single occupancy, with shared bath); additional bed on request*
Services & Amenities: *French, English and Spanish are spoken; rooms cleaned every 3 days; tourist information; kitchen use by request; smokers welcome*
Minimum stay: *2 nights*
Rates: *single €€€, double €€€€. Additional bed supplement €€. Discounts for extended stays*
Credit cards: *accepted*
Pets:

63. Euro
Marco Zurli
via Dei Mille 64, 00185 Rome
tel. 06 491279, mob. 340 2784650
fax 06 44704390
bedandbreakfast@bebenro.it
www.bebenro.it
Closed: 15 November-15 December

This B&B is on the 4th floor of a 19th-C building located just a few minutes from the Termini Station. The spacious rooms – with and without a private bathroom – have modern, functional furniture. The host, a hotel concierge, has considerable experience when it comes hospitality. This B&B is perfect for those who like complete autonomy.

Accommodation
Guestrooms: *3 doubles, also single occupancy, shared bath*
Services & Amenities: *English, Spanish, Polish, Russian spoken; rooms cleaned every day; tourist info; smokers welcome*
Rates: *single €, double €€*
Credit cards: *not accepted*
Pets:

64. Festa B&B
• B&B Association of Rome
tel. 06 55302248
fax 06 55302259
info@b-b.rm.it
www.b-b.rm.it
Closed: February, August and November

This B&B, which is in an apartment belonging to a family of four, is near the San Camillo hospital and 15 minutes by fast tram from Largo Argentina. The guest accommodation consists in a double bedroom (with TV on request) that shares a bathroom (equipped with shower) with the family. The room, which has both modern and period furniture, faces a large balcony that has a small table and a few chairs. The continental breakfast is generally served in the kitchen. When the weather's nice, it can be served on the terrace, which has a gazebo

Accommodation
Guestrooms: *1 double bedroom, also single occupancy, with shared bath; additional bed on request*
Services & Amenities: *French and English are spoken; rooms cleaned every day; complimentary tourist information; terrace; Internet access; smokers welcome*
Rates: *single €€, double €€€. Additional bed supplement €. Discounts for children and extended stays*
Credit cards: *not accepted*
Pets:

65. Fiori e Semi B&B

Lisa Tumino
via S. Telesforo 10
00165 Rome
tel. and fax 06 631120
mob. 336 615209
Closed: 11 November to 4 December and 5 to 31 January

This B&B is in a small, beautiful building just a 3-minute walk to St. Peter's. One of the rooms provides a view of the Cupola. The fresh furnishings include rattan furniture, light colors and lots of plants. The hostess is particularly focused on health and nature. In addition to the aesthetic aspects, she makes it a point, for example, to provide beds with wooden slats and excellent mattresses. Breakfast is served in a special room.

Accommodation
Guestrooms: *3 doubles, also single occupancy, 2 with private bath, 1 with shared bath; additional bed on request*
Services & Amenities: *English spoken; rooms cleaned every 3 days; complimentary tourist information; private parking*
Rates: *single €€, double €€€. Additional bed supplement €. Children under 5 free*
Credit cards: *not accepted*
Pets:

66. Giada B&B

• B&B Association of Rome
tel. 06 55302248, fax 06 55302259
info@b-b.rm.it
www.b-b.rm.it
Closed: November, January and February

This B&B occupies the 4th and 5th floors of an elegant 1950's building located near Villa Dona Pamphili, 15 minutes by tram from the old center. The small guest apartment, which is connected to the host apartment by an internal stairway, consists of double room with a panoramic terrace, a single room with a balcony, a small parlor area (with TV and telephone) and a bathroom (with a tub and shower). The continental breakfast is generally served in the family dining room, but it can also be served on the attic terrace. The host likes art, films, theater, painting and opera and is at the guests' disposal for making reservations to see exhibits and theatrical productions. Pay parking is available in the vicinity. On request, guests can be privately driven to and from the airport.

Accommodation
Guestrooms: *2 (1 double and 1 single, with shared bath)*
Services & Amenities: *French, English, German and Spanish are spoken; rooms cleaned every day; complimentary tourist information; terrace; smokers welcome*
Rates: *single €€, double €€-€€€. Discounts for children and extended stays*
Credit cards: *not accepted*
Pets:

67. Gioia B&B

• B&B Association of Rome
tel. 06 55302248, fax 06 55302259
info@b-b.rm.it
www.b-b.rm.it
Open all year

This B&B is in a '50s condo with garden in the San Giovanni district. The three guestrooms have air conditioning and modern, colored furnishings; two of them have a small parlor area. Breakfast is either served in the living room or in the garden.

Accommodation
Guestrooms: *3 double bedrooms, also single occupancy, with private bath; additional bed on request*
Services & Amenities: *French and English are spoken; rooms cleaned every day; complimentary tourist information; bike rental; Internet access; garden; smokers welcome; private parking*
Rates: *single €€, double €€€. Additional bed supplement €. Children under 10 free*
Credit cards: *not accepted*
Pets:

68. Il Fontanile
Corinne Dessaint
via del Fontanile Arenato 96
00163 Rome
tel. 06 6640064
ilfontanile@libero.it
www.bnbilfontanile.it
Closed: varies

This B&B, situated on the 2nd floor of a '60s building located near Villa Dona Pamphili, is 10 mins by bus from St. Peter's, and has a double room – with a private bathroom with tub and shower – that faces a large green area. The host family consists of 3 French-Italians. Breakfast is served in the family dining room. The hosts will also help the guests make arrangements and reservations, if required, for visits to the city's museums and other places of interest. Private parking is provided.

ACCOMMODATION
Guestrooms: *1 double, also single occupancy, with private bath; additional bed on request*
Services & Amenities: *French, English and Spanish are spoken; rooms cleaned every 3 days; tourist information; smokers welcome; private parking*
Rates: *single €€, double €€€. Additional bed supplement €. Children under 3 free*
Credit cards: *not accepted*
Pets:

69. Italian B&B
Mircea Marciu
via Emanuele Filiberto 161
00185 Rome
tel. 06 70451285
mob. 3477299890
www.italianbandb.com
Closed: 15 November to 15 December and 10 January to 1 March

This B&B is situated on the 1st floor of an early 20th-century building located near Viale Manzoni and is 150 m from the Colisseum. The two guestrooms – a double and a triple – have period furniture, a TV, and share the same bathroom, reserved for the guests, which has a shower. Guests also have the use of a small sitting room which has a TV. Breakfast, usually the continental type but can also be personalized as desired, is served in the guestrooms. The host, who's fond of music and sports, helps the guests make reservations for city tours, exhibits and theatrical productions. Underground pay parking is available in the vicinity.

ACCOMMODATION
Guestrooms: *2 (1 double and 1 triple room, also single occupancy, with shared bath)*
Services & Amenities: *French, English and Spanish are spoken; rooms cleaned every day; tourist information ; smokers welcome*
Rates: *single €€-€€€, double €€€, triple €€€-€€€€. Children under 5 free. Discounts for extended stays*
Credit cards: *not accepted*
Pets:

70. I Tetti di Roma
Gianpaolo Di Gangi
via Casale Monferrato 3
00182 Rome
tel. 06 70393798, mob. 338 9366938
fax 06 70393799
info@itettidiroma.it
www.itettidiroma.it
Open all year

ACCOMMODATION
Guestrooms: *2 doubles, also single occupancy, shared bath; additional bed on request*
Services & Amenities: *English, Spanish spoken; rooms cleaned every 3 days; tourist info; smokers welcome*
Minimum stay: *2 nights*
Rates: *single €€, double €€€. Additional bed supplement €. Discounts for children and extended stays*
Credit cards: *not accepted*
Pets:

The name of the B&B is given by its location on the 8th floor of a small, panoramic, '50s building. It's 15 mins from the Coliseum and the subway station is right outside the building. The guestrooms, which are in the part of the apartment that has an independent entrance (it's even off-limits for Goedel, "the world's tamest dog"), have colored, wooden doors, modern furniture, large windows and ceiling-mounted fans. The host, formerly a sommelier, is involved with refreshments and knows a lot of good addresses. He also prepares an excellent breakfast.

71. Laurentina B&B
• B&B Association of Rome
tel. 06 55302248, fax 06 55302259
info@b-b.rm.it, www.b-b.rm.it
Closed: 15 November to late December and February

This B&B is in a modernly-furnished apartment located in the Laurentina residential district. The guest accommodation offers 1 double room and includes modern furnishings. The Italian breakfast, enriched with bread and natural marmalades, is either served in the dining room or on the terrace. Smokers welcome.

ACCOMMODATION
Guestrooms: *1 double, also single occupancy, with private bath ♿*
Services & Amenities: *English spoken; rooms cleaned every 3 days; tourist info; terrace*
Minimum stay: *2 nights*
Rates: *single €€, double €€€*
Credit cards: *not accepted*
Pets: no

72. Le Terrazze B&B
• B&B Association of Rome
tel. 06 55302248, fax 06 55302259
info@b-b.rm.it
www.b-b.rm.it
Closed: 15 July to 31 August and 1 November to 15 December

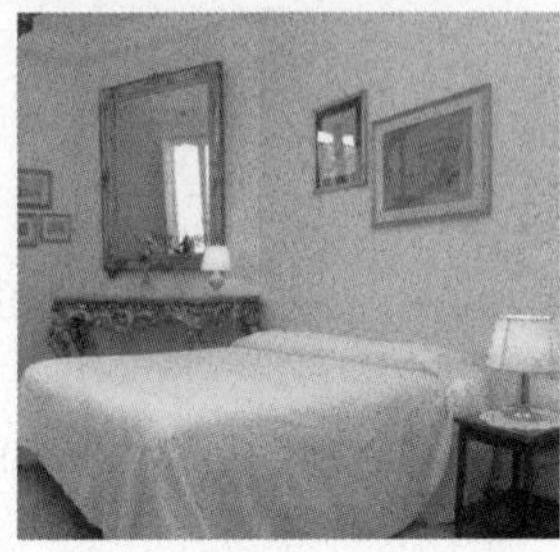

This B&B is in a 5th floor apartment located in a 1930's building which is 10 minutes from St. Peter's. The accommodation consists in three large double rooms and one single room, which are equipped with TV and share two bathrooms (with a shower). The rooms have period furniture and face a large terrace that provides a view of the city. Breakfast is served in the family spacious kitchen. A pay garage is available in the vicinity.

ACCOMMODATION
Guestrooms: *4 (1 single, 3 doubles, also single occupancy, shared bath); additional bed on request*
Services & Amenities: *French, English, German and Spanish are spoken; rooms cleaned every 3 days; tourist information; terrace; Internet access*
Rates: *single €€, double €€€. Additional bed supplement €. Discounts for extended stays*
Credit cards: *not accepted*
Pets: no

73. Maria & Paolo B&B
Maria Serra
via T. Omboni 21
00147 Rome
tel. and fax 06 5123287
mob. 338 4292556
paolomi@tiscali.it
www.mariaepaolo.it
Closed: January, August and November

TCI 10%

This B&B is near the Terme di Caracalla and is just 10 minutes by bus to the old center. The guestrooms have an independent entrance and a living room with a TV. The very large continental breakfast is served in the kitchen nook. The guest apartment is communicating with the host apartment.

ACCOMMODATION
Guestrooms: *2 doubles, also single occupancy, with shared bath*
Services & Amenities: *French, English and German are spoken; rooms cleaned every day; tourist info; kitchen use by request; terrace; smokers welcome; private parking*
Rates: *single €€, double €€€-€€€€*
Credit cards: *not accepted*
Pets: yes

74. Metella B&B
• B&B Association of Rome
tel. 06 55302248, fax 06 55302259
info@b-b.rm.it
www.b-b.rm.it
Closed: November, February and March

This apartment has a large terrace with plants. It's located in the vicinity of Villa Ada and is near Villa Borghese. The two guestrooms have classic furnishings and air conditioning. Breakfast is either served in the kitchen nook or on the terrace.

ACCOMMODATION
Guestrooms: *2 (1 double, 1 triple, also single occupancy, private bath)*
Services & Amenities: *English and Spanish are spoken; rooms cleaned every 3 days; tourist information; terrace; air conditioning; Internet access; smokers welcome*
Rates: *single €€, double €€€, triple €€€€*
Credit cards: *not accepted*
Pets: yes

75. Millenium B&B

Arianna Picconi
via Prati della Farnesina 57
00194 Rome
tel. and fax 06 3339301
mob. 339 6104048
p.aria@libero.it
www.bedinrome.com
• Latte e Miele
tel. and fax 06 3211783
info@sleepinitaly.com
www.sleepinitaly.com
Closed: 8 January to 9 March and 5 November to 5 December

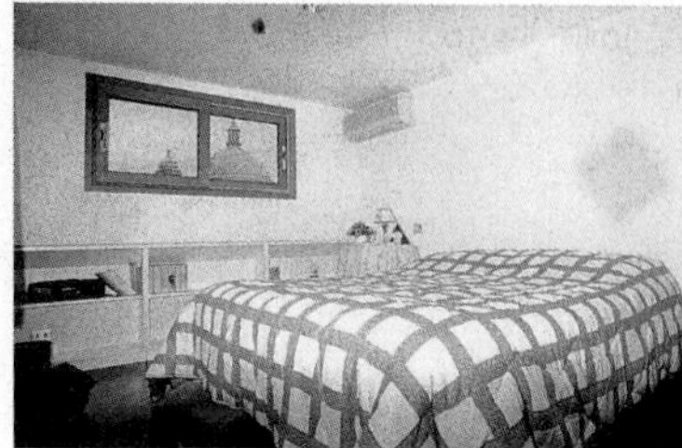

This B&B is in a small, modern building located in the Milvio bridge area, and is a 10-minute bus ride to the Ottaviano-San Pietro subway station. The guest accommodation consists in three, carefully-furnished, double rooms with TV. The rooms are divided between the attic and the upper attic. Two of the rooms have a terrace and a private bathroom, and one of them has a private bath. The two located in the upper level are air conditioned and share a bathroom (with a shower). The rich continental breakfast is served in the reserved room. Guests can use the refrigerator and the two internal parking spaces. Those who like cycling can enjoy the cycling path that runs along the Tiber and is only 100 meters away.

Accommodation
Guestrooms: *3 double bedrooms, also single occupancy, 1 with private bath and 2 with shared bath*
Services & Amenities: *English and Spanish are spoken; rooms cleaned every day; tourist information; terrace; air conditioning; smokers welcome; parking*
Rates: *single €-€€€, double €€-€€€. Children under 3 free*
Credit cards: *not accepted*
Pets:

76. My Home Trilussa

• My Home
tel. 06 3313347, fax 06 233212003
myhome@myhome.it
www.myhome.it
Open all year

This B&B in is a period building in a large, characteristic apartment that has wooden ceilings. The apartment is located 5 minutes from Piazza Campo dei Fiori and Piazza Navona. The three guestrooms – two doubles and a single – share the same bathroom, a large living room and an equipped kitchen.

Accommodation
Guestrooms: *3 (1 single and 2 double bedrooms, with shared bath); additional bed on request*
Services & Amenities: *English spoken; rooms cleaned every 3 days; tourist information; kitchen use by request; air conditioning; smokers welcome*
Rates: *€€€€. Children under 2 free, 3 to 6 -20%*
Credit cards:
Pets:

Piazza Navona.

77. New Rome Bed & Breakfast

Liana De Angelis and Giuseppe Morozzi
via del Boschetto 15
00184 Rome
tel. 06 4881693, mob. 333 3267313
Closed: 15 December to 15 January and 15 July to 15 September

This B&B is situated on the 1st floor of a late 19th-century building, located in the heart of the city, in the Quirinale area. The guest accommodation consists in two nicely-furnished double rooms and a single, which share the same two bathrooms (equipped with showers). The continental breakfast is served in the guestrooms directly by the hosts. On request, the hosts will also accompany the guests on guided visits of the city.

Accommodation
Guestrooms: *3 (2 double bedrooms and 1 single, with shared bath); additional bed on request*
Services & Amenities: *French spoken; rooms cleaned every day; complimentary tourist information; terrace; smokers welcome*
Minimum stay: *2 nights*
Rates: *single €, double €€. Additional bed supplement €€. Discounts for children*
Credit cards: *not accepted*
Pets:

78. Nicolini B&B Casa in Trastevere

Marta Nicolini
vicolo della Penitenza, 19
00165 Rome
tel. 06 69924722, mob. 335 6205768
fax 06 69787084
info@casaintrastevere.it
www.casaintrastevere.it
Closed: February, August and October

This B&B is in an apartment located in a small, characteristic alley in the Trastevere district, at the foot of the Gianicolo. Small families or groups of friends can have two rooms: one is a double, the other with

twin beds. Both rooms have TV and share two bathrooms, one of which is internal. The rooms are on the 1st floor of an early 19th-C building and have nice furnishings. Breakfast is served in the apartment's living room, which provides a view of a large, private garden. On request, the hostess can arrange to have the guests visit the city in the company of a guide from an accredited agency.

Accommodation
Guestrooms: *2 (1 double bedroom and 1 double, with private bath); additional bed on request*
Services & Amenities: *French and English spoken; rooms cleaned every three days; complimentary tourist information; kitchen use by request; smokers welcome*
Rates: *double €€€€. Additional bed supplement €. Discounts for groups*
Credit cards: *not accepted*
Pets:

79. Notti a Roma

TCI 10%

• ExpressRoome
tel. and fax 06 94289163
expressroome@libero.it
www.expressroome.itå
Open all year

This B&B is on the 1st floor of a 19th-C building and is just a short walk to the Termini Station and the Exposition Building. The guestrooms have modern, lacquered-wood furniture. Breakfast, which includes freshly-made croissants, is served in the guestrooms or in a small living room. On request, guests can have laundry service and the use of an Internet connection.

Accommodation
Guestrooms: *3 (2 doubles and 1 triple, 2 with private bath and 1 with shared bath)*
Services & Amenities: *English and Spanish are spoken; rooms cleaned every three days; complimentary tourist information; Internet access; smokers welcome*
Rates: *double €€-€€€, triple €€€-€€€€. Discounts for extended stays and groups*
Credit cards:
Pets:

80. Pamphili House B&B

• B&B Association of Rome
tel. 06 55302248
fax 06 55302259
info@b-b.rm.it
www.b-b.rm.it
Open all year

This B&B is in a large apartment that faces the Villa Pamphili park. The guest accommodation consists in three double rooms with modern, wooden furniture. The rich Italian breakfast is served in the family kitchen-dining room.

Accommodation
Guestrooms: *3 doubles, also single occupancy, with shared bath; additional bed on request*
Services & Amenities: *Spanish spoken; rooms cleaned every 3 days; tourist informaion; smokers welcome; private parking*
Rates: *single €€, double €€€. Additional bed supplement €*
Credit cards: *not accepted*
Pets:

81. Pierri B&B

Giovanni Pierri
via G. Giolitti 199
00185 Rome
mob. 347 8662395
Closed: February, March and November

This B&B is in an apartment on the top floor of a 1950's building. It's located in the Termini Station area and is 250 meters from Santa Maria Maggiore. This accommodation offers a double bedroom, which has a TV and the use of a shared bathroom (with a shower). The continental breakfast can either be served in the room or in the family kitchen. The host is fond of music and art and is at the guests' disposal for making reservations for visits to see the city's exhibits and theatrical presentations.

Accommodation
Guestrooms: *1 double, also single occupancy, with shared bath ♿*
Services & Amenities: *English spoken; rooms cleaned every 3 days; tourist info; smokers welcome*
Rates: *single €€, double €€. Additional bed supplement €*
Credit cards: *not accepted*
Pets:

82. Rap B&B

Anna Rap
via Adda 99
00198 Rome
tel. and fax 06 85352454
anna.rap@tiscali.it
Closed: November, February and 20 July to 20 August

This comfortable B&B, with its bright, spacious, comfortable rooms and classic and modern furniture, is located in a 3rd-floor apartment in a recently-restructured, 19th-century building, which is not far from Villa Borghese. The Italian breakfast is served in the very nice kitchen. Also sharing the apartment is a very gentle, affectionate cat.

Accommodation
Guestrooms: *2 double bedrooms, also single occupancy, with private bath; additional bed on request*
Services & Amenities: *French, English and Spanish are spoken; rooms cleaned every day; tourist information; smokers welcome*
Minimum stay: *3 nights*
Rates: *single €€, double €€€, triple €€€€. Discounts for extended stays*
Credit cards: *not accepted*
Pets:

83. San Giovanni B&B

• B&B Association of Rome
tel. 06 55302248
fax 06 55302259
info@b-b.rm.it
www.b-b.rm.it
Closed: November, January and February

This B&B, hosted in a 1930's building, is in the vicinity of San Giovanni in Laterano and is just 10 minutes on foot from the Coliseum. The guestroom has modern furnishings in shades of light blue. The Italian breakfast, which also includes cold cuts and cheese, is served in the dining room.

Accommodation
Guestrooms: *1 double bedroom, with private bath*
Services & Amenities: *French and English are spoken; rooms cleaned every 3 days; complimentary tourist information; Internet access; smokers welcome*
Minimum stay: *3 nights*
Prezzi: *€€€*
Credit cards: *not accepted*
Pets:

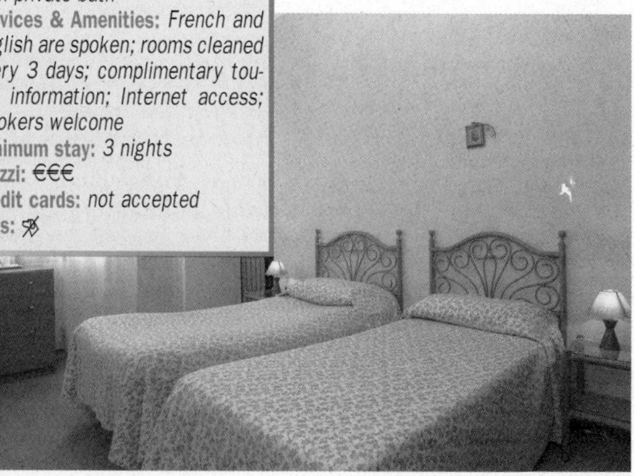

84. Sogno Roma B&B
• Home Express
tel. and fax 06 90129063
homeexpress@tiscalinet.it
www.home-express.it
Closed: February, August and November

This B&B, in a restructured, 1940's building located in the nice Prati district, is just a few bus stops from the Vatican Museums. This accommodation offers three guestrooms with modern, sober furnishings, and each room has its own bathroom. Breakfast, which can be either Italian or English, as desired, is served in the kitchen.

Accommodation
Guestrooms: *3 doubles, also single occupancy, with private bath*
Services & Amenities: *French, English and Spanish are spoken; rooms cleaned every 3 days; tourist information; smokers welcome*
Rates: *double €€€*
Credit cards: *not accepted*
Pets:

Detail of the School of Athens, *a masterpiece by Raphael conserved in the Vatican museums.*

85. The Cloister
• ExpressRoome
tel. and fax 06 94289163
expressroome@libero.it
www.expressroome.it
Closed: November and mid-January to late February

This B&B is located in a modern condominium and is just a 15-minute walk from St. Peter's basilica. This apartment is all at guests' disposal and consists in a double room, which is elegantly-furnished, a daytime area with TV and an equipped kitchenette. The Italian buffet breakfast is usually served in the small kitchen. Smokers are welcome.

Accommodation
Guestrooms: *1 double, also single occupancy, with private bath*
Services & Amenities: *English spoken; rooms cleaned every 3 days; tourist information; kitchenette; smokers welcome*
Minimum stay: *2 nights*
Rates: *single €€-€€€, double €€€-€€€€. Additional bed supplement €. Children under 3 free.*
Credit cards: *not accepted*
Pets:

86. Toia's B&B
• B&B Association of Rome
tel. 06 55302248
fax 06 55302259
info@b-b.rm.it
www.b-b.rm.it
Closed: February, August and November

This B&B is very centrally located in the enviable setting of the Piazza di Spagna, dominated by the majestic Scalinata della Trinità dei Monti. Guests have a modern room with air conditioning and a mini-bar. The Italian breakfast is served in the breakfast nook.

Accommodation
Guestrooms: *1 double bedroom, with private bath*
Services & Amenities: *English, German and Spanish spoken; rooms cleaned every three days; tourist information; air conditioning; smokers welcome*
Rates: *€€€€*
Credit cards: *not accepted*
Pets:

87. Tourist House
Fratelli Marinelli
via Cavour 211
00184 Rome
tel. 06 47824682
fax 06 48904681
touristhouse.rome@flashnet.it
www.alianet.it/clienti/thouse
www.touristhouse.it
Closed: November and February

This B&B, which is on the 5th floor of a 19th-century building, is located right in the old center and is just 500 meters from the Coliseum. It offers three modernly-furnished double rooms that provide a panoramic view. Properly equipped for preparing a continental breakfast, each room has a private, internal bathroom (with a shower), a TV, orthopedic beds and a ventilator. The hosts are glad to help their guests obtain reservations for visits to the city's shows and cultural events. They also provide lots of other information regarding, for example, the renting of bicycles and scooters.

Accommodation
Guestrooms: *3 doubles with private bath; additional bed on request*
Services & Amenities: *English and Spanish are spoken; rooms cleaned every day; tourist information; bike rental; air conditioning; smokers welcome*
Minimum stay: *only during holidays periods, 5 nights*
Rates: *double €€€€. Additional bed supplement €. Discounts for children and extended stays*
Credit cards: *accepted*
Pets: ✓

88. Un villino sulla Cassia
Gisella Emma
via Gradoli 19
00189 Rome
tel. 06 33262148
mob. 339 3230741
Closed: varies

This B&B is on the 2nd floor of a small, 1970's villa located in the Cassia-Nero's Tomb area, 10 kilometers from the Campidoglio. The guest accommodation consists in a double room with an independent entrance and the use of a small living room (with a TV and queen size sofa bed), as well as a shared bathroom (with a tub). The continental breakfast is served in the living room of this small apartment, which communicates with the main apartment and faces a large, sunny terrace. On request, scooters or other types of motorcycles can be rented through an agency. Smokers are welcome.

Accommodation
Guestrooms: *2 double bedrooms with shared bath*
Services & Amenities: *French and English are spoken; rooms cleaned every 3 days; tourist information; terrace; smokers welcome*
Rates: *€€€. Discounts for children*
Credit cards: *not accepted*
Pets: ✓

89. Vacanze Romane
Anselmo Cittadini
via Carlo Alberto 26
00185 Rome
tel. and fax 06 4441079
prenotazione@bbvacanzeromane.it
www.bbvacanzeromane.it
Closed: January, February, 1 to 15 August and 1 to 15 December

This B&B, on the 3rd floor of a period building located in the Santa Maria Maggiore area, has three double rooms with two shared bathrooms (one with a shower and the other with a tub and shower). The rooms, which can have a TV if desired, are decorated with collections of antique toys and French publicity posters. Breakfast, consisting of cappuccino and croissants, is generally served in the B&B's designated bar.

Accommodation
Guestrooms: *3 double bedrooms, also single occupancy, 1 with private bath and 2 with shared bath; additional bed on request*
Services & Amenities: *French and English are spoken; rooms cleaned every day; tourist information; smokers welcome*
Minimum stay: *2 nights*
Rates: *single €€, double €€€. Additional bed supplement €. Discounts for children*
Credit cards: *not accepted*
Pets: ✗

90. Villa Chiara
via P. Collussi 12,
località Casal Palocco
00125 Rome
tel. 06 52310583, 06 52311630
Closed: varies

This B&B is in a building that's surrounded by a 2,000 sq. meter garden and is located between EUR and Ostia. The three double guestrooms have period furniture. Each has a private, internal bathroom (with a shower), TV and a balcony. The continental breakfast is served in the family dining room. There are five members in this family. On request, the hosts will be happy to accompany the guests on a guided tour of the area. The visit most recommended is the one to the excavations of Ostia Antica, the marine city founded in 355 B.C. as the outpost of the Urbe on the mouth (ostium) of the Tiber.

A mosaic found in a necropolis in old Ostia.

Accommodation
Guestrooms: *3 doubles, also single occupancy, with private bath; additional bed on request* ♿
Services & Amenities: *French, English and German spoken; rooms cleaned every day; tourist info; garden; smokers welcome; parking*
Minimum stay: *3 nights*
Rates: *single €€, double €€€. Additional bed supplement. Discounts for children -30%*
Credit cards: *accepted*
Pets: 🐕

91. Villa Lucia
TCI 10%
Maria Ottavi
via Pomponia Grecina 6
00145 Rome
tel. 06 5139379
Closed: 10 January to 10 March and November

This B&B is in the vicinity of the Seven Churches, which is over 1 kilometer, as the crow flies, from the old center. Guests have a double room (with a TV and a terrace) and two single rooms with furniture in style. The double room and one of the singles have air conditioning. The continental breakfast is served in a breakfast nook reserved for the guests. The hosts recommend visiting the nearby San Paolo fuori le Mura basilica.

Accommodation
Guestrooms: *3 (1 double bedroom and 2 singles with private bath); additional bed on request*
Services & Amenities: *French spoken; rooms cleaned every day; tourist information; garden; smokers welcome; private parking*
Rates: *single €€, double €€€. Additional bed supplement €. Discounts for children and extended stays*
Credit cards: *not accepted*
Pets: 🐕

92. Villino Trieste
TCI 10%
• Latte e Miele
tel. and fax 06 3211783
info@sleepinitaly.com
www.sleepinitaly.com
Closed: 10 January to 10 March and 10 August to 10 September

Accommodation
Guestrooms: *2 doubles, also single occupancy, with private bath; additional bed on request*
Services & Amenities: *English spoken; rooms cleaned every day; tourist information; terrace; Internet access; garden; smokers welcome; private parking*
Minimum stay: *2 nights*
Rates: *single €€€, double €€€-€€€€. Additional bed supplement €€. Children under 2 free*
Credit cards: *not accepted*
Pets: not allowed

This B&B, in a small, elegantly-finished, early 20th-C villa located in a very green part of the town, near Villa Ada and Villa Chigi, along the Mura Aureliane, is just a 15-minute bus ride to the Piazza di Spagna and the Piazza del Popolo. Guests have two rooms with art déco furniture and antique paintings. Breakfast, consisting of pastries, cold cuts and cheese, as well as fresh fruit and homemade cakes, is served in the dining room.

93. Virginia B&B
• B&B Association of Rome
tel. 06 55302248, fax 06 55302259
info@b-b.rm.it
www.b-b.rm.it
Closed: November

This B&B is in a recently-renovated, 1960's condominium located in a tranquil residential district in the Colli Portuensi area. The guest accommodation consists in two modernly-furnished rooms and a large terrace where the Italian breakfast can be served.

ACCOMMODATION
Guestrooms: *2 (1 single and 1 double bedroom, with shared bath)*
Services & Amenities: *French and English are spoken; rooms cleaned every 3 days; complimentary tourist information; terrace; Internet access; smokers welcome*
Minimum stay: *2 nights*
Rates: *single €€, double €€€*
Credit cards: *not accepted*
Pets: 🚫

94. Vista di Roma
Sergio Salvucelli
via Nostra Signora di Lourdes 126
00167 Rome
tel. and fax 06 6634607
mob. 347 9117392
Closed: October, February and July

This B&B apartment is on the 5th floor of a '60s building (with an elevator) in the Aurelio district. The building is in front of the Parco del Pineto, 500 m from the subway station and 4 km from St. Peter's. The apartment has a marvelous panoramic view the goes from Monte Mario all the way to the Castel-li Romani. Guests also have the use of the TV room and the terrace. The rich continental breakfast is prepared by the hostess who, incidentally, likes to collect cigarette lighters, knives and all types of owls.

ACCOMMODATION
Guestrooms: *3 (1 single, 1 double and 1 double bedroom, with private bath)*
Services & Amenities: *French and Spanish are spoken; rooms cleaned every day; complimentary tourist information; terrace; air conditioning; smokers welcome*
Rates: *single €€€, double €€€-€€€€*
Credit cards: VISA MC
Pets: 🚫

95. • Bed & Breakfast Italia Tci 10%
Code L091
località Ostia
tel. 06 6878618, fax 06 6878619
info@bbitalia.it
www.bbitalia.it
Closed: varies

This is situated at Lido di Ostia. It has a double bedroom furnished in a modern and cheerful style; the bathroom with shower and tub is shared with the hosts. The city is famed for its crowded beaches, lively night entertainment, and for its numerous and well

preserved archaeological ruins. It is also well located to visit Rome, the center of which can be reached in 40 mins by bus. The hosts will provide a shuttle service to and from the airport by arrangement.

ACCOMMODATION
Guestrooms: *1 double bedroom*
Services & Amenities: *French, English and Spanish are spoken; rooms cleaned every 3 days; tourist information*
Minimum stay: *2 nights*
Rates: *€*
Credit cards: VISA MC *Bancomat*
Pets: 🐾

96. • Bed & Breakfast Italia
Code L109
località Ostia
tel. 06 6878618, fax 06 6878619
info@bbitalia.it
www.bbitalia.it
Closed: varies

This apartment is 500 m from the center of Ostia. It is simply and comfortably decorated with modern and convenient furniture and facilities. It has a double bedroom and a single bedroom; the private bathroom with shower and tub serves both rooms. Ostia is renowned for its bustling beaches, as well as for its archaeological site.

Accommodation
Guestrooms: *2 (1 single, 1 double)*
Services & Amenities: *English spoken; rooms cleaned every three days; tourist information*
Minimum stay: *2 nights*
Rates: €
Credit cards: VISA MC *Bancomat*
Pets: not allowed

97. • Bed & Breakfast Italia
Code L114
località Ostia
tel. 06 6878618
fax 06 6878619
info@bbitalia.it
www.bbitalia.it
Closed: varies

This apartment is in a modern building in Ostia. The B&B accommodation offers a double bedroom with TV, and bathroom shared with the lady of the house. Italian breakfast is served on the large balcony with a sea view. The city is famed for its beach, popular with the inhabitants of the capital. The hostess provides a shuttle service to and from Fiumicino Airport on request.

Accommodation
Guestrooms: *1 double bedroom*
Services & Amenities: *French and English are spoken; rooms cleaned every 3 days; tourist information*
Minimum stay: *2 nights*
Rates: €
Credit cards: VISA MC *Bancomat*
Pets: not allowed

98. • Bed & Breakfast Italia
Code R01
via dei Savorelli
tel. 06 6878618, fax 06 6878619
info@bbitalia.it
www.bbitalia.it
Closed: varies

An apartment situated on the second floor of an elegant building with elevator in the Aurelio district. It has a comfortable and cozy double bedroom. The bathroom with shower/tub is shared with the hosts. The lady of the house welcomes her guests, serves a rich and abundant breakfast, and provides valuable information on sightseeing and areas of interest. The old center can be reached quickly on foot.

Accommodation
Guestrooms: *1 double bedroom*
Services & Amenities: *French and English are spoken; rooms cleaned every 3 days; tourist information*
Minimum stay: *2 nights*
Rates: €
Credit cards: VISA MC *Bancomat*
Pets: allowed

99 • Bed & Breakfast Italia
Code R04
via Emanuele Filiberto
tel. 06 6878618, fax 06 6878619
info@bbitalia.it
www.bbitalia.it
Closed: varies

This B&B is 5 min from Rome's Termini station. The 4 rooms, 2 double bedrooms and 2 triples, are functionally furnished and

share one bathroom. Breakfast is served in the room. Its proximity to several bus lines and to the line A subway station, makes touring Rome easy for guests. The "Scuderie Papali" (Pope's Stables) is within walking distance.

Accommodation
Guestrooms: *4 rooms*
Services & Amenities: *French and English are spoken; rooms cleaned every 3 days; tourist information*
Minimum stay: *2 nights*
Rates: €
Credit cards: VISA MC *Bancomat*
Pets: no pets

100. • Bed & Breakfast Italia
Code R1001
via Luciano Zuccoli
tel. 06 6878618
fax 06 6878619
info@bbitalia.it
www.bbitalia.it
Closed: varies

This B&B is located in a third-floor apartment (with elevator) recently refurbished in the Montesacro district, 10 minutes from the center. The accommodation consists in a large, sunny single-bedroom decorated in soft colors, with a shared bathroom with tub/shower. The continental breakfast is

Accommodation
Guestrooms: *1 single*
Services & Amenities: *French and English are spoken; rooms cleaned every three days; tourist information; private parking*
Minimum stay: *2 nights*
Rates: €€
Credit cards: VISA MC *Bancomat*
Pets: no pets

served by the hostess in the lounge and on the large balcony in the summer. Private parking available for guests. This B&B is 100 meters from a bus stop to and from the center.

101.• Bed & Breakfast Italia
Code R1005
via Giuseppe Bertero
tel. 06 6878618, fax 06 6878619
info@bbitalia.it
www.bbitalia.it
Closed: varies

Accommodation
Guestrooms: *1 double*
Services & Amenities: *French, English, Spanish spoken; rooms cleaned every three days; tourist information*
Minimum stay: *2 nights*
Rates: €€
Credit cards: VISA MC *Bancomat*
Pets: pets welcome

This apartment is situated in the Nomentana district. Guests have a double bedroom with twin beds, TV and a private bathroom with shower. Breakfast is served in the lounge and on the large balcony in the summer. The building is 50 m from the number 311 and 342 bus stops, which reach the subway station in 10 minutes. The lady of the house will welcome pets.

102 • Bed & Breakfast Italia TCI 10%
Code R1010
via Casilina
tel. 06 6878618, fax 06 6878619
info@bbitalia.it
www.bbitalia.it
Closed: varies

This B&B is hosted in a first floor apartment surrounded by a garden, located in the

Accommodation
Guestrooms: *1 double*
Services & Amenities: *French and English are spoken; rooms cleaned every three days; tourist information; terrace; smokers welcome*
Minimum stay: *2 nights*
Rates: €€
Credit cards: VISA MC *Bancomat*
Pets: no pets

southeast area of Rome, in the Casilino district. The accommodation offers a double room with twin beds, classically furnished; the private bathroom has a shower. A terrace, where the continental breakfast is served in the summertime, is also available for guests. The tram stop to Termini station is 200 meters away.

103. • Bed & Breakfast Italia
Code R1015
via Pienza
tel. 06 6878618
fax 06 6878619
info@bbitalia.it
www.bbitalia.it
Closed: varies

This ground-floor apartment in an elegant building is located in the modern Montesacro district, near the center. The guest accommodation consists in a double room with two single beds and a private bathroom with tub. It is served by several buses, which reach the center in 20 minutes. This quiet area is full of shops and restaurants. Smokers are also welcome.

Accommodation
Guestrooms: *1 double*
Services & Amenities: *English spoken; rooms cleaned every three days; complimentary tourist information; smokers welcome*
Minimum stay: *2 nights*
Rates: €€
Credit cards: VISA MC *Bancomat*
Pets:

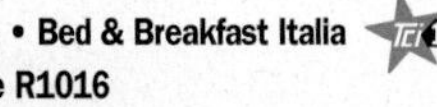

104. • Bed & Breakfast Italia
Code R1016
via Val di Lanzo
tel. 06 6878618
fax 06 6878619
info@bbitalia.it
www.bbitalia.it
Closed: varies

This apartment is located in the quiet Montesacro district, just outside the center. The guest accommodation consists in a double bedroom with two single beds (one is a folding bed). It is furnished in a cheerful, modern style. The private bathroom has a tub. The number 80 bus stop for the old center is 100 meters away.

Accommodation
Guestrooms: *1 double*
Services & Amenities: *French and English are spoken; rooms cleaned every 3 days; tourist information*
Minimum stay: *2 nights*
Rates: €€
Credit cards: VISA MC *Bancomat*
Pets:

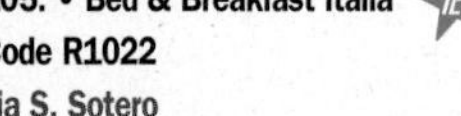

105. • Bed & Breakfast Italia
Code R1022
via S. Sotero
tel. 06 6878618, fax 06 6878619
info@bbitalia.it
www.bbitalia.it
Closed: varies

A penthouse situated in the Vatican area, behind St. Peter's. The double bedroom with twin beds is carefully furnished, and features a large balcony; bathroom with tub. Breakfast is served in the lounge. It is a central and very quiet area. The lady of the house, who is very friendly, provides guests with information on places to visit.

Accommodation
Guestrooms: *1 double*
Services & Amenities: *English and Spanish are spoken; rooms cleaned every 3 days; tourist info*
Minimum stay: *2 nights*
Rates: €€
Credit cards: VISA MC *Bancomat*
Pets:

106. • Bed & Breakfast Italia
Code R1028
via Divisione Torino
tel. 06 6878618, fax 06 6878619
info@bbitalia.it
www.bbitalia.it
Closed: varies

The B&B is hosted in a penthouse situated in the residential Laurentino district, a short distance from the center. The accommodation consists in a well-furnished attic-roof room with twin beds opening on to a large balcony facing the street and includes a shared garden; a private bathroom with shower is available. The subway station is 10 minutes away by foot.

Accommodation
Guestrooms: *1 double*
Services & Amenities: *French, English, German and Spanish are spoken; rooms cleaned every three days; complimentary tourist information; smokers welcome*
Minimum stay: *2 nights*
Rates: €€
Credit cards: VISA MC *Bancomat*
Pets:

107. • Bed & Breakfast Italia
Code R1029
viale Moliere
tel. 06 6878618, fax 06 6878619
info@bbitalia.it
www.bbitalia.it
Closed: varies

This apartment is located in the EUR residential area within a complex of terraced houses on three levels. The double-bed-

ded room (with the option of an extra bed for children) is furnished in a simple, lively style. The private bathroom has a shower. Guests can enjoy a patio and a very large balcony, where breakfast is served.

Accommodation
Guestrooms: *1 double bedroom*
Services & Amenities: *French, English and Spanish are spoken; rooms cleaned every three days; tourist information; terrace*
Minimum stay: *2 nights*
Rates: €€
Credit cards: VISA MC *Bancomat*
Pets: 🚫

108. • Bed & Breakfast Italia
Code R1034
via Giuseppe Sanarelli
tel. 06 6878618, fax 06 6878619
info@bbitalia.it
www.bbitalia.it
Closed: varies

This apartment is situated in the Monteverde district, near the large and stately Villa Pamphili Park. The accommodation offers a double-bedroom, large balcony and independent entrance. This quiet area is full of stores and picturesque shops; the surrounding area offers unlimited entertainment thanks to the wealth of restaurants and diners. Good public transport.

Accommodation
Guestrooms: *1 double bedroom*
Services & Amenities: *French and English are spoken; rooms cleaned every three days; tourist information; terrace*
Minimum stay: *2 nights*
Rates: €€
Credit cards: VISA MC *Bancomat*
Pets: 🚫

109. • Bed & Breakfast Italia
Code R1037
via Flaminia
tel. 06 6878618, fax 06 6878619
info@bbitalia.it
www.bbitalia.it
Closed: varies

This centrally located apartment is decorated with antiques, lamps and gilded mirrors. Guests are housed in an independent wing: a very large single room where an extra bed can be added on request; bathroom with shower. A fridge in the anteroom of the bathroom contains provisions for breakfast.

Accommodation
Guestrooms: *1 single; additional bed on request*
Services & Amenities: *French spoken; rooms cleaned every three days; tourist information*
Minimum stay: *2 nights*
Rates: €€
Credit cards: VISA MC *Bancomat*
Pets: 🚫

110. • Bed & Breakfast Italia
Code R1038
via San Melchiade Papa
tel. 06 6878618, fax 06 6878619
info@bbitalia.it
www.bbitalia.it
Closed: varies

An apartment situated near the center furnished with originality, flair and good taste. Two rooms are available for the guests: a double bedroom, with walls personally frescoed by the lady of the house, and a large single room, in which an extra bed can be added. Small garden.

Accommodation
Guestrooms: *2 (1 single, 1 double)*
Services & Amenities: *French and English are spoken; rooms cleaned every 3 days; tourist information; private parking*
Minimum stay: *2 nights*
Rates: €€
Credit cards: VISA MC *Bancomat*
Pets: 🚫

111. • Bed & Breakfast Italia TCI 10%
Code R1044
via dei Corazzieri
tel. 06 6878618, fax 06 6878619
info@bbitalia.it
www.bbitalia.it
Closed: varies

This B&B is situated in the Laurentino district, near EUR. The accommodation consists in two bedrooms, which share a bathroom with shower/tub and a kitchen with balcony. Guests will find breakfast provisions in the fridge, to enjoy it at their leisure.

EUR: Palazzo della Civiltà del Lavoro.

ACCOMMODATION
Guestrooms: *2 (1 double bedroom and 1 double)*
Services & Amenities: *French spoken; rooms cleaned every three days; tourist information*
Minimum stay: *2 nights*
Rates: €€
Credit cards: VISA MC *Bancomat*
Pets: allowed

112. • Bed & Breakfast Italia
Code R1050
via Prisciano
tel. 06 6878618, fax 06 6878619
info@bbitalia.it
www.bbitalia.it
Closed: varies

B&B situated in the elegant Balduina area. The accommodation offers a cozy and quiet double bedroom facing a courtyard planted with trees and a private bathroom with shower. Guests can enjoy a large balcony, where breakfast is served in the summer. The hosts are very warm and will provide useful tourist information.

ACCOMMODATION
Guestrooms: *1 double*
Services & Amenities: *English spoken; rooms cleaned every three days; tourist information*
Minimum stay: *2 nights*
Rates: €€
Credit cards: VISA MC *Bancomat*
Pets: not allowed

113. • Bed & Breakfast Italia
Code R1051
via della Stazione San Pietro
tel. 06 6878618, fax 06 6878619
info@bbitalia.it
www.bbitalia.it
Closed: varies

A central B&B situated on the fourth floor of a building (elevator available) 200 m from St. Peter's. A nice, homely apartment; the double bedroom with twin beds (which can be joined) is furnished with antiques, bathroom with shower. Informal atmosphere.

ACCOMMODATION
Guestrooms: *1 double*
Services & Amenities: *English spoken; rooms cleaned every three days; tourist information*
Minimum stay: *2 nights*
Rates: €€
Credit cards: VISA MC *Bancomat*
Pets: not allowed

114. • Bed & Breakfast Italia
Code R1052
via Roccaporena
tel. 06 6878618, fax 06 6878619
info@bbitalia.it
www.bbitalia.it
Closed: varies

An apartment on the second floor of an elegant building, centrally located in the quiet, residential Fleming district. It has a large double room with double bed, private bathroom with tub and a large balcony. The bus stop is 50 m away. The host's kindness and friendliness together with a comfortable atmosphere make this B&B a very homely choice.

ACCOMMODATION
Guestrooms: *1 double bedroom*
Services & Amenities: *French, English and German are spoken; rooms cleaned every 3 days; tourist information; terrace*
Minimum stay: *2 nights*
Rates: €€
Credit cards: VISA MC *Bancomat*
Pets: not allowed

115. • Bed & Breakfast Italia
Code R1054
via Francesco Pacelli
tel. 06 6878618, fax 06 6878619
info@bbitalia.it
www.bbitalia.it
Closed: varies

A first-floor B&B situated in a central area, 1 km from St. Peter's, in a narrow side street off Via Gregorio VII,

where silence and tranquility are assured. The double bedroom is spacious, light and classically furnished in keeping with the lounge, where

Accommodation
Guestrooms: *1 double bedroom*
Services & Amenities: *French and English are spoken; rooms cleaned every 3 days; tourist information*
Minimum stay: *2 nights*
Rates: €€
Credit cards: VISA MC *Bancomat*
Pets: allowed

breakfast is served. The bathroom has a shower/tub.

116. • Bed & Breakfast Italia
Code R1071
via Aldo Ballarin
tel. 06 6878618, fax 06 6878619
info@bbitalia.it
www.bbitalia.it
Closed: varies

A modern apartment set in a leafy area of the EUR residential district. A double room with twin beds (which can be joined on request), with the option of an extra bed for children, and a bathroom with shower are available. The hosts welcome guests in a

Accommodation
Guestrooms: *1 double*
Services & Amenities: *English and German are spoken; rooms cleaned every 3 days; tourist info*
Minimum stay: *2 nights*
Rates: €€
Credit cards: VISA MC *Bancomat*
Pets: not allowed

friendly and informal atmosphere. The house is 15 minutes from a romantic lake set in a park; the center can be reached by subway.

117. • Bed & Breakfast Italia
Code R1081
via Andrea Doria
tel. 06 6878618, fax 06 6878619
info@bbitalia.it
www.bbitalia.it
Closed: varies

A double bedroom with wardrobe, period chest of drawers, bookcase and small table with

Accommodation
Guestrooms: *1 double bedroom*
Services & Amenities: *French and English are spoken; rooms cleaned every 3 days; tourist info*
Minimum stay: *2 nights*
Rates: €€
Credit cards: VISA MC *Bancomat*
Pets: not allowed

TV; the bathroom with tub is for the exclusive use of guests. Breakfast is served in the lounge with a breathtaking view over St. Peter's dome. The Prati area is famed for its numerous shops and restaurants.

118. • Bed & Breakfast Italia
Code R1083
corso Rinascimento
tel. 06 6878618, fax 06 6878619
info@bbitalia.it
www.bbitalia.it
Closed: varies

This apartment is situated near Piazza Navona . It is on the second floor of an elegant building and has a double bedroom classically furnished

Accommodation
Guestrooms: *1 double bedroom*
Services & Amenities: *English spoken; rooms cleaned every 3 days; tourist information*
Minimum stay: *2 nights*
Rates: €€
Credit cards: VISA MC *Bancomat*
Pets: not allowed

with antiques; the private bathroom has a shower. The house is 5 minutes on foot from Campo dei Fiori, and 10 minutes from the Pantheon; several buses run to the center. Shops, typical restaurants, bars and coffee shops are a stone's throw away.

119. • Bed & Breakfast Italia
Code R1085
via Apuania
tel. 06 6878618, fax 06 6878619
info@bbitalia.it
www.bbitalia.it
Closed: varies

ACCOMMODATION
Guestrooms: *1 double bedroom*
Services & Amenities: *English spoken; rooms cleaned every 3 days; tourist information*
Minimum stay: *2 nights*
Rates: €€
Credit cards: VISA MC *Bancomat*
Pets: no

This apartment is located on the fifth floor of an elegant building with elevator. The accommodation consists in a double bedroom with a TV and a small balcony; the private bathroom has a shower. In summer, breakfast is served on the adjoining terrace; in winter it is served in the lounge.

120. • Bed & Breakfast Italia
Code R1086
via di Villa Pamphili
tel. 06 6878618, fax 06 6878619
info@bbitalia.it
www.bbitalia.it
Closed: varies

This apartment is located in a modern building in the Monteverde district. It is furnished in a cheerful style and has 2 bedrooms. One has a double bed and private bathroom with bathtub. The Villa Doria Pamphili Park, the Villa Sciarra Park, and the Gianicolo Park can be easily reached in 10 minutes on foot. Several buses stop just in front of the building and go to Piazza Venezia.

ACCOMMODATION
Guestrooms: *2 (1 double bedroom and 1 double)*
Services & Amenities: *German spoken; rooms cleaned every three days; tourist information; terrace; smokers welcome*
Minimum stay: *2 nights*
Rates: €€
Credit cards: VISA MC *Bancomat*
Pets: yes

121. • Bed & Breakfast Italia
Code R1095
via di Castelbarco
tel. 06 6878618, fax 06 6878619
info@bbitalia.it
www.bbitalia.it
Closed: varies

ACCOMMODATION
Guestrooms: *2 double bedrooms; additional bed on request*
Services & Amenities: *English and German are spoken; rooms cleaned every 3 days; tourist info; terrace*
Minimum stay: *2 nights*
Rates: €€
Credit cards: VISA MC *Bancomat*
Pets: no

A small detached house in a residential area of the Aurelio district, 15 minutes from the Vatican. The house is classically decorated with fine antiques; it has two large, quiet double bedrooms, both with en suite private bathroom, one with tub, one with shower.

122. • Bed & Breakfast Italia
Code R1098
via Giuseppe Valmarana
tel. 06 6878618, fax 06 6878619
info@bbitalia.it
www.bbitalia.it
Closed: varies

ACCOMMODATION
Guestrooms: *2 (1 single, 1 triple)*
Services & Amenities: *English spoken; rooms cleaned every three days; tourist information*
Minimum stay: *2 nights*
Rates: €€
Credit cards: VISA MC *Bancomat*
Pets: no

This fourth-floor apartment in an elegant building with elevator offers two warm, homely bedrooms; a single and a triple, and a private bathroom with shower/tub. It is a comfortable B&B with a relaxed air: the landlady cooks cakes, apple strudels and tarts for her guests' breakfast.

123. • Bed & Breakfast Italia
Code R1105
via Principe Eugenio
tel. 06 6878618, fax 06 6878619
info@bbitalia.it
www.bbitalia.it
Closed: varies

Accommodation
Guestrooms: *1 double*
Services & Amenities: *French and English are spoken; rooms cleaned every 3 days; tourist information*
Minimum stay: *2 nights*
Rates: €€
Credit cards: VISA MC *Bancomat*
Pets:

This B&B is in the central area of Piazza Vittorio, behind Santa Maria Maggiore Basilica. It is situated in an elegant building furnished in classic style with antiques. The simply decorated double room is large and light; its private bathroom has a shower. The Termini station is within walking distance

124. • Bed & Breakfast Italia
TCI 10%
Code R1109
via Filoteo Alberini
tel. 06 6878618, fax 06 6878619
info@bbitalia.it
www.bbitalia.it
Closed: varies

Accommodation
Guestrooms: *1 double*
Services & Amenities: *English spoken; rooms cleaned every three days; tourist information*
Minimum stay: *2 nights*
Rates: €€
Credit cards: VISA MC *Bancomat*
Pets:

This apartment, located in the Montesacro district, has a room with twin beds, TV and private bathroom with shower. Breakfast is served in the lounge and on a large balcony in the summer. The building is in a green, quiet neighborhood only 50m from a bus stop on a line that reaches the subway station in 10 minutes. The landlady welcomes pets.

125. • Bed & Breakfast Italia
Code R1110
via Carlo Dossi
tel. 06 6878618, fax 06 6878619
info@bbitalia.it
www.bbitalia.it
Closed: varies

Accommodation
Guestrooms: *1 double bedroom*
Services & Amenities: *French spoken; rooms cleaned every three days; complimentary tourist information; terrace; private parking*
Minimum stay: *2 nights*
Rates: €€
Credit cards: VISA MC *Bancomat*
Pets:

A self-contained apartment furnished with antiques on the third floor of a building, with an elevator, situated in the Montesacro district. This accommodation consists in a double bedroom with double bed, and a private bathroom with tub; in the summer, the continental breakfast is served on a large balcony overlooking a quiet street.

126. • Bed & Breakfast Italia
Code R1112
via Pio Emanuelli
tel. 06 6878618, fax 06 6878619
info@bbitalia.it
www.bbitalia.it
Closed: varies

The accommodation in this apartment consists in a double bedroom with twin beds furnished in a pleasant, informal style, and a private bathroom with shower. Although it is not very central, it is well served by transport: the subway station and bus stop are 10 meters away. The landlady serves the rich breakfast in the lounge and is always willing to offer helpful hints and tips.

Accommodation
Guestrooms: *1 double*
Services & Amenities: *French spoken; rooms cleaned every three days; tourist information*
Minimum stay: *2 nights*
Rates: €€
Credit cards: VISA MC *Bancomat*
Pets:

127. • Bed & Breakfast Italia
Code R1114
via Brennero
tel. 06 6878618, fax 06 6878619
info@bbitalia.it
www.bbitalia.it
Closed: varies

Accommodation
Guestrooms: *1 double*
Services & Amenities: *French and English are spoken; rooms cleaned every 3 days; tourist information*
Minimum stay: *2 nights*
Rates: €€
Credit cards: VISA MC *Bancomat*
Pets: no

This small self-contained apartment on the ground floor is situated in a street behind Piazza Sempione, in the Nomentano area. The accommodation consists in a double bedroom with twin beds, bathroom with shower and an equipped kitchenette, all furnished in a fresh, functional style. The bus stop is 100 m from the house.

128. • Bed & Breakfast Italia TCI 10%
Code R1121
largo Somalia
tel. 06 6878618, fax 06 6878619
info@bbitalia.it
www.bbitalia.it
Closed: varies

Accommodation
Guestrooms: *2 (1 single, 1 double)*
Services & Amenities: *French and English are spoken; rooms cleaned every 3 days; tourist information*
Minimum stay: *2 nights*
Rates: €€
Credit cards: VISA MC *Bancomat*
Pets: yes

The building is located in the African district. It has two rooms, informally furnished; the bathroom is exclusively for guests' use. Guests can choose to have breakfast in the kitchen or in the lounge. The atmosphere is homely and informal. This lively, crowded section of the city has good transport connections to the center.

129. • Bed & Breakfast Italia
Code R1125
via Catone
tel. 06 6878618, fax 06 6878619
info@bbitalia.it
www.bbitalia.it
Closed: varies

Accommodation
Guestrooms: *2 (1 double, 1 triple)*
Services & Amenities: *French and English are spoken; rooms cleaned every 3 days; tourist information*
Minimum stay: *2 nights*
Rates: €€
Credit cards: VISA MC *Bancomat*
Pets: yes

This apartment in hosted by an elegant building in the Prati district offers to its gusts two rooms, each with TV; private bathroom with shower/tub. It is 5 minutes on foot from St. Peter's as well as from the subway station.

130. • Bed & Breakfast Italia
Code R1130
viale Mura Aurelie
tel. 06 6878618, fax 06 6878619
info@bbitalia.it
www.bbitalia.it
Closed: varies

Accommodation
Guestrooms: *3 (2 doubles, 1 triple)*
Services & Amenities: *English spoken; rooms cleaned every 3 days; tourist information*
Minimum stay: *2 nights*
Rates: €€
Credit cards: VISA MC *Bancomat*
Pets: no

This B&B has three rooms: a triple with three beds, two doubles both with a double bed; two bathrooms are exclusively for guests. The furnishings are simple and functional. Just outside the front door, guests have a stunning view of St. Peter's dome; the Vatican can be reached in 5 minutes and both the Mole Adriana and the center are within walking distance.

131. • Bed & Breakfast Italia
Code R1131
via Foligno
tel. 06 6878618, fax 06 6878619
info@bbitalia.it
www.bbitalia.it
Closed: varies

Accommodation
Guestrooms: *1 double bedroom*
Services & Amenities: *English spoken; rooms cleaned every 3 days; complimentary tourist information*
Minimum stay: *2 nights*
Rates: €€
Credit cards: VISA MC *Bancomat*
Pets: 🚫

This apartment, located in a building in the San Giovanni district, is stylishly furnished with antiques. It offers a double room and a bathroom with shower/tub, sitting room and kitchen. It is 300 m from the subway station. Via Sannio, famed for its daily market, is 5 minutes away on foot.

132. • Bed & Breakfast Italia
Code R1139
via Sant'Angela Merici
tel. 06 6878618, fax 06 6878619
info@bbitalia.it
www.bbitalia.it
Closed: varies

Independent apartment on the first floor of an early twentieth-century building in the Bologna district. The house is furnished in a youthful and colorful style and consists in an entrance, a double bedroom, a kitchen and a bathroom with shower. Guests can enjoy an outdoor shared garden where they can have breakfast or just relax.

Accommodation
Guestrooms: *1 double bedroom*
Services & Amenities: *French and English spoken; rooms cleaned every 3 days; tourist information*
Minimum stay: *2 nights*
Rates: €€
Credit cards: VISA MC *Bancomat*
Pets: 🚫

133. • Bed & Breakfast Italia
Code R1141
via Luigi Pulci
tel. 06 6878618, fax 06 6878619
info@bbitalia.it
www.bbitalia.it
Closed: varies

Accommodation
Guestrooms: *2 (1 single, 1 double)*
Services & Amenities: *French, English and Spanish spoken; rooms cleaned every 3 days; tourist info; baby-sitting service; smokers welcome*
Minimum stay: *2 nights*
Rates: €€
Credit cards: VISA MC *Bancomat*
Pets: 🚫

The house is situated in the central area of Piazza Bologna. The room, furnished in a simple, lively style, is sunny and spacious; private bathroom with shower. Weather permitting, breakfast is served on the large balcony under a shady portico, otherwise it is served in the lounge.

134. • Bed & Breakfast Italia TCI 10%
Code R1155
via Suor Celestina Donati
tel. 06 6878618, fax 06 6878619
info@bbitalia.it
www.bbitalia.it
Closed: varies

Accommodation
Guestrooms: *2 (1 single and 1 double bedroom)*
Services & Amenities: *English spoken; rooms cleaned every three days; tourist information; terrace*
Minimum stay: *2 nights*
Rates: €€
Credit cards: VISA MC *Bancomat*
Pets: 🚫

Apartment on the 9th floor, without elevator, in a modern building in Prati. A single room with ensuite bathroom with shower is for guests. Elegant furnishings both antique and modern. Breakfast is served in the lounge or on the terrace (with wonderful view of the city). Guided tours organized by the owner on request.

135. • Bed & Breakfast Italia
Code R1156
via Novara
tel. 06 6878618, fax 06 6878619
info@bbitalia.it
www.bbitalia.it
Closed: varies

In the quiet area of Nomentano, this fourth floor apartment (elevator available) is tastefully furnished with an-

tiques. The guestroom, a sunny double bedroom, has a private bathroom. This elegant district is well served by transport: the subway station is 500 meters away and buses to the center are just 50 meters away.

Accommodation
Guestrooms: *1 double*
Services & Amenities: *French and English are spoken; rooms cleaned every 3 days; tourist information*
Minimum stay: *2 nights*
Rates: €€
Credit cards: VISA MC *Bancomat*
Pets:

136. • Bed & Breakfast Italia
Code R1160
viale Castrense
tel. 06 6878618, fax 06 6878619
info@bbitalia.it
www.bbitalia.it
Closed: varies

This fourth floor apartment (with elevator) is located in the central area of San Giovanni. It is classically decorated with antiques, and offers to its guests a double bedroom with TV and a bathroom with shower/tub. The rich continental breakfast is served by the lady of the house in the lounge. The subway station to the center is 5 minutes away on foot.

Accommodation
Guestrooms: *1 double bedroom*
Services & Amenities: *French and English are spoken; rooms cleaned every 3 days; tourist information*
Minimum stay: *2 nights*
Rates: €€
Credit cards: VISA MC *Bancomat*
Pets:

137. • Bed & Breakfast Italia TCI 10%
Code R1161
via Vitellia
tel. 06 6878618, fax 06 6878619
info@bbitalia.it
www.bbitalia.it
Closed: varies

Accommodation
Guestrooms: *1 double*
Services & Amenities: *rooms cleaned every three days; tourist info*
Minimum stay: *2 nights*
Rates: €€
Credit cards: VISA MC *Bancomat*
Pets:

B&B in one of the old districts of Rome and a favorite place for filmmakers, artists and writers. The owners chose the furniture carefully: soft colors, ceiling with stone vault. Breakfast provisions are left in the room. The bus stop, is 20 meters from the B&B.

138. • Bed & Breakfast Italia
Code R1164
largo Luigi Antonelli
tel. 06 6878618, fax 06 6878619
info@bbitalia.it
www.bbitalia.it
Closed: varies

This stylishly furnished apartment with antiques is situated in the EUR district. The accommodation consists in a doubleroom with TV, large balcony and air conditioning; the bathroom with shower is exclusively for the guests. The bus stop is 10 m from the accommodation; the subway station is 10 minutes away on foot.

Accommodation
Guestrooms: *1 double bedroom*
Services & Amenities: *French and English are spoken; rooms cleaned every 3 days; tourist information; terrace; air conditioning*
Minimum stay: *2 nights*
Rates: €€
Credit cards: VISA MC *Bancomat*
Pets:

139. • Bed & Breakfast Italia 
Code R1166
via Laurentina
tel. 06 6878618, fax 06 6878619
info@bbitalia.it
www.bbitalia.it
Closed: varies

Accommodation
Guestrooms: *2 (1 single, 1 double bedroom)*
Services & Amenities: *English spoken; rooms cleaned every 3 days; complimentary tourist information*
Minimum stay: *2 nights*
Rates: €€
Credit cards: VISA MC *Bancomat*
Pets: no

This 4th-floor apartment (with elevator) is located in the Laurentino district, well connected by public transport to the center. The accommodation includes 2 bedrooms, furnished in a modern, cheerful style; private bathroom with shower. It is 800 m from the subway station.

140. • Bed & Breakfast Italia
Code R1170
via del Grifone
tel. 06 6878618, fax 06 6878619
info@bbitalia.it
www.bbitalia.it
Closed: varies

Accommodation
Guestrooms: *1 triple*
Services & Amenities: *English spoken; rooms cleaned every 3 days; complimentary tourist information*
Minimum stay: *2 nights*
Rates: €€
Credit cards: VISA MC *Bancomat*
Pets: yes

A typical self-contained loft in the central Monti district, with modern furniture reflecting the landlady's New York origins. The room has three single beds, a bathroom with shower and a tiny kitchenette. The house is a 5-minute walk from the center. The subway station, shopping district and characteristic pubs and coffee shops are a stone's throw away.

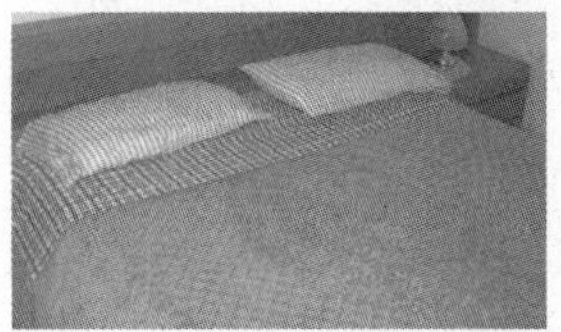

141. • Bed & Breakfast Italia 
Code R1171
via Erminia Frezzolini
tel. 06 6878618, fax 06 6878619
info@bbitalia.it
www.bbitalia.it
Closed: varies

Accommodation
Guestrooms: *2 (1 double bedroom and 1 double)*
Services & Amenities: *French, English and Spanish are spoken; rooms cleaned every 3 days; tourist info*
Minimum stay: *2 nights*
Rates: €€
Credit cards: VISA MC *Bancomat*
Pets: no

This ground floor accommodation is situated in northeast area of Rome, in the Montesacro district. The accommodation consists in two

double rooms, one with a double sofa bed and the other with twin beds; the private bathroom has a shower. In summertime guests can use the well tended garden where breakfast is served.

142. • Bed & Breakfast Italia
Code R1173
via Pietro Negroni
tel. 06 6878618, fax 06 6878619
info@bbitalia.it
www.bbitalia.it
Closed: varies

Accommodation
Guestrooms: *1 double*
Services & Amenities: *rooms cleaned every 3 days; complimentary tourist information*
Minimum stay: *2 nights*
Rates: €€
Credit cards: VISA MC *Bancomat*
Pets: no

This attic apartment is situated in the suburban area of Tiburtino in a small building surrounded by a communal garden. Its spacious and elegant interiors are furnished with period pieces of classical furniture. A double bedroom with twin beds and a bathroom with shower are available. The subway station, reaching the center in 20 min, is 5 min away on foot.

143. • Bed & Breakfast Italia Tci 10%
Code R1178
via Cariati
tel. 06 6878618, fax 06 6878619
info@bbitalia.it
www.bbitalia.it
Closed: varies

This cheery, modern apartment is situated in the suburbs of the Appio district. Two rooms are used for B&B purposes: one double and one single. In the summer, the rich continental breakfast is usually served on the large balcony facing the silent street below. The bus stop, which goes to the subway station in 20 minutes, is a 5-minute walk away.

Accommodation
Guestrooms: *2 (1 single, 1 double)*
Services & Amenities: *French spoken; rooms cleaned every 3 days; complimentary tourist information; terrace; smokers welcome*
Minimum stay: *2 nights*
Rates: €€
Credit cards: VISA MC *Bancomat*
Pets: no

144. • Bed & Breakfast Italia
Code R1179
via Eufrate
tel. 06 6878618
fax 06 6878619
info@bbitalia.it
www.bbitalia.it
Closed: varies

This accommodation is situated in the residential EUR district, a 5-minute walk from the Conference Center. This very silent, self-contained apartment is on the ground floor; the guest accommodation consists in a simply furnished double-room with ensuite bathroom. The guests can also use kitchen facilities. The subway station and bus stop running to the center in 20 minutes are 200 meters away. The host welcomes the guests and provides useful information about the town.

Accommodation
Guestrooms: *1 double bedroom*
Services & Amenities: *French and English are spoken; rooms cleaned every 3 days; complimentary tourist information*
Minimum stay: *2 nights*
Rates: €€
Credit cards: VISA MC *Bancomat*
Pets: no

145. • Bed & Breakfast Italia
Code R1182
via Lavinio
tel. 06 6878618, fax 06 6878619
info@bbitalia.it
www.bbitalia.it
Closed: varies

This independent apartment is in the San Giovanni area. It is classically furnished with antiques and has 3 rooms: a single and 2 triples, one with a double and a single bed, the other with three single beds; the bathroom with shower is shared by all rooms. It is a 10-min walk from St. Peter's and from the subway station.

Accommodation
Guestrooms: *3 (1 single, 2 triples)*
Services & Amenities: *rooms cleaned every 3 days; tourist info*
Minimum stay: *2 nights*
Rates: €€
Credit cards: VISA MC *Bancomat*
Pets: yes

146. • Bed & Breakfast Italia
Code R1184
via Luigi Cesana
tel. 06 6878618, fax 06 6878619
info@bbitalia.it
www.bbitalia.it
Closed: varies

The B& B is located in the Tiburtino district, just outside the center. It is furnished in a modern, cheerful style and offers two double bedrooms, both with a double bed, one with ensuite bathroom. Continental breakfast is served in the lounge. It is a 10-minute walk from the subway station to the Termini station and the center. The area is full of picturesque restaurants and nightlife.

Accommodation
Guestrooms: *2 double bedrooms*
Services & Amenities: *English spoken; rooms cleaned every 3 days; complimentary tourist information*
Minimum stay: *2 nights*
Rates: €€
Credit cards: VISA MC *Bancomat*
Pets: no

147. • Bed & Breakfast Italia
Code R1185
via Tembien
tel. 06 6878618, fax 06 6878619
info@bbitalia.it
www.bbitalia.it
Closed: varies

This fourth floor (with elevator) apartment situated in the Trieste district is sunny and tastefully furnished. It is independent and includes three double bedrooms; two have an ensuite bathroom with shower; the third has a private bathroom with tub. Guests can use the kitchen where breakfast provisions are left by the hosts.

Accommodation
Guestrooms: *3 doubles*
Services & Amenities: *English and Spanish are spoken; rooms cleaned every 3 days; complimentary tourist information; private parking*
Minimum stay: *2 nights*
Rates: €€
Credit cards: VISA MC *Bancomat*
Pets: no

148. • Bed & Breakfast Italia TCI 10%
Code R1190
via Portuense
tel. 06 6878618, fax 06 6878619
info@bbitalia.it
www.bbitalia.it
Closed: varies

This apartment is situated in a quiet street in the suburban Portuense district. This accommodation offers a double room with two single beds and modern, functional furnishings. The landlady makes cakes and jams for breakfast and will provide a shuttle service. The bus stop is 10 minutes away.

Accommodation
Guestrooms: *1 double, with private bath*
Services & Amenities: *French and English are spoken; rooms cleaned every 3 days; complimentary tourist information; private parking*
Minimum stay: *2 nights*
Rates: €€
Credit cards: VISA MC *Bancomat*
Pets: no

149. • Bed & Breakfast Italia
Code R1196
via Fiume Giallo
tel. 06 6878618, fax 06 6878619
info@bbitalia.it
www.bbitalia.it
Closed: varies

This accommodation is situated in the suburbs of the EUR district. The accommodation consists in a small residence with inner garden. The nice, tastefully furnished apartment is quiet and sunny and has a double bedroom and private bathroom with shower.

Accommodation
Guestrooms: *1 double bedroom*
Services & Amenities: *rooms cleaned every 3 days; complimentary tourist information; private parking*
Minimum stay: *2 nights*
Rates: €€
Credit cards: VISA MC *Bancomat*
Pets: no

Breakfast is served on the balcony in the warmer months, or in the lounge.

150. • Bed & Breakfast Italia
Code R1197
via Portuense
tel. 06 6878618, fax 06 6878619
info@bbitalia.it
www.bbitalia.it
Closed: varies

This third-floor apartment (with elevator) is situated in the suburban Portuense district, behind the Monteverde area. This accommodation consists in one double bedroom and one triple. The two rooms share a private bathroom with shower/tub. A bus, which makes the trip to the center in 20 minutes, stops at the front door. The area is full of shops, restaurants, and bars.

Accommodation
Guestrooms: *2 (1 double, 1 triple)*
Services & Amenities: *French and English are spoken; rooms cleaned every 3 days; tourist information; air conditioning*
Minimum stay: *2 nights*
Rates: €€
Credit cards: VISA MC *Bancomat*
Pets: no

151. • Bed & Breakfast Italia
Code R12
via Giuseppe Allievo
tel. 06 6878618, fax 06 6878619
info@bbitalia.it
www.bbitalia.it
Closed: varies

A large double room, with a dressing table with TV, an Art Nouveau chest-of-drawers and a Persian carpet. The bathroom

with shower/tub is shared with the owners. This B&B is in the Balduina district, connected to the center by the subway station and by buses stopping 200 m from the apartment. The hostess serves breakfast in the kitchen.

Accommodation
Guestrooms: *1 double bedroom*
Services & Amenities: *French spoken; rooms cleaned every 3 days; complimentary tourist information*
Minimum stay: *2 nights*
Rates: €
Credit cards: VISA MC *Bancomat*
Pets: not allowed

152. • Bed & Breakfast Italia
Code R1204
via Aleardo Aleardi
tel. 06 6878618, fax 06 6878619
info@bbitalia.it
www.bbitalia.it
Closed: varies

A fifth-floor (with elevator) self-contained apartment, simply and comfortably furnished, situated in the Appio-San Giovanni area. This accommodation offers has two double rooms; one has a double bed and is furnished in a fresh, modern style; the private bathroom has a shower. It is a 5-minute walk from St. Peter's Basilica, and 10 minutes from the subway to the center.

Accommodation
Guestrooms: *2 (1 double bedroom and 1 double)*
Services & Amenities: *English and German are spoken; rooms cleaned every 3 days; tourist information; smokers welcome*
Minimum stay: *2 nights*
Rates: €€
Credit cards: VISA MC *Bancomat*
Pets: allowed

153. • Bed & Breakfast Italia
Code R1208
via Boccardo
tel. 06 6878618, fax 06 6878619
info@bbitalia.it
www.bbitalia.it
Closed: varies

This second floor B&B is in a fairly central location in the Fleming residential area. The landlady offers her guests a double room with a double sofa bed, TV, private bathroom and a balcony where the rich continental breakfast is served in the summer. Guests can take part in the numerous activities organized by the landlady, who is a tango instructor. A pet lives in house.

Accommodation
Guestrooms: *1 double bedroom*
Services & Amenities: *French and English are spoken; rooms cleaned every three days; complimentary tourist information*
Minimum stay: *2 nights*
Rates: €€
Credit cards: VISA MC *Bancomat*
Pets: not allowed

154. • Bed & Breakfast Italia
Code R1211
via Battistini
tel. 06 6878618, fax 06 6878619
info@bbitalia.it
www.bbitalia.it
Closed: varies

This second floor apartment (with elevator) is located in the Aurelio district, a short distance from the center. It has two double rooms, one with a double bed and the other with twin beds, furnished in an informal, modern style; it has a bathroom with shower. Breakfast is served in the lounge. The subway station is a 5-minute walk away.

Accommodation
Guestrooms: *2 (1 double bedroom and 1 double)* ♿
Services & Amenities: *French, English and Spanish are spoken; rooms cleaned every three days; tourist information; terrace*
Minimum stay: *2 nights*
Rates: €€
Credit cards: VISA MC *Bancomat*
Pets: allowed

155. • Bed & Breakfast Italia
Code R1212
via Cola di Rienzo
tel. 06 6878618, fax 06 6878619
info@bbitalia.it
www.bbitalia.it
Closed: varies

A studio situated in the loft of an old building (with elevator). The accommodation includes an entrance, a bedroom with two single beds (one is a pull-out bed), kitchenette, bathroom with shower, and TV. The host, who lives next door, welcomes his guests and provides brochures and useful information. He leaves provisions for breakfast in the fridge.

Accommodation
Guestrooms: *1 double*
Services & Amenities: *French and English are spoken; rooms cleaned every 3 days; complimentary tourist information; smokers welcome*
Minimum stay: *2 nights*
Rates: €€
Credit cards: VISA MC *Bancomat*
Pets: 🚫

156. • Bed & Breakfast Italia
Code R1213
via Gregorio VII
tel. 06 6878618, fax 06 6878619
info@bbitalia.it
www.bbitalia.it
Closed: varies

This sixth floor apartment with elevator is just on the edge of the center in the Aurelio area. Two rooms, a double and a single, are available. The bathroom is shared. This warm and cozy house has simple fresh furnishings. The landlady provides advice and information on places to visit and things to do in town.

Accommodation
Guestrooms: *2 (1 single, 1 double)*
Services & Amenities: *English and Spanish are spoken; rooms cleaned every 3 days; tourist information; terrace; smokers welcome*
Minimum stay: *2 nights*
Rates: €€
Credit cards: VISA MC *Bancomat*
Pets: 🚫

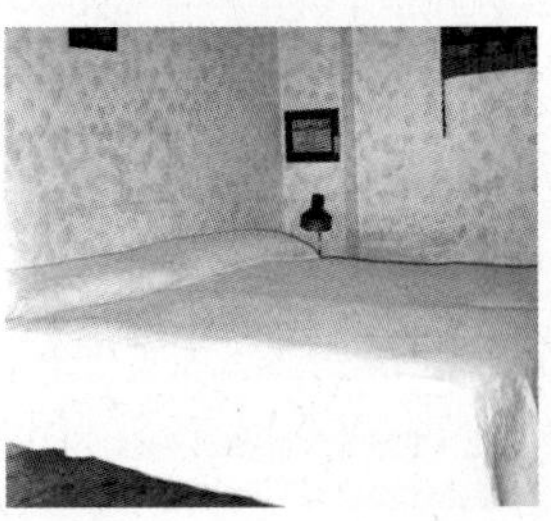

157. • Bed & Breakfast Italia
Code R1214
lungotevere Mellini
tel. 06 6878618, fax 06 6878619
info@bbitalia.it
www.bbitalia.it
Closed: varies

This room with three single beds and a private bathroom is independent and comfortably furnished in a functional style. It is situated in the Prati area, 1 km from Castel Sant'Angelo. The landlady welcomes guests and provides useful information about the town.

Accommodation
Guestrooms: *1 triple*
Services & Amenities: *English spoken; rooms cleaned every 3 days; complimentary tourist information*
Minimum stay: *2 nights*
Rates: €€
Credit cards: VISA MC *Bancomat*
Pets: 🐾

158. • Bed & Breakfast Italia
Code R1220
via degli Scolopi
tel. 06 6878618, fax 06 6878619
info@bbitalia.it
www.bbitalia.it
Closed: varies

This small, forty-square-meter, self-contained apartment is in the Balduina district, just on the edge of the center. It features a double room with double bed, bathroom with shower, a small lounge where breakfast is served and an extra bed can be added. This B&B is set in a leafy area next to the hosts' villa. The bus stop and the subway station are just 200 m away.

Accommodation
Guestrooms: *1 double bedroom; additional bed on request*
Services & Amenities: *French, English and Spanish are spoken; rooms cleaned every 3 days; tourist info; baby-sitting service; terrace; smokers welcome; private parking*
Minimum stay: *2 nights*
Rates: €€
Credit cards: VISA MC *Bancomat*
Pets: 🚫

159. • Bed & Breakfast Italia
Code R1221
via Stevenson
tel. 06 6878618, fax 06 6878619
info@bbitalia.it
www.bbitalia.it
Closed: varies

A fourth-floor apartment a short distance from the center in the Bologna district. A double bedroom with private bathroom complete with shower is available; the furnishings are comfortable, simple and cheerful. The subway station to Termini Station and the center is 300 m away.

Accommodation
Guestrooms: *1 double bedroom*
Services & Amenities: *French and English spoken; rooms cleaned every 3 days; tourist information; terrace; smokers welcome*
Minimum stay: *2 nights*
Rates: €€
Credit cards: VISA MC *Bancomat*
Pets: no

160. • Bed & Breakfast Italia
Code R1222
via Sant'Ippolito
tel. 06 6878618, fax 06 6878619
info@bbitalia.it
www.bbitalia.it
Closed: varies

Accommodation
Guestrooms: *2 (1 double, 1 triple)*
Services & Amenities: *English spoken; rooms cleaned every 3 days; tourist information; terrace*
Minimum stay: *2 nights*
Rates: €€
Credit cards: VISA MC *Bancomat*
Pets: yes

This B&B on the 4th floor of a building with elevator, is situated in an inner street in the Bologna district, 300 m from the "La Sapienza" University. It offers a triple room with a double bed and a single bed, a double room with a double sofa bed, and a bathroom with shower. The furnishings are colorful and cheerful. The bus stop and the subway station are 200 m away. Guests may use kitchen facilities.

161. • Bed & Breakfast Italia
Code R1224
viale Caduti per la Resistenza
tel. 06 6878618, fax 06 6878619
info@bbitalia.it
www.bbitalia.it
Closed: varies

Accommodation
Guestrooms: *1 double bedroom*
Services & Amenities: *French and English are spoken; rooms cleaned every 3 days; tourist information*
Minimum stay: *2 nights*
Rates: €€
Credit cards: VISA MC *Bancomat*
Pets: no

This small self-contained apartment on the eighth floor with elevator is located at EUR. It is decorated with modern furnishings and includes a double bedroom with TV, a sitting room with two sofa beds, a bathroom with shower and a fully equipped kitchenette. The bus stop to the subway is just outside the building.

162. • Bed & Breakfast Italia TCI 10%
Code R1226
via Ernesto Basile
tel. 06 6878618, fax 06 6878619
info@bbitalia.it
www.bbitalia.it
Closed: varies

This B&B is situated in the EUR residential area, in "Villaggio Azzurro". The accommodation consists in two double bedrooms, one with a double bed, the other with twin beds, each with TV, private bathroom with shower and large balcony. Fiumicino airport is 10 km away and the subway station is 2 km away. Host provides useful information about the town.

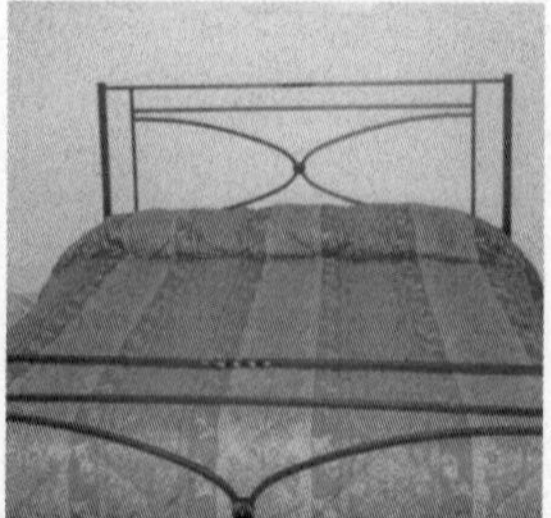

Accommodation
Guestrooms: *2 (1 double bedroom and 1 double)*
Services & Amenities: *English spoken; rooms cleaned every 3 days; tourist information; terrace*
Minimum stay: *2 nights*
Rates: €€
Credit cards: VISA MC *Bancomat*
Pets: yes

163. • Bed & Breakfast Italia
Code R1232
rampa Brancaleone
tel. 06 6878618, fax 06 6878619
info@bbitalia.it
www.bbitalia.it
Closed: varies

Accommodation
Guestrooms: *1 double bedroom*
Services & Amenities: *English and German are spoken; rooms cleaned every 3 days; complimentary tourist information*
Minimum stay: *2 nights*
Rates: €€
Credit cards: VISA MC *Bancomat*
Pets: no pets

This apartment is situated in the Vatican area, in a private street entered accessible by steps. It is on the first floor and offers to its guests a small veranda, a double room furnished in modern, fresh style, and a private bathroom with shower. The continental breakfast is generally served in the lounge. The bus stop for the center is 50 m away.The host welcomes his guests and provides information on places to visit.

164. • Bed & Breakfast Italia
Code R1236
via Eugenio Tanzi
tel. 06 6878618, fax 06 6878619
info@bbitalia.it
www.bbitalia.it
Closed: varies

Accommodation
Guestrooms: *3 (1 single, 1 double and 1 triple room)*
Services & Amenities: *French, English and German are spoken; rooms cleaned every 3 days; tourist information; private parking*
Minimum stay: *2 nights*
Rates: €€
Credit cards: VISA MC *Bancomat*
Pets: pets allowed

This apartment is located in the Monte Mario residential area. The accommodation consists in three rooms: a triple with a double bed and a single, a double with twin beds, and a single bedroom; a private bathroom with shower/tub. It is simply and practically furnished. Several buses going to the center and the subway station stop nearby.

165. • Bed & Breakfast Italia
Code R1238
via Galileo Ferraris
tel. 06 6878618, fax 06 6878619
info@bbitalia.it
www.bbitalia.it
Closed: varies

Accommodation
Guestrooms: *2 (1 single, 1 triple)*
Services & Amenities: *French, English and German are spoken; rooms cleaned every 3 days; complimentary tourist information*
Minimum stay: *2 nights*
Rates: €€
Credit cards: VISA MC *Bancomat*
Pets: pets allowed

This first-floor apartment is situated in an early twentieth-century building with elevator in the Testaccio district. The accommodation consists in a kitchen, a sitting room with TV, a triple room with a double bed and a single bed, a single bedroom, and a bathroom with tub; all the rooms are classically and simply furnished. Pets are welcome.

166. • Bed & Breakfast Italia
Code R1239
via Giuseppe Rosso
tel. 06 6878618, fax 06 6878619
info@bbitalia.it
www.bbitalia.it
Closed: varies

Accommodation
Guestrooms: *2 (1 double, 1 triple)* ♿
Services & Amenities: *rooms cleaned every 3 days; tourist information*
Minimum stay: *2 nights*
Rates: €€
Credit cards: VISA MC *Bancomat*
Pets: pets allowed

A first-floor apartment in a building situated in the residential district of Balduina. It has simple practical furnishings and offers two rooms, one with twin beds and a triple with a double and a single bed, are available; the private bathroom has a shower. An extra bed for children can be added on request.

167. • Bed & Breakfast Italia
Code R1240
via Giovanni da Castel Bolognese
tel. 06 6878618, fax 06 6878619
info@bbitalia.it
www.bbitalia.it
Closed: varies

The B&B faces the square where Rome's "Porta Portese" famous market is held on Sunday mornings. Guests can

enjoy the breakfast at their leisure. The kitchen is at the guests' disposal both for lunch and dinner. Guests will always find a bottle of wine and a packet of spaghetti, as well as all information about Rome.

Accommodation
Guestrooms: *1 double bedroom*
Services & Amenities: *French and English are spoken; rooms cleaned every 3 days; tourist information*
Minimum stay: *2 nights*
Rates: €€
Credit cards: VISA MC *Bancomat*
Pets: allowed

168. • Bed & Breakfast Italia
Code R1247
largo Riccardi
tel. 06 6878618, fax 06 6878619
info@bbitalia.it
www.bbitalia.it
Closed: varies

The spacious double room looks directly out onto St. Paul's Basilica and is classically furnished and with TV; the small but practical bathroom with shower is exclusively at the guests' disposal. The apartment is on the first floor with elevator. The subway for the center and the EUR district is 100 m away; in the area there are shops and workshops.

Accommodation
Guestrooms: *1 double bedroom*
Services & Amenities: *rooms cleaned every 3 days; complimentary tourist information; terrace; smokers welcome; private parking*
Minimum stay: *2 nights*
Rates: €€
Credit cards: VISA MC *Bancomat*
Pets: not allowed

169. • Bed & Breakfast Italia
Code R1250
via Napoleone III
tel. 06 6878618, fax 06 6878619
info@bbitalia.it
www.bbitalia.it
Closed: varies

This apartment is centrally located in the Termini district, midway between the railway station and Santa Maria Maggiore. On the sixth floor with lift, this accommodation comprises four rooms. It is simply furnished with match-

ing bedspreads and curtains, TV and safe in each room. Breakfast is served in the kitchen.

Accommodation
Guestrooms: *4 (2 singles, 2 triples)*
Services & Amenities: *rooms cleaned every 3 days; tourist info*
Minimum stay: *2 nights*
Rates: €€
Credit cards: VISA MC *Bancomat*
Pets: not allowed

170. • Bed & Breakfast Italia
Code R1251
via Prato della Corte
tel. 06 6878618, fax 06 6878619
info@bbitalia.it
www.bbitalia.it
Closed: varies

An extensively restored farmhouse in country style in the suburbs, 4 km from the Saxa Rubra area. Guests can use three double rooms and a private bathroom with tub; an

extra bed for children is available on request. Guests may use the park that surrounds the house.

Accommodation
Guestrooms: *3 doubles* ♿
Services & Amenities: *French, English and Spanish are spoken; rooms cleaned every 3 days; tourist information; private parking*
Minimum stay: *2 nights*
Rates: €€
Credit cards: VISA MC *Bancomat*
Pets: not allowed

171. • Bed & Breakfast Italia
Code R1252
via Trionfale
tel. 06 6878618, fax 06 6878619
info@bbitalia.it
www.bbitalia.it
Closed: varies

This first-floor apartment in an elegant building is situated a short distance from the center in the residential area of Balduina. The accommodation includes a double bedroom with a private bathroom. It is simply furnished with great attention to detail: the paintings, bedspreads, and curtains are all matching and feature soft shades of blue. The subway station is 800 m away; the bus stop is 200 m from the house.

ACCOMMODATION
Guestrooms: *1 double bedroom*
Services & Amenities: *French and English are spoken; rooms cleaned every 3 days; complimentary tourist information; smokers welcome*
Minimum stay: *2 nights*
Rates: €€
Credit cards: VISA MC *Bancomat*
Pets: not allowed

172. • Bed & Breakfast Italia
Code R1255
via Poggioli
tel. 06 6878618, fax 06 6878619
info@bbitalia.it
www.bbitalia.it
Closed: varies

This B&B is located in a private road near Piazza Bologna. The accommodation consists in a double room with TV. It is furnished in modern style; the private guest bathroom has a shower. It is a quiet, peaceful area. Several buses running to the center stop only 40 meters from the house.

ACCOMMODATION
Guestrooms: *1 double bedroom*
Services & Amenities: *French and English are spoken; rooms cleaned every 3 days; complimentary tourist information; smokers welcome*
Minimum stay: *2 nights*
Rates: €€
Credit cards: VISA MC *Bancomat*
Pets: not allowed

173. • Bed & Breakfast Italia TCI 10%
Code R1262
via Laurentina
tel. 06 6878618, fax 06 6878619
info@bbitalia.it
www.bbitalia.it
Closed: varies

A self-contained apartment in a villa dating from the early 90s, nestling in a leafy farm on Via Laurentina, at Montemigliore. The accommodation has country style furnishings, in keeping with the adjoining farmhouse and has colored curtains and bedspreads.

ACCOMMODATION
Guestrooms: *2 (1 double, 1 triple)*
Services & Amenities: *rooms cleaned every 3 days; tourist information; smokers welcome; parking*
Minimum stay: *2 nights*
Rates: €€
Credit cards: VISA MC *Bancomat*
Pets: not allowed

174. • Bed & Breakfast Italia
Code R1263
via Allegri da Correggio
tel. 06 6878618, fax 06 6878619
info@bbitalia.it
www.bbitalia.it
Closed: varies

Fifth-floor apartment in a building with elevator, centrally located in the Flaminio district, with a view of the Monte Mario observatory. The lady of the house offers to the guests an elegantly furnished double room with an ensuite bathroom. Fax, PC and Internet facilities are available on request.

ACCOMMODATION
Guestrooms: *1 double bedroom*
Services & Amenities: *English spoken; rooms cleaned every 3 days; tourist information; Internet access; smokers welcome*
Minimum stay: *2 nights*
Rates: €€
Credit cards: VISA MC *Bancomat*
Pets: not allowed

175. • Bed & Breakfast Italia
Code R1267
via B. Cerretti
tel. 06 6878618, fax 06 6878619
info@bbitalia.it
www.bbitalia.it
Closed: varies

The B&B is located in a self-contained ground-floor apartment, in a building in the central Aurelio district, 100 m from the subway station. It has air conditioning and TV and offers a triple bedroom with single beds, tastefully decorated in soft colors creating a warm atmosphere. The host lives on the first floor of the building and lets his guests use the kitchen. Pay parking.

Accommodation
Guestrooms: *1 triple*
Services & Amenities: *French and English are spoken; rooms cleaned every 3 days; complimentary tourist information; air conditioning; smokers welcome; private parking*
Minimum stay: *2 nights*
Rates: €€
Credit cards: VISA MC *Bancomat*
Pets: no

176. • Bed & Breakfast Italia
Code R1268
via Panfilo Castaldi
tel. 06 6878618, fax 06 6878619
info@bbitalia.it
www.bbitalia.it
Closed: varies

A self-contained apartment in a central district of the city featuring a twin-bedded room and private bathroom with shower. This accommodation is in the Trastevere district, near the Porta Portese Sunday market. The hostess welcomes guests on arrival, and leaves the provisions for breakfast in the fridge.

Accommodation
Guestrooms: *1 double*
Services & Amenities: *English spoken; rooms cleaned every 3 days; complimentary tourist information*
Minimum stay: *2 nights*
Rates: €€
Credit cards: VISA MC *Bancomat*
Pets: no

177. • Bed & Breakfast Italia
Code R1269
via Flaminia
tel. 06 6878618, fax 06 6878619
info@bbitalia.it
www.bbitalia.it
Closed: varies

A farmhouse surrounded by 70 hectares of cultivated fields on Via Flaminia. The double room has a TV, independent entrance and private bathroom with shower. The house is decorated with care for detail: tapestry wall hangings, Persian carpets, and period furniture create a romantic atmosphere. A large garden is at the guests' disposal. A car is recommended.

Accommodation
Guestrooms: *1 double bedroom*
Services & Amenities: *French and English are spoken; rooms cleaned every 3 days; tourist information; bike rental; smokers welcome; parking*
Minimum stay: *2 nights*
Rates: €€
Credit cards: VISA MC *Bancomat*
Pets: no

178 • Bed & Breakfast Italia
Code R1270
via Eurialo
tel. 06 6878618, fax 06 6878619
info@bbitalia.it
www.bbitalia.it
Closed: varies

The B&B is a self-contained apartment in the Appio district, 15 minutes from the old center by subway, which stops 200 m from the accommodation. The guest accommodation consists in a double room, a sitting room with a queen-size sofa bed and a bathroom. The hosts, who live upstairs, welcome guests on arrival.

Accommodation
Guestrooms: *2 (1 single and 1 double bedroom)*
Services & Amenities: *rooms cleaned every 3 days; tourist info*
Minimum stay: *2 nights*
Rates: €€
Credit cards: VISA MC *Bancomat*
Pets: no

179. • Bed & Breakfast Italia
Code R1271
via Rosa Govona
tel. 06 6878618, fax 06 6878619
info@bbitalia.it
www.bbitalia.it
Closed: varies

Accommodation
Guestrooms: *1 double*
Services & Amenities: *French spoken; rooms cleaned every 3 days; complimentary tourist information*
Minimum stay: *2 nights*
Rates: €€
Credit cards: VISA MC *Bancomat*
Pets: not allowed

The B&B is located in a small, self-contained ground-floor apartment in the central Gianicolense district, near the Trastevere area. This accommodation offers a room with twin beds, which be joined into a double on request, a bathroom with shower, a kitchenette and a small garden where breakfast can be served.

180. • Bed & Breakfast Italia

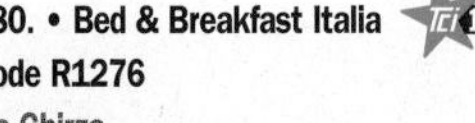

Code R1276
via Ghirza
tel. 06 6878618, fax 06 6878619
info@bbitalia.it
www.bbitalia.it
Closed: varies

The B&B is on the fifth floor of an elegant building with elevator, located in the Nomentano district, 100 meters from Corso Trieste. This studio apartment is complete with twin beds, bathroom with shower, kitchenette and large, scenic balcony. The furnishings are simple and elegant. Your hostess gives Italian lessons on request.

Accommodation
Guestrooms: *1 double*
Services & Amenities: *French and English are spoken; rooms cleaned every 3 days; tourist information; terrace; smokers welcome*
Minimum stay: *2 nights*
Rates: €€
Credit cards: VISA MC *Bancomat*
Pets: not allowed

181. • Bed & Breakfast Italia
Code R1277
piazza della Rovere
tel. 06 6878618, fax 06 6878619
info@bbitalia.it
www.bbitalia.it
Closed: varies

The B&B is between the Vatican City and the Trastevere district, 10-minutes' walk from St. Peter's Square. This 5th floor apartment in an old building without elevator offers a double room, which opens onto a large balcony with a view of the city rooftops, plus a bathroom with shower. The house is furnished in an original, personal style, with travel memorabilia. Breakfast is served in the lounge or on the balcony.

Accommodation
Guestrooms: *1 double*
Services & Amenities: *French and English are spoken; rooms cleaned every 3 days; complimentary tourist information; terrace; Internet access; smokers welcome*
Minimum stay: *2 nights*
Rates: €€
Credit cards: VISA MC *Bancomat*
Pets: not allowed

182. • Bed & Breakfast Italia
Code R1279
via Pinelli
tel. 06 6878618, fax 06 6878619
info@bbitalia.it
www.bbitalia.it
Closed: varies

An independent apartment with a single and two double rooms, one with double bed and one with two single beds, all with modern furnishings. Both the lounge and the dining room have balconies, where to have breakfast. The kitchen is available to guests. The apartment is located in the residential Balduina district.

Accommodation
Guestrooms: *3 (1 single, 1 double bedroom and 1 double)*
Services & Amenities: *French and English are spoken; rooms cleaned every 3 days; tourist information; smokers welcome*
Minimum stay: *2 nights*
Rates: €€
Credit cards: VISA MC *Bancomat*
Pets: not allowed

183. • Bed & Breakfast Italia
Code R1281
via Catel
tel. 06 6878618, fax 06 6878619
info@bbitalia.it
www.bbitalia.it
Closed: varies

The B&B is in a recently refurbished penthouse, made up of two rooms decorated in a modern style; it offers one double room with a queen-size bed, large windows with a view of Rome's rooftops, and a triple room with a bunk bed and a sofa bed. The guest bathroom has a shower. The B&B is located in the Monteverde district, an area full of shops and connected to the old center by tramway or bus in 20 minutes.

ACCOMMODATION
Guestrooms: *2 (1 double, 1 triple)*
Services & Amenities: *French and English are spoken; rooms cleaned every 3 days; tourist information*
Minimum stay: *2 nights*
Rates: €€
Credit cards: VISA MC *Bancomat*
Pets: not allowed

184. • Bed & Breakfast Italia
Code R1282
via degli Avignonesi
tel. 06 6878618, fax 06 6878619
info@bbitalia.it
www.bbitalia.it
Closed: varies

This third-floor apartment in a small building in the old center, 100 m from Piazza Barberini, offers a double room and a single room, sharing a bathroom with shower. The young hostess has given the furnishings her personal touch, decorating the apartment with antiques and bright colors. She serves continental breakfast in the kitchen.

ACCOMMODATION
Guestrooms: *2 (1 single, 1 double)*
Services & Amenities: *French and English are spoken; rooms cleaned every 3 days; complimentary tourist information; smokers welcome*
Minimum stay: *2 nights*
Rates: €€
Credit cards: VISA MC *Bancomat*
Pets: not allowed

185. • Bed & Breakfast Italia
Code R1283
via Festo Avieno
tel. 06 6878618, fax 06 6878619
info@bbitalia.it
www.bbitalia.it
Closed: varies

This apartment is located in an elegant building, in the Balduina residential district. The guest accommodation consists in a modernly furnished room with twin beds, a private balcony and a single room. The guest bathroom is equipped with tub and shower. The continental breakfast is usually served in the lounge. This B&B is situated in a quiet area connected to the rest of the city with efficient transport. The buses for the center stop nearby.

ACCOMMODATION
Guestrooms: *2 (1 single, 1 double)*
Services & Amenities: *French and English are spoken; rooms cleaned every 3 days; complimentary tourist information; terrace*
Minimum stay: *2 nights*
Rates: €€
Credit cards: VISA MC *Bancomat*
Pets: not allowed

186. • Bed & Breakfast Italia TCI 10%
Code R1284
via Ignazio Ribotti
tel. 06 6878618, fax 06 6878619
info@bbitalia.it
www.bbitalia.it
Closed: varies

This first-floor B&B is in a modern building with elevator, in the Portuense district. It is furnished in ethnic style, with personal touches and soft colors. It has one double room and one single room, which share a bathroom with shower.

ACCOMMODATION
Guestrooms: *2 (1 single, 1 double)*
Services & Amenities: *French and English are spoken; rooms cleaned every 3 days; tourist information; smokers welcome*
Minimum stay: *2 nights*
Rates: €€
Credit cards: VISA MC *Bancomat*
Pets: not allowed

187. • Bed & Breakfast Italia
Code R1285
via Premuda
tel. 06 6878618, fax 06 6878619
info@bbitalia.it
www.bbitalia.it
Closed: varies

Recently refurbished first-floor apartment in an 18th-C building with elevator in the Prati district. It has three rooms, one

of the double rooms has an en suite bathroom with shower; the other rooms share a large bathroom also with shower. The apartment is decorated

ACCOMMODATION
Guestrooms: *3 doubles*
Services & Amenities: *French, English spoken; rooms cleaned every 3 days; tourist info; smokers welcome*
Minimum stay: *2 nights*
Rates: €€
Credit cards: VISA MC *Bancomat*
Pets: no

in simple functional style. Provisions for breakfast can be found in the kitchen.

188. • Bed & Breakfast Italia
Code R1286
via Savastano
tel. 06 6878618, fax 06 6878619
info@bbitalia.it
www.bbitalia.it
Closed: varies

An elegant apartment in the Parioli district. Simply furnished, it features a double room with TV. The French window opens onto an extensive

ACCOMMODATION
Guestrooms: *1 double bedroom*
Services & Amenities: *French and English are spoken; rooms cleaned every 3 days; tourist information*
Minimum stay: *2 nights*
Rates: €€
Credit cards: VISA MC *Bancomat*
Pets: no

and well-tended garden-balcony. Breakfast can be served on that or in the lounge. The private bathroom for the exclusive use of guests has tub and shower. The area is connected to the old center by bus and by city train, stopping 50 m away.

189. • Bed & Breakfast Italia
Code R1287
via Attilio Friggeri
tel. 06 6878618, fax 06 6878619
info@bbitalia.it
www.bbitalia.it
Closed: varies

This apartment is in an elegant building in the Balduina district. It features one double room with TV and balcony, which is at

the guests' disposal. The private bathroom has a shower. Breakfast is served in the comfortable lounge. The bus stops 200 m away; the subway station is 800 m away.

ACCOMMODATION
Guestrooms: *1 double bedroom*
Services & Amenities: *French spoken; rooms cleaned every 3 days; complimentary tourist information; terrace; smokers welcome*
Minimum stay: *2 nights*
Rates: €€
Credit cards: VISA MC *Bancomat*
Pets: no

190. • Bed & Breakfast Italia
Code R1288
via Ruggero Fiore
tel. 06 6878618, fax 06 6878619
info@bbitalia.it
www.bbitalia.it
Closed: varies

This fourth-floor apartment is in a modern building with elevator, in the Prati district.The accommodation includes two

ACCOMMODATION
Guestrooms: *2 double bedrooms*
Services & Amenities: *French spoken; rooms cleaned every 3 days; tourist info; smokers welcome*
Minimum stay: *2 nights*
Rates: €€
Credit cards: VISA MC *Bancomat*
Pets: no

double guestrooms, one of which has a large balcony. The bathroom with tub is for

guests' use only. Breakfast is served by the hostess in the lounge. The subway station is 100 m away.

191. • Bed & Breakfast Italia
Code R13
via Prospero Colonna
tel. 06 6878618, fax 06 6878619
info@bbitalia.it
www.bbitalia.it
Closed: varies

Accommodation
Guestrooms: *2 (1 single, 1 double)*
Services & Amenities: *German spoken; rooms cleaned every 3 days; tourist information*
Minimum stay: *2 nights*
Rates: €
Credit cards: VISA MC *Bancomat*
Pets: not allowed

This apartment is on the fourth-floor of a building with elevator, in the Portuense suburb, and is furnished in a modern, cheerful style. It consists in a double and a single room, sharing a bathroom. The hostess makes a cot available. The old center is reached by bus and the nearest bus stop is 5 minutes away.

192. • Bed & Breakfast Italia
Code R20
via Pietro Cartoni
tel. 06 6878618, fax 06 6878619
info@bbitalia.it
www.bbitalia.it
Closed: varies

Accommodation
Guestrooms: *1 double bedroom*
Services & Amenities: *English spoken; rooms cleaned every 3 days; tourist info; smokers welcome*
Minimum stay: *2 nights*
Rates: €
Credit cards: VISA MC *Bancomat*
Pets: allowed

A second-floor apartment located in the Monteverde district that takes its name from the several parks in the area. One double room with TV and a large balcony is at the guests' disposal. The bathroom is shared with the owners. The accommodation is simply and elegantly decorated.

193. • Bed & Breakfast Italia
Code R2006
via degli Avignonesi
tel. 06 6878618, fax 06 6878619
info@bbitalia.it
www.bbitalia.it
Closed: varies

Accommodation
Guestrooms: *2 (1 single, 1 double)*
Services & Amenities: *French and English are spoken; rooms cleaned every 3 days; tourist information; smokers welcome*
Minimum stay: *2 nights*
Rates: €€
Credit cards: VISA MC *Bancomat*
Pets: not allowed

The B&B is located in a third-floor apartment in an elegant building. This accommodation offers one single room, one double room and a private bathroom. The refined furnishings all come from a movie set. In the warmer months, breakfast is served on the large balcony where guests can enjoy the view of Rome's rooftops.

194. • Bed & Breakfast Italia
Code R2007
via dei Banchi Nuovi
tel. 06 6878618, fax 06 6878619
info@bbitalia.it
www.bbitalia.it
Closed: varies

Accommodation
Guestrooms: *1 triple*
Services & Amenities: *French and English are spoken; rooms cleaned every 3 days; tourist information*
Minimum stay: *2 nights*
Rates: €€
Credit cards: VISA MC *Bancomat*
Pets: not allowed

This apartment is on the 2nd floor of an old building. The B&B is on two levels, with a mezzanine, exploiting all the room available, complete with modern furnishings. On the lower level there is a kitchenette, a sitting room with sofa bed and a bathroom with shower. The double room is in the mezzanine.

195. • Bed & Breakfast Italia
Code R2010
via Manfredi
tel. 06 6878618
fax 06 6878619
info@bbitalia.it
www.bbitalia.it
Closed: varies

This B&B is located in the Parioli district, in a ground-floor apartment that's tastefully furnished with antiques in a refined style. This accommodation offers one twin-bedded room with TV and bathroom with shower. The center can be reached by bus and tram, which stop 200 m away. This area has plenty of trendy shops and restaurants of all kinds. Pets live in the house.

ACCOMMODATION
Guestrooms: *1 double*
Services & Amenities: *French spoken; rooms cleaned every 3 days; complimentary tourist information; smokers welcome*
Minimum stay: *2 nights*
Rates: €€
Credit cards: VISA MC *Bancomat*
Pets: no

196. • Bed & Breakfast Italia
Code R2013
via di Santa Cornelia
tel. 06 6878618, fax 06 6878619
info@bbitalia.it
www.bbitalia.it
Closed: varies

A self-contained wing of an old mansion nestling in a park of centuries-old trees. Two double rooms are available: one with double bed and private bathroom with shower and the other with twin beds, sharing a bathroom with other rooms. The accommodation includes a lounge with TV, hall, kitchen and garden complete with swimming pool. The accommodation is decorated in a classic style with antiques.

ACCOMMODATION
Guestrooms: *2 (1 double bedroom and 1 double)*
Services & Amenities: *French, English and German are spoken; rooms cleaned every 3 days; tourist info; bike rental; horse-riding excursions; smokers welcome; private parking*
Minimum stay: *2 nights*
Rates: €€
Credit cards: VISA MC *Bancomat*
Pets: no

197. • Bed & Breakfast Italia
Code R2017
via Baccina
tel. 06 6878618, fax 06 6878619
info@bbitalia.it
www.bbitalia.it
Closed: varies

This B&B is located in the Monti district, near the Imperial Forum, on the 2nd floor of an old building and is decorated in a personal, bohemian style. It has a double room and ensuite bathroom with shower. The hostess welcomes her guests with a cocktail offered on the large balcony, in the shade of a pergola, where she also serves breakfast.

ACCOMMODATION
Guestrooms: *1 double bedroom*
Services & Amenities: *French, English, German and Spanish are spoken; rooms cleaned every 3 days; tourist information; terrace*
Minimum stay: *2 nights*
Rates: €€
Credit cards: VISA MC *Bancomat*
Pets: no

198. • Bed & Breakfast Italia
Code R2018
via Quintiliano
tel. 06 6878618, fax 06 6878619
info@bbitalia.it
www.bbitalia.it
Closed: varies

The host has personally designed and decorated the apartment in an original manner. It features a double room, which recalls the simple, Japanese style and a bathroom with tub for guests. In the morning, breakfast is served in the room or, in the summer, in the tiny garden. The B&B is located in the hilly Balduina residential district and has easy access to the center via transport, available 200 m away.

ACCOMMODATION
Guestrooms: *1 double bedroom*
Services & Amenities: *French and English are spoken; rooms cleaned every 3 days; tourist info; terrace*
Minimum stay: *2 nights*
Rates: €€
Credit cards: VISA MC *Bancomat*
Pets: yes

199. • Bed & Breakfast Italia
Code R2026
via L. Luciani
tel. 06 6878618, fax 06 6878619
info@bbitalia.it
www.bbitalia.it
Closed: varies

This apartment is located in the residential Parioli district, on the ground floor of a modern building. It features air conditioned rooms, one with TV and ensuite bathroom with shower; the other rooms share a bathroom. Beakfast is served in the room, which looks onto an internal garden.

ACCOMMODATION
Guestrooms: *3 doubles*
Services & Amenities: *French and English are spoken; rooms cleaned every 3 days; tourist information; air conditioning; private parking*
Minimum stay: *2 nights*
Rates: €€
Credit cards: VISA MC *Bancomat*
Pets:

200. • Bed & Breakfast Italia
Code R2036
vicolo del Cinque
tel. 06 6878618, fax 06 6878619
info@bbitalia.it
www.bbitalia.it
Closed: varies

This B&B is located in the Trastevere district, on the third floor of an old building. The accommodation offers a double room and a triple with a double and a single bed, furnished in a classic style with antiques. The bathroom is equipped with shower and is for the exclusive use of guests. A cot for children under two years of age is available. Pets live in the house.

ACCOMMODATION
Guestrooms: *2 (1 double, 1 triple)*
Services & Amenities: *French and English are spoken; rooms cleaned every 3 days; tourist information*
Minimum stay: *2 nights*
Rates: €€
Credit cards: VISA MC *Bancomat*
Pets:

201. • Bed & Breakfast Italia TCI 10%
Code R2041
via Ardeatina
tel. 06 6878618, fax 06 6878619
info@bbitalia.it
www.bbitalia.it
Closed: varies

A villa surrounded by a park on Via Ardeatina. The first floor with independent entrance is wholly at guests' disposal and is composed as follows: large lounge, one double room with TV and ensuite bathroom with tub, another double room and a triple with single beds, sharing a bathroom with shower.

ACCOMMODATION
Guestrooms: *3 (2 double bedrooms and 1 triple room)*
Services & Amenities: *English and German are spoken; rooms cleaned every 3 days; tourist info; parking*
Minimum stay: *2 nights*
Rates: €€
Credit cards: VISA MC *Bancomat*
Pets:

202. • Bed & Breakfast Italia
Code R2042
via Silvio Pellico
tel. 06 6878618, fax 06 6878619
info@bbitalia.it
www.bbitalia.it
Closed: varies

This elegant apartment is located in the Prati district. Classically furnished with antiques, it features a double room with double bed and ensuite bathroom with shower, for the exclusive use of the guests. Breakfast is served in the lounge, offering an enchanting view of St. Peter's basilica. The bus stop for the center is nearby.

ACCOMMODATION
Guestrooms: *1 double bedroom*
Services & Amenities: *French, English, Spanish spoken; rooms cleaned every 3 days; tourist info; terrace*
Minimum stay: *2 nights*
Rates: €€
Credit cards: VISA MC *Bancomat*
Pets:

203. • Bed & Breakfast Italia
Code R2045
via Lidia
tel. 06 6878618, fax 06 6878619
info@bbitalia.it
www.bbitalia.it
Closed: varies

This quiet and comfortably furnished apartment, with a view of the green park on the ancient Via Appia consists in two rooms: one double with twin beds and one triple with a double and a single bed. The private bathroom is equipped with a shower. It has a large balcony where the rich continental breakfast can be served.

ACCOMMODATION
Guestrooms: *2 (1 double, 1 triple)*
Services & Amenities: *German and Spanish are spoken; rooms cleaned every 3 days; tourist info; bike rental; terrace; air conditioning; parking*
Minimum stay: *2 nights*
Rates: €€
Credit cards: VISA MC *Bancomat*
Pets: 🚫

204. • Bed & Breakfast Italia
Code R2047
via delle Medaglie d'Oro
tel. 06 6878618, fax 06 6878619
info@bbitalia.it
www.bbitalia.it
Closed: varies

This second-floor apartment is in a building with elevator located in the Balduina residential district. The owner rents one double bedroom. The color of the headboard matches that of bedspreads and curtains. The room is furnished in a classic style with antiques. The bathroom with tub is reserved for the guests. Continental breakfast is served in the lounge.

ACCOMMODATION
Guestrooms: *1 double bedroom*
Services & Amenities: *French and English are spoken; rooms cleaned every 3 days; complimentary tourist information; private parking*
Minimum stay: *2 nights*
Rates: €€
Credit cards: VISA MC *Bancomat*
Pets: 🚫

205. • Bed & Breakfast Italia
Code R2053
via degli Scipioni
tel. 06 6878618, fax 06 6878619
info@bbitalia.it
www.bbitalia.it
Closed: varies

This apartment is on the third floor of an old building located in the Prati district. A double room and private bathroom with shower are reserved exclusively for guest use. The room is elegantly furnished in a personal style. Breakfast is served in the lounge.

ACCOMMODATION
Guestrooms: *1 double bedroom*
Services & Amenities: *French, English, German, Spanish spoken; rooms cleaned every 3 days; tourist info*
Minimum stay: *2 nights*
Rates: €€
Credit cards: VISA MC *Bancomat*
Pets: 🚫

206. • Bed & Breakfast Italia
Code R2058
via Rasella
tel. 06 6878618, fax 06 6878619
info@bbitalia.it
www.bbitalia.it
Closed: varies

Third-floor apartment is in the old center, just behind the Quirinale (the residence of the President of the Italian Republic) and not far from the Trevi Fountain. The twin-bedded room has a balcony and en suite bathroom with tub/shower. The atmosphere is friendly and casual. This area is full of restaurants and pubs.

ACCOMMODATION
Guestrooms: *1 double*
Services & Amenities: *French, English and Spanish are spoken; rooms cleaned every 3 days; tourist info; terrace; smokers welcome*
Minimum stay: *2 nights*
Rates: €€
Credit cards: VISA MC *Bancomat*
Pets: 🚫

207. • Bed & Breakfast Italia
Code R2066
via Buonarroti
tel. 06 6878618, fax 06 6878619
info@bbitalia.it
www.bbitalia.it
Closed: varies

Accommodation
Guestrooms: *1 double bedroom*
Services & Amenities: *English spoken; rooms cleaned every 3 days; tourist information; terrace; Internet access; smokers welcome*
Minimum stay: *2 nights*
Rates: €€
Credit cards: VISA MC *Bancomat*
Pets: 🐕

This elegant apartment is in a building dating from the late 19th and early 20th-century, within 5 minutes' walk of the Termini railway station. It features a double room, private bathroom with shower and a large balcony, where breakfast can be served with a breathtaking view over Rome's rooftops. It is just behind the Coliseum, easily reached on foot.

208. • Bed & Breakfast Italia
Code R2067
via di Monteverde
tel. 06 6878618, fax 06 6878619
info@bbitalia.it
www.bbitalia.it
Closed: varies

This fourth floor apartment, entirely at the disposal of guests, is in an apartment building with elevator, not far from the center. Furnished with valuable antiques, this accommodation consists in two double rooms with the option of a cot, two bathrooms with shower/tub, a large sitting room with sofa bed and free access to the kitchen. The area is quiet and well served by transport.

Accommodation
Guestrooms: *2 double bedrooms*
Services & Amenities: *French, English and Spanish are spoken; rooms cleaned every 3 days; tourist information; smokers welcome*
Minimum stay: *2 nights*
Rates: €€
Credit cards: VISA MC *Bancomat*
Pets: no

209. • Bed & Breakfast Italia
Code R2077
via della Balduina
tel. 06 6878618, fax 06 6878619
info@bbitalia.it
www.bbitalia.it
Closed: varies

Accommodation
Guestrooms: *2 double bedrooms*
Services & Amenities: *rooms cleaned every 3 days; tourist info; terrace*
Minimum stay: *2 nights*
Rates: €€
Credit cards: VISA MC *Bancomat*
Pets: no

This apartment is on the second-floor of an elegant building in the Balduina residential hill district. It boasts antique furnishings, marble floors and valuable carpets and includes one double room with TV, one room with double sofa bed and a large balcony. The private bathroom is equipped with shower/tub. The hostess offers her guests a stay in an informal, friendly environment.

210. • Bed & Breakfast Italia
Code R2080
via San Lucio
tel. 06 6878618, fax 06 6878619
info@bbitalia.it
www.bbitalia.it
Closed: varies

Accommodation
Guestrooms: *1 double bedroom*
Services & Amenities: *English spoken; rooms cleaned every 3 days*
Minimum stay: *2 nights*
Rates: €€
Credit cards: VISA MC *Bancomat*
Pets: no

The first-floor apartment is in an elegant building, centrally located within 15 minutes' walk from St. Peter's. A carefully furnished double room is available for guests. The private bathroom is equipped with shower/tub. Breakfast is served in the lounge.

211. • Bed & Breakfast Italia
Code R21
via Giorgio Scalia
tel. 06 6878618, fax 06 6878619
info@bbitalia.it
www.bbitalia.it
Closed: varies

Accommodation
Guestrooms: *1 double bedroom*
Services & Amenities: *rooms cleaned every 3 days; tourist info*
Minimum stay: *2 nights*
Rates: €€
Credit cards: VISA MC *Bancomat*
Pets: not allowed

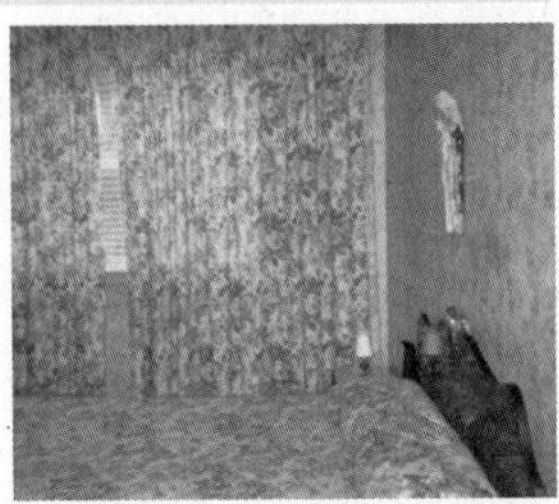

This recently restored apartment is in the Prati district. The owner offers guests one double room, furnished in a simple, functional style. The bathroom is shared with the host. It is possible to walk to the Vatican City and Castel Sant'Angelo. The subway station is 50 meters away. The host provides inside tips to Rome's visitors on request.

212. • Bed & Breakfast Italia
Code R2172
Via del Boschetto
tel. 06 6878618, fax 06 6878619
info@bbitalia.it
www.bbitalia.it
Closed: varies

Apartment on the 3rd floor of a building with elevator. Each room has TV and private bath with shower, and features classic furnishings. Breakfast is served in the livingroom. The bus stop is 100 m away. Piazza Barberini, Piazza Venezia, and Trevi Funtain can be reached on foot.

Accommodation
Guestrooms: *2 doubles & 1triple*
Services & Amenities: *French and English are spoken; rooms cleaned every 3 days; tourist information*
Minimum stay: *2 nights*
Rates: €€€
Credit cards: VISA MC *Bancomat*
Pets: allowed

213. • Bed & Breakfast Italia
Code R2107
via Sant'Agatone Papa
tel. 06 6878618, fax 06 6878619
info@bbitalia.it
www.bbitalia.it
Closed: varies

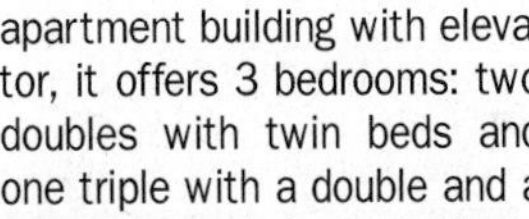

The B&B is located in the Aurelio district. On the fifth floor of an apartment building with elevator, it offers 3 bedrooms: two doubles with twin beds and one triple with a double and a single bed, sharing a bathroom with tub for the exclusive use of guests. All the rooms have TV and balcony. The apartment is furnished with antiques and warm colors. The bus station is 100 m away.

Accommodation
Guestrooms: *3 (2 doubles, 1 triple)*
Services & Amenities: *English spoken; rooms cleaned every 3 days; tourist info; terrace; Internet access*
Minimum stay: *2 nights*
Rates: €€
Credit cards: VISA MC *Bancomat*
Pets: not allowed

214. • Bed & Breakfast Italia
Code R2108
via Paolo II
tel. 06 6878618, fax 06 6878619
info@bbitalia.it
www.bbitalia.it
Closed: varies

Accommodation
Guestrooms: *1 double bedroom*
Services & Amenities: *English and Spanish are spoken; rooms cleaned every 3 days; tourist info*
Minimum stay: *2 nights*
Rates: €€
Credit cards: VISA MC *Bancomat*
Pets: not allowed

This B&B is located in a fifth-floor apartment situated in a building with elevator, in the central Vatican district. It is furnished with antiques and adorned with marble floors with salmon-pink grains matching the color of the upholstery. The guest accommodation consists in a double with wrought iron bed and TV. The bathroom is equipped with tub. A pet lives in the house.

215. • Bed & Breakfast Italia
Code R2115
via Canobi
tel. 06 6878618, fax 06 6878619
info@bbitalia.it
www.bbitalia.it
Closed: varies

The B&B, located in a 19th-C building, recalls the atmosphere of a Paris studio apartment since it is in the center of the Monteverde district, the area of artists and poets. It has two double rooms for guests, one of them with TV, furnished in perfect harmony with the host's style. The private bathroom is equipped with shower. The buses, which stop 200 m away, go to the old center in 15 mins.

Accommodation
Guestrooms: *2 double bedrooms*
Services & Amenities: *French and English are spoken; rooms cleaned every 3 days; tourist information*
Minimum stay: *2 nights*
Rates: €€
Credit cards: VISA MC *Bancomat*
Pets: 🚫

216. • Bed & Breakfast Italia
Code R2117
via Cunfida
tel. 06 6878618, fax 06 6878619
info@bbitalia.it
www.bbitalia.it
Closed: varies

Second-floor apartment in the Prati district owned by a lady who rents to women guests only. It has one single room with private bathroom equipped with tub. The style of furnishings is simple. A cot for children under two years of age can be added on request. The district is in a central position, within walking distance of St. Peter's basilica. The subway station is 400 m and the bus stop is at 50 m from the B&B.

Accommodation
Guestrooms: *1 single*
Services & Amenities: *English spoken; rooms cleaned every 3 days*
Minimum stay: *2 nights*
Rates: €€€
Credit cards: VISA MC *Bancomat*
Pets: 🚫

217. • Bed & Breakfast Italia
Code R2120
vicolo Silvestri
tel. 06 6878618, fax 06 6878619
info@bbitalia.it
www.bbitalia.it
Closed: varies

On the first floor of a Monteverde apartment building, the family offers two double rooms with parquet flooring. One of the rooms has a double bed and a single sofa bed; the other is a twin. The private guest bathroom is equipped with tub/shower. Breakfast is served in the lounge. The style of furnishings is simple. 50 m from the B&B is the entrance to Villa Pamphili, Rome's largest park.

Accommodation
Guestrooms: *2 (1 double bedroom and 1 double)*
Services & Amenities: *French and English are spoken; rooms cleaned every 3 days; tourist info; terrace*
Minimum stay: *2 nights*
Rates: €€
Credit cards: VISA MC *Bancomat*
Pets: 🚫

.218 • Bed & Breakfast Italia
Code R2124
via dei Gracchi
tel. 06 6878618, fax 06 6878619
info@bbitalia.it
www.bbitalia.it
Closed: varies

A self-contained apartment in a building with an internal portico. The apartment has been completely refurnished, and now boasts parquet flooring, white walls adorned with stuccowork, halogen spotlights, and elegant and modern furnishings. It offers a double room, a sitting room with double sofa bed, a bathroom with tub and shower and kitchen with provisions for breakfast in the fridge.

Accommodation
Guestrooms: *2 double bedrooms*
Services & Amenities: *English spoken; rooms cleaned every 3 days; tourist information*
Minimum stay: *2 nights*
Rates: €€
Credit cards: VISA MC *Bancomat*
Pets: 🚫

219. • Bed & Breakfast Italia
Code R2125
via Appia Antica
tel. 06 6878618, fax 06 6878619
info@bbitalia.it
www.bbitalia.it
Closed: varies

Accommodation
Guestrooms: *1 double bedroom*
Services & Amenities: *English spoken; rooms cleaned every 3 days; tourist info; private parking*
Minimum stay: *2 nights*
Rates: €€
Credit cards: VISA MC *Bancomat*
Pets: 🚫

This prestigious villa is located along the old Via Appia, in a residential dwelling complex. The family offers guests a large round room with double bed, private bathroom equipped with shower and a tiny kitchenette. The large French window, the main entrance to this small apartment, opens onto the park surrounding the villa. This area is famous for its archaeological sites.

220. • Bed & Breakfast Italia
Code R2129
via Cavour
tel. 06 6878618, fax 06 6878619
info@bbitalia.it
www.bbitalia.it
Closed: varies

This apartment located in the old center within 5 minutes' walk of the Imperial Forum. The apartment is roomy and

features country-style furnishings. The 3 rooms, one double, one twin-bedded and one with bunk bed, all have a safe. There are two bathrooms, one equipped with tub/shower, the other with just washbasin and WC. Provisions for breakfast can be found in the fridge.

Accommodation
Guestrooms: *3 doubles*
Services & Amenities: *French and English are spoken; rooms cleaned every 3 days; tourist information; air conditioning; smokers welcome*
Minimum stay: *2 nights*
Rates: €€
Credit cards: VISA MC *Bancomat*
Pets: 🚫

221. • Bed & Breakfast Italia
Code R2133
via della Marcigliana
tel. 06 6878618, fax 06 6878619
info@bbitalia.it
www.bbitalia.it
Closed: varies

Accommodation
Guestrooms: *2 (1 double, 1 triple)* ♿
Services & Amenities: *French and English spoken; rooms cleaned every three days; tourist information; horse-riding excursions; smokers welcome; private parking*
Minimum stay: *2 nights*
Rates: €€
Credit cards: VISA MC *Bancomat*

This villa is 500 m from the Settebagni highway exit. The accommodation offers a dou-

ble and a triple room, sharing a bathroom with shower. This house is furnished in a cheerful style. Breakfast is served in the lounge or in the portico.

222. • Bed & Breakfast Italia
Code R2135
via Ferrante Ruiz
tel. 06 6878618, fax 06 6878619
info@bbitalia.it
www.bbitalia.it
Closed: varies

Accommodation
Guestrooms: *3 (1 single, 1 double bedroom and 1 triple room)*
Services & Amenities: *French and English are spoken; rooms cleaned every three days; tourist info; air conditioning; private parking*
Minimum stay: *2 nights*
Rates: €€
Credit cards: VISA MC *Bancomat*
Pets: 🚫

A villa with garden, decorated with functional pieces of furniture, which make the accommodation comfortable and cozy. It is in a suburb of Rome, connected to the center by transport. Three bedrooms are available. The bathroom is for the exclusive use of guests. Breakfast is served in the lounge.

223. • Bed & Breakfast Italia
Code R2138
via del Babuino
tel. 06 6878618, fax 06 6878619
info@bbitalia.it
www.bbitalia.it
Closed: varies

This apartment is located in a prestigious building near Piazza di Spagna, within 5 minutes' walk of the Trinità dei Monti and the subway station. Self-contained and furnished in a classic style with antiques, this accommodation consists in a double room with

TV. The bathroom is equipped with shower and is for the exclusive use of the guests. The kitchenette is equipped for breakfast.

Accommodation
Guestrooms: *1 double*
Services & Amenities: *French spoken; rooms cleaned every 3 days; tourist information*
Minimum stay: *2 nights*
Rates: €€
Credit cards: VISA MC *Bancomat*
Pets: not allowed

224. • Bed & Breakfast Italia
Code R2139
via del Pié di Marmo
tel. 06 6878618, fax 06 6878619
info@bbitalia.it
www.bbitalia.it
Closed: varies

This apartment, consisting in a double room with ensuite bathroom and a queen-size bed, is comfortable and charming accommodation. It is conveniently located for the center; the Pantheon and Piazza Navona are 5 minutes' walk away. Breakfast is served in the lounge. The hostess, who has two cats, provides information brochures on Rome on arrival. The bus stop is 50 m away.

Accommodation
Guestrooms: *1 double*
Services & Amenities: *French, English and Spanish are spoken; rooms cleaned every 3 days; tourist information; smokers welcome*
Minimum stay: *2 nights*
Rates: €€
Credit cards: VISA MC *Bancomat*
Pets: not allowed

225. • Bed & Breakfast Italia
Code R2140
via Donatello
tel. 06 6878618, fax 06 6878619
info@bbitalia.it
www.bbitalia.it
Closed: varies

Fifth-floor apartment in an elegant building in the central Flaminio district. The accommodation consists in a single and a double with queen-size bed, which are sunny and spacious. The bathroom with shower is for the exclusive use of guests. Breakfast is served in the kitchen. It is close to Villa Borghese. The tram stops just outside the house and goes in 4 minutes to Piazza del Popolo.

Accommodation
Guestrooms: *2 (1 single, 1 double)*
Services & Amenities: *French and English are spoken; rooms cleaned every 3 days; tourist info; smokers welcome; private parking*
Minimum stay: *2 nights*
Rates: €€€
Credit cards: VISA MC *Bancomat*
Pets: not allowed

Architectural detail of Villa Borghese

226. • Bed & Breakfast Italia
Code R2143
via di Quarto Peperini
tel. 06 6878618, fax 06 6878619
info@bbitalia.it
www.bbitalia.it
Closed: varies

A villa located in the Flaminio suburb, nestling in a large park. The owners offer guests two self-contained wings of the house; one with two double rooms, the other, with a little overhead gallery with twin beds and a double sofa bed on the lower level. All the rooms have their private bathroom with shower, TV and air conditioning, and boast elegant furnishings with valuable antiques. The breakfast is served in a large garden in front of the swimming pool or in the lounge.

Accommodation
Guestrooms: *4 (3 double bedrooms and 1 double)*
Services & Amenities: *rooms cleaned every 3 days; tourist information; baby-sitting service; air conditioning; private parking; smokers welcome*
Minimum stay: *2 nights*
Rates: €€
Credit cards: VISA MC *Bancomat*
Pets: no pets

227. • Bed & Breakfast Italia Tci 10%
Code R23
via Alberto Asquini
tel. 06 6878618, fax 06 6878619
info@bbitalia.it
www.bbitalia.it
Closed: varies

Accommodation
Guestrooms: *1 double*
Services & Amenities: *English spoken; rooms cleaned every 3 days; tourist information*
Minimum stay: *2 nights*
Rates: €
Credit cards: VISA MC *Bancomat*
Pets: no pets

Located in the suburban Montesacro district, this second-floor apartment is hosted by a modern building with a large open space in front. The guest accommodation consists in a double room, which is decorated in a simple, functional style. Your hostess serves the continental breakfast in the family kitchen. The bus, which stops 50 meters away, reaches the subway station in 10 minutes.

228. • Bed & Breakfast Italia
Code R25
via Madonna dei Monti
tel. 06 6878618, fax 06 6878619
info@bbitalia.it
www.bbitalia.it
Closed: varies

Right in the heart of Rome, in a side street off Via dei Fori Imperiali, this small apartment is a 10-minute walk from the Coliseum, the Celio park and the Circo Massimo. It is located on the third floor of an apartment building without elevator. The guest accommodation consists in a double with twin beds, furnished in a simple style. The bathroom is shared with the hostess. The subway station is 400 m away. Only 100 m away are buses for Termini railway station and Piazza Venezia.

Accommodation
Guestrooms: *1 double*
Services & Amenities: *English and German are spoken; rooms cleaned every 3 days; tourist information*
Minimum stay: *2 nights*
Rates: €
Credit cards: VISA MC *Bancomat*
Pets: no pets

229. • Bed & Breakfast Italia
Code R37
via Pio Emanuelli
tel. 06 6878618, fax 06 6878619
info@bbitalia.it
www.bbitalia.it
Closed: varies

This accommodation is on the fourth floor of a building with elevator, in the Laurentino district. The family has chosen cheerful colorful furnishings in shades of blue. This accommodation offers two bedrooms, both with twin beds. The bathroom is shared. The continental breakfast is served in the family kitchen. A cat lives in the apartment. The center can be reached in 20 minutes by subway, 500 m away.

Accommodation
Guestrooms: *2 doubles*
Services & Amenities: *English spoken; rooms cleaned every 3 days; tourist information; terrace*
Minimum stay: *2 nights*
Rates: €
Credit cards: VISA MC *Bancomat*
Pets: no

230. • Bed & Breakfast Italia
Code R38
via Mameli
tel. 06 6878618, fax 06 6878619
info@bbitalia.it
www.bbitalia.it
Closed: varies

This apartment is located in the old part of the Trastevere district. The style of furnishings is modern and functional. A double room is available. The bathroom is shared with the owners. The bus stop is within 5 minutes' walk of the accommodation and buses run to the old center in 10 minutes. The hostess gives the keys of the apartment to her guests, so they feel completely independent during their stay.

The Lungotevere seen from Ponte Umberto

Accommodation
Guestrooms: *1 double bedroom*
Services & Amenities: *French, English and Spanish are spoken; rooms cleaned every three days; tourist information*
Minimum stay: *2 nights*
Rates: €€
Credit cards: VISA MC *Bancomat*
Pets: no

231. • Bed & Breakfast Italia
Code R49
via Paolo Alberà
tel. 06 6878618, fax 06 6878619
info@bbitalia.it
www.bbitalia.it
Closed: varies

A large double room consisting in twin beds, TV, and a large balcony full of flowers is available. The bathroom, with tub and shower, is shared with the host family. It is located in the Appio district, not far from the subway station, which connects the area to the center in 15 minutes. Nearby are shops and the small outdoor markets of Via Sannio and San Giovanni are just a couple of subway stops away.

Accommodation
Guestrooms: *1 double*
Services & Amenities: *French and English are spoken; rooms cleaned every 3 days; tourist information; terrace*
Minimum stay: *2 nights*
Rates: €€
Credit cards: VISA MC *Bancomat*
Pets: no

232. • Bed & Breakfast Italia
Code R52
via G. Sacchi
tel. 06 6878618, fax 06 6878619
info@bbitalia.it
www.bbitalia.it
Closed: varies

The B&B is in the central Tras-tevere district on the third floor of a building with elevator. It offers one room with a single bed, decorated with soft colors just like the rest of the house. A predominance of white and blue creates a relaxing atmosphere. The bathroom with shower and Jacuzzi tub is shared with the family. The bus stop is 200 m from the apartment and it is just 9 minutes to Campo dei Fiori.

Accommodation
Guestrooms: *1 single*
Services & Amenities: *English and Spanish are spoken; rooms cleaned every 3 days; tourist information; terrace; smokers welcome*
Minimum stay: *2 nights*
Rates: €€
Credit cards: VISA MC *Bancomat*
Pets: not allowed

233. • Bed & Breakfast Italia
Code R55
via Paola
tel. 06 6878618, fax 06 6878619
info@bbitalia.it
www.bbitalia.it
Closed: varies

Accommodation
Guestrooms: *2 (1 single and 1 double bedroom)*
Services & Amenities: *French and English are spoken; rooms cleaned every 3 days; tourist information*
Minimum stay: *2 nights*
Rates: €€
Credit cards: VISA MC *Bancomat*
Pets: not allowed

The B&B is in the old center of the town within 5 minutes' walk of Fontana dei Fiumi in Piazza Navona and St. Peter's Square, both by Bernini. The family lives on the fourth floor of a building without elevator and offers guests one double and one single room, furnished in a simple, functional style. The bathroom is shared. The owners, who have been Roman for generations, offer an informal, homely stay.

234. • Bed & Breakfast Italia
Code R59
via Statonia
tel. 06 6878618, fax 06 6878619
info@bbitalia.it
www.bbitalia.it
Closed: varies

Accommodation
Guestrooms: *1 double*
Services & Amenities: *French and English are spoken; rooms cleaned every 3 days; complimentary tourist information; terrace*
Minimum stay: *2 nights*
Rates: €
Credit cards: VISA MC *Bancomat*
Pets: not allowed

The house is in a central position in the San Giovanni district. The elderly but lively hostess lives on the sixth floor of a building with elevator dating from the nineteenth century, where she welcomes guests in a friendly, comfortable atmosphere. She offers guests one double room with twin beds and TV. The bathroom is shared. The style of furnishings is simple. In the summer, breakfast is served on a large balcony. The subway station is 200 m away.

235. • Bed & Breakfast Italia
Code R63
via Caltagirone
tel. 06 6878618, fax 06 6878619
info@bbitalia.it
www.bbitalia.it
Closed: varies

The B&B is a small apartment in an old building in the central San Giovanni district. The accommodation, furnished in a functional, simple style, includes one double bedroom. The bathroom is shared. It is close to Piazza San Giovanni in Laterano, next to the Via Sannio outdoor market. The area is very well served by transport: several buses run to the various Rome districts.

ACCOMMODATION
Guestrooms: *1 double bedroom*
Services & Amenities: *English spoken; rooms cleaned every 3 days; complimentary tourist information; terrace; air conditioning*
Minimum stay: *2 nights*
Rates: €€
Credit cards: VISA MC *Bancomat*
Pets: not allowed

A ceremony in front of San Giovanni in Laterano.

236.• Bed & Breakfast Italia TCI 10%
Code R66
via Acusilao
tel. 06 6878618, fax 06 6878619
info@bbitalia.it
www.bbitalia.it
Closed: varies

ACCOMMODATION
Guestrooms: *1 double bedroom*
Services & Amenities: *French, English and Spanish are spoken; rooms cleaned every 3 days; complimentary tourist information*
Minimum stay: *2 nights*
Rates: €€
Credit cards: VISA MC *Bancomat*
Pets: allowed

A villa in the Casal Palocco residential area, 30 minutes from the center of Rome and 10 minutes from Ostia and the Lazio beaches. The double room is quiet and bright and the bathroom is shared with the owners. Guests can enjoy the extensive garden of the house, as well as the swimming pool and the communal tennis court. A car is recommended.

Old Ostia, a decorated aedicula and the remains of a statue.

237. • Bed & Breakfast Italia
Code R68
via Emanuele Filiberto
tel. 06 6878618, fax 06 6878619
info@bbitalia.it
www.bbitalia.it
Closed: varies

This second floor apartment is a 10-minute walk from the main Termini railway station and the Basilica of San Giovanni in Laterano. The four guestrooms are spacious, bright, simply but tastefully furnished: they feature wooden bedsteads and period bedside tables, blue and rose colored drapes. The bathroom with tub is shared. The area is very well served by transport: several buses run to the various Rome districts. The subway station is 200 m away.

ACCOMMODATION
Guestrooms: *4 (1 double, 3 triples)*
Services & Amenities: *rooms cleaned every 3 days; tourist information; smokers welcome*
Minimum stay: *2 nights*
Rates: €
Credit cards: VISA MC *Bancomat*
Pets: not allowed

238. • Bed & Breakfast Italia TCI 10%
Code R70
via Guglielmo Albimonte
tel. 06 6878618, fax 06 6878619
info@bbitalia.it
www.bbitalia.it
Closed: varies

A bright apartment on the sixth floor of a building with elevator, within 5 minutes' walk of Porta Maggiore. It includes one double room with TV, one twin-bedded room, both decorated in a simple and functional style, complete with a large balcony. The bathroom is shared with the owners. It well located for several buses going to the center. The tram takes 10 mins to reach Termini railway station.

Accommodation
Guestrooms: *2 (1 double bedroom and 1 double)*
Services & Amenities: *French and English spoken; rooms cleaned every 3 days; tourist info; smokers welcome*
Minimum stay: *2 nights*
Rates: €
Credit cards: VISA MC *Bancomat*
Pets: no

239. • Bed & Breakfast Italia
Code R71
via Val Cristallina
tel. 06 6878618, fax 06 6878619
info@bbitalia.it
www.bbitalia.it
Closed: varies

This apartment is on the first floor of a building with elevator, not far from the center, in the lively Montesacro district. The guestroom is a double with simple, colorful furnishings; the bathroom is shared. The hostess welcomes her guests in a tranquil, friendly atmosphere. A bus takes 20 minutes to reach the Termini railway station. Nearby are Viale Libia, Viale Etiopia and Viale Somalia, some of the city's main shopping streets.

Accommodation
Guestrooms: *1 double bedroom*
Services & Amenities: *French and English are spoken; rooms cleaned every 3 days; tourist information*
Minimum stay: *2 nights*
Rates: €
Credit cards: VISA MC *Bancomat*
Pets: no

240. • Bed & Breakfast Italia
Code R72
via Paola
tel. 06 6878618, fax 06 6878619
info@bbitalia.it
www.bbitalia.it
Closed: varies

A third-floor apartment in an old Roman building without elevator, dating from the seventeenth century with a view of Castel Sant' Angelo. The furnishings are modern. The guest accommodation consists in a double and a single room, both with TV, looking onto the courtyard and, therefore, quiet. The large bathroom with tub/shower is shared with the young host.

Accommodation
Guestrooms: *2 (1 single and 1 double bedroom)*
Services & Amenities: *English spoken; rooms cleaned every 3 days; tourist info; smokers welcome*
Minimum stay: *2 nights*
Rates: €€
Credit cards: VISA MC *Bancomat*
Pets: no

241. • Bed & Breakfast Italia
Code R73
via Fonteiana
tel. 06 6878618, fax 06 6878619
info@bbitalia.it
www.bbitalia.it
Closed: varies

Accommodation
Guestrooms: *3 (2 doubles, 1 triple)*
Services & Amenities: *English and Spanish are spoken; rooms cleaned every 3 days; tourist information; terrace; smokers welcome*
Minimum stay: *2 nights*
Rates: €
Credit cards: VISA MC *Bancomat*
Pets: no

A fourth-floor apartment in a building with elevator 100 m from the Villa Pamphili park. This wholly refurbished accommodation includes three rooms, of which two doubles and one triple, decorated with warm colors in shades of blue, green and orange and lit with spotlights, thus creating a modern and functional style. The large, colorful bathroom is shared by all the rooms. Breakfast is served in the room.

242. • Bed & Breakfast Italia TCI 10%
Code R74
via Strozzi
tel. 06 6878618, fax 06 6878619
info@bbitalia.it
www.bbitalia.it
Closed: varies

Accommodation
Guestrooms: *1 double*
Services & Amenities: *French and English are spoken; rooms cleaned every 3 days; tourist information; smokers welcome*
Minimum stay: *2 nights*
Rates: €€
Credit cards: VISA MC *Bancomat*
Pets: no

This apartment is on the fourth floor of a building with elevator, located in the Garbatella district, not far from the center. The double bedroom with twin beds is bright and decorated in a modern, functional style. The bathroom with tub and shower cubicle is shared with the owners. Breakfast is served in the lounge or on the large balcony, which is at the guests' disposal.

243. • Bed & Breakfast Italia
Code R75
via Rocca Sinibalda
tel. 06 6878618, fax 06 6878619
info@bbitalia.it
www.bbitalia.it
Closed: varies

Accommodation
Guestrooms: *1 double*
Services & Amenities: *English spoken; rooms cleaned every 3 days; complimentary tourist information; smokers welcome*
Minimum stay: *2 nights*
Rates: €
Credit cards: VISA MC *Bancomat*
Pets: no

This B&B is on the second floor of a building with elevator, in the Trieste residential district. It offers a double room, decorated in shades of green and yellow. The bathroom is shared with the family. The area is well served by transport; the tourist center can be reached in 15 mins, passing via the Termini railway station. Within a short distance of the apartment are viale Somalia, viale Libia and viale Eritrea.

244. • Bed & Breakfast Italia
Code R76
via Giulio Braida
tel. 06 6878618, fax 06 6878619
info@bbitalia.it
www.bbitalia.it
Closed: varies

The house is in a private street in the Balduina residential district. A double room is offered for B&B purposes, decorated in a modern and cheerful style. The bathroom is shared with the host family. In summer, breakfast

is served on the large balcony; in winter it is offered in the dining room. The area is connected to the center by bus and subway.

Accommodation
Guestrooms: *1 double bedroom*
Services & Amenities: *rooms cleaned every 3 days; tourist information; smokers welcome*
Minimum stay: *2 nights*
Rates: €
Credit cards: VISA MC *Bancomat*
Pets: not allowed

245. • Bed & Breakfast Italia
Code R77
via Vittoria Colonna
tel. 06 6878618, fax 06 6878619
info@bbitalia.it
www.bbitalia.it
Closed: varies

This fourth-floor apartment is in an elegant building without elevator. A double room is allocated for B&B purposes. The apartment furnishings reflect the yoga philosophy practiced and taught by the hostess. White and wood are the dominating elements. The

bathroom is shared with the family. The rich continental breakfast is served in the room. Courses on cooking and Italian culture can be organized on request. The family provides information about the town.

Accommodation
Guestrooms: *1 double bedroom*
Services & Amenities: *French spoken; rooms cleaned every 3 days; tourist information*
Minimum stay: *2 nights*
Rates: €
Credit cards: VISA MC *Bancomat*
Pets: not allowed

Sacrofano (Rome)

B&B Villa dei Pini
via Monte Caminetto 7
00060 Sacrofano (RM)
tel. and fax 06 9084202
info@mylifting.com
utenti.tripod.it/benat/index.html
Closed: January, February and November

This B&B is in a house dating from the '70s. It's surrounded by a 1,000 sq. m garden that the guests are welcome to enjoy. The house is located in a residential area in the Monte Caminetto locality, at the Via Flaminia's 19th km point, 10 mins by bus from Rome. The two guestrooms, which have modern furniture and a TV, are located on the first floor and last mansard floor, respectively. The continental breakfast is served in the room. The hosts particularly recommend

taking a boat ride on Lake Bracciano, which is only 30 mins away by car

Accommodation
Guestrooms: *2 double bedrooms, also single occupancy, private bath; additional bed on request*
Services & Amenities: *French, English and Spanish are spoken; rooms cleaned every 3 days; tourist information; garden; smokers welcome; private parking*
Rates: *single €€, double €€€, Additional bed supplement €. Discounts for children -10%*
Credit cards: *not accepted*
Pets: not allowed

San Felice Circeo (Latina)

Isola di Eéa
Pyung Cha Min
via della Vasca Moresca 4
04017 San Felice Circeo (LT)
tel. 0773 548583
fax 06 5742839
mob. 339 8211502, 333 9738222
gf.ferretti@net-solution.tv
www.b-et-b.com
Open: 1 April to 30 September

Accommodation
Guestrooms: *6 doubles with private bath*
Services & Amenities: *French, English and Korean are spoken; rooms cleaned every day; complimentary tourist information; kitchenette; terrace; garden; smokers welcome; private parking*
Minimum stay: *1 week in August, 2 nights in other periods*
Rates: *single €€€€, double €€€€. Reduced prices for advance bookings (1 month).*
Credit cards: *not accepted*
Pets:

This B&B is in a villa built by the architect Sartogo. It's located in the heart of the Circeo promontory, in a park that has 6,000 sq. meters of Mediterranean scrub. The villa dominates the sea and the many natural pools among the rocks. Breakfast, which is actually a brunch, consists of fresh products obtained from reliable farms, as well as such oriental ingredients as soya and tofu.

• **Bed & Breakfast Italia**
Code L154
tel. 06 6878618, fax 06 6878619
info@bbitalia.it
www.bbitalia.it
Closed: varies

Accommodation
Guestrooms: *6 doubles*
Services & Amenities: *rooms cleaned every 3 days; tourist information; smokers welcome*
Minimum stay: *2 nights*
Rates: €€
Credit cards: VISA MC *Bancomat*
Pets:

This accommodation consists in six double rooms simply and comfortably furnished, with a communal garden where the rich breakfast is served. Bathrooms with shower. An extra bed can be added if needed. On request the family cooks local produce for meals. It is 300 m from the sea and a stone's throw from the old center, with its shops, restaurants, pubs and bars.

Santa Marinella (Rome)

Danny
Danny Englaro
via Leonardo da Vinci 10
00058 Santa Marinella (RM)
tel. 0766 510538, mob. 339 8831548
danny.rion@libero.it
Closed: 10 January to 15 February and 10 October to 10 December

Accommodation
Guestrooms: *3 (2 doubles and 1 single, which can be combined with 1 of the doubles, with private bath); additional bed on request*
Services & Amenities: *English and Spanish are spoken; rooms cleaned every 3 days; tourist information; kitchen use by request; terrace; garden; smokers welcome; private parking*
Minimum stay: *2 nights*
Rates: *double €€, triple €€-€€€, Additional bed supplement €. Discounts for extended stays*
Credit cards: *not accepted*
Pets:

This B&B, just a 10-minute walk to the center of Santa Mannella, is on the 1st floor of a small, 1970's villa located in a residential area. This apartment, which has an independent entrance, consists of three rooms, two bathrooms, a living room with TV and a fireplace, and a large terrace, as well as an equipped kitchen, which is where the buffet breakfast is served. The house, which is only 100 meters from the sea, is surrounded by a large garden, part of which is open to the guests.

• **Bed & Breakfast Italia**
Code L131
tel. 06 6878618, fax 06 6878619
info@bbitalia.it
www.bbitalia.it
Closed: varies

This apartment offers two doubles, one of which has double bed, and a single; the private bathroom with shower is shared. The house is surrounded by a well-kept garden where breakfast is served in summer. In winter, it is served in the lounge. Fast and frequent train service to Rome. The hosts provides useful information on places to visit.

ACCOMMODATION
Guestrooms: *3 (1 single, 1 double bedroom and 1 double)*
Services & Amenities: *rooms cleaned every 3 days; tourist info*
Minimum stay: *2 nights*
Rates: €€
Credit cards: VISA MC *Bancomat*
Pets: no

SEZZE (LATINA)

• **Bed & Breakfast Italia** TCI 10%
Code L038
tel. 06 6878618, fax 06 6878619
info@bbitalia.it
www.bbitalia.it
Closed: varies

A small detached house in Sezze, in close proximity to Latina. This accommodation offers a double bedroom, carefully furnished, with private bathroom with shower and includes a separate entrance that opens onto the well-kept garden. The lady of the house welcomes her guests in a homely and informal atmosphere.

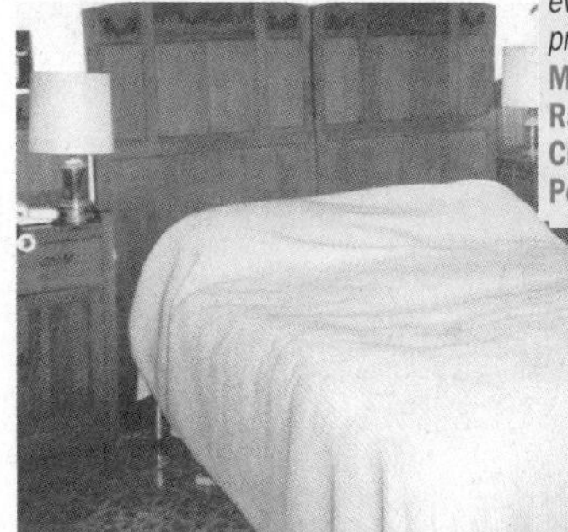

ACCOMMODATION
Guestrooms: *1 double bedroom*
Services & Amenities: *French and English are spoken; rooms cleaned every 3 days; tourist information; private parking*
Minimum stay: *2 nights*
Rates: €€
Credit cards: VISA MC *Bancomat*
Pets: yes

TIVOLI (ROME)

Al Seminario
via Teobaldi 2
00019 Tivoli (RM)
tel. 0774 318330, mob. 338 5960527
custer@libero.it
digilander.iol.it/alseminario
Closed: 5 November to 5 December, 1 August to 15 September and 15 to 31 January

This post-WW2 condominium located in the old center of Tivoli, near Villa d'Este and Villa Gregoriana, has two guestrooms with TV, a bathroom and a beautiful terrace. The continental breakfast is served in the dining room. The hostess and her son will gladly provide useful tourist information and advice.

ACCOMMODATION
Guestrooms: *2 (1 double with shared bath and 1 double bedroom with private bath, also single occupancy); additional bed on request*
Services & Amenities: *English spoken; rooms cleaned every three days; complimentary tourist information; baby-sitting service; terrace; smokers welcome*
Rates: *single €-€€, double €€-€€€*
Credit cards: *not accepted*
Pets: yes

A mosaic conserved in Villa Adriana, Tivoli.

B&B La Panoramica

Giuseppina Malagreca
viale Arnaldi 45
00019 Tivoli (RM)
tel. and fax 0774 335700
mob. 338 4971221
Closed: January

Accommodation
Guestrooms: *3 (2 double bedrooms and 1 triple room, also single occupancy, 1 with private bath and 2 with shared bath); additional bed on request*
Services & Amenities: *French, Englishand German are spoken; rooms cleaned every day; tourist information; lunch & dinner reservations; smokers welcome*
Rates: *single €€, double €€-€€€. Additional bed supplement €. Children under 6 free*
Credit cards: *not accepted*
Pets:

This B&B is on the 2nd-floor of a small, late 19th-C villa located in a green, panoramic residential area in the center of Tivoli, just a short distance from Villa D'Este. Guests have three rooms with an independent entrance. Breakfast is either served on the large terrace that provides a splendid view of Rome, or in the family living room, which has period furniture, a TV, a piano and a telescope. Guests are welcome to use this room at any time during the day. The family is at the disposal of the guests for providing guided visits of Rome. Guests can be privately driven to and from the airport or train station. The host also offers the guests the possibility of having lunch or dinner in the B&B's designated restaurant.

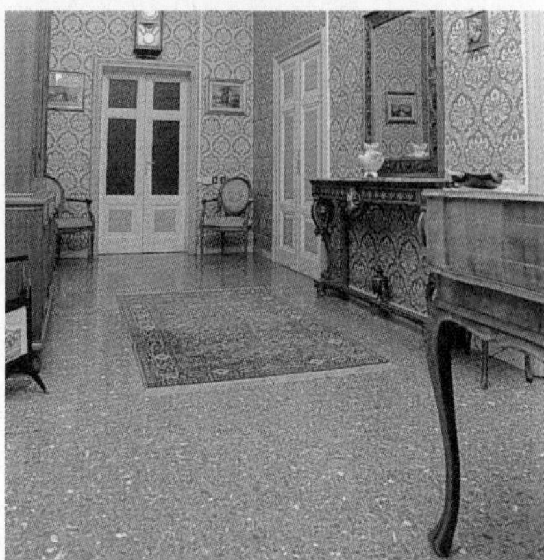

• Bed & Breakfast Italia
Code L007
tel. 06 6878618, fax 06 6878619
info@bbitalia.it
www.bbitalia.it
Closed: varies

Accommodation
Guestrooms: *6 doubles*
Services & Amenities: *French and English are spoken; rooms cleaned every 3 days; complimentary tourist information; private parking*
Minimum stay: *2 nights*
Rates: *€€*
Credit cards: *VISA MC Bancomat*
Pets:

A modern villa surrounded by a well-tended garden of olive trees. The six large sunny double rooms with wide balcony and a scenic view are furnished with exquisite taste; an extra bed for children can be added. The rooms are in an attic-wing of the villa with a separate entrance. An outdoor swimming pool and parking are available. The atmosphere is homely and informal.

• Bed & Breakfast Italia
Code L141
tel. 06 6878618, fax 06 6878619
info@bbitalia.it
www.bbitalia.it
Closed: varies

This B&B is located in an apartment, furnished in a cheerful modern style. The accommodation consists in a triple bedroom, with a double and a single bed. It shares the bathroom with the family. Private parking available for the guests. The lady of the house offers a baby-sitting service on request. Rome is 20 km away and can be reached by bus or train in 40 minutes.

Accommodation
Guestrooms: *1 triple room*
Services & Amenities: *French and English are spoken; rooms cleaned every 3 days; tourist info; baby-sitting service; smokers welcome*
Minimum stay: *2 nights*
Rates: *€*
Credit cards: *VISA MC Bancomat*
Pets:

• Bed & Breakfast Italia
Code L148
tel. 06 6878618, fax 06 6878619
info@bbitalia.it
www.bbitalia.it
Closed: varies

Accommodation
Guestrooms: *2 doubles*
Services & Amenities: *French and English are spoken; rooms cleaned every 3 days; tourist information; bike rental; private parking*
Minimum stay: *2 nights*
Rates: €
Credit cards: VISA MC *Bancomat*

A small and sunny attic wing in a villa surrounded by a well-kept garden. This accommodation consists in two double rooms – one of which has a double bed – and a shared bathroom with shower. The lady of the house provides a shuttle service to and from the nearest station on request. Rome can be reached by bus in 40 minutes.

Trevignano Romano (Rome)

Casa Plazzi
Gianni Plazzi
via Olivetello 23
00069 Trevignano Romano (RM)
tel. 06 9997597, mob. 335 6756250
fax 06 900910196
welcome@casaplazzi.com
www.casaplazzi.com
Open all year

This B&B is in a large, recently-built villa located in Trevignano, on the shore of Lake Bracciano. It has a swimming pool, a dressing room and a deck chair, and is immersed in the green of a large garden. Guests have a few comfortable rooms – one of which has a fireplace and a terrace with a view of the lake – and a small apartment with a kitchen. The Italian breakfast is served on the veranda that faces the lake. On request, guests can have meals and laundry service. Furthermore, Trevignano has a number of sports organizations for going sailing, playing tennis, going horseback riding, practicing archery or playing golf.

Accommodation
Guestrooms: *6 (5 double bedrooms, also single occupancy, and 1 triple room, with private bath)* ♿
Services & Amenities: *English spoken; rooms cleaned every three days; tourist information; lunch & dinner reservations; terrace; garden; private parking*
Rates: *single €€€, double €€€€, triple €€€€*
Credit cards: *not accepted*
Pets: not allowed

• Bed & Breakfast Italia
Code L023
tel. 06 6878618, fax 06 6878619
info@bbitalia.it
www.bbitalia.it
Closed: varies

This small romantic B&B is on the ancient Via Cassia in the center of the picturesque hamlet of Trevignano Romano. This apartment is entirely at the disposal of guests; it is carefully furnished with an attic roof and exposed beams, and offers a double bedroom, a pullout sofa in the lounge with fireplace on the lower floor, from where a wrought iron staircase leads to the bedroom, and a bathroom with shower.

Accommodation
Guestrooms: *2 double bedrooms*
Services & Amenities: *English spoken; rooms cleaned every 3 days; complimentary tourist information*
Minimum stay: *2 nights*
Rates: €€
Credit cards: VISA MC *Bancomat*
Pets: not allowed

Velletri (Rome)

B&B In Villa
Tommaso Conti
via del Boschetto 32
00049 Velletri (RM)
tel. 06 9632952, 800 252999
www.velletri.it/b&b
Closed: Mondays and Thuesdays

This B&B is located 500 meters from the center of Velletri. Guests have three rooms, two of which face the same terrace. The continental breakfast is generally served in the family living room, which has a TV and is open to the guests. When the weather's nice, breakfast can be served in the large garden.

Accommodation
Guestrooms: *3 doubles, also single occupancy, with private bath; additional bed on request*
Services & Amenities: *rooms cleaned every day; terrace; garden; smokers welcome; private parking*
Rates: *single €€, double €€. Additional bed supplement €. Discounts for extended stays -10%*
Credit cards: *not accepted*
Pets:

Santa Maria dell'Orto
contrada Paganico
00049 Velletri (RM)
tel. 06 9634460
fax 06 9626022
mocivita@tin.it reals@libero.it
Closed: varies

This B&B is in a small, independent, 1970's villa located on the edge of town, on the southern side of the Albani Hills. The hosts live on the 1st-floor and the guestrooms are on the 2nd-floor and in the mansard. The living room and dining room are on the ground floor. All the rooms have plain, functional furniture. The Italian breakfast is served in the dining room.

Accommodation
Guestrooms: *3 doubles (also single occupancy) with private bath outside the room; additional bed on request* ♿
Services & Amenities: *French and English are spoken; rooms cleaned every day; tourist information; baby-sitting service; kitchen use by request; terrace; garden; smokers welcome; private parking*
Minimum stay: *3 nights*
Rates: *single €€, double €€€. Discounts for children -25% and extended stays*
Credit cards: *not accepted*
Pets:

The Torre del Trivio, Tivoli.

• Bed & Breakfast Italia
Code L160
tel. 06 6878618, fax 06 6878619
info@bbitalia.it
www.bbitalia.it
Closed: varies

The B&B is in a villa surrounded by an extensive park. It has three double rooms: one with twin beds and the others with double beds, all with private bathroom with shower; three triple rooms: one with single beds and private bathroom with shower, the others with a double bed and a single sharing one bathroom. It is furnished with country-style antiques, terracotta flooring, and precious carpets. Other facilities include Internet, fax, baby-sitting service, and private parking.

Accommodation
Guestrooms: *6 (2 double bedrooms, 1 double and 3 triple rooms)*
Services & Amenities: *French and English are spoken; rooms cleaned every three days; complimentary tourist information; baby-sitting service; Internet access; smokers welcome; private parking*
Minimum stay: *2 nights*
Rates: *€€*
Credit cards: VISA MC *Bancomat*
Pets:

• Bed & Breakfast Italia
Code L161
tel. 06 6878618, fax 06 6878619
info@bbitalia.it
www.bbitalia.it
Closed: varies

This B&B is in a villa surrounded by a garden. Guests may use two single rooms: one with private bathroom with tub/shower, the other with shared bathroom; two double rooms, one with private bathroom, the other with shared bathroom; and a quadruple room with a double bed and two single beds, with private bathroom. A large lounge is at the disposal of guests. The rooms are elegantly furnished with antiques. The hosts offer a baby-sitting service, private parking, fax and phone facilities.

ACCOMMODATION
Guestrooms: *5 (2 single, 2 double bedrooms and 1 quadruple room)*
Services & Amenities: *French and English are spoken; rooms cleaned every three days; tourist information; baby-sitting service; Internet access; smokers welcome; private parking*
Minimum stay: *2 nights*
Rates: €
Credit cards: VISA MC *Bancomat*
Pets:

VETRALLA (VITERBO)

Bed & Breakfast Vetralla
Enrica Sanetti and Gino Ferri
Ufficio Turistico
01019 Vetralla (VT)
tel. 0761 460006
fax 0761 460475
ufficioturistico@thunder.it
www.comune.vetralla.vt.it
Open all year

The commune of Vetralla has united about 15 B&Bs that amount to a total of 60 beds. A few of these are in the town, while others are in the countryside. However, they all provide friendly hospitality in comfortable, tranquil rooms that have independent entrances and private bathrooms. Special arrangements can be made for guests who are traveling with dogs or horses.

ACCOMMODATION
Guestrooms: *60 beds in doubles or triple rooms with private bath; additional bed on request* ♿
Services & Amenities: *rooms cleaned every 3 days; tourist information; horse-riding excursions; garden; smokers welcome; parking*
Rates: *single €, double €€. Discounts for children and extended stays*
Credit cards: *not accepted*
Pets:

La Vecchia Stalla
Giuseppina Pippi Cianfana
01019 Vetralla (VT)
tel. 0761 481750, mob. 338 5694995
info@personalguide.it
www.personalguide.it
• Friendly Home-Gli Amici del B&B
tel. 02 860147, fax 02 875860
friendlymilano@dada.it
tel. and fax 011 9536376
fhrivoli@virgilio.it
Closed: 15 January to 15 February and July-August

This B&B is in what used to be the stalls of this restructured, early 19th-C farmhouse surrounded by lots of greenery. The stalls were converted into living quarters without, however, making them lose their original rustic character, which is reflected in their very nice furnishings. Breakfast is served in the kitchen of the apartment reserved for the guests. The hostess is at the guests' disposal for visiting the surrounding area.

ACCOMMODATION
Guestrooms: *1 apartment (4 beds)*
Services & Amenities: *English spoken; rooms cleaned every three days; complimentary tourist information; kitchen use by request; garden; smokers welcome; private parking*
Rates: *€€-€€€ per person. Children under 2 free. Discounts for extended stays*
Credit cards: *not accepted*
Pets:

Viterbo

Bed & Breakfast Farinella

Maurizio Makovec
via Capodistria 14
01100 Viterbo
tel. and fax 0761 304784
mob. 339 3655617
makcvt@yahoo.it
www.villafarinella.it
Open: March to November

This B&B is in a transformed, 18th-century, manor villa located just 2 kilometers from the old center of Viterbo. The hostess, who loves gardening, and her son, who likes tourism, preserved the original structure,

together with its period furniture and romantic tranquil atmosphere. The bathrooms have been completely restructured. The Italian breakfast is served in the 19th-century living room. The adjoining farm dépendance, which used to be a storage barn, has been converted into an independent apartment. The large garden has very old chestnut trees.

Accommodation
Guestrooms: *3 double bedrooms, with private bath; additional bed on request*
Services & Amenities: *English spoken; rooms cleaned every 3 days; tourist info; terrace; garden; smokers welcome; private parking*
Rates: *single €€€, double €€€, triple €€€. Discounts for children and extended stays*
Credit cards: *not accepted*
Pets:

Il Mandorlo

Alberto and Paola Cappelli
strada Tuscanese 36, località Santa Caterina
01100 Viterbo
tel. 0761 250705, 051 330472
mob. 335 7057067
bebelmandorlo@libero.it
space.tin.it/clubnet/hbfcap
Closed: 7 January to Easter holidays

This B&B's guestrooms, with their modern and classic furniture, are on the ground floor of a farmhouse that's immersed in the countryside along the Tuscanese, just 4 km from Viterbo and 300 m from the Terme dei Papi complex, the natural thermal baths that permit free access. This is a good place to start visits to Villa Lante, Lake Bolsena, Tarquinia and Vulci. The place also provides hospitality for about ten cats. Guests must please only smoke outside.

Accommodation
Guestrooms: *2 (1 double bedroom and 1 single, with private bath)* ♿
Services & Amenities: *French spoken; rooms cleaned every 3 days; tourist information; baby-sitting service; kitchenette; bike rental; garden; private parking*
Rates: *single €€, double €€€. Discounts for extended stays*
Credit cards: *not accepted*
Pets:

La Meridiana

Strada Cimina km 3500
01100 Viterbo
tel. 0761 308282, 0761 306230
fax 0761 304004
vecchiameridiana@libero.it
www.lameridianastrana.com
• Friendly Home-Gli Amici del B&B
tel. 02 860147, fax 02 875860
friendlymilano@dada.it
tel. and fax 011 9536376
fhrivoli@virgilio.it
Closed: 9 January to 9 April

This B&B is in a restructured, 1690 farmhouse located just outside Viterbo. It's in the middle of a farm that has olive and fruit trees. The guestrooms are nicely furnished with period furniture and restored items. Besides a swimming pool, there's also a riding school on the property that also organizes excursions on horseback.

Accommodation
Guestrooms: *5 (3 double bedrooms, 1 double and 1 triple room, also single occupancy, with private bath)*
Services & Amenities: *French and English are spoken; rooms cleaned every day; tourist info; kitchenette; horse-riding excursions; garden; smokers welcome; private parking*
Rates: *single €€, double €€€*
Credit cards: *accepted*
Pets:

Villa Lucia
Francesca and Alessandra Corbucci
strada Roncone 7/B
01100 Viterbo
tel. 0761 341975
mob. 335 7565013, 328 7646728
rancy@libero.it
Closed: December to February

This B&B is in a small, recently-built villa located in a residential area, just 1 km from the city's old center. Guests have rooms with independent entrances, as well as a large living room with a TV and a fireplace. The host family, which consists of four persons who love their collection of very friendly cats and dogs, provides a continental breakfast that includes different types of pastries.

Accommodation
Guestrooms: *2 doubles with private bath; additional bed on request*
Services & Amenities: *French and English are spoken; rooms cleaned every day; tourist information; baby-sitting service; garden; smokers welcome; private parking*
Rates: *single €€, double €€€. Discounts for children and extended stays*
Credit cards: *not accepted*
Pets: *not allowed*

• Bed & Breakfast Italia
Code L058
tel. 06 6878618, fax 06 6878619
info@bbitalia.it
www.bbitalia.it
Closed: varies

TCI 10%

A villa in the old center of Viterbo, which has an important Etruscan museum, on Via Francigena, once a place of transit for pilgrims returning from Rome. The two double rooms, one with a double bed and one with bunk beds, have TV and a large balcony. The surrounding park is exclusively for the use of guests. Breakfast is served under a gazebo or by the fireplace in the large lounge. Homely and cozy atmosphere. The Etruscan necropolis, the Borgia Castle, the Cathedral, Santa Sivinilla catacombs, Lake Vico are well worth a visit.

Accommodation
Guestrooms: *2 (1 double bedroom and 1 double)*
Services & Amenities: *French and English are spoken; rooms cleaned every three days; complimentary tourist information; terrace*
Minimum stay: *2 nights*
Rates: *€€*
Credit cards: *Visa MC Bancomat*
Pets: *allowed*

Zagarolo (Rome)

• Bed & Breakfast Italia
Code L157
tel. 06 6878618, fax 06 6878619
info@bbitalia.it
www.bbitalia.it
Closed: varies

A country house set in 500 square meters of parkland with high trunk trees, cyclamens and daisies. Guest accommodation consists in two rooms, one with twin beds and one with double bed, with the option of an additional fold-up bed for children under two. Each room has its own private bathroom with shower. Zagarolo is famous for its wine festival, held in September.

Accommodation
Guestrooms: *2 doubles*
Services & Amenities: *French spoken; rooms cleaned every 3 days; tourist information; baby-sitting service; bike rental; smokers welcome; private parking*
Minimum stay: *2 nights*
Rates: *€€*
Credit cards: *Visa MC Bancomat*
Pets: *not allowed*

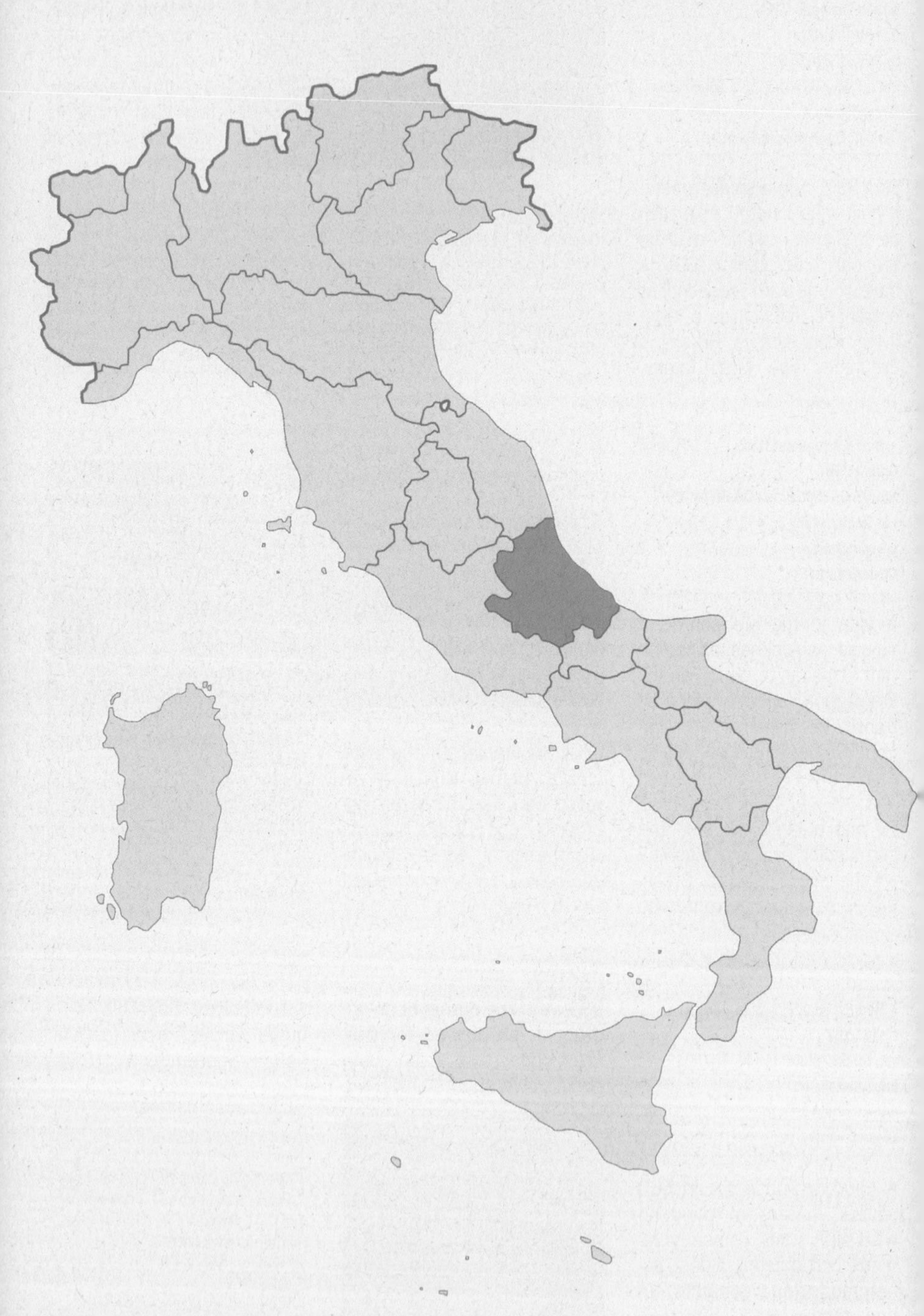

Abruzzo

ANCARANO (TERAMO)

• **Bed & Breakfast Italia**
Code AB10
tel. 06 6878618, fax 06 6878619
info@bbitalia.it
www.bbitalia.it
Closed: varies

This B&B is located on the southern side of the Tronto valley. This farmhouse is situated on a hill and is country style with elegant furnishings. The accommodation offers four rooms; the furniture is in perfect keeping with the rest of the house: four-poster beds, timber-beamed ceilings, matching bedspreads and curtains. The village of Ancarano is 15 km from San Benedetto del Tronto and Ascoli Piceno.

ACCOMMODATION
Guestrooms: *4 (2 singles, 2 doubles); additional bed on request*
Services & Amenities: *English and French are spoken; rooms cleaned every 3 days; tourist information; smokers welcome; private parking*
Minimum stay: *2 nights*
Rates: €€
Credit cards: VISA MC *Bancomat*
Pets: no

ATRI (TERAMO)

• **Bed & Breakfast Italia**
Code AB6
tel. 06 6878618, fax 06 6878619
info@bbitalia.it
www.bbitalia.it
Closed: varies

This farm-holiday residence in the province of Teramo offers a panoramic view of the vineyards and olive groves of the Maiella mountains. The accommodation offers two double and one triple room, all furnished in the rustic style of old farmhouses. Guests can enjoy the services offered by the owners: a swimming pool and outings on horseback and a riding-school with instructor. The seaside resort of Silvi Marina is just 6 km away.

ACCOMMODATION
Guestrooms: *3 (2 doubles, 1 triple)*
Services & Amenities: *English and French are spoken; rooms cleaned every 3 days; tourist information; horse-riding excursions; educational courses by request*
Minimum stay: *2 nights*
Rates: €
Credit cards: VISA MC *Bancomat*
Pets: yes

Cagnano Amiterno (L'Aquila)

• **Bed & Breakfast Italia**
Code AB2
tel. 06 6878618, fax 06 6878619
info@bbitalia.it
www.bbitalia.it
Closed: varies

This B&B is located 25 km from the Campofelice mountain ski resort, in a small independent house. The accommodation consists in a triple room furnished in a simple, comfortable style with a view of the Abruzzi Apennines. Meals can be booked at the nearby farm restaurant. Guests can also go on trips organized by the "Riserva della Cascina".

Accommodation
Guestrooms: *1 triple room*
Services & Amenities: *English and Spanish are spoken; rooms cleaned every 3 days; tourist information; private parking*
Minimum stay: *2 nights*
Rates: €
Credit cards: VISA MC *Bancomat*
Pets: allowed

Castel di Sangro (L'Aquila)

• **Bed & Breakfast Italia**
Code AB11
tel. 06 6878618, fax 06 6878619
info@bbitalia.it
www.bbitalia.it
Closed: varies

TCI 10%

This B&B is located in the National Park of Abruzzi, near the Roccaraso mountain ski resort, and consists in three independent cottages each with a double bedroom or a triple. Rooms are furnished in a simple and comfortable style. In the area there are several tennis courts, a water park, a lake for anglers, soccer fields and a sports hall. Nature lovers can go on excursions within the park.

Accommodation
Guestrooms: *3 doubles or triples*
Services & Amenities: *rooms cleaned every 3 days; complimentary tourist information; smokers welcome; private parking*
Minimum stay: *2 nights*
Rates: €€
Credit cards: VISA MC *Bancomat*
Pets: not allowed

Loreto Aprutino (Pescara)

• **Bed & Breakfast Italia**
Code AB13
tel. 06 6878618, fax 06 6878619
info@bbitalia.it
www.bbitalia.it
Closed: varies

This B&B is in a building located in the center of the medieval hamlet. The accommodation comprises a single and a double room, decorated in pastel colors, period furniture and wrought-iron beds. The internal garden, where breakfast is served in summertime, is a fine example of 13th-century architecture. Pescara is 25 km and Montesilvano 15 km away.

Accommodation
Guestrooms: *2 (1 single, 1 double)*
Services & Amenities: *English and French are spoken; rooms cleaned every 3 days; tourist information; terrace; private parking*
Minimum stay: *2 nights*
Rates: €€
Credit cards: VISA MC *Bancomat*
Pets: not allowed

ORICOLA (L'AQUILA)

• Bed & Breakfast Italia
Code AB4
tel. 06 6878618, fax 06 6878619
info@bbitalia.it
www.bbitalia.it
Closed: varies

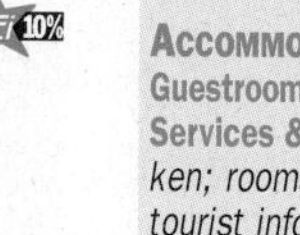

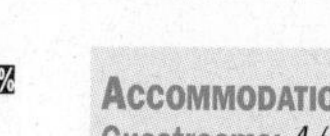
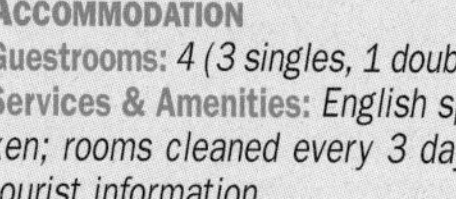

ACCOMMODATION
Guestrooms: *4 (3 singles, 1 double)*
Services & Amenities: *English spoken; rooms cleaned every 3 days; tourist information*
Minimum stay: *2 nights*
Rates: €€
Credit cards: VISA MC *Bancomat*
Pets: not allowed

Located in a medieval hamlet in the province of l'Aquila, this B&B occupies a wing of a castle overlooking the village. The accommodation consists in three singles and one double-bedded room with period country style furniture and coffered ceilings. Two bathrooms with shower/tub are at guests' disposal. In summer, the generous breakfast is served on the large balcony surrounding the house.

PESCARA

Maria Burlini B&B
Maria Burlini
via Campo Felice 13
65125 Pescara
tel. and fax 085 413861
m.burlini@virgilio.it
Open all year

ACCOMMODATION
Guestrooms: *1 double bedroom, also single occupancy, private bath*
Services & Amenities: *rooms cleaned every 3 days; tourist information; smokers welcome; Internet access; terrace; garden; private parking*
Minimum stay: *2 nights*
Rates: *single €–€€, double €€–€€€. Children under 3 free*
Credit cards: *not accepted*
Pets: not allowed

The B&B is in a small villa with garden, situated in a quiet, residential area. Guests have a room in which to relax, as well as a large terrace, which is where the hostess serves breakfast consisting of pastries and natural marmalades. On request, a crib for infants can also be provided. Interesting places to visit in the heart of the old city include the house in which Gabriele D'Annunzio was born.

• Bed & Breakfast Italia
Code AB12
tel. 06 6878618, fax 06 6878619
info@bbitalia.it
www.bbitalia.it
Closed: varies

ACCOMMODATION
Guestrooms: *2 (1 single, 1 double)*
Services & Amenities: *English, French and Spanish are spoken; rooms cleaned every 3 days; tourist information; baby-sitting service; bike rental; horse-riding excursions; air conditioning; private parking*
Minimum stay: *2 nights*
Rates: €€
Credit cards: VISA MC *Bancomat*
Pets: not allowed

Art Nouveau villa built on a baronial estate located in the Pescara hills, 500 m from the town center, surrounded by a large garden of centuries-old trees. Guest-rooms, a single and a double, are furnished in a simple and comfortable style. In the warmer months breakfast is served on the large terrace with solarium. This B&B is just 200 m from the railway station. Toddlers welcome. Baby-sitting service available.

Pescocostanzo (L'Aquila)

Pescocostanzo
• Dolce Sonno Bed & Breakfast
tel. 081 2451317
mob. 338 4916755
b.dolcesonno@tiscalinet.it
Open all year

This B&B is located at the town's entrance and provides a nice view of the typical mountain landscape. On the first floor of the two-story guest apartment there's a living room with a fireplace and a TV, an equipped kitchen corner, a double bed, and a bathroom with a shower. The second floor has a mansard with four beds. All the rooms have warm, mountain-style wooden furniture. The town, which is only 15 minutes from the ski slopes, also makes an ideal base for going on summer excursions.

Accommodation
Guestrooms: *2 (1 double bedroom, 1 quadruple, private bath)*
Services & Amenities: *English spoken; rooms cleaned every three days; complimentary tourist information; kitchenette*
Minimum stay: *1 week*
Rates: *€€€–€€€€. Children under 3 free*
Credit cards: *not accepted*
Pets:

Pescasseroli (L'Aquila)

• Bed & Breakfast Italia
Code AB3
tel. 06 6878618, fax 06 6878619
info@bbitalia.it
www.bbitalia.it
Closed: varies

Accommodation
Guestrooms: *3 (2 doubles, 1 triple)*
Services & Amenities: *English and French are spoken; rooms cleaned every three days; complimentary tourist information; horse-riding excursions; private parking*
Minimum stay: *2 nights*
Rates: *€€*
Credit cards: VISA MC *Bancomat*
Pets:

A villa located in Pescasseroli, 1 km from the ski runs, surrounded by a garden exclusively at guests' disposal. This accommodation offers two doubles and one triple room with the option of an extra bed, all furnished in a simple and elegant style. A sports center with tennis courts and a swimming-pool easily reached nearby. Trekking on horseback is organized by the nearby riding-school.

Pianella (Pescara)

• Bed & Breakfast Italia TCI 10%
Code AB9
tel. 06 6878618
fax 06 6878619
info@bbitalia.it
www.bbitalia.it
Closed: varies

Accommodation
Guestrooms: *3 (2 doubles, 1 triple)*
Services & Amenities: *English and French are spoken; rooms cleaned every 3 days; tourist information; bike rental; private parking*
Minimum stay: *2 nights*
Rates: *€€*
Credit cards: VISA MC *Bancomat*
Pets:

This B&B is hosted by an 19th-century mill, restored preserving its original structure, and located 20 kilometers from Pescara. The accommodation consists in three rooms, two doubles and a triple, with prestigious

furnishings in inlaid wood; they have no heating and are generally used in summer. This B&B is a few kilometers from the Pescara railway station and airport. A private car park is available. Guests can also borrow bicycles to explore the surrounding area.

Sant'Omero (Teramo)

• **Bed & Breakfast Italia**
Code AB5
tel. 06 6878618, fax 06 6878619
info@bbitalia.it
www.bbitalia.it
Closed: varies

A two-story villa that overlooks the countryside on the Marche-Abruzzi border. The upper floor is exclusively at the disposal of guests. The accommodation consists of three double rooms, all boasting nineteenth-century furnishings. In summertime, breakfast is served in the surrounding garden which faces the Marche hills. Easily reached nearby, besides the Adriatic Coast, are the towns of Fermo, Offida and Ascoli Piceno.

Accommodation
Guestrooms: *3 doubles*
Services & Amenities: *English and French are spoken; rooms cleaned every three days; tourist information; private parking*
Minimum stay: *2 nights*
Rates: €€
Credit cards: VISA MC *Bancomat*
Pets

Vasto (Chieti)

• **Bed & Breakfast Italia** Tci 10%
Code AB8
tel. 06 6878618, fax 06 6878619
info@bbitalia.it
www.bbitalia.it
Closed: varies

Two-story house in the middle of a park with a sea view. Guest accommodation includes a double and a single room, both with TV and safe, all with modern furnishings. In summer months, the rich continental breakfast is served on the large balcony overlooking the vineyards and orchard; in wintertime, in the kitchen by the fireplace. Babysitting service available. Guests can also borrow bicycles to visit the surrounding area.

Accommodation
Guestrooms: *2 (1 single, 1 double)*
Services & Amenities: *English and French are spoken; rooms cleaned every 3 days; tourist information; baby-sitting service; bike rental; private parking*
Minimum stay: *2 nights*
Rates: €€
Credit cards: VISA MC *Bancomat*
Pets:

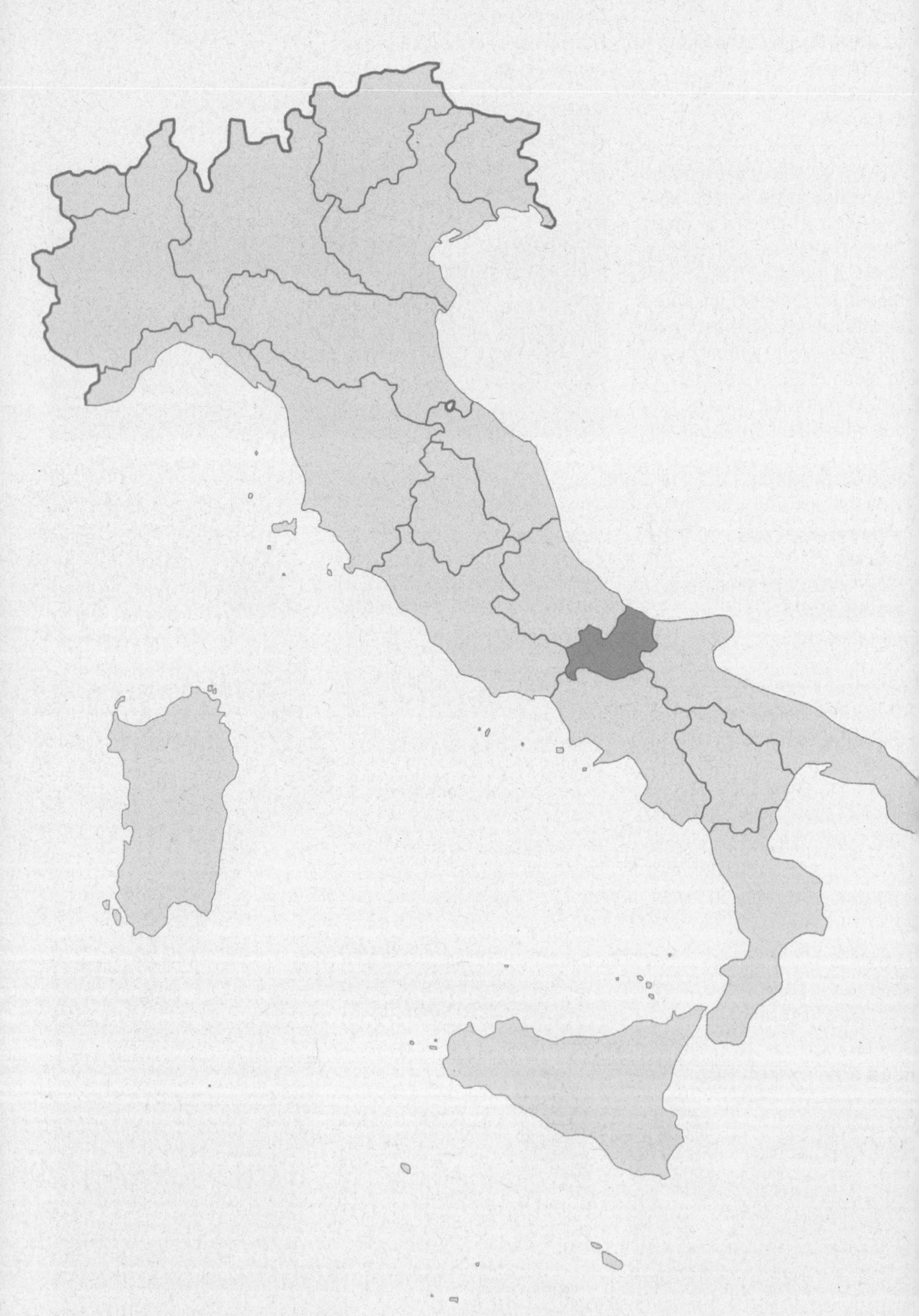

Molise

Montecilfone (Campobasso)

• **Bed & Breakfast Italia**
Code M03
tel. 06 6878618
fax 06 6878619
e-mail: info@bbitalia.it
sito: www.bbitalia.it
Closed: varies

Accommodation
Guestrooms: *1 double*
Services & Amenities: *English spoken; rooms cleaned every three days; tourist information; smokers welcome; terrace; private parking*
Minimum stay: *2 nights*
Rates: €€
Credit cards: VISA MC *Bancomat*
Pets: not allowed

In Montecifone, in the province of Campobasso, a double bedroom with TV and a spacious balcony are available. The bathroom has shower and Jacuzzi tub. The continental breakfast is served by the landlady on the balcony under a shady pergola. The bathroom is decorated in shades of yellow and the room has classic, elegant wood furnishings. The village is 18 km from Termoli, 45 km from Vasto, and 18 km from the Adriatic coast.

Venafro (Isernia)

Dimora del Prete di Belmonte TCI 10%
Dorothy Volpe
via Cristo 49
86079 Venafro (IS)
tel. and fax 0865 900159
e-mail: info.dimora@tin.it
sito: www.dimoradelprete.it
Open all year

Accommodation
Guestrooms: *4 doubles with private bath; additional bed on request*
Services & Amenities: *English and French are spoken; rooms cleaned every day; tourist info; dinner reservation; smokers welcome; Internet access; garden*
Rates: *double €€€€. Additional bed supplement €. Children under 2 free*
Credit cards: *Bancomat*
Pets: allowed

In 1860, this ancient dwelling, now carefully restored, was created by putting together several 16th-century houses. In fact, it has marvelous marble stairs, high-quality furniture, and walls are either frescoed or covered with original silk tapestry. In 1973, the owners

converted the house into an open residence, with four double guestrooms, a large terrace and a beautiful garden that has several very old palm trees. Guests can also enjoy regional specialties and the family farm's production of wine and organic products.

Campania

Agropoli (Salerno)

La Colombaia
Luigi Botti
via Piano delle Pere
84043 Agropoli (SA)
tel. 0974 821800, fax 0974 823478
colombaia@tin.it
www.web.tiscali.it/lacolombaia
Open: March to October

TCI 10%

Once an old farm house and now made into a beautiful villa with an extra wing, this B&B sits up on a hill with a panoramic view of the Gulf of Salerno and the Isle of Capri. All the guestrooms have double beds and are furnished in the late 18th-century English style. The English breakfast is served either in a reserved dining room or out in the garden. The hosts also propose evening meals, which can be enjoyed next to the large swimming pool.

Accommodation
Guestrooms: *3 doubles with private bath; additional bed on request*
Services & Amenities: *English spoken; rooms cleaned every day; tourist information; dinner reservation; terrace; air conditioning; Internet access; smokers welcome; private parking*
Minimum stay: *2 nights*
Rates: *double €€-€€€. Children under 2 free; 2 to 6 -30%. Additional bed supplement -20%*
Credit cards: *Visa MC Bancomat*
Pets: *not allowed*

Amalfi (Salerno)

Villa Adriana
Adriana Di Stasio
via dei Martiri d'Ungheria 46
84011 Amalfi (SA)
tel. 081 282520, mob. 348 7319244
fax 081 289780
serpone@hotmail.com,
myhomeyourhome@virgilio.it
www.myhomeyourhome.it
Open all year

Stasio Palace, a fine early 20th-century villa located in Amalfi's old center, now accommodates B&B guests. It has an elegant atmosphere, a typical seashore character, Vetri ceramic floors and a large panoramic terrace. An Italian breakfast is served in the dining room. The hosts offer the possibility of enjoying a private beach and special rates for renting a scooter or a boat.

Accommodation
Guestrooms: *2 doubles, with private bath; additional bed on request*
Services & Amenities: *French, English and Spanish are spoken; rooms cleaned every three days; tourist information; terrace; Internet access; smokers welcome*
Minimum stay: *2 nights*
Rates: *€€€€*
Credit cards: *accepted*
Pets: *allowed*

BENEVENTO

• Bed & Breakfast Italia
Code C35
tel. 06 6878618, fax 06 6878619
info@bbitalia.it
www.bbitalia.it
Closed: varies

A self-contained apartment consisting in three rooms, all with TV: two double bedrooms and a triple with three beds, which share a bathroom with tub. Furnishings are simple and comfortable. The hosts will personally accompany guests on tours of the city and the surrounding areas. Witnesses to Benevento's history are the monuments in the old center, such as the church of Santa Sofia, with its unique dodecagonal plan. Local culinary specialties, such as "torrone" (a kind of nougat) and "Strega", the liqueur inspired by the legendary Benevento witches, should be tasted.

ACCOMMODATION
Guestrooms: *3 (2 double bedrooms and 1 triple room)*
Services & Amenities: *French, English and Spanish are spoken; rooms cleaned every 3 days; tourist information; private parking*
Minimum stay: *2 nights*
Rates: €€
Credit cards: VISA MC *Bancomat*
Pets: 🐕

CASAMARCIANO (NAPLES)

• Bed & Breakfast Italia
Code C8
tel. 06 6878618, fax 06 6878619
info@bbitalia.it
www.bbitalia.it
Closed: varies

A small house with private parking and garden, this B&B consists in two large double bedrooms and a single; each room has TV and a private bathroom with shower. The furnishings are modern and functional. In the summer, a continental breakfast is served in the garden. The house is only 2 km from the Circumvesuviana railway line to the most famous Campania towns such as Naples, Sorrento and Pompei.

ACCOMMODATION
Guestrooms: *3 (1 single and 2 double bedrooms, all with private bath)*
Services & Amenities: *French, English and Spanish are spoken; rooms cleaned every three days; complimentary tourist information; private parking*
Minimum stay: *2 nights*
Rates: €€
Credit cards: VISA MC *Bancomat*
Pets: 🐕

CASERTA

B&B Caserta
Gianni Centore
via San Michele 3
località Casertavecchia
81100 Caserta
tel. 0823 329455
0823 371330
fax 0823 323550
mob. 348 51101976, 348 5109491
info@bedandbreakfastcaserta.it
www.bedandbreakfastcaserta.it
Closed: November to February

Located in the village of Casertavecchia, which is just 5 km from the Reggia and 20 mins from Naples, this B&B is a converted 14th-century Franciscan convent that was completely reconstructed in the early part of the 20th century. There are two independent guest suites, elegantly furnished with early-20th century furniture, that have a terrace with a solarium and a hydromassage. For enjoying some relaxing moments, there's also a small, hilltop farm just a short distance away, with equipped farmland and a splendid view of the Amalfi coastline.

ACCOMMODATION
Guestrooms: *2 suites, also single occupancy, with private bath*
Services & Amenities: *French and English are spoken; rooms cleaned every three days; tourist information; terrace; garden; smokers welcome; private parking*
Minimum stay: *2 nights*
Rates: €€€€
Credit cards: *not accepted*
Pets: 🐕

Castellammare di Stabia (Naples)

• Bed & Breakfast Italia TCI 10%
Code C10
tel. 06 6878618, fax 06 6878619
info@bbitalia.it
www.bbitalia.it
Closed: varies

This B&B is situated in a centrally-located town near all the major resorts on the Amalfi coast: Positano, Ravello, Sorrento and Amalfi. The three rooms are elegantly furnished, have satellite TV and all face the sea. Your hosts provide a shuttle service to and from the beach. The Pompeii archaeological site is 3 kilometers away. Boats to the islands of Ischia and Capri leave from the port of Castellamare.

Accommodation
Guestrooms: *3 triple rooms*
Services & Amenities: *English spoken; rooms cleaned every three days; complimentary tourist information*
Minimum stay: *2 nights*
Rates: €
Credit cards: VISA MC *Bancomat*
Pets: not allowed

Cicciano (Naples)

Il Cortile TCI 10%
Arturo Nucci
via Roma 43
80033 Cicciano (NA)
tel. and fax 081 8248897
dupon@libero.it
Open all year

This 18th-C house has a large courtyard – which was once used for agricultural purposes – and a surrounding Mediterranean type garden with rare magnolias, palm trees, camellias and citrus fruit. The rooms, which overlook the garden, are divided into two separate parts and have independent entrances and epoch furniture. Breakfast, which is served in the courtyard consists of various marmalades, fruit, local sweet and non-sweet products from the adjoining farm.

Accommodation
Guestrooms: *3 (1 single and 2 doubles with shared bath); additional bed on request* ♿
Services & Amenities: *French, English, German and Dutch are spoken; rooms cleaned every day; tourist info; educational courses by request; Internet access; garden; smokers welcome; parking*
Minimum stay: *2 nights*
Rates: *€€ per person. Discounts for groups*
Credit cards: *not accepted*
Pets: allowed

Comiziano (Naples)

A Casa di Felicetta
• A Casa di Parthenope
tel. 081 7944186, mob. 338 6880058
fax 081 7944186
info@casadiparthenope.it
www.casadiparthenope.it
Closed: August

This B&B is in a modern villa, located just few kilometers from Nola. It's surrounded by a large, well-kept garden and has three bright guestrooms with independent entrances. Guests have the use of kitchen, and the Italian breakfast, which features natural sweet products, is served either in the family's apartment or in the kitchen reserved for the guests. The hostess loves ceramics and the house is decorated with quite a number of them.

Accommodation
Guestrooms: *3 (1 double bedroom, with private bath and 2 doubles with shared bath); additional bed on request*
Services & Amenities: *rooms cleaned every day; tourist information; terrace; garden; smokers welcome; private parking*
Minimum stay: *2 nights*
Rates: *double €€€, triple €€€€. Discounts for children*
Credit cards: *not accepted*
Pets: not allowed

Corbara (Salerno)

• **Bed & Breakfast Italia**
Code C24
tel. 06 6878618, fax 06 6878619
info@bbitalia.it
www.bbitalia.it
Closed: varies

This B&B is located in villa immersed in vegetation. The guest accommodation consists in five double bedrooms, all furnished in a simple and comfortable style. In summertime, the rich continental breakfast is served in the shady garden. Several places

of interest, such as Amalfi, Positano, Sorrento, Naples, and Ercolano, are easily reached on the highway. Private parking is available for the guests.

Accommodation
Guestrooms: *5 doubles*
Services & Amenities: *English spoken; rooms cleaned every three days; complimentary tourist information; private parking*
Minimum stay: *2 nights*
Rates: €€
Credit cards: VISA MC *Bancomat*
Pets:

Giffoni Sei Casali (Salerno)

Palazzo Pennasilico
Luigi Pennasilico
via Le Piazze 27, località Sieti
84090 Giffoni Sei Casali (SA)
tel. and fax 089 881822
mob. 328 9480172
Open all year

This 17th-C palace, now a B&B with a magic, fascinating atmosphere, is located in the heart of the historic village of Sieti. The "alcove" suite with its wall decorations and living room with 16th-century frescos are certainly well worth visiting. For perfect relaxation there are the small rooms that have fireplaces, and there is also the old park. Breakfast, consisting of natural sweets, is served on the large panoramic terrace. Arriving guests are welcomed with baskets of typical sweets. Bicycles are placed at their disposal.

Accommodation
Guestrooms: *3 (2 double bedrooms and 1 suite, with private bath)*
Services & Amenities: *French spoken; rooms cleaned every 3 days; tourist information; bike rental; horse-riding excursions; terrace; Internet access; garden; smokers welcome; private parking*
Rates: *double* €€€€, *suite* €€€€
Credit cards: *accepted*
Pets:

Isola d'Ischia - Barano (Naples)

Residenza Mezzogiorno B&B
Pietro di Iorio
via Pendio del Gelso 19
80070 Barano d'Ischia (NA)
tel. 081 990175, mob. 347 9007879
info@vacanzeaischia.it
www.vacanzeaischia.it
• **Bed & Breakfast Italia**
tel. 06 6878618, fax 06 6878619
info@bbitalia.it
www.bbitalia.it
Closed: November, January and February

Accommodation
Guestrooms: *2 mini-apartments, with private bath*
Services & Amenities: *English spoken; rooms cleaned every three days; complimentary tourist information; terrace; smokers welcome*
Minimum stay: *in August, 2 weeks*
Rates: € *per person*
Credit cards: *not accepted*
Pets:

Located in a recently built house in the southern part of the Isle of Ischia, just a few minutes from the main port and 5 minutes on foot from the Maronti Lido, this B&B has two guest apartments. The family occupies part of the building and prepares breakfast, which consists of genuine, homemade sweets. Breakfast is generally served on the large terrace, which is also provided with large umbrellas. Guests who love to fish can also practice this sport in the company of the host.

• **Bed & Breakfast Italia**
Code C26
tel. 06 6878618, fax 06 6878619
info@bbitalia.it
www.bbitalia.it
Closed: varies

This B&B is hosted by a two-story villa, located in the hilly Ischia area, between Punta Sant'Angelo and the Punta San Pancrazio beaches. The guests accommodation includes two small apartments on the first floor with two double bedrooms, and a triple room, classic furnishings and telephone.

The bus stops serving the beach is a few meters away. The host provides useful information on places to visit.

ACCOMMODATION
Guestrooms: *3 (2 doubles, 1 triple)*
Services & Amenities: *English and German are spoken; rooms cleaned every 3 days; complimentary tourist information; private parking*
Minimum stay: *2 nights*
Rates: €€
Credit cards: *Bancomat*
Pets:

• **Bed & Breakfast Italia**
Code C51
tel. 06 6878618, fax 06 6878619
info@bbitalia.it
www.bbitalia.it
Closed: varies

This B&B is located in a residential complex at Il Capo. The guest accommodation consists in four different-sized apartments for two to six guests in a two-story house. Each apartment has TV, washing machine, safe, fully equipped bathroom and well-equipped kitchen. Rooms afford a magnificent sea view and overlook the swimming pool. Provisions for breakfast, which can also be taken in the garden, can be found in the kitchen. Guests can use the fax on request.

ACCOMMODATION
Guestrooms: *6 rooms*
Services & Amenities: *English and German are spoken; rooms cleaned every three days; complimentary tourist information*
Minimum stay: *2 nights*
Rates: €€
Credit cards: *Bancomat*
Pets:

ISOLA D'ISCHIA - CASAMICCIOLA TERME (NAPLES)

B&B Martinetti
Fortunato Martinetti
• **Friendly Home-Gli Amici del B&B**
tel. 02 860147, fax 02 875860
friendlymilano@dada.it
tel. and fax 011 9536376
fhrivoli@virgilio.it
Open: 15 March-15 November

This independent house, with its many colorful flowers, is located in Ischia's old center, just a few meters from the thermal baths and the sea. The island's typical architecture is reflected in the large panoramic terrace, where the guests have the abundant Italian breakfast. There are bicycles for rent for the guests, as well as the use of the kitchen and, on request, the guests can also rent a boat.

ACCOMMODATION
Guestrooms: *3 double bedrooms, also single occupancy, with private bath; additional bed on request*
Services & Amenities: *French and German are spoken; rooms cleaned every three days; complimentary tourist information; kitchen use by request; dinner reservation; bike rental; terrace; smokers welcome*
Rates: *single €€, double €€€. Additional bed supplement €. Discounts for children, students and honeymooners*
Credit cards: *not accepted*
Pets:

• Bed & Breakfast Italia
Code C12
tel. 06 6878618, fax 06 6878619
info@bbitalia.it
www.bbitalia.it
Closed: varies

Accommodation
Guestrooms: *2 double bedrooms*
Services & Amenities: *German spoken; rooms cleaned every three days; complimentary tourist information; private parking*
Minimum stay: *2 nights*
Rates: *€€*
Credit cards: *Bancomat*
Pets:

This villa is located on the island of Ischia. This accommodation offers two double rooms with simple comfortable furnishings. The house has a large flowered balcony, personally cared for by the lady of the house, where breakfast is served in the warmer months. The spa and mineral waters of Ischia have special therapeutic properties and Casamicciola has two of the best spa pools on the island.

Isola d'Ischia - Forìo (Naples)

Casa Lora
Mirella Covatta
località La Costa
80075 Forìo (NA)
tel. 081 907389, mob. 335 5849988
fax 049 8643394
mirella.covatta@tin.it
• Associazione Koko Nor
tel. 049 8643394, mob. 338 3377912
fax 049 8643394
kokonor@bandb-veneto.it
www.bandb-veneto.it/kokonor
Open: April to September and Christmas holidays

Accommodation
Guestrooms: *6 doubles, also single occupancy, with private bath; additional bed on request*
Services & Amenities: *French and English are spoken; rooms cleaned every day; tourist information; dinner reservation; terrace; Internet access; smokers welcome; parking*
Minimum stay: *2 nights*
Rates: *single €€, double €€€. Additional bed supplement €. Children under 6 -50%.*
Credit cards: *not accepted*
Pets:

The ancient rural house, which was originally used during the wine harvest, faces Mount Epomeo and its Poseidon gardens. The house, surrounded by a vegetable garden and citrus trees, has a natural Turkish bathroom. The ground floor leads directly into the garden, which has a pergola with a view of the sea. Breakfast, consisting of natural products and fruit juice, is served under this pergola or in the living room. Guests can also enjoy local dishes for dinner.

Epomeo
Elsa Almasio
via Casa di Maio
Primo Vicolo 1
80075 Forìo (NA)
tel. 06 9642309, mob. 347 7960091
fax 06 96153261
e.almasio@yahoo.it
Open: March to October

Accommodation
Guestrooms: *2 doubles, with shared bath; additional bed on request*
Services & Amenities: *English and German are spoken; rooms cleaned every day; tourist information; terrace; smokers welcome*
Minimum stay: *3 nights*
Rates: *double €€€, triple €€€€. Discounts for children*
Credit cards: *not accepted*
Pets:

This apartment, located inside a typical Ischian building in the old center of Forio, is just a short walk from the sea. The guest accommodation consists in two double rooms and includes a large panoramic terrace, provided with table, deck chair and large umbrella, where the breakfast is served. The guests can also receive help in organizing island excursions and boat rides.

Villa Spinavola
Elsa Almasio
via Spinavola 2
80075 Forio (NA)
tel. 06 9642309, mob. 347 7960091
fax 06 96153261
e.almasio@yahoo.it
Open: March to October

This two-story, '50s building, surrounded by a garden, is just a short walk from the center of Forio. This accommodation offers three guestrooms each furnished in marine style. The rich breakfast, which is served in the B&B dining room, consists of brioches, sweet products, sliced ham and salami and various types of cheese. The hosts are available for organizing island and sea excursions.

Accommodation
Guestrooms: *3 double bedrooms (1 with private bath, 2 with shared bath)*
Services & Amenities: *English and German are spoken; rooms cleaned every day; tourist information; garden; smokers welcome*
Minimum stay: *3 nights*
Rates: *€€€-€€€€. Discounts for children*
Credit cards: *not accepted*
Pets:

• **Bed & Breakfast Italia**
Code C13
tel. 06 6878618, fax 06 6878619
info@bbitalia.it
www.bbitalia.it
Closed: varies

A recently built apartment block, set in the green vineyards of Forio d'Ischia, 6 kilometers from the Poseidon Gardens and 1.5 kilometers from Sant'Angelo, a scenic village on the rocky headland of the same name. It is a stone's throw from the nearest town (Panza), and close to the Bay of Sorgeto, reached via a long flight of steps. Each flat has a double room, a well-equipped kitchen area, a bathroom and a large balcony or a portico with garden.

Accommodation
Guestrooms: *2 doubles*
Services & Amenities: *French, English and German are spoken; rooms cleaned every three days; complimentary tourist information*
Minimum stay: *2 nights*
Rates: *€€*
Credit cards: VISA MC *Bancomat*
Pets:

• **Bed & Breakfast Italia**
Code C30
tel. 06 6878618, fax 06 6878619
info@bbitalia.it
www.bbitalia.it
Closed: varies

Accommodation
Guestrooms: *3 double bedrooms*
Services & Amenities: *English and German are spoken; rooms cleaned every 3 days; tourist information*
Minimum stay: *2 nights*
Rates: *€€*
Credit cards: VISA MC *Bancomat*
Pets:

A villa with garden and outdoor swimming-pool. There are three very sunny double bedrooms with independent entrances and local-style furnishings. Each has a balcony with a sea view and a private bathroom with shower. The hosts offer guests a warm relaxing welcome. Forio has the beaches of Chiaia, Citara, and Punta del Soccorso with the sixteenth-century sanctuary church of the same name.

Licusati (Salerno)

• **Bed & Breakfast Italia**
Code C23
tel. 06 6878618, fax 06 6878619
info@bbitalia.it
www.bbitalia.it
Closed: varies

Accommodation
Guestrooms: *3 (2 doubles, 1 triple)*
Services & Amenities: *French and English are spoken; rooms cleaned every 3 days; tourist information; lunch & dinner reservations*
Minimum stay: *2 nights*
Rates: €€
Credit cards: VISA MC *Bancomat*
Pets: no

This B&B is hosted by a sixteenth-century historic home, located in the medieval hamlet of Licusati, in the Cilento valley Park, 8 kilometers from the Marina di Camerota beach. The hosts offer one triple room and two double rooms, furnished in the same style as the rest of the house. The bus stop for links to the nearby cities is beside the house.

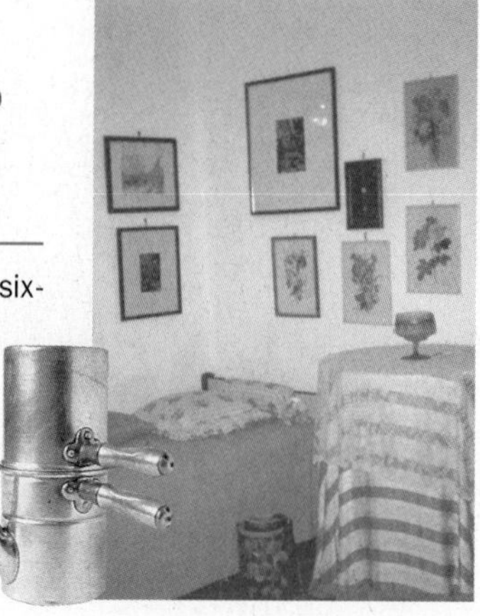

Marcianise (Caserta)

• **Bed & Breakfast Italia**
Code C50
tel. 06 6878618, fax 06 6878619
info@bbitalia.it
www.bbitalia.it
Closed: varies

Accommodation
Guestrooms: *1 triple room*
Services & Amenities: *English spoken; rooms cleaned every 3 days; tourist information; smokers welcome; private parking*
Minimum stay: *2 nights*
Rates: €€
Credit cards: VISA MC *Bancomat*
Pets: no

The B&B is located in a semi-detached house built recently, 6 kilometers from the Reggia of Caserta. The guestroom is on the top attic floor used only by guests, and is reached up a convenient winding staircase. It is simply furnished with a double bed plus a queen-size sofa bed. The continental breakfast is served in a small bright lounge with TV. The house nestles in Andromeda Park, which has a walled area with car park for guests.

Massa Lubrense (Naples)

Villa Bellini TCI 10%
• **Dolce Sonno Bed & Breakfast**
tel. 081 2451317, mob. 338 4916755
b.dolcesonno@tiscalinet.it
Open: March to September

Accommodation
Guestrooms: *4 (2 singles and 2 doubles, with shared bath)*
Services & Amenities: *English spoken; rooms cleaned every three days; complimentary tourist information; garden; smokers welcome; private parking*
Minimum stay: *2 nights*
Rates: *double* €€€€
Credit cards: *not accepted*
Pets: no

Although close to the sea, this house is actually like being out in the country. Located in the center of town, just a short way from the little port and 6 kilometers from Sorrento, the villa is surrounded by a large garden containing olive and lemon trees. There are two guestrooms with double beds. One room is the "sea" room and has a fireplace. The other is the "country" room and has Campania and Sicilian furnishings. The rich continental breakfast, or a breakfast of Sorrentine products, is served in the garden. Boat service is available on request.

Melizzano (Benevento)

Boscarello
Giovanna Florena
contrada Boscarello 10,
località Torello
82030 Melizzano (BN)
tel. 0824 945100 and 081 414189
fax 081 403886
info@boscarello.com and
giovanna@boscarello.com
www.boscarello.com
Closed: Christmas holidays

This B&B is located in a refurbished old farmhouse in the heart of the Sannino countryside, just a few km from the Telese thermal baths. Surrounded by a large garden, the house has elegantly furnished guestrooms and a dépendance with a nice living room and a fireplace. Breakfast consists of both sweet and non-sweet items and is served either in the kitchen or in the garden. In the summertime, guests can use the swimming pool with its hydromassage section.

Accommodation
Guestrooms: *2 double bedroom, also single occupancy, with shared bath; 1 mini-apartment (2-4 beds)*
Services & Amenities: *French and English are spoken; rooms cleaned every 3 days; tourist information; dinner reservation; garden; smokers welcome; parking*
Rates: *single €€, double €€€, mini-apartment €€€€.*
Children under 2 free
Credit cards: *not accepted*
Pets: ✓

Minori (Salerno)

• **Bed & Breakfast Italia**
Code C48
tel. 06 6878618, fax 06 6878619
info@bbitalia.it
www.bbitalia.it
Closed: varies

On the Amalfi coast, three studio apartments furnished in a simple, comfortable style, consisting in a sitting room with sofa bed, kitchenette and small bathroom with shower. Breakfast is prepared with regional products and served by the hosts. The apartments are located at Maiori, the oldest inhabited coastal village, known for its Roman villa where a costume festival is held every 25 August. The hosts live in the same building and will provide tourist information.

Accommodation
Guestrooms: *3 doubles*
Services & Amenities: *rooms cleaned every three days; complimentary tourist information; smokers welcome; private parking*
Minimum stay: *2 nights*
Rates: €€
Credit cards: VISA MC *Bancomat*
Pets: ✗

Montecorice (Salerno)

• **Bed & Breakfast Italia**
Code C19
tel. 06 6878618, fax 06 6878619
info@bbitalia.it
www.bbitalia.it
Closed: varies

Accommodation
Guestrooms: *3 (2 doubles, 1 triple)*
Services & Amenities: *French and English are spoken; rooms cleaned every 3 days; tourist information; smokers welcome; private parking*
Minimum stay: *2 nights*
Rates: €€
Credit cards: VISA MC *Bancomat*
Pets: ✓

This house, overlooking the hills of the National Park of Cilento, is about 70 kilometers from Salerno and near the Cilento trunk-road, which links all the Amalfi coastal resorts. The guest accommodation consists in two double bedrooms and a triple room. Private parking is available for the guests. The host provides useful information on places to visit.

Montecorvino Rovella (Salerno)

• **Bed & Breakfast Italia**
Code C16
tel. 06 6878618, fax 06 6878619
info@bbitalia.it
www.bbitalia.it
Closed: varies

This accommodation consists in two rooms located on the upper floor of an old seventeenth-century farmhouse. One has original family furnishings; the other is more modern and has a private bathroom with a Jacuzzi. Guests can enjoy the large trellised balcony and the living room with fireplace. It is 2 km from Battipaglia highway exit, and 20 km from the Amalfi coast, Paestum and the National Park of Cilento.

Accommodation
Guestrooms: *2 doubles*
Services & Amenities: *Spanish spoken; rooms cleaned every three days; complimentary tourist information; private parking*
Minimum stay: *2 nights*
Rates: €€
Credit cards: VISA MC *Bancomat*
Pets:

Mugnano del Cardinale (Avellino)

• **Bed & Breakfast Italia**
Code C44
tel. 06 6878618, fax 06 6878619
info@bbitalia.it
www.bbitalia.it
Closed: varies

Mugnano del Cardinale is in the green mountains of lower Irpinia. The B&B is located in a nice apartment. This accommodation offers three rooms: a single, a double bedroom, and a twin, each with TV. Two private bathrooms, one with shower and the other with shower/tub, are available. The house is connected to all major Campania towns, such as Naples, Avellino, Salerno and Caserta, either by bus or the Circumvesuviana railway line. Private parking is available for the guests.

Accommodation
Guestrooms: *3 (1 single, 1 double bedroom and 1 double)*
Services & Amenities: *English and German are spoken; rooms cleaned every three days; tourist information; baby-sitting service; air conditioning; smokers welcome; private parking*
Minimum stay: *2 nights*
Rates: €€
Credit cards: VISA MC *Bancomat*
Pets:

Naples

Antiche Terrazze
Mimma Mortilli
salita Capodimonte 147
80136 Naples
tel. and fax 081 293726
mob. 338 1605483
anticheterrazze@hotmail.com

Accommodation
Guestrooms: *3 doubles, with private bath; additional bed on request*
Services & Amenities: *French and English are spoken; rooms cleaned every 3 days; tourist information; dinner reservation; terrace; Internet access; smokers welcome*
Minimum stay: *2 nights*
Rates: €€ *per person. Additional bed supplement* €€*. Discounts for extended stays*
Credit cards: *not accepted*
Pets:

• **Le Finestre sul Golfo B&B**
tel. 081 7712978, mob. 333 2440156
pinarusso@tin.it, www.bbitaly.it
Open all year

This B&B, located in Capodimonte, is on the 4th floor of a 17th-C building. There's no passenger elevator, but it does have a hoist elevator for the luggage. The terrace provides an outstanding view of the Gulf of Naples and Mt. Vesuvius. The breakfast, including homemade products, is served in the living room with fireplace. TV, safe and laundry service availables on request.

B&B Casa Azulejos
• Associazione Koko Nor

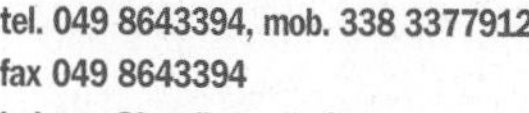

tel. 049 8643394, mob. 338 3377912
fax 049 8643394
kokonor@bandb-veneto.it
www.bandb-veneto.it/kokonor
Open all year

This B&B is located on the top floor of an 18th-century building in the center of Naples and is just 5 minutes from the National Museum. The rooms have refined, period furnishings and majolica floor tiles. The continental breakfast is served in a living room that has a nice view of Mt. Vesuvio. On request, the hostess will provide the guests with short courses on regional cuisine, and is more than happy to let them taste the rich flavors of traditional Campania dishes.

Accommodation
Guestrooms: *2 doubles, also single occupancy, with shared bath*
Services & Amenities: *French and English are spoken; rooms cleaned every day; tourist information; dinner reservation; educational courses by request; Internet access; smokers welcome*
Minimum stay: *2 nights*
Rates: *single €€, double €€€. Children under 3 free*
Credit cards: *not accepted*
Pets:

Casa del Mar
Paolo Serpone
corso Vittorio Emanuele 749
80122 Naples
tel. 081 282520, mob. 348 7319244
fax 081 289780
serpone@hotmail.com
and myhomeyourhome@virgilio.it
www.myhomeyourhome.it
Open all year

In the heart of Mergellina, this B&B is a large loft with eclectic furnishings that mix antique objects with design and ethnic items. Breakfast is served in the living room with fireplace, or on the furnished, panoramic terrace. This B&B is centrally located and also very close to the hydrofoil boat landing that provides transportation to the islands. This makes it ideal for visiting the city and the islands of Capri, Ischia and Procida.

Accommodation
Guestrooms: *1 double bedroom, private bath; additional bed on request*
Services & Amenities: *French, English and Spanish are spoken; rooms cleaned every 3 days; tourist information; terrace; Internet access; smokers welcome*
Minimum stay: *2 nights*
Rates: *€€€€*
Credit cards: *accepted*
Pets:

Posillipo
• Dolce Sonno Bed & Breakfast
tel. 081 2451317, mob. 338 4916755
b.dolcesonno@tiscalinet.it
Open all year

This rather small villa (300 sq. meters) with its independent entrance is located very panoramically on the Posillipo hill near Marechiaro and Cordoglio. This accommodation offers two rooms with double beds, luxuriously finished, and with period furniture as well as modern items. The rich breakfast features local products and is served either on the veranda with its garden or, weather permitting, out on the panoramic terrace.

ACCOMMODATION
Guestrooms: *2 double bedrooms with shared bath*
Services & Amenities: *English spoken; rooms cleaned every day; tourist information; terrace; smokers welcome; private parking*
Minimum stay: *2 nights*
Rates: €€€€. *Children under 3 free*
Credit cards: *not accepted*
Pets: not allowed

SeeYouAtHome
• Le Finestre sul Golfo B&B
tel. 081 7712978, mob. 333 2440156
pinarusso@tin.it
www.bbitaly.it
Closed: January, February and August

This single-room B&B, which has a small kitchen and bath, is located right in an 18th-C building in the old center. This is one of the city's most elegant districts. The room is on the 4th floor, but there's an elevator. The room's early 20th-C furniture and exposed ceiling beams give the B&B a warm, slightly rétro atmosphere. The classic continental breakfast is served in the room and, on request, the hostess can provide some of this territory's typical dishes. Laundry service, as well as special rates with the restaurants, is also available.

ACCOMMODATION
Guestrooms: *1 studio apartment (3-4 beds)*
Services & Amenities: *French, English and German are spoken; rooms cleaned every 3 days; tourist information; kitchen use by request; lunch & dinner reservations; Internet access; smokers welcome*
Minimum stay: *2 nights*
Rates: €€ *per person. Discounts for children and extended stays*
Credit cards: VISA MC *Bancomat*
Pets: not allowed

Spaccanapoli
Diego Serpone
largo Paparelle 13
80100 Naples
tel. 081 282520, mob. 348 7319244
fax 081 289780
serpone@hotmail.com and
myhomeyourhome@virgilio.it
www.myhomeyourhome.it
Open all year

ACCOMMODATION
Guestrooms: *5 doubles, also single occupancy, with private bath; additional bed on request*
Services & Amenities: *French, English and Spanish are spoken; rooms cleaned every 3 days; tourist info; terrace; air conditioning; Internet access; smokers welcome*
Minimum stay: *2 nights*
Rates: *single* €€€, *double* €€€€
Credit cards: *accepted*
Pets: allowed

This B&B occupies 3 floors in a 17th-C building, located in the most picturesque part of the city, with craftsman's shops, the most beautiful churches and buildings, Greco-Roman traces, and the most famous trattorias and pizzerias. Besides rooms furnished in modern style, the guests have the use of kitchen with a dining area where breakfast is served, and living room and a terrace. On request, a garage is also available and transportation to and from the airport.

Via Egiziaca Attico

• Dolce Sonno Bed & Breakfast
tel. 081 2451317, mob. 338 4916755
b.dolcesonno@tiscalinet.it
Open all year

This large attic apartment is located in the city's old center, close to the San Carlo Theater and the Umberto I gallery. The rooms with their offset ceilings, ancient travertine windows, and Florentine brickwork fireplace and floors, provide a charming atmosphere. It has three rooms. The breakfast, which is either continental or, on request, consisting of organic products, can be served either in the living room or out on the terrace, which permits the guests to enjoy a view of a corner of the ancient city.

Accommodation
Guestrooms: *3 double bedrooms, 1 with private bath and 2 with shared bath; additional bed on request*
Services & Amenities: *English spoken; rooms cleaned every day; complimentary tourist information; terrace; smokers welcome*
Minimum stay: *2 nights*
Rates: €€€€. *Additional bed supplement* €-€€
Credit cards: *not accepted*
Pets: 🚫

• Bed & Breakfast Italia
Code C28
via Santa Teresa degli Scalzi
tel. 06 6878618, fax 06 6878619
info@bbitalia.it
www.bbitalia.it
Closed: varies

Small two-story house with private parking and garden located in the Stella district. The first floor, entirely at the disposal of guests, is composed of two double rooms. Furnishings are elegant and refined. Bus stops to Piazza del Plebiscito, the Duomo, San Carlo Theater, and Maschio Angioino are 10 minutes away on foot. The old center, centered around Piazza del Gesù, is within short walking distance. Private parking available.

Accommodation
Guestrooms: *2 doubles*
Services & Amenities: *English and Spanish are spoken; rooms cleaned every 3 days; tourist information; private parking*
Minimum stay: *2 nights*
Rates: €€
Credit cards: VISA MC *Bancomat*
Pets: 🚫

• Bed & Breakfast Italia
Code C42
salita Capodimonte
tel. 06 6878618, fax 06 6878619
info@bbitalia.it
www.bbitalia.it
Closed: varies

In an old mansion in Capodimonte, this third floor apartment without elevator consists in two double bedrooms, one with ensuite bathroom, and a furnished balcony overlooking vegetation and the other with a large bathroom with a Jacuzzi. In summertime, a continental breakfast is served on a terrace with a solarium offering a stunning view. Other services are available: dinner by request, laundry and ironing.

Accommodation
Guestrooms: *2 double bedrooms*
Services & Amenities: *French spoken; rooms cleaned every 3 days; complimentary tourist information; smokers welcome*
Minimum stay: *2 nights*
Rates: €€
Credit cards: VISA MC *Bancomat*
Pets: 🚫

• Bed & Breakfast Italia
Code C47
via P. Castellino
tel. 06 6878618, fax 06 6878619
info@bbitalia.it
www.bbitalia.it
Closed: varies

A large apartment (115 square meters) on the first floor of a building in the Vomero residential district. This accommodation offers three spacious double bedrooms with antique furnishings and TV; a cot for children under two can be added in one of the rooms.

Shared bathroom with shower. The apartment is surrounded by a large balcony. Bicycles are available for guests who want to ride around Naples.

ACCOMMODATION
Guestrooms: *3 double bedrooms*
Services & Amenities: *rooms cleaned every three days; complimentary tourist information; bike rental; smokers welcome*
Minimum stay: *2 nights*
Rates: €€
Credit cards: VISA MC *Bancomat*
Pets: no

• Bed & Breakfast Italia
Code C49
via Duomo
tel. 06 6878618, fax 06 6878619
info@bbitalia.it
www.bbitalia.it
Closed: varies

ACCOMMODATION
Guestrooms: *3 (1 single, 2 doubles)*
Services & Amenities: *English spoken; rooms cleaned every three days; complimenrary tourist information*
Minimum stay: *2 nights*
Rates: €€
Credit cards: VISA MC *Bancomat*
Pets: no

On the 3rd floor of a historic building with elevator, in the very heart of the town, 3 small apartments recently restored with early 19th-C furnishings. The first apartment consists in an entrance hall, a sitting room with sofa and kitchenette, bathroom with

shower. The second and third are studio apartments divided into a sitting room with kitchenette, a bedroom and a bathroom. Large balcony overlooking Via Duomo and parquet flooring in all rooms. The San Lorenzo district is well served by the number 1 and 2 bus lines and the subway – the stop is 150 m away.

NOLA (NAPLES)

• Bed & Breakfast Italia
Code C21
tel. 06 6878618, fax 06 6878619
info@bbitalia.it
www.bbitalia.it
Closed: varies

ACCOMMODATION
Guestrooms: *3 (1 double, 2 triples)*
Services & Amenities: *French and English are spoken; rooms cleaned every 3 days; tourist information; private parking*
Minimum stay: *2 nights*
Rates: €€
Credit cards: VISA MC *Bancomat*
Pets: yes

This B&B, about 20 kilometers from Naples, is located in Silvana Park, a residential area easily reached on the Circumvesuviana line. The accommodation offers 2 triple rooms and a double, each

with TV and a large balcony facing the nice garden. Italian breakfast is served in the family kitchen. Private parking is available for guests.

Ogliastro Cilento (Salerno)

Bed & Breakfast Borghi del Cilento
Filippo Crisci
via San Donato 28
84061 Ogliastro Cilento (SA)
tel. 0974 833728, mob. 330 461044
filcrisci@tiscali.it
www.amicibedandbreakfast.it
Open all year

TCI 10%

This refined, 17th-C building has several floors and still has its original structures, including an oil press and its brick and stone roof. The guestrooms are furnished with antiques that testify to the house's history. Breakfast, which includes marmalade and homemade sweets, is served either on the large terrace or in the kitchen, where there is an old fireplace. The guests are welcome to enjoy the garden, with its orange trees, and the internal courtyard.

Accommodation
Guestrooms: *2 doubles, 1 with private bath and 1 with shared bath; 1 mini-apartment (2-4 beds)*
Services & Amenities: *French spoken; rooms cleaned every day; tourist information; terrace; Internet access; smokers welcome; private parking*
Minimum stay: *2 nights*
Rates: *€ per person. Children under 2 free*
Credit cards: *not accepted*
Pets: ✓

Paestum (Salerno)

• Bed & Breakfast Italia
Code C31
tel. 06 6878618, fax 06 6878619
info@bbitalia.it
www.bbitalia.it
Closed: varies

Located in Capaccio, the seat of the Paéstum town hall, the B&B has three triple rooms and a double with independent entrances, simply furnished and all with private bathroom and shower. A large balcony and garden with parking are at the guests' disposal. The village of Capaccio is 1.5 km from the archaeological site of Paestum, the ancient Greek colony (6th C BC) of which famous remains survive in the open air (sanctuary of Hera, temple of Neptune), and also in the National Archeological Museum in front of the excavations (Tomba del Tuffatore). The area is also renowned for its mozzarella made from the milk of black buffalos.

Accommodation
Guestrooms: *4 (1 double, 3 triples)*
Services & Amenities: *English spoken; rooms cleaned every 3 days; tourist information; private parking*
Minimum stay: *2 nights*
Rates: *€€*
Credit cards: VISA MC *Bancomat*
Pets: ✓

Palinuro (Salerno)

• Bed & Breakfast Italia
Code C18
tel. 06 6878618, fax 06 6878619
info@bbitalia.it
www.bbitalia.it
Closed: varies

This B&B is located 2 kilometers from Palinuro, a few meters from the sea, and is run by an expert cook fond of diet cuisine. It has two double rooms and two single rooms, all furnished in a simple and comfortable way. In summertime, breakfast is served on the large balcony or in the garden. The bus stop for Palinuro is just in front of the house. Horseback excursions are available.

Accommodation
Guestrooms: *4 (2 singles, 2 doubles)*
Services & Amenities: *French and English are spoken; rooms cleaned every three days; complimentary tourist information; private parking*
Minimum stay: *2 nights*
Rates: *€€*
Credit cards: VISA MC *Bancomat*
Pets: ✗

Pisciotta (Salerno)

• **Bed & Breakfast Italia**
Code C22
tel. 06 6878618, fax 06 6878619
info@bbitalia.it
www.bbitalia.it
Closed: varies

Seventeenth-century home, restored preserving its original structure, located in the National Park of Cilento, between Naples and Palinuro. Each guestroom – three double rooms and three triple rooms – is furnished in rustic marine style and affords a stunning sea view. 2 km from the railway station connecting Pisciotta to Palinuro. A shuttle service from the station to the accommodation is available.

Accommodation
Guestrooms: *5 (3 doubles, 2 triples)*
Services & Amenities: *English and Spanish are spoken; rooms cleaned every three days; complimentary tourist information*
Minimum stay: *2 nights*
Rates: €€
Credit cards: VISA MC *Bancomat*
Pets:

Policastro Bussentino (Salerno)

• **Bed & Breakfast Italia**
Code C1
tel. 06 6878618, fax 06 6878619
info@bbitalia.it
www.bbitalia.it
Closed: varies

A cottage 500 m from the sea, located near the National Park of Cilento and from Palinuro, facing on the delightful Policastro Gulf. The accommodation offers three light, airy double rooms, with classic furnishings. Continental breakfast is served in the lounge, featuring a stone vaulted ceiling and a large glass window facing the Campania hills. Private parking available.

Accommodation
Guestrooms: *3 doubles*
Services & Amenities: *English spoken; rooms cleaned every three days; complimentary tourist information; private parking*
Minimum stay: *2 nights*
Rates: €€
Credit cards: VISA MC *Bancomat*
Pets:

Pompei (Naples)

• **Bed & Breakfast Italia**
Code C11
tel. 06 6878618, fax 06 6878619
info@bbitalia.it
www.bbitalia.it
Closed: varies

The house is situated in a small residential area in the very heart of the modern hamlet, which has grown up near the Archeological Park. One single and two double rooms are available. Furnishings are simple and comfortable. The archaeological site and the ruins of ancient Pompeii are just 1 km away. Naples, Sorrento, Amalfi and links to the islands of Ischia and Capri are 30 km away.

Accommodation
Guestrooms: *3 (1 single, 2 doubles)*
Services & Amenities: *German spoken; rooms cleaned every 3 days; tourist information; parking*
Minimum stay: *2 nights*
Rates: €€
Credit cards: VISA MC *Bancomat*
Pets:

Pontelandolfo (Benevento)

• **Bed & Breakfast Italia**
Code C46
tel. 06 6878618, fax 06 6878619
info@bbitalia.it
www.bbitalia.it
Closed: varies

Accommodation
Guestrooms: *6 (1 single, 3 doubles, 2 triple rooms)*
Services & Amenities: *French, English and Spanish are spoken; rooms cleaned every 3 days; tourist information; Internet access; smokers welcome; private parking*
Minimum stay: *2 nights*
Rates: €€
Credit cards: VISA MC *Bancomat*
Pets:

This small familyrun hotel offers to its guests three double, two triple and one single bedrooms. Four bathrooms with shower are exclusively for guest use; two more bathrooms are shared. The six rooms have a small fridge. Guests can take advantage of special offers at the first floor restaurant. The hosts provide all kinds of facilities, including car and coach rental, and guided tours. Private parking available.

Quadrelle (Avellino)

• **Bed & Breakfast Italia**
Code C2
tel. 06 6878618, fax 06 6878619
info@bbitalia.it
www.bbitalia.it
Closed: varies

A B&B located in in the Mount Partenio foothills, 30 mins from Naples. The house has two double rooms, furnished in a simple and comfortable style. Guests can enjoy a large fenced garden and car parking. Naples, Pompei, Salerno, Mt Vesuvius, Reggia di Caserta, and the Amalfi coast are easily reached thanks to its proximity to the highway and to the local Circumvesuviana railway station.

Accommodation
Guestrooms: *2 doubles*
Services & Amenities: *English spoken; rooms cleaned every three days; complimentary tourist information; private parking*
Minimum stay: *2 nights*
Rates: €€
Credit cards: VISA MC *Bancomat*
Pets:

Ravello (Salerno)

• **Bed & Breakfast Italia**
Code C39
tel. 06 6878618, fax 06 6878619
info@bbitalia.it
www.bbitalia.it
Closed: varies

The B&B is hosted by a castled villa, in a park, on several floors, one entirely at guests' disposal. The apartment consists in two double bedrooms and one bathroom. A small swimming pool and a rose garden may be used by guests. 150 stone steps lead up to the villa. It is about 5 kilometers from Amalfi, 15 kilometers from Salerno, 25 kilometers from Sorrento. The nearest railway station is at Vietri, 8 kilometers away.

Accommodation
Guestrooms: *2 doubles*
Services & Amenities: *French and English are spoken; rooms cleaned every three days; tourist information; air conditioning; smokers welcome*
Minimum stay: *2 nights*
Rates: €€
Credit cards: VISA MC *Bancomat*
Pets:

Roccamonfina (Caserta)

• **Bed & Breakfast Italia**
Code C32
tel. 06 6878618, fax 06 6878619
info@bbitalia.it
www.bbitalia.it
Closed: varies

Two double and one triple rooms with independent entrances, in a country house with all modern conveniences and simple furnishing. The triple room has a private bathroom with shower; the double rooms share one bathroom. All rooms have TV. The coast, the old sanctuary church of Lattani and the Reggia di Caserta are a 15 km drive from Roccamorfina. A chestnut and mushroom festival is held in autumn. This accommodation has a cozy atmosphere.

+Accommodation
Guestrooms: *3 (2 doubles, 1 triple)*
Services & Amenities: *French and English are spoken; rooms cleaned every three days; tourist information; private parking*
Minimum stay: *2 nights*
Rates: €€
Credit cards: VISA MC *Bancomat*
Pets: not allowed

Rofrano (Salerno)

• **Bed & Breakfast Italia**
Code C37
tel. 06 6878618, fax 06 6878619
info@bbitalia.it
www.bbitalia.it
Closed: varies

This typical country-house, restored bearing in mind the environment and using ecological materials, is situated in the heart of the National Park of Cilento The accommodation consists in two triple and one single bedrooms furnished in a functional and personal style. The triple rooms share a bathroom with shower; the single has a private bathroom. The entrance is independent. The hosts serve organic breakfast. Visitors can take part in rural activities and excursions led by professional guides.

Accommodation
Guestrooms: *3 (1 single, 2 triple)* ♿
Services & Amenities: *English spoken; rooms cleaned every 3 days; tourist information; baby-sitting service; smokers welcome*
Minimum stay: *2 nights*
Rates: €€
Credit cards: VISA MC *Bancomat*
Pets: not allowed

San Sebastiano al Vesuvio (Naples)

A Casa di Maria Paola
viale dei Platani 36
80040 San Sebastiano al Vesuvio (NA)
tel. 081 7717461
• **A Casa di Parthenope**
tel. 081 7944186, mob. 338 6880058
fax 081 7944186
info@casadiparthenope.it
www.casadiparthenope.it
Open all year

This B&B is located in a modern villa surrounded by a garden. The guestroom is simply furnished. Breakfast is served in the bright living room, which the guests are also welcome to use for relaxing and where the hosts take pleasure in visiting and chatting with their guests

Accommodation
Guestrooms: *1 double, with private bath; additional bed on request*
Services & Amenities: *English and Spanish are spoken; rooms cleaned every three days; complimentary tourist information; Internet access; garden; smokers welcome; private parking*
Rates: *double €€€, triple €€€€*
Credit cards: *not accepted*
Pets: allowed

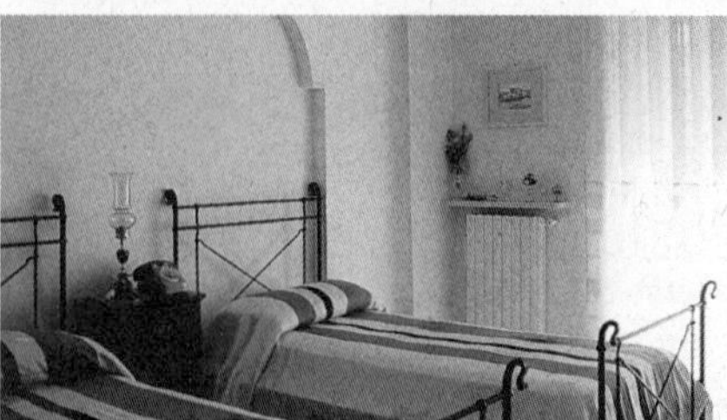

A Casa di Mariarosaria
via Palmieri 73
80040 San Sebastiano al Vesuvio (NA)
tel. 081 7711974
• A Casa di Parthenope
tel. 081 7944186, mob. 338 6880058
fax 081 7944186
info@casadiparthenope.it
www.casadiparthenope.it
Closed: August

This B&B is in a small, recently constructed villa located in the center of town. The guests have the use of a stylishly furnished room and a small garden. The hostess is particularly fond of preparing exquisite Neapolitan dishes and revealing a few of her very secret recipes to her guests. The Italian breakfast is served in the living room.

ACCOMMODATION
Guestrooms: *1 double bedroom, also single occupancy, with private bath*
Services & Amenities: *English spoken; rooms cleaned every 3 days; tourist info; Internet access; garden; smokers welcome; private parking*
Rates: *single €€, double €€*
Credit cards: *not accepted*
Pets: *(not allowed)*

SAVIANO (NAPLES)

A Casa di Giuseppe
• A Casa di Parthenope
tel. 081 7944186, mob. 338 6880058
fax 081 7944186
info@casadiparthenope.it
www.casadiparthenope.it
Closed: August

ACCOMMODATION
Guestrooms: *1 double bedroom, also single occupancy, private bath*
Services & Amenities: *French and English are spoken; rooms cleaned every day; complimentary tourist information; garden; smokers welcome; private parking*
Minimum stay: *2 nights*
Rates: *single €€, double €€€*
Credit cards: *not accepted*
Pets: *(not allowed)*

This B&B is in an antique building located in the town that's noted for its Carnival. This refined and tastefully furnished apartment consists of a room with classic furnishings, and a charming living room with fireplace, where the host enjoys chatting with his guests. He particularly likes to give them advice regarding the places of interest in the area. The Italian breakfast is served in the dining area.

SESSA AURUNCA (CASERTA)

• Bed & Breakfast Italia TCI 10%
Code C38
tel. 06 6878618, fax 06 6878619
info@bbitalia.it
www.bbitalia.it
Closed: varies

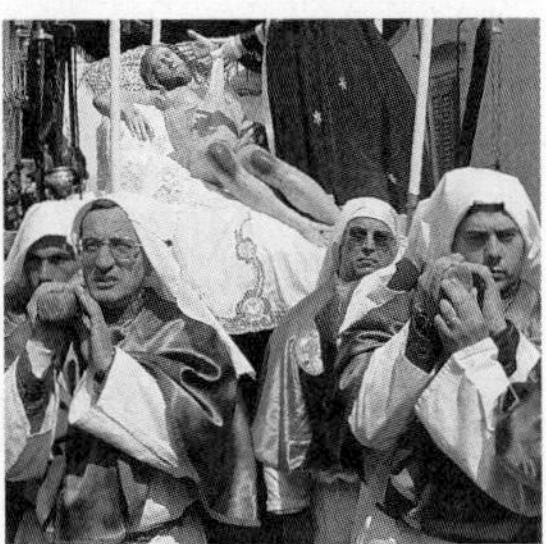
The confraternity of Sessa Aurunca in procession on Good Friday.

ACCOMMODATION
Guestrooms: *2 (1 double bedroom and 1 double)*
Services & Amenities: *French, English and Spanish are spoken; rooms cleaned every 3 days; tourist information; baby-sitting service; horse-riding excursions; smokers welcome; private parking*
Minimum stay: *2 nights*
Rates: *€€*
Credit cards: VISA MC *Bancomat*
Pets: *(not allowed)*

A self-contained apartment with two bedrooms, one with a double bed and one with twin beds, a sitting room, kitchen and bathroom with shower. The landlady, who lives upstairs, serves breakfast and cleans the rooms. Sessa Aurunca is 203 meters above sea level and is the ancient Suessa, the city of the Aurunci. The ruins of a theater and its Roman Baths bear witness to its past; the twelfth-century Cathedral is outstanding.

Sorrento (Naples)

B&B Villa Oriana
Pasquale d'Esposito
via Rubinacci 1
80067 Sorrento (NA)
tel. 081 8782468, mob. 335 6384718
villaoriana@tiscali.it
digilander.iol.it/villaoriana
• Associazione Turisti per Casa
tel. and fax 0532 63066
buccimg@libero.it
www.turistipercasa.it
Open: March to October and New Year's Day

TCI 10%

This panoramic villa, a few mins from the city center, is immersed in the fragrance and colors of the citrus orchards. It offers a suite with 18th-C furnishings and two large bright rooms – the "tangerine room" and the "lemon room" – each provided with every comfort. The traditional English breakfast also includes typical specialties of the Sorrento peninsula. In warm weather, breakfast is served on the terrace, which provides a nice view of the Gulf of Naples. There's a swimming pool 50 m away, and transportation from the station is "on the house".

Accommodation
Guestrooms: *3 doubles, also single occupancy, with private bath; additional bed on request*
Services & Amenities: *French and English are spoken; rooms cleaned every day; tourist information; baby-sitting service; lunch & dinner reservations; educational courses by request; terrace; air conditioning; Internet access; garden; smokers welcome; private parking*
Rates: *single and double €€€€. Suite supplement €€. Additional bed supplement €€. Discounts for extended stays*
Credit cards: VISA MC
Pets: no

Palazzo Starace
Home Express
tel. and fax 06 90129063
homeexpress@tiscalinet.it
www.home-express.it
Open all year

This restructured, early 20th-C building is located in Sorrento's old center, just a short walk from the port and the sea. The hosts provide 3 guest bedrooms, each furnished in modern, Mediterranean style and in shades of light blue. Two of these rooms have a terrace. Classic Italian breakfast is normally offered at the bar adjoining the B&B. A crib is also available for those who have a child.

Accommodation
Guestrooms: *3 (2 doubles and 1 triple room, with private bath)*
Services & Amenities: *English and spoken; rooms cleaned every day; tourist information; terrace; smokers welcome; private parking*
Minimum stay: *3 nights*
Rates: *double €€€-€€€€, triple €€€€. Children under 2 free. Discounts for extended stays.*
Credit cards: VISA MC *Bancomat*
Pets: yes

• Bed & Breakfast Italia
Code C27
tel. 06 6878618, fax 06 6878619
info@bbitalia.it
www.bbitalia.it
Closed: varies

This small house with a panoramic view is located about 2 kilometers from the town center. The guest accommodation consists in two double rooms with ensuite shower/bathroom with sauna and Jacuzzi and includes TV, air conditioning and balcony. The bus stop for the town center is 300 meters from the B&B. Guests can play ping-pong in the games room or relax by the swimming-pool in summertime. Optional cot for children under two. Private parking available for guests.

Accommodation
Guestrooms: *2 doubles*
Services & Amenities: *French, English and German are spoken; rooms cleaned every three days; complimentary tourist information; air conditioning; private parking*
Minimum stay: *2 nights*
Rates: *€€*
Credit cards: VISA MC *Bancomat*
Pets: no

Torre del Greco (Naples)

A Casa di Annamaria e Riccardo
• A Casa di Parthenope
tel. 081 7944186, mob. 338 6880058
fax 081 7944186
info@casadiparthenope.it
www.casadiparthenope.it
Open all year

This B&B is located on the coastline between Naples and Sorrento. Years ago, this coast was where the Neapolitan elite spent their holidays. It provides a large living room with period furniture, bright rooms, and terraces where the guests can enjoy a beautiful view of the Gulf of Naples. In the kitchen with fireplace, the hostess offers a rich breakfast consisting of hot beverages, local sweets and traditional cakes.

Accommodation
Guestrooms: *3 (1 single and 2 double bedrooms, with private bath); additional bed on request*
Services & Amenities: *French and English are spoken; rooms cleaned every day; tourist information; terrace; Internet access; garden; smokers welcome; private parking*
Minimum stay: *2 nights*
Rates: *single €€, double €€€. Children under 12 -50%*
Credit cards: *not accepted*
Pets: *not allowed*

Tramonti (Salerno)

B&B Nirvana TCI 10%
Gloria Giordano
via Sclavo 61
84010 Tramonti (SA)
tel. 089 876649
pidima@inwind.it
• Associazione Turisti per Casa
tel. and fax 0532 63066
buccimg@libero.it
www.turistipercasa.it
Open all year

In a restructured villa surrounded by vegetation, and just 10 km from Amalfi, this B&B makes the ideal base for visiting the tourist attractions of the Amalfi coast, as well as for hiking through the Lattari Mountains. The villa is furnished with antiques, has brickwork flooring and offers a large room and a terrace. Breakfast features local products and organically cultivated fruit in season.

Accommodation
Guestrooms: *1 double bedroom, also single occupancy, with private bath; additional bed on request*
Services & Amenities: *French, English and German are spoken; rooms cleaned every day; tourist information; baby-sitting service; lunch & dinner reservations; bike rental; educational courses by request; terrace; garden; smokers welcome; private parking*
Minimum stay: *3 nights*
Rates: *single €€, double €€€. Additional bed supplement €. Children under 3 free. Discounts for extended stays*
Credit cards: *not accepted*
Pets: *not allowed*

Vico Equense (Naples)

Astapiana
Giovanna Rispoli
via Camaldoli
80069 Vico Equense (NA)
tel. 081 403797
astapiana@tin.it
Open: April to October

This 17th-C house, located on the hills of the Sorrento peninsula, was once a Camaldolite hermitage. Surrounded by olive trees and grapevines, it still has the ancient columned walkway of the hermits that permits a panoramic view of the Gulf of Naples. The rooms are furnished with antiques. The kitchen, where guests are served a rich breakfast of cottage cheese and "diavulilli" (small Italian cheese with red pepper), still has the original 18th-C majolicas, the water well, the fireplace with its copper pans and the marble work surfaces.

Accommodation
Guestrooms: *3 doubles, private bath*
Services & Amenities: *French and English are spoken; rooms cleaned every 3 days; tourist information; terrace; Internet access; smokers welcome; private parking*
Minimum stay: *3 nights*
Rates: *€€-€€€. Discounts for extended stays*
Credit cards: *not accepted*
Pets: *not allowed*

Puglia

Alberobello (Bari)

• **Bed & Breakfast Italia**
Code PU13
tel. 06 6878618, fax 06 6878619
info@bbitalia.it
www.bbitalia.it
Closed: varies

B&B located in "trulli" houses, the typical Apulia dwellings of prehistoric origin. They are characterized by whitewashed walls and a distinctive conical roof made up of gray stones. Five small apartments furnished in a cheerful style are available: 3 with a double bed and 2 with three beds, private bathroom with shower. An extra bed for children can be added on request. The hosts provide information about tours and wine and culinary haunts in the area.

Accommodation
Guestrooms: *5 (3 doubls, 2 triples)*
Services & Amenities: *English and German are spoken; rooms cleaned every 3 days; tourist informations; terrace; private parking*
Minimum stay: *2 nights*
Rates: €€
Credit cards: VISA MC *Bancomat*
Pets:

Andria (Bari)

La Ualanìa
Pina Stolfa
strada statale 170 al km 18,500
località Citulo
70031 Andria (BA)
tel. 0883 569850, fax 080 8984091
Closed: 15 to 31 August

This B&B is hosted in a restructured, stone farmhouse, situated in the heart of the Alta Murgia, which is just 1 km from Castel del Monte. The guest house is where the "ualano" used to live. He was the man who worked in the vineyard. Now it has a small living room with a kitchenette and a surrounding garden. Breakfast, which also includes bread with tomato and oil, and a cream that's typical of this area, made from sheep-milk cottage cheese, is either served in the apartment or in the main house.

Accommodation
Guestrooms: *1 mini-apartment (2-4 beds)*
Services & Amenities: *English spoken; rooms cleaned every 3 days; tourist information; kitchenette; bike rental; horse-riding excursions; garden; smokers welcome; private parking*
Rates: *double €€, quadruple €€€€. Discounts for children and extended stays*
Credit cards: *not accepted*
Pets:

BARI

• **Bed & Breakfast Italia**
Code PU3
tel. 06 6878618, fax 06 6878619
info@bbitalia.it
www.bbitalia.it
Closed: varies

This apartment is situated on the fifth floor of an old building in the old center of Bari where important monuments are found in its winding streets. The accommodation consists in a single room with TV, large balcony and private bathroom with shower. It is traditionally and elegantly furnished with antiques, matching curtains and bedspread. Your hostess serves generous breakfasts with typical local produce in the spacious lounge and is happy to provide useful information about the town. This B&B is 200 meters from the beach.

ACCOMMODATION
Guestrooms: *1 single*
Services & Amenities: *French and English are spoken; rooms cleaned every 3 days; tourist information*
Minimum stay: *2 nights*
Rates: €€
Credit cards: VISA MC *Bancomat*
Pets: 🚫

CASTELLANA-GROTTE (BARI)

• **Bed & Breakfast Italia**
Code PU15
tel. 06 6878618, fax 06 6878619
info@bbitalia.it
www.bbitalia.it
Closed: varies

This small, detached house is set in the countryside 25 km from the Apulia sea. It has two rooms: one with a double bed and one with three single beds, furnished in a modern and functional style, with an independent entrance and large balcony. The bathroom with shower is shared by the two rooms. The B&B is 30 km from Alberobello, famous for its original houses, and 20 km from Monopoli.

ACCOMMODATION
Guestrooms: *2 (1 double bedroom and 1 triple room)*
Services & Amenities: *French and English are spoken; rooms cleaned every 3 days; tourist information; terrace; private parking*
Minimum stay: *2 nights*
Rates: €€
Credit cards: VISA MC *Bancomat*
Pets: 🚫

CASTRIGNANO DEL CAPO (LECCE)

Villa La Meridiana TCI 10%
Attilio Caputo
lungomare C. Colombo 61
località Santa Maria di Leuca
73040 Castrignano del Capo (LE)
tel. 0833 758242, fax 0833 758246
lameridiana@attiliocaroli.it
www.lameridiana.it
Open all year

ACCOMMODATION
Guestrooms: *1 suite (5 beds)*
Services & Amenities: *French and English are spoken; rooms cleaned every day; tourist info; kitchenette; terrace; air conditioning; garden; smokers welcome; private parking*
Rates: €€€€
Credit cards: DC VISA MC *Bancomat*
Pets: ✓

This B&B, on the ground floor of a 19th-C villa that's bound by the Art Superintendence, consists of an elegant suite that has an independent entrance, 2 bedrooms, living room, kitchenette, fireplace, period furniture, air conditioning, satellite TV and telephone. Breakfast, consisting of pastries made by the hostess, can also be served outside in the park among the bougainvillaea shrubs, palms and pine trees. Besides the park's swimming pool, guests can also enjoy the use of a private beach, a bathing hut, and a boat.

Castro Marina (Lecce)

La Casetta
• Latte e Miele Salento
tel. 0836 484242, mob. 347 8182786
salento@sleepinitaly.com
www.sleepinitaly.com/salento
Open: June to October

This B&B, which is at the Castro Marina inlet – 45 kilometers from Lecce – and has a large terrace facing the sea, is perfect for enjoying a nice, relaxing vacation. The small, guest apartment, which has three beds and modern, functional furnishings, is located in a small, recently-restructured villa that has private access to the sea. The hostess prepares a small, self-service, buffet breakfast consisting of fruit juices, natural marmalades, homemade pastries and, if desired, cold cuts and various types of cheese.

Accommodation
Guestrooms: *1 mini-apartment with 3 beds*
Services & Amenities: *French and English are spoken; rooms cleaned every three days; complimentary tourist information; kitchen use by request*
Minimum stay: *2 nights*
Rates: €€€€
Credit cards: *not accepted*
Pets:

Cisternino (Brindisi)

I Tramonti di Calongo
Michaela Beckert
località Calongo
72014 Cisternino (BR)
tel. 080 4449140, fax 080 4443273
beckert@tin.it
Open all year

This B&B is in a 19th-C complex consisting of a small chapel and 4 trullies (typical cone-roofed dwellings of Puglia). Guests have independent apartments in two of the trullies and the use of the chapel. Each trulli is furnished in a different style and has an equipped kitchen. The breakfast of organic and natural products is served on the shared patio. Guests have the use of scooters, and also have access to a 7-passenger-car shuttle service.

Accommodation
Guestrooms: *3 mini-apartments (2-4 beds each)* ♿
Services & Amenities: *French, English and German are spoken; rooms cleaned every 3 days; tourist information; kitchen use by request; bike rental; Internet access; garden; private parking*
Minimum stay: *3 nights*
Rates: *double* €€-€€€, *quadruple room* €€€€
Credit cards: *not accepted*
Pets:

Conversano (Bari)

• Bed & Breakfast Italia
Code PU24
tel. 06 6878618, fax 06 6878619
info@bbitalia.it
www.bbitalia.it
Closed: varies

This apartment is situated on the top (third) floor of a building in an area facing a public garden with playground and indoor sports facilities. It consists in a double bedroom with TV and independent entrance; a single bedroom with large balcony, all simply and comfortably furnished. The house is equipped with air conditioning. The town of Conversano preserves an outstanding artistic and archaeological heritage represented by several churches and by its famous castle.

Accommodation
Guestrooms: *2 (1 single and 1 double bedroom, with private bath)*
Services & Amenities: *French and English are spoken; rooms cleaned every three days; tourist information; bike rental; air conditioning; smokers welcome; private parking*
Minimum stay: *2 nights*
Rates: €€
Credit cards: VISA MC *Bancomat*
Pets:

GALATONE (LECCE)

Masseria Lo Prieno
Maria Grazia Castriota
contrada Orelle, 73044 Galatone (LE)
tel. 0833 865898, 0833 865443
fax 0833 861879
Closed: October

This B&B is located in a 19th-C farmhouse – located 10 km from the sea – that's surrounded by a large area with olive trees and a pine grove. Rooms have modern furnishings and an independent entrance. Breakfast of natural products and genuine pastries, is served in the dining room, where guests can also have lunch and dinner. Guests are free to use the bocce court, tennis court and mare-drawn carriage for taking rides in the vicinity.

ACCOMMODATION
Guestrooms: *6 doubles with private bath; additional bed on request*
Services & Amenities: *English spoken; rooms cleaned every three days; complimentary tourist information; lunch & dinner reservations; bike rental; horse-riding excursions; garden; smokers welcome; private parking*
Minimum stay: *2 nights*
Rates: *double €€€. Additional bed supplement €. Discounts for children and extended stays*
Credit cards: MC *Bancomat*
Pets:

GRAVINA IN PUGLIA (BARI)

Agri Biologica delle Murge
Capone Michele
località Dolcecanto
70024 Gravina in Puglia (BA)
tel. 0803 269717, 0803 267566
mob. 348 3812083
fax 0803 262860
mcapone@murge.it
www.murgia.it/abm
Open: Easter holidays to September

This B&B is located in an old, restructured farmhouse that has a furnished garden complete with games for children, and offers 3 double rooms. The place is surrounded by cultivated fields of crops that are strictly organic. The rich breakfast, consisting of products from this farm, is either served under the portico or in the dining room. Guests also have the use of a barbecue, a swimming pool for children, a camping area and an equipped camper. The hosts offer their guests the opportunity of participating in the farm's activities, as well as engaging in various sports.

ACCOMMODATION
Guestrooms: *3 doubles, also single occupancy, with shared bath; additional bed on request*
Services & Amenities: *English spoken; rooms cleaned every three days; tourist information; baby-sitting service; kitchen use by request; horse-riding excursions; educational courses by request; garden; smokers welcome; private parking*
Minimum stay: *2 nights*
Rates: *single €, double €€. Additional bed supplement €. Children under 3 free*
Credit cards: *not accepted*
Pets:

• Bed & Breakfast Italia
Code PU20
tel. 06 6878618, fax 06 6878619
info@bbitalia.it
www.bbitalia.it
Closed: Easter holidays to September

ACCOMMODATION
Guestrooms: *1 double bedroom*
Services & Amenities: *English spoken; rooms cleaned every three days; complimentary tourist information; baby-sitting service; bike rental; Internet access*
Minimum stay: *2 nights*
Rates: €
Credit cards: MC *Bancomat*
Pets:

A rustic farmhouse, the home of an organic farm, situated in Dolcecanto, a hilltop village about 450 meters above sea level. The guest accommodation consists in a double bedroom; the bathroom is shared with the hosts. The furnishings are rustic and functional. This small village can be reached by bus from Gravina (two daily services) or by train (Foggia-Gravina-Gioia line). The Metaponto Ionian coast is 75 kilometers away, and the Bari Adriatic coast is 75 kilometers away. The hostis happy to provide useful information about the surrounding area

ISCHITELLA (FOGGIA)

• Bed & Breakfast Italia
Code PU28
tel. 06 6878618, fax 06 6878619
info@bbitalia.it
www.bbitalia.it
Closed: varies

A farmhouse situated in the Park of Gargano, 5 km from the sea, in the province of Foggia. It has six rooms furnished in a cheerful and comfortable style, each with TV and private bathroom with shower. Guests can enjoy the swimming pool, tennis court and garden, offering a stunning view of Lake Varano. The Tremiti Islands can be reached by boat; Vieste and Rodi Garganico are within half an hour's drive.

ACCOMMODATION
Guestrooms: *6 (4 double bedrooms, 2 quadruples, private bath)* ♿
Services & Amenities: *French and German are spoken; rooms cleaned every 3 days; tourist information*
Minimum stay: *2 nights*
Rates: €
Credit cards: VISA MC *Bancomat*
Pets: no

LECCE

B&B Centro Storico
Mauro Bianco
via A. Vignes 2b
73100 Lecce
tel. 0832 242727, 0832 242828
mob. 338 5881265, fax 0832 242727
bed_breakfast.lecce@libero.it
www.bedandbreakfast.lecce.it
Open all year

This B&B is located in a restructured building that dates from the year 1500. The guestrooms have star-vaulted ceilings, classic-style furniture and all the comforts, including air conditioning, mini-bar and private balconies. Guests also have the use of a reading room with a library of tourist information, where breakfast is also served. Guests are welcome to relax on the terrace. Arrangements can be made for boarding animals and for taking various excursions.

ACCOMMODATION
Guestrooms: *5 (3 doubles also single occupancy, with shared bath, 1 triple and 1 suite with private bath); additional bed on request* ♿
Services & Amenities: *French and English are spoken; rooms cleaned every day; tourist info; terrace; air conditioning; smokers welcome*
Rates: *single €, double €€. Additional bed supplement €. Children under 3 free*
Credit cards: *accepted*
Pets: yes

B&B Dolce Casa
Andreina Goffredo
viale Marche 15
73100 Lecce
tel. and fax 0832 231724
b.and.b_goffredo@tin.it

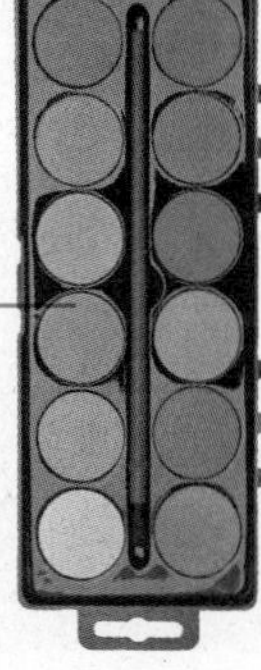

This B&B is located in a 1st-floor apartment of a '70s building situated on the outer edge of Lecce's old center. Guests have six large double rooms with modern furnishings and air conditioning, and each room has a different color. The Breakfast is served in the guestrooms. The hostess, an artist, has hung some her paintings in the guestrooms and in the small, shared living room.

ACCOMMODATION
Guestrooms: *6 doubles, also single occupancy, with private bath; additional bed on request*
Services & Amenities: *French and English are spoken; rooms cleaned every day; tourist info; terrace; air conditioning; Internet access; smokers welcome*
Rates: *single €, double €€. Additional bed supplement €. Discounts for children -10%*
Credit cards: *not accepted*
Pets: no

Il Portoncino
• Latte e Miele Salento
tel. 0836 484242, mob. 347 8182786
salento@sleepinitaly.com
www.sleepinitaly.com/salento
Open all year

This B&B, near the Cathedral, in the heart of the old part of Lecce, is ideal for anyone wanting to experience the typical peace and quiet of an old village. The accommodation offers a small guest apartment with period furniture, a bedroom, a small living room with a kitchenette, and a wooden, intermediate level where a 3rd bed can be located. Breakfast is the continental type.

Accommodation
Guestrooms: *1 mini-apartment with 3 beds*
Services & Amenities: *rooms cleaned every day; complimentary tourist information; kitchenette; smokers welcome*
Rates: €€€
Credit cards: *not accepted*
Pets: 🚫

La Casa al Campanile
• Latte e Miele Salento
tel. 0836 484242, mob. 347 8182786
salento@sleepinitaly.com
www.sleepinitaly.com/salento
Open all year

This B&B, located in the old center, in a 17th-C building situated at the foot of the Cathedral bell tower, has refined period furniture that adds further charm to the place and gives it a classic, traditional look. Besides enjoying the very tranquil, reserved atmosphere, guests can also enjoy such comforts as a tub with a hydromassage, a TV in the room, and a flowery terrace, which is especially nice on pleasant, summer evenings. Breakfast features local pastries and is served in the elegant dining room, which has a typical, vaulted, Lecce ceiling and a stone fireplace.

Accommodation
Guestrooms: *1 double with private bath; additional bed on request*
Services & Amenities: *rooms cleaned every 3 days; tourist information; terrace; Internet access; smokers welcome; private parking*
Minimum stay: *2 nights*
Rates: €€€€. *Additional bed supplement* €
Credit cards: *not accepted*
Pets: 🚫

The base of a column of the baroque aedicula of the Olivetan convent in Lecce.

Manfredonia (Foggia)

• Bed & Breakfast Italia
Code PU12
tel. 06 6878618, fax 06 6878619
info@bbitalia.it
www.bbitalia.it
Closed: varies

Accommodation
Guestrooms: *3 (1 single, 1 double bedroom and 1 triple room)*
Services & Amenities: *French and English are spoken; rooms cleaned every three days; complimentary tourist information; terrace*
Minimum stay: *2 nights*
Rates: €
Credit cards: VISA MC *Bancomat*
Pets: 🚫

A first-floor recently restored house in a leafy area directly on the sea. Outside parking available. The accommodation consists in a single room with shared bathroom, a double room with double bed, TV and private bathroom with shower, a triple with a single and a double bed and private bathroom with shower and an independent entrance. This B&B is about 18 kilometers from San Giovanni Rotondo and Monte San Giovanni.

Martina Franca (Taranto)

• **Bed & Breakfast Italia**
Code PU26
tel. 06 6878618, fax 06 6878619
info@bbitalia.it
www.bbitalia.it
Closed: varies

The B&B is in a small countryhouse 1.5 km from Martina Franca, an old town in the Murge area founded in 1300. This accommodation offers a triple room with double and single bed, large balcony and private bathroom with shower. The furnishings are modern, colorful and cheerful. The breakfast is served by the lady of the house in the lounge. An extra bed for children under two, a garden and private parking are available.

Accommodation
Guestrooms: *1 triple*
Services & Amenities: *French, English and German are spoken; rooms cleaned every three days; complimentary tourist information; terrace; smokers welcome; private parking*
Minimum stay: *2 nights*
Rates: *€€*
Credit cards: VISA MC *Bancomat*
Pets: 🚫

Monopoli (Bari)

Curatori
Onofrio Contento
contrada Cristo delle Zolle 227
70043 Monopoli (BA)
tel. and fax 080 777472
agricurcont@libero.it
Open all year

This farmholiday B&B is hosted by an 18th-century farmhouse situated in the open country, just 2 kilometers from the center of Monopoli. The accommodation consists in a suite and double rooms, all provided with a private bathroom and an independent entrance. Rooms, some of which are in the main house and others in the dépendance, have rustic furniture. The continental breakfast, which consists of natural products, is served in a room that's shared with the hosts. There's also a riding stable on the property. Private parking available for the guests.

Accommodation
Guestrooms: *2 doubles, also single occupancy, and 3 suites, with private bath*
Services & Amenities: *English spoken; rooms cleaned every 3 days; tourist info; lunch & dinner reservations; horse-riding excursions; garden; smokers welcome; parking*
Rates: *single €, double €€-€€€. Children under 12 -10%*
Credit cards: *not accepted*
Pets: 🚫

Mottola (Taranto)

• **Bed & Breakfast Italia**
Code PU25
tel. 06 6878618, fax 06 6878619
info@bbitalia.it
www.bbitalia.it
Closed: varies

The B&B is a complex of apartments thoroughly restored respecting the local architecture. The guest accommodation includes six triple rooms, all with double and single beds, TV, and private bathroom equipped with shower, featuring period country-style furniture. The rich continental breakfast is served in the rooms. Guests may have lunch or dinner by reservation at the restaurant below. The village is 15 km from the sea. Baby-sitting service available.

Accommodation
Guestrooms: *6 triple rooms*
Services & Amenities: *English spoken; rooms cleaned every 3 days; tourist information; baby-sitting service; air conditioning*
Minimum stay: *2 nights*
Rates: *€€*
Credit cards: VISA MC *Bancomat*
Pets: 🚫

NARDÒ (LECCE)

• **Bed & Breakfast Italia**
Code PU6
tel. 06 6878618, fax 06 6878619
info@bbitalia.it
www.bbitalia.it
Closed: varies

ACCOMMODATION
Guestrooms: *4 double bedrooms; additional bed on request*
Services & Amenities: *French and English are spoken; rooms cleaned every 3 days; tourist information*
Minimum stay: *2 nights*
Rates: €€
Credit cards: VISA MC *Bancomat*
Pets: allowed

The B&B is hosted by a comfortable and functional cottage. The accommodation consists in two double bedrooms, each with private bathroom, and two double bedrooms sharing one bathroom. All the rooms feature a wardrobe, chest-of-drawers, dresser, writing desk, and table. Garden with parking is also available for the guests. Breakfast is prepared and served by the hosts in the lounge or under the pergola.

OSTUNI (BRINDISI)

Il Frantoio
strada statale 16 al km 874
72017 Ostuni (BR)
tel. and fax 0831 330276
ilfrantoio@pugliaonline.it
www.trecolline.it
Open all year

ACCOMMODATION
Guestrooms: *6 (2 doubles, 2 triples, 1 quadruple and 1 with 5 beds, with private bath)*
Services & Amenities: *French and English are spoken; rooms cleaned every day; tourist information; dinner reservation; bike rental; horse-riding excursions; garden; smokers welcome; parking*
Minimum stay: *2 nights*
Rates: €€€ *per person. Discounts for children -40%*
Credit cards: VISA
Pets: not allowed

This B&B is just a short distance from the sea. It's located in an ancient fortified farmhouse, surrounded by olive trees, and it has an underground olive press, as well as a citrus orchard and a garden. It still has its original courtyard, where the guests can enjoy the shade in the daytime or nice candlelight dinners in the evening. The hosts raise small farm animals and horses. Breakfast includes family products like organic oil, marmalades, pastries and yoghurt, while the refined dinners feature vegetable preserves and meat.

• **Bed & Breakfast Italia**
Code PU17
tel. 06 6878618, fax 06 6878619
info@bbitalia.it
www.bbitalia.it
Closed: varies

ACCOMMODATION
Guestrooms: *2 (1 double bedroom and 1 double); additional bed on request*
Services & Amenities: *French spoken; rooms cleaned every 3 days; tourist information; terrace; smokers welcome; private parking*
Minimum stay: *2 nights*
Rates: €€
Credit cards: VISA MC *Bancomat*
Pets: not allowed

An old complex of "trulli", the famous Apulia dwellings of prehistoric origin, characterized by whitewashed walls and a typical conical roof made of gray stones. They are set in the leafy area of Selva Ostunense, a quiet and panoramic area, 2 km from town and 6 km from the sea. The furnishings are in bright lively colors. They consist in double or twin rooms, large balcony, TV, private bathroom with shower. Garden and private parking available. On request, the hosts provide guided tours or car rental for visiting the area.

• **Bed & Breakfast Italia**
Code PU29
tel. 06 6878618, fax 06 6878619
info@bbitalia.it
www.bbitalia.it
Closed: varies

The villa and the studio situated 5 km from the sea are both entirely for guest use. It consists in two bedrooms, a double-bed and a twin-bed, a large sitting room with a fireplace and TV, a kitchen, bathroom with washing machine, veranda and parking. The studio includes a double bedroom, a kitchen, TV, veranda and parking. Tennis courts, a swimming pool and several bathing establishments are located in the area. Guests can use the B&B bicycles.

Accommodation
Guestrooms: *3 doubles*
Services & Amenities: *English and Spanish are spoken; rooms cleaned every three days; tourist information; smokers welcome; private parking*
Minimum stay: *2 nights*
Rates: €€
Credit cards: VISA MC *Bancomat*
Pets: allowed

Otranto (Lecce)

Palazzo delli Falconi
• **Latte e Miele Salento**
tel. 0836 484242, mob. 347 8182786
salento@sleepinitaly.com
www.sleepinitaly.com/salento
Open all year

This tranquil B&B is located in the Palazzo delli Falconi, a 16th-C building that has considerable architectural value. It's only a short distance from the Cathedral of Otranto, where one can see the only religious mosaic existing in southern Italy. The B&B has four large double rooms, all furnished in the classical style with period furniture. The panoramic terrace, which provides an impressive view of the church, is where the hostess serves breakfast, consisting of warm beverages, marmalades and homemade pastries.

Accommodation
Guestrooms: *4 doubles, with private bath*
Services & Amenities: *French and English are spoken; rooms cleaned every day; tourist information; kitchen use by request; terrace; Internet access; smokers welcome; private parking*
Minimum stay: *3 nights*
Rates: *double €€€€*
Credit cards: *not accepted*
Pets: not allowed

Peschici (Foggia)

Villa Passiaturo TCI 10%
Franco Losito
viale Libetta 30
71010 Peschici (FG)
tel. and fax 0884 963040
Open: Easter holidays to late October

This recently-reconstructed villa, located in the center of Peschici, is only 1 km from the sea. It provides a convenient base for taking trips to the Gargano or going to the Tremiti Islands. Guestrooms have modern furniture, a private bathroom, TV and refrigerator. Beakfast, which consists of pastries, cold cuts and various types of cheese, is either served on the terrace or in a small dining room.

Accommodation
Guestrooms: *3 (2 doubles, also single occupancy, 1 triple; private bath)*
Services & Amenities: *English and German are spoken; rooms cleaned every day; tourist information; terrace; garden; smokers welcome*
Rates: *single €€€, double €€€€. Children under 6 -50%*
Credit cards: *not accepted*
Pets: not allowed

Polignano a Mare (Bari)

Villa Annamaria
Diego Altomonte
Case Sparse 49
70044 Polignano a Mare (BA)
tel. and fax 080 4240302
daltomonte@mail.media.it
Open all year

This recently-built villa, which provides a magnificent view, is surrounded by pine trees and cactus plants. It's just outside of Polignano a Mare (which is 33 kilometers from Bari) and only a short distance from the small Cala Paguro port. The guest apartments have a kitchen and a fireplace and two rooms: a double and one with four beds. The rich breakfast, consisting of genuine pastries, crêpes and marmalades, is served on the family terrace. The family has been passionately constructing balloons for several years.

Accommodation
Guestrooms: *2 mini-apartments (2 and 4 beds)*
Services & Amenities: *French, English and Arabic are spoken; rooms cleaned every 3 days; tourist info; kitchen use by request; terrace; garden; smokers welcome*
Minimum stay: *2 nights*
Rates: €€€
Credit cards: *not accepted*
Pets: 🐾

Pulsano (Taranto)

• Bed & Breakfast Italia
Code PU5
tel. 06 6878618, fax 06 6878619
info@bbitalia.it
www.bbitalia.it
Closed: varies

Five studio apartments with vaulted ceilings in "tufa" rock in an old Ionian farmhouse thoroughly refurbished to preserve its Mediterranean tradition. It offers four double bedrooms and a triple furnished in simple rustic style; all have private bathrooms with shower, large balcony and kitchenette. A tennis court, soccer field, bocce court ground and jogging track are exclusively available to guests; bicycles may be rented. Smokers are welcome. A private car park is also available.

Accommodation
Guestrooms: *5 (4 double bedrooms and 1 triple room)*
Services & Amenities: *French, English, German and Spanish are spoken; rooms cleaned every 3 days; tourist information; horse-riding excursions; terrace; smokers welcome; private parking*
Minimum stay: *2 nights*
Rates: €€
Credit cards: VISA MC *Bancomat*
Pets: no pets

• Bed & Breakfast Italia
Code PU8
tel. 06 6878618, fax 06 6878619
info@bbitalia.it
www.bbitalia.it
Closed: varies

Accommodation
Guestrooms: *3 doubles*
Services & Amenities: *French and English are spoken; rooms cleaned every 3 days; complimentary tourist information ; horse-riding excursions; terrace; smokers welcome; private parking*
Minimum stay: *2 nights*
Rates: €€
Credit cards: VISA MC *Bancomat*
Pets: no pets

This accommodation is hosted in a house built in the fifties and offers three double bedrooms with single beds and two bathrooms with tub/shower. All the rooms have a balcony and TV. An extra bed for children under two is available. In summer, guests can take courses in sailing, windsurfing and flying ultra-light planes and they can enjoy concerts such as the operatic music festival of Valle d'Itria and the jazz festival of Cisternino. Marina di Pulsano is 20 km from Taranto.

Rodi Garganico (Foggia)

• **Bed & Breakfast Italia**
Code PU16
tel. 06 6878618, fax 06 6878619
info@bbitalia.it
www.bbitalia.it
Closed: varies

High above the sea, this villa is surrounded by woodlands and colorful orange-blossom. The sea is 300 meters away. The accommodation offers five rooms, three with double beds and two triples, all with TV, private bathroom with shower and large, panoramic balcony. The furnishings are bright, simple and functional. The rich breakfast is served on a large, scenic veranda. A garden and private parking are also available. Folk-shows are held for the guests.

Accommodation
Guestrooms: *5 (3 doubles, 2 triples)*
Services & Amenities: *English and Spanish are spoken; rooms cleaned every 3 days; tourist information; terrace; private parking*
Minimum stay: *2 nights*
Rates: *€€*
Credit cards: VISA MC *Bancomat*
Pets:

San Giovanni Rotondo (Foggia)

Famiglia Morcaldi
corso Nazionale 30
71013 San Giovanni Rotondo (FG)
tel. 0882 456835, mob. 347 0963917
Open all year

This B&B, which can host up to 8 persons, is in a recently-constructed building located in center of town and 20 kilometers from the Gulf of Manfredonia. Guests have a plainly-furnished apartment with two bedrooms, a living room, a bathroom and a kitchen. And guests also have the use of one parking space under cover. Breakfast, which the hostess prepares as requested by her guests, is served in the house. However, if preferred, guests can prepare their own breakfast. San Giovanni Rotondo is especially noted for its many faithful followers of Padre Pio.

Olive groves on the Gargano coast.

Accommodation
Guestrooms: *2 (4 beds with shared bath)*
Services & Amenities: *French, English and Spanish are spoken; rooms cleaned every day; tourist information; smokers welcome; private parking*
Rates: *€ per person*
Credit cards: *not accepted*
Pets:

• **Bed & Breakfast Italia**
Code PU18
tel. 06 6878618, fax 06 6878619
info@bbitalia.it
www.bbitalia.it
Closed: varies

Accommodation
Guestrooms: *3 (1 double bedroom and 2 triple rooms)*
Services & Amenities: *English spoken; rooms cleaned every 3 days; tourist info; smokers welcome*
Minimum stay: *2 nights*
Rates: *€€*
Credit cards: VISA MC *Bancomat*
Pets:

A first-floor apartment in a building in the old center, 600 m from the Santa Maria delle Grazie cloister, on the main road to the monastery. The accommodation consists in a double bedroom and two triple rooms with single beds, both with TV. The two private bathrooms are equipped with shower. The village, the destination of pilgrims visiting Padre Pio's birthplace, is adjacent to the National Park of Gargano, 40 km from the sea. The seaside resorts of Vieste and Rodi Garganico are easily reached.

San Pietro Vernotico (Brindisi)

Solange Marzano Pedrini TCI 10%
via Rizzo 24
72027 San Pietro Vernotico (BR)
tel. 0831 653882, fax 0831 655159
solange@tiscalinet.it
Open: Easter holidays to late October

This early 20th-C villa, located in the center of town, has a large garden with several trees. Guests have the use of a two-story dépendance, which has a double room, a living room with TV, a kitchen, a bathroom, a sofabed and a terrace. Breakfast is by request (the family produces alimentary preserves) and can either be served in the garden or in the main house. Alternatively, the guests can serve themselves in the apartment.

Squinzano, the abbey of Santa Maria delle Cerrate (12th cent.), 10 km from San Pietro Vernotico.

Accommodation
Guestrooms: *1 mini-apartment (4 beds); additional bed on request*
Services & Amenities: *French, English and German are spoken; rooms cleaned every day; tourist information; kitchen use by request; garden; smokers welcome; private parking*
Rates: *€€€. Discounts for extended stays*
Credit cards: *not accepted*
Pets: allowed

San Severo (Foggia)

• Bed & Breakfast Italia
Code PU27
tel. 06 6878618, fax 06 6878619
info@bbitalia.it
www.bbitalia.it
Closed: varies

A nineteenth-century farmhouse with riding-ground in the province of Foggia, 25 km from the sea. It has two rooms with French windows opening onto the garden of the house: one is a double bedroom with twin beds, and the other is a triple with a double bed and a single; both are classically furnished with antiques. The rooms share a private bathroom with shower. The continental breakfast is served in the garden.

Accommodation
Guestrooms: *2 (1 double, 1 triple)* ♿
Services & Amenities: *English spoken; rooms cleaned every 3 days; tourist information; bike rental; horse-riding excursions*
Minimum stay: *2 nights*
Rates: €€
Credit cards: Visa MC *Bancomat*
Pets: not allowed

Spongano (Lecce)

La Corte del Mito
Anna Addario Chieco
via Congregazione 53
73038 Spongano (LE)
tel. 0832 246255, 0836 945023
mob. 339 5451307, fax 0832 246255
antonioriz@libero.it
www.lamacchiola.it
Closed: February and March

This B&B is 50 kilometers from Lecce, in an aristocratic, 19th-century building situated in the Salento countryside, in a small, rural village that's next to a organic farm. Two of the guestrooms, which have classic Tuscan furnishings, are in an independent apartment. Breakfast, which consists of natural and local products, is either served in the large garden or in the dining room.

Accommodation
Guestrooms: *2 double bedrooms, also single occupancy, private bath; 1 mini-apartment (4 beds)*
Services & Amenities: *French and English are spoken; rooms cleaned every 3 days; tourist information; kitchen use by request; lunch & dinner reservations; bike rental; Internet access; garden; smokers welcome; private parking*
Minimum stay: *2 nights*
Rates: *single €€€, double €€€€, quadruple €€€€*
Credit cards: *not accepted*
Pets: not allowed

Turi (Bari)

• **Bed & Breakfast Italia**
Code PU19
tel. 06 6878618, fax 06 6878619
info@bbitalia.it
www.bbitalia.it
Closed: varies

A villa in the suburbs of Turi, a village in the Murgia area, near Bari. The house, which boasts a large outer space, is simply and comfortably furnished. It has four guestrooms: two singles, one double, one triple with a double and a single bed; all rooms are

with TV and large panoramic balcony. The three bathrooms have shower/tub. A private parking is also available for the guests. The coast can be reached in an hour's drive.

Accommodation
Guestrooms: *4 (2 singles, 1 double bedroom and 1 triple room)*
Services & Amenities: *French and English are spoken; rooms cleaned every three days; complimentary tourist information; smokers welcome; private parking*
Minimum stay: *2 nights*
Rates: €€
Credit cards: VISA MC *Bancomat*
Pets: no

Ugento (Lecce)

Villa Edy
Alessandro Coti
via Principe Amedeo 99
località Torre San Giovanni
73059 Ugento (LE)
tel. 0593 46233, 0833 931386
mob. 348 6043668
info@cabotobedandbreakfast.com
www.caabotobedandbreakfast.com
Open: March to October

This B&B, which consists of a modern villa with three independent trullies for the guests, is located in the Salento countryside. It's just a short distance from the sea and has a sailing school next to it. The room furnishings are very nice and the furnished garden, which is very well kept, also has a barbecue. Guests can also use the kitchen, take sailboat trips, make excursions and go fishing.

Accommodation
Guestrooms: *3 'trulli' (2-3 beds)* ♿
Services & Amenities: *French, English and Spanish are spoken; rooms cleaned every 3 days; tourist information; kitchen use by request; bike rental; educational courses by request; garden; smokers welcome; private parking*
Rates: *double €€, triple €€€€. Children €*
Credit cards: *not accepted*
Pets: yes

Vernole (Lecce)

• **Bed & Breakfast Italia**
Code PU23
tel. 06 6878618, fax 06 6878619
info@bbitalia.it
www.bbitalia.it
Closed: varies

Stay in farming surroundings in a Mediterranean-style villa in Vanze, in the heart of Salento, 3 km from the sea. It is set in an olive grove adjoining the "Le Cesine" WWF park. This accommodation offers five rooms: three double rooms and two triple rooms with double bed and single bed, all with TV, private bathroom, large balcony and independent entrance. Simple and comfortable furnishings. A large garden and private parking are also available. Meals served by the family on request are prepared with their homegrown products.

Accommodation
Guestrooms: *5 (3 double bedrooms and 2 triple rooms)* ♿
Services & Amenities: *English and Spanish are spoken; rooms cleaned every 3 days; tourist information; smokers welcome*
Minimum stay: *2 nights*
Rates: €€
Credit cards: VISA MC *Bancomat*
Pets: no

Basilicata

Abriola (Potenza)

La Dolce Vita
Maria Rosaria Robilotta
via Gelsi 16, contrada Valloni
85010 Abriola (PZ)
tel. 0971 923067, 0971 923524
Open: Easter and Christmas holidays, 14 February and May to October

This B&B is located at 900 m in a forest. The house is surrounded by almost 20 acres of cultivated farmland, which also makes it suitable for farm-holiday. Breakfast consists of natural pastries and organic marmalades made from the farm's products. On request, a typical Lucanian dinner can be provided. The family farm produces a particularly noteworthy mulberry syrup, which is also used for making excellent aperitifs and thirst-quenching beverages.

Accommodation
Guestrooms: *4 doubles, private bath; additional bed on request*
Services & Amenities: *French, English spoken; rooms cleaned every 3 days; tourist info; dinner reservation; terrace; garden; smokers welcome; private parking*
Minimum stay: *2 nights*
Rates: *double €€*
Credit cards: *not accepted*
Pets:

Avigliano (Potenza)

• Bed & Breakfast Italia TCI 10%
Code B1
tel. 06 6878618, fax 06 6878619
info@bbitalia.it, www.bbitalia.it
Closed: varies

This B&B is located in the old center of a small village, 15 kilometers from Potenza and 30 from Melfi, where the large Norman castle with polygonal towers deserves a visit. The area can be explored by bicycle or on horseback. A car is needed to reach the house. Private parking available.

Accommodation
Guestrooms: *4 (1 single, 2 doubles and 1 triple room)*
Services & Amenities: *French and English are spoken; rooms cleaned every 3 days; tourist information; baby-sitting service; private parking*
Minimum stay: *2 nights*
Rates: €€
Credit cards: VISA MC *Bancomat*
Pets:

Lagonegro (Potenza)

Valsirino
Mario Civale
~~contrada Niella, 85042 Lagonegro (PZ)~~
mob. 338 8158496
Open all year

Accommodation
Guestrooms: *huts, cottages (1-5 beds)*
Services & Amenities: *rooms cleaned every day; complimentary tourist information; kitchenette; lunch & dinner reservations; horse-riding excursions; garden; smokers welcome; private parking*
Rates: *€ per person. Discounts for children -50%*
Credit cards: *not accepted*
Pets:

This B&B is located at an altitude of 1200 m, 4 km from the ski lifts and 30 mins from the sea. Guests have the option of several huts and small houses with rustic furnishings and kitchen facilities. Breakfast, consisting of typical products and genuine pastries, is served in the dining room. The hosts, on request, can also provide lunch and dinner. On the adjoining terrain (on which there are also small farm animals) guests can go horseback riding or dog-sledding.

Calabria

Bova (Reggio di Calabria)

B&B Betty

• Calabria in Famiglia
tel. 0965 626840, mob. 328 9094209
fax 0965 626840
info@bbcalabria.it, www.bbcalabria.it
Open all year

This B&B is hosted in an early 20th-C house located in the middle of a village that's perched on a panoramic hill in the Greci di Calabria area. Breakfast consists of pastries, honey, natural marmalades and "scaddhatteddhe": typical local ring-shaped buns. The hostess is more than willing to make her kitchen available for those wishing to learn the secrets of making pasta and bread. There are various places in the vicinity that are full of natural beauty, history, legends and traditions.

Accommodation
Guestrooms: *2 doubles with shared bath; additional beds on request*
Services & Amenities: *English, French, Spanish and Greek are spoken; rooms cleaned every 3 days; tourist information; kitchen use by request; educational courses by request; smokers welcome; terrace*
Rates: *€ per person. Discounts for children and extended stays*
Credit cards: *not accepted*
Pets:

B&B Margherita

• Calabria in Famiglia
tel. 0965 626840, mob. 328 9094209
fax 0965 626840
info@bbcalabria.it
www.bbcalabria.it
Open all year

This B&B, hosted by a restructured, 19th-C house, situated at an altitude of 800 m and 11 km from the sea, has period furniture and provides a nice view of the sea. Breakfast, consisting of typical local products, is served in the kitchen. Guides are available for tours to see the natural beauties, as well as for visiting the historic and archeological sights. Donkeys can be hired for trekking into the protected areas.

Accommodation
Guestrooms: *2 doubles, also single occupancy, with shared bath*
Services & Amenities: *Greek spoken; rooms cleaned every day; complimentary tourist information; smokers welcome; Internet access; terrace*
Rates: *€ per person*
Credit cards: *not accepted*
Pets:

B&B Marino

• Calabria in Famiglia
tel. 0965 626840, mob. 328 9094209
fax 0965 626840
info@bbcalabria.it
www.bbcalabria.it
Closed: December to February

This BB, with its very friendly atmosphere, is located in ancient, carefully-restructured farmhouse situated in the old center. The guestrooms have classic furnishings and typical fabrics of local tradition. Breakfast consists of genuine products and local specialties. The location offers the possibility of making excursions into the surrounding area.

Accommodation
Guestrooms: *2 doubles, also single occupancy, with shared bath*
Services & Amenities: *rooms cleaned every day; complimentary tourist information; kitchen use by request; smokers welcome; terrace; private parking*
Rates: *€ per person. Discounts for children*
Credit cards: *not accepted*
Pets:

Cassano allo Jonio (Cosenza)

• **Bed & Breakfast Italia**
Code CA10
tel. 06 6878618
fax 06 6878619
info@bbitalia.it
www.bbitalia.it
Closed: varies

A modern villa with garden consisting in six double rooms, all complete with a small fridge. Four rooms have a private bathroom with shower; the other two share one. Breakfast is served in the garden. Guests can pay to use a sports complex with tennis courts, volleyball and golf course. The beach is 300 meters away.

Accommodation
Guestrooms: *6 (3 double bedrooms and 3 doubles)*
Services & Amenities: *English and French are spoken; rooms cleaned every three days; complimentary tourist information; horse-riding excursions*
Minimum stay: *2 nights*
Rates: €€
Credit cards: VISA MC *Bancomat*
Pets:

Cirò Marina (Crotone)

• **Bed & Breakfast Italia**
Code CA11
tel. 06 6878618, fax 06 6878619
info@bbitalia.it
www.bbitalia.it
Closed: varies

Accommodation
Guestrooms: *2 (1 double bedroom and 1 double)*
Services & Amenities: *English spoken; rooms cleaned every 3 days; tourist information; private parking*
Minimum stay: *2 nights*
Rates: €€
Credit cards: VISA MC *Bancomat*
Pets:

The guest accommodation consists in an apartment with a double room and a twin room, each with private bathroom with shower. It has simple and comfortable furnishings and includes an independent entrance. In summertime, breakfast is served by the hosts in the small garden of the house. Private parking and two bicycles available for guests. The host provides useful information on places to visit.

Condofuri (Reggio di Calabria)

B&B Il Bergamotto
località Amendolea
• **Calabria in Famiglia**
tel. 0965 626840, mob. 328 9094209
fax 0965 626840
info@bbcalabria.it
www.bbcalabria.it
Open: March to October

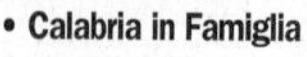

This B&B is located in Aspromonte, which is inside the Aspromonte National Park, in an ancient, restructured farmhouse that has rustic style furnishings. Breakfast, which consists of genuine products from the family farm, is served in the dining room or on the patio. Guests can also purchase some of these products. There are many trails and excursion routes in the vicinity for those who would like to do some riding on the back of a donkey.

Accommodation
Guestrooms: *1 mini-apartment with 3 beds*
Services & Amenities: *English and German are spoken; rooms cleaned every day; tourist information; kitchenette; lunch & dinner reservations; garden; private parking*
Rates: € *per person. Discounts for children*
Credit cards: *not accepted*
Pets:

Corigliano Calabro (Cosenza)

Aranciera
Antonio Romio
contrada Cozzo Giardino
87064 Corigliano Calabro (CS)
tel. 0983 82730
e-mail: maria51lf@libero.it
Open: May to October

Accommodation
Guestrooms: *3 (2 doubles, and 1 triple room, with shared bath)*
Services & Amenities: *English spoken; rooms cleaned every three days; complimentary tourist information; bike rental; smokers welcome; terrace; garden; private parking*
Rates: *double €€, triple €€€. Children under 2 free*
Credit cards: *not accepted*
Pets: ✓

This B&B is located in a small, modern villa out in the country in the middle of an orange orchard and 10 kilometers from the Sibari archeological site. Breakfast, consisting of local products, cold cuts and various types of cheese, is served in the living room.

• **Bed & Breakfast Italia**
Code CA8
tel. 06 6878618
fax 06 6878619
info@bbitalia.it
www.bbitalia.it
Closed: varies

TCI 10%

Accommodation
Guestrooms: *4 (1 double, 3 triples)*
Services & Amenities: *rooms cleaned every three days; complimentary tourist information; private parking*
Minimum stay: *2 nights*
Rates: €€
Credit cards: VISA MC *Bancomat*
Pets: ✗

Just 150 m from the sea, this B&B offers three small apartments with independent entrance; they consist in three triple rooms with a double bed and a single bed, and a double room with twin beds. Each has a private bathroom with shower and air conditioning, TV and small fridge. Other facilities are offered by the hosts, such as a restaurant and a dance floor on the sea. The castle, and the churches of Carmine and S. Antonio are well worth a visit. Private parking available.

Crotone

• **Bed & Breakfast Italia**
Code CA7
tel. 06 6878618
fax 06 6878619
info@bbitalia.it
www.bbitalia.it
Closed: varies

Accommodation
Guestrooms: *2 (1 single and 1 double bedroom)*
Services & Amenities: *English and Franch are spoken; rooms cleaned every three days*
Minimum stay: *2 nights*
Rates: €€
Credit cards: VISA MC *Bancomat*
Pets: ✗

This B&B is located in an old building in the center of town. The accommodation offers a double and single room decorated with original and elegant furnishings. The two rooms share a bathroom with shower. Breakfast is served in the large parquet-floored lounge. Crotone was one of the main ancient Greek settlements in southern Italy, was the birthplace of Pythagoras. Its center is still enclosed by ramparts built by Naples' viceroy in 1500.

Diamante (Cosenza)

Famiglia Tosto
Donatella Tosto
contrada San Francesco 1
località Cirella
87023 Diamante (CS)
tel. 0985 86704
Open all year

This B&B, located in a restructured, 18th-century house, in a particularly nice position. It provides a splendid view and has three guestrooms in the main building and two of which are in the dépendance. All have classic furnishings enriched with numerous paintings done by the hostess, who is a lover of art. The traditional breakfast, which also includes typical pastries, is generally served outdoors. Smokers welcome.

Accommodation
Guestrooms: *3 doubles, shared bath; additional bed on request*
Services & Amenities: *French spoken; rooms cleaned every 3 days; tourist info; garden; private parking*
Minimum stay: *2 nights*
Rates: *€ per person. Discounts for children under 6*
Credit cards: *not accepted*
Pets:

Fuscaldo (Cosenza)

• Bed & Breakfast Italia
Code CA12
tel. 06 6878618,fax 06 6878619
info@bbitalia.it
www.bbitalia.it
Closed: varies

An eighteenth-century farmhouse, formerly a mill, 5 minutes from the sea. All built in stone, it has two double rooms with brass beds for guests. Breakfast is served under a gazebo in the garden or in the lounge. Guests can enjoy soccer and bocce court and sample typical Calabrian products cooked by their hosts at their nearby restaurant.

Accommodation
Guestrooms: *2 doubles*
Services & Amenities: *rooms cleaned every 3 days; complimentary tourist information; smokers welcome; private parking*
Minimum stay: *2 nights*
Rates: *€€*
Credit cards: *Visa MC Bancomat*
Pets:

Longobucco (Cosenza)

B&B Annamaria
• Calabria in Famiglia
tel. 0965 626840, mob. 328 9094209
fax 0965 626840
info@bbcalabria.it
www.bbcalabria.it
Open: May to December

Accommodation
Guestrooms: *2 doubles, also single occupancy, with shared bath*
Services & Amenities: *German spoken; rooms cleaned every day; complimentary tourist information; kitchen use by request; lunch & dinner reservations; private parking*
Rates: *€ per person. Discounts for children and extended stays.*
Credit cards: *not accepted*
Pets:

This B&B, with its warm, friendly atmosphere and its comfortable period furniture, is in a modern house located in the old center. The traditional breakfast also includes pastries and homemade biscuits.

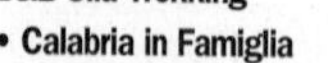

B&B Sila Trekking
• Calabria in Famiglia
tel. 0965 626840, mob. 328 9094209
fax 0965 626840
info@bbcalabria.it
www.bbcalabria.it
Open all year

This B&B, with its period furniture and loom-woven tapestries, is located in the heart of the Sila National Park. The surrounding area has an abundance of natural beauty, and guests can enjoy it on foot or by taking mountain-bike excursions. There are riding stables 10 km away where guests can arrange to go horseback riding.

Accommodation
Camere: *2 doubles, shared bath*
Services & Amenities: *German spoken; rooms cleaned every day; complimentary tourist information; kitchen use by request; smokers welcome; Internet access*
Rates: *€ per person. Discounts for children and extended stays*
Credit cards: *not accepted*
Pets:

B&B Vela

• Calabria in Famiglia
tel. 0965 626840, mob. 328 9094209
fax 0965 626840
info@bbcalabria.it
www.bbcalabria.it
Open all year

This very friendly B&B, located at an altitude of 700 m in a characteristic, carefully-restructured, 19th-century house, is an excellent base from which to do some challenging hiking or to take nice hikes to enjoy nature from close up. Breakfast, consisting of round buns and genuine biscuits, is served in the dining room with fireplace.

Accommodation
Guestrooms: *1 double bedroom, also single occupancy, private bath*
Services & Amenities: *rooms cleaned every day; tourist info; kitchen use by request; lunch & dinner reservations; smokers welcome; terrace*
Rates: *€ per person. Discounts for children and extended stays*
Credit cards: *not accepted*
Pets: not allowed

Lungro (Cosenza)

• Bed & Breakfast Italia
Code CA6
tel. 06 6878618, fax 06 6878619
info@bbitalia.it
www.bbitalia.it
Closed: varies

This B&B is set in a green park of old oaks, pine-trees and cypresses at Con-trada Sant'Angelo. The rooms reflect the special attention devoted to the house, which extends over 500 sq. m and has a portico where breakfast is served. Guests are encouraged to relax at the swimming pool and the nearby park, and are invited to see the owner's fine collection of vintage cars.

Accommodation
Guestrooms: *4 doubles*
Services & Amenities: *English and French are spoken; rooms cleaned every three day; complimentary tourist information; private parking*
Minimum stay: *2 nights*
Rates: €€
Credit cards: VISA MC *Bancomat*
Pets: not allowed

Rossano (Cosenza)

• Bed & Breakfast Italia
Code CA5
tel. 06 6878618, fax 06 6878619
info@bbitalia.it
www.bbitalia.it
Closed: varies

A 17th-C farmhouse nestling in 16 hectares which offers two quadruple rooms with fireplace and private bathroom/shower, and two double rooms sharing a bathroom with shower. All rooms look out onto the inner courtyard and face the equipped garden. Breakfast is served in the garden or in the dining room by the fireplace. Guests can play bocce or enjoy hiking and rafting.

Accommodation
Guestrooms: *2 quadruple rooms and 2 double bedrooms*
Services & Amenities: *French, English, Spanish are spoken; rooms cleaned every 3 days; tourist info*
Minimum stay: *2 nights*
Rates: €
Credit cards: VISA MC *Bancomat*
Pets: allowed

San Nicola Arcella (Cosenza)

• Bed & Breakfast Italia

Code CA1
tel. 06 6878618, fax 06 6878619
info@bbitalia.it
www.bbitalia.it
Closed: varies

The B&B is hosted by a seaside home, dominating the Gulf of Policastro. This accommodation includes three comfortable bedrooms with antique furnishings and TV. The entrance is independent; from the large balcony guests can admire the inlet below dominated by the island of Dino. A continental breakfast served by the hosts on the large balcony or in the lounge.

Accommodation
Guestrooms: *3 double bedrooms*
Services & Amenities: *French and English spoken; rooms cleaned every 3 days; tourist info*
Minimum stay: *2 nights*
Rates: €€
Credit cards: VISA MC *Bancomat*
Pets: not allowed

Sicily

Acireale (Catania)

• **Bed & Breakfast Italia**
Code S37
tel. 06 6878618, fax 06 6878619
info@bbitalia.it
www.bbitalia.it
Closed: varies

Accommodation
Guestrooms: *3 double bedrooms*
Services & Amenities: *French, English and German are spoken; rooms cleaned every 3 days; tourist information; air conditioning; private parking*
Minimum stay: *2 nights*
Rates: €€
Credit cards: VISA MC *Bancomat*
Pets:

A prestigious villa, furnished in a simple, refined style, adorned with antiques and matching details and surrounded by a garden with a view of the sea. It consists in three double rooms, all with air conditioning, three bathrooms with shower for the use of the guests only. It is located at Loreto, within 10 minutes' walking distance of the old center of Acireale. Catania is 5 km away. A car is necessary.

Agrigento

Casa Lerux
Ruggero Casesa
via Callicratide 164
92100 Agrigento
tel. 0922 27203, mob. 333 2059606
lerux@libero.it
Open all year

This B&B, which is located in a large, classical-type apartment situated in a completely-restructured building dating from the '70s, is just a few minutes from the center of town and is close to a supermarket, a pharmacy a newsstand and various stores. It's also in a perfect location for making visits to the Valley of the Temples. Breakfast is served in the dining room. The guestrooms have large balconies on both sides.

Accommodation
Guestrooms: *4 (2 singles, 1 double, 1 double bedroom, shared bath)*
Services & Amenities: *French, Spanish and Dutch are spoken; rooms cleaned every day; complimentary tourist information; kitchenette; smokers welcome*
Rates: *single €-€€. Children under 3 -50%*
Credit cards: *not accepted*
Pets:

• **Bed & Breakfast Italia**
Code S27
tel. 06 6878618, fax 06 6878619
info@bbitalia.it
www.bbitalia.it
Closed: varies

ACCOMMODATION
Guestrooms: *2 (1 double bedroom and 1 double)*
Services & Amenities: *French, English and German are spoken; rooms cleaned every 3 days; tourist info*
Minimum stay: *2 nights*
Rates: €
Credit cards: VISA MC *Bancomat*
Pets: no

This unpretentious and simply furnished apartment, with a view of the town, is in a privileged position in the heart of Agrigento, renowned for its cultural and art attractions. It includes one double and one twin-bedded room, both with TV. The private guest bathroom is equipped with tub/shower. Several buses connect the area to the Valley of Temples and to the archaeological site.

The Cathedral of San Nicola in Agrigento.

• **Bed & Breakfast Italia**
Code S33
località San Leone
tel. 06 6878618, fax 06 6878619
info@bbitalia.it
www.bbitalia.it
Closed: varies

A detached house in a seaside resort, 5 km from the old heart of Agrigento. The first floor is completely at the disposal of guests and features comfortable, simple furnishings. It includes three rooms, a double, a twin and a triple with three single beds, plus a private bathroom with shower. The sea is 200 m away, and the famous Valley of Temples is 4 km away. A car is recommended for visiting the surrounding area.

ACCOMMODATION
Guestrooms: *3 (1 double bedroom, 1 double and 1 triple room)*
Services & Amenities: *rooms cleaned every three days; tourist information; bike rental; smokers welcome; private parking*
Minimum stay: *2 nights*
Rates: €€
Credit cards: VISA MC *Bancomat*
Pets: no

A moment during the San Calogero procession in Agrigento.

• **Bed & Breakfast Italia** TCI 10%
Code S34
tel. 06 6878618, fax 06 6878619
info@bbitalia.it
www.bbitalia.it
Closed: varies

This villa is situated on the hills around Agrigento, in the Angeli Park. It is simply and tastefully decorated for the guests' comfort. The guest accommodation includes a large balcony, where it is possible to have breakfast, one double room and one triple with a double and a single bed, both complete with TV. The private bathroom has a shower. It is 15 minutes from the sea. Private parking is available.

ACCOMMODATION
Guestrooms: *2 (1 double bedroom and 1 triple room)* ♿
Services & Amenities: *French spoken; rooms cleaned every three days; complimentary tourist information; smokers welcome; private parking*
Minimum stay: *2 nights*
Rates: €€
Credit cards: VISA MC *Bancomat*
Pets: no

• **Bed & Breakfast Italia**
Code S54
tel. 06 6878618, fax 06 6878619
info@bbitalia.it
www.bbitalia.it
Closed: varies

The B&B is located halfway between the Valley of Temples and the sea. It is on the second floor of a villa, 3 km from Agrigento. Three small apartments including two double rooms, each with its own private bathroom with shower, and one small apartment, consisting of two single

rooms, each with private bathroom as well, are allocated for B&B purposes. All the apartments have a kitchen, lounge and simple furnishings. The bus stop is 50 m from the accommodation.

ACCOMMODATION
Guestrooms: *8 (2 singles and 6 doubles)*
Services & Amenities: *French, English and German are spoken; rooms cleaned every 3 days; tourist information; smokers welcome; private parking*
Minimum stay: *2 nights*
Rates: €€
Credit cards: VISA MC *Bancomat*
Pets: no

BALESTRATE (PALERMO)

• **Bed & Breakfast Italia**
Code S26
tel. 06 6878618, fax 06 6878619
info@bbitalia.it
www.bbitalia.it
Closed: varies

A villa of 350 sq. m, surrounded by a well-tended garden and a large, old olive grove. The owners offer guests a double room, including a cot, furnished in a classic style in shades of white and pink, complete with TV and independent entrance. Telephone, fax, solarium and private parking are available for the con-

ACCOMMODATION
Guestrooms: *1 double bedroom* ♿
Services & Amenities: *rooms cleaned every 3 days; tourist information; private parking*
Minimum stay: *2 nights*
Rates: €€
Credit cards: VISA MC *Bancomat*
Pets: no

venience of guests. On request, your hosts will prepare meals using their homegrown produce.

BUSETO PALIZZOLO (TRAPANI)

Baglio Case Colomba
Fabio and Anna Maria Bertolazzi
borgo Murfi
91012 Buseto Palizzolo (TP)
tel. 091 6841211, mob. 347 2116470
info@casecolomba.com
www.casecolomba.com
Open: May to October
and Easter holidays

This B&B – located in the Trapani countryside between Erice and Segesta – is in a late 19th-century farmhouse situated on an old farm that's still operating. Guests have two independent rooms with rustic furnishings, as

well as a kitchen that still has its traditional characteristics. The breakfast, which consists of fresh local products, is either served in the home or in the patio.

ACCOMMODATION
Guestrooms: *1 apartment with 4 beds* ♿
Services & Amenities: *French, English and Spanish are spoken; rooms cleaned every three days; complimentary tourist information; kitchen use by request; garden; smokers welcome; private parking*
Rates: *€ per person. Children under 6 -30%. Discounts for extended stays*
Credit cards: *not accepted*
Pets: yes

Caltagirone (Catania)

Antico Palmento
via Fela 99
95041 Caltagirone (CT)
tel. 0933 23898
mnessuno@tin.it
Open all year

This 19th-century house, with its garden, is 1 kilometer from Caltagirone and gets its name from the room on the ground floor that has an ancient Arabian "palmento" press for squeezing grapes. This is one of the few such presses remaining in Sicily. The continental breakfast (or English type if requested), which is served in this room, also includes some local fruit. The guestrooms have air conditioning, a mini-bar and a TV. Guided tours of the vicinity can be arranged.

Accommodation
Guestrooms: *3 (2 doubles, also single occupancy and 1 triple room, with private bath)* ♿
Services & Amenities: *French and English are spoken; rooms cleaned every 3 days; tourist info; terrace; air conditioning; Internet access; garden; smokers welcome; parking*
Rates: *single €, double €€-€€€, triple €€€-€€€€. Children under 2 free; 2 to 12 -50%*
Credit cards: *not accepted*
Pets:

• **Bed & Breakfast Italia**
Code S49
tel. 06 6878618, fax 06 6878619
info@bbitalia.it
www.bbitalia.it
Closed: varies

The B&B is a completely restored villa, decorated with antiques and coffered ceilings; each room has a charming view and features TV, air conditioning and a small fridge. The house includes a lounge with satellite TV and ample parking for the use of guests. It is within 1.5 km distance of

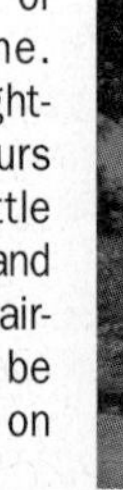

the center of Caltagirone. Guided sightseeing tours and a shuttle service to and from the airport can be arranged on request.

Accommodation
Guestrooms: *3 (2 doubles, 1 triple)* ♿
Services & Amenities: *French and English are spoken; rooms cleaned every 3 days; tourist info; bike rental; air conditioning; private parking*
Minimum stay: *2 nights*
Rates: €€
Credit cards: VISA MC *Bancomat*
Pets:

Castelvetrano (Trapani)

• **Bed & Breakfast Italia**
Code S7
tel. 06 6878618, fax 06 6878619
info@bbitalia.it
www.bbitalia.it
Closed: varies

Accommodation
Guestrooms: *4 (2 doubles, 2 triples)*
Services & Amenities: *French spoken; rooms cleaned every 3 days; complimentary tourist information; private parking*
Minimum stay: *2 nights*
Rates: €€
Credit cards: VISA MC *Bancomat*
Pets:

A complex of self-contained apartments, fully furnished and with a half-board option. It includes two double rooms with bathroom with shower, and two triple rooms with bathroom equipped with tub. Castelvetrano, an old village, which started to develop under Arab rule, is in the Belice valley, 5 minutes from Selinunte, one of the island's most important archeological zones dating from the Greek epoch. Private car park available.

Castiglione di Sicilia (Catania)

• Bed & Breakfast Italia
Code S48
tel. 06 6878618, fax 06 6878619
info@bbitalia.it
www.bbitalia.it
Closed: varies

This B&B is hosted by a typical country-house, recently restored, surrounded by a large orchard and at the foot of Mt Etna. This accommodation includes a double room with balcony, furnished in a rustic style, TV, bathroom with shower and independent entrance. The rich breakfast is served in the lounge or, in the warmer months, in the orchard. Castiglione di Sicilia is 5 kilometers from the Alcantara Gorges, hollowed out by the river Alcantara in the layers of lava from Etna. Private parking is also available for guests.

Accommodation
Guestrooms: *1 double bedroom*
Services & Amenities: *English spoken; rooms cleaned every 3 days; tourist information; bike rental; smokers welcome; private parking*
Minimum stay: *2 nights*
Rates: €€
Credit cards: VISA MC *Bancomat*
Pets: 🚫

Catania

Casamia
Silvana Puglisi
via D'Annunzio 48
95128 Catania
tel. 095 445682
fax 095 50997
casamia48@tin.it
Open all year

This B&B is in a large apartment inside an early 20th-century building located in the center of Catania. The comfortable guestrooms have plain furniture and lively-colored, coordinated fabrics. Guests share the use of a comfortable living room that has a hi-fi system, TV and a library. The Italian breakfast is served in the family kitchen.

Accommodation
Guestrooms: *6 (1 single and 5 doubles, with private bath);* ♿
Services & Amenities: *French and English are spoken; rooms cleaned every 3 days; tourist info; bike rental; Internet access; smokers welcome; private parking*
Rates: *single* €€, *double* €€€. *Additional bed supplement* €. *Discounts for children, groups and extended stays*
Credit cards: *accepted*
Pets: 🚫

• Bed & Breakfast Italia
Code S46
tel. 06 6878618, fax 06 6878619
info@bbitalia.it
www.bbitalia.it
Closed: varies

This B&B is a penthouse in a recently restored eighteenth-century building, in the old center of the city. The guest accommodation consists in two twin-bedded rooms, one double room, two triple rooms, both with a single and a double bed, sharing two bathrooms with showers. The large balcony affords a view of the Catania Duomo, the baroque church of San Placido, the Mt Etna and the port. The sea and the art and shopping areas of the city are 100 m away. Smokers are welcome.

Accommodation
Guestrooms: *5 (1 double bedroom, 2 doubles and 2 triple room)*
Services & Amenities: *rooms cleaned every 3 days; tourist information; smokers welcome*
Minimum stay: *2 nights*
Rates: €€
Credit cards: VISA MC *Bancomat*
Pets: 🚫

Cattolica Eraclea (Agrigento)

• Bed & Breakfast Italia
Code S23
tel. 06 6878618, fax 06 6878619
info@bbitalia.it
www.bbitalia.it
Closed: varies

This B&B is in the old center of the small town, 20 minutes away from the famous archaeological site of the Valley of Temples. Available to the guests is a 25 sq.meter mezzanine apartment consisting in a simply and tastefully furnished double room (with the option of a third bed), bathroom with shower, TV and independent entrance. Catto-lica Eraclea, rich in art and culture, hosts festivals and public events throughout the year. Agrigen-to (40 km), Sciacca (40 km), Lake Arancio, the Eraclea Minoa archaeological site and the sandy beaches are easily reached.

Accommodation
Guestrooms: *1 double*
Services & Amenities: *German spoken; rooms cleaned every three days; tourist information*
Minimum stay: *2 nights*
Rates: €€
Credit cards: VISA MC *Bancomat*
Pets:

Chiaramonte Gulfi (Ragusa)

• Bed & Breakfast Italia
Code S51
tel. 06 6878618, fax 06 6878619
info@bbitalia.it
www.bbitalia.it
Closed: varies

A nineteenth-century farmhouse, at Roccazzo. Recently restored but preserving its original structure, it is made up of three small apartments each consisting in one double room with TV, one twin-bedded room, bathroom with shower and equipped kitchenette. All the apartments are self-contained and furnished in rustic style. Guests can enjoy the swimming pool, table tennis, tennis court and five-a-side soccer pitch. The area is within a short distance of Caltagirone, Noto, Syracuse and Ragusa Ibla, which can only be visited by car; private car park available.

Accommodation
Guestrooms: *6 doubles*
Services & Amenities: *English spoken; rooms cleaned every three days; tourist information; bike rental; private parking*
Minimum stay: *2 nights*
Rates: €€
Credit cards: VISA MC *Bancomat*
Pets:

Collesano (Palermo)

B&B Gargi di Cenere
Donatella Pucci
contrada Gargi di Cenere
90016 Collesano (PA)
tel. and fax 0921 428431
gargidicenere@libero.it
• Friendly Home-Gli Amici del B&B
tel. 02 860147, fax 02 875860
friendlymilano@dada.it
tel. and fax 011 9536376
fhrivoli@virgilio.it
Open all year

This B&B is located in a farmhouse surrounded by a citrus grove. It has period furniture and many family mementos. Breakfast, consisting of fresh products, is served in the dining room. Guests have the use of a swimming pool that's like the typical tubs that were used in the 18th C for irrigating the citrus trees

Accommodation
Guestrooms: *5 (2 double bedrooms, also single occupancy, 1 triple and 2 quadruples, with private bath); additional bed on request*
Services & Amenities: *French spoken; rooms cleaned every three days; complimentary tourist information; kitchen use by request; dinner reservation; garden; smokers welcome; private parking*
Rates: *single €, double €€€, triple and quadruple room €€€-€€€€*
Credit cards: *accepted*
Pets:

Masseria Abazia
tel. 091 6167839, mob. 360 406016
abaziafloris@hotmail.com
• Friendly Home-Gli Amici del B&B
tel. 02 860147, fax 02 875860
friendlymilano@dada.it
tel. and fax 011 9536376
fhrivoli@virgilio.it
Closed: July and December or January

This B&B is hosted by a beautiful, completely-restructured farmhouse, located in the hills of the Cefalù hinterland, in the middle of a large grove of olive trees. The accommodation offers large, fresh rooms with furniture belonging to the family. The family makes organic olive oil with its ancient, traditional press. The rich breakfast consists of fresh products gathered from the farm.

ACCOMMODATION
Guestrooms: *1 double bedroom, with private bath and 1 mini-apartment (3 beds)*
Services & Amenities: *French and English are spoken; rooms cleaned every 3 days; tourist information; kitchen use by request; bike rental; horse-riding excursions; educational courses by request; garden; private parking*
Minimum stay: *2 nights*
Rates: *double €€€, mini-apartment €€€€*
Credit cards: *not accepted*
Pets: ✓

ENNA

Residenza il Mandorleto TCI 10%
Saida Crea and Maurizio Stellino
contrada Gerace
• ANBBA
tel. 041 731429
fax 041 2769546
info@anbba.it
www.anbba.it
• Friendly Home-Gli Amici del B&B
tel. 02 860147
fax 02 875860
friendlymilano@dada.it
tel. and fax 011 9536376
fhrivoli@virgilio.it
Open: 15 May to 15 October

This perfectly-restructured, typical farmhouse is surrounded by a large, fenced-in garden and has a large, panoramic terrace. The comfortable guestrooms have ceiling fans and traditional furniture. There is also a living room with a corner in which to relax. The continental breakfast, which consists of local products, is enriched with almonds from the organic farm during the September harvest period.

ACCOMMODATION
Guestrooms: *3 (1 double and 2 triples, with private bath); cot or child's bed available*
Services & Amenities: *English spoken; rooms cleaned every three days; tourist information; lunch & dinner reservations; horse-riding excursions; garden; smokers welcome; private parking*
Rates: *double €€, triple €€€. Additional cot or child's bed supplement. Children under 2 free. Discounts for extended stays and for honeymoon trips*
Credit cards: *not accepted*
Pets: ✓

• Bed & Breakfast Italia TCI 10%
Code S29
tel. 06 6878618, fax 06 6878619
info@bbitalia.it
www.bbitalia.it
Closed: varies

This is a country-house on the edge of Enna. The owners offer the whole first floor to guests. Decorated with period furniture, it includes a private bathroom with shower and a kitchenette. The house is within 10 mins' distance of the Enna railway station and 2 km from the Calascibetta Arab-Norman village. Nearby are important archaeological sites and Piazza Armerina is 30 mins away. A car is absolutely necessary to tour and visit these sites.

ACCOMMODATION
Guestrooms: *1 double bedroom*
Services & Amenities: *French and English are spoken; rooms cleaned every three days; complimentary tourist information; private parking*
Minimum stay: *2 nights*
Rates: *€€*
Credit cards: VISA MC *Bancomat*
Pets: ✗

Giardini Naxos (Messina)

• **Bed & Breakfast Italia**
Code S56
tel. 06 6878618, fax 06 6878619
info@bbitalia.it
www.bbitalia.it
Closed: varies

The guest accommodation of this B&B consists in four studio apartments within a residential complex, each offering a room with a double sofa bed, bathroom with shower, a kitchenette and a large scenic balcony. The furnishings are simple, functional and colorful. On arrival, guests find mineral water and cold drinks in the fridge. Your hostess leaves provisions for breakfast in the kitchen. The bus stop is 50 meters from the house and it takes 15 minutes to reach Taormina. Two parking spaces are available. Smokers are welcome.

Accommodation
Guestrooms: *4 doubles*
Services & Amenities: *rooms cleaned every 3 days; tourist information; smokers welcome; private parking*
Minimum stay: *2 nights*
Rates: €€
Credit cards: VISA MC *Bancomat*
Pets: not allowed

Giarre (Catania)

• **Bed & Breakfast Italia** TCI 10%
Code S39
tel. 06 6878618, fax 06 6878619
info@bbitalia.it
www.bbitalia.it
Closed: varies

This B&B is hosted by a villa in rustic Sicilian style, surrounded by a garden of palms, Mediterranean plants and centuries-old oaks. The accommodation offers three double rooms with TV, balcony and air conditioning, that are furnished with antiques and share two bathrooms, one of which with a Jacuzzi. It is located at Giarre, a village of the Catania hinterland, 20 km from Acireale and 30 km from Taormina. A car is absolutely necessary. Private car park is available.

Accommodation
Guestrooms: *3 double bedrooms*
Services & Amenities: *French spoken; rooms cleaned every 3 days; tourist information; baby-sitting service; air conditioning; smokers welcome; private parking*
Minimum stay: *2 nights*
Rates: €€
Credit cards: VISA MC *Bancomat*
Pets: not allowed

Isola di Pantelleria (Trapani)

• **Bed & Breakfast Italia**
Code S2
tel. 06 6878618, fax 06 6878619
info@bbitalia.it
www.bbitalia.it
Closed: varies

Accommodation
Guestrooms: *4 (2 doubles, 2 triples)*
Services & Amenities: *English spoken; rooms cleaned every three days; complimentary tourist information; private parking*
Minimum stay: *2 nights*
Rates: €€€
Credit cards: VISA MC *Bancomat*
Pets: not allowed

In the Bugeber district, overlooking Lake Venere, the owners offer guests four small apartments, suitable for 2/4 persons, all self-contained, complete with equipped kitchen and bathroom with shower. These are traditional cubical stone dwellings called "dammusi". In the communal space guests can use the log-fire oven, the open kitchen and parking. Capers, sweet wine, jams and dried tomatoes can be supplied by your host on request, who will also provide useful information.

• **Bed & Breakfast Italia**
Code S3
tel. 06 6878618, fax 06 6878619
info@bbitalia.it
www.bbitalia.it
Closed: varies

The accommodation of this B&B includes five mini-apartments in so-called "dammusi", the island's traditional cubical stone dwellings. Four consist in a sitting room, double bedroom and bathroom with shower. The fifth apartment has two double bedrooms, one with twin beds, and a bathroom with shower. Each apartment is self-contained, equipped and has a view of the sea. Among the attractions of the island are the hot sea spa at Nikà, the natural sauna on the Montagna Grande and the sulfur mud in Lake Venere.

Accommodation
Guestrooms: *5 mini-apartments*
Services & Amenities: *French and English are spoken; rooms cleaned every three days; complimentary tourist information; terrace*
Minimum stay: *2 nights*
Rates: €€
Credit cards: VISA MC *Bancomat*
Pets:

Isole Egadi - Marettimo (Trapani)

• **Bed & Breakfast Italia** 
Code S12
tel. 06 6878618, fax 06 6878619
info@bbitalia.it
www.bbitalia.it
Closed: varies

A group of houses on the small island of Egadi. The guest apartments have been recently refurbished, in perfect keeping with the original Arab style, and are in colorful courtyards or on the cliffs over the sea. The rooms, doubles or triples, have cots and are decorated in a simple, functional way, opening onto a large balcony. The bathrooms have showers. Private parking is also available for the guests.

Accommodation
Guestrooms: *5 (1 single, 3 doubles and 1 triple room)*
Services & Amenities: *English spoken; rooms cleaned every 3 days; tourist information; smokers welcome; private parking*
Minimum stay: *2 nights*
Rates: €€
Credit cards: VISA MC *Bancomat*
Pets:

Marettimo, the main center of the island, is 686 meters above sea level and offers both sea and mountain attractions.

Isole Eolie - Lipari (Messina)

Marcello Saltalamacchia 
via Munciarda
98055 Lipari (ME)
tel. 090 9811692
tel. and fax 090 9880541
Closed: November to February

This Aeolian style house, with its characteristic "epulera" (a terrace colonnade), is located 1 km from the center of Lipari (close to the tennis courts), 50 m from the sea and 4 km from the beaches. This accommodation offers three double rooms, which have modern furniture and private bathrooms, lead directly into a large garden that has stone pathways and lemon trees. The guests enjoy a very cordial atmosphere and the traditional breakfast is enriched with crushed ice beverages and fresh brioches. The hosts are always happy to organize boat trips to allow the guests to fully enjoy the beauties of this island.

Accommodation
Guestrooms: *3 doubles, private bath*
Services & Amenities: *English and French are spoken*
Rates: € *per person. Discounts for children*
Credit cards: VISA MC *Bancomat*

Isole Eolie - Salina (Messina)

• **Bed & Breakfast Italia**
Code S5
tel. 06 6878618, fax 06 6878619
info@bbitalia.it
www.bbitalia.it
Closed: varies

A nineteenth-century mansion with frescoes, surrounded by a garden. The family lives on the first floor and the ground floor is reserved for guests. The rooms, two doubles, two triples and one quadruple, are comfortable and decorated with valuable furniture; each room has a large balcony and an ensuite bathroom with shower. Breakfast is prepared and served by the hostess and guests can choose between a traditional continental breakfast and sweet or savory omelets and fresh fruit.

Accommodation
Guestrooms: *5 (2 double bedrooms, 2 triples and 1 quadruple)*
Services & Amenities: *French and English are spoken; rooms cleaned every three days; tourist information; private parking*
Minimum stay: *2 nights*
Rates: €€
Credit cards: VISA MC *Bancomat*
Pets: no

• **Bed & Breakfast Italia**
Code S22
tel. 06 6878618, fax 06 6878619
info@bbitalia.it
www.bbitalia.it
Closed: varies

A wing of a small Mediterranean-style villa with garden. The two guestrooms, a double and a triple, are both carefully furnished, have independent entrances and a panoramic view of the sea. Private parking is available. This accommodation is in the village of Malfa, within 20 mins' walk of the tiny harbor and beach, immersed in a landscape where grapes and prickly pears are cultivated. The other villages on the island are within easy reach.

Accommodation
Guestrooms: *1 double and 1 triple*
Services & Amenities: *English spoken; rooms cleaned every three days; tourist information; terrace; private parking*
Minimum stay: *2 nights*
Rates: €€
Credit cards: VISA MC *Bancomat*
Pets: yes

Marsala (Trapani)

• **Bed & Breakfast Italia**
Code S14
tel. 06 6878618, fax 06 6878619
info@bbitalia.it
www.bbitalia.it
Closed: varies

A house with garden, completely at the guests' disposal, is 7 km from Marsala. It includes six double rooms with TV and large balcony, and a sitting room with kitchenette. Each room has a private bathroom with shower and the option of a cot for children under the age of two. The old center contains the Archeological Museum, with a relic of a Punic ship, the Museum of Flemish Tapestries and the Duomo, which houses important sculptures by the Gaginis. There is a large necropolis at nearby Mozia.

Accommodation
Guestrooms: *6 double bedrooms*
Services & Amenities: *French and English are spoken; rooms cleaned every three days; tourist information; smokers welcome; private parking*
Minimum stay: *2 nights*
Rates: €€
Credit cards: VISA MC *Bancomat*
Pets: yes

Mascali (Catania)

• **Bed & Breakfast Italia**
Code S28
tel. 06 6878618, fax 06 6878619
info@bbitalia.it
www.bbitalia.it
Closed: varies

Hilltop detached house at Mascali, in the province of Catania, surrounded by a garden and an orchard. It has two double rooms, each with its own balcony and TV. The private bathroom is equipped with tub and shower. The garden, with a small swimming pool, overlooks the volcano on one side and the town of Taormina on the other. A car is recommended. It is 25 km from Giardini Naxos and 50 from Catania.

Accommodation
Guestrooms: *2 double bedrooms*
Services & Amenities: *French and English are spoken; rooms cleaned every three days; complimentary tourist information; smokers welcome; private parking*
Minimum stay: *2 nights*
Rates: €€
Credit cards: VISA MC *Bancomat*
Pets: not allowed

Modica (Ragusa)

Giogaia
Pietro Iacono
via Modica Giarratana 83/a
97015 Modica (RG)
tel. and fax 0932 751769
mob. 339 7693623
lagiogaia@tin.it
www.giogaia.it
Open all year

This B&B is in a recently-constructed farmhouse located near the slopes of the Iblei Mountains. It's just a few kilometers from the center of Modica and the sea. Guests have a large, air-conditioned mansard with a sunny terrace and a living room with a kitchen corner. Breakfast, consisting of local specialties and natural products, is either served in the family dining room or on the terrace. The garden has play area for the children.

Accommodation
Guestrooms: *3 (2 doubles, also single occupancy, shared bath; 1 double bedroom, private bath). Additional bed on request*
Services & Amenities: *English and Spanish are spoken; rooms cleaned every 3 days; tourist information; kitchenette; educational courses by request; terrace; air conditioning; garden; smokers welcome; private parking*
Rates: *single €€, double €€. Additional bed supplement €. Children under 2 free. Discounts for extended stays*
Credit cards: *not accepted*
Pets: allowed

Monreale (Palermo)

• **Bed & Breakfast Italia**
Code S41
tel. 06 6878618, fax 06 6878619
info@bbitalia.it
www.bbitalia.it
Closed: varies

These two small self-contained apartments are in the historic Pozzillo area. Each apartment has a twin-bedded room and a triple with a double and a single bed, plus a bathroom with shower. The style of furnishings is simple and functional. They are within 5 minutes' walk of the Duomo of Monreale, an admirable example of Arab-Norman art. The small town is 10 kilometers from Palermo, easily reached on public transport, and it is close to the renowned Mondello beach. A car is recommended. Bicycles are available for the guests.

Accommodation
Guestrooms: *4 (2 doubles, 2 triples)*
Services & Amenities: *French spoken; rooms cleaned every 3 days; tourist information; bike rental; terrace*
Minimum stay: *2 nights*
Rates: €€
Credit cards: VISA MC *Bancomat*
Pets: not allowed

Nicolosi (Catania)

• Bed & Breakfast Italia
Code S30
tel. 06 6878618, fax 06 6878619
info@bbitalia.it
www.bbitalia.it
Closed: varies

This villa, built in the forties and furnished in simple, functional style, consists in three triple rooms, each with a double and a single bed. The bathroom has tub/shower. It is ideally situated in the last inhabited village on the route to the crater of Etna, the starting point for expeditions close to the volcano summit. The sea is 10 kilometers away and is easily reached by bus.

Accommodation
Guestrooms: *3 triple rooms*
Services & Amenities: *English spoken; rooms cleaned every 3 days; tourist information; private parking*
Minimum stay: *2 nights*
Rates: €
Credit cards: VISA MC *Bancomat*
Pets: no

Noto (Syracuse)

Centro Storico
Antonietta Scrofani
corso Vittorio Emanuele 64
• ANBBA
tel. 041 731429
fax 041 2769546
info@anbba.it
www.anbba.it
Closed: January to February

Accommodation
Guestrooms: *2 (1 double and 1 suite with 4 beds, private bath)*
Services & Amenities: *English spoken; tourist information; kitchenette; smokers welcome*
Rates: *€€ per person. Discounts for children*
Credit cards: *not accepted*
Pets: no

This B&B is located in a restructured, 18th-century building in the old center of Noto. This area is, in part, restricted to pedestrians. Noto is the capital of Sicilian baroque and is famous for its churches and fabulously-decorated, tufo buildings. Moreover, it's only 30 kilometers from Syracuse and just 5 kilometers from the sea. Guests have a room with a refrigerator and TV, and a suite with a kitchen corner and a washing machine. The Italian breakfast is served in the guestroom.

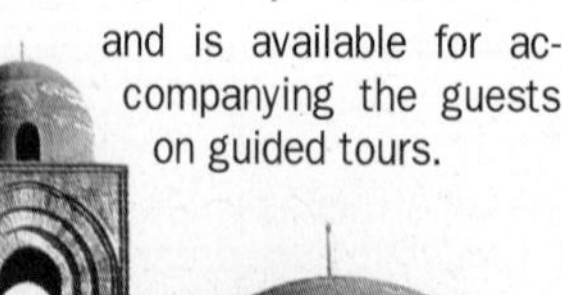

The face of Medusa, symbol of Trinacria. Below, the domes of the church of San Giovanni degli Eremiti in Palermo.

Palermo

B&B Castiglione
Maria Castiglione and Giuseppe Galanti
piazza Stazione Lolli 3
90141 Palermo
tel. and fax 091 335300
mob. 339 7805328
md4095@mclink.it
www.primitaly.it
Open all year

Accommodation
Guestrooms: *3 (1 single, 1 double and 1 triple with shared bath)*
Services & Amenities: *French and English are spoken; rooms cleaned every day; tourist information; air conditioning; garden; smokers welcome; private parking*
Rates: *single €€, double €€€. Children under 5 free*
Credit cards: *not accepted*
Pets: no

This B&B is in an apartment located on the first floor of a late 18th-century building. One of the three large guestrooms is decorated with fine friezes and frescoes. The large breakfast, which consists of freshly-baked items, fruit and yoghurt, is usually served in the guestroom. Guests have the use of the family refrigerator. The hostess is well informed on the artistic treasures located in the city and surrounding area, and is available for accompanying the guests on guided tours.

B&B Palermo
• Friendly Home-Gli Amici del B&B
tel. 02 860147, fax 02 875860
friendlymilano@dada.it
tel. and fax 011 9536376
fhrivoli@virgilio.it
Closed: 13 November
to 13 December

This B&B is hosted in a large, elegant apartment situated in a condominium, right in the center of town, next to the Villa Trabia Park. The accommodation consists in two rooms with a mixture of family furniture and modern items collected by the hostess. When the weather is nice, breakfast is served on the terrace, which provides a beautiful view of the historical park.

ACCOMMODATION
Guestrooms: *2 (1 single, 1 double private bath)*
Services & Amenities: *English and Spanish are spoken; rooms cleaned every 3 days; tourist information; terrace; smokers welcome*
Minimum stay: *2 nights*
Rates: *single €€€, double €€€€. Children under 2 free*
Credit cards: *not accepted*
Pets: 🚫

Il Glicine La Piana dei Colli
località Mondello
90121 Palermo
tel. 091 454565
ilglicine.pa@pronet.it
www.ilglicine.net
• Friendly Home-Gli Amici del B&B
tel. 02 860147, fax 02 875860
friendlymilano@dada.it
tel. and fax 011 9536376
fhrivoli@virgilio.it
Open all year

Il Glicine is a large, 18th-century villa that has a typical Sicilian shape. It's located near the Mondello beach and

is only a few minutes from the center of town. The three guestrooms, located in a large apartment situated inside the complex, have the same antique charm. They have terracotta floors, fine wood paneling and a large fireplace. Breakfast, which is prepared and served by the hostess, also includes freshly picked fruit from the garden.

ACCOMMODATION
Guestrooms: *3 (1 single, 2 doubles, private bath); additional bed on request*
Services & Amenities: *French, English and German are spoken; rooms cleaned every 3 days; tourist info; garden; smokers welcome*
Minimum stay: *2 nights*
Rates: *single €€€, double €€€€. Discounts for extended stays*
Credit cards: *not accepted*
Pets: ✓

Il Glicine. Mondello
località Mondello
• Friendly Home-Gli Amici del B&B
tel. 02 860147, fax 02 875860
friendlymilano@dada.it
tel. and fax 011 9536376
fhrivoli@virgilio.it
Open all year

This beautiful, typically-Mediterranean house, wrapped by a large wisteria vine and surrounded by pine trees, is located close to the city, just a short distance from the famous Mondello beach. It provides a very nice, panoramic view of the gulf. The warm furnishings also include some family items. Guests have a double room and a small, independent apartment for 4 persons and a kitchen corner. The very well-prepared breakfast is either served in the family dining room or outdoors.

ACCOMMODATION
Guestrooms: *1 double bedroom, with private bath and 1 mini-apartment (4 beds)*
Services & Amenities: *French and English are spoken; rooms cleaned every 3 days; tourist info; kitchenette; garden; smokers welcome*
Minimum stay: *2 nights in double bedroom and 4 nights in mini-apartment*
Rates: *double €€€, mini-apartment €€€€*
Credit cards: *not accepted*
Pets: ✓

• **Bed & Breakfast Italia**
Code S24
tel. 06 6878618, fax 06 6878619
info@bbitalia.it
www.bbitalia.it
Closed: varies

Tenth-floor apartment in an old building near the Politeama theater, in the very heart of the town. It consists in six double rooms with independent climate control, furnished in the style of the 60s, offering a panoramic view of the city. A third bed and/or cot can be added on request. There are three bathrooms with shower, one of which has wheelchair access. A spacious lounge is at guests' disposal, including TV, a reading corner and a fireplace. On request, your hosts prepare meals with typical Sicilian products.

Accommodation
Guestrooms: *6 doubles ♿*
Services & Amenities: *English spoken; rooms cleaned every 3 days; tourist information; air conditioning; smokers welcome*
Minimum stay: *2 nights*
Rates: *€€*
Credit cards: *VISA MC Bancomat*
Pets: *not allowed*

Pettineo (Messina)

Casa Migliaca
Teresa Allegra
contrada Migliaca
98070 Pettineo (ME)
tel. 0921 336722, fax 0921 391107
info@casamigliaca.com
www.casamigliaca.com
Open all year

This ancient, 18th-C, Sicilian house, whose panoramic position provides a view of the sea, has always been kept in excellent condition. Its ancient olive press is particularly interesting, as well as its olive storage facilities, the grindstone – which is now used as a dining table – the perfectly kept bedrooms and the antique furnishings. Breakfast, which consists of pastries, cold cuts and cheese, is served in the kitchen. The dinner, if desired, consists of products from the farm, all prepared in accordance with Sicilian recipes.

Accommodation
Guestrooms: *6 doubles with private bath; additional bed on request*
Services & Amenities: *French and English are spoken; rooms cleaned every 3 days; tourist information; dinner reservation; air conditioning; garden; smokers welcome; private parking*
Rates: *single €€, double €€€€. Children under 3 free; 3 to 10 -50%*
Credit cards: *accepted*
Pets: *not allowed*

• **Bed & Breakfast Italia**
Code S6
tel. 06 6878618, fax 06 6878619
info@bbitalia.it
www.bbitalia.it
Closed: varies

Old stone-built house recently restored. Five rooms with twin beds, two of which have the option of a cot for children under the age of two, are used for B&B purposes. All the rooms are large and sunny, and have a private balcony, heating and bathroom with shower. Besides the breakfast, the hosts offer half-board, serving homemade produce. Horse riding and guided excursions of the area and to the nearby Park of Nebrodi are possible but must be arranged in advance.

Accommodation
Guestrooms: *5 doubles*
Services & Amenities: *rooms cleaned every 3 days; tourist information; terrace; private parking*
Minimum stay: *2 nights*
Rates: *€€*
Credit cards: *VISA MC Bancomat*
Pets: *not allowed*

Piedimonte Etneo (Catania)

• **Bed & Breakfast Italia**
Code S53
tel. 06 6878618, fax 06 6878619
info@bbitalia.it
www.bbitalia.it
Closed: varies

This detached house is furnished in a personal style with colored walls and valuable furniture. On the first floor there are two double rooms, sharing a bathroom with tub/ shower. On the ground floor there are two more double rooms, each with private bathroom equipped with tub/shower, and TV. Guests can use the large garden in front of the house and the swimming pool. Hostess serves breakfast in the first-floor lounge.

Accommodation
Guestrooms: *4 doubles*
Services & Amenities: *rooms cleaned every 3 days; tourist info*
Minimum stay: *2 nights*
Rates: €€
Credit cards: VISA MC *Bancomat*
Pets:

Ragusa

• **Bed & Breakfast Italia**
Code S35
tel. 06 6878618, fax 06 6878619
info@bbitalia.it
www.bbitalia.it
Closed: varies

A detached house built in the thirties, recently restored, in a small country village, in the province of Ragusa, on a hill facing southeast. With lovely and rustic furnishings, it is not far from the sea (just 10 kilometers). It features two double rooms, one of which with twin beds, and a private guest bathroom with shower. The area is renowned for its wines and culinary products. Wonderful excursions by sailing boat can be arranged. A car is absolutely necessary.

Accommodation
Guestrooms: *2 (1 double bedroom and 1 double)*
Services & Amenities: *French and English are spoken; rooms cleaned every 3 days; tourist information; baby-sitting service; bike rental; smokers welcome; private parking*
Minimum stay: *2 nights*
Rates: €€
Credit cards: VISA MC *Bancomat*
Pets:

Randazzo (Catania)

• **Bed & Breakfast Italia**
Code S42
tel. 06 6878618, fax 06 6878619
info@bbitalia.it
www.bbitalia.it
Closed: varies

Two small apartments, each consisting in a triple room with double bed plus a single bed. Both have rustic furnishings, exposed beams and stonewalls, evoking a medieval atmosphere. They are located at Randazzo, a small village at the foot of the Etna volcano, between the Etna Park and the Nebrodi Park, two places surrounded by woods of great interest for nature enthusiasts.

Accommodation
Guestrooms: *2 triple rooms*
Services & Amenities: *French and English are spoken; rooms cleaned every 3 days; tourist information; bike rental; Internet access; smokers welcome*
Minimum stay: *2 nights*
Rates: €€
Credit cards: VISA MC *Bancomat*
Pets:

Rosolini (Syracuse)

• Bed & Breakfast Italia
Code S50
tel. 06 6878618, fax 06 6878619
info@bbitalia.it
www.bbitalia.it
Closed: varies

A two-story villa in the heart of the village, surrounded by a garden carefully tended by the hostess, who offers guests a room with modern cheerful furnishings, twin beds, a large bookcase, rocking-chair, balcony and TV. The bathroom has a shower.

The rich breakfast is usually served in the large comfortable lounge. Smokers are welcome. The several wineries in the area make Rosolini a vintage wine-tasting center.

Accommodation
Guestrooms: *1 double*
Services & Amenities: *French spoken; rooms cleaned every 3 days; tourist information; baby-sitting service; air conditioning; smokers welcome*
Minimum stay: *2 nights*
Rates: €€
Credit cards: VISA MC *Bancomat*
Pets:

Salemi (Trapani)

• Bed & Breakfast Italia
Code S43
tel. 06 6878618, fax 06 6878619
info@bbitalia.it
www.bbitalia.it
Closed: varies

A two-story house dating from the 19th century in the small town, which was under Arab rule and experienced major expansion in the Norman age. The rooms, three doubles and two singles, are decorated with antique wooden furnishings and share two bathrooms. A car is needed to reach the main tourist attractions: Agrigento and Porto Empedocle.

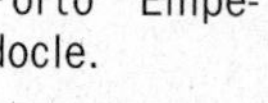

Accommodation
Guestrooms: *5 (2 singles and 3 double bedrooms)*
Services & Amenities: *French, English and German are spoken; rooms cleaned every 3 days; tourist information; smokers welcome; private parking*
Minimum stay: *2 nights*
Rates: €€
Credit cards: VISA MC *Bancomat*
Pets:

San Giovanni la Punta (Catania)

• Bed & Breakfast Italia
Code S45
tel. 06 6878618
fax 06 6878619
info@bbitalia.it
www.bbitalia.it
Closed: varies

Accommodation
Guestrooms: *2 (1 double bedroom and 1 triple room)*
Services & Amenities: *French and English are spoken; rooms cleaned every 3 days; complimentary tourist information; smokers welcome; private parking*
Minimum stay: *2 nights*
Rates: €€
Credit cards: VISA MC *Bancomat*
Pets:

The B&B is in a village 10 km from the sea. It is a comfortable house, with warm country-style furnishings. It consists in a double room with TV and balcony and a single room, sharing a bathroom with shower. In summer months, a continental breakfast is served in the shade of the gazebo; in winter it is offered in the dining room. The B&B is half an hour's drive from Catania and Taormina. A car is absolutely necessary.

San Gregorio di Catania (Catania)

• **Bed & Breakfast Italia**
Code S15
tel. 06 6878618, fax 06 6878619
info@bbitalia.it
www.bbitalia.it
Closed: varies

A small villa nestling in vegetation. Three bedrooms are allocated for B&B purposes: two twin-bedded rooms with private bathroom, balcony and TV and one double room with a large, furnished balcony looking onto the tropical garden. On request, the hosts prepare meals with local produce, served in the garden or on the large patio under the wonderful gazebo. They also organize lively evenings with karaoke or barbecues. The atmosphere is homely and friendly. Private parking is available.

Accommodation
Guestrooms: *3 (1 double bedroom and 2 doubles)*
Services & Amenities: *French and English are spoken; rooms cleaned every three days; complimentary tourist information; terrace; private parking*
Minimum stay: *2 nights*
Rates: €€
Credit cards: VISA MC *Bancomat*
Pets:

• **Bed & Breakfast Italia**
Code S31
tel. 06 6878618, fax 06 6878619
info@bbitalia.it
www.bbitalia.it
Closed: varies

A perfect old Sicilian-style villa, with a small annexed chapel dating from 1300, decorated with original, antique furniture and surrounded by a well tended park. The guest accommodation includes three double rooms with TV, two of which have a balcony, and two private bathrooms. It is 5 kilometers from the sea and from Catania. A car is recommended to explore the artistic and historical beauties of the area, such as Taormina, 40 kilometers away. Private parking is also available for the guests.

Accommodation
Guestrooms: *3 double bedrooms*
Services & Amenities: *French and English are spoken; rooms cleaned every 3 days; tourist information; bike rental; smokers welcome; private parking*
Minimum stay: *2 nights*
Rates: €€
Credit cards: VISA MC *Bancomat*
Pets:

Sant'Agata li Battiati (Catania)

• **Bed & Breakfast Italia**
Code S9
tel. 06 6878618, fax 06 6878619
info@bbitalia.it
www.bbitalia.it
Closed: varies

The B&B is an apartment not far from the center. The rooms offered to guests are a double and a twin, each with private bathroom. The refined furnishings show attention to quality and details. The bus stops right before the house, and takes 20 minutes to reach the center of Catania, a perfect example of baroque style and still preserving the signs of its Greek and Norman past.

Accommodation
Guestrooms: *2 (1 double bedroom and 1 double)*
Services & Amenities: *English spoken; rooms cleaned every 3 days; tourist info; terrace; private parking*
Minimum stay: *2 nights*
Rates: €€
Credit cards: VISA MC *Bancomat*
Pets:

An excursion exploring Mt Etna is an unforgettable part of a stay in Catania

San Vito lo Capo (Trapani)

Baglio La Luna
Daniela Jaforte
contrada Calampiso
91010 San Vito lo Capo (TP)
mob. 335 8362856
www.bagliolaluna.com
Open: June to September

This B&B, in an old building, surrounded by a lot of vegetation, is located on a high point overlooking the sea with a view of the cape. The guestrooms have both modern and rustic furniture, and there's also a living room and a garden with barbecue. Breakfast is served in the dining room. On request, the hosts can organize hikes and give lessons in how to prepare local dishes.

Accommodation
Guestrooms: *3 doubles, also single occupancy, with private bath*
Services & Amenities: *English and Spanish are spoken; rooms cleaned every day; tourist information; kitchen use by request; lunch & dinner reservations; educational courses by request; terrace; garden; smokers welcome; private parking*
Minimum stay: *2 nights*
Rates: *single €€-€€€, double €€€-€€€€. Children under 2 free; 2 to 6 -50%. Discounts for extended stays*
Credit cards: *not accepted*
Pets:

• **Bed & Breakfast Italia**
Code S16
tel. 06 6878618, fax 06 6878619
info@bbitalia.it
www.bbitalia.it
Closed: varies

A typical Mediterranean villa with garden, on a hill adjoining the Natural Reserve of the Gipsy, a site of tourist excursions to the beach inlets, golden sandy beaches and nature paths, 7 km from the village. It features a double and triple room with single beds. Each room has a private bathroom with shower and separate entrance. The B&B is a 30 minutes' drive from the village of Erice. The sea is 3 km away. A well tended garden and private parking are available.

Accommodation
Guestrooms: *2 (1 double bedroom and 1 triple room)*
Services & Amenities: *English, German and Spanish are spoken; rooms cleaned every three days; complimentary tourist information; private parking*
Minimum stay: *2 nights*
Rates: *€€*
Credit cards: VISA MC *Bancomat*
Pets:

Sciacca (Agrigento)

• **Bed & Breakfast Italia**
Code S52
tel. 06 6878618, fax 06 6878619
info@bbitalia.it
www.bbitalia.it
Closed: varies

Accommodation
Guestrooms: *2 (1 double bedroom and 1 triple room)*
Services & Amenities: *French and English are spoken; rooms cleaned every three days; complimentary tourist information; air conditioning*
Minimum stay: *2 nights*
Rates: *€€*
Credit cards: VISA MC *Bancomat*
Pets:

The house is located on the outskirts of Sciacca, a well-known seaside resort in the province of Agrigento. It includes two large rooms furnished in classic style with antiques: one double room and one triple room with a double and a single bed, both with ensuite bathroom with shower and independent entrance. A tropical plant nursery is annexed to the house, as well as a well tended garden, at the guests' disposal. The bus takes 10 mins to reach the town's old center. A car is absolutely necessary.

Syracuse

Archè
Rosa Giallombardo
via Faro Massoliveri 6
96100 Syracuse
tel. 0931 721094, mob. 338 3892273
bandb.arche@tiscali.it
web.tiscali.it/BandBArche/index/html
Closed: February and March

This beautiful, '50s villa built of stone is very close to the sea and faces the Ortigia Island. Its period and early 20th-C furniture create a very nice atmosphere. Breakfast, consisting of natural and homemade products, is served in the kitchen or out in the garden's gazebo. Guests are welcome to use the living room with fireplace and large picture window. They can also use the path leading to the private beach.

Accommodation
Guestrooms: *4 (3 doubles/triples, also single occupancy, and 1 quadruple room, with private bath)*
Services & Amenities: *English and Spanish are spoken; rooms cleaned every 3 days; tourist information; terrace; air conditioning; garden; smokers welcome; private parking*
Minimum stay: *2 nights*
Rates: *single €-€€, double €€-€€€, quadruple €€€€*
Credit cards: *not accepted*
Pets:

Dolce Casa - Bed & Breakfast TCI 10%
Rossella Regolo
via Lido Sacramento 4, contrada Isola
96100 Syracuse
tel. and fax 0931 721135
mob. 338 2935995
dolce.casa@tin.it
www.iblea2000.com/dolcecasa
Open all year

This B&B, which is near the Arenella Lido, is in a residential section that's just a few minutes from the city. This large, modern villa is surrounded by a garden with lots of flowers, palm and pine trees, and a terrace. The guests accommodation consists in six, air-conditioned, country-style-furnished double rooms all on the upper floor, and includes a living room. The hostess prepares breakfast, which also consists of homemade cakes, biscuits, buns and fresh fruit juice.

Accommodation
Guestrooms: *6 doubles, with private bath; additional bed on request*
Services & Amenities: *English spoken; rooms cleaned every day; tourist info; terrace; garden; smokers welcome; private parking*
Rates: *single €€, double €€€. Additional bed supplement €. Children under 5 free*
Credit cards: *not accepted*
Pets:

Dolce Silenzio
Bruna Mantovani Borghese
via Mirabella 18
96100 Syracuse
tel. and fax 0931 64201
dolcesilenzio@inwind.it
Closed: half of August and December

Accommodation
Guestrooms: *1 double/quadruple room, also single occupancy, with private bath*
Services & Amenities: *French, English, German and Spanish are spoken; rooms cleaned every three days; complimentary tourist information; terrace; Internet access; smokers welcome*
Rates: *single €€, double €€, quadruple €€€€. Children under 3 free*
Credit cards: *not accepted*
Pets:

This B&B, located in a 17th-century building situated on the Ortigia Island, in the most interesting part of the city, has a double room (with the possibility of making it a 4-bed room by adding extra beds), which is located in a mansard and has both modern and period furniture. The rich Italian breakfast is either served on the terrace or in the kitchen.

Villa Lucia
Lucia and Maria Luisa Palermo
trav. Mondello 1, contrada Isola
96100 Syracuse
tel. 0931 721007, mob. 336 888537
fax 0931 721587
www.villalucia/siracusa.it
Open all year

Accommodation
Guestrooms: *6 double bedrooms, also single occupancy, with private bath* ♿
Services & Amenities: *French spoken; rooms cleaned every day; tourist info; terrace; air conditioning; Internet access; garden; smokers welcome; private parking*
Rates: *single €€€€, double €€€€*
Credit cards: *accepted*
Pets: not allowed

This manor villa, surrounded by a large Mediterranean park with palm trees, citrus trees and flowers, is on the Plemmirio promontory that faces the Ortigia Island. The guestrooms have a classic atmosphere, and three of them are in the dépendance situated in the park. The buffet breakfast, which also consists of cold cuts and cheese, is served in the winter garden overlooking the vegetation. Guests also have the use of a nice conference room located in a pleasant pavilion.

• Bed & Breakfast Italia
Code S4
tel. 06 6878618, fax 06 6878619
info@bbitalia.it
www.bbitalia.it
Closed: varies

Accommodation
Guestrooms: *2 (1 single and 1 double bedroom)*
Services & Amenities: *English spoken; rooms cleaned every three days; complimentary tourist information; private parking*
Minimum stay: *2 nights*
Rates: *€€*
Credit cards: VISA MC *Bancomat*
Pets: not allowed

The B&B is hosted by a villa on the edge of Syracuse, on three levels, with a well tended garden facing the sea. The accommodation consists in two rooms, one single and one double, that are decorated with wicker furniture and colorful bedspreads; they feature ensuite bathrooms, air conditioning and a balcony. Although the bus, which takes 15 minutes to get the center, stops 300 meters away, a car is recommended. Private parking is available for the guests.

• Bed & Breakfast Italia
Code S10
tel. 06 6878618, fax 06 6878619
info@bbitalia.it
www.bbitalia.it
Closed: varies

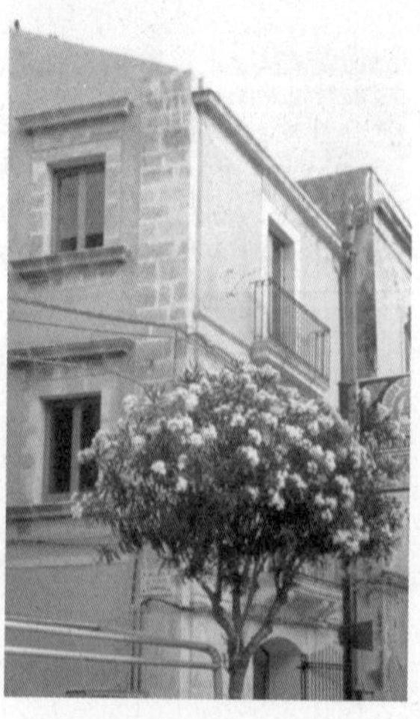

Accommodation
Guestrooms: *1 double bedroom and 1 triple room*
Services & Amenities: *rooms cleaned every three days; tourist information; smokers welcome*
Minimum stay: *2 nights*
Rates: *€€*
Credit cards: VISA MC *Bancomat*
Pets: allowed

This second-floor apartment in an old building with elevator, in the old center, is available for guests. The rooms, a double and a triple, are large and cozy, complete with TV and open onto a comfortable, large balcony. They share a bathroom with shower. Cultural and art sights can all be reached by foot: the Duomo, the temple of Apollo, the ruins of the Greek theater and of the amphitheater. The sea is 15 kilometers away by car.

• **Bed & Breakfast Italia**
Code S40
tel. 06 6878618, fax 06 6878619
info@bbitalia.it
www.bbitalia.it
Closed: varies

An old mansion in the center of Syracuse which offers four guestrooms, all featuring balcony, TV, ceiling fan, ensuite bathroom with shower. It is within a short distance of the archaeological site, where it is possible to visit the ancient Greek theater, still almost intact, and where the ancient authors' tragedies are performed annually. Also the island of Ortigia is easily reached. A car is necessary. Smokers are welcome.

Accommodation
Guestrooms: *4 double bedrooms*
Services & Amenities: *English spoken; rooms cleaned every three days; complimentary tourist information; smokers welcome*
Minimum stay: *2 nights*
Rates: €€
Credit cards: VISA MC *Bancomat*
Pets: [no pets]

• **Bed & Breakfast Italia** TCI 10%
Code S47
tel. 06 6878618, fax 06 6878619
info@bbitalia.it
www.bbitalia.it
Closed: varies

A house with an independent entrance and a view of the sea, in the city's old center. A double room with parquet flooring, balcony and a bathroom with shower is used for B&B purposes. PC and fax facilities are available. In summer months, breakfast prepared

Accommodation
Guestrooms: *1 double bedroom*
Services & Amenities: *French and English are spoken; rooms cleaned every three days; tourist information; smokers welcome*
Minimum stay: *2 nights*
Rates: €€
Credit cards: VISA MC *Bancomat*
Pets: [no pets]

with typical Sicilian specialties is served by your hostess on a large, scenic balcony. Right in front of the house there is a tiny beach, where guests can sunbathe.

Taormina (Messina)

• **Bed & Breakfast Italia**
Code S21
tel. 06 6878618, fax 06 6878619
info@bbitalia.it
www.bbitalia.it
Closed: varies

This stone villa on three levels, built in the fifties, very well kept and comfortable, is in the center. At the entrance there is an old iron gate; the two large glass windows in the lounge open onto the large balcony, adorned with marbles and friezes. The floors are tiled in terracotta and with Caltagirone ceramics. The four guestrooms are on the second floor: three doubles and a triple, all with private bathroom, bright and carefully decorated,

Accommodation
Guestrooms: *4 (3 doubles and 1 triple room)*
Services & Amenities: *English spoken; rooms cleaned every 3 days; tourist info; terrace; private parking*
Minimum stay: *2 nights*
Rates: €€
Credit cards: VISA MC *Bancomat*
Pets: [pets allowed]

boasting a panoramic view. Thanks to its hilltop position guests can enjoy a view of the whole town: the rooftops, the creeks, the Naxos Gardens and the open sea.

Terrasini (Palermo)

• **Bed & Breakfast Italia**
Code S55
tel. 06 6878618, fax 06 6878619
info@bbitalia.it
www.bbitalia.it
Closed: varies

A two-story villa with park and swimming pool. The family offers guests four double rooms, two of which are twins, each with private bathroom with shower. The apartments are elegantly furnished with antiques. In summer, continental breakfast is served in the shade of the large patio and, in the winter months, guests can have breakfast on the veranda. Private parking is available. Use of the swimming pool is possible in July and August.

Accommodation
Guestrooms: *4 (2 double bedrooms and 2 doubles)*
Services & Amenities: *rooms cleaned every 3 days; tourist information; baby-sitting service; air conditioning; smokers welcome; private parking*
Minimum stay: *2 nights*
Rates: €€
Credit cards: VISA MC *Bancomat*
Pets: no

Trecastagni (Catania)

• **Bed & Breakfast Italia**
Code S32
tel. 06 6878618, fax 06 6878619
info@bbitalia.it
www.bbitalia.it
Closed: varies

A 19th-century villa in typical Sicilian style, furnished with antiques, surrounded by an orchard and a vineyard, which produces grapes for organic wine. It consists in two double rooms, one with twin beds, and a private bathroom with shower for the guests. The hostess makes cakes, which are served for breakfast. This villa is at the foot of the Mt Etna, 15 km from the sea and Acireale. A car is recommended for transfers.

Accommodation
Guestrooms: *2 (1 double bedroom and 1 double)*
Services & Amenities: *English spoken; rooms cleaned every three days; complimentary tourist information; bike rental; smokers welcome; private parking*
Minimum stay: *2 nights*
Rates: €€
Credit cards: VISA MC *Bancomat*
Pets: no

Tremestieri Etneo (Catania)

B&B Dolina
Valeria Carastro
via Cardinale Francicanava 44
95030 Tremestieri Etneo (CT)
tel. 095 7410600, mob. 347 8137063
dolina_bb@hotmail.com
• **Friendly Home-Gli Amici del B&B**
tel. 02 860147, fax 02 875860
friendlymilano@dada.it
tel. and fax 011 9536376
fhrivoli@virgilio.it
Open all year

This B&B is in a two-story villa situated in a residential area of the city at the foot of Mt Etna. It's surrounded by hills that have many vineyards. The guestrooms, which have modern, light-colored furniture, lead onto a large terrace. Guests are also welcome to enjoy the garden with its equipped relaxation area.

Accommodation
Guestrooms: *3 (1 double bedroom and 2 doubles, also single occupancy, with shared bath)*
Services & Amenities: *English spoken; rooms cleaned every 3 days; tourist information; lunch & dinner reservations; educational courses by request; garden; smokers welcome*
Rates: *single €, double €€. Children under 2 free. Discounts for students and for honeymoon trips*
Credit cards: *not accepted*
Pets: yes

Valderice (Trapani)

• **Bed & Breakfast Italia**
Code S44
tel. 06 6878618, fax 06 6878619
info@bbitalia.it
www.bbitalia.it
Closed: varies

Accommodation
Guestrooms: *2 doubles; additional bed on request*
Services & Amenities: *rooms cleaned every 3 days; tourist info; smokers welcome; private parking*
Minimum stay: *2 nights*
Rates: €€
Credit cards: VISA MC *Bancomat*
Pets: not allowed

A ground floor apartment, self-contained, consisting in a double room and a twin-bedded room, both tastefully and simply furnished, with the option of a third bed. The bathroom has a shower. Guests can use the lounge, the large courtyard in front of the house and the parking area. The host family is very friendly and full of concern for their guests' needs. A car is necessary.

Viagrande (Catania)

Consorzio "Casali dell'Etna"
Ignazio Barbagallo and Fabio Bonaccorsi
via Garibaldi 387
95029 Viagrande (CT)
tel. and fax 095 7890656
mob. 347 7631613
natour@ctonline.it
• **Friendly Home-Gli Amici del B&B**
tel. 02 860147, fax 02 875860
friendlymilano@dada.it
tel. and fax 011 9536376
fhrivoli@virgilio.it

Accommodation
Guestrooms: *45 beds*
Services & Amenities: *rooms cleaned every 3 days; tourist information; lunch & dinner reservations; educational courses by request; smokers welcome; transport to/from airport, minibus trips, angling*
Rates: €€ *per person*
Credit cards: *not accepted*
Pets: allowed

This consortium unites various rural-tourism operators whose work concerns the commune of Viagrande. This lovely little town, set in the foothills, is particularly attractive because of its ancient summer villas surrounded by luxurious gardens. The sculptured lava decorations, the black basalt masks on the front portals and the plaster work done with the use of volcanic sand blend perfectly with the Etna landscape. The consortium arranges sojourns in these residences.

Azienda Agricola Blandano
This B&B, located in a rural complex, complete with manor house, dépendance and adjoining farmland, is surrounded by fine vineyards and orchards. Guests can enjoy wine-tasting and can also become acquainted with the local cuisine.

Azienda Agricola Di Bella
This interesting, 18th-C villa, with its Italian garden and surrounding 15 acres of land, is situated between Etna and the sea. Hospitality is offered in the ancient residence that forms part of the complex. The host gives lessons in Tai Chi.

Azienda Agricola L'Annunziata
Hospitality is offered in the rooms of a typical, 18th-century, manor house, which has balconies with lava-stone, baroque decorations and an ancient millstone.

Azienda Brucato
Guests have the use of the dépendance of this beautiful, now restructured, late 19th-C residence, which is surrounded by vineyards and orchards.

Azienda Condorelli
This 19th-C manor house has an annexed residence for the guests. The residence has a garden and a beautiful patio, which is where the generous breakfast is served.

Azienda L'Albero Lungo
This 19th-C residence, which is a perfect example of baronial residences found in Etna, is surrounded by countryside and offers hospitality in its annexed guest accommodations.

Azienda Sorbello
This 17th-C villa, located in Viscalori, a community consisting of ancient summer homes, offers hospitality in an apartment located on the upper floor of the building, which also includes a nice terrace.

Società Cucina del Sole
This school, which has been teaching aspiring cooks from various parts of the world how to prepare Sicilian dishes, can provide hospitality in a small house next to the building. This small house is surrounded by a flourishing garden.

Sardinia

Alghero (Sassari)

B&B da Anna Rita
località Fertilia
• Sardegna B&B Reservation
tel. 070 4520011, fax 070 4520403
bedsardegna@tiscali.it
Open: June to September and Easter holidays

This B&B is located 7 kilometers from Alghero in a small, recently-constructed villa situated in the Monte Doglia National Park. Guest accommodation consists in three rooms with modern, functional furniture. The continental breakfast is either served on the veranda or in the kitchen. The family can provide transportation to and from the airport.

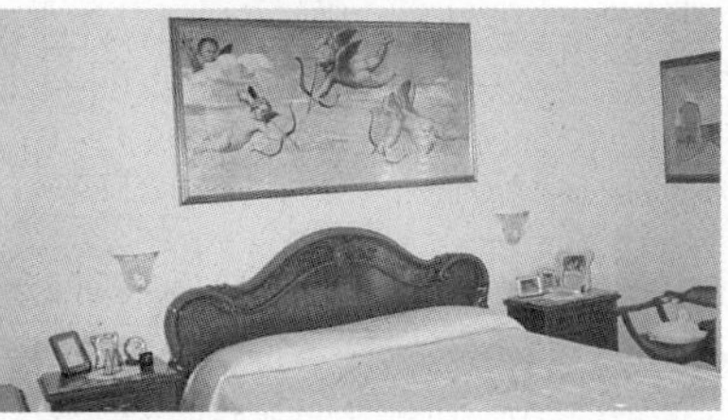

Accommodation
Guestrooms: *3 (1 single and 2 double bedrooms, with shared bath)*
Services & Amenities: *French and English are spoken; rooms cleaned every day; complimentary tourist information; bike rental; terrace; garden; private parking*
Minimum stay: *3 nights*
Rates: *€ per person. Children under 3 free, 4 to 8 -50%*
Credit cards: *not accepted*
Pets: 🐾

Monte Doglia TCI 10%
località Fertilia
• Associazione "Sardegna Ospitale"
tel. 079 2595061, mob. 347 7773072
fax 079 2592241
info@bbsardegna.com
www.bbsardegna.com
Closed: varies

This house, situated in the countryside, just 2,5 km from the sea, is very close to the natural oasis of Capo Caccia. The accommodation includes a garden and internal parking. This place is particularly suitable for children. In fact, the hostess is a very active and hospitable grandmother. The vicinity provides many opportunities for hiking and excursions.

Accommodation
Guestrooms: *3 doubles, also single occupancy, 2 with private bath and 1 with shared bath; additional bed on request*
Services & Amenities: *English spoken; rooms cleaned every 3 days; tourist info; baby-sitting service; garden; smokers welcome; parking*
Rates: *single €-€€, double €€-€€€. Children under 3 free, 4 to 12 -50%*
Credit cards: *not accepted*
Pets: 🐾

Vista sul Golfo Tci 10%

• Associazione "Sardegna Ospitale"
tel. 079 2595061, mob. 347 7773072
fax 079 2592241
info@bbsardegna.com
www.bbsardegna.com
Closed: varies

ACCOMMODATION
Guestrooms: *3 doubles, also single occupancy, with shared bath*
Services & Amenities: *English and Spanish are spoken; rooms cleaned every 3 days; complimentary tourist information; kitchen use by request; terrace; smokers welcome*
Rates: *single €-€€, double €€-€€€. Children under 6 free; 7 to 12 -50%*
Credit cards: *not accepted*
Pets: ✓

This attic, which is completely restructured and has refined finishings, also has a terrace facing the sea. There's a parking space right in front of the house, and the equipped beach is only 30 m away. On request, the guests can use the family kitchen. There are various archeological sites as well as a natural reserve in the vicinity that are well worth visiting.

ARZACHENA (SASSARI)

B&B Oasi di Gallura
• Sardegna B&B Reservation
tel. 070 4520011, 070 4520403
bedsardegna@tiscali.it
Open: April to September

ACCOMMODATION
Guestrooms: *3 (2 doubles, also single occupancy, shared bath; 1 double bedroom, private bath). Additional bed on request*
Services & Amenities: *French and English are spoken; rooms cleaned every day; tourist information; terrace; garden; private parking*
Minimum stay: *2 nights*
Rates: *€€€€-€€€€€. Additional bed supplement €€. Children under 3 free: 4 to 8 -50%*
Credit cards: *not accepted*
Pets: ✗

There's a splendid, pastel-colored villa with an English lawn located just outside of Arzachena. This villa, surrounded by a park with tall trees, old olive trees and Mediterra-nean scrub, is ideal for a vacation close to nature while, at the same time, being just a few minutes from the fashionable Costa Smeralda and Gallura beaches. The hostess serves the continental breakfast either in the dining room or on the veranda. Just a few kilometers away, guests can enjoy horseback riding and visiting particularly interesting archeological sites.

Ca' La Somara
Alberto Lagattolla
località Sarra Balestra
07021 Arzachena (SS)
tel. and fax 0789 98969
calasomara@libero.it
Closed: 15 January to 15 March

ACCOMMODATION
Guestrooms: *3 doubles, private bath*
Services & Amenities: *French and English are spoken; rooms cleaned every three days; tourist information; dinner reservation; Internet access; garden; smokers welcome; private parking*
Minimum stay: *3 nights*
Rates: *€€-€€€*
Credit cards: *not accepted*
Pets: ✓

This B&B, which is out in the country, just a few minutes from the Porto Cervo sea, is located in an ancient, reconstructed stall, which is next to a donkey-breeding farm. The three double rooms have upper levels, are furnished in the Mexican style, and lead directly into the garden. Breakfast, consisting of natural products and genuine pastries, is served outside under the portico. The hosts can also offer dinner and organize energetic treatments (carried out under an arabesque tent that comes from the desert), as well as relaxing excursions.

Bosa (Nuoro)

B&B Bosa
• Associazione "Sardegna Ospitale"
tel. 079 2595061, mob. 347 7773072
fax 079 2592241
info@bbsardegna.com
www.bbsardegna.com
Open: Easter holidays to October

This B&B, located in a 4-story house with no elevator, was built in 1850. It faces a small square reserved for pedestrians in Bosa's old center. The guestrooms, which have modern, functional furniture, are located on the 2nd and 3rd floors. The 4th floor has a terrace that the guests are welcome to use. Breakfast can also include typical Sardinian products on request. The kitchen is also available.

Accommodation
Guestrooms: *3 (1 double bedroom and 2 singles, with shared bath); additional child's bed on request*
Services & Amenities: *French, English and Spanish are spoken; rooms cleaned every three days; complimentary tourist information; baby–sitting service; kitchen use by request; lunch & dinner reservations; bike rental; terrace; smokers welcome*
Rates: *single €-€€, double €€-€€€. Children under 3 free; 4 to 12 -50%*
Credit cards: *not accepted*
Pets: no pets

Budoni (Nuoro)

B&B da Carmela
• Sardegna B&B Reservation
tel. 070 4520011, 070 4520403
bedsardegna@tiscali.it
Closed: November

Very careful restructuring has transformed what was once a secular rustic abode into this very nice bare-stone house, which is embellished with a splendid bougainvillea plant. The house, that has two guestrooms on the first floor, is situated on the east coast, 30 kilometers from Olbia and 4 kilometers from the sea. The vicinity offers the possibility of going horseback riding or hiking. Any children accompanying the guests must be at least 8 years old.

Accommodation
Guestrooms: *2 doubles with private bath; additional bed on request*
Services & Amenities: *rooms cleaned every day; tourist information; private parking*
Rates: *€ per person*
Credit cards: *not accepted*
Pets: no pets

B&B Miosotis
Caterina Dui
località S'Iscala
08020 Budoni (NU)
tel. 070 664240, 0784 837329
mob. 330 430422
ale.silvia@tiscali.it
budoni.interfree.it
Open: April to October, Easter and Christmas holidays

This small, recently-constructed, duplex villa is located in a hilly area near the sea. Its three guestrooms have modern furnishings. The Italian breakfast, which also includes such typical local products as sausages and cheese, is served in the kitchen. The hostess, a shiatsu and reflexology therapist, can provide therapeutic treatment.

Accommodation
Guestrooms: *3 (2 double bedrooms and 1 double, also single occupancy, with shared bath)*
Services & Amenities: *French, English and Spanish are spoken; rooms cleaned every three days; complimentary tourist information; kitchenette; garden; smokers welcome; private parking*
Minimum stay: *2 nights*
Rates: *single €-€€, double €€-€€€*
Credit cards: *not accepted*
Pets: pets allowed

Cagliari

B&B Villa Cao
• Sardegna B&B Reservation
tel. 070 4520011, 070 4520403
bedsardegna@tiscali.it
Closed: 20 December to 7 January and August

This villa is situated in the old center of Villanova and is surrounded by a quiet garden. There's one guestroom and a suite, both air conditioned and both very carefully and elegantly furnished. Breakfast consists of warm beverages, marmalades and homemade pastries. In the wintertime, breakfast is either served in the guestroom or in a nice living room. In the summertime, it's served in the patio that provides a view of the garden. The house isn't suitable for hosting children.

Accommodation
Guestrooms: *2 (1 single and 1 suite, with private bath)*
Services & Amenities: *English and Spanish are spoken; rooms cleaned every day; tourist information; baby-sitting service; air conditioning; Internet access; garden; private parking*
Rates: *€€-€€€€ per person. Discounts for extended stays*
Credit cards: *not accepted*
Pets:

Casa di Maria Rosa
Maria Rosa Rapetti
via Pontida 40, località Pirri
09134 Cagliari
tel. 070 502391, fax 070 553739
sardacam@iol.it
www.casadimariarosa.com
Open all year

This B&B is in a small, modern building just 10 minutes by car from the port and the airport. The house is surrounded by a large, equipped garden, and also has a children's swimming pool. The three guestrooms have modern furnishings, colored murals and a leisure room. The rich breakfast, consisting of typical products, is either served in a room that has a fireplace, or in the garden. The hostess can provide shiatsu therapeutic treatment.

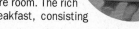

Accommodation
Guestrooms: *3 doubles, private bath*
Services & Amenities: *English spoken; rooms cleaned every three days; tourist information; baby-sitting service; lunch & dinner reservations; garden; smokers welcome; parking*
Minimum stay: *in summer, 1 week*
Rates: *single €€, double €€€. Discounts for extended stays*
Credit cards: *not accepted*
Pets:

• Bed & Breakfast Italia
Code SA6
tel. 06 6878618, fax 06 6878619
info@bbitalia.it
www.bbitalia.it
Closed: varies

A detached house furnished in a cheerful, modern style, surrounded by a large and well tended garden. It includes a twin-bed room, independent entrance and TV. The private bathroom for the use of guests has a shower. In the summer months, a continental breakfast is served on the veranda; in winter it is offered in the lounge. The house is within 20 minutes' walk of Cagliari's old center, renowned for the Elephant's Tower. Private parking is available.

Accommodation
Guestrooms: *1 double*
Services & Amenities: *English and Spanish are spoken; rooms cleaned every three days; tourist information; private parking*
Minimum stay: *2 nights*
Rates: €€
Credit cards: *Bancomat*
Pets:

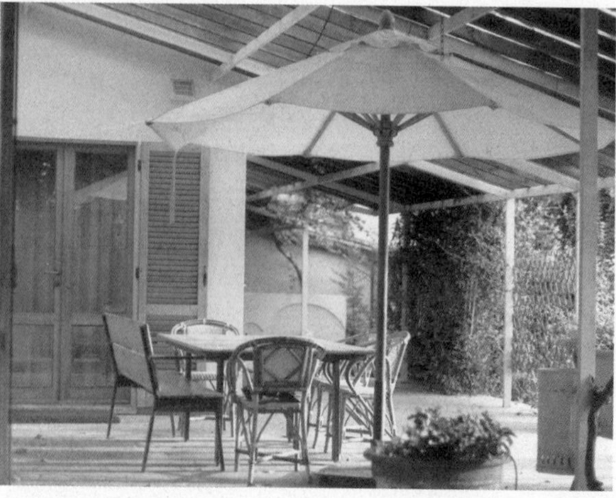

Carbonia (Cagliari)

B&B Annacarla
Annacarla Flore
via Catania 3, 09013 Carbonia (CA)
tel. 0781 662046, 0781 61978
mob. 338 3922179
annacarla.flore@tiscali.it
www.bedbreakfast.cjb.net
Open all year

This B&B is on the first floor of an apartment surrounded by a garden. The guestrooms have modern wooden furniture. The Italian breakfast, which includes natural pastries, is served in the kitchen reserved for the guests. This B&B is ideal for visiting the archeological coal mines park and the Siris Punic archeological site.

Accommodation
Guestrooms: *3 (2 doubles, 1 double bedroom, shared bath); additional bed on request ♿*
Services & Amenities: *French and English are spoken; rooms cleaned every 3 days; tourist info; kitchen use by request; terrace; air conditioning; Internet; smokers welcome; parking*
Minimum stay: *3 nights*
Rates: €€-€€€
Credit cards: *accepted*
Pets: no

Domus de Maria (Cagliari)

B&B La Torre
• **Sardegna B&B Reservation**
tel. 070 4520011, 070 4520403
bedsardegna@tiscali.it
Open all year

Accommodation
Guestrooms: *2 doubles, also single occupancy, with shared bath*
Services & Amenities: *rooms cleaned every day; tourist information; baby-sitting service; kitchenette; lunch & dinner reservations; terrace; garden; smokers welcome; private parking*
Minimum stay: *3 nights*
Rates: €-€€ *per person. Children under 3 free; 4 to 8 -50%*
Credit cards: *not accepted*
Pets: yes

This B&B, which is in a modern villa with garden, is 700 m from the Torre di Chia beach, which is famous for its long stretches of white sand. It has 2 nice rooms and a living room with kitchenette. They are also welcome to use the garden. Breakfast is served on the veranda. Guests are also invited to taste a few local dishes.

Dorgali (Nuoro)

B&B Su Romasinarzu
località Cala Gonone
• **Sardegna B&B Reservation**
tel. 070 4520011, 070 4520403
bedsardegna@tiscali.it
Open: April to October

Accommodation
Guestrooms: *3 (1 single and 2 doubles, with shared bath)*
Services & Amenities: *rooms cleaned every day; tourist information; terrace; garden; private parking*
Minimum stay: *2 nights*
Rates: € *per person. Children under 3 free, 4 to 8 -50%*
Credit cards: *not accepted*
Pets: no

This B&B is in a restructured 30s house with a panoramic view and is in an area famous for its beautiful beaches. The accommodation also includes a living room, furnished in the rustic style, and with large windows. The traditional breakfast, with its local pastries, is served in this living room.

Fluminimaggiore (Cagliari)

B&B Domus Liscia
Rosaria Liscia
località Su Trabì
09010 Fluminimaggiore (CA)
tel. 0781 580160
lisciadomus@tiscalinet.it
• **Associazione Domus Amigas**
tel. and fax 0781 36319
Open: April to August

This B&B is located in Costa Verde – 15 kilometers from the famous Piscinas dunes – in a rustic house surrounded by a large, verdant garden with fruit trees. Its furnishings and ceilings made of bare beams and reeds create a nice atmosphere. The rich breakfast consists of homemade cakes and natural marmalades. On request, the hostess can also take care of the kids.

Accommodation
Guestrooms: *2 (1 single and 1 double, with shared bath)*
Services & Amenities: *French and English are spoken; rooms cleaned every three days; tourist information; baby-sitting service; garden; smokers welcome; parking*
Minimum stay: *2 nights*
Rates: € *per person. Children under 4 free. Discounts for extended stays*
Credit cards: *not accepted*
Pets: no

Goni (Cagliari)

B&B La Casa delle Fate
• Sardegna B&B Reservation
tel. 070 4520011, 070 4520403
bedsardegna@tiscali.it
Open all year

This B&B is on the 1st floor of a modern building with elevator, which makes accessing it easy for handicapped people. The building is located on the main street of Goni, a small town whose inhabitants are farmers and animal breeders. It's also where important archeological sites are found, such as the Domus de Janas (the house of the fairies) and the Pranu Mutteddu necopolises. The guestrooms, which share the bathroom, have Sardinian style furnishings. Breakfast, of homemade pastries, is served in the dining room, where guests can also have lunch and dinner.

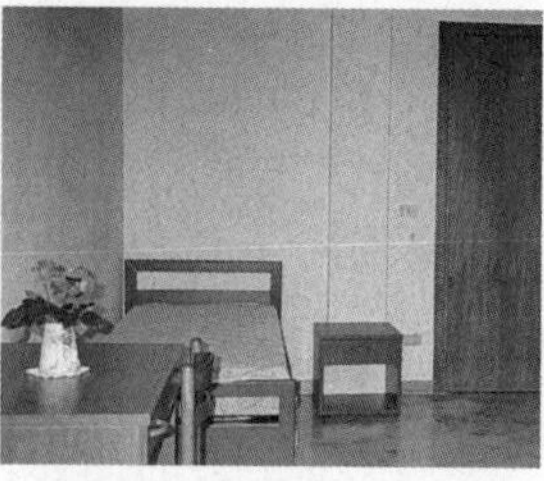

Accommodation
Guestrooms: *3 doubles, also single occupancy, shared bath* ♿
Services & Amenities: *rooms cleaned every day; tourist information; baby-sitting service; lunch & dinner reservations; garden; smokers welcome*
Minimum stay: *2 nights*
Rates: *€ per person. Children under 3 free; 4 to 8 -50%*
Credit cards: *not accepted*
Pets: no

Gonnesa (Cagliari)

L'Elicriso Tci 10%
Umberto Delussu
località S'Ortu de Coccu
09010 Gonnesa (CA)
tel. 0781 36412
web.tiscalinet.it/csa_sardegna
• Associazione Domus Amigas
tel. and fax 0781 36319
Open all year

The Elicriso is located in a farmhouse that's surrounded by a large garden. It sits at foot of Mount San Giovanni, inside the Sulcis Geomineral Park, less than 2 kilometers from the sea. Its guestrooms have period furnishings and face a communicating terrace.

Accommodation
Guestrooms: *2 doubles, also single occupancy, 1 with private bath and 1 with shared bath*
Services & Amenities: *French and English are spoken; rooms cleaned every day; tourist information; terrace; garden; smokers welcome; private parking*
Rates: *single €, double €-€€. Children under 5 free*
Credit cards: *accepted*
Pets: yes

Breakfast, consisting of typical Sardinian products, is served in the farmhouse's large dining room. In the shop next to the property, guests can take part in the making of bread, which involves an ancient natural leavening method.

Maria Teresa Contu Figus Tci 10%
San Giovanni Miniera Normann 12
09010 Gonnesa (CA)
tel. 0781 45567
• Associazione Domus Amigas
tel. and fax 0781 36319
Open all year

This part of Sardinia has a lot of old mines, many of which have now become parks containing archeological sites. This duplex has two guestrooms with rustic furnishings. The traditional breakfast, enriched with homemade blackberry and quince or Sardinian black-cherry marmalades, is served in a room that has a kitchenette and a fireplace. The garden has a barbecue facility and a wood-burning oven. Private parking is also available.

Accommodation
Guestrooms: *2 doubles, also single occupancy, with 1 private bath and 1 shared bath; additional bed on request*
Services & Amenities: *rooms cleaned every day; tourist info; garden; smokers welcome; private parking*
Minimum stay: *2 nights*
Rates: *single €€, double €€. Children under 6 -50%*
Credit cards: *not accepted*
Pets: yes

Paola Delussu
tel. and fax 0781 36319
• Associazione Domus Amigas
tel. and fax 0781 36319
Open: March to October

This house is located in the center of Gonnesa, the Iglesiente town just 3 kilometers from the coast. Guests have a mansard – surrounded by a large terrace – that has two double rooms with rustic style furnishings. The hostess, an herbalist, is happy to introduce her guests to the world of herbs and arranges excursions, provides consulting and prepares special brews. Breakfast, which can be enriched with Sardinian pastries, is served in the kitchen or in the dining room. There's a covered garage in which guests can keep any bicycles they may have.

Accommodation
Guestrooms: *2 doubles with shared bath; additional bed on request*
Services & Amenities: *French spoken; rooms cleaned every day; tourist information; terrace; garden; smokers welcome; private parking*
Rates: *double €. Discounts for children*
Credit cards: *not accepted*
Pets:

Isola di Sant'Antioco (Cagliari)

B&B Giardini Mediterranei
Paolo Balia
via Belvedere 97
09017 Sant'Antioco (CA)
tel. 0781 800359
paolofranco.balia@tin.it
• Associazione Domus Amigas
tel. and fax 0781 36319
Closed: January and February

This Mediterranean style B&B is located on a organic farm in the Isola di Sant'Antioco. With is verdant surroundings, vineyards, orchards and Mediterranean scruff, this is the ideal place for spending a nice vacation in close contact with nature. The guestrooms are in the rustic style and have plain furniture. Breakfast consists of pastries, natural marmalades and warm beverages. On request, guests can use the kitchen and also make arrangements for having lunch and dinner. Gardening lessons and bicycles are also available.

Accommodation
Guestrooms: *3 (1 single and 2 doubles, with shared bath)*
Services & Amenities: *French and English are spoken; rooms cleaned every 3 days; tourist information; kitchen use by request; lunch & dinner reservations; bike rental; educational courses by request; garden; smokers welcome; private parking*
Rates: *€ per person. Discounts for children and extended stays*
Credit cards: *not accepted*
Pets:

La Rosa dei Venti B&B
via Goceano 30
09017 Sant'Antioco (CA)
tel. 0781 828010
mob. 347 6364566, 349 8752537
rosaventi@hotmail.com
www.rosaventi.it
• Friendly Home-Gli Amici del B&B
tel. 02 860147, fax 02 875860
friendlymilano@dada.it
tel. and fax 011 9536376
fhrivoli@virgilio.it
Open all year

This villa, with its large Mediterranean garden, is located just a short distance from the island's small touristic port and beaches. Guests have three rooms with TV and a beautiful garden. The furnishings include both antiques and local, handmade items. The breakfast, which consists of typical pastries and natural cakes, is served in the patio or in the living room.

Accommodation
Guestrooms: *3 doubles or double bedrooms, with private bath*
Services & Amenities: *French and English are spoken; rooms cleaned every day; tourist information; bike rental; air conditioning; garden; smokers welcome; parking*
Minimum stay: *2 nights*
Rates: *€€ per person. Children under 2 free; 3 to 12 -30%*
Credit cards: *not accepted*
Pets:

Iglesias (Cagliari)

Giancarlo Rinaudo
corso Colombo 116
09016 Iglesias (CA)
tel. 0781 23997
allori.allori@tiscalinet.it
• Associazione Domus Amigas
tel. and fax 0781 36319
Open all year

This B&B, which is on the state road that leads to Villamassargia, is located in a small villa 3 kilometers from the center of Iglesias. The family consists of four persons. Guests have a double room with plain, modern furnishings and an adjoining private bathroom. The continental breakfast is served in the family dining room. Guests are welcome to enjoy the living room with its TV. A private, internal parking is also provided.

Accommodation
Guestrooms: *1 double with private bath*
Services & Amenities: *French and English are spoken; rooms cleaned every day; tourist information; garden; smokers welcome; private parking*
Minimum stay: *3 nights*
Rates: *double €€. Discounts for children*
Credit cards: *not accepted*
Pets: (no pets symbol)

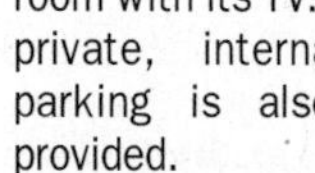
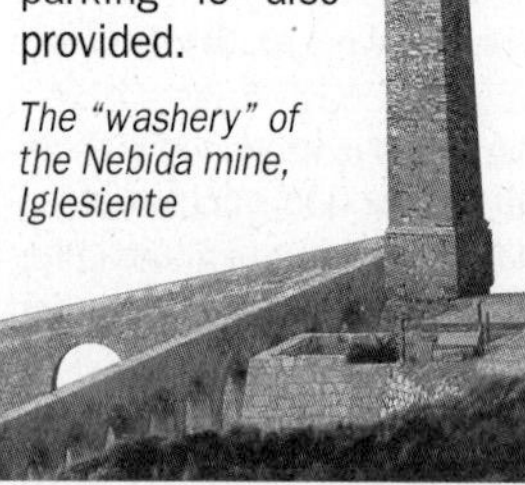

The "washery" of the Nebida mine, Iglesiente

• Bed & Breakfast Italia
Code SA3
tel. 06 6878618, fax 06 6878619
info@bbitalia.it
www.bbitalia.it
Closed: varies

This recently built villa, surrounded by a well tended Mediterranean garden, is on the outskirts of Cagliari, 10 kilometers from the sea. This accommodation includes one triple room, with a double and a single bed, and one single room, both complete with TV; there are two bathrooms, one of which equipped with tub/shower, the other with shower only. A cot for children under the age of two is available on request. A car is needed to visit the area.

Accommodation
Guestrooms: *2 (1 single, 1 triple)*
Services & Amenities: *English spoken; rooms cleaned every 3 days; tourist information*
Minimum stay: *2 nights*
Rates: €€
Credit cards: VISA MC *Bancomat*
Pets: (no pets symbol)

Mamoiada (Nuoro)

Villa Barone
• Sardegna B&B Reservation
tel. 070 4520011, 070 4520403
bedsardegna@tiscali.it
Open all year

Accommodation
Guestrooms: *3 doubles, with shared bath*
Services & Amenities: *French spoken; rooms cleaned every 3 days; tourist information; dinner reservation; garden; smokers welcome; private parking*
Rates: *double €€-€€€. Children under 3 free; 4 to 8 -50%*
Credit cards: *not accepted*
Pets: (pets allowed symbol)

This B&B is in villa that's surrounded by a verdant cultivation of vegetables and fruit. The guestrooms, which have plain, comfortable furnishings, are on the 1st and 2nd floors. Breakfast, which consists of typical, local bread and pastries, is either served in the living room or in the small tavern. Mamoiada is famous for its "mamuthones," the ancient, bizarre, masked characters who parade on the streets of the city during the Carnival period.

Masainas (Cagliari)

Monica Joanni e Elio Caboni
via Pascoli 2
09010 Masainas (CA)
tel. 0781 964648
• Associazione Domus Amigas
tel. and fax 0781 36319
Open: March to October, Christmas holidays and New Year's day

This house is located in the country, near the southwestern coast, just a short distance from Sant'Antioco and the connections for San Pietro. The guests have an independent house with an external stairway. The rooms are exclusively furnished with natural materials, and two of them have large upper levels that provide additional bed space. There are also two cribs, as well as a room with a fireplace, two large terraces and a garden with a barbecue. Some of the family's farm products are served at breakfast and, on request, guests can also try the homemade bread.

Accommodation
Guestrooms: *3 doubles with shared bath; additional bed on request*
Services & Amenities: *French, English and German are spoken; rooms cleaned every three days; tourist information*
Rates: € *per person*
Credit cards: *not accepted*
Pets: 🚫

Monastir (Cagliari)

B&B Sa Domu de Su Meri Cristou
• Sardegna B&B Reservation
tel. 070 4520011, 070 4520403
bedsardegna@tiscali.it
Open all year

This typical, very ancient Sardinian house is mainly made of mud bricks. It has a stone foundation, just like the other ancient homes in the area. It's located in Monastir, among the hills and plains of this rural center called "campidano." That's why these houses are called "campidanesi" houses. The guestrooms have elegant, tasteful, 19th-century furnishings.

Accommodation
Guestrooms: *2 doubles, 1 with private bath and 1 with shared bath*
Services & Amenities: *French and English are spoken; rooms cleaned every day; tourist information; dinner reservation; garden; smokers welcome; private parking*
Minimum stay: *3 nights*
Rates: € *per person. Children under 3 free; 4 to 8 -50%*
Credit cards: *not accepted*
Pets: 🚫

The continental breakfast is enriched with homemade cakes and is served in the large living room that has a fireplace. Arrangements can also be made for having lunch and dinner.

Narbolia (Oristano)

B&B Casa Pisanu
• Sardegna B&B Reservation
tel. 070 4520011, 070 4520403
bedsardegna@tiscali.it
Open: May to October

This completely-restructured, early 20th-C house, with its frescoed vaults, is located in the center of town. It's in the Gulf of Oristano, 15 km from the S'Archittu and San Giovanni beaches and 10 km from the place where the boat leaves for the Mal di Ventre Island. Guests have

three functionally-furnished rooms on the ground floor and a large kitchen. Breakfast consists of typical, local products. There's a riding stable and a well-known golf course in the vicinity.

Accommodation
Guestrooms: *3 double bedrooms, also single occupancy, shared bath* ♿
Services & Amenities: *French and English are spoken; rooms cleaned every three days; tourist information; kitchen use by request; terrace; smokers welcome*
Minimum stay: *3 nights*
Rates: € *per person. Children under 3 free; 4 to 8 -50%*
Credit cards: *not accepted*
Pets: 🐾

Olbia (Sassari)

B&B Domus de Rocas
• Associazione "Sardegna Ospitale"
tel. 079 2595061, mob. 347 7773072
fax 079 2592241
info@bbsardegna.com
www.bbsardegna.com
tel. 070 4520011, 070 4520403
bedsardegna@tiscali.it
Closed: July and August

This B&B, with its refined atmosphere, is located in a "stazzu" – a stone-paneled, rural building – with a Mediterranean-scrub garden. It's 2 km from Porto Rotondo, 10 km from Porto Cervo and just 300 m from the sea. Very nicely furnished with local furniture and fabrics, this house also has kilm carpets, carved-cedar doors and a panoramic terrace. Breakfast consists of typical, local products.

Accommodation
Guestrooms: *3 doubles, also single occupancy, with shared bath*
Services & Amenities: *French and English are spoken; rooms cleaned every 3 days; tourist information; dinner reservation; educational courses by request; terrace; air conditioning; Internet access; garden; private parking*
Minimum stay: *3 nights*
Rates: *single €€-€€€, double €€€*
Credit cards: *not accepted*
Pets:

B&B Il Carrubo
Giovannella Degortes
località Porto Rotondo
07026 Olbia (SS)
tel. 0789 34022, mob. 347 6380316
deg.eva@tiscalinet.it
web.tiscalinet.it/ilcarrubo
• Associazione Turisti per Casa
tel. and fax 0532 63066
buccimg@libero.it
www.turistipercasa.it
Open: June to September

This B&B, located in a rural, 18th-century house, surrounded by a old vineyard, is situated on the Costa Smeralda, 1 kilometer from Porto Rotondo. This house, with its tranquil, friendly atmosphere, is very close to the sea and just a short distance from the archeological sites. Its three guestrooms have a large terrace, and the breakfast is the continental type.

Accommodation
Guestrooms: *3 doubles, also single occupancy, 2 with private bath and 1 with shared bath*
Services & Amenities: *English spoken; rooms cleaned every day; tourist info; dinner reservation; terrace; garden; smokers welcome; private parking*
Minimum stay: *3 nights*
Rates: *€€-€€€ per person. Children under 3 free*
Credit cards: *not accepted*
Pets:

• Bed & Breakfast Italia
Code SA5
tel. 06 6878618, fax 06 6878619
info@bbitalia.it
www.bbitalia.it
Closed: varies

The B&B is situated in the typical rural homes of the Gallura area called "stazzi". It features small self-contained apartments that have a double bedroom, a lounge with kitchenette where guests can prepare their breakfast, a veranda and a bathroom with shower. A garden and private parking are available. It is possible to walk along the coast to the spot of Punta Volpe.

Accommodation
Guestrooms: *2 doubles*
Services & Amenities: *French and English are spoken; rooms cleaned every three days; tourist information; private parking*
Minimum stay: *2 nights*
Rates: *€€*
Credit cards: VISA MC *Bancomat*
Pets:

Posada (Nuoro)

I Gerani

• Associazione "Sardegna Ospitale"
tel. 079 2595061, mob. 347 7773072
fax 079 2592241
info@bbsardegna.com
www.bbsardegna.com
Closed: varies

This villa, with its classic furnishings and garden, is located in a small community that's just 2 km from the sea. In the summertime, the village has various activities, including folklore exhibits, festivals and open-air movies. A beach umbrella and an ice chest are available for the guests, who can also enjoy various archeological and naturalistic sites, horseback riding, sailboat racing and skin-diving.

Accommodation
Guestrooms: *3 doubles, also single occupancy, with shared bath*
Services & Amenities: *French and English are spoken; rooms cleaned every three days; tourist information; garden; smokers welcome; private parking*
Minimum stay: *2 nights*
Rates: *single €-€€, double €€-€€€*
Credit cards: *not accepted*
Pets: ✗

Quartu Sant'Elena (Cagliari)

B&B A&A

• Sardegna B&B Reservation
tel. 070 4520011, 070 4520403
bedsardegna@tiscali.it
Closed: November

This B&B is in a multilevel villa that was designed by a famous architect. It's 12 miles from Cagliari, on the coastal road for Villasimius. The accommodation consists in three double rooms. The hostess is a jazz fan and likes to organize musical evenings for her guests. For those who like sports activities, this place is ideal because they can enjoy skin-diving, sailing and horseback riding. The hostess can provide lessons in cooking. Children under 10 years of age are not accepted.

Accommodation
Guestrooms: *3 (1 double, also single occupancy, with private bath, and 2 doubles, with shared bath); additional bed on request*
Services & Amenities: *English spoken; rooms cleaned every day; tourist information; dinner reservation; bike rental; educational courses by request; terrace; Internet access; garden*
Minimum stay: *3 nights*
Rates: *€€-€€€ per person*
Credit cards: *not accepted*
Pets: ✗

B&B Le Giare

• Sardegna B&B Reservation
tel. 070 4520011, 070 4520403
bedsardegna@tiscali.it
Closed: November

This B&B is located on the coast road for Villasimius, 12 kilometers from Cagliari and 2 kilometers from the sea. There are lots of inlets and white beaches, such as the Mari Pintu, Torre delle Stelle and Porto sa Ruxi beaches. The guestrooms in this rustic house, which, however, has an elegant air, have period furniture, paintings by well-known artists and antique prints. The breakfast is served in the family living room.

Accommodation
Guestrooms: *3 (2 singles, shared bath; 1 double, private bath). Additional bed on request*
Services & Amenities: *French, English and Spanish spoken; rooms cleaned every 3 days; tourist info; baby-sitting service; lunch & dinner reservations; terrace; garden; parking*
Minimum stay: *2 nights*
Rates: *€ per person. Children under 3 free; 4 to 8 -50%*
Credit cards: *not accepted*
Pets: ✓

• **Bed & Breakfast Italia**
Code SA7
tel. 06 6878618, fax 06 6878619
info@bbitalia.it
www.bbitalia.it
Closed: varies

A villa nestling among pines, 250 meters from the sea, in a tourist/residential holiday village. The owners offer guests the first floor that consists in two double rooms, a bathroom with shower, an equipped kitchen where breakfast is served, a lounge with TV and a veranda. The furnishings are simple and elegant. The guests can use the garden, which has a typical Sardinian oven and a barbecue. Private parking is available. Smokers are welcome.

ACCOMMODATION
Guestrooms: *2 doubles*
Services & Amenities: *rooms cleaned every 3 days; tourist information; smokers welcome; private parking*
Minimum stay: *2 nights*
Rates: €€
Credit cards: VISA MC *Bancomat*
Pets: 🚫

RIOLA SARDO (ORISTANO)

B&B da Paola e Giorgio
• **Sardegna B&B Reservation**
tel. 070 4520011, 070 4520403
bedsardegna@tiscali.it
Open: March to November

This B&B, which is located in an early 20th-century house that has both modern and period furnishings, is situated in a small, Oristano agricultural community, 12 kilometers from the sea. The continental breakfast is enriched with a selection of cakes and organic marmalades.

ACCOMMODATION
Guestrooms: *3 doubles, also single occupancy, with shared bath*
Services & Amenities: *French, English and Portuguese are spoken; rooms cleaned every day; tourist information; kitchen use by request; terrace; Internet access; garden; smokers welcome; private parking*
Minimum stay: *3 nights*
Rates: € *per person. Children under 3 free, 4 to 8 -50%*
Credit cards: *not accepted*
Pets: 🚫

SANTADI (CAGLIARI)

B&B S'Andriana
Silvana Camboni
località S'Andriana
09010 Santadi (CA)
tel. 0781 955107, 0781 954146
mob. 339 8279713
silvanacamboni@libero.it
• **Associazione Domus Amigas**
tel. and fax 0781 36319
Open all year

This B&B is located in a pastel-colored house out in the countryside at the foot of some charming hills. The house is situated in the lower Sulcis area, which is 15 km from Portu su Trigu, a small, rock-enclosed beach, and 20 km from the white Portopino beach. Guests have a small, comfortable apartment with modern furnishings and large terraces. Breakfast consists of typical local products, and the hostess is happy to reveal some of her secrets on regional Sardinian cooking. For the guests who like hiking, there's the Pantaleo Forest, with its springs and Is Zuddas grottos.

ACCOMMODATION
Guestrooms: *1 mini-apartment with 4 beds*
Services & Amenities: *English spoken; rooms cleaned every day; tourist information; baby-sitting service; kitchenette; dinner reservation; bike rental; educational courses by request; terrace; Internet access; garden; smokers welcome; private parking*
Rates: € *per person. Discounts for children and extended stays*
Credit cards: *not accepted*
Pets: 🐾

San Teodoro (Nuoro)

Gli Olivastri
• Associazione "Sardegna Ospitale"
tel. 079 2595061, mob. 347 7773072
fax 079 2592241
info@bbsardegna.com
www.bbsardegna.com
Open all year

Tci 10%

This villa, with its young couple and 2 little children, has a garden and a lawn and is situated in a very panoramic position 1 kilometer from town and 1,5 kilometers from the sea. The rich Italian breakfast is served in the shared living room. On request, guests can also use the kitchen. Private parking available.

Accommodation
Guestrooms: *2 doubles, with shared bath*
Services & Amenities: *English spoken; rooms cleaned every day; complimentary tourist information; kitchen use by request; terrace; garden; smokers welcome; private parking*
Rates: *single €€, double €€€. Children under 3 free; 4 to 8 -50%*
Credit cards: *not accepted*
Pets:

Santu Lussurgiu (Oristano)

• Bed & Breakfast Italia
Code SA4
tel. 06 6878618, fax 06 6878619
info@bbitalia.it
www.bbitalia.it
Closed: varies

Tci 10%

The B&B is in an old noble stone mansion. It has 4 double rooms, 3 twins and one double. The furniture of each room has its own style, valuable antiques in the double room; colorful, modern furnishings in the others. There are two private bathrooms, one with shower and one with tub. The other two bathrooms are shared with the other rooms. Horse riding and guided excursions can be arranged.

Accommodation
Guestrooms: *4 (1 double bedroom and 3 doubles)*
Services & Amenities: *German spoken; rooms cleaned every 3 days; tourist information*
Minimum stay: *2 nights*
Rates: *€€*
Credit cards: VISA MC *Bancomat*
Pets:

San Vito (Cagliari)

B&B I Glicini
• Sardegna B&B Reservation
tel. 070 4520011, 070 4520403
bedsardegna@tiscali.it
Open all year

This typical, 19th-century manor house, with its characteristic "lolla" – arched loggia – facing the cobblestone courtyard, is located in the center of town, 6 kilometers from the sea. It's

also near places of touristic and archeological interest. The rooms are still original and the floors are either made of wood or paved with mosaic-decorated tiles. The rich breakfast consists of typical, local products.

Accommodation
Guestrooms: *3 doubles, also single occupancy, with private bath* ♿
Services & Amenities: *English and Spanish are spoken; rooms cleaned every 3 days; tourist information; kitchen use by request; dinner reservation; garden; smokers welcome*
Rates: *€ per person. Children under 6 free*
Credit cards: *not accepted*
Pets:

Sassari

Il Casale
località Canaglia
• Associazione "Sardegna Ospitale"
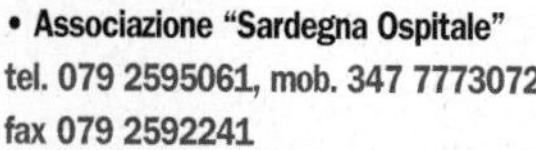
tel. 079 2595061, mob. 347 7773072
fax 079 2592241
info@bbsardegna.com
www.bbsardegna.com
Closed: varies

This independent, recently-restructured house, has a garden, is surrounded by countryside, and has plain, functional furniture. Guest accommodation consists in three double rooms and includes a TV room and a barbecue. The vicinity offers horseback riding, skin diving and visits to archeological sites. Private parking available.

Accommodation
Guestrooms: *3 doubles, also single occupancy, with shared bath; additional bed on request*
Services & Amenities: *French and English are spoken; rooms cleaned every 3 days; tourist information; garden; smokers welcome; private parking*
Rates: *single €-€€, double €€-€€€. Children under 3 free; 4 to 8 -50%*
Credit cards: *not accepted*
Pets:

La Mimosa
località Monte Oro
• Associazione "Sardegna Ospitale"
tel. 079 2595061, mob. 347 7773072
fax 079 2592241
info@bbsardegna.com
www.bbsardegna.com
Closed: varies

This modern, very nicely finished villa, with its classic, elegant furnishings, is 3,5 kilometers from Sassari and 15 kilometers from the sea. The hostess, who has two grown children, prepares a large Italian breakfast, which is usually served in the garden. The vicinity offers excursions on horseback.

Accommodation
Guestrooms: *2 doubles, also single occupancy, with private bath; additional bed on request*
Services & Amenities: *French spoken; rooms cleaned every 3 days; tourist information; garden; smokers welcome; private parking*
Rates: *single €-€€, double €€-€€€. Children under 3 free; 4 to 8 -50%*
Credit cards: *not accepted*
Pets:

Pink House
località Platamona
• Associazione "Sardegna Ospitale"
tel. 079 2595061, mob. 347 7773072
fax 079 2592241
info@bbsardegna.com
www.bbsardegna.com
Closed: varies

Accommodation
Guestrooms: *3 doubles, also single occupancy, 2 with private bath and 1 with shared bath*
Services & Amenities: *English spoken; rooms cleaned every 3 days; tourist information; kitchen use by request; garden; smokers welcome; private parking*
Rates: *single €-€€, double €€-€€€. Children under 3 free; 4 to 8 -50%*
Credit cards: *not accepted*
Pets:

This recently-constructed villa, with its very courteous family, consisting of three persons, has classic furnishings and a garden, it's located in a very interesting archeological area, and the sea is only 4 kilometers away. On request, the guests can use the family kitchen. The vicinity offers horseback riding, hiking and boat excursions.

Serri (Nuoro)

B&B Sa Corti
• Sardegna B&B Reservation
tel. 070 4520011, 070 4520403
bedsardegna@tiscali.it
Open: March to October

This B&B is located in a late 18th-C house situated in a small village of farmers and shepherds. The house is on a "giara" plateau (the Sardinian name for a basaltic volcanic prominence) in the southeastern part of Sardinia. Rooms have wrought iron beds, ancient wooden cupboards, and

characteristic bare-beamed ceilings. Breakfast consists of local products. There are many archeological points of interest in this area: one of the most actractive is the Santa Vittoria Sanctuary nuraghe. The vicinity also offers horseback riding.

Accommodation
Guestrooms: *3 doubles, also single occupancy, with private bath ♿*
Services & Amenities: *French and English are spoken; rooms cleaned every day; tourist information; garden; private parking*
Minimum stay: *1 week*
Rates: *€ per person. Children under 3 free; 4 to 8 -50%*
Credit cards: *not accepted*
Pets: *not allowed*

Sinnai (Cagliari)

Vignetta B&B
Ugo and Lucia Masala
strada litoranea per Villasimius
km 27,100, località Solanas
09048 Sinnai (CA)
tel. 070 7500002, mob. 349 2973461
ugaccios@tiscali.it
Closed: July and August

This B&B, in a single-family house that's just a few minutes away by car from the well-known Villasimius beaches, provides a nice view of the sea. It offers four rooms with handmade local furniture, as

well as a reading room with a library and corner for relaxing. Breakfast, which consists of pastries, as well as cold cuts and cheese, is served in a dining area or outdoors.

Accommodation
Guestrooms: *4 (1 single, 2 double bedrooms and 1 double, with shared bath)*
Services & Amenities: *French and English are spoken; rooms cleaned every 3 days; tourist information; bike rental; air conditioning; Internet access; garden; smokers welcome; private parking*
Minimum stay: *2 nights*
Rates: *single €, double €€*
Credit cards: *not accepted*
Pets: *allowed*

• Bed & Breakfast Italia
Code SA1
località Solanas
09048 Sinnai (CA)
tel. 06 6878618, fax 06 6878619
info@bbitalia.it
www.bbitalia.it
Closed: varies

A charming rose cottage, nestling in a green area. The landlords offer for B&B purposes three double rooms and two singles, furnished in a simple and functional style. It is situated in a park, on a hilltop with a view of the Sola-

Accommodation
Guestrooms: *5 (2 singles, 3 doubles)*
Services & Amenities: *French and English are spoken; rooms cleaned every 3 days; tourist information; smokers welcome; private parking*
Minimum stay: *2 nights*
Rates: *€€*
Credit cards: *Visa MC Bancomat*
Pets: *not allowed*

nas beach, one of the main beaches on the Villasimius coastline. Cagliari is 30 minutes away by car. Private parking is also available.

Thiesi (Sassari)

Sa Mesaluna
Maria Francesca Demontis
via Lamarmora 35
07047 Thiesi (SS)
tel. 079 889716, mob. 349 7817143
samesaluna@jannas.it
Open all year

This B&B is in an ancient, recently-restructured, 18-century house whose guestrooms each have a different color, sedate, rustic furnishings and air conditioning. The Italian breakfast is either served in the kitchen or on the terrace. This place makes an excellent base for visiting the nuraghe and Domus de Janas archeological sites in the Sardinian hinterland.

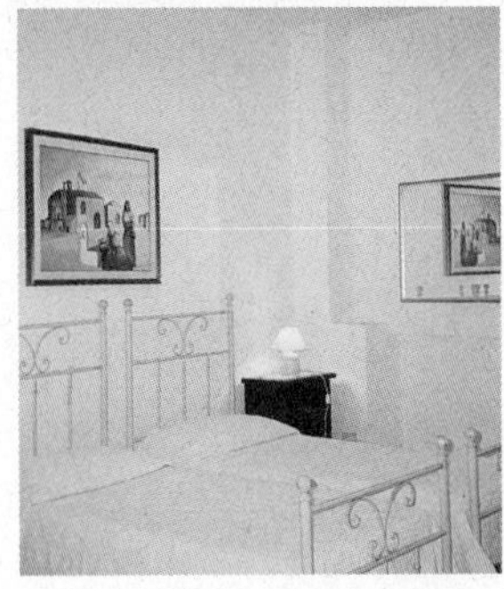

Accommodation
Guestrooms: *3 (1 single, 1 double and 1 triple room, with private bath)*
Services & Amenities: *English spoken; rooms cleaned every 3 days; tourist information; kitchen use by request; bike rental; air conditioning; terrace; garden; smokers welcome*
Rates: *single €, double €€. Children under 3 free; 4 to 12 -50%*
Credit cards: *not accepted*
Pets:

Torralba (Sassari)

B&B Casa Pirisi
• Sardegna B&B Reservation
tel. 070 4520011, 070 4520403
bedsardegna@tiscali.it
Open: June to September

This B&B, 50 kilometers from Alghero, is in an ancient, two-story, completely-restructured house that's located in the town's old center and faces a small, charming square. The nice guestrooms occupy the first floor and have plain, functional furniture. This particular locality has very important archeological testimonials. In fact, there's the Sant'An-tine nuraghe, which is Sardi-nia's second most important megalith, and the Communal Museum of the Valley of the Nuraghi of Logudoro and Meijlogu. The Italian breakfast is served in the family dining room.

Accommodation
Guestrooms: *3 doubles, also single occupancy, with shared bath*
Services & Amenities: *rooms cleaned every 3 days; tourist information; kitchen use by request; lunch & dinner reservations*
Rates: *€ per person. Children under 3 free, 4 to 8 -50%*
Credit cards: *not accepted*
Pets:

Uta (Cagliari)

B&B da Mariella
• Sardegna B&B Reservation
tel. 070 4520011, 070 4520403
bedsardegna@tiscali.it
Open all year

Accommodation
Guestrooms: *3 doubles, also single occupancy, with private bath*
Services & Amenities: *French and English are spoken; rooms cleaned every day; tourist info; dinner reservation; air conditioning; garden; smokers welcome; private parking*
Rates: *€ per person. Children under 3 free; 4 to 8 -50%*
Credit cards: *not accepted*
Pets:

This B&B, in an area that has several nuraghe villages, is 50 minutes from the dunes of the Chia and Capospartivento beach. The rich breakfast, which consists of fresh fruit, typical handmade pastries and warm beverages, is served in the family garden. Especially noteworthy is the WWF oasis at the foot of Mount Arcosu and the Santa Gilla pond, a protected area where one can enjoy observing the beautiful flamingoes.

Villacidro (Cagliari)

B&B Oasi Verde

• B&B Liguria e... non solo
tel. 010 3291204
fax 010 3299774
oltrelazzurro@libero.it
www.bbitalia.net
Open all year

This B&B is in a small, modern villa located in a hilly area just a few minutes from the center of town. Guests have a double room and share the family bathroom. The room, which has classic furnishings and a TV, opens onto a panoramic balcony. The breakfast, which can either be the continental type or another type as desired, is generally served in the living room. In the summertime, it can be served in the garden, under the gazebo.

Accommodation
Guestrooms: *1 double, also single occupancy, with shared bath; additional bed on request*
Services & Amenities: *English, German and Spanish are spoken; rooms cleaned every day; complimentary tourist information; garden; smokers welcome*
Rates: *single €€, double €€€. Additional bed supplement €. Children under 2 free; 2 to 12 -50%. Discounts for extended stays*
Credit cards: *not accepted*
Pets: no

Villamassargia (Cagliari)

I Castello di Gioiosa Guardia
Betty Mascia
via XXV Aprile 21
09010 Villamassargia (CA)
tel. and fax 0781 75011
• Associazione Domus Amigas
tel. and fax 0781 36319
Open all year

Accommodation
Guestrooms: *3 doubles, also single occupancy, with private bath*
Services & Amenities: *rooms cleaned every day; tourist information; garden; smokers welcome*
Rates: *single €, double €€*
Credit cards: *not accepted*
Pets: no

This area is well-known for its production of carpets and fabrics, as well as for its rich archeological and historic testimonials. This large, recently-constructed house, is not far from the center of town, and is surrounded by an olive grove. Rooms have handmade, Sardinian furniture and an independent entrance. The continental breakfast, which consists of typical pastries, is served in a dining room or in the kitchen. The hostess willingly teaches her guests how to prepare local dishes. Guests can also taste the oil, wine and various cheeses made by the family.

Villanova Monteleone (Sassari)

B&B Su Cantaru
• Sardegna B&B Reservation
tel. 070 4520011, 070 4520403
bedsardegna@tiscali.it
Open all year

This B&B is located in an early 20th-century house situated in the center of Villanova Monteleone. This town, 24 km from Alghero and 10 km from the sea, is an important center for breeders from Nurra. The stark, wild landscape, with its groves of holm and cork oaks, create a splendid contrast with the colors of the sea. The guestrooms have Sardinian style furnishings, including loom-woven tapestries, drapes and bedcovers. The continental breakfast, served by the hostess, is enriched with local honey, tarts and organic marmalades.

Accommodation
Guestrooms: *3 (1 single and 2 double bedrooms, with private bath); additional bed on request*
Services & Amenities: *rooms cleaned every day; tourist information; kitchen use by request; garden; smokers welcome*
Rates: *single €€, double €€€. Children under 10 free*
Credit cards: *not accepted*
Pets: no

Mendulas

• **Associazione "Sardegna Ospitale"**
tel. 079 2595061, mob. 347 7773072
fax 079 2592241
info@bbsardegna.com
www.bbsardegna.com
Closed: varies

This farmhouse, with its very friendly atmosphere, is situated just 2,5 km from town in an area that's full of important archeological and naturalist sites. The guestrooms have rustic-style furnishings. The host family – which consists of four persons – is the owner of a riding stable. On request, guests can taste the local culinary specialties.

ACCOMMODATION
Guestrooms: *2 doubles, also single occupancy, 1 with private bath and 1 with shared bath*
Services & Amenities: *rooms cleaned every 3 days; tourist information; lunch & dinner reservations; horse-riding excursions; garden; smokers welcome; private parking*
Rates: *single €, double €€. Children under 3 free*
Credit cards: *not accepted*
Pets:

VILLASIMIUS (CAGLIARI)

B&B da Adriana

• **Sardegna B&B Reservation**
tel. 070 4520011, 070 4520403
bedsardegna@tiscali.it
Open: March to November

ACCOMMODATION
Guestrooms: *3 doubles, private bath*
Services & Amenities: *French and English are spoken; rooms cleaned every 3 days; tourist information; baby-sitting service; kitchen use by request; lunch & dinner reservations; terrace; garden; smokers welcome; private parking*
Minimum stay: *2 nights*
Rates: *€€-€€€ per person. Children under 12 -50%*
Credit cards: *not accepted*
Pets:

This B&B, which is 5 km from the center of town, is in the Capo Carbonara Geomarino park and only 300 m from the white Porto Sa Ruxi beach. The small hosting villa, which has a large Mediterranean garden, is part of a residence complex that has a swimming pool and tennis court. There's and extra charge for using the pool or court. Breakfast is served in the garden or on the patio.

I Gigli

• **Associazione "Sardegna Ospitale"**
tel. 079 2595061, mob. 347 7773072
fax 079 2592241
info@bbsardegna.com
www.bbsardegna.com
Closed: varies

This small, independent villa is located in a very panoramic position. In fact, it's right in front of the sea. The beach is only 50 m away and is, therefore, easily reached on foot. Breakfast is served in the garden. On request, guests can use the family kitchen. The vicinity offers horseback riding, sea and land excursions, skin diving and sailing.

ACCOMMODATION
Guestrooms: *2 doubles, also single occupancy, with shared bath*
Services & Amenities: *English spoken; rooms cleaned every 3 days; tourist information; kitchen use by request; garden; smokers welcome; private parking*
Rates: *single €€, double €€€€. Children under 3 free; 4 to 8 -50%*
Credit cards: *not accepted*
Pets:

Index of Places

T

U

V

W

Z

Update contributions

For the next edition of *Italian Bed & Breakfasts*

Would you like to send us details of a Bed & Breakfast you visited? Is your B&B in this guide but details have changed (telephone, e-mail, website, services)? Did you visit a B&B that is not included in this guide? Do you have any suggestions that would increase the number and quality of inclusions? There is a simple and effective way to help us update the *Italian Bed & Breakfasts* guide: fill in the form below and add your comments (please print). Photocopy this page and send it by post or fax to:

Touring Editore – Redazione Guida B&B
Via Adamello 10 – 20139 Milan – fax 02 8526215

Bed & Breakfast notification

Bed & Breakfast name..
Owner..
Address..
Town.. Province..
Telephone....................................fax..............................e-mail..............................
Room prices..
Is it already mentioned in the guide? Yes No

Details

1 Location (old town centre or major attractions)...
....
2 B&B appearance and maintenance...
....
3 Number of rooms and beds...
4 Number of guest bathrooms..
5 Type of breakfast offered..
....
6 Terrace, garden, parking available...
7 Tourist info provided...

Comments and remarks..
....

Surname...
Name...
TCI member no. (if any)..
Town/City.............................Street.. Country..........
Telephone..............................fax...................... e-mail..
Date and signature

LUCCA
Via SS. Annunziata, 1070
Tel./Fax +39 0583 426314
Mobile +39 339 4116840
e-mail: biancalana@tin.it
www.casabiancalana.it

Casa Biancalana is a beautiful old country house built in the XVII century on the original unit of an ancient monastery of the XIII century. It is formed by a main central unit, where the owners live, and by small flats and rooms, available for the guests; the rooms have antique furniture, and all the units have shower, heating system and satellite TV. The house is surrounded by a wide garden and has a swimming pool, and an area for children amusement. It is possible to rent bicycles and to use Internet connection.

Situated a stroll away from the art of Florence, the Fortezza da Basso, the Congress Palace and near Santa Maria Novella Station and the Airport Amerigo Vespucci.
I DUE LEONI Bed & Breakfast aims to reproduce the warmth and cosiness of your own home, yet providing you with all the comforts of a good hotel.
This friendly B & B has its own garden to help you relax after work or a day on the town, or siply enjoy a sunny day in the warmest months of the year.

Via delle Ghiacciaie, 41 - FIRENZE - Tel. +39 055 3245033
Tel. / Fax +39 055 579118 - E-mail: info@idueleonifirenze.it

Viale Cavour 134 -SIENA- Tuscany - ITALY
Tel & Fax 0039 057740374 *e-mail:* iris02@tiscali.it
http:// **www.soggiornoiris.com**

BED & BREAKFAST IRIS
is located to 300 metres from historical centre of ***Siena,*** *near* ***Antiporto Camollia.*** *Situated in the ancient* ***"SAPORI Palace"*** *- completely restored in* ***2002*** *- it's consisting of rooms that offer all the possible comforts.*

The homely welcome is a guarantee of a pleasant and relaxed stay. You are invited to taste a delicious breakfast in our original dining-room where is present a caratteristic cooking area decorated with a beatiful variety of italian marbles.

Tel. +39(0)583 496872 - Fax. +39(0)583 957600
www.villaromantica.it - info@villaromantica.it
Via N. Barbantini, 246 S.Marco
55100 Lucca A11, exit Lucca est, (Stadio)

Villa Romantica hides among trees within two minutes walk to the medieval Centre of Lucca, has comfortable double bedrooms with private bathroom, one junior suite with jacuzzi tub and one four poster suite with drawing-room all equipped with every comforts such as: satellite TV, direct telephone, air conditioning. Breakfast room, bar and meeting room complete our facilities. Ample private car parking, bicycles and swimming pool are free.

VILLA ANNA

53027 San Quirico d'Orcia
(SIENA)
Via Sano di Pietro, 9
Phone/Fax: +39 0577 897278
Mobile: +39 347 7748732
E-mail: annamaria101@supereva.it

Built in the style of the Fifties, villa with garden and private parking, just a few steps away from the historical town center. Villa Anna offers excellent hospitality with breakfast in comfortable apartments equipped with kitchenette and furnished with period furniture. Lovely view over Siena Montalcino and the surrounding hills thick with Brunello and Chianti vineyards.

Bed and Breakfast

At only 10 minutes drive from the Medieval walls of Florence, the **Borgo Ponte dell'Asse Bed and Breakfast** rests amidst an old village in existence since 1400. Surrounded by a thick vegetation with tall cypresses, the village is characterized by a cluster of buildings that are typical of the rural Tuscan landscape. Guest accommodations with two bedrooms with double beds, bathroom with double wash-basin and shower cabin, wide terrace for breakfast in the open air, with an independent entrance. From the village one can easily reach other tour sites in Tuscany (Chianti, Siena, Pisa, Lucca etc.) even with public means of trasport. English and French spoken.

Via della Greve, 12 - 50018 - Scandicci (Firenze) - Tel. and fax +39 055 2048650 - e-mail: p.andreotti1@tin.it
www.agriturismo.net/borgo_ponte_dell_asse/indexita.shtml

via L. Da Vinci, 47/49
Calcinaia - Lastra a Signa (FI)
Tel./fax +39 055 8723629
www.farmhousecupoli.it

An old farmhouse, tipical of the tuscan country side, is called as "casa colonica". Our colonica has been totaly restored, inside and out, conserving the original and unique architectural features.

Seven rooms are available for guests who wish to have a holiday in the beautiful hills that sorround Florence. All the rooms have en-suite bathrooms, and are furnished with family heirooms to create a simple, confortable and rustic atmosphere.

Relaxing reading room, spacious sitting room, swimming pool, laundry service, mountain-bike hire. We produce our own extra virgin olive oil, jams, fresh fruit and vegetables. Horseback riding (3 Km), fishing (600 mts), shooting range (2 Km) and trekking. Paths for long hikes or leisurly walks.

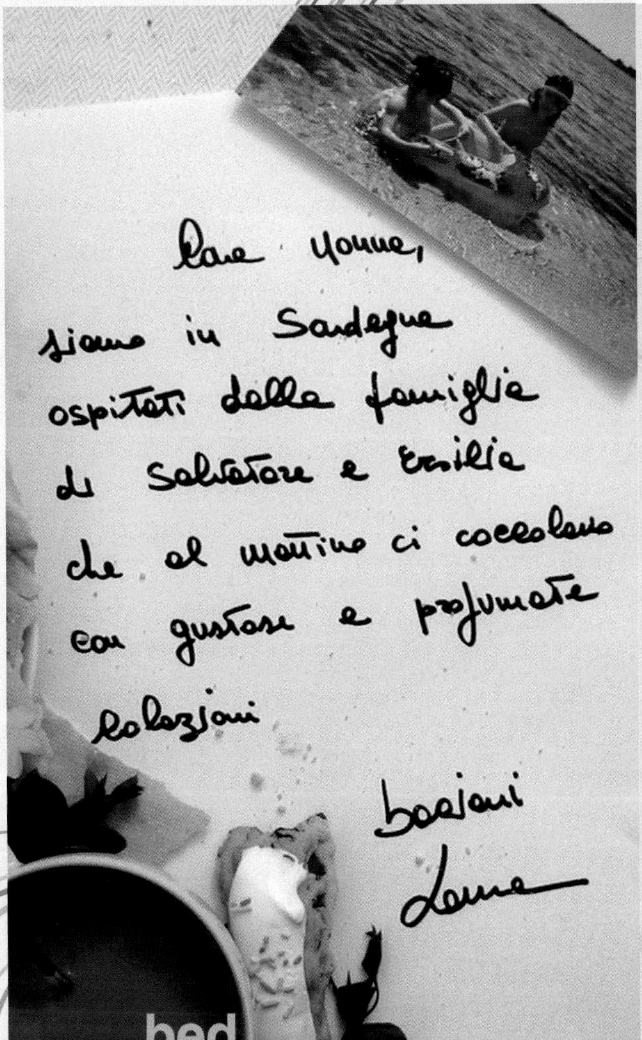

siamo in Sardegna
ospitati dalla famiglia
di Salvatore e Emilia
che al mattino ci coccolano
con gustose e profumate
colazioni

bacioni
Laura

bed and breakfast within the family

Sardegna B&B Reservation has recently set up and organized the first group of families willing to host you in their own houses in order to let you enjoy the magical atmosphere of the island.

Our families will always welcome you as a friend in compliance with the quality standards of the "reception charter", so at breakfast you will taste our traditional Sardinian cuisine.

B&B TOURS IN SARDINIA

GUESTS OF THE SEA AND MINES

In the Sulcis area near Iglesias, signs from the Neolithic era are never far away from the abandoned mines located on white beaches or within impervious cliffs.

GUESTS OF OUR HISTORY

Period houses and real personal life stories where families have chosen to make you enjoy the roots of an ancient land.

SEARCHING FOR SAVOURS

In this area of the Mediterranean, the sun, sea, land and heritage are the main ingredients of the wine and food tradition.

Prices from 145.00 Euros per person per week based on two people sharing; breakfast included.

RESERVATION CENTRE

Our reservation centre will help you to choose and book the best location according to your needs and advise on the most interesting area for your holiday.

CALL CENTER

tel +39 070 7265007
fax +39 070 7269608
e-mail:
bedsardegna@tiscali.it
www.sardegna.com